THE HISTORY OF LATIN AMERICA

PALGRAVE ESSENTIAL HISTORIES

General editor: Jeremy Black

This series of compact, readable, and informative national histories is designed to appeal to anyone wishing to gain a broad understanding of a country's history.

THE HISTORY OF LATIN AMERICA

COLLISION OF CULTURES

Marshall C. Eakin

First published in 2007 by
PALGRAVE MACMILLAN™
175 Fifth Avenue, New York, N.Y. 10010 and
Houndmills, Basingstoke, Hampshire, England RG21 6XS
Companies and representatives throughout the world.

PALGRAVE MACMILLAN is the global academic imprint of the Palgrave Macmillan division of St. Martin's Press, LLC and of Palgrave Macmillan Ltd. Macmillan® is a registered trademark in the United States, United Kingdom and other countries. Palgrave is a registered trademark in the European Union and other countries.

ISBN-13: 978–1–4039–8081–6
ISBN-10: 1–4039–8081–0

Library of Congress Cataloging-in-Publication Data is available from the Library of Congress.

A catalogue record of the book is available from the British Library.

Design by Newgen Imaging Systems (P) Ltd., Chennai, India.

First edition: June 2007

10 9 8 7 6 5 4 3 2 1

Printed in the United States of America.

For Lacy and Lee
who came of age with this book

Contents

Part III   Forging a New Order

Part IV   Democracy, Development, and Identity

List of Illustrations

Acknowledgements

This book has been a lifetime in the making. Growing up in a former province of Mexico (Texas) that once lay on the northern frontier of the Spanish Empire in the New World surely shaped my outlook on Latin America long before I became aware that the region existed. My elementary school Spanish lessons from Señora González and Señor Cuellar no doubt subtly moved me (at a very early age) in the direction of my career in Latin American studies. A summer doing public health work with the Amigos de las Americas in the highlands of Guatemala in 1970 hooked me definitively on Latin America, creating a passion that grew during the year and a half (1973–74) I was a student at the Universidad de Costa Rica. Charles Stansifer, Elizabeth Kuznesof, William J. Griffith, Robert Gilmore, and Anita Herzfeld began my formal (and informal) training as a historian of Latin America while I was an undergraduate and then masters student at the University of Kansas in the 1970s. I had the privilege of studying with James Lockhart at UCLA in the late 1970s as he carried out pathbreaking work in the colonial history of Latin America. I owe an enormous debt to the late E. Bradford Burns, my mentor at UCLA, a brilliant and charismatic teacher, and one of the few academic historians of Latin America with the audacity to write about big themes for audiences beyond the academy.

My life and work in Latin America since 1970 would not have been possible without the generous financial support of many institutions and organizations. The National Defense Education Act (Title VI), the University of Kansas, the University of California at Los Angeles, the Tinker Foundation, the Fulbright-Hays program, the Fundação João Pinheiro, and the National Endowment for the Humanities have all funded my education as a Latin Americanist over the last 35 years. I have been extraordinarily lucky to work at Vanderbilt University since 1983. The administration of the university has been wonderfully supportive of Latin American studies, and that support has grown dramatically in recent years. I owe a special thanks to Gordon Gee and Richard McCarty for their continuing encouragement and help. An exceptional group of colleagues in the Department of History and the Center for Latin American and Iberian Studies has profoundly influenced my outlook on Latin America, and life in general. Caroline Knobloch read and critiqued the entire draft of the manuscript as it took shape and gave me invaluable advice on my prose and ideas. Thank you, Caroline. Thousands of students in my classes have pushed me continually to think and rethink my ideas and they have taught me as much as I have taught them. A long experience working with other groups—churches, public schools, community groups, retirement learning programs, and Vanderbilt alumni—has helped shaped my outlook on the presentation of my knowledge about Latin America. To all of these former "students," many thanks for your tough questions and comments over the years.

My wife, Michelle Beatty-Eakin, has been a constant and unflagging source of support in my career and in our family. When I began serious work on this book some five years ago, our two daughters were barely teenagers. Now they are in the process of becoming independent young women. As important as my "work" is to me, they have been constant reminders that my life with them has always been even more precious and enriching. This book is dedicated to them. I hope they are as lucky as I have been to find a career filled with passion and commitment that is both enormously satisfying and constantly challenging.

In the end, I owe my greatest debt to all those Latin Americans with whom I have talked, argued, laughed, danced, drank, cried, and celebrated over the last four decades. In my travels and studies from Mexico to Patagonia, from Puerto Rico to Rio de Janeiro, I have had the great privilege of sharing a substantial part of my life with an incredibly diverse group of peoples who have taught me more about their world and mine than I can ever convey in one book, or even one life. I hope that this book does some justice to the peoples and places I have come to know in Latin America, and helps non-Latin Americans understand why the region and its peoples are so compelling, complex, and important.

xii

Map 1. Latin America Today

Introduction

Unity and Diversity

"Nothing more than a geographical reality? And yet it moves. In actions, unimportant at times, Latin America reveals each day its fellowship as well as its contradictions; we Latin Americans share a common space, and not only on the map. . . . Whatever our skin color or language, aren't we all made of assorted clays from the same multiple earth?"

—Eduardo Galeano
Uruguayan writer

The collision of three peoples—Native Americans, Europeans, and Africans—gave birth to Latin America. We know with great certainty that the moment of conception was October 12, 1492. Before the arrival of Christopher Columbus to the "New World," there was no Latin America. On that warm Caribbean morning in October 1492, Columbus unwittingly brought together two worlds and three peoples, initiating a violent and fertile series of cultural and biological clashes that continue today. For thousands of years the Native Americans had lived in isolation from the inhabitants of what became known as the "Old World." The peoples of Asia, Africa, and Europe had fought, traded, and otherwise intermingled since the rise of the human species throughout those regions, but they had lost any sustained contact with the populations of the Americas for millenia. On October 12, 1492, Columbus "reunited" the inhabitants of the Old World and the New World and initiated an ongoing exchange of humans, plants, animals, and microbes that created (and continually re-creates) Latin America. The collision of Native Americans, Europeans, and Africans, like three powerful streams converging to produce a roaring river, mixed these three peoples into a dazzling variety of combinations, producing something new and unique in world history. As the decades and centuries passed, the turbulent river gradually split into many different streams, but all had their origins in the great waterway formed by the initial clash of these three groups.

It is these dramatic collisions and convergences that provide Latin America with both its unity and its diversity. A common process of conquest, colonization, resistance, and accommodation across the region provides the unity that allows us to speak of something so mislabeled as "Latin" America. Five hundred years after that instance of conception, the descendants of the "Columbian Moment" bear the highly visible reminders of this common process: they live in nation-states formed out of western and southern European political and legal traditions; they speak Romance languages (Spanish, Portuguese, French) as the dominant tongues; overwhelmingly, they practice varieties of Christianity (especially Roman Catholicism); and they are integrated into the capitalist system that arose out of the North Atlantic world. Yet, at the same time, it has become harder and harder to speak of a common experience for Latin America as the centuries pass. Despite this impressive unity in traditions and history, beneath the European façade lay astonishingly rich and diverse variations that increasingly divide the region. The most obvious is racial and cultural diversity. In Mexico, Central America, and the Andean world (especially Ecuador, Peru, and Bolivia), the presence of large, dense Indian populations has produced a racial and cultural mixture that, on closer scrutiny, makes these countries very unlike Europe and very distinct from the rest of Latin America. In the Caribbean and Brazil, the massive importation of millions of Africans from the sixteenth to the nineteenth centuries makes these countries very different from "Indo-America." The massive immigration of Europeans to Argentina and Uruguay in the late nineteenth and early twentieth centuries, and absence of large Indian or African populations in those countries, has produced yet another major variation on the Latin American heritage. In short, there are many Americas within Latin America.

When I speak of conquest and collision in this book I am really speaking of multiple conquests and collisions, as Native Americans, Europeans, and Africans came together throughout Latin America in a variety of combinations and locales. To complicate matters further, in the nineteenth and twentieth centuries the peoples of the Middle East and Asia also began to enter the region in significant numbers, once again reshaping and redefining the racial and cultural character of Latin America. Yet, despite the multiplicity of collisions and peoples, I firmly believe that the initial encounters in the century after 1492 provided—and continue to provide—Latin America with a unity and coherence that allows us to write about the region as a whole. Latin America has a common core of characteristics that allows us to speak about it as a whole, yet we must always remember that its dimensions have been constantly shifting and evolving since the moment of conception in October 1492.

Even the name for the region has shifted over the centuries. Although often referred to as the "New" World or the "Indies" in the decades and centuries after the voyage of Columbus, the combined American colonies of Spain, Portugal, and (eventually) France had no common generic name until the mid-nineteenth century. The awkward term "Latin America" appeared for the first time in the 1850s, in Colombia, and was taken up by the French, who had colonial ambitions in the region during the 1860s. Clearly, it is a Eurocentric term that emphasizes the "Latin" (Spanish, Portuguese, French) heritage of the region while ignoring the important African and Indian cultures in the Americas. Like many others, I will continue to use the term for lack of a better one, while recognizing its limitations. At the same time, it is also important to recognize that "Latin America" has many definitions. The most traditional definition is a political one that includes 20 countries that gained their independence from Spain, Portugal (Brazil), and France (Haiti) in the nineteenth century (and at the turn of the twentieth century in the cases of Cuba and Panama). This is a convenient and handy definition, but it leaves the historian with the quandary of what to do with places like the British West Indies, Guyana, Suriname, or Curaçao. All were once part of the Spanish Empire, and hence, part of colonial Latin America, but once seized by Britain and the Netherlands they are no longer a part of Latin America politically. Even more complex is Puerto Rico, by all cultural and linguistic standards a part of Latin America, but not an independent country. Even if one sticks to political boundaries as the defining characteristic, then a sizable chunk of the western United States was a part of Latin America until the mid-nineteenth century, as was Florida.

From my perspective, Latin America is both a political and a cultural construct that is constantly evolving. In 1493, Latin America consisted of a small settlement (Santo Domingo) on the island of Hispaniola. This was the first place where the two worlds and three peoples converged. By 1600, Latin America had expanded to include most of the islands of the Caribbean, central Mexico, parts of Central America, much of the Andean world, and settlements along the coast of Brazil. The military conquest had spread the cultural collisions to ever-widening spaces across the Americas. By 1700, the Spanish had lost control of many islands in the Caribbean, but had extended their presence (along with the Portuguese) deeper into the interior of the American continents. Latin America was both expanding and contracting. In the nineteenth century, Latin America (as a political unit) shrunk even more as the United States conquered and annexed Texas, California, and much of the so-called Far West. In a larger, cultural sense, however, Latin America continues to expand and thrive with the centuries-old movement of peoples from South to North. Arguably, south Florida, southern California, much of Texas, and even areas of New York City or Washington, D.C., today form part of Latin America. (Los Angeles has a larger Spanish-speaking population than some Latin American countries!) For the purposes of this book, I will generally stick to the political boundaries of Latin America (the traditional 20 countries) while always recognizing that areas like the British West Indies, Puerto Rico, or Texas at times form a part of Latin America, and they continue to be linked to it culturally, if not politically. The 20 traditional countries (plus Puerto Rico) today form the core of an always evolving and shifting region.

My goal in this book is to tell the story of Latin America from its creation to the present. More precisely, it is "a" story of Latin America, for the region has a multiplicity of "stories"—not only of the individual countries, but also within those nation-states. While recognizing the extraordinary diversity of voices and stories across a vast region that today is home to half a billion people, I do believe that I can and must construct a clear narrative line. A narrative history, despite its flaws, brings a unity to this exceptional diversity, and a coherence to a cacophony of voices. I seek to provide a sweeping overview to a multiplicity of stories while recognizing the problems of constructing this "big picture." This concise, one-volume, synthetic history gives substantial attention to the pre-Columbian roots of both the New World and the Old. Roughly one-half of the book covers the period up to the early nineteenth century, and the second half surveys the last two hundred years. Although I have built a strong social and cultural historical narrative, this text also features an analysis of institutions and structures. I emphasize the processes as well as many of the individuals who forged the history of Latin America. More than a simple chronicle of politics, this is the story of the birth and emergence of Latin American civilizations.

A series of themes forms the core of the analysis and narrative throughout the book. The principal theme, the one I have already introduced, is the clash of peoples and cultures—Native Americans, Europeans, Africans— that defines Latin America and gives it both its unity and diversity. The other major organizing themes are: (1) "hierarchy and power," focusing on politics and political culture; (2) "poverty and plenty," that is, the pronounced social and economic inequities that arose in the conquest phase and that continue to plague Latin America today; (3) "the fruits of the land," concentrating on patterns of economic development; (4) "the power of the spirit," highlighting the importance of spirituality and religious beliefs; and, finally, (5) "the search for identity," emphasizing the changing meaning and nature of Latin American identity(ies), especially as seen through art, literature, and popular culture. Although the focus in the colonial period will be largely on Mesoamerica (Mexico and Central America), the Caribbean, the Andes, and Brazil, I cover other regions as well. The coverage of the region for the nineteenth and twentieth centuries is very sweeping, but concise. This is not, by any means, an encyclopedic history of Latin America, but rather a synthetic and interpretive overview.

I have divided this story into five parts. Part I, "Three Peoples Converge," opens with a brief description of the physical features of Latin America. Geology, geography, and climate have deeply shaped the development of the region, from the routes of the conquistadors to the exploitation of the great silver and gold mines of Mexico, Peru, and Brazil, to the expansion of plantation, export-oriented agriculture. Geography is not destiny, but it does profoundly shape historical trajectory. I then introduce the three groups who came to create Latin America after 1492. Despite their extraordinary biological homogeneity, the Native Americans, the first group I discuss, were an exceptionally diverse group of peoples ranging from simple hunters and gatherers to the inhabitants of the formidable Aztec, Mayan, and Incan empires. The native peoples, migrating from Asia, had begun to settle the Americas possibly as far back as 40,000 years ago. (The inhabitants of Europe and Africa have much more ancient roots in their homelands, going back to the emergence of the human species.) The second group discussed are the Europeans, more specifically the Spanish and Portuguese. In the centuries before the Columbian Moment, Spain and Portugal had become a vibrant cultural intersection of the Christian, Jewish, and Islamic worlds, and a geographical intersection of Europe, Africa, and the Middle East. Islamic invaders swept across North Africa and then the Iberian peninsula in the eighth century. For the next 800 years the Spanish and Portuguese slowly reconquered the peninsula, created the first nation-states in Europe, and forged a powerful alliance between Church and State. All of this would set the stage for their conquest of the Americas. Even more so than the Native Americans and the Europeans, the Africans, the third of the groups under discussion, were a kaleidoscope of peoples, cultures, and political units who happened to inhabit the same continental landmass. When the Europeans began to explore the coast of West Africa in the fifteenth century, they encountered civilizations that were their military equals. For nearly a century before 1492, the Europeans and the Africans traded and sparred along the entire west coast of Africa as they initiated the creation of an "Atlantic world."

Led by the Portuguese in the fourteenth and fifteenth centuries, European overseas expansion was the driving force that brought all three peoples together. The rise of nation-states, the emergence of commercial capitalism, Western science, and a militant Christianity all drove the Europeans outward, using ships that they had created through innovative technologies that had filtered into the Mediterranean from the Middle East, the Indian Ocean, and China. The Europeans sailed in search of gold, glory, and to spread the gospel. The much-discussed "rise of the West" in the fifteenth century began a process of expansion and eventual European world domination that would not be seriously challenged until the twentieth century. The voyage of Columbus in 1492 is one of the definitive moments in this process of overseas expansion, and it initiates the dramatic military conquest of Latin America in the sixteenth century. The Spanish came in waves, sweeping across the islands of the Caribbean by 1520, and from there across Mexico and Central America in the 1520s and 1530s. Another wave of conquest moved across Panama and down through the Andes in the 1530s and 1540s. The Caribbean became the gateway to the Spanish Empire in the Americas, with Mexico and Peru the two "core" regions flush with large Indian populations, fertile lands, and rich silver mines. Less dramatically, the Portuguese stumbled onto the coast of Brazil in 1500 on their way to India. After some fitful efforts, the Portuguese Crown had established a permanent presence on the northeastern coast of Brazil by 1550.

In Part II, "Building Empires and Societies in a New World," I turn to the key institutions that the Iberians (the inhabitants of the Iberian peninsula, i.e., Spain and Portugal) constructed in the Americas to rule their new colonies, and the ways Native Americans and Africans struggled to resist and shape the imposition of these institutions. The Spanish and Portuguese had to harness the labor of large numbers of Indians and Africans to extract wealth from the newly conquered lands. In Spanish America, the Crown devised mechanisms to force Indians to work for the Spanish landowners, and they occasionally resorted to enslaving Indians. In the Caribbean and Brazil, with the destruction and disappearance of the native populations, the Spanish and Portuguese turned to African slave labor. Large landed estates, worked by forced Indian labor and African slaves, had emerged by the late sixteenth century, and is perhaps the most damaging and enduring legacy of Iberian colonialism. The hunger for larger and larger numbers of slaves in the Caribbean and Brazil fueled the rise of the Atlantic slave trade for three centuries. A diaspora of some 12–15 million Africans crossed the Atlantic to reshape the Americas, Africa, and Europe, binding their destinies in an increasingly interconnected Atlantic world. The discovery of silver in Mexico and Upper Peru (Bolivia) in the sixteenth century, and gold in the Brazilian interior in the eighteenth century, intensified the demand for "unfree" Indian and African laborers and funneled immense wealth into an expanding European economy.

The Iberians brought across the Atlantic the legal and political institutions they had developed through centuries of Roman and Islamic conquest and reconquest. In the Americas they adapted them and created new institutions. I want to emphasize that although these institutions were Spanish and Portuguese, the Indians and Africans, and their descendants, resisted them and forced the Iberians to alter and revise them. The process was a tug-of-war, albeit a very unequal one. The empires and chiefdoms on both sides of the Atlantic had developed political cultures that were very hierarchical and with a strong sense of collective identity and responsibility. The Spanish and Portuguese imposed their collectivist, racist, and hierarchical cultural systems on the Indians and Africans in the Americas, often upon large populations that were already highly stratified, hierarchically structured, and racially unequal. The Iberians put into place empires that eventually developed into complex bureaucracies that were (at least in theory) highly centralized and built on privilege. Mexico City and Lima became the capitals of the two Spanish American viceroyalties, with Havana serving as the gateway to this vast empire. Salvador became the viceregal capital and center of Portugal's sugar empire in Brazil. Power radiated from these imperial cities following a simple rule: the farther one was physically located from the central plaza in the capital, the less power and influence one had. By 1700, northern Mexico, the gulf coast of North America, and the plains of southern South America were the frontiers on the periphery of this vast empire. The interior of South America, Spanish or Portuguese, was unconquered and largely untouched by Europe.

Although the military conquest of the core regions had been completed by 1600, the spiritual conquest of the Americas was incomplete and only partially successful. That most of Latin America today is overwhelmingly Catholic is powerful testimony to the success of the Church's ability to spread the word of a Christian God. The process of conversion, however, was bitterly resisted by non-Europeans, both openly and surreptitiously. The result was the rise over the centuries of new religions and religious mixtures that fused the ancient religious beliefs and practices of Native Americans and Africans with Catholicism. Folk Catholicism, vodun, candomblé, and macumba are just a few of the religious traditions that emerged out of the efforts to impose Christianity on highly resistant Indians and Africans, who already had their own ancient religious systems. It proved far harder to impose European religion on the hearts and souls of the Africans and Indians than it was to subdue them physically and militarily.

The formation of new peoples, cultures, and societies is at the heart of Part II. The struggle among the three peoples that begins in October 1492 was complex and took on many forms across the Americas. Racial and cultural mixture took place from the first moments of contact, whether by consent or coercion, through conscious or unconscious efforts to impose or adopt new languages, diet, dress, values, or religious beliefs. The collisions eventually produced a rainbow of skin tones, and in the case of the Iberians, they imposed an explicit and enduring racial hierarchy. In the most general terms, three new, "intermediate" racial groups emerged by the end of the sixteenth century. The offspring of Europeans and Indians became known as mestizos, the children of Europeans and Africans as mulattos, and the descendants of the mixing of Indians and Africans as zambos (the origin of the U.S. term "sambo"). In the racial and cultural hierarchy the Europeans imposed, in general, the more one looked, acted, and sounded like a European the higher one's position. Indians and African slaves were at the bottom of the social pyramid, while the mestizos and mulattos occupied the middle level. At the top of the social pyramid, a distinction would eventually emerge among those of Spanish descent, between those born in Spain (known as peninsulars), and those born in the Americas (known as creoles). By the mid-seventeenth century, the creole population had grown steadily and, especially around the viceregal capitals of Lima and Mexico, one could see the emergence of an "American" culture that had the Iberian peninsula as its principal roots. Increasingly, these American-born Spaniards began to see themselves as a common group with an identity distinct from their peninsular-born compatriots. Although something similar developed in Portuguese America, the process was slower, later, and weaker.

In the mid- to late eighteenth century the Bourbon monarchs in Spain and the Marquis of Pombal in Portugal reorganized and revamped the American empires in the face of two centuries of decline. The seventeenth century had seen the rise of the Dutch, English, and French as colonial powers who carved out colonies in the Americas, ending the Iberian near monopoly in the New World colonies. In Canada, North America, and the Caribbean, the new powers claimed territory and challenged Spain. The discovery of gold in Brazil and the revival of a long-stagnant silver mining economy in Spanish America helped revive the Iberian empires in the eighteenth century. The economic and political reforms were not enough to meet the challenge (especially of England) and, ironically, they alienated the creoles. The reassertion of imperial control after nearly a century of lax rule angered the American Spaniards, but they were not yet ready to assert their own autonomy. Strangely enough, it was the Napoleonic invasions of Spain and Portugal in 1807–08 that forced the issue of self-rule and triggered the bloody wars for independence. Between 1808 and 1825 Spain and Portugal lost nearly all of their colonies in the Americas. By the 1830s, 18 new republics had begun to take shape (with Cuba and Panama emerging as independent nations at the turn of the twentieth century).

Part III of this history describes the efforts of these new nations to "forge a new order" in the nineteenth century. Two major political groups emerged out of the destruction of the old colonial regime: Liberals and Conservatives. The latter looked back to Spain and Portugal for guidance, holding on to hopes for a strong, centralized government, the continuing influence of the Catholic Church, an unchanging social order, and an economy that would remain highly regulated. They looked back to the past and wanted to conserve as much of the pre-independence order as possible. Their bitter antagonists, the Liberals, looked to the future—to England, France, and the United States—for their inspiration. Their heroes were the founding fathers of the United States; the ideals of liberty, fraternity, and equality; and the founders of classical liberalism: Locke, Montesquieu, Mill, and Bentham. At least in theory, they wanted decentralized government, equality in social and political relations, a free market economy, and they despised the traditional values of the Catholic Church. Throughout much of the nineteenth century, Liberals and Conservatives battled for control of the new nations, with the Liberals eventually gaining the upper hand across the region by the 1870s. In some countries, these battles wreaked havoc, destruction, and chaos. At one extreme, Mexico had 50 presidents between the1820s and the 1870s, experienced three foreign invasions, and lost half of its national territory in wars with the United States. At the other end of the political spectrum, Brazil and Chile achieved relative political stability by the 1830s and 1840s and moved forward with the process of nation-building and economic development.

The ascendancy of the Liberals in the last quarter of the nineteenth century transformed Latin America as profoundly as did the conquest of the sixteenth century. In many ways, the period was the "second conquest" of the region. The Liberals opened their nations to the international economy through the production and export of raw materials and foodstuffs: silver, copper, tin, guano, coffee, bananas, sugar, beef, and wheat (to name just a few products). After participating as subordinates in the closed Iberian economic empires for centuries, the nations of Latin America turned outward, and their insertion into the rapidly expanding Atlantic economy had profound consequences for the great masses of Latin Americans. As the demand for primary products in Europe and the United States accelerated, the production of cash crops and the extraction of raw materials in Latin America expanded, intensifying the power of large landowners and concentrating greater and greater lands and resources in the hands of a small landholding elite. The construction of railroads, telegraph lines, roads, and the expansion of shipping opened up the vast interior of Latin America to immigration, by newly arriving Europeans (especially Spaniards and Italians) and by the more

Europeanized citizens of the coastal cities. The power of the central State, along with the economic penetration, spread deep into the interior, producing a cultural and social clash between the great masses who were largely of Indian, African, and racially mixed origins, and the more European elites and their allies from the cities. From the perspective of the Europeanized elites, this was a clash between "civilization and barbarism." From the perspective of the masses of the interior it was a struggle to hold on to their lands and their way of life. The price of "progress" across Latin America in the nineteenth century was the destruction of these non-European cultures and societies. Until about 1900, many Indians, runaway slaves, and especially those of racially and culturally mixed heritage had been able to live relatively free from the ways of the "modern" world. After 1900, the inexorable pressure of European culture and civilization was inescapable.

In the aftermath of independence, Great Britain, the United States, and France quickly emerged as the most important foreign influences on Latin America. In South America, the British had a powerful financial and cultural presence. In the Caribbean, Central America, and Mexico, the United States established an equally powerful presence. French culture mesmerized nearly all Latin American elites. British influence in these regions diminished throughout the century as U.S. influence grew. The First World War would signal the decline of British influence globally, and in Latin America the United States would replace Great Britain as the dominant power in South America by the Second World War. In the Caribbean and the Gulf of Mexico the direct economic and military power of the United States became overwhelming in the first decades of the twentieth century. The United States had announced its intention to exercise power in the region with the Monroe Doctrine (1823), declaring that it would henceforth not tolerate the interference of European powers in the Americas. As the most powerful nation on the planet, England could generally ignore this U.S. declaration. The expansionism of the United States cost Mexico nearly half its territory in what is now the U.S. Southwest. The United States exploded on to the world scene in 1898 during the Spanish American War, seizing Cuba, Puerto Rico, and the Philippines from Spain. For the next four decades, the military and economic power of the United States in the Caribbean basin surged as it sent troops into Cuba, Puerto Rico, the Dominican Republic, Haiti, Nicaragua, Venezuela, and Mexico. In 1903, Theodore Roosevelt "took Panama" in order to build an interoceanic canal. South of Panama, U.S. military presence was minimal, but its financial and economic power continued to grow.

Even before the wars for independence, the cultural influence of Great Britain, the United States, and France had begun to supplant the centuries-old cultural hegemony of Spain and Portugal. In the century after independence,

British and French cultural influence grew. In most of Latin America, it would not be until after the Second World War that the United States would become the most important foreign cultural influence. For centuries, the Latin American elites had imitated and emulated the cultural values and aspirations flowing across the Atlantic from Madrid, Lisbon, London and Paris. By the end of the seventeenth century, especially in the viceregal courts in Mexico City and Lima, an "American" sense of identity had begun to emerge. By the end of the eighteenth century, cultural developments and the rising political grievances of the creoles (and their counterparts in Brazil) heightened the growing sense of identity as separate from Spain and Portugal. Increasingly, the elites (but not necessarily the great masses) saw themselves as Mexicans, Peruvians, or Brazilians even if they remained loyal Spanish or Portuguese subjects.

These elites fought for and achieved their political independence in the era of European Romanticism, an age that glorified heroic individualism, national identity, emotion, and the power of nature. As in Europe, the Latin American elites in the Age of Romanticism sought to define themselves by writing (some would say inventing) their own history and literature. In the first half of the nineteenth century, Latin American Romantic novels and historical works emulated European patterns, but gave them a special twist as they took place in American locales, with Native Americans playing a highly romanticized role in the storylines. Romanticism gave way in the last third of the century to the rise of Realism and Naturalism, again following the cultural patterns of Europe. Again, the novels and historical works sought to define national character and traditions, but not with the highly sentimentalized portrayals of the Romantics. Realist and Naturalist writers tried to depict the nitty-gritty reality of life in Latin America, and they turned to the brutality of class conflict in the cities, the exploitation of Indians and Africans in the countryside, and the clash of cultures and peoples. While the Romantics told a tale of the heroic convergence of peoples and cultures, the Realists and Naturalists painted a picture of nation-building through conflict and bloodshed.

In the last decades of the nineteenth century and the first decades of the twentieth century, parallel cultural movements known as Modernism emerged in both Spanish America and Brazil. In Spanish America this movement began in the 1860s and, once again, was imitating the latest trends in Europe, especially Paris. Its great hallmark was poetry and its greatest figure was Rubén Darío, an extraordinary Nicaraguan poet of humble origins. Harkening back to Romanticism, Spanish American Modernism emphasized emotion, spirituality, and intuition. It had run its course by the First World War. Brazilian Modernism, on the other hand, emerges about the time of the First World War and represents a turning point in Latin American cultural history. As with all these previous literary and artistic movements in Brazil, the Modernists sought to define themselves as Brazilians. Unlike previous movements, this one declared its independence from European culture. By the 1920s, the Brazilian cultural elites, and the Spanish American ones as well, had begun to see themselves as peoples of Native American and African descent as well as Europeans. They saw themselves as a unique people that blended three peoples into one new "cosmic race" (to use the words of the Mexican intellectual José Vasconcelos). Nearly a century after declaring their political independence from European colonial powers, the Latin Americans declared their cultural independence from Europe.

By the early twentieth century, the "story" of Latin America becomes more difficult to narrate. In many ways the sixteenth century is an easier task for the historian. The collision of the three great streams of peoples produced a series of patterns with many variations, but there are patterns nonetheless: conquest, colonization, the clash of cultures, the emergence of new societies. This is a story that takes shape across all of the Americas and, in this sense, all of the Americas share a common history. For the historian, then, the colonial era has a powerful coherence and unity, to a large extent created by European conquest and colonialism. By the eighteenth century, the mighty river of Latin America has already begun to branch off into many streams, and the wars for independence accelerate this process. Nevertheless, the common processes of independence, early nation-building, and entry into the international economy continue to provide the historian with a common set of themes even as the emerging nations forge increasingly divergent paths.

We can still speak of common patterns in the twentieth century in politics, economics, society, and culture, but the variations become more pronounced and the story more fragmented. Rather than try to produce an encyclopedic history of all the countries of Latin America, Part IV instead focuses on the themes of "democracy, development, and identity." Chapters 18 to 22 concentrate primarily on the theme of "hierarchy and power" as I survey two major paths in the twentieth century. In Mexico (1910), Guatemala (1944), Bolivia (1952), Cuba (1959), and Nicaragua (1979), men and women who wanted to change their nations in profound and fundamental ways attempted to destroy the old regimes and build socialist societies that would bring an end to the enormous social and economic inequities that have plagued Latin America since the Conquest. Uruguay, Argentina, Chile, and Costa Rica, on the other hand, built long-term reform processes that largely succeeded in creating societies that share many features with the social democratic movements in Western Europe. These nine cases are the clearest examples of reform and revolution in twentieth-century Latin America, and the other countries in the region follow paths that are less clearcut and more difficult to classify. The rest of the countries of Latin America have not experienced successful revolutions, and their reform movements are less successful—and less clearcut—than those in Uruguay, Argentina, Chile, and Costa Rica.

All political regimes in twentieth-century Latin America, regardless of ideological orientation, pursued paths to economic development. Economic security and "rights" have had a higher priority in Latin America than the pursuit of political rights. The heritage of agrarian economies built on the export of raw materials and foodstuffs was one of the most pronounced legacies of the nineteenth century. In the most extreme cases, Latin American economies in the early twentieth century depended almost entirely on a single crop or mineral for their success: sugar in Cuba; coffee in much of Central America, Colombia, and Brazil; tin in Bolivia; copper in Chile; wheat and beef in Argentina. These "monocultural" economies had successfully entered into the international trading system, and the revenues from exports fueled the economic growth and expansion of infrastructure all across Latin America. Yet, it also made these economies extremely vulnerable to the rise and fall of commodities prices in Europe and the United States. These economies became rollercoasters lurching up and down with the shifting demand for their products in the North Atlantic world. The Great Depression of 1929 shattered most of the economies of Latin America as the demand for the exports of the so-called economy of desserts (coffee, sugar, bananas) plummeted.

In nearly all of Latin America, most noticeably in the larger nations, political and economic elites turned the economies inward, and from the 1930s to the 1980s the general pattern in the region was one of increasing government intervention to promote diversification and industrialization. This was done through protectionism, the creation of state-controlled enterprises, and large-scale public financing of key sectors of the economy. By the 1960s this process of replacing imported manufactured goods with domestically produced ones had helped create substantial industrial parks in the larger nations—Brazil, Mexico, Argentina—and to a lesser extent in many other countries. The oil shocks of the 1970s and the debt crisis in the 1980s, however, brought an end to this half-century-old cycle. By the end of the twentieth century nearly all the nations of Latin America had made a pronounced move toward more open economies with fewer trade barriers, they had substantially reduced government intervention in the economy, and had privatized hundreds of state-controlled corporations. This return to the classical liberal economics of the early nineteenth century—free trade, reduced government intervention, laissez faire policies—became known as neo-liberal economics in Latin America (and ironically, as neo-conservative in the United States). It has been accompanied by a paradoxical parallel trend, the creation of trading blocs through regional integration: the North American Free Trade Agreement or NAFTA (Canada, U.S., Mexico); the "Southern Market" or Mercosul (Brazil, Argentina, Uruguay, Paraguay); as well as others. As nations reduce barriers to trade within their regional blocs, they make it more difficult for those nations outside the trading blocs to gain entry. For many of the smaller nations of Latin America (the Caribbean islands or the nations of Central America, for example), these regional trading blocs offer the opportunity to seek an economic future that would not be possible with their small national markets and few resources.

Despite the widespread image of Latin America as poor and underdeveloped, the region experienced impressive economic growth in the 30 years after World War II. By the 1980s, Brazil had become one of the ten largest economies in the world. Mexico and Argentina had also built substantial industrial economies, and even the smallest countries in the region had established some type of industrial base. Yet, despite the economic growth, Latin America remains a "rich land full of poor people." The persistence of pronounced socioeconomic inequities remains the most striking feature of all Latin America. Wealthy Brazil, with its enormous resources, in the 1990s had the most unequal distribution of income of any country in the world. The huge social, economic, and cultural divide between a relatively small elite and the masses of impoverished peoples that emerged out of the Iberian conquest in the sixteenth century has not only persisted for centuries, but it has also intensified. Contrary to what many would expect, economic development and the emergence of democracy in Latin America have not done much to close this enormous social and economic divide. It has been one of the most powerful constants in Latin American history across the constantly changing political and economic regimes.

By the early twenty-first century, however, the enormous racial and cultural diversity of Latin America has also been reinforced by a growing economic diversity. The industrial economies of Brazil and Mexico, for example, are in a different economic universe from the (still) impoverished agrarian economies of Haiti or Honduras. Chile, Argentina, Uruguay, and Costa Rica (societies that are overwhelmingly of European descent) have attenuated the socioeconomic divide more successfully than most of the nations of Latin America. The large indigenous populations of Guatemala, Ecuador, Peru, and Bolivia, on the other hand, continue to face grinding poverty and discrimination. These diverse nations have emerged out of five centuries of common historical processes and patterns, yet each now pursues its own identity and distinctiveness. Most of the peoples of these traditional 20 nations, and many others beyond their borders, see themselves as "Latin Americans." At the beginning of the twenty-first century, close to half a billion people identify themselves as participants and the descendants of a common history and heritage.

This is seen most clearly in the vibrant and influential literature that has come out of Latin America in the second half of the twentieth century. By the 1960s and 1970s the so-called "boom" in Latin American literature made it the most influential in the world. Writers like Jorge Luis Borges (Argentina), Mario Vargas Llosa (Peru), Octavio Paz (Mexico), Gabriel García Márquez (Colombia), and Alejo Carpentier (Cuba) forged a literature that was both self-consciously Latin American and universal. By the end of the twentieth century, Latin Americans no longer sought to define themselves through cultural models imported from Europe and the United States. Instead, they redefined world culture by grappling with the meaning of the collision of three peoples in the Americas. In each country and region of Latin America, writers, artists, and composers created new cultural contributions that had their roots in the collisions that began in the late fifteenth century.

At the beginning of the twentieth century, Latin America does have a common history and, perhaps, a common future. The processes of collision, conquest, and colonization that began in 1492 defined the region, and continue to provide it with common roots. Yet, more than 500 years of historical processes in this vast region have also produced 20 very different nations (and Puerto Rico) and emigrants beyond their borders who stretch the boundaries and reach of Latin America. In spite of their shared roots, Argentina today looks very little like Guatemala, and Costa Rica is a world apart from Brazil. These diverging paths will be even more pronounced when other historians attempt to survey the region at the beginning of the twenty-second century. Yet, despite these increasing differences, Latin America today shares a common present, one that is more democratic and participatory than at any time in its history. For all its flaws, the pursuit of democracy, social justice, cultural pluralism, and economic development in Latin America is stronger than ever before. The drive for regional economic integration, ironically, may run counter to diverging cultural and social trajectories. If regional integration continues, we may one day see that Latin America—indeed, all of the Americas—will have not only a common past, but also a common future.

Part I

Three Peoples Converge

1

The Lay of the Land—and the Water

Tens of millions of years before the dramatic clashes of peoples that gave birth to Latin American cultures and societies, the almost imperceptible collisions of enormous tectonic plates forged the landmasses of what we now call the Americas. The physical features of Mexico, Central America, the Caribbean, and South America have emerged out of the encounters of six massive tectonic slabs or plates drifting imperceptibly across the surface of the Earth. For hundreds of millions of years the landmasses that we recognize today as continents have been slowly migrating across the face of the Earth—separating, drifting, and colliding. Around 600 million years ago, "South America" lay on the opposite side of the globe in an "upside-down" position, forming part of a collection of landmasses known to geologists as Gondwanaland. Some 400 million years later, all of the modern continents had rammed together, creating a single landmass known as Pangea. What today is the northeastern "bulge" of Brazil jutting into the Atlantic was nestled up against the lands that now constitute the coast of the Bight of Benin in West Africa, and the southern coastline of South America stretched out alongside the African coastline from modern-day Nigeria to South Africa. "North America" was nestled up against the northwestern coast of the African continent and southwestern Europe, at the entrance of what today is the Mediterranean.

At the end of the geological age known as the Jurassic period (about 135 to 100 million years ago), the North American and South American landmasses had begun to slide to the west as Pangea gradually split apart. The space between the two continents opened up, initiating the formation of what would become the Gulf of Mexico and the North Atlantic Ocean. As South America and Africa separated, the South Atlantic also began to take shape. Between 90 and 60 million years ago, North and South America had begun to move closer together, near their present locations. As the two enormous plates migrated westward, they collided with the Cocos Plate in the gap between the two continents. This geological confrontation thrust the islands of the Greater Antilles upward, in the region now occupied by Central America. The Cocos Plate continued pressing up against the North American and Caribbean Plates while sliding down and under the Caribbean Plate to the east. This collision sheared apart the largest piece of the Greater Antilles, creating Cuba and Hispaniola and gradually pushed the islands into their present locations. It also thrust upward Central America as a land bridge between North and South America, while forming the Gulf of Mexico and the Caribbean Sea. As these three plates pushed up against each other, they also created a series of volcanic arcs along their edges, through southern Mexico, Central America, and across the Lesser Antilles. The colliding plates produced a violent venting of molten magma creating the classic volcanic cones in central Mexico—Orizaba, Popocatepetl, and Ixtacihuatl—rising some 17,000 to 19,000 feet above sea level.

The collision of tectonic plates was even more violent in western South America. Beginning about 15 million years ago, and continuing for some 10 million years, the Nazca Plate pushed eastward up against the South American Plate, creating extraordinary volcanic activity that gave birth to the various ranges of the Andes along the length of western South America. This continuing collision warped, folded, and thrust the crust of the Earth upward, forming spectacular mountains second only to the Himalayas in altitude. The Andean range is rarely more than 200 miles wide (except in Bolivia where its width doubles), and the highest peaks range from 18,000 to nearly 23,000 feet. (Mt. Aconcagua on the Argentine-Chilean border is the highest peak in the Americas at 22,835 feet above sea level.) The continuing eastward movement of the Cocos, Nazca, and Antarctic Plates up against the west coast of Latin America produces constant volcanic instability from Mexico to southern Chile. The earthquakes that have devastated Latin American cities since the sixteenth century are but the most recent episodes in millions of years of geological instability produced by the continuing movement of these plates.

When the human species began to emerge hundreds of thousands of years ago, the shifting tectonic plates had already given form to the continents as we know them today. The Americas, North and South, are two enormous landmasses (stretching from nearly the North to the South Pole) connected by the Central American isthmus and the islands of the Caribbean. Each continent covers about eight million square miles, and combined they account for one-quarter of the Earth's land surface. They are separated from Asia by the vast Pacific Ocean, except at the northernmost point where the narrow stretch of waters in the Bering Strait flows between Siberia and Alaska. For millions of years the equally enormous Atlantic Ocean formed a formidable barrier between the Americas, Europe, and Africa, with the large islands of Greenland and Iceland serving as stepping stones across the waters in the far north.

Today, Latin America spans some 7,000 miles (roughly the distance from northern Finland to South Africa) from the Rio Grande to Cape Horn, across more than 60 degrees of latitude. Most of the people in the region, however, live in the 40 degrees of latitude between the Tropic of Cancer and the Tropic of Capricorn. (The tropics in the Americas are called the "neotropics" by scientists.) At its widest east-west axis, from Peru to the Brazilian bulge, South America spans some 3,200 miles (roughly the distance from San Francisco to Nova Scotia). As Jared Diamond has pointed out in his Pulitzer-prize-winning book *Guns, Germs, and Steel*, the enormous extension of Latin America (and Africa) on a north-south axis across such great distances has profoundly shaped its history and development. The vast, hot lowlands of Central and South America acted as barriers to the spread of crops and livestock as they were domesticated in the temperate uplands of central Mexico and the Andes. Unlike the peoples of Europe, the United States, and the core of Asia, the peoples of Latin America and Africa have had to contend with much greater diversity in their environments, and greater challenges to movement across these environments. The end result in both Africa and the Americas was the much later and slower development and diffusion of agriculture capable of sustaining more complex societies and civilizations. The peoples of the Northern Hemisphere, especially in the Old World and in North America, have moved along an east-west axis through roughly similar climatic zones, facilitating the spread of "development" (to use a modern term).

The enormous geological and latitude range have shaped the formation of a wide variety of geographic and climatic zones across Latin America. Geographers have divided up the region into Middle America (Mexico, Central America, and the West Indies) and South America. (To be very precise, geographically, North America ends at the Isthmus of Tehuantepec in Southern Mexico and South America begins at the Isthmus of Panama, with Central America in between.) The two most impressive physical features of all the Americas are enormous mountains and large river systems. From the Alaskan Arctic down through the western United States, Mexico, Central America, and western South America, two lines of mountain ranges—thrust upward from the age-old pressure of the Pacific tectonic plates pressing up against the continents—form the backbone of the Americas, North and South. In the western United States and Mexico, the Rocky Mountains and the Sierra Madre Mountains define much of the region. Between the Rockies and the Pacific Mountains along the West Coast are plateaus and desert basins extending from Canada down into central Mexico, wrapping around the Sierra Madres. Several smaller mountain ranges through southern Mexico and Central America dominate the landscape. Geological instability and frequent volcanic activity have scarred the region and made its peoples "sons and daughters of the shaking earth" (to steal Eric Wolf's beautiful phrase). The Andean chain of mountains has two branches in northern South America, one beginning in Panama and the other in western Venezuela. Both converge in central Colombia and two roughly parallel ranges extend down through Ecuador, Peru, Bolivia, western Argentina, and Chile. Although there are true coastal lowlands in western Colombia and Ecuador, the coastal plain from northern Peru to southern Chile is often very narrow and arid. In contrast with the young and rugged Andes, the eastern highlands of South America are old and worn down. The Amazon basin splits them into two large pieces. To the north are the Guiana Highlands or Shield, and to the south the highlands that cover much of eastern Brazil. Both sets of mountains gradually decline in altitude as they move inland, eventually disappearing into the Amazonian lowlands. At their highest points (in the east), the Guiana and Brazilian Highlands reach only a few thousand feet above sea level.

If the Pacific mountain ranges form the backbone of Latin America, the great river systems are its arteries. Stretching more than 4,000 miles from its source in the Peruvian Andes until it empties into the Atlantic, the Amazon is the greatest of all the rivers of the Americas, dwarfing even the mighty Mississippi River. More than 15 miles across at some points, it reaches depths of 250 feet, deeper than any other river in the world. The early explorers were so impressed with this river, with its volume of water eight times that of the Mississippi, that they called it a river-sea. The Amazon River Valley consists of some 25,000 miles of rivers and streams draining much of the interior of South America. With the Andes to the west, and the Guiana and Brazilian Highlands to the northeast and southeast, the Amazon is something of a giant funnel system channeling waters from the interior into the equatorial Atlantic. To the north and south of the Amazon lie two more great river systems, the Orinoco and the Paraná-Paraguay. Both river systems originate in the interior of the continent. The Orinoco winds eastward through northern South America for some 1600 miles, emptying into the Atlantic on the northeastern coast via an enormous delta that begins some 250 miles inland. The Paraná-Paraguay basin drains the interior of South America and spans parts of Bolivia, Brazil, Paraguay, Argentina, and Uruguay. The two rivers converge near the Argentine city of Corrientes, eventually joining the Río de la Plata and then flowing into the South Atlantic. Unlike the Mississippi in temperate North America, these three great river systems of South America have been sparsely inhabited and undeveloped tropical frontiers for centuries. The great rivers of South America have never been the thriving transportation axes of development like the Mississippi, the Nile, the Yangtze, or the Indus. Equally important, the great population centers of Latin America since pre-Columbian times—Mexico, Central America, the Andes—have no significant river systems. It is one of the great ironies of the geography of Latin America that where there are great rivers there are few people, and where there are many people there are no great rivers.

The densest populations in Latin America developed in the temperate highlands of central Mexico and the Andes. In central Mexico, civilization emerged in the valleys at altitudes of 6,000 to 9,000 feet. In the Andes, populations were much more fragmented in the mountain valleys with the high plain (*altiplano*) in Bolivia bordering Lake Titicaca playing a role similar to the Valley of Mexico. The *altiplano*, however, is above 10,000 feet and much colder and more arid than the Valley of Mexico. The cool highlands of Mexico and the Andes became the two great centers for the emergence of agriculture in the New World with the domestication of maize in Mesoamerica and the potato in the Andes. The tropical lowlands of eastern South America produced the third area where food production arose independently, in this case, around the domestication of the tuber known as manioc or cassava. Despite the dispersal of food cultivation across much of tropical America, the lowlands of South America never developed dense populations. The interior lowlands of South America form its "empty heart," in the words of one geographer. In pre-Columbian times, much of the interior lowlands and the coastal plains of eastern South America were covered by forest and jungle, as was much of the Caribbean basin, both the islands and the coastal mainland.

While latitude and altitude contribute to the great diversity of climatic zones in Latin America, this variety is also shaped by wind systems and the influence of the surrounding oceans and seas. In the lowland tropical regions the general rule is high rainfall and hot temperatures, with little variation in temperature range. Despite its popular image, temperatures in the Amazon average only in the high eighties, and rarely fluctuate more than ten degrees higher or lower. The temperature range is much greater in the mountains, dropping to freezing levels on the Bolivian *altiplano*. As one old saying goes, "Night is the winter of the tropics." The warm South Equatorial Current feeds into the Caribbean Sea and the Gulf of Mexico, helping create hot cauldrons of water. As the northeast trade winds sweep across the Caribbean from June to October, the air becomes hot, moist, and volatile, creating the hurricanes that plague the region. The hot, moist air masses moving into South America from the equatorial Atlantic provide the enormous rainfall that characterizes the Amazon River Valley. Moderate ocean temperatures in the South Atlantic help create subtropical to warm temperatures through southern Brazil, Paraguay, Uruguay, and northern Argentina. In the Pacific, contending currents clash. The Equatorial Counter Current flows eastward before splitting north toward Central America and south toward Ecuador and Peru. It brings warm, moist air and rain to southern Central America. From the north, the cool California Current helps insure moderate temperatures in western Mexico. From the south, the cold Peru Current flows upward from Chile. As the mild winds from the south Pacific pass over this cold water, they cannot absorb moisture and the result is arid conditions along the South American coast. In the Atacama Desert in northern Chile, there are areas where no rainfall has ever been recorded. Every three to seven years, the ocean along the western coast of South America reaches unusually warm levels, normally beginning around December. Known as El Niño ("the Christ child"), this warming reverses normal wind flows and brings enormous rainfall and flooding to South America, especially the desert regions of Peru.

The enormous variations in latitude, altitude, rainfall, and temperature have produced an astonishing array of flora and fauna throughout Latin America. In the tropical lowlands of the Caribbean and eastern South America, the change of "seasons" is largely confined to a wet season and a dry season, creating lush and fertile environments for flora that flourish year-round. The tropical forests of Amazonia are home to the most diverse collection of plant and animal species on the planet. At the other extreme, the deserts of northern Mexico and the Pacific coast of South America are arid and hostile to the proliferation of both flora and fauna. These deserts, however, have some of the richest mineral deposits in the world, including silver, nitrates, and copper. Altitude shapes the ecology of the mountains. At higher elevations in the Andes, the terrain is barren and arid. In both Mesoamerica and the Andes, civilizations have flourished at altitudes from 3,000 to 13,000 feet, exploiting the rich volcanic soils of Central America and the melting snow in the Andes. In some mountainous regions (like Costa Rica), tropical latitudes and altitude have produced an enormous array of ecological zones in very small areas. Costa Rica is home to about 800 species of birds, more species than are found in all of North America.

Geography and geological history, especially the isolation of the New World from the Old, have also profoundly shaped the flora and fauna of Latin America. When the Europeans arrived in 1492, the Americas had no cattle, horses, oxen, or camels—in short, no significant beasts of burden. (A species of prehistoric horse had died out thousands of years before 1492.) The alpacas and llamas of the Andes were the closest thing to a beast of burden, but ones that refuse to carry more than 80 kilograms. The largest beasts in Latin America were tapirs in the tropical lowlands. Jaguars and mountain lions were the largest predators. Over thousands of years, the crops emerged that would feed most Native Americans, and that were native only to the Americas: maize in Mesoamerica, cassava in the Caribbean and Amazonian lowlands, the potato in the Andes. Chile peppers, pineapples, cacao (chocolate), and tobacco are just a few of the American flora that were unknown in the Old World. (Imagine an Old World before 1492 with no tobacco, no chocolate, and no readily available form of sugar!)

Just as it is difficult to speak of Latin America as a cultural unit, the extraordinary diversity of climates, geographic zones, and physical features make the region even more complex. Again, although geography is not destiny, we should keep in mind the underlying geographical features of the various regions of Latin America as its history unfolds. Small tropical islands, for example, will operate under serious constraints, compared to the fertile lands of southern South America or the enormous mineral resources of Mexico. These very diverse geographical and geological features played, and continue to play, a key role in the development and underdevelopment of the countries of Latin America.

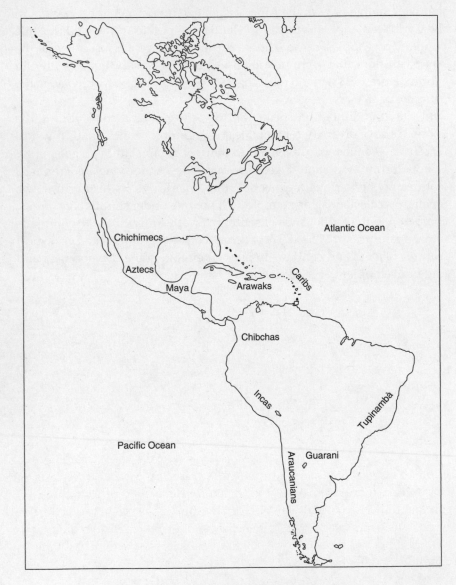

Map 2. Major Indigenous Groups before 1492

2

American Peoples and Cultures

The "first Americans" arrived in a series of migrations from the Asian continent across the Bering Strait possibly as far back as 40,000 years ago. The last wave of migrants was the Eskimo, or Inuit, who traveled across the frozen expanses of the Arctic about 4,000 years ago. Archaeologists have long debated the dates of the earliest arrivals, with more traditional and conservative scholars arguing against any clear proof of migration before about 12,000 years ago. Although not an archaeologist, I believe there is growing and convincing evidence, especially from Chile, that the dates should be pushed back to at least 20,000 years ago. All agree, however, that by 10,000 years ago humans occupied most of the Americas from Canada to Tierra del Fuego. The islands of the Caribbean and the plains of southern South America were probably the last major regions to be populated, only about 2,000 years before the arrival of Columbus. In contrast to the striking diversity of their languages and cultures, Native Americans were extraordinarily homogenous in genetic or biological terms. (The blood type of most Native Americans, for example, is O, a type common to more than 80 percent of them.) For reasons that are not entirely clear, these early migrants did not bring with them the diseases of the Old World. (Some have hypothesized that the cold Arctic passage served as a sort of "filter," killing off dangerous microbes.) None of the Native American populations had exposure to diseases that ravaged the Old World: influenza, smallpox, measles, malaria, yellow fever, plague, typhus. For this lack of exposure and immunity, they would pay a very high price during the European invasion and conquest.

We do not know with any great certainty how many people lived in the Americas in 1492. A long and ongoing debate has led to widely divergent estimates of the indigenous population prior to the European conquest. Estimates range from as low as 25 million to as high as 125 million. Most specialists would probably put the figure somewhere around 50 to 75 million. The most densely populated regions were Mesoamerica (central Mexico to northern Costa Rica), with a population possibly as high as 25 to 30 million, and the Andes, with some 10 to 15 million inhabitants. Estimates for other regions are highly unreliable and largely guesses. For 1550, for example, the usual guesses are from one to five million people in North America and the same estimate for Brazil. At the moment of European contact, over 350 major tribal groups, divided into more than 150 major linguistic groups, spread across the Americas.

When Columbus arrived in the Caribbean in1492, he believed that he had reached the "Indies," something of a generic term for Asia in his day. He called the natives *"indios"* and this word stuck, entering into the vocabulary of many languages. The term "Native Americans" has gained wide accep-tance in the last few decades, but it is also problematic. The term "America" is also Eurocentric. It is a name given to the New World by a German cartog-rapher in the early sixteenth century to honor Amerigo Vespucci, one of the best-known early explorers. I will use these terms interchangeably. Most native groups before the Conquest simply called themselves "the people" and they saw the rest of the peoples around them as the "Other," to use the parlance of contemporary academics. There is no "politically correct" term to employ here. One of the most radical groups of the 1970s, for example, was called the American Indian Movement. One growing movement now pro-motes the term "indigenous peoples." From my perspective, it is one of the great ironies of the early twenty-first century that the term "Indian" has now become a generic label adopted by native peoples all across the Americas to create a sense of solidarity. In effect, they have accepted the lumping of all native peoples together, something the Europeans artificially did in the sixteenth century to peoples with no sense of common identity or solidarity.

Although this is the standard story of the peopling of the Americas, controversies have challenged this narrative in recent decades. Some (most prominently, Ivan van Sertima, a linguist at Rutgers University) have argued for the key role of African migrants in the rise of American civiliza-tions. Others (such as the Scandinavian anthropologist, Thor Heyerdahl) have made the case for transpacific voyages. Ironically, the trouble with these theories is that they produce a mirror image of the racism of the nineteenth-century European scholars who attempted to explain the origins of the great pre-Columbian ruins of Mesoamerica and the Andes in this way. They believed that the native peoples of the Americas were too ignorant and unfit to have produced what were clearly the remains of incredibly sophisticated civilizations. They theorized that these cultures must have originated from transatlantic voyages by the Greeks, the Egyptians, or the lost tribes of Israel. The theories that Africans provided the origins of the great Native American civilizations make the same mistake, reversing the racial bias of the nineteenth century from "white" to "black." Those who would argue that the great American civilizations arise from a black African origin make the same assumption that the Native Americans were incapable of creating these great cultures on their own.

More significantly, recent archaeological finds have pushed back the dates of first occupation and raised interesting possibilities of transoceanic contacts. More and more finds, such as those at Monte Verde in Chile, and the discovery of skeletal remains in the state of Washington, make it harder and harder to hold to the Asiatic immigrants after 12,000 B.C. theory. Clearly, the dates are going to be pushed back, and there is growing evidence for the presence of non-Asiatic influences and genes. Nevertheless, I will stand by the gist of the traditional explanation. I still believe that the Asian migrants formed the basic genetic stock of the Native Americans, but there probably were some transoceanic contacts. They were just not fundamental to cultural developments. I believe that these transoceanic arrivals were not only possible, but that some did make the voyages. There was not, however, a back and forth exchange. The (very small) traffic was all "inbound."

VARIETIES OF CULTURES

An amazing array of cultures and peoples emerged in the Americas before 1492, and there are many different frameworks for grouping Native American peoples. Some of the most important have divided these peoples by language groups, levels of political organization, or by their relationships to ecological systems. Using language groups is fairly non-controversial, but it does not tell us much about differences among the many diverse peoples. We need to categorize so we can differentiate among the many cultures, but we must be very careful not to fall into the dangerous moral judgments of the nineteenth century that assumed some sort of moral superiority for the more highly organized groups. Looking at the complexity of political organization tells us a great deal about differences, but does not necessarily lead us to judgments of moral superiority or inferiority. One of the great advantages of the ecological analysis is that it divides peoples up by how they respond to their environments, and provides us with useful ways to understand varying levels of social, economic, and political organization.

I will use a simple scheme, first suggested by the eminent historian James Lockhart, that divides all the native peoples into three basic types.

The first of these groups is "nonsedentary" or nomadic peoples. These are very small groups that live by hunting and gathering. With few members, they do not produce a surplus of food. These tribes cannot develop even the most basic social divisions: gender roles, age divisions, someone recognized for their special religious powers, such as a shaman. Good examples of nonsedentary peoples are the Cheyenne and Apaches of the Great Plains of North America and the Gê peoples in the forests and prairies of eastern South America.

"Semisedentary" peoples settle for periods in a single location, but then move on to new lands. They develop some limited knowledge of domesticating animals and growing crops. They may have dogs, or herding animals, and basic knowledge about planting some crops. This rudimentary form of agriculture produces a small surplus. "Slash-and-burn" agriculture is typical of many semisedentary peoples. Sometimes called swidden agriculture, it involves clearing the forest with stone tools, and then burning everything. This is, on a small scale, the same procedure employed on a massive scale in Amazonia today to deforest the region. The ash serves as fertilizer, but after a couple of seasons the poor tropical soils force the tribes to move on and repeat the process. In an era of small, widely dispersed tribes, the forest eventually grows back and the millions of acres of tropical forest could support slash-and-burn indefinitely. Even this low level of agricultural productivity frees some to engage in activities other than food production. Tribes can grow into the hundreds, with many families and large huts. Groups sometimes grow large enough to split or fission into two separate groups. The division of labor becomes more complex, but still limited to hunters, those who tend the crops (generally women), and those with special religious duties. Good examples of semisedentary peoples are the Tupí, who once inhabited the long coastal region of Brazil, and the peoples of the Brazilian rain forest who continue to live this way. The Yanomami, who today straddle the Brazilian-Venezuelan border, are perhaps the most famous example. They provide us with a glimpse of how many of the native peoples of lowland regions probably lived for thousands of years.

"Sedentary" peoples, as the name suggests, are rooted in a single place on a permanent basis. These are cultures that have mastered the domestication of plants and animals. They joined the exclusive group of peoples in the Old World who moved into sophisticated manipulation of their surrounding environment. Unlike those in the Old World, however, the sedentary peoples of the Americas had no large beasts of burden—no horses, oxen, water buffalo, or pack animals. (As Jared Diamond has pointed out, this absence of large domesticated animals also probably shielded the Native Americans from the kinds of diseases that developed in the Old World. Smallpox, plague, and the like seem to have arisen in domesticated animals and then spread to the domesticators.) The development of more accomplished agriculture allows the population of sedentary peoples to grow and to develop very complex social structures. Rather than remaining in the hundreds, tribes could grow into the thousands and tens of thousands with the production of greater and greater surpluses of food. As in industrial societies today, greater productivity per farmer freed more and more people to leave farming and engage in a wide array of non-food-producing activities.

Although the most sophisticated of these sedentary peoples had complex social structures and urban centers, I should emphasize that (as in Europe) the vast majority of the people continued to live on the land in the countryside. But the shift to settled agriculture was a revolutionary one, just as it had been in the Old World. Some good examples of these sedentary peoples are the tribes in the eastern woodlands of North America, or the Arawaks in the Caribbean. Agriculture had developed enough in these regions to produce networks of villages and tribes. Although not as complex as the three greatest empires in the Americas, these societies did form chiefdoms and confederations that enlarged their power and ability to make war and dominate others. When Columbus arrived in the Caribbean, it was large villages and chiefdoms that he encountered, peoples in between the great empires, on the one hand, and hunters and gatherers, on the other.

HIGH CIVILIZATIONS: MAYAS, AZTECS, INCAS

The most highly developed of the sedentary peoples were the Mayas, Aztecs, and Incas. The first to develop were the Mayas, who reached two "peaks" (A.D. 250–900 and A.D. 1200–1450) in two different areas of Mesoamerica. As with all great civilizations, although the eventual focal point of development was in a particular region (southern Mexico, Guatemala, Honduras, and El Salvador) the Maya arose out of the convergence and borrowing over centuries of many techniques and practices in Mesoamerica. The great "mother" culture of Mesoamerica was that of the Olmecs, who flourished along the Gulf of Mexico from about 1200 to 400 B.C. Many of the peoples of Mesoamerica inherited from the Olmecs their religious traditions, notions of time, and artistic styles. After the decline of the Olmecs, and up until around A.D. 900, central Mexico became a powerful cultural influence across the region, first from the great city of Teotihuacan (on the outskirts of present-day Mexico City) and then Tula, the home of the Toltecs.

What is perhaps most striking about the Maya is how intensively they exploited the extremely inhospitable lowland forests of Guatemala and southern Mexico. In contrast to the great river civilizations of the Middle East and Asia, the Maya overcame extraordinary ecological challenges to create a very sophisticated and productive agriculture that was the key to their development. The Aztecs (central Mexico) and the Incas (Ecuador, Peru, Bolivia) were late bloomers, emerging as impressive empires in the fifteenth century. In each case, the focal point of development was eventually at altitudes above 7,000 to 8,000 feet and through the harnessing of waters from lakes and mountain streams and rivers. For both the Aztecs and the Incas, the empires were the culmination of centuries of agricultural and cultural developments. All three civilizations (Aztecs, Incas, Maya) shared common features: highly sophisticated irrigation and farming, complex social and cultural organization, sophisticated calendar and astronomical knowledge, highly developed religions, and militant ideologies of conquest and empire-building. When the Europeans encountered the Aztecs and the Incas, they confronted peoples who were their equals in nearly all realms of life.

The earliest Americans had begun to make tools and settle into villages by 8000 B.C., in the period often called Paleo-Indian (just a fancy way of saying "old Indian"!) or the Archaic. Unlike the people of the Old World, the peoples of the Americas had no large draft animals (except the rather finicky llamas and alpacas in the Andes), and they never developed the use of the wheel, plows, iron, or the so-called true keystone arch. The earliest tools that appear are named after the site of Clovis, New Mexico, where archaeologists first found them. During several thousand years, humans spread out across all of the Americas, living largely by hunting, fishing, and gathering. From about 8000 to 2500 B.C., in the Archaic period, we see the first signs of agriculture, simple pottery, and the domestication of maize and the potato.

At least four places emerge as centers for the development of agriculture in the Americas: Mesoamerica, the Andes, Amazonia, and possibly in the Caribbean basin. Over the next two thousand years, the cultures that form the basis of the great civilizations begin to take shape in Mesoamerica and the Andes, with the origins of sophisticated agriculture, social stratification, and the emergence of the first great ceremonial centers.

Agriculture was the key to the emergence of complex civilizations in the Americas, just as it was in the Old World in China, India, Egypt, and Mesopotamia. These cultures not only developed sophisticated means of domesticating plants and animals; they also developed elaborate systems of irrigation that formed the backbone of the emerging states and empires. Water is the key to agriculture, and control of water requires increasingly sophisticated organization of people and political power. In central Mexico this meant controlling the waters of Lake Texcoco around what became the Aztec capital of Tenochtitlan. In the Andean world it meant controlling the water coming down out of the high mountains. In the words of a famous scholar of the 1950s, Karl Wittfogel, these were "hydraulic" civilizations. The central crops were maize in Mesoamerica and potatoes in the Andes. Both are indigenous to the Americas and today form two of the four major crops that feed the vast majority of the world's population. (The other two are Old World crops—rice and wheat.) In the Caribbean basin and lowland South America, the main crop was a tuber that went by many names and varieties: yucca, manioc, or cassava. The peoples of Mesoamerica also domesticated cacao (chocolate), various squashes and chilis, and pineapple, all crops that did not exist in the Old World.

As we have seen, the Maya were the first of these three great civilizations to emerge. Maya civilization was, in reality, a series of city-states and empires that rose and fell over nearly 2000 years. Unlike the Aztecs and the Incas, the Maya never constructed a unified and extensive empire. Across Mesoamerica, several key cultures emerged in the formative or pre-Classic period from 2500 B.C. to A.D. 250. During this era, the Maya developed a sedentary society around sophisticated agriculture and the domestication of plants and animals. They also developed fine pottery, weaving, and stone work. The first great ceremonial centers emerged, especially in the central highlands of Guatemala. With their linear and angular architecture, these centers became the origins of Maya city-states. An intensive agriculture made possible the rise of urban centers that contained upwards of 50,000 inhabitants. As in Spain and Portugal, Maya society was built on hierarchy and inequality, with a small class of nobles and an enormous class of commoners who lived and worked on the land. Like the Old World societies, the Maya had a complex social hierarchy based on wealth, prestige, and family lineage. Slavery was also a part of Maya society, especially the enslavement of war captives.

The first Maya civilization reached full development during the Classic period, from about A.D. 250 to 900. All the accomplishments for which the Maya are known flourished during these centuries. This is the era of the great explosion of artistic, intellectual, and architectural endeavors. In particular, building on the achievements of the Olmecs, the Maya developed an impressive astronomical knowledge that rivaled that of the Old World, and a form of mathematics based on a vigesimal system (based on the number 20, not 10). The Maya had two calendars that moved in sync over centuries. One was a solar calendar divided into 18 months with 20 days each, concluding with 5 days of dread and uncertainty at the end of each year. The other was divided into 13 months with 20 days each. These calendars began at the same mythical moment of origin, and every 52 (365-day) solar years, both ended at the same time in a period of tremendous uncertainty and foreboding. In addition, the Maya maintained what archaeologists have dubbed a "long count" calendar that began at the moment of creation—3114 B.C. on the Christian calendar. The Maya also developed a writing system, which was rare among the native peoples of the Americas. Based on a system of glyphs, most surviving examples are carved into the stone monuments of Mesoamerica, and these public statements provide us with an official history of Maya nobles and kings. The Spanish systematically hunted down and destroyed Maya "books" during the sixteenth century and only four of these have survived.

Perhaps the most famous symbols of this era are the restored ruins of great pyramids and palaces where the nobles and priests staged elaborate religious and political rituals. Most striking are the steeply stepped pyramids with their temples at the top. Amazingly, the Maya built these great stone cities with no beasts of burden and no metal tools. The exploitation of human labor must have been enormous. The partially restored ruins at Tikal in Guatemala and Palenque in southern Mexico are prime examples of the power and glory of the massive Maya structures. Only three of the pyramids in the region have yielded royal tombs. Bloodletting and drug-induced trances were central to the religious worldview of the Maya, and these temples served as the primary locus of religious ritual and cosmology. Some of the most powerful scenes from surviving paintings and carvings show Maya nobles drawing blood through the ritual mutilation of their own tongues and genitals. This sacrificial blood offered to the gods helped keep the great cycle of life moving forward.

One of the great mysteries of pre-Columbian America is the collapse of Classic civilizations all across Mesoamerica around A.D. 900. Scholars have suggested a variety of causes: disease, ecological disaster, and war, but none has achieved any kind of consensus. After the demise of the great city-states across Mesoamerica, another great Maya civilization emerges in the lowlands of the Yucatán peninsula and northern Guatemala after A.D. 1200 and collapses in the mid-1400s. In the so-called Post-Classic period, we see the rise of the great city-states such as Chichén Itzá and Uxmal in northern Guatemala and the Yucatán. These cities and their architecture have clear influences from the Classic cultures of central Mexico, the most visible example being the presence of the "feathered serpent" known as Kukulkán in the Yucatán and Quetzalcóatl in central Mexico. The most powerful of these city-states was Mayapán, which was at the peak of its power from around A.D. 1200 to 1450. This second great Maya period, however, ended nearly a half-century before the arrival of the Spanish invaders, probably a victim of intense civil wars among competing city-states. With their sophisticated knowledge of astronomy, mathematics, calendars, and a writing system, the Maya are perhaps the most impressive of the three high civilizations of the Americas. Yet, the lack of any overarching imperial authority after 1450 left the Maya much more dispersed and decentralized than the Incas or the Aztecs. Ironically, this may have made them more difficult to conquer than their other two counterparts.

The Aztecs emerge late in the post-Classic period (A.D. 900–1500) in the Valley of Mexico. They built on the great cultural accomplishments of the Maya and other Mesoamerican peoples. In particular, they consciously traced their lineage back to the Toltecs of Tula, a city that sat on the periphery of the Valley of Mexico. Toltec power had peaked around the year A.D. 1000 under the ruler Quetzalcóatl. In Aztec cosmology, Quetzalcóatl was expelled from Tula and he was expected to return some day to reclaim his kingdom. (The year of his expected return in the Aztec calendar coincided with the year 1519 on the Christian calendar.) The Toltec state collapsed in the twelfth century, but its influence was widespread across central Mexico. The Aztecs probably arrived in the region at about the time of the collapse of Toltec power. They were a nomadic people who settled around a lake in the Valley of Mexico in the twelfth century. As the old founding myth goes, they left their original homeland of Aztlan (probably in what would become the Southwest of the United States) and their gods had instructed them to settle when they found an eagle perched on a cactus with a serpent in his beak. (This is now the symbol on the Mexican flag.) After serving as mercenaries, they forged alliances with other cities around the marshy lake and began to build their own center, Tenochtitlan, on an island in the lake in the mid-fourteenth century. (Speaking Nahuatl, these people are more accurately known as the Mexica or Nahuas, but I will use their more familiar name here. The region the Spanish would eventually refer to as Mexico was the homeland of the Mexica.) In the fifteenth century under Itzcoatl, they began to expand outwards, forging a "triple alliance" with the nearby cities of Texcoco and Tlacopan. Eventually, they reduced their two allies to subordinates and within fifty years conquered nearly all of central Mexico from coast to coast. Only a few peoples managed to resist domination, most notably the Tlaxcalans to the east of Tenochtitlan. Unlike the Incas, the Aztecs did not develop an extensive bureaucratic system. They preferred to extract tribute and to let local rulers serve as their intermediaries. As they became increasingly powerful in the fifteenth century, they destroyed their old histories and rewrote their "official" history to link their origins directly to the celebrated Toltecs.

Their complex religion required them to offer fresh human blood to appease the war god, Huitzilopochtli (often translated as "hummingbird on the left" or "hummingbird from the south"). In the Aztec worldview, Huitzilopochtli and the warrior sun, Tonatiuh, are engaged in a perpetual struggle against the stars. To fuel this fight, and to keep the sun moving across the sky each day, Huizilopochtli and Tonatiuh require fresh human blood. The pursuit of blood from larger and larger numbers of sacrificial victims both drives and accompanies empire-building. When the great pyramid in Tenochtitlan was dedicated in 1487, the Aztecs are believed to have ritually slaughtered as many as twenty thousand victims. The empire reached its peak in the early sixteenth century under Montezuma II, who ascended to the throne in 1502.

As in other major civilizations, intensive agriculture made the growth and diversification of their society possible. Through the construction of extensive dams, canals, and flood channels, the Aztecs harnessed the waters of the Valley of Mexico. In the surrounding lakes they developed a system of "gardens" that were, in effect, fertile patches of land built up by filling in small sections of the lake with soil and vegetation. These patches (or *chinampas*) were built in gridlike patterns with canals running through them. Perhaps as many as one hundred thousand farmers worked in the *chinampas* by the time of the Conquest. The highly productive agriculture of the Valley of Mexico and the spoils of empire fueled the growth of Tenochtitlan. By 1519 the city had perhaps a quarter of a million inhabitants. Massive stone temples rose above the central plaza and eight major canals crisscrossed the city. A series of major causeways connected the island capital with the lakeshores to the north, west, and south.

The Incas also emerged as a great empire in the fifteenth century. The development of the Inca empire parallels many of the developments in Mesoamerica. Several cultures developed in the two millennia before the Incas and contributed to the key elements of their civilization. One of the most important of these precursors emerged around Chavín de Huántar, a city above 10,000 feet in northern Peru. Chavín flourished at roughly the same time as the Olmecs and developed complex architectural styles, textiles, and religious practices that would diffuse across the Andean region. The most distinctive feature of Chavín's artwork is a feline being (most likely originating from the influence of the Amazonian lowlands and its jaguar cults) whose impact can be seen throughout the Andean world. The Mochica, on the arid northern Peruvian coast, played the role of Teotihuacan and Tula from about A.D. 200 to 700. They developed an impressive empire with sophisticated pottery, metallurgy, pyramids, and irrigation systems. While Chavín and the Mochica thrived in the north and the coastal lowlands, after A.D. 600 the most important influences in the Andean world were in the central highlands—at Tiahuanaco on the high plain around Lake Titicaca in modern-day Bolivia, and the Wari Empire radiating outward from the area around Ayacucho in southern Peru. By around A.D. 1000, both the Mochica and Chavín civilizations had disintegrated. Another powerful new group—the Chimú—emerged in the mid-thirteenth century and their influence would be widespread until they were conquered by the Incas in the mid-fifteenth century. Their capital at Chan-Chan in the arid northern Peruvian coastal lowlands may have had a population of some 150,000.

Like the Aztecs, the Incas had humble origins in the mid-thirteenth century in a small village called Cuzco in the southern highlands of modern-day Peru. Their rise was even quicker and more sweeping than that of the Aztecs. Beginning in the 1430s under Pachacuti Inca and his son, Topa Inca, they moved outwards from Cuzco, conquering the *altiplano* in Bolivia, the cities of the coastal lowlands (including Chan-Chan), and as far north as the highlands of modern-day Ecuador. By the early sixteenth century, the Inca empire stretched from Ecuador to northern Chile and Argentina and across the highlands of Bolivia. Somewhere between five to ten million people fell under Inca rule. As with the Aztecs, Inca expansion essentially halted at the fringes of sedentary society. The equivalent of the deserts and nomads of northern Mexico for the Incas were the tropical hunters and gatherers of the lowlands east of the Andes.

Inca civilization developed at very high altitudes in the Andes (above 8,000 feet). The terrain of the region is stunning, with towering mountains rising very quickly from an arid coast. Steep river valleys cut through the mountains, bringing the melting snowpack down to the coast. Like the Mesoamericans, the Incas developed a very sophisticated terraced agriculture. The so-called "Irish" potato, in fact, is native to the Andes and, like maize in Mesoamerica, became the primary foodstuff. The Incas also raised maize. They raised alpacas and llamas to serve as beasts of burden, and to provide meat and wool. Small rodents, known to us today as guinea pigs, were native to the region and provided another basic food source.

The Incas developed a complex religion with many gods and an imperial ideology. More so than in Mesoamerica, the Incas pursued a process of cultural imperialism. As they conquered peoples and forced them to pay tribute, they also imposed on them their language (Quechua) and religion. As with all great empires, the Incas both imposed their own gods and, along the way, absorbed many of the gods and practices of those they conquered. In the Bolivian *altiplano*, they facilitated the spread of the other major indigenous language in the Andes, Aymara. They built the most extensive empire in the Americas. Astonishingly, the Incas ran this vast empire without any system of writing. An extensive and impressive road system linked all regions of the empire and an enormous bureaucracy. Two main roads, one along the coast and another in the mountains, ran from the northern to the southern fringes of the empire. A series of roads running east-west connected up these two great axes of transportation. Some of the Inca bridges across deep mountain gorges survived into the nineteenth century, and sections of these roads are still in use. The Incas imposed a forced rotary draft labor system (known as the *mit'a*) to build and maintain roads, bridges, public buildings, and an extensive network of granaries.

The northern capital of the empire was in Quito (contemporary Ecuador) and the southern capital in Cuzco (present-day Peru). As in central Mexico, the basic social unit was a sort of clan or *ayllu*. In a vast system of reciprocity, the *ayllu* provided labor for the empire and the state provided the *ayllu* with goods, especially foodstuffs. Civil war broke out in this vast empire shortly before the arrival of the Spanish. After the death of Huayna Cápac (possibly from smallpox) in 1525, two of the Inca ruler's many sons, Huáscar and Atahualpa, engaged in a bloody struggle for control of the empire. This struggle over control of the Inca Empire would play into the hands of the Spanish and facilitate the conquest of the Incas.

3

Iberians and Africans

Three continents—Africa, Europe, and Asia—formed the "Old World," and for thousands of years the peoples of these continents developed in almost complete isolation from the peoples of the Americas. In the ancient and medieval worlds the Mediterranean Sea formed the center of an economic and political network that linked Europe, North Africa, and the Middle East. The primary axes of trade came out of the East (the Indian Ocean and China, across the Middle East, then across the eastern Mediterranean), and the South (from sub-Saharan Africa northward across the desert) to the cities of the Italian peninsula. In turn, this trade then moved across the Mediterranean and the European continent to the Atlantic, the North Sea, and the Baltic. Goods and peoples moved back and forth along this dense and complex set of trading networks that ultimately linked the major cultures and peoples of the Old World. Gold and ivory from sub-Saharan Africa, spices from the Indian Ocean, silks from East Asia, and silver from central Europe were just a few of the most important goods moving along these trade routes.

In the fifteenth century, the city-states of Florence, Genoa, and Venice were among the most vibrant and dynamic trading centers in the world, as goods flowed out of Asia, across the Middle East, into the eastern Mediterranean, and then to the Italian peninsula. In the second half of the thirteenth century, when Marco Polo, his father, and his uncle left Venice, they moved across Iran to the Persian Gulf, then to Kashgar in central Asia. From there they took the old Silk Road across China to Peking. Another major trade route connected Peking with Canton in south China and then Malacca in the "Spice Islands" (what we today call Indonesia and the East Indies). From there, ships moved to southwestern India, where traders

linked up with trade routes into the Persian Gulf, the Red Sea, and East
Africa. Another strong stream of commerce moved across North Africa
into the Mediterranean. Gold from the mines, ivory and pepper from the
forests, and salt from the desert moved northward and eastward across
the vast Sahara to Fez, Tunis, Tripoli, and Cairo.

With the gradual development of a dynamic trading core in northwestern
Europe around England and the Low Countries (today's Netherlands and
Belgium), the Italian city-states became important intermediaries between
emerging Atlantic trading centers (London, Antwerp, Amsterdam) and
the trading centers in Asia and Africa. The Italian city-states became the
incubators for the rise of modern capitalism in the fifteenth and sixteenth
centuries. What we think of as capitalism arose as a system of trade and
exchange by men and women taking great risks in pursuit of profit.
Entrepreneurs risked their savings buying and selling over long distances
with the ever-present possibility that, quite literally, their ship might not
come in, and they could lose everything. (This scenario was immortalized
in the plot of Shakespeare's *The Merchant of Venice*, 1598.) In this sense, the
early conquistadores and voyagers were engaged in commercial ventures.
They were not simply explorers; they were also entrepreneurs. The Italian
city-states were hotbeds for breeding capitalist merchants and traders.

The exchange of goods, diseases, and peoples followed these extensive
trading networks across three continents. Gold, ivory, silks, and spices were
the luxury goods that came out of the East and Africa, and commanded the
highest profits and prices in Europe. Silver was the primary European good
moving east. It was these luxury items that produced the highest profits, not
the bulk items such as foodstuffs and grains. All of these items came to
Europe through many intermediaries, a process that raised the price of
purchase at each step of the way. A long-standing dream of European
merchants in the Middle Ages was to seek more direct contact with the
producers. The failure of the Crusades in the Middle Ages demonstrated
the futility of reaching the East via a land route. With access across the
Middle East blocked, the water route to Asia became the logical, yet
immensely daunting, path for direct trade with Asia.

The peoples of the Old World also (unwittingly) traded their diseases.
Although the Old World was really a series of relatively isolated regions,
the trade networks linked them together via merchants and armies of
conquest. Deadly microbes followed the paths of merchants and soldiers
as smallpox, influenza, plague, and measles (to name just a few examples)
moved through the populations of all three continents over millennia.
Although these diseases continued to be deadly for centuries, the populations
of the Old World developed some levels of immunity. The descendants of
survivors were not as likely to die in succeeding epidemics. The biological isolation of the peoples of the Americas protected them from these

Old World scourges, and allowed them to grow and thrive in a world exceptionally free of major diseases. As we shall see, one of the most devastating consequences of the European discovery of the Americas was the introduction of the diseases of the Old World and the near annihilation of Native Americans.

Different forms of slavery also arose on all three continents, usually the enslavement of people considered ethnically distinct from the captors. Although we tend to think of slavery as an aberration, it has existed throughout history and on nearly all continents. The ancient Greeks built Athenian democracy on the backs of slaves. Both Christians and Moslems enslaved and sold African peoples. When Columbus lived in Portugal in the late fifteenth century, African slaves made up perhaps 10 percent of the population of Lisbon. Black Africans also engaged in slavery and the slave trade with both Europeans and peoples of the Islamic world long before 1492. In each of the regions of the Old World, slavery took on different meanings. The Africans, for example, did not have the concept of private property and their slaves were not viewed as chattel, as they were in Europe. Slavery also existed in the high civilizations of the New World. The conquest of the Americas would radically transform slavery and create new forms out of those that existed in the Old World. The modern Atlantic slave trade created slave systems on a scale that was unprecedented in world history.

The peoples of the Old World were numerous and diverse, with many different power centers. During the Renaissance (roughly 1350 to 1550) the first nation-states began to emerge in Europe. In the Middle Ages, Europe was politically fragmented into geographically small duchies, principalities, and kingdoms. In one sense, the Renaissance is partly defined by the political transformations that lead to the emergence of the first European nations. Machiavelli's famous political tract, *The Prince* (1515), is a call to his Italian patrons to take note of this process and bring the Italian peninsula together as a single nation-state. Unfortunately for the Italians, others would take Machiavelli's advice long before the Italian princes.

CREATING SPAIN AND PORTUGAL

The first nations began to emerge around weak monarchies that gradually extended their control over larger and larger territories. In essence, the monarch was simply the most powerful noble among many nobles. He had to assert his supremacy over his fellow lords and gain their allegiance. The key to power at the end of the Renaissance (and, for that matter, ever since) has been for states to gain control of more and more resources. In medieval and Renaissance Europe this meant gaining control over the land and a portion of the agricultural wealth produced by the peasants. The rulers who saw this and succeeded in accumulating the allegiance of more and more lords (through persuasion or force) became the first great monarchs in Europe. Spain and Portugal were at the forefront of this process. By the mid-twelfth century, a monarchy had begun to emerge in Portugal, and, by the mid-thirteenth century, the House of Burgundy had gained control over roughly the area of modern Portugal. Several kingdoms emerged in Spain in the late Middle Ages, and a unified Spain would emerge under Fernando and Isabel in the last quarter of the fifteenth century.

The Iberian peninsula lay on the western periphery of the ancient world during the glory days of the Greeks and the rise of the Roman Empire. The Romans conquered the peninsula in the second century B.C. They divided the peninsula into administrative units, naming the eastern portion Iberia, a term that has come to refer to the entire peninsula. (It is a nice, short way to refer to both Spain and Portugal.) The northern half of what today is Portugal was known as Portucale, which eventually was transformed into the name Portugal. With the fall of Rome in the fifth century, Roman control disintegrated, but the Romans left behind a powerful legacy. Latin would gradually evolve across the peninsula into a series of languages and dialects. By 1492, Portuguese and Castilian Spanish had clearly evolved into distinct languages, supported, systematized, and promoted by the emerging new nations. The Romans imposed Christianity on local peoples just as the Spanish and Portuguese would impose it on the peoples of the Americas a thousand years later, and, by the eighth century, Roman Catholicism had become the dominant Iberian religion. Roman law would survive and endure as the basis for the legal systems of Spain and Portugal (and eventually Latin America). Many Roman settlements would eventually become some of the principal Iberian cities.

In the early eighth century, Islamic peoples from North Africa overran and conquered most of the peninsula. Although referred to generically as Moors, the single unifying characteristic was that all of these peoples were followers of Mohammed and Islam. Over centuries, waves of different Islamic peoples conquered and reconquered the peninsula. The "Reconquest" by the Christian rulers would take nearly 800 years. It began in the early eighth century in the mountainous region of northwestern Spain, an area never conquered by the Moors. Slowly but surely, over centuries, the Christian lords reconquered territory from the "infidels," leading to the formation of a series of kingdoms on the peninsula. Like modern conflicts in the Middle East or Northern Ireland, this long war was both a religious and a political conflict, a war for both God and King.

The process of territorial consolidation and reconquest had been completed in Portugal by 1253 and it had emerged by then as the first nation-state in Europe. It consisted, in fact, of two kingdoms—the northern section, the old Roman Portucale, and the southern half, the region known by the Arabic name, the Algarve. Afonso Henriques of the House of Burgundy declared himself king of Portugal in 1139, and his successors would eventually be recognized by the Vatican as a *rex* or king. With the conquest of the Algarve completed in 1253, Portugal had by then taken on more or less the boundaries we recognize today. By the mid-fifteenth century, the last Moorish stronghold on the Iberian peninsula was the area around the city of Granada in the south. The two most powerful kingdoms on the peninsula were Castile (basically central Spain) and Aragón (much of eastern Spain). With the marriage of Isabel of Castile and Fernando of Aragón in 1469, and their rise to their respective thrones in the 1470s, most of what we consider Spain today had come under their joint control, except Granada. The long reconquest of Spain ended in January 1492 with the fall of Granada (after a ten-year siege) and the retreat of the last Moorish ruler, Boabdil, across the Strait of Gibraltar. (Legend has it that, as he retreated from the city and sorrowfully looked back, his mother observed, "You do well my son, to weep as a woman for the loss of what you could not defend as a man.")

The Islamic invasions and Christian reconquest had long linked Iberia and Africa through war, trade, and religion. Spain and Portugal served as a transition zone between Europe and Africa. The Iberian peninsula was a vibrant and dynamic crossroads of ethnic groups, religions, and cultures. It was a very different world from the rest of Europe (and even gave rise to the witticism that Europe ended at the Pyrenees!). The Iberians, unlike most Europeans, had access to the advances in science, mathematics, astronomy, and navigation in the Islamic world. This was a world that stretched in a sweeping arc across North and East Africa, through the Middle East, into central Asia, across the Indian subcontinent, and into the East Indies. While most of Europe fell into economic and political fragmentation and stagnation in the centuries after the fall of Rome, Islam spread outward from the Arabian peninsula beginning in the sixth century. Over the next thousand years, the Islamic world expanded militarily, economically, and culturally. While much of Europe lost direct contact with the knowledge of the ancient Greek and Roman world, Iberia never did, and it continually absorbed the developments of the Islamic world throughout the Middle Ages. In this sense, Spain and Portugal had an enormous head start on the other European peoples in the process of overseas expansion. Nearly all of the key technology in shipping and navigation would come out of the Middle East and the Indian Ocean during the Middle Ages. The Portuguese, more so than any other Iberian people, had honed and accumulated knowledge about astronomy, cartography, shipbuilding, and sailing. As is so often true in history, the great point of encounter for diverse peoples would produce a dynamic center of creativity and expansion, in this case, in tiny Portugal. The Portuguese would expand westward into the Atlantic and southward along the coast of West Africa.

PEOPLES AND CULTURES OF AFRICA

Even more so than the populations of Europe and the Americas, the peoples of Africa were incredibly diverse in ethnicity, religion, and language. In a fundamental sense, there were no Africans, just as there were no Native Americans or Europeans. Instead, there were hundreds of societies and cultures who did not see themselves as one people or the inhabitants of a continent (most were not even aware of the existence of the continent). To see them all as one people or one race is to project (mistakenly) our present notions about Africa and Africans back into the past. As with the other continents, Africa was a name dreamed up by European mapmakers for an enormous landmass. Among the many peoples of the continent, there was certainly no sense of being part of some larger entity known as Africa. The Tuareg of North Africa were profoundly different from, say, the Khoisan of southern Africa. As with the Native American peoples, each of these groups generally saw themselves as the center of the universe, and they saw most other peoples as very different from themselves.

As on the other two continents of the Old World, there was also a wide variety of levels of political and economic development, from small tribes to empires, ranging across a vast array of environments from desert to tropical forest to mountains. The peoples of Africa speak hundreds of languages that linguists have grouped into six major families. By the late fifteenth century, the populations of North Africa had several thousand years of experience dealing with the cultures of Europe. The great civilizations of Egypt and the Nile, the Phoenicians, and the Carthaginians had played prominent roles in the Mediterranean world for millennia. The ancient "eastern" civilizations in Egypt and the Fertile Crescent in the Near East, in a very direct sense, were the cradle of what we now call Western Civilization, with its roots in ancient Greece and Rome. Between the seventh and eleventh centuries, the spread of Islam across North Africa in a sweeping arc from modern-day Kenya to Nigeria provided the region with a common dominant language (Arabic) and religion (Islam). The vast Sahara Desert formed a formidable barrier between North and West Africa. In much of West and central Africa, the languages are distinct from those of North Africa and form part of a completely different linguistic family. Through most of southern Africa, Bantu languages predominate.

Religious diversity also characterized the cultures of Africa. Although Islam dominated across North Africa, it was often split by major internal divisions. Across most of West, central, and southern Africa, many groups held beliefs that are crudely lumped together as "animist," essentially meaning that they believed that all living things were animated by spirits. Most of these cultures also placed great emphasis on reverence for, and worship of, their ancestors. This sacred worldview was very similar to that of many Native Americans, and not unlike some Christian notions. In the ancient Abyssinian kingdom (Ethiopia), a variant of Christianity predominated.

The two regions that would have the greatest contact with Europeans in the fifteenth and sixteenth centuries were West and central Africa. As noted earlier, when the Europeans began to appear on the coast of West Africa in the fifteenth century, they encountered peoples who were their technological and military equals. As in ancient Mesoamerica, powerful states had risen and fallen long before the arrival of Europeans. The kingdom of Mali, centered around the Niger River, dominated much of the interior of West Africa in the thirteenth and fourteenth centuries and helped spread the influence of Islam. In the late fifteenth century the Songhai established an empire in the same region around Gao and the legendary Timbuktu. Before the rise of the Atlantic shipping networks, Songhai dominated the trade routes from the southern fringes of West Africa across the Sahara to the Mediterranean. Much of the gold circulating in Europe during the Middle Ages came across the Sahara from the interior of West Africa. When the Portuguese began to trade along the coast in the last half of the fifteenth century, they encountered dozens of small states and peoples. These ranged from powerful kingdoms such as Kongo in central Africa and the Akan states in West Africa to small city-states similar to those on the Italian peninsula. The Europeans had to learn to deal with each one individually. As in Europe, the boundaries and definitions of these states and peoples were fluid and changing. In West Africa alone, the process of conquest and warfare was constantly shifting boundaries and the balance of power among states.

For historians, the biggest problem in understanding just what the Europeans confronted is a lack of sources. Most of the cultures in Africa were preliterate and so did not leave written accounts of these first encounters with Europeans. For centuries, our view of the early encounters has been primarily through the eyes of the Europeans who wrote down their impressions of the Africans, and all of these sources are problematic, bringing with them all the prejudices and racial stereotypes that the Europeans carried with them around the globe. As I have pointed out, the most important point to make here is that most of the African peoples in the fifteenth and sixteenth centuries met the Europeans as equals. The Portuguese, and those Europeans who followed them, had to negotiate with African peoples along the coast to set up fortified trading posts. The Europeans did not have any significant goods that the Africans needed, while the Africans had gold, ivory, pepper, and (eventually) slaves that the Europeans desperately desired. Our notions of pillage and imperialism in Africa arise out of the events of the late nineteenth century. But at least until the late seventeenth century, the Europeans did not have a military or technological advantage over the Africans. That advantage was really a development of the industrial revolutions of the nineteenth century: steamships, repeating rifles, machine guns, quinine, and the railroad dramatically altered the balance of power in the nineteenth century and led very quickly to the partition of Africa among the European powers in the 1880s and 1890s. In earlier centuries, West and central African states were the political, military, and technological equals of the Europeans. The greatest evidence of this is the inability of the Europeans to penetrate inland until the late nineteenth century.

The areas that would feel the impact of European expansion most powerfully stretched from modern-day Senegal to Angola. Senegambia was a series of Mande-speaking states that provided access to the vibrant trade with the interior of West Africa via the Senegal and Gambia Rivers. To the south were numerous small states in the region the Portuguese called Upper Guinea and Sierra Leone. Moving southeastward, the Europeans named the regions after the dominant exports—the Grain Coast, Ivory Coast, and Gold Coast. The latter (more or less the location of Ghana today) would become one of the major staging grounds of European powers for centuries, first as an outlet for gold, and then for slaves. Farther east is the Bight of Benin, a region the Europeans called the Slave Coast because of the fundamental role it would play in the transatlantic slave trade. Covering roughly the region of modern-day Togo, Benin, and western Nigeria, the region was densely populated and home to several powerful kingdoms. In the western section of this region was the Kingdom of Dahomey. To the east was the Kingdom of Benin, stretching from Lagos in the west to the Niger River delta in the east. It was primarily an inland state that reached its peak of power in the sixteenth century. Sandwiched in between the two was the Oyo kingdom, extending from the coast inland to dense forests and farther north to woodland savanna. The most important ethnic group in Oyo were the Yoruba, whose impact upon Latin American society and culture would be profound. Deeper inland (today, northern Nigeria) were Hausa kingdoms that had come under Islamic influence centuries earlier.

East and south of the Kingdom of Benin was the Niger River delta and a region that came to be known as the Cameroons (an English corruption of the Portuguese name "Camarões" Coast or shrimp coast). This is an area of mangrove swamps and countless streams and rivulets. In the fifteenth century, vibrant trading networks crisscrossed the region, connecting numerous independent villages. Farther south along the coast of Equatorial Africa, the Kingdom of Kongo had emerged as an impressive and powerful state by the time the Portuguese arrived in the 1480s. Encompassing 250,000 people, Kongo spanned some 250 miles from the Congo River south and another 250 miles inland from the coast. On the north side of the river were two other substantial kingdoms—Loango on the coast and Tio to the east. The interior of central Africa contained numerous other kingdoms, the most famous centered around the city of Great Zimbabwe. A city of perhaps 20,000 inhabitants at its height, Great Zimbabwe covered some 60 acres and had protective walls 30 feet high and 15 feet thick. The surrounding kingdom disintegrated in the fifteenth century and was not known to Europeans until an explorer came across the ruins in the late nineteenth century.

Below the tropical equatorial zone, southern Africa contains a diversity of environments. The Kalihari Desert in the southwest has always been sparsely inhabited, and was home to scattered groups of nomadic hunters known today as the Khoisan. Across much of southern Africa, Bantu-speaking peoples farmed and raised livestock. Three main groups predominated: the Shona, Sotho-Tswana, and Nguni (to use their modern names). The Shona occupied the area of modern Zimbabwe and Mozambique while the Sotho-Tswana spread across much of what today is South Africa. The Nguni lived to the east, from the mountains down to the Indian Ocean. Great mineral riches lie beneath the soils of southern Africa. Gold, copper, tin, and iron have been mined and traded for centuries. As in the case of West Africa, the peoples of southern Africa exported gold, in this case down the Zambezi River to Sofala on the East African coast. This trade connected the black Africans of central and southern Africa with the Arabs along the coast of East Africa from the Red Sea to Mozambique. Thriving commercial centers spanned the coast of East Africa—Mogadisho, Malindi, Mombasa, and Kilwa were the most notable.

Africa, like the Americas and Europe, was a diverse region of many peoples, languages, and kingdoms in the late fifteenth century. Like the Americas, trade networks connected the various regions within much of Africa, to Europe via the Mediterranean Sea, and to Asia via the Indian Ocean. In some ways, Africa formed one side of a triangular trading network with Europe and Asia that had linked the continents of the Old World for millennia. As the Europeans moved steadily out into the Atlantic in the fifteenth and sixteenth centuries, the growing trade between Europeans and Africans initiated a profound transformation that would shift the axis of power in the world. For the Europeans it would shift the locus of their civilization out of the Mediterranean and into the Atlantic. The Portuguese trading posts along the African coast in the fifteenth century would form the foundation for the construction of an

Atlantic trading network that would eventually link up with the Americas. Portuguese expansion into the Indian Ocean, and Spanish and Portuguese expansion into the Americas in the sixteenth century, would make the Atlantic the dynamic new center of international trade. They began to create an Atlantic economy that would fundamentally alter the future of all peoples on all continents. European overseas expansion would become the driving force behind the collision of peoples that would give birth to Latin America in the late fifteenth century.

4

Moving Out across the Oceans

The early history of Latin America unfolded as a dramatic chapter in the rise of a truly global history that began to take shape with the aggressive expansion of European peoples across the earth during the Renaissance. Beginning in the fifteenth century, the Europeans crisscrossed the globe, eventually subduing most of the peoples they encountered and establishing the global supremacy of the West. The nations of the Western Hemisphere began as colonial enterprises, and Europe played the central role in the formation and development of New World societies for centuries. European expansion eventually created a truly global economic system linking up all societies and cultures. As I have emphasized, Latin American history began in the late fifteenth century when a group of small, newly emerging nations in Europe embarked on overseas voyages in pursuit of trade with Africa and Asia. This expansion drove them out across the Atlantic and into a series of dramatic collisions with new peoples and continents. Five hundred years later, Latin America continues to grapple with the legacies of European colonialism and the consequences of those collisions.

The "rise of the West" to world domination from the fifteenth to the nineteenth centuries was by no means an inevitable process. Prior to 1500, the peoples of the globe were scattered and relatively isolated, and Europe was but one of many power centers in the world. The Chinese had constructed a highly developed civilization over millennia in East Asia, and the Moguls were about to establish a vast empire on the Indian subcontinent. The Ottoman dynasty controlled much of North Africa, the Middle East, and southeastern Europe, while the Persian empire stretched from present-day Iran across the Arabian peninsula. Russian rulers had forged a powerful kingdom centered around Moscow. Substantial empires in Africa (Abyssinia, Oyo, Kongo) were as impressive as any monarchy in Europe. The great trade routes connected Europe with Asia via Muslim merchants in the Middle East, and black Africa with Europe via Muslim traders in North Africa. Europeans had only vague and fanciful ideas of the dimensions of the lands beyond the Mediterranean rim, mostly from the writings of a few adventurous travelers like Marco Polo (1254–1324). On the other side of the Atlantic, the Aztecs dominated central Mexico and the Incas controlled an empire in the Andes. While all these empires had expanded and gained control of vast territories, only the Europeans, with their newly-emerging and fragile monarchies, moved so relentlessly outward across the oceans.

WHY THE EUROPEANS?

Complex and interacting factors drove the Europeans outward and made their success possible. Europe, in 1492, was politically fragmented and splintered. Germany and Italy would not come together as unified nations until the nineteenth century. France and England were wracked by civil wars. England would not begin to emerge as a unified nation until the conclusion of the War of Roses in the late fifteenth century, and did not really get going until the reign of Elizabeth I (1558–1603). France would be bitterly divided, especially by the religious wars throughout the sixteenth century. Only Portugal and Spain had begun to emerge as nations, and they were small compared to the other empires around the world. In 1500, Portugal had perhaps one million to a million and a quarter inhabitants, and Lisbon had a population of about 100,000. Spain was significantly larger and had perhaps eight million inhabitants, and its principal port, Seville, was about the same size as Lisbon. By the late fifteenth century, the first of the new nation-states had begun to consolidate around a handful of the numerous and dispersed feudal monarchies. Portugal (in the twelfth and thirteenth centuries) and Spain (in the fifteenth century) pioneered this process of state-building. England, France, and the Netherlands followed in the sixteenth century. Once these monarchies had established centralized authority and consolidated control over the land, they could then turn their attention to overseas expansion. The continual competition among these relatively small states created a dynamic of innovation in politics, society, and economics. Ironically, the power struggles among the Spanish, Portuguese, French, English, and Dutch would make European civilization dynamic, strong, and tenacious.

An aggressive and expansive culture with the Judeo-Christian worldview and the emergence of modern science at its core propelled the Europeans across the seas. The cultural factor is perhaps the most difficult to pin down, and the most elusive. It is what some historians would call the "fudge" factor. My own view is that the Judeo-Christian vision of a world created by an omnipotent God, a world with a clear beginning point, and moving upward and progressively toward an end point, is crucial to understanding European civilization and its expansion. Most of the rest of the cultures of the world (Asian and American, for example) see history as cyclical and circular. So much of the fate or destiny of humans has been determined by the great cycles of life. In contrast, the Europeans see history as linear and progressive, not cyclical. Men such as Columbus and Cortés had a much greater faith in their ability to make their own destiny as humanity moves toward that end point. The Europeans also felt compelled to bring the opportunity for salvation to all peoples. Christianity is an aggressively proselytizing religion. Furthermore, the rise of modern science, a process that is intimately linked to Christianity in the sixteenth and seventeenth centuries, also gave the West dynamism. The desire to understand the natural world (for the likes of a Newton or a Kepler) was a desire to reveal God's design for the universe. Christianity and Western science share the notion that the natural world is ours to understand and to dominate and manipulate. "Be fruitful and multiply," as it says in the opening passages of the Bible, "and replenish the earth, and subdue it; and have dominion over" it (Genesis 1:28). It is a utilitarian view of the natural world. Christianity, then, drove the Europeans out across the globe to bring the word of God to those who had not yet been saved. Modern science provided them with the rationale for discovering, understanding, and exploiting the fruits of nature. In many ways, this was the most distinct factor in the process of European expansion.

With the prominent exception of the Jews (mainly concentrated in Eastern Europe), Europe was a Christian civilization. And in 1500 there was but one church, one Christianity, in Western Europe, the Catholic (i.e., universal) Church headquartered in Rome. Although bloody wars dramatically and irrevocably shattered this religious unity in the sixteenth century, Protestants and (even more so) Catholics shared an aggressive zeal to convert all peoples and to save their souls. In large part due to a centuries-long battle to drive the Muslims from Spain and Portugal, Iberian Catholicism became the most militant and aggressive in Europe. Although often mixed with other motives, the desire of Europeans to find and save new souls was sincere and profound. Overseas expansion offered an unprecedented opportunity to carry the message of Christ to other peoples. Bernal Díaz del Castillo, one of the conquistadores of Mexico, captured this mixture of motives when he observed that he and his compatriots embarked upon their mission "in the service of God and His Majesty, and to give light to those who sat in darkness—and also to acquire that gold which most men covet." The spiritual conquest played a central role in the construction of Latin American culture. The Iberians set out to conquer the Native Americans with both the sword and the cross.

Innovations in science and technology provided the new nations with the means for expansion. Europeans gradually assimilated astronomical knowledge, and the compass and navigational tools that had been developed in China, India, and the Middle East. By the late fifteenth century, they had also developed the ships that would take them around the globe—most notably, the caravel. Unlike the ancient square-masted Roman galleys that plied the relatively calm Mediterranean, the caravel had a potent combination of technology: a large hull for sailing the high seas, a sternpost rudder and triangular sails for directional mobility, and artillery to intimidate those who challenged or refused to cooperate with them. Knowledge of the stars and navigational instruments gave the Europeans the means to chart their course. The caravel provided them with the means to sail it.

Science, technology, and the consolidation of nation-states paved the path to expansion; cultural and economic forces propelled Europeans down the path. Western culture is peculiar in its emphasis on the systematic pursuit of practical knowledge about the natural world. Many civilizations up to modern times have contributed to the growth of science and technology, but only the West brought together the disparate contributions of other civilizations to produce the revolution that gave birth to modern science in the sixteenth century. Only in the West was technological innovation so aggressively promoted and revolutionized. The pursuit of scientific and technological advances became both an end in itself and the means to other ends. Science and technology became instruments for expansion, and for colonial exploitation.

Greed was also a powerful motive driving Western expansion. In the Renaissance (1350–1550), the most revolutionary economic system in world history—capitalism—had begun to emerge in Europe. The very essence of what we consider to be the core features of capitalism were taking shape. The self-interested pursuit of profit, the development of markets for the relatively free exchange of goods and services, the consolidation of the notion of private property and legally binding contracts, all developed around trading networks that crisscrossed Europe by 1500. The instruments that were essential for the rise of capitalism also took shape in these years, especially in the Italian city-states: notions of credit, banking, accounting techniques, and the pooling of capital in "companies." By 1500, the complex and growing trading system in Europe had laid the basis for the birth of a capitalist economy driven by the pursuit of profit. The most impressive profits came from the trade of luxury goods and rare spices from the East. Middle Eastern and North African intermediaries stood in the way of the Europeans and the suppliers. Given the difficulties (vividly demonstrated by the Crusades in the late Middle Ages) of trying to wrest control of the overland trade from the intermediaries by force, the logical alternative was to establish sea routes to the East. Portugal, Europe's "window to the Atlantic," was strategically positioned to serve as an intermediary in the trade between the Mediterranean and northern Europe, and to become a jumping-off point to the East.

Pursuit of profit and souls drove the Europeans out onto the high seas and around the globe, while the new science, technology, and monarchies provided them with the means to find their way. In the fourteenth and fifteenth centuries, the small city-states of northern Italy pioneered the expansion. Strategically located between the growing European economy and the overland routes to the East, Venice, Florence, and Genoa had developed sophisticated trading economies, and pioneered credit and financial tools such as double-entry bookkeeping and banking. In the sixteenth century, Portugal and Spain, the first of the centralized monarchies, left the Italian city-states behind. After 1492, the Iberian empires in the Americas and the East shifted the axis of the European economy out of the Mediterranean and into the Atlantic.

The combination of these four factors—political will, economic dynamism, religious zeal, and technological innovation—emerged in Europe (and nowhere else) and they emerged first in Spain and Portugal. The Iberians were the leaders in this process because they combined all four factors. They put their houses in order through the consolidation of a national monarchy. The unification of the kingdoms of Castile and Aragón under Fernando and Isabel effectively created modern Spain, and the fall of Granada in 1492 completed the process. Spain was the cutting edge in state formation and nation-building in the Renaissance, as Machiavelli so astutely pointed out in *The Prince* (1515). Portugal was at the forefront of the trade revolution. The Portuguese had consolidated their monarchy and boundaries two centuries before Spain, and the new nation was at the crossroads of trade from the Mediterranean, Africa, and northern Europe. Both monarchies were militant and aggressive at spreading Christianity. Centuries of reconquering territory from the Moors had forged a religious militancy, especially in Spain, unlike anything in the rest of Europe. The Iberians fervently and sincerely wished to spread the gospel far and wide.

CREATING AN ATLANTIC WORLD

Their Islamic experience also put Spain and Portugal far ahead of the rest of Europe in scientific and technical developments in navigation. Portugal, in particular, was at the cutting edge of maritime expertise by the fifteenth century. Under Prince Henry (1394–1460), known to history as "The Navigator," the Portuguese monarchy promoted voyages and expeditions beginning in the early fifteenth century. Henry, third in line for the throne, brought together mapmakers, astronomers, and other experts at Sagres in southern Portugal to push the process of overseas expansion. These voyages were not state-directed in the same sense as, say, the space program in the United States in the 1960s and 1970s. The monarchy sometimes provided funds and support, but often the voyages were undertaken by entrepreneurs acting with nothing more than royal support and blessing.

The Portuguese pioneered the process of expansion into the Atlantic. They had a favored geographical position as Europe's window to the Atlantic. They were at the midpoint on the axis of trade from the Mediterranean to the dynamic and growing economies of northwestern Europe. Under the House of Avis (1383–1578), they had consolidated their nation two hundred years before the Spanish. In the fourteenth century they were already out in the Atlantic discovering and conquering islands. As early as the 1340s they had explored the Canary Islands. In the 1420s they conquered Madeira, and in the 1430s they moved into the Azores. Under the Avis dynasty in the fifteenth century, they began to work their way down the coast of West Africa. The Portuguese usually date the beginning of their empire-building to the capture of the North African city of Ceuta in 1415. Over the next century they would construct a global trading empire stretching from Brazil to Africa, to the Indian Ocean, and to China and Japan. Although their short-term goal was trade in the Atlantic, the long-term dream was to establish direct trade with the Indies. In effect, they would do an "end run" by water around the many Middle Eastern and North African intermediaries who sold them goods from sub-Saharan Africa and the Far East. By 1434 an expedition had rounded Cape Bojador on the West African coast, a point long considered impassable. In 1482, the Portuguese established a fortified trading post, or factory, at São Jorge da Mina (better known as Elmina) on the coast of modern-day Ghana. Over the next two years, Diogo Cão led an expedition that explored the mouth of the Congo River and regions to the south. In 1488, Bartolomeu Dias rounded the tip of Africa and entered the Indian Ocean, although his crew nearly mutinied and forced him to turn back to Portugal.

In many ways, the Portuguese were the primary instigators in the creation of an "Atlantic world." In the fifteenth century, they established regular trade with peoples down the entire length of the Atlantic coast of Africa. They became the principal agents connecting not only Europe and sub-Saharan Africa, but also many African peoples. They were interested in trade, not military conquest. The tactics they followed were the same around the globe: establish trade with the locals, build a fortified trading post on the coast, then become the dominant traders between European and non-European peoples. Ironically, they did this in pursuit of a longer-term goal of establishing trade directly with Asia. It was an eminently practical plan. Trade with everyone in your path while you work your way to the bigger prize—the Indies. The Portuguese would eventually achieve this goal, but their key role in the movement out into the Atlantic would lead directly to the European discovery of the Americas and the creation of an Atlantic world.

The "discovery" of the Americas, what I call the "Columbian Moment," was arguably the most important event in world history in the last one thousand years. It brought together two worlds, the "Old World" of Europe, Africa, and Asia, and the "New World" of the Americas. Both had lived in biological and cultural isolation for thousands of years. Columbus's voyage began the process of *sustained* exchange between these two worlds in an irreversible process that continues today—it was a momentous step in the creation of a "global village." This moment had enormous consequences for both worlds. It lead to the invasion, conquest, and decimation of the peoples of the Americas. It was the beginning of the process of European expansion and the creation of a world dominated by European powers. The biological exchange of plants, animals, and diseases profoundly reshaped global ecology and culture.

This moment and its meaning are also very controversial. First, there has been intense debate over the very term "discovery." Clearly, from the Native American perspective there was no "discovery" of the Americas. They were already well aware of the existence of their own homeland. This is why a lot of scholars have taken up the term "encounter" to describe what happened on October 12, 1492. This is a nice, neutral term, and it is fine, but from the European perspective this was clearly a profound and decisive discovery of a world and peoples they did not know. Within a few years, it became clear to Europeans that Columbus had not reached Asia, but new lands and peoples that were nowhere to be found in their most important sources of knowledge: the Bible and the writings of the ancient Greeks and Romans. It took about a century and a half before European intellectuals and theologians were able to assimilate and explain these lands and peoples, and to fit them into their religious and intellectual worldview. All the same, it was also a moment of "discovery" for the Native Americans, who, much to their dismay, and without seeking it out, discovered the Europeans.

The voyage of Columbus in 1492 would forever end the cultural and biological isolation of the Americas and the Old World, and it brought together these two worlds that had developed separately for millennia. Columbus took the first and most dramatic step in the creation of a single, interconnected world. One of the great chroniclers of the Spanish conquest in the sixteenth century, Francisco López de Gómara, called it "[t]he greatest event since the creation of the world (excluding the incarnation of Him who created it)." Unwittingly, Columbus initiated the collision that gave birth to

Latin America. Bartolomé de las Casas, who witnessed the remarkable discoveries and the conquest in the Caribbean, believed that, "Everything that has happened since the marvelous discovery of the Americas has been so extraordinary that the whole story remains incredible to anyone who has not experienced it at firsthand. Indeed, it seems to overshadow all the deeds of famous people in the past, no matter how heroic, and to silence all talk of other wonders in the world."

Some see Columbus as a visionary at the vanguard of Western civilization. Others portray him as an evil destroyer and the epitome of all that is wrong with the West. We should not argue so much about the man, but rather we should come to grips with the importance of the process he began. Although he is one of the most famous figures in world history, Columbus remains an elusive, shadowy, chameleonlike figure. We have about as much information on Columbus as any person who lived in the late fifteenth and early sixteenth centuries, but nearly all of it is controversial, uncertain, and flawed. As one of his biographers (Salvador de Madariaga) has said, Columbus is "Like a squid, he oozes out a cloud of ink around every hard square fact of his life. This ink, multiplied by the industry of his historians, has made but blacker and thicker the mystery which attaches to him."

Even Columbus's origins are disputed. It is fairly clear that he was from the Italian port city of Genoa, although many nations claim him (Spain, France, even Russia). He was probably born to a family of weavers in 1451 and in the Genoese dialect his name would have been Cristoforo Colombo. In the 1470s, as a young man, he began to ship out on voyages to the eastern Mediterranean. In 1476, at the age of 25, he arrived in Portugal, then the most advanced seafaring country in the Western world. As we have seen, Portugal had already begun to construct a global empire. In this bustling crossroads to the Atlantic and Mediterranean, Columbus became part of a thriving Italian immigrant community. He developed extensive contacts in shipping and commerce, and he learned Portuguese and Latin, as well as Castilian Spanish. (Nearly all his surviving writings are in Spanish.) This very learned man would eventually adopt the Spanish name Cristóbal Colón. He signed official documents with the name Christoferens—the bearer of Christ—a clear indication of his deep and abiding Christian devotion. In 1478 or 1479 he married Felipa Moniz, whose family owned islands in the Atlantic, and also had connections at the Portuguese court. They had one son, Diego, born in 1480. (His wife apparently died not long after. Columbus later had a romantic liaison with Beatriz Enríquez de Arana, producing a second son, Hernando, who would become his father's biographer.)

It is in Portugal that Columbus developed what he called the "enterprise of the Indies," that is, the single-minded belief that by sailing west across the Great Western Sea one could arrive safely in Asia, or the "Indies," as the region was called. His originality was not in showing that the earth was round. This is a fictional story created by Washington Irving in his great nineteenth-century biography of Columbus. All educated people since ancient times had known that the world was a sphere, and a Greek astronomer in Egypt had calculated the circumference of the globe with great accuracy in the third century B.C. Columbus's originality, strangely enough, was in his great mistake. He miscalculated the size of the globe, and we have a reasonably good idea of how he made this mistake. Columbus was very well read in astronomy, navigation, and geography, but he undercalculated the length of a single degree of longitude, and, when multiplied by 360, it shrank the earth from its correct circumference of nearly 25,000 miles (at the equator) to about 19,000 miles. His second miscalculation was that he believed China was much larger than it actually is. Combining these two mistakes led Columbus to estimate the distance across the Atlantic to Asia to be about 2,400 miles. Ironically, this mistake is the basis both of his great discovery, and his vilification. It led him to the Americas, and has led those who despise him to portray him as a stubborn and misguided fool.

But why do it? Why would Columbus, or anyone else, want to cross the Atlantic? In essence, the Europeans coveted the highly profitable spice trade to Asia, and they wanted a direct sea route as an alternative to paying intermediaries who brought the goods across Asia, India, the Middle East, and North Africa. Columbus was driven by the usual motives of the time: the pursuit of wealth, the desire to spread Christianity, and fame. Or, as the famous litany goes—he went in pursuit of gold, glory, and gospel. For years he attempted to persuade the Portuguese to back his plan, but they (quite correctly) rejected his calculations. In 1485, he gave up on the Portuguese and traveled to Spain to try to persuade Fernando and Isabel to back his enterprise. Columbus was also rebuffed by the experts of the Spanish crown, but they did not completely reject him. While Fernando and Isabel engaged in the last stages of the reconquest of the peninsula from the Moors, they provided him with occasional grants. In 1491, a royal commission once again rejected Columbus's calculations, but, at the last moment, the Queen decided to take a chance on him. As one old story goes, planning to leave Spain, he was already well down the road, completely dejected, when a rider overtook him to say that the Queen had changed her mind. What most likely motivated her was the chance to invest a little, with the chance of gaining more. It was a gamble. Isabel, however, did not hock the royal jewels. (That is another bogus children's story.) She did provide some funds for the expedition, and then levied a tax on the southern port city of Palos to finance and man three ships. Columbus and some friends provided the rest of the capital. This was truly an enterprise of venture capitalists.

Part of the reason for the reluctance of the monarchs to back him may have been the exorbitant demands Columbus made for his services. In the agreement he signed with them in 1491, they agreed to give him a share of all profits, to name him "governor general and admiral of the ocean sea" should he succeed, and to ennoble him—some strikingly bold demands for a foreigner with little formal education, wealth, and no family connections to the Spanish elite!

THE COLUMBIAN MOMENT

In August of 1492, Columbus sailed from Palos in three ships: the legendary *Niña*, *Pinta*, and *Santa Maria* with some 90 men. Two brothers, Martín Alonso and Vicente Yáñez Pinzón, commanded the *Niña* and the *Pinta*. Talk about daring, or foolhardy—these ships were only 90 feet long, about the size of a yacht. The three ships stopped in the Canary Islands, made some repairs, replenished supplies, and headed due west into the unknown in early September. Columbus, like many great figures in history, was also incredibly lucky. He encountered perfect sailing conditions, and, by moving as far south as he did, he caught the prevailing westerly winds across the Atlantic. We know a fair amount about the voyage because Columbus kept a daily log or diary, and parts of that account have survived. About four weeks later and 2,400 miles west, he spotted land, probably one of the islands of the Bahamas. Believing he was in the Indies, he called the locals "Indians," and proceeded to scout among the islands. Columbus could not have imagined the enormous consequences of this landing on a small island on the morning of October 12, 1492.

As he spotted islands, he claimed them for Castile, and named them after his patrons (San Salvador or "the Savior," Fernandina, Isabela, and Española). Martín Alonso Pinzón and his crew disappeared with the *Pinta*. On Christmas Eve, as a drunken crew slept, the *Santa Maria* ran aground on the coast of Española (better known in English as Hispaniola, modern-day Haiti and the Dominican Republic). Columbus would eventually decide to leave forty men (nearly half his crew) behind at a settlement he christened La Navidad (Christmas) to remember the ill-fated ship grounding. As he prepared to return to Spain, Martín Alonso reappeared with the *Pinta*, offering excuses for his departure. It must have been a testy reunion. In February, both ships headed north, and, as luck would have it again, they caught the prevailing easterly winds that carried them home. Terrible winter storms separated the two ships. Columbus managed to stop in the Azores before sailing into the harbor at Lisbon in the first days of March 1493. Columbus spent several days with the king who must have (eventually) lamented the enormous lands and opportunity that had slipped through his grasp. Columbus then sailed back to southern Spain, completing a journey that had taken eight months. Right on his heels, Pinzón arrived in the *Pinta*. Depressed and ailing, Pinzón immediately rowed ashore without so much as greeting Columbus or his brother Vicente, and he died soon after. Columbus proceeded overland some 800 miles to Barcelona to present his findings (including some six unfortunate Indians) to Fernando and Isabel.

March of 1493 is Columbus's great moment. On his return, Fernando and Isabel receive him as a hero and name him Duke of Veragua, Admiral of the Ocean Sea, and Governor General of the Indies. A less ambitious man would have retired in glory. Instead, Columbus immediately outfitted a much larger fleet, and, in late 1493, headed back across the Atlantic. He would make three more voyages across the "Great Western Sea" over the next decade. He would never find China or Japan, and he would die in 1506, embittered and in disgrace for his error and his mismanagement of Spanish possessions in the Caribbean. His remains were buried and moved on several occasions in succeeding centuries, and today, four cities (Santo Domingo, Havana, Seville, and Valladolid) all claim to have his bones. Even in death, Columbus remains a mystery.

So what are we to make of all this? Here was a man with a single-minded purpose, or put more bluntly, a fanaticism, that drove him across the Atlantic in search of Asia, only to stumble upon the Americas. He wanted to seek a direct sea route to the spice trade in the East, and he ended up among an unknown people in the West. But, in the end, the debate over whether Columbus was hero or villain, a crazed (and lucky) medieval figure or a visionary (and prophetic) Renaissance man, misses the point.

In the final analysis, it is not the man, but the process he initiated, that matters most. In October of 1492, these two worlds began a process of exchange—of plants, animals, peoples, and germs—that reshaped both worlds, and created a single world. As we have seen, of the four major crops that feed the world today—wheat, rice, corn, and potatoes—the first two were known only in the Old World, and corn and potatoes only in the New. The animals of the Old World, cattle, horses, pigs, sheep, and chickens (to name a few) would transform life and the diet of the Americas. Tobacco and chocolate, to mention just two plants, would revolutionize diet, and vice, in the Old World. And finally, the microbes of the Old World would wreak havoc among the peoples of the Americas. Smallpox, influenza, and measles, in particular, annihilated millions. The standard estimate of the impact of Old World disease on Native Americans is that 85 to 90 percent of the population of the Americas had disappeared within 50 years. This is the largest demographic catastrophe in human history. And that is why, when all is said and done, Christopher Columbus, and the Columbian Moment, are so central, not only to the history of the Americas, but also to the history of all peoples of the world.

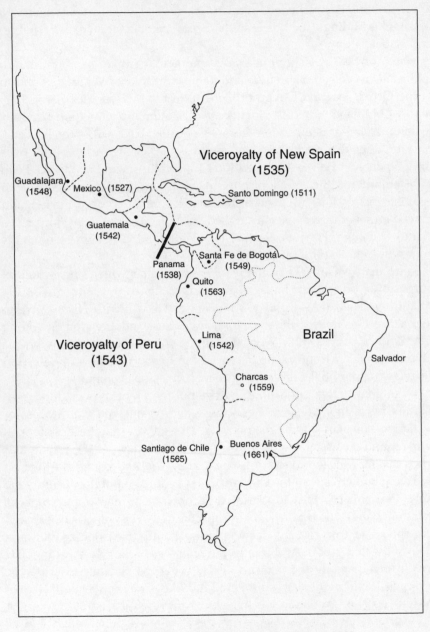

Map 3. Spanish and Portuguese America ca. 1700

5

The First Conquest

THE CARIBBEAN CRUCIBLE

Following the lead of Columbus, the Spanish swept across the Caribbean within a generation, conquering and destroying the native peoples in their path. The Spanish moved through the conquest of the islands in what I call a "stepping-stone" process. They would conquer an island, establish a base of operations, and then move outward from there in a step-by-step pattern. Hispaniola, for example, became the staging ground for invading Cuba, and then Cuba for the conquest of Mexico. From island to island the Spanish replicated the original process on Hispaniola, while adding new features to respond to the different lands and peoples they encountered. In a pattern that would be reproduced across Latin America for the next century, the conquerors divided the spoils—plunder, land, and Indians—among themselves. The conquest operated on something of a seniority system. The senior members of the expeditions got the best spoils, and those who got the smaller shares, along with those who arrived in the later waves of conquistadors, were pushed outward to find their own riches and to conquer their own lands. Unlike the Portuguese, who consciously set out to build their factories, or trading posts, the Spanish came to conquer, pillage, and then settle in as colonists. After the initial conquest, they recognized that all future wealth would have to come from the land, and the key to producing on the land was the exploitation of non European labor.

In so many ways, the Caribbean was the "crucible of the Americas"—a proving ground for methods and processes that the Spanish then replicated and developed in many other regions. In the military conquest, they would seize the local Indian chief in order to "decapitate" the "nation" they were fighting. The Arawak word for leader or chief was corrupted into Spanish as "*cacique*," and this became the generic term used by the Spanish across the Americas to refer to Indian leaders. (The Arawak language also contributed a large number of words to Spanish, such as: *canoa* [canoe], *barbacoa* [barbeque], *huracán* [hurricane], and *hamaca* [hammock].) After subjugating the Indian peoples, the conquistadors put them to work on the land to produce tribute. The system they put into place in the Caribbean was derived from one developed in the Reconquest of Spain. Eventually known as the *encomienda*, it was a grant from the Crown of the *use* of land, and the labor on it, in exchange for developing the land, protecting it, and Christianizing the Indians. In theory, the Crown retained ownership of the land. The *encomienda* would spread with the conquest to the rest of Spanish America.

Whether through force or consent, the Spanish mated with Indian (and then African) women, immediately creating a new generation of racially-mixed peoples (mestizos and mulattoes). The first cataclysmic collisions between peoples produced this cultural and biological mixture. In a very profound sense, Latin America begins with the birth of this first generation of racially-mixed children. The mestizos and mulattoes are the living, breathing embodiment of this new culture and people. These "multicultural" children born of the first moments of the Conquest, quite literally, are the first Latin Americans. The cultures and societies of Latin America begin with them. At its core, the history of Latin America for the past five hundred years has been a story of miscegenation (racial mixing), so that today this racial and cultural mixture defines most of Latin America.

The Spanish also created legal and religious institutions to control and regulate the lives of the non-European majority they dominated. Again, they first turned to their experience conquering the Moors, but then they had to create new institutions that did not exist in Iberia to deal with these new lands and peoples. In the Americas, the Spanish created two parallel worlds—what they called the "republic" of the Spaniards, and a "republic" of Indians. In good medieval fashion, each world was explicitly and clearly hierarchical, racist, and built on inequalities and privileges. These were the basic patterns of the Spanish conquest.

The greatest prizes in the Caribbean were the larger islands: Hispaniola, Puerto Rico, and Cuba. The island of Hispaniola became the first major staging ground for conquest and colonization in 1492–93. The first settlement on the north side of the island failed after Columbus returned to Spain. No one knows why, but all of the men left behind at La Navidad (Christmas) were dead when the Admiral returned. The most common theory is that they mistreated the local Indians and brought massive retaliation and annihilation down on the settlement. When he returned in 1493, Columbus founded Santo Domingo on the south side of the island.

This settlement became the first center of operations for the Spanish conquest and colonization. It has the distinction of being the oldest European settlement in the Americas. Santo Domingo became the first Spanish city in the Americas, and the founding point of the key legal, political, economic, and cultural institutions. It became the prototype for the founding and design of other Spanish American cities. Laid out on a grid plan, it had the cathedral on one side of the main square, and the governor's palace on another, with the city council quarters on a third side. The residences of the most important families in the community would always be on or near the main plaza.

The Spanish moved across the island, subduing all the native peoples in a ferocious series of battles. The conquistadores very quickly abandoned nearly all efforts at negotiation and alliance. In most cases, they simply employed brutal force and bloody destruction of the Indians. Despite bitter opposition and the Indians' numerical superiority, Spanish weapons and tactics overwhelmed them. Spanish cannons, firearms, and steel swords provided a technological edge for the Europeans. Horses and dogs of war proved enormously effective. Disease also began to annihilate the Indians. Almost with the first waves of Europeans, epidemics appeared, ravaging the Indian peoples. Smallpox was especially devastating. Syphilis also appeared, although its origins remain hotly contested. It appears that the bacillus for the disease existed in both the Old and New Worlds, but the Conquest somehow triggered a virulent new form that killed and crippled both Native Americans and Europeans. (The first outbreak of syphilis in Europe was among Spanish armies in the mid-1490s.) In the half-century after 1492, Old World diseases struck down possibly 85 to 90 percent of the native population of the Americas! The carnage was appalling —some 40 to 45 million people died within two generations. (As a comparison, an equivalent demographic catastrophe for the United States today would be the deaths of 240 to 250 million people.) The Native Americans paid a very high price for their long isolation from the microbes of the Old World.

Bartolomé de las Casas, one of the greatest figures in Latin American history, witnessed the conquest of the island of Hispaniola and wrote scathing denunciations of Spanish methods. Born around 1474, Las Casas had come to the Caribbean as a merchant and conquistador. As a mature adult, he took his vows as a Dominican priest and then dedicated the rest of his long life to defending the Indian peoples of the Americas. He crossed the Atlantic 14 times in the sixteenth century, surely an extraordinary accomplishment in itself! His *Short Account of the Destruction of the Indies* (1542), a passionate denunciation of Spanish treatment of the Indians, remains in print and widely read today. According to Las Casas, the conquistadores counted "it as nothing to drench the Americas in human blood and to dispossess the people who are the natural masters and dwellers in those vast and marvellous kingdoms, killing a thousand million of them, and stealing treasures beyond compare." (The Dutch and English, in particular, happily translated the works of Las Casas and promoted the so-called Black Legend—the notion that the Spanish were an especially evil, bloodthirsty, and rapacious people. This anti-Spanish prejudice continues to pervade many accounts of the Conquest in writings, especially in English, up to the present.)

From Hispaniola, the Spanish moved out in all directions, stumbling onto other islands, and the mainland of North, South, and Central America. By 1506, they had overrun Puerto Rico, and by 1511 they had swept across Cuba. The smaller islands also fell like dominoes. Cuba, the largest and richest of the islands, soon eclipsed Hispaniola as the key staging ground. The Spanish crown divided up the best lands in Cuba and awarded them (and the Indians on them) to the conquistadores. The largest island of the Caribbean, Cuba substantially magnified the scale of the conquest and the need to develop institutions to deal with more and more lands and Indians. The size of *encomiendas* rose dramatically as landholdings became enormous. On these islands, in these first three decades of the Conquest, the large, landed estate emerged. It would prove to be perhaps the most enduring, and insidious, legacy of the Iberian conquest of the Americas. The institutions developed in Hispaniola were put into place on other islands.

By 1519, the Spanish had swept across the Caribbean, conquering, annihilating, and establishing the institutions for a growing colonial empire. The rapidity of the conquest of the Caribbean and the devastation to native peoples were appalling. As the Spanish hopped across the islands, they also landed on and explored the coastlines of the American mainland. Several expeditions moved northward into Florida, the Mississippi River Valley, and the southeast of what would become the United States. Those who chose to move north from the Caribbean failed to find riches even equal to those of the Caribbean conquest. Those who moved southward from the islands also had little luck, as they explored and colonized what became known in English as the Old Spanish Main. This region stretched from modern-day Venezuela to Panama. As with the northward expeditions, these unlucky conquistadores failed to find the riches and spoils equal to those of the Caribbean.

The greatest spoils of conquest lay to the west (in Mexico and Central America) and to the south (in the Andes of western South America). By 1519, a series of voyages to the west, especially from Cuba, had probed the long coastline of Central America. In particular, they had moved along the Yucatán Peninsula, bringing back stories of a great empire to the west. In 1517, Francisco Hernández de Córdoba led an expedition from Cuba to the Yucatán. The Yucatec Maya resisted the invaders ferociously, killing half of the expedition and fatally wounding Hernández de Córdoba. The governor of Cuba, Diego Velázquez, then dispatched Juan de Grijalva with an expeditionary force. The Maya again drove the Spanish back to Cuba, but Grijalva brought back the first reports of a great empire on the mainland. A generation after the arrival of Columbus in Hispaniola, the Spanish had conquered the Caribbean islands, and they had stumbled upon the gateway to one of the two greatest prizes in the Americas—the Aztec empire in Mexico.

THE CONQUEST OF MEXICO

The conquest of Mexico is an epic tale of the catastrophic collision of two powerful and aggressively expanding empires. The tale has all the elements of high drama. It is the story of how a thousand Spaniards toppled a mighty civilization of millions. Two heroic and tragic figures provide the drama with a personal focus—Montezuma, the Aztec ruler, and Hernán Cortés, the ruthless leader of the Spanish conquistadores. Daring military tactics and tragic miscalculations combined to bring down a powerful empire. This tale has been chronicled several times—in classic accounts by Cortés himself in his letters back to the Spanish emperor; by his lieutenant, Bernal Díaz del Castillo; by the Aztecs themselves in the aftermath of the Conquest; in the nineteenth century by William Hickling Prescott; and, most recently, by Sir Hugh Thomas. We should always keep in mind that this is the story of the clash of two powerful and expanding civilizations and empires, and not of the destruction of some idyllic, egalitarian Native American people living in harmony with nature. Both empires had emerged over the previous century. Both were monarchies led by powerful leaders. Militant and aggressive religions drove both empires outward through conquest, and both were built on very complex social and cultural systems.

In many ways, the conquest of Mexico is a classic example of the old view that great events take shape when the "man and the hour meet." Hernán Cortés was that man, and he brilliantly exploited the opportunities that the historical moment provided him. He is certainly the greatest and most famous of the Spanish conquistadores of the sixteenth century. We know that Cortés was from a family in the small town of Medellín in Extremadura, the southwestern region of Spain that produced so many of the conquistadores. Born in 1484 or 1485, he wanted to fight in Italy but instead headed to the Caribbean as a teenager in 1504, participating in the conquest of Cuba after 1509. Most likely he came from a family that was down on its luck, and he was probably on the fringes of the lower nobility. He probably studied law at the University of Salamanca, but most likely was not a graduate. Like many of the conquistadores, he came from a relatively privileged position in Spanish society. They had the training and the means to have options in life that were not available to the great rural masses, but were unable to live a sufficiently comfortable life among the nobility. The Americas offered these ambitious men the opportunity for increased wealth and social mobility. Those in the upper reaches of the nobility had little incentive to leave Spain and take any risks in the conquest. Those at the bottom of the social hierarchy had little opportunity to take those risks, but seized the opportunity when it came along.

Cortés tied his fortunes to the new governor of Cuba, Diego Velázquez, and prospered as an estate owner, local magistrate, and owner of gold mines. With a reputation as a womanizer and gambler, he apparently seduced Catalina Suárez Marcaida and then reluctantly married her in 1515 and had one son with her, Martín. In his early thirties, he could have remained a successful landowner and local figure, but he did not choose to settle down. Cortés was a restless man. When word came back from expeditions in 1517–18 about powerful and wealthy empires in lands to the west, Velázquez began to mount a large expedition to confront and conquer these peoples. Velázquez had to find a leader, but he feared that anyone capable of leading the expedition might also eventually strike out on his own. He was right, and he made the wrong choice: Hernán Cortés. A large share of the financing for the mission came from the personal fortune of Cortés. At the last minute, in February 1519, hearing that he was to be removed from his post by a nervous Velázquez, Cortés ordered his 11 ships and 500 men to embark for the westward voyage. (There were also eight women aboard.) He defied royal authority in the process.

The first stages of the conquest of Mexico are the story of serious miscalculations by Montezuma, and ruthlessly cunning maneuvers by Cortés. His first moves were to establish a base of operations, consolidate his control over his men, and to begin to exploit divisions among the Indians of Mexico. In one of his first encounters with the Maya along the coast of Yucatán, Cortés stumbled upon Gerónimo de Aguilar, a Spaniard who had been shipwrecked years earlier and had "gone native," marrying into local society and learning the language. He provided Cortés with an interpreter, and extremely valuable information about local society. The expedition moved along the coast of the Yucatán peninsula to its western base at Tabasco where the Spanish had their first serious battle and victory. The Tabascans gave Cortés 20 women as a present. Among them was a young, noble Aztec captive, Malintzin, baptized Marina by the Spanish. Probably about 15 years of age, Marina came from southern Mexico. Various accounts of her origins and enslavement exist, but none are considered definitive. Initially, Cortés gave her to another conquistador, Alonso Hernández Portocarrero, but when he returned to Spain in June 1519,

Doña Marina, or La Malinche, as she is also known, became Cortés's mistress, and eventually his interpreter. (She spoke Nahuatl, the language of the Aztecs, and she learned Spanish very quickly.) She would bear him a son, also named Martín, in 1522. Cortés would eventually have him legally recognized as a legitimate son and heir. Marina played a crucial role in the Conquest, providing Cortés with the ability to understand the Aztecs. She had knowledge of the Aztec empire and their political system and worldview that she could convey to the Spaniards. She also could listen to the Aztecs and give Cortés a sense of their deliberations and disagreements. The Aztecs had no equivalent of Marina, and this created an important asymmetry in their knowledge about each other.

On Easter Sunday, April 21, 1519, Cortés established the city of Vera Cruz (the "true cross"), where he spent the next four months ferreting out his enemies and cultivating his friends, among both Indians and Spaniards. Here Cortés exhibited his legal knowledge and training. By creating his own town and town council, he placed his men and himself directly under the control of the Spanish monarch, and not that of the governor of Cuba. He immediately sent emissaries to the court in Madrid to make an appeal on his behalf to the young king, Charles or Carlos I. Charles I was a central figure in the emergence of Spain as the greatest power in the world in the sixteenth century. His mother, Juana, was the daughter of Fernando and Isabel. His father was the son of the Hapsburg ruler of the Austrian Empire. Born in Ghent in 1500, he grew up speaking Flemish. His grandmother, Isabel, died in 1504, and Fernando in 1516. His father died before Fernando, and his mother had been declared mentally incapacitated (she is known in Spanish history as Juana la Loca). When Charles ascended to the throne in 1516, he inherited an impressive empire: from his mother's side of the family he acquired Spain and its possessions in the Americas, and from the Hapsburgs, the Low Countries and parts of southern Italy. He was elected Holy Roman Emperor, and is best known by the title Charles V (the fifth Charles to rule the Holy Roman Empire), although he was the first Charles to rule Spain. Cortés wrote a series of lengthy letters to the emperor and they are one of the great sources for understanding the Spanish view of the conquest of Mexico—vivid accounts of the conquistador in the heat of the conquest.

Cortés bullied and persuaded the coastal Indians, the Totonacs, to join up with him, and he was careful not to challenge the Aztecs directly. He followed the same strategy with each Indian group he encountered. Gradually, he added hundreds of Indian warriors to his 500 Spanish troops. His most effective weapons were the deadly, powerful crossbow, steel swords, a crude firearm called the harquebus (something akin to a rifle or musket), and small cannons. Ferocious mastiffs would tear Indian warriors to shreds, and enormous war horses initially frightened and perplexed the

Indians, who had never seen quadrupeds larger than a deer. Early on, they seemed to believe that the mounted Spaniard and the horse were a single being, something like the ancient centaur. The most effective Indian weapons were arrows and projectiles, especially sharpened stones. Very quickly the Spaniards adopted the Indians' thick, tightly-woven cotton vests as better protection against these projectiles than their own chain mail.

The Spaniards and their Indian allies marched toward the center of the Aztec empire. Located on an island on Lake Texcoco in the Valley of Mexico, Tenochtitlan was connected to the lakeshores on the north, west, and south, by impressive causeways. A highly developed urban center, the city had a population of perhaps 250,000, making it one of the largest cities in the world, certainly much larger than any city in Spain. Montezuma, hearing of the arrival of the strangers, hesitated in his response, and sealed his fate. Montezuma had become the Aztec emperor in 1502, when he was probably around 35 years of age. (Also known in Spanish as Moctezuma, the most accurate transliteration of his name from Nahuatl is Motecuhzuma, but I will stick with the traditional spelling.) He was described by one of the early Spanish chroniclers as "a man of medium stature, with a certain gravity and royal majesty, which showed clearly who he was even to those who did not know him."

Cortés arrived in Mexico at the end of the Aztec 52-year calendar cycle, a period of immense apprehension and dread in the Aztec religion. At the end of each cycle, the Aztecs believed that the world might be destroyed before a new cycle could begin. It is also possible that Montezuma feared that Cortés was an exiled god, returning to claim his lands. (Historians have long been skeptical of the Aztec sources for this line of argument. All of them were written after the Conquest and can easily be read as ex post facto rationalizations of the Aztec failure to defeat the Spanish.) According to Aztec religious tradition, the feathered serpent god, Quetzalcóatl, had long ago been exiled to the east, and one day he would return to claim his lands. There are indications that Montezuma may have thought, at least initially, that Cortés was Quetzalcóatl. In the months and years preceding the arrival of the Spanish, strange omens appeared in central Mexico, including a flaming ear of corn in the sky, a bird with a mirror embedded in his head, and a temple bursting into flame. The Spanish had arrived in the year of 1-Reed, the predicted date for the return of Quetzalcóatl!

In August 1519, Cortés set out for the Aztec capital. Over nearly three months, the conquistadores moved up into the mountains of central Mexico, covering more than 200 miles. Before departing from Vera Cruz, Cortés dramatically stripped and scuttled his ships, leaving his small army no alternative but to forge ahead. As a warning to those who might challenge his authority, he hanged one challenger and cut off the feet of another. The Spanish rose through the mountain valleys of central Mexico, passing peaks that reached 17,000–18,000 feet above sea level. They fought and negotiated with various Indian groups, drawing them into their struggle against the Aztec imperialists. The most important of these allies was the Tlaxcalans, living around a city-state some 50 miles to the east of Tenochtitlan. In September, Cortés reached Tlaxcala and he marveled at the size and sophistication of the city: "This city is so big and so remarkable that . . . the little I will say is, I think, almost unbelievable, for the city is much larger than Granada and very much stronger, with as good buildings and many more people than Granada had when it was taken. . . . There is in the city a market where each and every day upward of thirty thousand people come to buy and sell . . ."

After fierce fighting, he persuaded the Tlaxcalans (who were bitter enemies of the Aztecs) to join his cause. The battles against the Tlaxcalans are vividly described in Bernal Díaz's classic account, *The True History of the Conquest of New Spain*:

> We were four hundred, of whom many were sick and wounded, and we stood in the middle of a plain six miles long, and perhaps as broad, swarming with Indian warriors. Moreover we knew that they had come determined to leave none of us alive except those who were to be sacrificed to their idols. When they began to charge the stones sped like hail from their slings, and their barbed and fire-hardened darts fell like corn on the threshing floor, each one capable of piercing any armor or penetrating the unprotected vitals. Their swordsmen and spearmen pressed us hard, and closed with us bravely, shouting and yelling as they came.

From Tlaxcala, the Spaniards moved 30 miles south to subdue Cholula. Possibly to cement their pact with the Tlaxcalans (who were also bitter enemies of the Cholulans), the Spanish massacred the nobility of Cholula and possibly as many as 3,000 others. All along the way, Montezuma's emissaries had attempted to persuade the Spaniards not to approach the Aztec capital. Gifts of gold and other precious items failed to buy off the Spanish, but their reaction to the gold shocked the Aztecs. According to one famous Aztec chronicle, "The Spaniards appeared much delighted . . . they seized upon the gold like monkeys, their faces flushed. For clearly their thirst for gold was insatiable; they starved for it; they lusted for it; they wanted to stuff themselves with it as if they were pigs." Undeterred by the pleadings of the emissaries, Cortés prepared to enter the Valley of Mexico and the Aztec capital.

The Spanish entry into the Valley of Mexico in November 1519, and their reception by Montezuma as they entered the Aztec capital, is one of the great moments in the conquest of the Americas. Fortunately, we have

accounts, both by the Spanish and the Aztecs. We have the impressions of
Bernal Díaz as the Spaniards approached the city on the lake:

> when we saw all those cities and villages built in the water, and other great
> towns on dry land, and that straight and level causeway leading to Mexico,
> we were astounded. These great towns and temples and buildings rising
> from the water, all made of stone, [and it] seemed like an enchanted
> vision. . . . Indeed, some of our soldiers asked whether it was not all a
> dream. It is not surprising therefore that I should write in this vein. It was all
> so wonderful that I do not know how to describe the first glimpse of things
> never heard of, seen or dreamed of before.

A post-Conquest Aztec account describes the initial encounter this way:

> Motecuhzoma now arrayed himself in his finery . . . [and] went out to meet
> them. . . . He presented many gifts to the Captain [Cortés] and his com-
> manders, those who had come to make war. He showered gifts upon them
> and hung flowers around their necks; he gave them necklaces of flowers
> and bands of flowers to adorn their breasts. . . . Then he hung gold neck-
> laces around their necks and gave them presents of every sort as gifts of
> welcome.

Much to his later chagrin, Montezuma lodged the Spanish in one of his
palaces. Within days, the daring Spaniards took Montezuma as their
hostage, "decapitating" the empire. This daring move of "seizing the
cacique" provoked a crisis at the highest levels of the empire. With their
ruler as prisoner, the Aztecs hesitated to attack the invaders, but Cortés
could do no more than demand an enormous ransom in gold, while
unable to attack the tens of thousands of Aztec subjects around him. With
this bold capture, Cortés paralyzed the Aztecs for several months. It was
the beginning of the end of the mighty empire.

In less than a year, Cortés and his men had moved from vague notions
of an expedition to the west, to traveling to the heart of the Aztec capital.
He had cunningly exploited divisions among the Indian enemies of the
Aztecs, and manipulated the hesitant Montezuma. From February to
August 1519, he had surveyed the coast, acquired Marina, founded a city,
and then consolidated control over his men. From August to November,
he marched inland to the Aztec capital, adding thousands of Indian warriors to his band of about 500 Spaniards. Cortés and his men were also
risking everything, should they fail to conquer and acquire great riches
for the king. With his flight from Cuba, he had defied the king's representative, the governor of Cuba. He had committed treason, and his only
hope was to make a case for establishing his own legal authority independent of Cuba. This was his reason for founding Vera Cruz, and his
famous letters back to Charles V, in essence, were making a case that his
success should overshadow any charges of insubordination.

Sitting in the center of Tenochtitlan, surrounded by hundreds of thousands of hostile Indians, Cortés faced an even greater challenge from his own people. From the moment of his hurried departure from Cuba, Diego Velázquez had tried to bring Cortés back to face the consequences of his defiance of the governor's authority. Cortés had adeptly countered the efforts to stop him in Vera Cruz, eventually sinking his own ships to prevent any retreat or second thoughts. A small group had arrived in Mexico in July 1519 and news of Velázquez's displeasure had instigated conspiracies against Cortés by Velázquez's supporters. As Cortés moved into central Mexico, Velázquez prepared to chase him down. Surrounded now in Tenochtitlan, Cortés learned that a larger, second expedition led by Pánfilo Narváez had landed on the coast in April 1520. With nearly a thousand troops, including 80 horsemen, 120 crossbowmen, and 80 harquebusiers, the expedition presented a formidable challenge for Cortés.

In a daring move, Cortés left 120 of his men under the command of Pedro de Alvarado in Tenochtitlan, and, with the other two-thirds of his men, he marched back to the coast, where he brilliantly outmanuevered and defeated Narváez in late May 1520. With fewer than 300 men, he launched a surprise midnight attack, capturing Narváez (who lost an eye in the battle). He then persuaded hundreds of the soldiers to join him, and those who showed hostility were imprisoned in Vera Cruz. As Cortés returned to Tenochtitlan with hundreds more men, Alvarado had brought down the wrath of the Aztecs on the Spanish in the capital. In a massacre whose origins are bitterly contested, the Spaniards fell upon the Aztecs during a religious ceremony, slaughtering them in droves. Hundreds, perhaps thousands, were trapped in a courtyard while celebrating the festival of Toxcatl in honor of the Aztec god, Huitzilopochtli. Spanish steel cut to pieces many of the elite warriors and nobles, contributing to the weakening of the Indians' ability to respond. The Aztecs allowed the Spaniards to reenter the capital, probably hoping to entrap and annihilate the entire Spanish force. The Spanish forces that reentered the Aztec capital in June 1520 now numbered some 1300 men, nearly 100 horses, 80 crossbowmen, and 80 harquebusiers. This force was joined by nearly 2,000 Tlaxcalan warriors.

With Montezuma's authority nearly completely spent, the Aztecs declared war and laid siege to the Spaniards and their allies for three weeks. It appears that the Spanish garroted the now useless Montezuma, along with many other Aztec nobles, and threw their bodies into the surrounding streets. The surviving Aztec nobles selected Cuitlahuac as the new emperor (or *tlatoani*) and an all-out war ensued. Running out of food, water, and gunpowder, Cortés decided to flee the city. After failing to break out of the capital several times, he made one last desperate attempt. On the infamous "Sad Night" (*Noche Triste*, sometimes translated as "Night of Tears"), June 30, 1520, the Spanish battled their way across the shortest causeway to the western side of Lake Texcoco. Cortés hoped to sneak out of the city in the middle of the night. The Spanish had built a portable bridge to span the gaps in the causeway the Aztecs had created to trap them in the capital. Initially, the escape was aided by a fierce rainstorm, but the alarm was quickly sounded. Attacked by thousands of Aztec warriors on the causeway, and from canoes on the lake, the Spaniards and their Indian allies suffered staggering losses. Nearly all the Tlaxcalans were killed and many Spaniards died from wounds or drowned after falling into the surrounding waters. Some Spaniards were cut off and forced to barricade themselves again in the city's center. (They were later captured, forced to dance naked on the great pyramid in the center of the city, and then sacrificed to Huitzilopochtli.) Most of the Spaniards' horses and all their artillery were lost, and many Spaniards drowned in the lake, pulled down by the gold they had accumulated from Montezuma's ransom. For five days the Spanish fought their way around the lake to Tlaxcala. The Spanish managed to survive annihilation, but they lost nearly 900 men (and 5 women who had arrived with Narváez). Over 1,000 Tlaxcalan warriors died alongside the Spanish. Cortés, Marina, Aguilar, Alvarado, and other key lieutenants survived the disastrous retreat.

At this darkest moment for Cortés and the Spanish, they began to plan another military campaign that would eventually bring them total victory. With his forces decimated, his weapons advantage blunted, and still facing challenges from Cuba, Cortés embarked on a series of brilliant diplomatic manuevers in the second half of 1520. He astutely balanced the factions within his own people, and the complex relations among the multiple peoples in central Mexico. With the help of the Tlaxcalans, he brought many of the Indian peoples of central Mexico into an anti-Aztec alliance. These allies, who had fought so fiercely against the Aztecs, now had their fate tied closely to the Spaniards. Should the Aztecs regroup and defeat the Spanish, these allies would surely go down with the invaders. The destruction and political disarray in Tenochtitlan bought Cortés time to regroup and the remaining 450 Spaniards time to heal from their wounds.

As he moved to lay siege on Tenochtitlan in early 1521, another deadly ally emerged—smallpox. One of Narváez's expedition had arrived infected with smallpox. The disease rapidly spread throughout the empire, striking down some 40 percent of the people of central Mexico within a year. Although the disease weakened the Aztecs, it also laid waste to the Spanish allies. More important, it devastated the Aztec nobility and potential leaders, leading to further disarray. Known as the "great rash" in Aztec accounts, smallpox killed Montezuma's successor, Cuitlahuac. The psychological and cultural dislocation must have been enormous, as the Indians surely seriously questioned the power of their own gods, and the strength of the invaders.

New men drawn to Mexico by news of the advancing conquest, the growing number of Indian allies, and disease gradually tightened the siege. Amazingly, Cortés ordered the building of some thirteen small ships (40 feet in length) to press the siege of Tenochtitlan. (The shipwright, Martín López, became one of the most important assets of the Spaniards.) A thousand Indian porters brought from Vera Cruz the sails and riggings that Cortés had stripped from his own fleet before sinking it. In late December 1520, Cortés marched back to the Aztec capital with 550 Spanish soldiers, and 10,000 Tlaxcalan warriors. Through political and diplomatic maneuvering, Cortés brought the city of Texcoco to his side, and it provided him with a base of operations for the siege. Through selective acts of terror, he bullied his Spanish and Indian antagonists. At this point, Cortés discovered a plot against him by some of the men from the Narváez expedition. He hanged one of the key culprits as a lesson to the others.

The Aztec resistance was ferocious in its final stages under the leadership of the last Aztec leader, Cuauhtemoc. In January and February 1521, another 10,000 Tlaxcalans arrived with timbers for the shipbuilding. Controlling the surrounding lakes would be critical to the fall of Tenochtitlan. The final assault began in late April with the launching of 13 flat-bottomed brigantines. (Forty thousand Indians had to dig a channel 12 feet wide and 12 feet deep to launch the ships!) Cortés divided his force of more than 700 Spaniards and thousands of Indians into three groups under the commands of Pedro de Alvarado, Cristóbal de Olid, and Gonzalo de Sandoval. In one fierce naval battle, Cortés was wounded in the leg and was nearly dragged off by the Aztecs before being saved by his men. Ten captured Spaniards were taken to the top of the Great Temple and faced, in the words of the Aztec chronicles, the "sweet death of the obsidian knife" as an open challenge to the Spanish forces. The Aztecs tanned the faces of the sacrificed Spaniards, beards included, and sent them to surrounding towns to demonstrate Aztec power and Spanish mortality. Nevertheless, the Spanish and their allies gradually closed the circle, advancing through the city, street by street, encountering bitter resistance.

The city finally fell on August 13, 1521, after 80 days of siege warfare, the Spanish having razed nearly all the major structures in the process. The last successor to Montezuma, Cuauhtemoc, surrendered, and he was then tortured and executed. The Spanish continued to attack and pillage for several more days. Possibly as many as 100,000 Indians died in the battle for Tenochtitlan. Cortés had defeated the Aztecs with a force of a thousand Spaniards, 80 horses, 16 artillery pieces, and 13 brigantines. But they would never have succeeded without the tens of thousands of Indian allies who fought alongside them. The empire had not been conquered from without, but from within. The top of the pyramid had been lopped off, and the Spanish replaced the Aztecs as the rulers of the Mexican heartland. The Indian population would never again pose any serious military threat to the Spanish. Beyond the fringes of the Aztec empire, however, especially in the northern deserts and in the Yucatán, the Spanish would face tenacious resistance. Eloquent Aztec accounts written after the Conquest described the feeling of defeat and despair: "And all these misfortunes befell us. We saw them and wondered at them: we suffered this bitter fate. Broken spears lie in the roads; we have torn our hair in grief. . . . We have beat our heads in despair against the adobe wall for our inheritance is lost and dead."

In central Mexico, Cortés and his men quickly moved to divide up the spoils of victory—gold, land, and Indians. Back in Spain, his phenomenal success had turned the legal battle in his favor, and in October 1522, Charles V named Hernán Cortés governor and captain general of "New Spain." Three and one-half years after his insubordinate flight from Cuba, he was vindicated and rewarded. He had moved from a rebellious adventurer to an enormously wealthy royal governor over a vast new empire larger than Spain itself. He married Marina off to another conquistador, but she died soon after. Arguably, she is the most important woman in Mexican history. Cortés would make other forays into southern Mexico and Central America. Ennobled as the Marquis of the Valley of Oaxaca, he eventually returned to Spain and died near Seville in 1547 at the age of 62. He remains the most fascinating figure of all the conquistadores—cunning, ruthless, tenacious, and ambitious. No other conquistador would ever match him.

THE CONQUEST OF PERU

The conquest of the Incas is another epic tale of a struggle between two powerful and expanding empires. Despite the broad similarities with the conquest of Mexico, there are significant differences. Like the conquest of Mexico, the conquest of Peru pits a ruthless Spanish conquistador and his small army against a powerful Indian ruler and his millions of subjects. In both cases, the Spanish exploited the divisions among the Indians to bring down the empire. The Spanish very quickly seized the *cacique* and held him for ransom, paralyzing his armies. They then marched to the capital high in the mountainous interior, eventually capturing the main center of power. But the conquest of Peru is also a tale of betrayals and bloody, divisive struggles inside the two contending groups. Shortly before the arrival of the Spanish, the Inca ruler had died, and two of his sons, Atahualpa and Huáscar, were at war over control of the empire. Once the Spanish succeeded in the initial phase of the conquest, they split into bitter factions and civil war wracked Spanish Peru for years. In the end, nearly all the major leaders of the conquest of Peru were killed by this factional warfare.

Francisco Pizarro, moreover, never achieved the enormous reputation that has always surrounded Hernán Cortés.

The so-called "men of Cajamarca" were a smaller group than the army that began the conquest of Mexico, and they faced enormous problems at every step of the process. The conquest of the Incas began as a partnership among three key figures in Panama, but the dominant figure was clearly Francisco Pizarro. He was the illegitimate son of a minor noble from Trujillo, also in Extremadura in southern Spain. Like Cortés, he was a veteran of the conquest of the Caribbean, but with even more experience. He had also fought in Italy. He fought and then settled in Panama after 1509, becoming one of the more important settlers. In 1513, he accompanied Balboa on his sighting of the Pacific. Born around 1478, he was older than Cortés, but lacked his education or sophistication. Along with Diego de Almagro and a priest, Hernando de Luque, Pizarro raised funds for expeditions to a land to the south called Peru (probably the corruption of an Indian word) spurred by the successes of Cortés in Mexico.

Several expeditions probed the coast of western South America in the 1520s, moving Pizarro and his men to the fringes of a powerful empire. In 1524, he led a small expedition of 80 men to the south, but ran into horrendous problems. The group ran out of food and they battled with hostile Indians. In 1526–27, he tried again, this time with 160 men, and once more faced difficult times. The expedition was stranded on an island and Almagro returned to Panama for help. Some 13 men chose to stay with Pizarro on the island, enduring extreme isolation and starvation. When Almagro reappeared with more men and supplies seven months later, they managed to capture an Indian raft full of gold and silver, precious stones, and textiles. After pushing on south to Tumbez, on the northern fringe of the Inca empire, the expedition once again had to turn back.

Pizarro returned to Spain in 1528 and met with the triumphant Cortés—an historic encounter between the newly lionized conqueror of Mexico and the future conqueror of Peru. Charles V granted Pizarro a royal license to discover and conquer "Peru." The 13 men who had stayed on with Pizarro in the earlier, ill-fated expedition were ennobled, but Almagro received only a minor title, something that he would long hold against Pizarro. Returning triumphant to Trujillo, Francisco Pizarro recruited four of his half-brothers (Hernando, Gonzalo, Juan, and Pedro), along with other relatives and neighbors, for his expedition. (Some 38 were "gentlemen," 90 came from what we might call the middle class, and another 20 came from the lower class.) In late 1530, Pizarro's expedition left Panama, landing on the coast of Ecuador. With fewer than two hundred men, he advanced on Tumbez once again. Physical destruction and depopulation everywhere alerted them to the ongoing civil war in the empire. As Cortés had done, Pizarro expertly gathered information and learned of the divisions and the politics of the empire. He brought with him Indians captured on earlier expeditions who were native speakers of Quechua (the language of the Inca empire) and were now also fluent in Spanish. After nearly two years of wanderings and hardships in southern Ecuador and northern Peru, in late 1532 Pizarro finally moved to confront the Inca empire with 62 horsemen and 106 foot soldiers. Almagro returned to Panama for more men and supplies.

At the moment the Spaniards moved inland, a bloody civil war was drawing to a close in an empire of some five to ten million Indians. The Inca ruler since 1498, Huayna Cápac, had died around 1526, possibly from smallpox, a disease that had swept through the Caribbean and Mexico after 1518. He had many sons by various wives and no clear line of succession. Huayna Cápac had expanded the Inca Empire through conquest and had built a powerful professional army that was now controlled by his son, Atahualpa, in the northern half of the empire. The elite of the court in Cuzco selected another son, Huáscar, as the successor to Huayna Cápac. Atahualpa rallied forces around him in the north in Quito. Huáscar controlled the southern section centered around the capital of Cuzco. Eventually, Atahualpa rebelled against his half-brother. Although briefly imprisoned by Huáscar, Atahualpa ultimately turned the tables and captured Cuzco. Most of his troops were from ethnic groups to the north who occupied Cuzco and treated the local Indian tribes brutally. The brutality of the Conquest was not restricted to Spanish treatment of Indians.

About the time he received news of the arrival of the strange foreigners, Atahualpa had made camp near the town of Cajamarca. Atahualpa's spies reported back on these strange, bearded foreigners and severely underestimated them. The spies told the Inca ruler that the Spaniards could easily be taken prisoner. Pizarro communicated with the two warring Indian camps. Atahualpa allowed the small Spanish force to approach him in the Valley of Cajamarca in November 1532. A small force of horsemen met with Atahualpa. The always hotheaded Hernando de Soto even charged his horse toward Atahualpa, halting only inches from him. The Inca ruler, reportedly, did not even flinch. The Spanish settled into the buildings around the Cajamarca square after Atahualpa agreed to meet with Pizarro the following day.

Much like Montezuma before him, Atahualpa foolishly underestimated this force of 160 Spaniards in the face of some 40,000 Inca troops. Overconfident, Atahualpa left behind most of his armed soldiers as he approached the Spaniards across an open plain in front of the town. He entered the town with some 5,000 to 6,000 lightly armed retainers and servants. Hidden in the narrow streets around the plaza, the Spaniards waited nervously for Atahualpa to move into their midst. In no hurry, the Inca ruler mounted an enormous and slow ceremonial procession. Finally, with daylight disappearing, the Spaniards persuaded Atahualpa to approach the plaza. In the description of one Spanish eyewitness:

> In a very fine litter with the ends of its timber covered in silver, came the figure of Atahualpa. Eighty lords carried him on their shoulders, all wearing a very rich blue livery. His own person was richly dressed, with his crown on his head and a collar of large emeralds around his neck. He was seated on the litter, on a small stool with a rich saddle cushion. He stopped when he reached the middle of the square, with half his body exposed.

A Dominican priest, Friar Vicente de Valverde, then stepped forward with a Bible in hand and began to give a capsule explanation of Christianity and the Spanish Crown. According to one account, Atahualpa then "told him to give him the book to examine. . . . After examining it, he threw it angrily down among his men, his face a deep crimson." Valverde fled back to the Spaniards, calling for them to punish the "barbaric" Indians. Pizarro gave the signal and the Spaniards charged the stunned Incas after firing harquebuses and cannons into the packed square. Pizarro and a group of horsemen quite literally cut their way through the thousands of Indians and dragged the astonished Atahualpa back into their fortified position in the city. One Spaniard wrote that: "In the space of two hours—all that remained of daylight—all those troops were annihilated . . . six or seven thousand Indians lay dead on the plain and many more had their arms cut off and other wounds." Each Spaniard had cut down an average of 14 or 15 unarmed or lightly armed Indians in two horrible hours. Spanish steel and horses had done their job. According to the great Andean chronicler, Huamán Poma de Ayala, "They killed the Indians like ants."

Probably believing that the invaders planned to plunder and leave Peru, Atahualpa agreed to pay them an enormous ransom. (According to tradition, he reached high on the wall of his room and made a mark, promising to fill the room up to that level with gold and silver. The purported room still stands off the square in Cajamarca.) Although a prisoner, he was allowed regular communication with his subordinates, in an arrangement much like the earlier one between Montezuma and Cortés in Mexico. When Pizarro attempted to have the captive Huáscar brought to him, Atahualpa had him executed, further inflaming the divisions among the Indians. With the help of Atahualpa's supporters, the Spaniards collected quite literally a room full of gold and silver. Under royal protection, a group of Spaniards led by Hernando Pizarro scoured the countryside for plunder. Eventually the Spaniards melted down 11 tons of gold and 13 tons of silver, with a standard share of 45 pounds of gold and 90 pounds of silver! Pizarro, as the leader, received seven shares. When Almagro arrived with 150 new men, they were given tiny shares, spurring deep resentment. (According to one Inca chronicler, the Spanish would never be satisfied, no matter how much gold they received: "Even if all the snow in the Andes turned to gold, still they would not be satisfied.")

In 1533, the Spanish decided to march on to Cuzco, the center of the universe in Incan cosmology. Known as Tawantinsuyo, the "navel of the universe," Cuzco was located at 11,000 feet above sea level in the Andes Mountains to the southeast and had a population of some 50,000. Pushed by Almagro and fears that Atahualpa was plotting against them, Pizarro and his captains sentenced the Inca to death by burning. Father Valverde ostensibly persuaded the condemned monarch to accept Christian baptism, and he was then strangled, rather than burned, on July 26, 1533, an ignominious death for the once powerful Inca. (In the Andean world there is no afterlife for those without a physical body at death.) Pizarro installed a puppet ruler, Manco Inca (another son of Huayna Cápac), who eventually realized that the Spanish were not allies but exploiters. The embittered followers of Huáscar joined Pizarro and they took control of Cuzco in November 1533, seizing an even greater prize. The division of the spoils once again produced bitterness between the Pizarro and Almagro factions. Almagro and his men decided to head south in July 1535 in search of greater conquests. They would eventually cover some 3,000 miles over a period of 18 months, returning tattered and empty-handed. Worried about the vulnerability of Cuzco to Indian attacks, Pizarro returned to the coast and founded a capital for his new conquests. Named the City of Kings, because it was founded on January 6 (Epiphany, or the Day of the Three Kings, in the Christian calendar), it eventually became known as Lima, a corruption of its Indian name (Rimac).

At the same time, Atahualpa's supporters in Quito, to the north, continued to fight the Spanish. Pizarro sent his captain, Sebastián de Benalcázar, north to Quito where the Spanish and their Indian allies quickly defeated the remainder of Atahualpa's armies. The defeated Incan army burned and abandoned the city, and Benalcázar built a new Spanish city on the ruins. Manco Inca secretly amassed an army of 200,000 and in May 1536 turned on his former allies and laid siege to the 190 Spaniards and about 1,000 of their Indian allies in Cuzco. Juan Pizarro was killed in an expedition to relieve the besieged city. After a ten-month siege and the arrival of reinforcements, the Spanish lifted the siege and Manco Inca and his supporters fell back into the mountains. The inability of tens of thousands of Indians to overwhelm the small Spanish contingent in Cuzco signaled the complete inability of the Incas to defeat the Spaniards. Manco Inca withdrew to the mountains and a tiny, independent Inca kingdom survived there until the 1570s.

Even more so than Cortés, Pizarro faced serious challenges from within his own people. Diego de Almagro, who had left Peru to explore Chile, returned in April 1537 to help lift the siege of Cuzco. Almagro reentered

Cuzco and arrested Francisco Pizarro's brothers, Gonzalo and Hernando. Gonzalo managed to escape and Hernando was ransomed and freed. Both sides then prepared for battle. On the plain of Salinas (near Cuzco), the forces of the Pizarros triumphed in April 1538. Hernando Pizarro then executed Almagro in July. Three years later, in July 1541, Almagro's supporters avenged his death. Twenty heavily armed supporters of Almagro's son attacked Francisco Pizarro's palace in Cuzco, assassinated him with knife thrusts, and forced the city council to appoint the young Diego Almagro as the new governor. Manco Inca offered refuge to the assassins, who then killed him in 1544 in an effort to curry favor with the Crown.

Charles V sent out a new governor, Cristóbal Vaca de Castro. He organized the forces of the Pizarros, and in September 1542 they defeated and killed the young Almagro. Shortly afterward, Charles issued the infamous New Laws to protect the Indians and rein in the growing power of the Spanish *encomenderos* (landowners). One notorious clause called for taking Indians away from "the persons responsible for the disturbances between Pizarro and Almagro." The conquistadores quickly realized that this would effectively include all of them. King Charles sent out a new viceroy, Blasco Núñez Vela, to enforce the New Laws, and he met with immediate opposition from the conquistadores led by Gonzalo Pizarro. Gonzalo defeated and killed the new viceroy in battle in January 1546, a clear act of treason. Rather than taking the truly radical step of asserting independence from the king, Gonzalo unleashed a reign of terror on all Spaniards he suspected of disloyalty. He executed 340 Spaniards during his short rule, more than had died in the conquest! A new royal emissary, Pedro de la Gasca, astutely won over many of Gonzalo's supporters and then defeated him in April 1548. On a plain in front of Cuzco, Pizarro's surrounded forces chose to accept pardons in exchange for crossing over to the loyalist forces. Pizarro's followers abandoned him without a fight. Gonzalo and other rebel leaders were tried for treason and then beheaded. One last revolt, led by Francisco Hernández Girón, broke out in 1553 and lasted nearly a year. With his defeat and subsequent execution, the tragic Spanish conquest of Peru came to an end. The subjugation of rebel Spaniards had taken far longer to accomplish than the defeat of the Incas, and they had killed more of each other than the Incas had been able to kill of them. The conquerors of the Incas had conquered themselves.

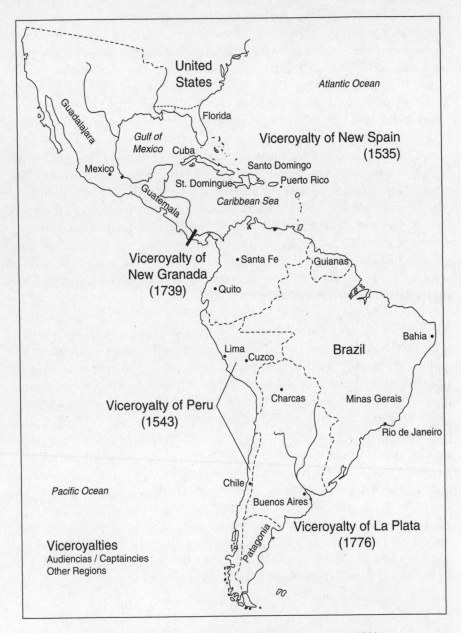

Map 4. Major Political Divisions in Latin America ca. 1800

6

The Conquest on the Peripheries

FROM THE CORE TO THE FRONTIERS

With the completion of the conquest of Peru, the three "core" regions of the Spanish empire in the Americas were in place by the 1550s. Spain's empire in the Americas would radiate outward from Mexico City in the Viceroyalty of New Spain; from Lima in the Viceroyalty of Peru; and, from the gateway to the empire, Havana, Cuba. The first two were the centers of dense Indian populations that the Spanish would harness to exploit the land. These regions were also, as it turned out by the 1550s, blessed with enormous silver deposits in the deserts of northern Mexico and the arid mountains of Upper Peru (modern-day Bolivia). Although it did not have the population density or the mineral deposits, Havana took on a key role in Spain's empire as the entry and exit point for the American colonies. The Caribbean shipping lanes became the lifeline of the American empire.

These three "core" regions served as the principal stepping-stones to the conquest of other regions. From Cuba, conquistadores had moved westward to the conquest of Mexico. Others were not as fortunate as Cortés. Rather than rich and densely populated empires, they mostly found much smaller groups of people and little mineral wealth. Some of these conquistadores left Cuba for the southeast of the future United States, and others moved along the northern coast of South America (*Tierra Firme*, or "solid ground"). Panama became the staging ground for the conquest of Peru. Almagro moved south from Peru into Argentina and Chile, and Benalcázar northward into Ecuador and northern South

America. Some even had the misfortune of moving east into Amazonia, only to be swallowed up by the dense equatorial forests. From Mexico, expeditions moved into the future southwest of the United States. Pedro de Alvarado was the luckiest of the later conquistadores, heading into the old Maya regions of Guatemala and southern Mexico.

As the Spanish hopped across the islands, they landed on and explored the coastlines of the American mainland. The most important expeditions to the north moved into Florida, the Mississippi Valley, and the southeast of what would become the United States. Juan Ponce de León, a leading figure in the conquest of Puerto Rico, died after exploring what today is Florida. He had participated in the conquest of Puerto Rico in 1508, and then became the governor of the island (called San Juan at that point) from 1509 to 1511. Hungry for more conquests, he led an expedition into the Bahamas and then to the coast of the North American mainland in 1513. His arrival coincided with the Feast of Flowers (Easter Holy Week), so he called the new territory La Florida. This was the first official Spanish expedition on the North American mainland. In 1521 he returned with another expedition and was fatally wounded in a battle with Indians.

An expedition led by the one-eyed Pánfilo de Narváez to Florida also ended disastrously for the Spanish. Narváez was one of the great losers among the early conquistadores. In the 1510s he participated in the conquest of Jamaica and Cuba. As we have seen, he led a failed expedition to arrest Hernán Cortés in 1520. After spending more than two years in prison for his failures in Mexico, he managed to redeem himself in the eyes of the Crown and the king granted him a contract to explore Florida in 1526. Shipwrecked in West Florida (near present-day Tampa Bay) in 1528, the survivors eventually built rafts and tried to sail westward along the coast. Narváez and nearly 300 men disappeared into the warm waters of the Gulf of Mexico without a trace. A handful of survivors led by Alvar Núñez Cabeza de Vaca, the expedition's treasurer, washed ashore on the coast of Texas (near the present location of Galveston). They must have been a pitiful sight. In his poignant account of his travails, Cabeza de Vaca (*cowhead*) described their first encounter with the Indians: "And at the hour of dusk the Indians came looking for us . . . and when they saw the disaster which had come upon us, and with the grief and great pity they felt for us, all of them began to cry . . . And to see those uncivilized and savage men, like brutes, were so sorry for us, caused me and the others in our company to feel even deeper grief, and to fully understand the nature of our misfortune."

Gradually, the small band worked its way across Texas, New Mexico, and northern Mexico in the 1520s in one of the epic sagas of the Spanish conquest. Cabeza de Vaca and three others, including a slave of Moroccan origin, Estebanico, made their way across this hostile and difficult terrain for eight years! This is a classic story of the so-called "civilized" European "going native." Eventually, the four of them became traders and Cabeza de Vaca gained fame as a shaman or medicine man. Very few Europeans would so completely assimilate into Native American society—and then live to tell about it. He came as close to complete empathy with the Indians as was probably humanly possible for a European of the early sixteenth century. He described one group of Indians as "wonderfully handsome folk, very lean and extremely strong and agile." In April 1536, the four men came across a contingent of Spanish soldiers on the west coast of Mexico. They had mixed feelings about their "rescuers," who promptly enslaved and sold their Indian companions. The ever restless Alvar Núñez Cabeza de Vaca quickly returned to Spain and was awarded a contract to explore southern South America. His account of his wanderings was published in the 1540s as the *Naufragios* (Shipwrecks; translated into English as *Castaways*). He later experienced another grueling trek across Paraguay.

Those who chose to move north from the Caribbean failed to find riches equal even to those of the Caribbean conquests. Those who moved southward from the islands explored and colonized what is known in English as the Old Spanish Main. This region stretched from modern-day Venezuela to Panama. In addition to settlements along the northern South American coast, the most important of these expeditions went to Panama. In 1513, Vasco Núñez de Balboa managed to cut his way across the deadly jungles and mountains of Panama to become the first European to see the Pacific Ocean. Balboa led an expedition of nearly 200 Spaniards and a thousand Indians through the dense jungles and mountains of the isthmus. In late September, he reached the continental divide and gazed across what he called the "South Sea." This feat was immortalized (albeit incorrectly) by the great Romantic poet John Keats when he wrote "On First Looking into Chapman's Homer": "Then I felt like some watcher of the skies/When a new planet swims into his ken;/Or like stout Cortez when with eagle eyes/He stared at the Pacific—and all his men/Looked at each other with a wild surmise—/Silent, upon a peak in Darien."

Many of the most ill-fated expeditions of conquest moved into the North American mainland. Hernando de Soto died while exploring the lower Mississippi Valley in 1542. De Soto had participated in the conquest of Central America in the 1510s and 1520s, and the conquest of Peru in the 1530s. Ever restless and infamous for his cruelty, he led an expedition to Florida and through what today is the U.S. South beginning in 1539 (after conferring with Cabeza de Vaca about his experiences in the region). He died in Louisiana and his companions tossed his body into the great Mississippi River. The general rule in the Conquest, ironically, was that the least developed Indian peoples were the most difficult to conquer.

Seminomadic and nomadic tribes would be the most difficult to control and subdue (the Plains Indians of North America and the peoples of the Amazon are classic examples). All along the Gulf Coast region, the conquistadores failed to find other complex and developed states they could conquer. Those Spaniards who moved into the Southwest faced even worse results.

Cabeza de Vaca's trek across Texas, New Mexico, and northern Mexico in the late 1520s and early 1530s demonstrated the futility of expending large amounts of money and men on the northern frontier of New Spain. The long and unproductive expedition of Francisco Vásquez de Coronado in the 1540s simply underscored the wisdom of the Aztecs in ending their efforts at conquest where the deserts of northern Mexico began. Wandering through what would later become the states of Arizona, New Mexico, Texas, Oklahoma, and Kansas, Coronado stumbled upon the Zuñi Indians and the Grand Canyon in his search for the fabled golden city of Cíbola. Nuño de Guzmán led expeditions into the northwest of Mexico (1529–36) in a region that became known as New Galicia. In 1546, the Spanish would find rich silver strikes in the northern deserts. The nomadic tribes of the region, known in Nahuatl as the *Chichimecs* (the dog people), battled the Spaniards into late in the sixteenth century. Even Cortés, after all his conquests in central Mexico, was foolish enough to lead an expedition westward into Baja California, encountering very little of value, but leaving his name on the Sea of Cortés. Like the Aztecs and the Incas, the Spanish would focus their attention on the densely populated regions. They needed labor to succeed, and without large populations to exploit, they soon moved on. Not until the eighteenth century would the Spanish make any headway in settling and trying to control this northern frontier, and even then their efforts were insignificant in the larger picture of the empire.

The tropical environments of northern South America proved no more hospitable to the conquistadores than the deserts of northern Mexico. In 1530, with more than 600 men, one of the lieutenants of Cortés, Diego de Ordas, explored the Orinoco River after hearing tales of gold growing in the jungle. Like so many other forays into the tropical jungles, disease and hostile Indians decimated the expeditions and they returned starving and in rags. The Welser family, the bankers of Charles V, contracted to colonize what today is Venezuela ("little Venice"), but forays led by their German agents, Ambrosius Dalfinger and Nicolás Federman, accomplished little. Somewhat more successful was Gonzalo Jiménez de Quesada, who led an expedition of some 500 men into the interior of Colombia in 1537–38. Within months, only 170 remained alive. The expedition came across the Muisca, a complex confederation with perhaps a million people near the present location of Bogotá. Attracted by tales of an Indian chief who painted himself with gold dust, the Spanish scoured the region for the so-called "golden one" (*El Dorado*). They did not find him, but they did locate a region that was (and still is) rich in gold and emeralds.

The Spaniards in Peru had heard stories of El Dorado—a land of gold and spices. In 1541, Gonzalo Pizarro set out for the east from Quito with some 200 Spaniards and several thousand Indian porters and supplies. The expedition was one of the great disasters of the conquest. As the Spanish descended from the towering Andes into the tropical Amazonian lowlands, the mountain Indians died in droves—from disease and abuse by their Spanish overseers. With their supplies gone and nearly all their Indian porters dead, the Spaniards decided to send one of their leaders, Francisco de Orellana, with some 57 men, downriver on makeshift boats in search of food. Once Orellana set off, the powerful current prevented him from returning. Pizarro and his men ate their dogs and horses, eventually gave up on Orellana, and staggered back to Quito in August 1542, returning to the fratricidal wars among the conquerors of Peru. Orellana eventually made his way 2,000 miles down the Amazon to the Atlantic, and in late 1542 he and his men found their way back to Santo Domingo. Inadvertently, these Spaniards had become the first Europeans to navigate the Amazon. The immense waterway became known as the River of the Amazons when Orellana reported a fierce battle on the river with a tribe led by women warriors who had cut off one breast to facilitate the expert use of a bow. These warriors were compared to the Amazons of Greek mythology. No one else has seen them since Orellana.

Central America was perhaps the most important exception to the lack of results of those who moved outward from the core regions. Pedro de Alvarado's conquest of the Maya in the 1540s was a smaller-scale version of the conquests in Mexico and Peru. Passionate, impetuous, and often lacking any self-control, Alvarado was a complete contrast to the coldly rational and calculating Cortés. Alvarado left Mexico in December 1523. Smallpox preceded him, greatly diminishing Indian resistance to Spanish troops and their Indian allies (mainly Tlaxcalans from central Mexico). After fighting their way through Chiapas in southern Mexico, Alvarado found the Cakchiquel and Quiché Maya at war with each other. He allied with the Cakchiquel, who stood by as the Spanish defeated the Quiché. According to tradition, Alvarado himself defeated the Quiché ruler, Tecúm-Umán, in hand-to-hand combat. An old Indian legend says that a proud and distraught quetzal bird landed on the bloodied ruler to protect his body. When he flew off, he had a bright, blood-red chest of feathers to go with his brilliant green feathers. (The quetzal today is the national bird of Guatemala and the name of its currency.)

Alvarado spent the rest of the 1520s conquering the remainder of Guatemala and El Salvador. He subdued the Cakchiquel, burned their chiefs at the stake, and then branded and sold many of their people into slavery. In 1527, Alvarado and his brother built a Spanish capital (Santiago or St. James) at the base of a volcano in the central highlands of Guatemala. Alvarado made a triumphant visit to Spain in 1527, receiving the title of Governor of Guatemala. He ruled over a "captaincy-general" that stretched from Chiapas and Guatemala down to Costa Rica. (Guatemala and Nicaragua are both Spanish corruptions of Indian words for the regions. Costa Rica ("rich coast"), El Salvador ("the savior"), and Honduras ("depressions") are all names created by the Spanish.)

The irrepressible Alvarado, hearing of Pizarro's exploits in Peru, rushed to join in the conquest of the Incas. Alvarado was an irritant to both Pizarro and Almagro, and, after they paid him a substantial sum, he left Peru. Alvarado then returned to Spain and married Francisca de la Cueva, the daughter of a prominent Spanish family. She died shortly after arriving in Guatemala. Pizarro then went back to Spain and married her sister, Beatriz. He returned to Guatemala in 1539 before heading off in search of the fabled golden cities of Cíbola in northern Mexico. Alvarado died on this futile expedition after a horse fell on him. One of his critics summed up Alvarado's life by observing "that every plan he made was begun with impetuosity, continued with cruelty, and ended in disaster." In a very unusual move, Doña Beatriz succeeded him as Governor of Guatemala. Her rule was short-lived—two days. On the night of 10 September 1541, a massive mud slide and flood destroyed the capital and drowned Doña Beatriz. Construction of a new capital began in 1543 (at a site now known as Antigua). Destroyed by an earthquake in 1773, the Guatemalan capital was then moved to its present site.

In addition to the forces moving down from Guatemala and Mexico, Spanish conquistadores moved from Panama up into Central America. Pedro Arias de Ávila (better known as Pedrarias Dávila), ruthlessly seized control of the Spanish possessions on the isthmus of Panama in the 1510s. A controversial and brutal figure, Pedrarias has not been treated kindly by historians. One early historian of the region remarked: "The whole story of the occupation of Central American lands . . . is, in fact, one of the most miserable chapters in the history of the Spanish Empire. It contains no outstanding achievements; it is but a chronicle of jealousy and self-seeking, of sordid scrambling for territory and gold." He goes on to say that "the infamy of Pedrarias, his rivals and associates, makes the greatness of Cortés stand forth in clearer light." And this from a traditional historian who generally admired the conquistadores!

Pedrarias sent expeditions into Costa Rica and Nicaragua in the 1520s, eventually taking up residence in the latter after subduing the Nicarao Indians. After convicting (on trumped-up charges) and executing Balboa in 1519, and consolidating his control over Panama, Pedrarias tried to stop the explorations of Gil González Dávila into what today are Costa Rica, Nicaragua, and Honduras. Pedrarias dispatched Francisco Hernández de Córdoba into Nicaragua at almost the same time as Alvarado was moving into Guatemala in 1523. One of Cortés's lieutenants, Cristóbal de Olid, moved into Honduras by sea shortly afterward in 1524. In the aftermath of many failures and the decimation of his forces, Olid tried to break free of his commander's authority (as Cortés himself had done in Cuba and Mexico). Cortés appeared on the scene in 1525 and reined in his lieutenant. Pedrarias seized Córdoba after he appeared to be staking out on his own claims, and executed him. Although the Crown eventually removed Pedrarias from his position in Panama, the king named him governor of Nicaragua. Pedrarias Dávila died there in 1531 at the age of 90. The historian Roger Bigelow Merriman summed up Pedrarias as "one of the ablest but most repellent figures in the ranks of the conquistadores; proud, selfish, treacherous, and vengeful."

Francisco de Montejo, another of the lieutenants of Cortés, began the conquest of the Yucatán in 1527. Montejo had known Doña Marina (the famous mistress of Cortés) well during the conquest of Mexico, and he had a great deal of information on the Yucatec Maya. The highly fragmented Maya in the region lived in a harsh, hot, and humid land covered with scrub forest. Montejo spent until late 1534 tromping across the peninsula, finding no great cities and no gold. For the next five years, the Spanish abandoned and ignored Yucatán. When they returned in 1540, the object of their desire was not gold and riches. These determined and disillusioned conquistadores simply sought what they saw as a modest recompense (land and Indians) for years of fruitless soldiering. As in other conquests, they allied with one Indian group against another. Although the Spanish established permanent settlements, the Maya of Yucatán remained among the most rebellious of the native peoples of the Americas. In 1542 the Spanish founded Mérida and then Valladolid, both named after cities in Spain. Franciscan priests, in particular the legendary Diego de Landa, moved into the region to Christianize the Indians.

THE "CONQUEST" OF BRAZIL

Colonized by the Portuguese, Brazil was a late starter in the Conquest, in comparison to Spanish America. Covering nearly 40 percent of the landmass of South America today, Brazil is sometimes referred to as the "other" Latin America. Brazil has historically faced Africa and Europe, with its back to Spanish America. With no large, dense Indian civilizations, the process of conquest and colonization was more like the one that occurred in the Caribbean than the ones in Mexico or Peru. But, like the core regions in Spanish America, Brazil developed densely populated centers with elaborate administrative and political structures. Somewhat like the Spanish and Columbus, the Portuguese stumbled onto a continent on their way to the Orient. As noted earlier, the Portuguese were the great pioneers in the Atlantic. For the entire fifteenth century, they had moved into the islands of the Atlantic and down the west coast of Africa. By 1488, Bartolomeu Dias had rounded the Cape of Good Hope (in southern Africa) and found a sea route to Asia. Quite rightly, the Portuguese monarchy had rejected Columbus's plan to head west to arrive in Asia. Portuguese cartographers and geographers recognized that Columbus had underestimated the size of the earth. They understood that no sailing vessel of the late fifteenth century could survive what would have been a ten-thousand-mile sea voyage without the crew succumbing to starvation. Fortunately for Columbus and Spain, the Americas blocked the route to Asia—and at a viable sailing distance.

In 1497, the Portuguese king, Manoel I (1495–1521), sent a large expedition around the Cape to India under the command of Vasco da Gama. Historians still have no good explanation as to why the Portuguese waited nearly ten years to follow up the momentous voyage of Dias. In the meantime, Columbus sailed to the New World, and in 1493 returned via Portugal. (I sometimes wonder what the Portuguese must have been thinking when Columbus appeared, claiming to have found the Indies and showed them the handful of Caribbean Indians he had dragged back with him across the ocean!) When da Gama returned to Portugal in 1499, he fulfilled the old European dream of direct trade with the East. In effect, he achieved what Columbus had set out to accomplish by traveling in the other direction. Despite the loss of several ships, the estimated profit on the India cargo was 700 percent! The king immediately outfitted another large expedition under the command of Pedro Álvares Cabral, a minor nobleman in his 30s with little overseas experience.

The expedition of Cabral ventured too far west as they moved out into the Atlantic, attempting to catch the prevailing winds to southern Africa, and in April 1500 they spotted what they thought was a large island, but was actually the South American mainland. Many have long suspected that the Portuguese knew where they were going. In 1494, after the return of Columbus, the Spanish and Portuguese had signed a treaty at Tordesillas (in southern Spain), dividing up the world between themselves. They drew an imaginary line from pole to pole some 370 leagues west of the Cape Verde Islands, agreeing (with some exceptions) that all lands west of the line should be Spanish and all those to the east would be Portuguese. Strangely enough, the eastern section of South America lies on the eastern side of the line, leading many to believe that the Portuguese had knowledge of the South American landmass when they signed the treaty. No documentation has ever been found to prove this suspicion.

King Francis I of France demanded to see "the will of our father Adam, that I may see if he has really made you [the Spanish and Portuguese] his only universal heirs."

Fortunately, a royal scribe wrote an eyewitness account of the landing in Brazil and the nine days Cabral's fleet tarried on the South American coast. Pedro Vaz de Caminha's letter is one of the most important accounts we have of the moment of initial contact—the first encounter, if you will, between Native Americans and Europeans. It is also one of the most important sources for the creation of the myth of the "noble savage." "They seem," he wrote, "to be such innocent people that, if we could understand their speech and they ours, they would immediately become Christians, seeing that, by all appearances, they do not understand about any faith . . . these people are good and have a fine simplicity. Any stamp we wish may be easily printed on them, for the Lord has given them good bodies and good faces, like good men." Now, there is a bold statement for someone fresh off the boat with no knowledge of the local language or culture! The account reveals indigenous peoples with very low levels of technology and political organization. Caminha noticed that they did not have plows, cattle, goats, or sheep and that they depended on cassava as the staple of their diet.

The Portuguese held religious services on the beach and exchanged glass beads and bells for some exotic animals and a few pieces of jewelry. Seeing little gold and no large cities, after nine days, with fresh water supplies and some Indian trinkets the fleet returned to their original route and headed east to southern Africa. One ship took Caminha's letter back to Lisbon to alert the king to the discovery. A storm off the coast of Africa divided the fleet and sent several ships to the bottom of the ocean. Cabral's remaining ships regrouped, reached India (using an Arab pilot from east Africa), and headed home with rich cargoes of spices and luxury goods. The Indian trade around Africa soon became regularized, with fleets leaving Lisbon in March or April and arriving in India in September or October. The fleet then left India in late December arriving back in Portugal by midsummer.

The Portuguese experienced enormous success establishing a trading empire in Africa, the Indian Ocean, and East Asia. By the 1520s, the Portuguese had forcefully taken control of the key access points in the Indian Ocean: Ormuz at the entrance to the Persian Gulf, the Straits of Malacca in the East Indies (but not the entrance to the Red Sea). By the 1550s, they had settled into Macao on the south coast of China and Nagasaki in southern Japan. By the mid-sixteenth century the Portuguese had created the largest trading empire in world history, stretching from Brazil to Japan. For the next two centuries, the Portuguese monarchy would be one of the richest in the world, with a wealth harvested from the trade of foods and spices: nutmeg, clove, cinnamon, sugar, and the like. The ever witty Francis I derisively referred to his Portuguese counterpart, Manoel I, as "the grocer king."

With this success, the Portuguese paid minimal attention to the Brazilian coast over the first half of the sixteenth century. They were content to enrich themselves off the Asian and African trade, rather than bother with the lowly "savages" of the Brazilian coast. Even more so than the Aztecs or Incas, the Asian peoples the Portuguese encountered were easily their technological and military equals on land (but rarely on the water). There would be no significant European conquests in Asia for another two centuries. The only significant product the Portuguese could extract from the Indians was a hard wood that produced a dark red dye. It was known as brazilwood, and the coastal colony from which it came soon became known on maps as Brazil. It was not until the last third of the sixteenth century that the Portuguese colony began to develop, with rapidly expanding sugar plantations and slave labor at its core. The semi-sedentary and nonsedentary Indians of the South American coast resisted Portuguese control, moved deeper into the interior, or died from European diseases. There would be no dramatic clash and conquest of complex empires in eastern South America.

The initial phases of Portuguese conquest and colonization were tentative and weak. Almost all their efforts were eventually concentrated in the northeast. In the 1510s and 1520s, the handful of Portuguese factories, or trading posts, along the lengthy Brazilian coast could do little to prevent competition from the French. In 1530, the Crown sent out an expedition under Martim Afonso de Sousa to establish a more permanent and secure presence. With four ships, soldiers, royal officials, priests, and settlers, he set up the town of São Vicente along the southern coastline of what today is Brazil, and then the king divided the coast into 12 captaincies. Just eight were settled in the sixteenth century, and initially, São Vicente in the south and Pernambuco in the north were the only two that flourished. This proprietary system of colonization (as with the *encomienda* in Spanish America) created the seeds of a burdensome colonial legacy (examined in later chapters). The large landed estate controlled by a small white elite has its origins in the captaincy system.

Not until 1549 did the Portuguese establish a serious colonial presence, with its capital in Bahia. In 1549, the king sent out Tomé de Sousa as the governor general over all the captaincies. Sousa's expedition of 1200 men and women brought an even larger presence of settlers, soldiers, royal officials, and merchants. He also brought with him six young priests from the recently established Society of Jesus, better known as the Jesuits. Sousa founded a new colonial capital at a stunning location on the northeastern coast in the captaincy of Bahia. Named Salvador, or "The Savior," it would serve as Brazil's capital until 1763. Not until the governorship of Mem de Sá (1558–72) did the Portuguese really assert control over the colonies and expel the French along the coast. Rather than carrying out the dramatic conquest of dense Indian populations in the interior (as in Mexico and Peru), the Portuguese carved out tiny coastal enclaves. For most of the colonial era, they would "cling to the coast like crabs," in the words of one of Brazil's first historians, Vicente do Salvador.

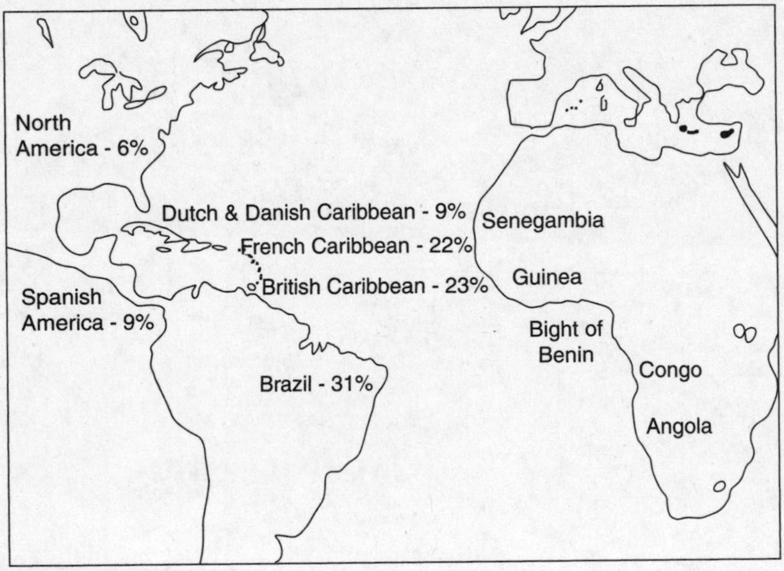

Map 5. Transatlantic Slave Trade—Major Sending and Receiving Areas

Part II

Building Empires and Societies in a New World

7

Land and Labor

THE GREAT ESTATES

As the military conquest in the core regions drew to a close in the sixteenth century, the Spanish and Portuguese turned to making their new possessions productive, long-term enterprises. Cultivation and exploitation of the land became the primary objective of the developing colonial regimes. Land without labor, however, was useless to the Spanish and Portuguese. The populations of Spain and Portugal were not very large, perhaps some 10 to 11 million, combined, in the early sixteenth century. The monarchies of both had little interest in a large out-migration of their subjects; rather, they needed them to provide an adequate and compliant labor force in Iberia. Mexico and Peru, on the other hand, had populations that were each possibly double that of Spain and Portugal combined. The migration of Iberians across the Atlantic in the sixteenth century was probably around 2,000 per year, not enough to make a large impact on the labor supply. The key to success in the new American empires then hinged on the mobilization of a large and compliant labor force. This was accomplished primarily through the exploitation of forced Indian labor in Mexico and Peru. In the Caribbean and Brazil, the Spanish and Portuguese eventually turned to African slave labor. The estates then used the *unfree* labor force to produce the wealth of the land that made the colonial economies work. Quite literally, the Americas were built from the sweat and blood of Indians and Africans. And much of the economic expansion in Europe after 1500 was fueled by the wealth of the Americas produced by this sweat and blood. Out of this coercive labor system emerged the most burdensome legacy of the colonial period—the large landed estate.

The large landed estates were one of the three pillars of the early Latin American economies. The large estates produced the commodities (grains, meats, and supplies) that fed Latin Americans, and they supplied the cash crops for export to Europe (sugar, chocolate, dyestuffs). The second major pillar was also a form of landed estate—gold and silver mines that generated the financial fuel for the Spanish and (later) the Portuguese empires. The third pillar was a large and complex commercial system that moved goods throughout the empires.

The great estates were the dominant economic institution in Latin America for nearly three hundred years (and in some regions even longer). The very nature of these estates has been debated for nearly five hundred years, and in some ways this discussion has directed the attention of scholars away from other types of landholdings. Although they were the dominant type of landholding, they have always been fewer in number than the many landholdings of all sizes, and in the hands of a very small percentage of landholders (small and medium plots of land with few workers). This is a fundamental point, and I want to emphasize it for a moment. Although the general image of Latin America is often of a place with huge haciendas and plantations worked by the masses of poor laborers, this is only partially true. Quite clearly, the large estates and their owners dominated the economy, monopolized political power, and stood at the top of the social pyramid. They were a very small minority of landholders (with great power), and the vast majority of landholdings were small and medium plots. In effect, the large estates were at the center of a complex network of properties, with many small landholders dependent upon the large estates for their very survival. Control of these large estates has historically been the key to control of the economy and the political system. In Latin America, those who controlled the fruits of the large estates ruled all the land.

Throughout the colonial era, and well into the nineteenth and twentieth centuries in some countries, the most powerful local, regional, and national political positions were filled by men whose wealth came from the land. The second most powerful group was merchants engaged in overseas commerce, a trade driven by exports from the land. In the least economically developed regions of Latin America, Central America being the prime example, this domination of the landed elite families lasted into the late twentieth century. Land was power—economic, social, and political.

These estates have gone by many names—*haciendas, estancias, fincas, fazendas. Hacienda* comes from the Spanish verb, *hacer*, "to do" or "to make." In Portuguese, the same verb is *fazer*, which becomes *fazenda* for the estate. It was a place where something was made or produced. *Hacienda* is a common term for estates in Mexico; *estancia* is widely used in southern South America; and *finca* is widely used in Central America.

(The list of terms is long and varies by location.) For many years, the traditional scholarly approach divided the estates into two main types: haciendas and plantations—a useful, but misleading, dichotomy. The traditional argument goes something like this. There were two major types of large estate—haciendas were located in temperate climates, employed Indian labor, produced foodstuffs for local and regional markets, were largely self-sufficient, and were not profit-oriented enterprises. Plantations, on the other hand, were in tropical climates, used African slave labor, produced cash crops for export, had to bring in their own food, and were profit-oriented enterprises. This is a nice, convenient theoretical dichotomy, but it fails to hold up in practice. In some places, Indians produced sugar cane, African slaves produced food crops for local consumption, and plantations were sometimes self-sufficient in food production. And it is completely wrong to argue that somehow owners of haciendas were not motivated by profit. All of these estates were business enterprises. In short, it is a useful dichotomy, but one that has limitations that we must keep in mind.

The land and labor systems the Spanish and Portuguese developed are key to understanding the evolution of Latin America, and how it has been very different from the colonial experience of the United States. In the Caribbean crucible during the first years of the Conquest, the Spanish turned to the *encomienda* system. Once the initial pillaging was over, and the Crown had to settle in for the long haul, the royal administrators had to develop the instruments for regulating the new society. The logical tendency was to take Spanish and Portuguese institutions and then adapt them to the needs of the Americas. The *encomienda* is a classic example. It had been used to some extent in the Reconquest. In the Caribbean it developed into an important and central instrument of Spanish colonial society. At its simplest, the *encomienda* was a grant—of the use of the land and the Indian labor on it to a Spaniard, in exchange for certain obligations. The grantee, or *encomendero*, had to protect the land for Spain, develop it, pay taxes, and Christianize the Indians. I want to emphasize that it was a grant for the use of the property; it was not a title to it. In theory, the King remained the owner, and the *encomendero* was a concessionary whose rights could be revoked at any time. In practice, many of these initial grants would eventually evolve into privately-owned estates.

The *encomienda* system emerged full-blown in the Caribbean, Mexico, and Peru as a system of land grants in the first half of the sixteenth century. Along with the division of spoils, such as gold and silver, the conquistadores were given *encomiendas* for their service to the Crown. As the King moved down through the ranks of the conquistadores, he granted *encomiendas* that reflected their importance. Cortés, for example, was Marquis of the Valley of Oaxaca, an enormous, heavily populated and rich agricultural region. His new domain included the entire Zapotec kingdom of Tehuantepec. With each new wave of conquistadores and conquests, the process was repeated. It became increasingly unworkable, and the Crown then turned to the *repartimiento* system, a means of dividing up available Indian labor among the Spanish landowners. Several factors undermined the *encomienda* system. First, those who arrived later and later discovered that the best lands had been given out. This was an important factor in pushing the latecomers out into new areas for conquest. Second, in the first half of the sixteenth century, disease struck down millions of Native Americans, annihilating entire villages. In the Caribbean, this annihilation was nearly total by 1550. As a consequence, the *encomenderos* found themselves losing their labor force. In varying degrees, this also happened in Mexico and Peru. Finally, as early as the 1530s, the Crown began to worry about the growing power of the *encomenderos*, and wanted to rein them in. The civil wars and rebellions among the Spaniards in Peru simply reinforced this fear.

All of these factors pushed the Crown to shift from the use of the *encomienda* and to replace it with the *repartimiento* system. From the Spanish verb, *repartir*, "to divide up," the *repartimiento* was aimed at just that—dividing the remaining Indian labor force among the landowners. Under this system, Indian villages were given labor quotas, and they had to provide specified numbers of workers to the Crown on a regular basis. A royal official in each region would then be in charge of the regular division of Indian labor. As always, the most powerful landowners (many of them previously *encomenderos*) would get the best allocations, and the less powerful ones would get the leftovers. Legally, the landowners had to recompense the Indian workers but, in reality, this rarely occurred. The *repartimiento* was, in effect, a rotary draft labor system, one that had pre-Columbian roots. Both the Aztec and Inca empires were built on rotary draft labor, known as the *coatequitl* in Mexico and the *mit'a* in Peru (known as the *mita* in Spanish). In a sense, the Spanish redesigned an old form of coerced labor already familiar to the Indians. The local village leaders now had to ensure a supply of workers on a regular basis to the Spaniards rather than the Aztecs or Incas.

The *mita* in the Andes was established by the "founding father" of the Viceroyalty of Peru, Francisco de Toledo, who served as viceroy from 1569 to 1581. Toledo issued laws that regulated the size and frequency of labor levies, the "wages" to be paid, and the landowner's "responsibilities." In the 1570s, he organized the *mita* to supply labor to the silver mines in Potosí, and each year it mobilized more than 10,000 Indians. The *repartimiento* was an enormous regime for the systematic exploitation of the Indians across Spanish America. It provided the Spanish with a reasonably secure and cheap labor force, and it (at least in theory) kept that labor under Crown control rather than under the control of the landowners. Forced Indian labor would persist in Mexico, Central America, and the Andes in some form or fashion until the twentieth century. Most of Latin America would gradually move toward some sort of free wage labor system after 1600. The *mita* system in Peru was not abolished until 1812.

In the Caribbean and Brazil, the near-complete destruction of the Indians (from conquest and disease), or their flight, turned the Spanish and Portuguese toward the growing use of African slave labor. The Spanish and Portuguese could not turn to the use of large, organized Indian populations to work the land as in Mexico and Peru. Instead, they turned to the Atlantic slave trade. Beginning with the Portuguese in Brazil in the late sixteenth century, and then in the seventeenth century in the islands of the Caribbean, African slave labor became the principal labor force on the large estates. The Brazilian sugar plantations on the northeastern coast around Salvador and in Pernambuco were modeled on the much smaller versions in Madeira and Cape Verde. They became the model for the other plantations that would emerge in the Caribbean in the seventeenth century, and the southern British colonies (Virginia and the Carolinas) in the eighteenth century.

It was not until the last third of the sixteenth century that Brazil began to develop, with rapidly expanding sugar plantations and slave labor at its core. The Portuguese created the first great plantation society in the Americas, a pattern all the other European powers would emulate. The Portuguese colonies in the islands of the Atlantic gave them a century of experience with sugar and slavery before they transferred the model on a vast scale to Brazil. Sugar cane was a luxury crop, originally from the East Indies, that the Portuguese transplanted to Madeira and the Azores in the fifteenth century. The king had granted Madeira to Prince Henry as a lifetime fief and he promptly divided it into several captaincies. The islands were settled in the 1440s and the colonists brought in wheat, grapes, and cane sugar. By 1500, sugar had become the principal local crop, and nearly everything else, including wheat, was imported. Eventually, Madeira had nearly 100 sugar mills. Facing shortages of labor, the Portuguese turned in the mid-fifteenth century to importing captive black Africans. In the early sixteenth century, more than 10 percent of the population of Lisbon—some 10,000 people—was African slaves. (After 1550, the sugar industry rapidly declined and grapes and wine would become Madeira's most famous export by the seventeenth century.) By the early sixteenth century, the Portuguese had a long and valuable experience with growing a cash crop for export to Europe. The Atlantic islands had become the successful prototypes of the plantation societies that would spring up all across the Americas in the sixteenth and seventeenth centuries.

The sugar and slavery complex developed after 1560 around Bahia and Pernambuco, on a vast scale. The Indians died off from disease, fled, or resisted European contact. In the Native American societies, women engaged in agricultural labor, not men. The settlers turned increasingly to the enslavement of Indians to guarantee a labor supply. In the 1560s, however, smallpox and measles epidemics reduced the Native American population in Bahia around the capital. Furthermore, the Jesuits were concentrating surviving Indians into villages under their control and away from the settlers. The growing plantations drove the demand for African slaves and fueled the growth of the Atlantic slave trade. In the last quarter of the sixteenth century, Brazil would become the first major importer of African slaves in the Americas. Within a few decades, the sugar zone along the northeastern coast had become a land of blacks and mulattoes rather than Indians and Portuguese. Brazil became the engine of growth in the rise of the Atlantic slave trade. The Brazilian northeast became the core of Portuguese presence in the Americas, as sugar and slavery became the engine of economic expansion.

THE TRANSATLANTIC SLAVE TRADE

The transatlantic slave trade was the largest forced migration in world history (until the Second World War). Although slavery has been called a "peculiar institution," it has existed in nearly all periods of history and in all regions of the world. Here we are focusing on the modern, Atlantic slave trade that arose in the mid-fifteenth century, moving millions of black Africans to all regions of the Americas. Africans arrived in the New World via the so-called "middle passage" from capture in Africa to delivery in the Americas. The trade took place for four hundred years and involved many nations and peoples on both sides of the Atlantic. All the major European powers were involved—Spain, Portugal, England, France, and Holland, and every country in the Americas participated in the trade. What often goes unspoken was the participation of many African peoples and states in the trade. As we have seen, the view that somehow all peoples in Africa saw themselves as one or that they had a single sense of identity is misguided. "Africa" did not exist. Much like the native peoples of the Americas, the numerous groups on the African continent saw themselves as distinct peoples, and they had no concept of Africa or African, concepts created by Europeans in modern times. The transatlantic slave trade drew together hundreds of peoples and political units in Europe, Africa, and the Americas. It would be hard to find anyone who did not participate in this extraordinarily inhumane episode in world history.

The transatlantic slave trade began in the 1440s and lasted until the 1860s. Best estimates place the number of black Africans arriving in the Americas in slavery at some 12 to 15 million. For every African who arrived alive on our shores, probably another had died between the point of capture in Africa and disembarkation in the New World. In other words, we are really talking about some 24 to 30 million Africans initially enslaved and destined for the Americas. This would be roughly 8 to 10 million people each century from a continent that had somewhere between 80 to 120 million inhabitants during this time period. The study of the trade has become very sophisticated, with a large body of literature that provides serious responses to many of the popular and sometimes ludicrous claims in the press. Understandably, there are problems that historians confront in trying to reconstruct this sordid chapter in world history. Our best quantitative sources are the shipping records of the European merchants, and these are spotty and often deceptive. They are highly dispersed and unevenly preserved. In the United States, for example, the records were scattered among a large number of ports and traders. In Brazil, the largest importer, many of the records were destroyed. The best evidence comes from British consular officials in Brazil, who carefully tracked imports in the first half of the nineteenth century.

The first black Africans were shipped to Lisbon in the 1440s. We have, in fact, an excellent eyewitness account of the arrival of one of the first shipments, which arrived at Lagos on the coast of southern Portugal in August 1444. Gomes Eannes de Zurara, a courtier attached to Prince Henry the Navigator, described the arrival of 235 Africans as "a marvelous sight, for, amongst them, were some white enough, fair enough, and well-proportioned; others were less white, like mulattoes; others again were as black as Ethiops, and so ugly, both in features and in body, as almost to appear . . . the images of a lower hemisphere." He went on to add, "What heart could be so hard as not to be pierced with piteous feeling to see that company? For some kept their heads low, and their faces bathed in tears, looking one upon another. Others stood groaning very dolorously, looking up to the height of heaven, fixing their eyes upon it, crying out loudly, as if asking help from the Father of nature; others struck their faces with the palms of their hands, throwing themselves at full length upon the ground; while others made lamentations in the manner of a dirge, after the custom of their country. . . ." Forty-six of these slaves were handed over to Prince Henry, who watched the unloading from nearby on his horse.

With the discovery of the Americas in the 1490s, African slaves began to cross the Atlantic. For about two decades Fernando and Isabel debated whether or not to allow the shipment of African slaves to their new possessions in the Americas. Only in 1510 did Fernando begin to authorize slave shipments, to be regulated by the Crown, to the islands of the Caribbean. This is the true beginning of the transatlantic slave trade. It was the rise of sugar plantations that gave the trade its first great push after 1560. Black slaves were everywhere in the Americas from the very beginning. Diego Velázquez had slaves in Cuba by 1511; a black slave was with Balboa when he first saw the Pacific; and Estebanico, as you will remember, was at the side of Cabeza de Vaca in his eight years wandering across what today is the Southwest of the United States. Juan Garrido (a free black) was at the side of Cortés in the conquest of Mexico.

Perhaps 100,000 Africans were brought to Spanish America as slaves in the period before 1575. It was not until after 1550 that the trade to the Americas surpassed the shipments of Africans into Europe. With the rise of sugar plantations in the Caribbean in the 1600s, the trade accelerated dramatically to Spanish, English, and French colonies. The rising curve of imports on the charts begins after 1570 with the emergence of the first great sugar plantations on the northeastern coast of Brazil. By the 1650s, the Dutch, English, and French had copied the Portuguese and thriving plantations on the islands of the Caribbean continued to escalate the demand for slave labor. Nearly two-thirds of the slaves who crossed the Atlantic made the passage in the eighteenth century. The reason for this is simple: every European plantation society in the Americas was in full swing, all with high labor demands. Portuguese Brazil, and Spanish, French, and British colonies in the Caribbean and what today is the U.S. South, were all operating at full tilt. (In Brazil the greatest demand was in the gold fields of the southeast.) Although every European maritime power was engaged in the trade, it was the English who carried most of the slaves across the Atlantic in the eighteenth century, supplying not only their own colonies, but those of the other European powers as well.

With the rise of an antislave trade and antislavery movement in the late eighteenth century, the trade would gradually decline until its extinction in the 1860s. What is perhaps most striking to the modern mind about this episode in world history is how easily the Europeans and Africans took up this trade in human cargo, and how long it endured before anyone really questioned the morality of it. It was not until the last half of the eighteenth century that the first sustained cries for the end of the trade began in earnest. Ironically, it was spearheaded by English Quakers, who themselves had been major traders earlier. With growing English pressure, especially after 1800, the trade, and slavery in the Americas, were squeezed out of existence by the last half of the nineteenth century. The last known slave shipment arrived in Cuba in January 1870, and Brazil has the ignominious distinction of being the last nation in the Americas to abolish slavery—in May 1888.

Although all regions of the Atlantic world felt the impact of the trade, several key regions played the most important roles. The region around the Bight of Benin in West Africa became the first great exporter of human cargo. The early trade back to Europe had focused on the region of West Africa around what today is Senegal and Gambia, a region immediately south of the Sahara. In the sixteenth century, the focus of the trade shifted south and east to what the Europeans generically referred to as Guinea, the modern-day nations of Guinea and Sierra Leone. By the end of the sixteenth century, this trading zone extended along the coasts of modern day Ghana, Benin, Nigeria, and the Cameroons. All the European powers had trading posts in the Bight of Benin, beginning with the Portuguese at Elmina in the 1480s. The Angola/Congo region supplied many Bantu peoples to the Americas. Central Africa contributed slaves from the early sixteenth century, but Angola did not become a major supplier until the seventeenth century. Angola became a virtual appendage of Brazil's sugar economy as slaves moved westward and sugar, molasses, tobacco, and cane alcohol from Brazil supplied African markets. In the late eighteenth century, the Portuguese turned increasingly to Mozambique in East Africa for slaves. In part this was due to the growing demand for more and more slaves. It was also a reaction to the growing competition with the English and French in the traditional exporting centers in West and central Africa. The length of the voyage from Mozambique to Brazil was ten weeks, as opposed to the usual four from West or central Africa.

In the Americas, the single largest importer of slaves was Brazil, absorbing possibly 33 percent of all the trade. Unlike that of any other region, the Brazilian trade was constantly increasing, right to the very end in 1850, when the Brazilian parliament abolished the trade under heavy British pressure. In the first half of the nineteenth century, the Brazilians were importing about 50,000 slaves per year to work on the expanding coffee plantations of the southeast. This is nearly double the rate of the eighteenth century. The Caribbean basin devoured around 50 percent into Spanish, English, French, and Dutch possessions. Although a much larger importer than Brazil, the Caribbean was politically and geographically fragmented. As in Brazil, the demographic impact in the region was enormous. The imprint of African heritage is more pronounced in these two regions today than anywhere else in the Americas. The Thirteen Colonies (the future United States) came into the trade late and ended it early, taking in perhaps 6 percent of all imports, some 750,000 Africans. Although African slaves came into the North American mainland with the Spanish as early as the sixteenth century, the first shipments of enslaved Africans to the Thirteen Colonies arrived in Virginia in 1619. Plantation society did not really enter into full flower until the eighteenth century, and slave imports ended in 1808. Slavery was largely (but not exclusively) concentrated in the Old South, the region of North America that, consequently, has been most deeply imprinted by Africa. Nevertheless, this African influence in the U.S. South has never been as pronounced as it has been in the Caribbean and Brazil.

The "middle passage" was a journey that is almost beyond the comprehension of peoples living in the comfort of developed nations in the early twenty-first century. The first stage of the journey began with the capture of prisoners in the interior of Africa. We have some classic personal accounts of this journey in the writings of Gustavus Vassa and Mahommam Baquaqua. Vassa, also known by his African name, Olaudah Equiano, was born around 1745 in what is now eastern Nigeria. Captured and then sent to the West Indies, he eventually traveled all over the Atlantic world in both slavery and freedom. His autobiography, *The Interesting Narrative*, appeared in England in 1789 and it is a powerful condemnation of the slave trade. "Let the polished and haughty European," observes Equiano, "recollect that *his* ancestors were once, like the Africans, uncivilized, and even barbarous. Did Nature make *them* inferior to their sons? And should *they too* have been made slaves? Every rational mind answers, No." [Emphasis in the original.] Baquaqua tells a harrowing tale of his capture by other Africans (through trickery), probably from the area of what today is Burkina Faso, his trek to the coast, then his transatlantic journey. "Its horrors, ah!" he bemoans, "who can describe. . . . Oh! the loathsomeness and filth of that horrible place will never be effaced from my memory. . . . My heart even at this day, sickens at the thought of it . . ."

Slavery existed in Africa before the Europeans arrived, and captives had been moved around the continent, but on a much smaller scale than the massive forced relocation of peoples that would take place after 1600. The arrival of European traders dramatically reoriented the trade from the interior trading networks on the continent to destinations westward across the Atlantic. Captives often traveled great distances and changed hands several times before arriving at the European trading posts on the coast. At places like Elmina (Ghana) and Luanda (Angola), the captives were placed in pens, branded, and often nominally baptized. For most, it was their first experience with the ocean and Europeans. The passage across the Atlantic was harrowing at best. The average ship probably held around 400 slaves chained in groups and stacked like wood on shelves below decks. With minimal food and water, disease, punishments, and tropical temperatures above 100 degrees below deck, on a typical voyage probably some 15–20 percent of the passengers died en route. Upon arrival in the Americas, whether in Baltimore, Charleston, Havana, or Rio de Janeiro, the processing procedure was similar. Exhausted and weakened Africans were placed in pens, groomed, and then put on the auction block. The vast majority went to work in the fields and mines of the American South, the Caribbean, and Brazil. They and their descendants then quite literally built the new societies of the Americas.

The Brazilian plantations were large and complex systems connecting many parcels of land and peoples. Generally, they were not single, contiguous lands, but many pieces, often with smaller landholders located around the pieces. The smallholders and the big planters were closely linked to each other in relations of codependency. In years when the planter could not fully utilize all his lands, he would lease them out to the smallholders in something of a sharecropping arrangement. The small-holder, or *lavrador*, would plant and harvest, but had to process his cane at the mill of the big planter. They would then split the profits, according to some sort of agreed-upon percentages. The planters, or *fazendeiros*, would often provide the *lavradores* with work or lease out surplus slaves to them. In tough times, the *fazendeiro* would lend the *lavradores* food, medical help, and would sometimes serve as the godfather for children. With both slaves and freemen, the *fazendeiros* became powerful patrons for their "clients." They all lived in what some historians have referred to as a "moral economy"—everyone had certain rights and responsibilities. The most basic was that the patron took care of his clients, and they, in turn, offered him their loyalty and obedience. It was not unlike feudalism in the Middle Ages: the plantation complex bound planters, peasants, and slaves into complex relationships of inequality and dependency. They were rela-tionships that were much more complicated than the usual simplistic notions of powerful planters employing naked force to keep the peasants and slaves in place. It was a world bound together by a strong sense of col-lective connections, but ones built on hierarchy and inequality, a world very different from the one we are accustomed to in early twenty-first century North America.

Across the Americas, the Spanish and Portuguese built colonial societies on a clear and harsh hierarchy: a social structure where a small, white elite controlled economic and political power through their control of land and a non-European labor force. The pronounced inequities built into these structures of exploitation are the most enduring and burdensome legacy of the conquest and colonization of Latin America.

8

State and Empire

Throughout the sixteenth and seventeenth centuries, the Spanish and Portuguese by fits and starts conquered and colonized larger and larger areas of the Americas. Moving outwards from the core regions in the Caribbean, Mexico, Peru, and the northeastern coast of Brazil, they constructed their American empires. At the same time, they relentlessly continued their global expansion. By 1600, the Portuguese had built an empire of trading posts from Brazil to East and West Africa to India, the East Indies, and the coast of China and Japan. This "trading post" empire spanned four continents and circled the Earth. The Spanish moved into the Philippines and North Africa, and fought for control of the Low Countries and sections of Italy. In the sixteenth century, Portugal and Spain established the first truly global empires. The increasing scale and complexity of the Iberian possessions around the world presented enormous administrative and bureaucratic challenges for the two monarchies. Not since the empires of the ancient world had any rulers faced such daunting challenges. For the Portuguese, these challenges came largely outside of the Americas before 1700. The Portuguese monarchy strained to control and administer colonial outposts on four continents from Brazil to Japan. Spain's greatest assets, however, clearly lay in the Americas and focused the monarchy's attention on its empire in the New World. Throughout the first two centuries of conquest and colonization, Spain and Portugal extended the power of their nation-states through the creation and extension of Iberian administrative, legal, and political institutions to their growing possessions in the Americas.

CORPORATISM AND HIERARCHY

The political and administrative system the Spanish and Portuguese created in the aftermath of the conquest in Latin America grew out of a statist and centralist political culture that faced few checks on its power before overseas expansion, or during centuries of colonial rule. Latin American politics have been molded over the centuries by a medieval, Iberian Catholic tradition that diverged from the path taken by Protestant Western Europe in the aftermath of the Middle Ages. Western Europe witnessed the emergence of growing checks on the power of the monarchy, a growing emphasis on the rights of the individual, and a mechanistic vision of politics. The Reformation in the sixteenth century and the Scientific Revolution in the sixteenth and seventeenth centuries profoundly influenced and intermingled with the rise of the western European political heritage. These two extraordinary processes, one religious and the other intellectual, contributed to the erosion of the power of established authority in Europe, both sacred and secular.

Powerful monarchs in Spain and Portugal kept the Reformation north of the Pyrenees, and Iberia remained on the periphery of the Scientific Revolution. The medieval Catholic vision of Thomas Aquinas (1224–74) maintained its grip on the Iberian world, and it was a vision of hierarchy, order, and community. Rather than a mass of individuals who somehow managed to come together into a fine-tuned machine, the Iberians envisioned society as a body (*corpore*) in which everyone had a place and function. Individuals knew their place and their function, and, by performing their ascribed duties, they kept the body politic healthy. A growing and complex bureaucracy formed the skeleton of this body politic, a bureaucracy in which power flowed upward to the king, who headed the system. Powerful landowners, merchants, military officers, the clergy, and public functionaries kept the masses in check by dominating the state machinery, and the patronage it dispensed. The state controlled and channeled resources (patrimony) to allies and friends, denying patronage to enemies. The state bureaucracy took on a life of its own, certifying, verifying, and acting as the buffer between the powerful and the powerless. This patrimonial system, with its corporatist ethos of hierarchy, stability, and concentration of power, stood in stark contrast to the shifts taking place in Western Europe, especially in England, by the sixteenth and seventeenth centuries.

Richard Morse, one of the most astute thinkers on things Latin American, pointed out long ago the powerful imprint that the Middle Ages left on Latin American culture. As he noted, the patrimonial system was pluralistic, but not representative. It compartmentalized privilege, rather than promoting equality before the law. The components of society interacted with each other through the paternalistic state rather than relating directly to each other. The result is that Iberians and Ibero-Americans have a stronger attachment to the "natural order" and the "human community" than do Anglo-Americans. As Morse observed, the belief that "man makes and is responsible for his world is less deep or prevalent" than in other parts of the West. Whereas North Americans have historically delegated power to their leaders, Latin Americans up to the present still prefer to deliver power to their leaders.

This corporatist, collectivist ethos converged in important ways with the conquered cultures. The cultures of Native Americans and Africans also had strong traditions of collectivism, corporatism, and hierarchy. In Mesoamerica and the Andes, in particular, the Spanish system of hierarchy and privilege replaced those of the Aztecs, Mayas, and Incas. In many ways, the social and political pyramid in these old empires paralleled the highly stratified Iberian societies. The non-European peoples may have resisted the new imperial order, but they certainly must have recognized much of its logic and structure. The Spanish, especially in the defeated Indian empires, consciously attempted to incorporate the social and political hierarchies of pre-Columbian America into the new order they constructed.

LINES OF POWER AND AUTHORITY

The early modern state was small, ill-defined in its functions, and weak. In Iberia, the state had gradually emerged out of the Reconquest around monarchies across the peninsula. By 1492, the multiple monarchies and states on the peninsula had been reduced to just two powerful emerging nations. In a sense, the royal families in Spain and Portugal were simply the most powerful noble families, the ones that had managed to emerge victorious in the struggle among powerful lords. In Portugal, for example, war between the Portuguese and Castilian nobles in the 1380s led to the rise of the House of Avis under João (or John) I in 1385. After King Sebastião died on the battlefield in North Africa in 1578—without an heir—Philip (Felipe) II of Spain managed to dominate the Portuguese nobility and impose himself and the House of Hapsburg on Portugal. (Philip's mother was a Portuguese princess.) When Columbus arrived in the Caribbean in 1492, he was sailing for Queen Isabel and the Kingdom of Castile as her personal emissary. She ruled over a kingdom of several million inhabitants in central Spain, without a fixed seat of government, and under constant threat of rebellion by powerful nobles and restless peasants. Lisbon and Madrid did not become the permanent homes of the two monarchies until the mid-sixteenth century.

These tenuous and fragile Iberian states had arisen to handle the most basic functions of governance: external defense, internal security, the administration of justice, and the collection of taxes. This latter function was the most important, for it generated the revenue to carry out all the others. These states did not have standing professional armies in the modern sense, but rather mobilized large numbers of men (at best, in the tens of thousands), normally through the lords who were loyal vassals of the king. These armies defended against foreign invasion, often engaged in incursions of their own to conquer adjacent kingdoms, and (in the case of Spain) spent much of the sixteenth century fighting across southern and central Europe during the Counter-Reformation. Keeping the peasants in their place and the lords from each other's throats was the most important internal security issue. Peasant rebellions presented the most serious internal threat to monarchies in the sixteenth and seventeenth centuries (after the internal conspiracies of noble lords). Roman law provided the basis for Iberian legal culture, and the most important issue facing the courts was the adjudication of property rights. Clearly, the system evolved under the control of the nobility, who used it to defend their rights and privileges. Hierarchy, privilege, and inequality formed the basis of Iberian legal culture. Nobles, commoners, clergy, and military all had their own rights and privileges (*fueros*, in Spain), and their own courts.

The administrative apparatus of the early modern state was small and its functions were often ill-defined and overlapping. In principle, all power flowed downward from the monarch and information and wealth flowed upward to him. The primary lines of administration were parallel bureaucracies for justice, tax collection, and military affairs. As with all his subjects, from peasants to nobles, royal officials ultimately had a bond of allegiance and loyalty directly to the king. He was quite simply the most powerful patron in the land and the lords were his most important clients. Appointment to a royal office, from the most powerful to the most humble, ultimately depended on networks of patronage and influence. The modern notion of a rational bureaucracy staffed by civil servants who gain their positions through merit, and who are not supposed to use public office for private gain, has little in common with the early modern state. In the Iberian empires, officials had a proprietary notion of office holding. As long as they did not overstep certain norms and bounds, officeholders used their positions to enhance their own wealth and power. Indeed, applicants sought public office as a means to improve their status and move to an ever higher position.

Perhaps the most striking difference between the early modern state and states in the twenty-first century is the absence of social services. Education, health care, and other social services in sixteenth-century Iberia were the functions of the Catholic Church, not the monarchy. The close relationship of church and state after the *patronato real* (or *padroado real* in Portuguese) in the late fifteenth century made the church in the

Iberian empires a virtual arm of the state. The crown appointed church officials and often even collected the tithe. Priests and nuns educated the privileged, ministered to the sick and infirm, cared for wayward young women, and sheltered orphans. In the Spanish and Portuguese empires, the Catholic Church formed a separate and distinct line of administration and bureaucracy. It was unusual in that its most powerful officials had a dual allegiance—to king and pope—one that was often strained and difficult. These men and women owed their careers and advancement to both the monarchy and the papacy, and this must have made their lives much more complicated than their counterparts in other sectors of the early modern state.

In this Iberian world of the late fifteenth century, God was a male who resided in Heaven with unquestioned power, the pope was his temporal, religious representative, and the king derived his authority and power, in theory, from divine right. On rare occasions, a female served as the head of state (Isabel being the most prominent example), but it was clearly a man's world ruled by patriarchy. Men filled all key positions of authority in royal government, and male priests dominated the church administration. Although women had inheritance rights and certain privileges, men controlled the legal system and made all the important decisions in the public sphere.

In the immediate aftermath of the voyages of Columbus and Cabral, the Spanish and Portuguese monarchies gradually created institutions to manage their growing overseas dominions. In the Portuguese empire, centered primarily on the Asian trade, the crown created an Overseas Council (*Conselho Ultramarinho*) to supervise the maritime empire. Eventually, the Portuguese monarchy created two parallel bureaucracies, one for administration and the other for commerce, and the Spanish followed a similar path. In Spain, the Board of Trade (*Casa de la Contratación*) controlled the flow of goods and people in and out of Spain to the empire in the New World. Created in 1503, the Casa became a very powerful institution. For nearly three centuries, the city of Seville served as the official (and only) port for all trade with the American territories. This exclusive monopoly made Castilian merchants very rich and powerful and made Seville the commercial center of the Atlantic world for two hundred years.

In 1524, the Emperor Carlos (Charles) V created the Council of the Indies (*Real y Supremo Consejo de las Indias*) to administer imperial affairs in the Americas. Originally composed of a president and a handful of councillors, over the years the Council expanded, adding a variety of posts, including a treasurer, secretaries, accountants, and even a historian and cosmographer. As with most royal posts, these positions were usually filled by men from elite families with training in law, or by clergy, the so-called *letrados*, or men of letters. (Nearly 250 councillors passed through the Council between 1524 and 1700.) In the seventeenth and eighteenth centuries, a financially strapped monarchy increasingly appointed wealthy individuals who could purchase their office or those who were favorites of the Court. Every conceivable function of government fell under the jurisdiction of the Council. It blended executive, judicial, and legislative activities as well as commercial, military, and ecclesiastical functions. Directly appointed by the king, the members of the Council exercised supreme authority over all Spanish America. The enormous distance from the colonies, the legalistic nature of Iberian governance, and the mentality of councillors who very rarely had any direct experience in the Americas, produced a constant and substantial flow of paper. The wheels of administration turned slowly and deliberately. As J. H. Elliott has pointed out, "This made for careful rather than imaginative government, more inclined to regulate than to innovate."

With the rapid expansion of the conquest after 1520, Charles V created two large administrative units to handle the vast and densely populated regions of Mesoamerica and the Andes. Created in 1535, the Viceroyalty of New Spain stretched (at least in theory) from the southern tier of the present United States through Mexico and Central America to Panama, across the Caribbean and into northern South America (and even included the Philippines after the 1570s). Charles followed with the creation of the Viceroyalty of Peru in 1540, roughly spanning the newly conquered Inca Empire. In the words of the New Laws of 1542, "the kingdoms of Peru and New Spain are to be ruled and governed by viceroys who represent our royal person." Not until the late eighteenth century would the Spanish Crown finally create (two) additional viceroyalties to accommodate the growth of the empire in the New World. (These viceroyalties were modeled on those in Spain and the Mediterranean—Aragón, Catalonia, Valencia, Navarre, Sardinia, and Naples.) The earliest viceroys played a very powerful role in the consolidation of royal authority and control, and in the creation of the basic institutions of the Spanish American Empire.

The viceroys reproduced on a smaller scale the court of the king in Mexico City and Lima. Wary of the influence of the most powerful nobles in Castile, the king generally turned to the younger members of the powerful elite families or to nobles of lesser rank to serve as viceroys. (Nearly one hundred men served as viceroys in colonial Spanish America.) Antonio de Mendoza, the first viceroy of New Spain (1535–49)—and one of the greatest—was one of the younger children of a marquis. He was named to this powerful and central position at the age of 40. Luis de Velasco (1550–64) followed a series of unimpressive early choices for viceroys in Peru, and like Mendoza became the founding father of the administrative machine in his viceroyalty. Both men left a powerful imprint on their domains, imprints that would endure for centuries.

Below the viceroys, the Crown in Spanish America gradually established regional administrative units known as *audiencias*. By the seventeenth century, there were ten *audiencias* (see map 3) each with eight or nine *oidores* or *fiscales*, again largely men with legal training. The president-governor of the *audiencia* was often a military man, especially after 1600, with the rising threat to the American colonies from other European powers. Although the *audiencias* were supposed to exercise largely judicial functions, they often took on other administrative functions, especially in the absence of a viceroy. Along with the viceroys, they formed the elite of the Spanish American imperial bureaucracy. (About a thousand men served on the *audiencias* before 1700.) Ever suspicious (and usually with good reason), the king regularly sent out independent judges to conduct visits (*visitas*) to check up on royal officials. At the end of his term of office, every royal official experienced a *residencia*, a sort of review of performance. Its principal purpose was to see if the official had upheld standards and had not violated royal guidelines in the exercise of his authority.

Below the regional authority of the *audiencias* were towns and their surrounding countryside, divided into *alcadías mayores* or *corregimientos*. The king appointed an *alcalde mayor* or *corregidor*, often a local landowner, as his representative. All officially recognized towns had a town council (*cabildo*) dominated by powerful local notables—landowners, priests, merchants. As Mark Burkholder and Lyman Johnson have pointed out, the municipality was the "cornerstone of Spanish rule and settlement" in the Americas. The local aldermen and judges exercised the most direct influence and power over the lives of the peoples of the empire. Municipalities were the first and most direct face of royal authority and power, regulating everything from weights and measures to the division of lands. Despite the economic power of the large rural estates, as in Spain and Portugal, citizens in the two empires were defined in relation to their nearest urban center.

The greater the distance from Madrid and the viceregal capitals, the greater the leeway of local officials to exercise their own discretion and power. At best, correspondence from Madrid to Lima in the mid-seventeenth century took eight months to arrive. An immediate response (a rarity, no doubt) took another eight months on the return. An equivalent turnaround to more remote regions of the empire (Paraguay or Bolivia) could take years. The wheels of the empire turned very slowly! Contact between Lisbon and the Brazilian settlements was much better, with a transatlantic voyage taking about a month. The Portuguese monarchy, however, often waited years to get a response to messages sent out to East Asia and India. These enormous communication delays, combined with the fragmented and widely dispersed authority in the Iberian empires, meant that state presence, in the words of John Elliott, "while all pervasive, was not all-commanding."

MONARCHIES, NATIONS, EMPIRES

By the close of the sixteenth century, the Spanish and Portuguese monarchies had created global empires on a scale never seen before in the history of the world. The rise of the Spanish and Portuguese nations and empires was neither an inevitable nor a linear process. Both Spain and Portugal had emerged in the late Middle Ages out of the Reconquest, a process that was fitful, full of surprises and false turns. Although seldom recognized, Portugal was the first nation-state to emerge in Europe out of the chaos and political fragmentation of the Middle Ages. In the late eleventh century—roughly the same time the French Normans crossed the Channel and conquered England—a French noble, Henri of Burgundy, asserted control over the region around Oporto, known as Portucale in Roman times (hence the origin of the name "Portugal"). Henri married the illegitimate daughter of Alfonso VI of Castile and pledged allegiance to him. In the 1120s and 1130s, Henri's son, Afonso Henriques, rebelled against Castilian rule. By the 1140s, he proclaimed himself king of Portugal, independent of Castile. It would take Afonso Henriques nearly 40 years to persuade the Pope and other kings to recognize the House of Burgundy and Portugal as a kingdom in 1179. By the mid-thirteenth century (1245) the Burgundians completed the reconquest of southern Portugal (the Algarve), extending the emerging nation to its modern borders. The monarch became known as the King of Portugal and the Algarve.

In 1383, civil war broke out in Portugal as both peasants and lords rebelled against the crown. Out of the resulting chaos, João (John), an illegitimate prince and Master of the religious Order of Avis emerged triumphant to establish a new monarchy, the House of Avis. John I (1385–1433) had to fight off an invasion from Castile in 1385 to consolidate his power. He turned to another tiny Atlantic kingdom—England—as his chief ally. The Anglo-Portuguese Alliance was sealed with a treaty in 1386 at Windsor Castle. John I then married Phillipa (the daughter of Edward III) and began a binational relationship that would continue for centuries. Under the House of Avis (1385–1578), Portugal experienced its greatest days of glory. John and Phillipa's three legitimate sons—Duarte, Pedro, and Henrique—led Portugal into the modern world. Although his older brothers would become king and regent, respectively, Henrique turned to other interests. As the Duke of Viseu and Master of the Order of Christ, he used his wealth and influence to promote overseas voyages and is known best as Prince Henry the Navigator. (He had a hand in perhaps a third of all the overseas voyages in the first half of the fifteenth century.) The illegitimate son of John I (also named John) founded a very powerful family of dukes (the Braganzas), who would one day assume the throne (in 1640).

Under Manoel I (1495–1521) and John III (1521–57), Portuguese overseas expansion climaxed. The Portuguese and Spanish royal families also frequently forged marriage alliances. Charles I of Spain (Carlos V, 1517–56) married Manoel's daughter (Isabel) and John III married Catarina, Charles's sister. Philip II (1556–98), the eldest son of Charles and Isabel, married Maria (in 1543) the daughter of John and Catarina (and his cousin). After the death of Catarina, John III married Philip's sister Juana (in 1552). She was John's niece. Juana gave birth to one child, Sebastião, in 1554 not long before the death of John III. Often described as sick in both body and mind, Sebastião assumed power at the age of 14. Possessed of a dream to resume the Reconquest, Sebastião mounted an ill-fated expedition to North Africa in 1578. Undisciplined and disorganized, 20,000 Portuguese troops (including Spanish, German, and Italian mercenaries) attacked a force of some 50,000 Muslims near Alcácer Quibir in Morocco. In what has been described as the worst defeat in Portuguese military history, the Muslims slaughtered the cream of Portugal's nobility, including Sebastião. Nearly all of the remaining expeditionary force fell prisoner to the local sultan. This military fiasco brought an end to the House of Avis (Sebastião was unmarried and childless) and Portugal's independence. (The young king's body was never recovered, leading some to argue that he had not died and would one day return to lead Portugal to new days of glory.)

The creation of the Spanish nation under a single monarchy was also a tortured process full of historical contingencies, a process that took nearly eight centuries, beginning with the first steps of the Reconquest in the early eighth century. A series of kingdoms (Asturias, Catalonia, León, and Navarre, to name a few) emerged on the peninsula and by the mid-fifteenth century the two most powerful—Aragón to the east and Castile in central Spain—had gobbled up the others. The unification of the two kingdoms eventually resulted from the marriage of Fernando of Aragón and Isabel of Castile, although neither was in line to inherit the throne when they married in 1469. Both were astute and careful strategists and Isabel claimed the throne of Castile in 1474 while Fernando became king of Aragón in 1479. Together they ruled the dual kingdoms (although each was ruled as a separate entity), forming the basis for the modern Spanish nation. They married their daughter (Juana) to Philip, the son of Maximilian, the Austrian Hapsburg emperor. Isabel died in 1504 and her son-in-law died suddenly in 1506. Tragically, Juana had become increasingly erratic and was judged completely mad by 1509 (she is best known in Spanish history as Juana la Loca or Joana the Mad) when she retired to a monastery, where she would spend 46 years in seclusion. When Fernando died in early 1516, the crown passed to his grandson Charles, the son of Juana and Philip. Born in Ghent in 1500, the awkward and odd-looking Charles arrived on the northern coast of Spain in 1517, setting foot on the peninsula for the first time. Raised in Flanders, speaking Flemish, Charles was wholly ignorant of conditions in Spain and did not speak Castilian Spanish. Despite a rather shaky start, however, he would emerge as one of the greatest figures of the sixteenth century and in world history over the last millennium.

The first of the Spanish Hapsburg dynasty (1517–1700), Charles inherited vast domains from all four of his grandparents. From his maternal grandmother (Isabel), he inherited the crown of Castile (stretching from Galicia and Navarre in the north through central Spain to Granada and Andalusia in the south). Through his maternal grandfather (Fernando) he became King of Aragón (essentially the eastern third of the peninsula including Valencia and Catalonia) and ruler of the Kingdom of Naples (southern Italy), Sardinia, Sicily, and the Balearic Islands. His paternal grandmother (Mary of Burgundy) left him control of the Low Countries (modern day Netherlands, Belgium, and Luxembourg) and the Franche Comté in eastern France. From his paternal grandfather (Maximilian of Austria) Charles inherited substantial territories in Central Europe (including Innsbruck, Vienna, and Trieste). When Maximilian died in 1519, Charles was named Holy Roman Emperor through the machinations of his Austrian relatives. This teenage ruler became at once Holy Roman Emperor, King of Castile and León, King of Aragón, Duke of Burgundy, and Count of Barcelona! (He became Emperor Charles V of the Holy Roman Empire, and King Charles I of Spain. He is best known as Charles V.) Within two decades, he would add the Aztec and Inca Empires to his domain, becoming the most powerful and richest monarch the world had known to that point.

Charles V transformed Spain from a nation into an empire that spanned Europe and the Atlantic. His diplomatic and military forays across Europe made him an absentee monarch. During his 40-year reign he resided in Spain for less than 16 years. In 1526, he married his cousin Isabel, the daughter of Portugal's Manoel I, and she would serve as regent during many of her husband's lengthy absences. Charles would exhaust much of the wealth of Spain and Spanish America in wars across Europe and the Mediterranean. The rise of the Ottoman Empire in Turkey by the 1520s presented an enormous threat to European Christendom through the next two centuries. Although Charles would fight the "Turk," it would be his son Philip who faced the brunt of Ottoman expansion. The Spanish victory at the Battle of Lepanto (off the Greek coast) in 1571 definitively secured peace for the western Mediterranean. The rise of Martin Luther and the Reformation in central Europe proved the more costly and difficult challenge for Charles and the Catholic Church. At the very moment of Charles's ascent to power in Spain, Luther proclaimed his break with Rome and touched off decades of religious warfare in Europe. Charles V became the great warrior for the Counter-Reformation, and the price for Spain was staggering. Charles borrowed heavily from German, Genoese, Flemish, and Spanish bankers, and the wages of warfare were ultimately multiple bankruptcies (1557, 1575, and 1596) for the Spanish monarchy in the second half of the sixteenth century.

If Charles was the great warrior, his son Philip was the quintessential bureaucrat. While his father spent much of his life in the saddle on the battlefield in the midst of soldiers, Philip spent most of his tucked away at his desk in the Escorial Palace surrounded by paper and bureaucrats. Raised by his Portuguese mother, Philip probably spent his early years speaking her native language, as well as Castilian Spanish. His first wife, yet another Portuguese princess, died in childbirth, leaving Philip a widower at 21. Charles arranged his son's marriage to Mary Tudor in 1554, hoping to unite the monarchies of England and Spain. The brilliant plan collapsed with the death of Mary in November 1558. The Protestant forces stymied Charles on the battlefield in central Europe and through diplomatic and dynastic maneuvers in England. Charles abdicated the Spanish crown in favor of Philip II in 1556 (his mother Juana had died the previous year), and then retired to a monastery at Yuste in Extremadura. He spent the last two years of his life surrounded by a hundred retainers nursing a serious case of gout. With his death in 1558, the title of Holy Roman Emperor passed back to an Austrian Hapsburg and, in the words of the clever John Elliott, he left his son Philip II a legacy of "bankruptcy and heresy."

Philip II reoriented Spain's destiny from the eastward-looking continental perspective of his father to a westward-looking transatlantic empire. At the very moment of his ascent to power, the costly religious wars in Europe bankrupted the monarchy and the rich silver deposits of Mexico and Peru began to flow across the Atlantic in increasingly large quantities. While the Spanish kingdoms financed the regime of Charles V in the first half of the sixteenth century, American silver funded the empire of Philip II in the second half of the century. Known for his cold, austere, and controlled personality, Philip faced a personal life of continual tragedy. He buried four wives and twice as many children. Fearing a conspiracy, he felt compelled to imprison his son Charles (by his first wife, Maria, of Portugal), who soon died under questionable circumstances. His fourth wife, Anna, of Austria, bore him five children, yet only one (the future Philip III) lived beyond the age of eight. It was Philip I who finally halted the peripatetic wanderings of the court and made Madrid the permanent Spanish capital in 1561. In the hills above the capital he built the Escorial, between 1563 and 1584, as "part-mausoleum, part-monastery, and part-royal residence." The embodiment of his reign, the Escorial, in the words of J. H. Elliott, has a "cold symmetry, classicism, imperial, dignified, and aloof—a fitting symbol of the triumph of constraint in the Spain of the Counter-Reformation, and the triumph of authoritarian kingship over the disruptive forces of anarchy."

With the death of the young and misguided King Sebastião of Portugal, Philip II moved to assert his claim to the Portuguese throne. He had, after all, married Maria, the daughter of John III (d. 1557), and Sebastião was

Philip's nephew. Much of the Portuguese nobility had been killed or held
for ransom in the ill-fated invasion of Morocco. With the help of large
amounts of American silver and an invading army, Philip "persuaded"
the Portuguese to "offer" him the crown. He did, however, make some
concessions. Portugal and its empire would continue to operate as an
independent entity run by a viceroy who reported to a Council of Portugal.
Crowned Philip I of Portugal in 1580, he spent very little time in the country before returning to Spain. The unification of the two nations and
empires under one king created the largest and richest empire in world
history, one that would only be eclipsed in the eighteenth century by the
British. From 1580 to 1640, Spain and Portugal were ruled by the Spanish
Hapsburgs in an era sometimes referred to as the "Babylonian Captivity"
by the Portuguese. Internal problems in Spain and an uprising in Portugal
in 1640 would separate the empires once again, and lead to the ascendancy
of the Braganza dynasty in Portugal.

THE END OF IBERIAN SUPREMACY

The last two decades of the sixteenth century marked the height of Iberian
power in the Atlantic world, and the beginning of a long period of decline for
both nations, a decline that would not be reversed until the late twentieth
century. By 1600, new European powers had begun to emerge and to challenge Iberian supremacy in Europe, in the Atlantic, and across the globe. The
English under Elizabeth I (1558–1603) began their rise to power, especially
on the sea. More immediate, and initially more powerful, was the challenge
to Spain and Portugal from the Dutch and the rise of the Dutch Republic.

The emergence of the Dutch Republic is one of the great stories in
world history. In the sixteenth century, the Low Countries consisted
roughly of modern-day Belgium, Luxembourg, and the Netherlands
(and parts of what is now northeastern France). To the north, the people
spoke an evolving dialect of German that would become Dutch. To
the south, they spoke dialects of French. The Low Countries had come to
Philip II as an inheritance from his father. Unlike his father (born in
Flanders), Philip was a foreign ruler. With the explosion of the Reformation,
many of the inhabitants turned to Protestantism, especially the version
preached by Jean Calvin of Geneva. Along with Martin Luther, Calvin is
one of the two giants of the Reformation in the sixteenth century.
Calvin's message was much more radical than Luther's. According to
Calvin, it was not enough to be a devout believer, a good Christian had
to demonstrate his belief through actions and behavior. If one lived in a
society that did not permit a person to live outwardly a Christian life, he
argued, then a good Christian should act to change the society. This was

a revolutionary message in the sixteenth century. (Indeed, it would be truly revolutionary today if people acted on their most deeply held beliefs!) While Martin Luther had broken with Rome and told men to follow their own consciences and to speak directly with God, Calvin now told them to create a society that would allow them to live out their beliefs. Calvin believed deeply in the individual's responsibility to reform society according to God's divine (Calvinist) plan. Calvin's message was a call to his Dutch followers to challenge their Spanish Catholic rulers (or their oppressors, as they would have said). By the 1560s, perhaps two-thirds of the "Dutch" had converted to Calvinism. The efforts of the Spanish Catholic Philip II to impose his rule on the Dutch Protestants produced a long and bloody conflict full of atrocities that would last for decades.

For more than 40 years, Philip II and his son Philip III (1598–1621), sent waves of Spanish troops and mercenaries into the Low Countries. In 1566, Calvinists throughout the country rioted, prompting Philip to send in ten thousand men under the command of the Duke of Alba. The Duke ruthlessly suppressed any rebellion and publicly executed several thousand suspected heretics, including very powerful nobles. After Spanish mercenaries ran amok, killing thousands in Antwerp in 1576, most of the provinces united against Spanish rule. In 1581, William of Orange denounced Philip II and declared independence from Spanish rule. Ultimately, the northern provinces succeeded in holding off Spain's armies.

The region had long been a hotbed of trade, finance, fishing, and shipping. What was emerging in the Low Countries in the fifteenth and sixteenth centuries, in fact, was revolutionary in economic terms. Unlike most of the powerful men of Europe, the elite in the Low Countries did not derive their wealth from the land and control of peasants. Instead, they made their money from banking, fishing, trade, and shipping. The Dutch developed one of the largest maritime fleets in world history, bringing in revenue from fishing and shipping. They became experts in the handling of long-distance financial transactions. Much like the Genoese in the fifteenth century, the Dutch had become the great overseas merchants and financiers of the sixteenth and seventeenth centuries. The famous burghers of Amsterdam, immortalized in the great paintings of Rembrandt and the other Dutch Masters, were men of the city and trade. They were not feudal lords tied to the land and landed estates. The Dutch formed the cutting edge of modern economic development. They were the advance guard in the emergence of modern capitalism, a preindustrial capitalism built on trade and exchange. By 1598, Spain was forced to concede the de facto independence of the Dutch Republic, and recognized the new nation by the Twelve Years Truce in 1609. The seven northern provinces became

Dutch, and the ten southern ones continued under Hapsburg control and were known as the Spanish Netherlands.

The rise of the Dutch Republic at the beginning of the seventeenth century initiated a series of global struggles among the European powers. Both Spain and Portugal paid a high price for the conflict in the Netherlands. It marked the beginning of powerful challenges—first from the Dutch and then the English and French—and a centuries-long slide from world-power status to weak and backward economies and political systems. England crushed Spain's "invincible" armada in 1588, capturing or destroying some 40 to 50 ships and 15,000 men. After 1600, Dutch, French, and English pirates and privateers attacked Spanish and Portuguese possessions in the Atlantic, Pacific, and Indian Oceans while expeditions established colonial settlements in North, South, and Central America, as well as the islands of the Caribbean.

The Spanish and Portuguese had exercised a near-monopoly on European conquest and colonization in the Americas for nearly a century. The rise of the English, French, and Dutch nations in the late sixteenth and early seventeenth centuries brought that monopoly to an end after 1600. It was the Dutch who were the first great catalyst in the challenges to the Iberians, and in their decline. In the case of all three newcomers, they moved from harassing the Spanish and Portuguese to becoming a permanent presence and challenge. The French began this process in South America in the mid-sixteenth century, followed by the English shortly thereafter. The Dutch appeared on the scene in the last two decades of the sixteenth century in a spectacular fashion. In retrospect, it was the beginning of a long decline for Spain and Portugal, even though they managed to hold on to their possessions in the Americas.

The Dutch emerged as the great maritime power in the first half of the seventeenth century and immediately struck at Spanish and Portuguese possessions on both sides of the Atlantic, in the Indian Ocean and in East Asia. Portuguese possessions were, in fact, more vulnerable than places like Mexico and Peru. As a global trading network of ports, the Portuguese possessions were much more exposed to Dutch naval power than the silver mines of Potosí or central Mexico. Spain was most vulnerable in the Caribbean basin, especially Havana, Cartagena, and Portobello. The Dutch seized Rio de Janeiro, Salvador, and Recife, as well as Elmina and Luanda in the 1620s and 1630s. Bahia fell under Dutch control and was retaken by the Portuguese in 1625. The most devastating blow was the loss of Olinda and Recife in 1630. For a quarter of a century, the Dutch occupied the coast of Pernambuco, their "Netherlands Brazil." It was during these years that the Dutch ended the Portuguese domination of the Asian trade by establishing bases in Ceylon, Indonesia, and Japan. The great weakness of the Spanish was their fleet system, the lifeline of the

American empire. In 1628, Piet Heyn captured the entire fleet as it left Havana.

Dutch supremacy lasted until midcentury, when the English emerged as the greatest maritime power ever. The Dutch had challenged the English with settlements on Manhattan Island, in the Caribbean, and South America. In a series of Anglo-Dutch wars in the 1650s, 1660s, and 1670s, the English replaced the Dutch as the great naval power on the oceans. Much like the Portuguese empire, the Dutch empire endured for centuries, but primarily as a trading and maritime empire.

With the rise of the new challengers, the Caribbean became a battleground for imperial rivalries in the seventeenth century. The English were the most successful challenger to the Spanish in the West Indies. As the power struggles emerged, Spain concentrated its forces in the larger islands: Cuba, Hispaniola, Puerto Rico, and Jamaica. When Spain and the Dutch Republic went to war in the 1620s, English pirates began seizing islands vacated by the Spanish. In 1655, an English fleet captured Jamaica and held it. By the late seventeenth century, the English held some 20 colonies, from the Mosquito Coast in Central America, to British Guiana in South America, to the Bahamas. Well into the eighteenth century, they would have to fight Indians, rebellious slaves, pirates, and their European rivals to hold on to them.

The French and Dutch had less dramatic success conquering and colonizing, but they did establish permanent settlements. In the long run, Saint Domingue (the western portion of Hispaniola) would become the French prize colony, emerging as the richest colonial possession in the world in the mid-eighteenth century. The Dutch were the "also-rans" in this grab for territory, seizing Curaçao in 1634. With the English, French, and Dutch conquests, the Caribbean became a multinational, multilingual, multiracial region, a microcosm of the larger struggles among Europeans, Indians, and Africans in the conquest of the Americas.

As Spain, Portugal, and their colonies in the Americas entered into the seventeenth century, they moved into a new phase in their relationships, and in the consolidation of new societies in the Americas. The rise of powerful military and diplomatic challenges from other European nations— England, France, the Netherlands—severely hampered the transatlantic connection, especially the fleet system, and initiated a long period of looser metropolitan control. This would mean greater local autonomy in the colonies and the emergence of a growing creole society run more and more by those born in the Americas. What many historians have called the "long" seventeenth century (from about 1580 to 1720) was characterized by declining silver shipments across the Atlantic (especially after 1620), the rise of the great estates in the Americas, the emergence of societies and cultures that blended Iberian, Amerindian, and African traditions into new forms that were neither Iberian, nor Amerindian, nor African. In short, declining Iberian power translated into increasing local autonomy, and the gradual emergence of "American" societies and cultures. This is perhaps most visible in the evolution of religion and religious cultures in seventeenth-century Latin America.

9

Religion and Empire

Military conquest and religious conversion advanced together throughout the Americas—the sword and the cross marched side by side. In early modern Europe, church and State—the sacred and the secular worlds—closely intertwined and could not be disentangled. For the men and women in sixteenth-century Europe, there was no separation of the sacred and the secular as we think of them today. For most, if not all peoples, religious significance imbued all life and all actions. This was as true for Native Americans as it was for Africans and Europeans. Only the most devoutly religious today come close to this early modern mentality. For these people, there is no distinction between religion and "the rest of life." For the closest modern equivalent, we would have to look at fundamentalist regimes such as the Taliban in Afghanistan.

Unlike the military conquest, the spiritual conquest was incomplete and imperfect, and it will never be completed. Although the vast majority of Latin Americans today call themselves Catholics, large numbers of them engage in religious rituals and practices that are clearly of non-Western origin. With somewhere around 400 million believers, Latin America today is the largest concentration of Catholics in the world. Brazil, a country of 185 million, is now the largest Catholic country on earth. Yet, millions of these Catholics, and those who do not call themselves Catholic, hold beliefs and practice rituals that have their origins in African or Native American cultures. With the end of the religious intolerance and the Catholic monopoly on Latin America after independence in the nineteenth century, the religious pluralism of Latin America has gradually increased, and the dream of imposing a single, Catholic religion will now never be accomplished. Although Catholicism remained the official state religion in much of Latin America after independence in the early nineteenth century, the new nations allowed other religions to worship openly and freely for the first time. For all intents and purposes, the original, naive dream of the conquistadores and the Iberian kings that they would convert all the peoples of the Americas through persuasion or force, had long since been proven fruitless.

THE SPIRITUAL CONQUEST

For the Spanish and the Portuguese, their conquest of the Americas was an extension of the centuries-long religious and military struggle against the Moors. Conquest was both military and spiritual, pitting the "true believer" against the "infidel." There was, quite simply, no doubt in the minds of the Spanish and Portuguese that they were doing God's work, and that the Moors, or the Native Americans, or Africans were engaging in the work of the Devil. From our early twenty-first-century perspective, shaped by relativism and cynicism, this is very often hard for us to understand. Christianity, by its very nature, is an aggressive and militant religion that has always sought to make new converts. Christianity has been, since its beginnings with Jesus, a religion founded on the need to spread the "Word" to all peoples. In an era of unyielding certainty about truth and righteousness, the Spanish and Portuguese took very seriously Luke 14:23, "Go out into the highways and hedges, and compel them to come in."

The Spanish, in particular, were perhaps the most militant and proselytizing of all Christians in Europe. The experience (over eight centuries) of driving the Muslims back across Spain, and then the Straits of Gibraltar, forged a deeply militaristic mentality. By the fifteenth century, this would have been unfamiliar terrain for Christians in western and northern Europe who did not face a powerful or threatening religious adversary. The closest parallel was in southeastern Europe, where Muslim armies fought for centuries with Christians, creating deeply rooted animosities that resurfaced with a vengeance in the region at the end of the twentieth century. For the Iberians, the sword and the cross conquered new peoples together, hand in hand, for the one true God and the one true king.

In Spain and Portugal, the church and the state were intimately intertwined, in contrast to our contemporary view of the two institutions. The Reconquest forged this linkage on the Iberian peninsula. The king ultimately received his authority from God via the Pope's blessing. Despite the frequent disagreements, and even wars, between the Vatican and monarchs, all European kings ultimately wanted to have their rule validated by the blessing of the Church in Rome. Conversely, the Pope lacked troops and needed the financial resources of the monarchies to survive and grow. In the early sixteenth century, in Spain and Portugal, the monarchy forged a special relationship with the Vatican known as "royal patronage" (*patronato real* in Spanish or *padroado real* in Portuguese). In exchange for financial and military support for the Vatican, the Pope granted the two monarchies the right to appoint Church officials. A series of papal bulls gave the two monarchies effective control of the administration of Church jurisdictions, the collection of revenues (the tithe), and the payment of salaries. The evangelization of the Americas was an enterprise on a scale never before faced by Rome, and the Pope essentially handed over the task to the Iberian monarchies. The Catholic Church in the Spanish and Portuguese empires became a virtual arm of the state. The Council of the Indies, in practice, administered and executed the privileges of the *patronato* in Spanish America. In effect, the clergy became servants of the state, placing them in a difficult position as they answered to two masters. High Church officials, in particular, such as bishops and archbishops, owed their appointments to the king, but they ultimately answered to Rome.

When the Reformation broke out in central and northern Europe in the early sixteenth century, it did not cross the Pyrenees. The German princes of central and northern Europe were fighting a political as well as a theological battle with Rome. By challenging the Vatican on religious belief, they could also seize the assets of the Catholic Church in their domains, and establish control over this powerful parallel organization in their territories. Having already effectively seized control over the Church on the peninsula, the Iberian monarchs had no reason to challenge Rome on theological or political grounds. On the contrary, it was in their best interest vigorously to support the religious orthodoxy of Rome against all challenges. The creation of the Inquisition in the late fifteenth century, and the expulsion of Muslims and Jews from Spain and Portugal, provide vivid examples of the pursuit of religious orthodoxy. These were early modern forms of what we would now call "ethnic cleansing."

With the discovery of the Americas, the Catholic Church faced a serious theological and practical question: what to do about the Indians? The Native Americans and the American continents did not appear in either of the two great sources of authority: the Bible and the ancient Greek and Roman writers. The Europeans wrestled with this problem for decades (if not for centuries) before coming up with ways to get around this problem. In a worldview built on authority, what was one to make of peoples and lands who were not even mentioned in the two most important and authoritative sources of knowledge? As strange as it may sound to us today, the Spanish engaged in a debate over the nature of the Indian to determine if he or she had a soul and the faculty of reason. This is no small matter, for without rational faculties, one cannot discern the difference between good and evil. One cannot make the reasoned choice between salvation and damnation. Without a soul, there would be nothing to save. Pope Paul III issued a bull, *Sublimis Deus* (1537), declaring the Indians rational beings with souls. Eventually, Charles V decided that the indigenous peoples were humans with souls and the faculty of reason, but they were to be treated as wards of the Crown.

One of the greatest figures in colonial American history, Bartolomé de las Casas, emerged as the great defender of the Indians in this debate. Born around 1474 to a merchant family in Seville, Las Casas witnessed the return of Columbus to Spain with a handful of Indians. In 1502, he sailed to the Caribbean, worked for his father supplying military expeditions, and witnessed the Conquest firsthand. While in his twenties, he experienced a religious awakening and was ordained a priest. (Eventually he became a Dominican.) He accompanied Velázquez and Narváez in the conquest of Cuba in 1513, converting Indians and becoming an *encomendero*. The decimation of the Indians in the Conquest deeply moved Las Casas and he spent the rest of his long life condemning Spanish treatment of the native peoples of the Americas. His *A Short Account of the Destruction of the Indies* (1539) was widely translated and used by Protestants (especially the Dutch and English) to condemn the Catholic monarchy of Spain. The book is still in print today, and is one of the most important statements on human rights ever written. In 1550, he engaged the humanist Juan Ginés de Sepúlveda in a highly publicized debate in Valladolid. While Las Casas argued that Spain's only justification in conquering the Americas was to convert the native peoples, and that the only true means to accomplish this conversion would be through persuasion and not force, Sepúlveda countered with arguments based on Aristotle and Saint Thomas Aquinas that a war against the Indians was just one of superior men over inferior beings. Although the debate had no official conclusion or decision, the position of Las Casas became the prevailing one (at least in legal theory). For his energetic and extraordinary missionary work and defense of the native peoples, he is known as "Protector of the Indians." Las Casas crossed the Atlantic 14 times, moving between his religious work in the New World, and defending the Indians before the court in Spain. He died in Madrid in 1566 at the age of 91.

An extraordinary group of men and women were the principal religious conquistadores. These priests and nuns moved into Latin America in the sixteenth and seventeenth centuries to bring the word of their God to Native Americans and Africans. Two kinds of clergy engaged in the construction of the Catholic Church in the Americas: regular and secular. All the clergy went through seminaries for their religious training and were then ordained, taking vows of poverty, chastity, and obedience to the Church. Priests and nuns trained in the seminaries and schools of the dioceses are known as secular clergy. The religious orders within the Church have their own training and the priests and nuns owe loyalty and obedience to the order as well as the Church. Those from the orders are known as regular clergy (from the Latin *regula*, for they carefully regulated their lives in their training). In the process of the Conquest, the monarchs favored the regular clergy, believing them to be more capable and less corrupt than the secular clergy. With their own well-defined organizations within the Catholic Church, the regulars became powerful interest groups within the Iberian empires, and always presented more serious challenges to royal authority than the secular clergy. The most important religious orders in the conquest of Latin America were the so-called mendicant orders, those who emulated the work of Jesus, preaching the gospel among the masses. The most important of these were priests from the Jesuits, Dominicans, and Franciscans. The Franciscans dated back to their founding father, St. Francis, in the Middle Ages, as did the Dominicans, named after St. Dominic. Many of the first priests sent out to the Caribbean were Dominicans and Franciscans. A group of 12 Franciscans arrived in Mexico in 1524, followed by the Dominicans and Augustinians in 1526 and 1533. By midcentury there were probably some 800 priests and nuns in New Spain.

Whatever one thinks of their theology and methods, these clergy spread their gospel under some of the most extraordinary conditions imaginable. Never numbering more than a few thousand across all of the Americas, they moved into a sea of Indians and Africans, learning their languages and customs. Their strategy was to baptize first and then educate the Africans and Indians in the word of God. This led to many unintended consequences, including cultural and religious misunderstandings and blending. In many ways, these priests were the first anthropologists in the Americas. They learned the Indian languages, at times so well that they were able to create a written language, dictionaries, and grammars. Nahuatl, for example, the language of the Aztecs, was given a Roman alphabet, and the written language was then taught in schools to the Indian elites. Pedro de Gante, an extraordinary Flemish Franciscan, organized a school for sons of the Indian nobles in Mexico City. Gante quickly became fluent in Nahuatl (the language of instruction) and began the process of creating a written language with a Latin alphabet. Some of the most valuable documents we have today for the study of colonial and pre-Columbian Mexico were written down in Indian communities across central Mexico throughout the colonial era. Another Franciscan, Bernardino de Sahagún, devoted most of his life to amassing a twelve-volume encyclopedia of Aztec life written in Nahuatl, Spanish, and Latin. In the early sixteenth century, Sahagún was able to interview survivors of the Conquest about life before the Spanish invasion, and his *Florentine Codex* is one of the monumental sources for the study of Aztec society before the

Conquest. Diego de Landa, the bishop of Yucatán, and another Franciscan, produced a similar work on the Maya, and there are other equally important examples.

Yet, we must remember that the reason these dedicated priests so conscientiously learned languages and customs was to eradicate them and to turn Native Americans into good, Europeanized Christians. The objective was to understand the mind and worldview of the Indians so as to know best how to change them. Landa, for example, once he had collected and researched every possible Maya book (codex), then burned all of his sources! Success, for the missionaries, was the complete and total annihilation of pre-Columbian religious beliefs and practices. This was a world of absolutes, of truth and heresy, of the right way, and the wrong path. The missionaries were engaged in a struggle for the hearts and souls of the Indians, and they showed no quarter, and expected none in return.

The Jesuits and Franciscans are but two of the most striking examples of these religious orders. While the Franciscans were founded in the Middle Ages, the Jesuits were a very new order founded in 1536. Both set out to serve as the vanguard of Christian missionaries. The Franciscans played the key role in the creation of the Catholic Church in Mexico. The Jesuits were central to the creation of the Church in Brazil. The Jesuits are, from my perspective, the most interesting religious order in the Catholic Church. Unlike the other major orders, the Jesuits were created in the sixteenth century in the heat of the Reformation and Counter-Reformation. A Spanish soldier, Ignatius of Loyola, formed around him a group of followers in the 1530s. While recovering from wounds, he had a religious vision and dedicated his life to saving souls for Christ. Organized along military lines, these devout disciples of Christ called themselves the Company of Jesus. In 1540, the Pope approved the establishment of their group as a religious order that eventually came to be known as the Society of Jesus, or the Jesuits. By the time of Ignatius of Loyola's death in 1556, the order had nearly 1,000 members, growing to more than 15,000 by the early seventeenth century. Jesuits arrived in Brazil in 1549 and played a key role in the construction of the Church there. Francis Xavier, an early Jesuit, began missionary work in India and the Far East in the 1540s, and the Jesuits would play a powerful role in China and Japan in the late sixteenth and early seventeenth centuries. They arrived in Canada in 1611. The Jesuits became the great educators of the Catholic Church, establishing colleges in Mexico City, Lima, and Córdoba, Argentina. Highly centralized, increasingly wealthy from their plantations and haciendas in the Americas, very well connected politically, the Jesuits would, by the eighteenth century, come to be feared by kings. The Spanish and Portuguese monarchies expelled the Jesuits from their territories in the mid-eighteenth century to rein them in. More than 2,000 personnel in the empires were exiled to Italy. The Pope suppressed the order in 1773, only to "resurrect" it in 1814. The order did not return to Latin America until the mid-nineteenth century. Along with the Franciscans, the Jesuits were the "shock troops" of the Catholic Church in the spiritual conquest of Latin America. Both would have a powerful influence across the Americas, but they would fail in their ultimate objective, to Christianize all of the native peoples of the Americas.

The institutional presence of the Church began to expand quickly after the conquest of Mexico and Peru. In the 1530s and 1540s the Vatican created a series of bishoprics in New Spain (Mexico City, Oaxaca, Michoacán, Guadalajara) and the extraordinary Franciscan, Juan de Zumárraga, became the first bishop in the new colonial capital. A similar process followed in Peru and Central America. By 1550, there were 22 dioceses in Spanish America. By the end of the colonial period, this number had doubled to 45. The first Brazilian bishopric did not come until the establishment of the colonial capital at Salvador da Bahia in 1549. As in fifteenth-century Spain and Portugal, Philip II eventually expanded the Inquisition to Spanish America. The Holy Office for the Propagation of the Faith, as it was known, arrived in Mexico City and Lima in the early 1570s. Indians were generally exempted from the authority of the Inquisition and its wrath fell primarily upon the Spanish and racially-mixed groups, as well as the unfortunate Protestants who might be captured during battles with the English and Dutch. The Inquisition operated very sporadically in Brazil through three visitations (all in the north and northeast) in the 1590s, 1680s, and finally in the 1760s.

BLENDING RELIGIOUS TRADITIONS

The efforts to impose Christianity on millions of non-Europeans, and their efforts to resist the new religion, produced a religious mixing that defines much of Latin America today. The blending of old symbols with new meanings, or new symbols with old meanings, is known as "syncretism" among anthropologists. This blending was sometimes the product of conscious resistance and, at times, of unconscious resistance. Elements of Christianity and non-Christian beliefs mixed to produce new religions that are not indigenous, nor African, nor European, but truly American. Spain and Portugal won the political battle to impose a European system on the peoples of Latin America, but they only partially conquered their hearts and souls. Today, the dominant languages, legal systems, and political structures are European. And, as we have seen, some 85 to 90 percent of Latin Americans are nominally Catholics, but the spiritual conquest was partial and incomplete. Two prime examples of the failure of the spiritual conquest, and the blending of religious traditions are folk Catholicism in Mexico, Central America, and the Andes, and African-influenced religions in the Caribbean and Brazil, such as *candomblé* in Brazil.

Folk Catholicism in Mesoamerica is one of the most striking examples of the failure of the spiritual conquest. It should come as no great surprise that the native peoples of Mesoamerica would fight tenaciously to hold on to their age-old religious worldview. They had a centuries old cosmology built on the notion of cyclical and circular time and history. The Aztecs and Maya saw time as a series of 52-year cycles, a sort of great wheel of life. Although they had a creation story much like that of Christianity and other world religions, the world was repeatedly being destroyed and regenerated in cycles. This was very different from the Christian notion of linear time: creation, the fall of man, redemption and salvation through the Son of God, and then an eventual, final moment of reckoning, the end of history. They had many gods that animated the forces of the natural and supernatural worlds. Powerful forces were behind the elements and the movements of nature. Understandably, then, much of religious ritual aimed at appeasing or influencing these powerful forces, especially through sacrifices of some type.

Their universe included realms similar to heaven and hell in Christianity. The Maya world had three layered domains: (1) the starry arch of heaven, (2) the stony Middleworld of earth made to flower and bear fruit from the blood of kings, and, (3) the dark waters of the Underworld below. The world of humans was connected to the Underworld by a center axis that ran through the center of existence and that materialized in the person of the king who brought it into existence while in a trance atop a pyramid. The beings of the Underworld could be materialized through ritual bloodletting.

Given the large Indian populations in Mesoamerica and the few hundred Catholic priests among them, it is not surprising that the conversion of the native peoples was slow, imperfect, and that blending took place. Perhaps the most striking example of the process of syncretism is the cult around the Virgin of Guadalupe, Mexico's patron saint. The Virgin is said to have appeared to an Indian peasant, Juan Diego, in December 1531, on a hill north of Mexico City. She commanded the building of a church on the site, Tepeyac, a hill associated with the Aztec goddess of the earth, Tonantzin. When the Franciscan bishop of Mexico, Juan de Zumárraga asked for more proof, the Virgin told Juan Diego to gather roses in his mantle. When Juan Diego opened the mantle for Zumárraga, the Virgin's image was imprinted on it. According to tradition, this is the same image that hangs above the altar of the Basilica of Guadalupe today. This sacred story is doubly fascinating, not only because it represents a blend of a prehispanic deity with a major Catholic figure, but also because of the way it has been passed along. The Virgin of Guadalupe became the rallying figure for Indians in colonial Mexico and for the so-called creoles (Spaniards born in Mexico). Yet, when historians attempt to reconstruct this story, the first undisputed evidence is no earlier than the mid-seventeenth century. In other words, this history may have been dreamed up in the seventeenth century, and become a prime example of blending that had never happened, but was later accepted by the Indians as a story of blending. It might be a fabricated account made to appeal to those who wanted to claim a Mexican identity of blending, and then the claim took on a life of its own. The Virgin of Guadalupe became a powerful national symbol in the nineteenth century, and is today a national cult.

Another vivid example of this blending is in the celebration of the Day of the Dead. Celebrated across much of what might be called Indo-America, the *Día de los Muertos* is a nearly one-week celebration in late October and early November. The central idea is to bring together both living and dead family members and friends in an atmosphere of communion and spiritual revival. As David Carrasco has pointed out, the celebration emphasizes preparations for the ceremonies, the creation of family altars, and a ceremonial feast of the dead. Sahagún's *Florentine Codex* contains a description of the Aztec cult of the dead that could easily describe contemporary ceremonies. In both these examples, we see the emergence of peoples who eventually describe themselves as Catholics, but whose religious rituals and beliefs also include many influences from pre-Hispanic times. Anthropologists have labeled this blending among the large masses of Indians in Mesoamerica as "folk Catholicism"—a Catholicism of the people.

Afro-Brazilian religions are another powerful example of this religious syncretism. The African peoples brought with them many different religions to the Americas: animism, Islam, and Christianity. The followers of Islam had swept across East, North, and some of West Africa long before the arrival of the European slave traders. The Portuguese had converted some African peoples to Christianity, most notably in the Kingdom of Kongo. The most powerful religious influences to come across the Atlantic, especially from West Africa, were animist—based on the belief that powerful spirits are ever-present in the world around us. The hundreds of African gods or deities were eventually reduced to about 15 to 20 in the Caribbean and Brazil. The most influential came from the areas of modern day Nigeria and Benin.

Candomblé in northeastern Brazil is one of the most notable examples of the mixtures of African and Christian beliefs. Its origins are primarily from Yoruba peoples in West Africa. About a dozen African deities eventually merge with Catholic saints, Jesus, and Mary. While suppressed for centuries, Afro-Brazilian religions are freely practiced today, and are widely accepted within Brazil by nonbelievers. As with vodun in Haiti, and folk Catholicism in Spanish America, Afro-Brazilian religions are vivid testimony to the resistance of Indians and Africans to the spiritual conquest. They are also witness to the creativity and ingenuity of those people and their descendants.

10

Race, Culture, and Society

The Europeans conquered the Americas and forcibly transported millions of Africans across the Atlantic, but they did not completely subdue or annihilate the cultures of the Indians and Africans. Military imperialism advanced for centuries. Cultural imperialism only partially succeeded. By 1700, the military conquest of Latin America was over except for the frontiers of Central and South America (and some of these frontiers would not be subdued militarily until the beginning of the twentieth century). The European empires were in place all across the Americas and would last, in some cases, into the late twentieth century. The nation-states of our time, the legal and political systems of these countries, and their economies are the direct descendants of the European conquistadores and colonists of the sixteenth and seventeenth centuries. Beneath this European political, legal, and economic veneer, however, lies the legacy of non-European peoples' resistance to complete Westernization. Through intense resistance and calculated accommodation, Native Americans and Africans held on tenaciously to much of their precontact cultures. We have seen the best example of this through the religious struggle and the failure of the spiritual conquest. Yet, we can also see this in language, music, dance, and many other areas of the culture of the great majority of Latin Americans in 1700 and today. Perhaps the most powerful legacy of the conquest and colonization of the Americas is the extraordinarily complex racial and cultural mixture that defines nearly all of the Americas.

Initially, the Spanish and Portuguese tried to enforce a very elaborate and complicated racial tracking system in the Americas. This scheme attempted to classify everyone by every conceivable mix of ancestors. Spanish artists captured the system beautifully in a series of paintings illustrating numerous racially mixed couples and their offspring. The elaborate classification scheme quickly collapsed for a simple reason: one had to know the complete genealogy of a person to be certain of his or her precise racial classification, and for all but the elite the records were scarce to nonexistent. How could one possibly know all the various ancestors of an individual and their racial categories? In the end, the Spanish were very conscious of racial gradations, but these very nuanced gradations were really only important for those higher up in the social pyramid, or those aspiring to rise in the social hierarchy.

I always visualize the racial intermixing by using the image of a triangle with each of the three main groups at different corners: Europeans, Indians, and Africans. Although there were many, many categories, each of the sides of the triangle can be seen as one of the major intermediate racial groups. The offspring of Europeans and Africans were mulattoes; of Europeans and Indians, mestizos; and, less common, the children of Africans and Indians were known in Spanish as zambos (the origin of the word *sambo* in English). Mulattoes and mestizos increased in numbers throughout the Conquest and the colonial eras and, in Latin America and the Caribbean, the racially mixed eventually became the second largest racial group. In the more constrained society of British North America, the racially mixed were pushed down into the ranks of the Africans and Indians. The United States eventually developed a two-tier racial structure of white and nonwhite. In much of Latin America, a three-tier society emerged, of white, nonwhite, and those in between, with no clear boundaries, but rather ambiguities. The United States eventually moved toward a bipolar system based on "race," while Latin America evolved a continuum based on "color."

The identities that all of these people constructed were complex and often fluid. What it meant to be Indian was fairly clear, but even that evolved as Indians gradually adopted and adapted customs and traditions from other peoples. "Indian," in many ways, is the perfect example of the fluidity of categories. What truly defined an Indian was not simply physiognomy, that is, facial and physical features. It also meant wearing traditional tribal dress, speaking an indigenous language, living in a village with other Indians, and self-identifying with the tribal group. The influence of contact with Spaniards, the pull of towns and cities, and sometimes the destruction of the surrounding Indian community gradually worked toward the cultural assimilation of the Indians into Hispanic culture and society. An "Indian" who left his village, spoke Spanish, and took on the dress of the European masses became a mestizo. Culture, in effect, overrode biology.

The Europeans also borrowed from Indians and Africans, developing their own "European" identity in the Americas, a "creole" identity. By the end of the seventeenth century in Spanish America, and the late eighteenth century in British America, the descendants of Europeans, born in the Americas, increasingly saw themselves as not just Spaniards or English. In Spanish America, they became known as creoles, a term originally used to denote the child of an African born in the New World. The creoles—and this would also apply to people like Benjamin Franklin and George Washington—may have been European in biology and culture, but they had gradually absorbed the foods, some of the vocabulary, and practices of the Indians and Africans. This is why, when the English or Spaniards came out to the Americas in the eighteenth century, they saw the "Americans" as exotic and crude compared to their compatriots in London, Paris, Lisbon, or Madrid.

Perhaps the most interesting groups, however, were those "in between," both culturally and ethnically, for they truly created American identities that blended cultural traits in new and unique ways. African influences in music and speech patterns, and Indian influences in diet and language, are but some of the most visible examples of this mix. We need to remember that the vast majority of the peoples of the Americas, for most of their history, have been Africans, Indians, and their racially mixed descendants. They are closer to a "typical" American identity (if there is such a thing) than our traditional European vision of "Americans." In this very fundamental sense, we can say that the European peoples were clearly the victors of the Conquest, but the Indians and Africans were never completely vanquished. Indeed, they are still with us, and a part of us.

THREE CONVERGING CULTURES AND RACES

Cultural and racial mixing took place across the Americas in Spanish, Portuguese, British, French, and Dutch colonies. Each of these colonial societies gradually developed differing approaches in dealing with this mixture. In Brazil and much of the Caribbean, the mix of Africans and Europeans produced many societies that were overwhelmingly racially mixed. Both regions had white minorities throughout the colonial era and beyond. Brazil, for example, had a population of perhaps three million in the early nineteenth century. Best estimates are that half, or 1.5 million, were slaves, many of them African-born. Of the other 1.5 million, half were racially mixed, primarily of blacks and whites. In other words, only a quarter of the Brazilian population was "white," and the Brazilian definition of white is less rigorous than in the United States. Even with a more expansive definition of "white," Brazil did not become a predominantly white population until the beginning of the twentieth century. Some of the Caribbean islands (Haiti, for example) today are overwhelmingly composed of people of African descent, while others, such as Puerto Rico and the Dominican

Republic, have incredibly mixed and racially diverse populations. In the heavily indigenous regions of Mesoamerica and the Andes, miscegenation also took place, but the result was a mix primarily of Indians and Europeans. The prime examples here are Mexico, Guatemala, Peru, Ecuador, and Bolivia. These are nations whose populations remained majority Indian well into the twentieth century. The mixing of Europeans and Indians over centuries has been creating an ever larger mestizo population. In this century, the mixing has been most dramatic and pronounced in Mexico, creating a nation that has consciously defined itself as a mestizo society.

In British North America, especially in the southern colonies, racial mixture also took place, but the "racial" system that developed looked very different from the first two examples. For complicated reasons that are still debated among historians and anthropologists, in British North America the racial mixture that occurred was largely denied or publicly suppressed. All agree that it took place, especially among blacks and whites, and recent DNA studies seem to indicate that anywhere from a quarter to a third of African Americans in the United States have "white" ancestors. The United States developed a system that became increasingly rigid in the nineteenth century, and recognized no middle ground of racial mixture, but only the categories "black" and "white." With the rise of Jim Crow and racial segregation in the late nineteenth century, the last official vestiges of the recognition of intermixing disappeared. After 1910, the census category of mulatto was removed, further solidifying the official recognition of a bipolar, black or white, racial system. The "one drop rule" prevailed. Any person with any black ancestry was considered black. Major figures in American history such as Frederick Douglass were considered "black," even though his father had been white. The Indian peoples in North America were annihilated or eventually relegated to isolated reservations, and the black population was primarily concentrated in the southern colonies. With the exception of colonial South Carolina, none of the Thirteen Colonies ever had a black majority.

As we have seen, in Latin America, the system that emerged was one of a "color continuum" rather than the North American "racial bipolarity." Clearly, then, race is a social construct that has no genetic basis, since every culture defines what we call "race" in different ways. Contemporary notions of race arise out of nineteenth-century social science that attempted to define races scientifically. Scientists today, especially those working in genetics, almost universally reject the notion of biologically defined categories of race. They tell us, in effect, that there are no clear biological or genetic boundaries that separate the human species sufficiently to define racial groups. What we tend to call race, is, in fact, our own culture's reading of physical appearance, in particular, skin tones. And these readings are highly subjective and variable.

In much of Latin America, for example, racial mixture was acknowledged, and the categories were multiple and flexible. The "reading" of appearance varies widely, but, in many Latin American societies, race is generally on a continuum of colors, and one's place on the continuum depends on many factors in addition to skin color. As in all the societies in the Americas, race and social class interact to determine one's position in the social hierarchy. Here are a couple of vast overgeneralizations, ones that overwhelm the complexities of the many societies in the Americas. First, what gradually developed in the United States, especially after 1865, was a system where race always trumps class. Until the civil rights revolution of the 1960s, blacks were excluded from the privileges of the upper class in U.S. society, regardless of their economic success. Second, in Latin America, historically, class trumps race. In contrast to the situation in the pre-1960s United States, economic success in Latin America could translate into social ascent, and racial "bleaching." As an old saying goes in Brazil, "money whitens." One can quite literally change one's standing in society and others' perception of color through economic success.

For complex reasons, in the Thirteen Colonies the mixture was often denied, the categories were fewer, and, as time passed, they became less and less flexible. A number of factors in British North America probably influenced the creation of a more rigid, bipolar system that did not recognize intermediary racial groups. More women and families immigrated earlier, and despite their subordinate position, women had a greater voice in discouraging their men from offering recognition to their offspring by slave women. The demographic ratios in North America meant there were more white women to marry and mate with and this lessened the possibilities of interracial unions. Although British North America may have looked somewhat like the rest of the Americas in its racial profile in the eighteenth century, slavery became more rigid in the nineteenth century, and "black" became synonymous with "slave." (In 1860, less than 2 percent of blacks in the South were free.)

The British Caribbean is a good counterpoint to British North America, because it also developed a mix and set of perceptions more like those of Latin America. There is good evidence to show that the differing racial systems in the United States and Latin America are not simply a result of the differences between English and Iberian cultures. The British colonists who settled the West Indies came from the same backgrounds as those who settled the colonies on the North American mainland. Some, in fact, were the very same people. (Alexander Hamilton, for example, was born in St. Kitts.) The demography in the British Caribbean, however, was more like Brazil and less like the Thirteen Colonies, with very large percentages of blacks and small numbers of whites. The resulting racial profiles are more diverse and more on a continuum than bipolar. The mix of English settlers and large numbers of blacks could not evolve into the same kind of racial and social hierarchy as in New England, where the English colonists brought in very few blacks and drove off or killed the Indians.

These differing constructions came to have very powerful, and often devastating, consequences for people of color. To be dark-skinned in South Carolina versus northeastern Brazil meant very different things. Despite the discrimination and prejudice against nonwhites all across the Americas, they faced legal and social systems with greater flexibility in Latin America than in what would become the United States. Although all American societies were built on racist hierarchies, the dark-skinned peoples of Latin America and the Caribbean had greater flexibility and possibilities for advancement than their counterparts in British North America.

All of these American societies were built on systems of hierarchy and inequality. All developed a sort of racial and social pyramid. In those societies with large African and Indian populations, they formed the very large base. In Mesoamerica and the Andean world, Indians were the most downtrodden and discriminated against. As with peasants in Europe, the elites and those more privileged on the social scale depicted the Indians and Africans as beasts who were subhuman. As so often happens in history, those with power and privilege worked to rationalize and reinforce their "superiority" by promoting ideologies that demeaned and dehumanized those over whom they had power. Right to the present, the classification *indio* remains a term as powerful as "nigger" in American English. (Again, there is no generally accepted term for the native peoples of the Americas. In some places in Latin America they refer to themselves as *naturales* or *indígenas*.) At the top of the social pyramid were those who looked, acted, and sounded European. At the very top of the pyramid in Spanish America, for example, were those who truly were European, born in Spain (the so-called *peninsulares*), with wealth, education, excellent family background, and political connections. Yet, a poor Spaniard, with no education, no money, and no social connections could also sink far down the social pyramid (but he would still have an advantage over his darker-skinned, poor compatriots).

The large middle ground was occupied by the racially and culturally mixed: mestizos, mulattoes, and zambos. These groups would eventually come to define most of Latin America by the nineteenth and twentieth centuries. In much of Latin America today, Mexico and Brazil being the prime examples, the vast majority of the population come from racially mixed backgrounds. All the Europeans came from societies with very strong senses of racial hierarchy and superiority. Fifteenth-century Spain, in fact, is a classic case that demonstrates that having peoples of many different cultural and ethnic backgrounds living side by side *does not* necessarily lead to tolerance. Spain and Portugal were profoundly racist societies. Witness the expulsion of the Moors and the Jews in the late fifteenth century. They were, however, societies with very nuanced and complex racial hierarchies.

CREATING LATIN AMERICAN SOCIETIES AND CULTURES

In the aftermath of conquest came the more long-term process of colonization and the construction of new societies and cultures in the Americas. The clash of cultures during the Conquest gave way to the convergence of, and struggles among, peoples over the succeeding centuries. In the core regions of Spanish America, the military conquest was complete and the basic institutions of colonial society in place by the 1570s. Portuguese Brazil reached this stage around 1600. The English, French, and Dutch did not have their colonies in place until well into the 1600s. In comparative terms, then, the core regions of Latin America developed for more than a century before English, French, and Dutch America began to take shape. The roots of Latin American societies and cultures are deeper and more distant than those of the United States.

As we have already seen, the large landed estates became the main economic sustenance of the Iberian colonies, and the vast majority of the population lived in the countryside. Along with the great estates, the conquistadores built cities and towns. Despite the importance of the countryside, power was concentrated in the urban centers of Latin America. The cities, in many ways, were European islands amidst a sea of Indians and Africans. From these urban centers, European culture and power radiated outward. The great wealth from the land eventually flowed inward into the cities, and much of it, across the Atlantic to Europe. The goods that came in from Europe flowed through the ports, into the major cities, and then outward into the hinterlands of the core regions. Town and country were inextricably linked together through an ebb and flow of goods, services, and peoples.

Until the nineteenth century, the cities of Latin America far outstripped those of North America. In Spanish and Portuguese America, most of the "European" population lived in urban centers, and the countryside was overwhelmingly Indian or African. The conquistadores sometimes built their principal cities on the ruins of ancient indigenous cities. Mexico City, built on the razed Aztec city of Tenochtitlan, was the second largest city in the Americas until the mid-eighteenth century. On the ruins of Tenochtitlan, the Spanish built a classic grid plan as prescribed by the Crown and later codified in the Laws of the Indies by Philip II. Around the central plaza were the cathedral and the main government buildings, and, as with all the principal Latin American cities, the residences of the wealthiest and most powerful families were located on the streets around and near the plaza. By 1620, Mexico City had a population of about 100,000. We have a detailed description of the city in the early seventeenth century from the Englishman Thomas Gage, a Dominican priest. It gives us a very nice picture of the wealth and splendor of the greatest city of the Americas at the time.

> The streets of Christendom [i.e. Europe] must not compare with those in breadth and cleanliness, but especially in the riches of the shops which do adorn them. . . . There are not above fifty churches and chapels, cloisters and nunneries, and parish churches in that city; but those that are there are the fairest that ever my eyes beheld, the roofs and beams being in many of them all daubed with gold, and many altars with sundry marble pillars, and others with brazil-wood stays standing one above another with tabernacles for several saints richly wrought with golden colours, so that twenty thousand ducats is a common price of many of them.

Lima and Havana, unlike Mexico City, were completely Spanish cities created fresh out of the Conquest. In the early seventeenth century, Lima had some 10,000 property-owning residents, which probably meant a population of around 50,000. Havana was much smaller, but by the mid-eighteenth century was the second largest city in Spanish America with some 80,000 inhabitants. By 1580, there were more than 200 Spanish American towns and cities, and more than 300 by 1630. Nearly every major urban center of Latin America had been founded by 1600. Jamestown and Plymouth were still 10 and 20 years in the future. In Brazil, Salvador was the largest city, with smaller urban centers at Olinda and Recife. Salvador probably had a population of about 20,000 in the mid-seventeenth century and would be the largest city in Brazil until the middle of the nineteenth century. The twin northeastern cities of Olinda and Recife probably had half the population of Salvador. Rio de Janeiro was just a sleepy little port that would not begin to grow until the discovery of gold in the interior in the 1690s.

In the mid-seventeenth century, the largest urban center in the Americas was the Peruvian mining city of Potosí. The mountain of Potosí is located in a cold and inhospitable region of modern Bolivia. It rises some 2,000 feet above the plain below, which is itself at an altitude of 13,000 feet above sea level. In the mid-sixteenth century, when the Spanish discovered that this mountain contained vast silver deposits, it became a magnet for people and economic activity. Potosí mushroomed into the richest mining center in the world. A census in the late sixteenth century registered 120,000 inhabitants, making Potosí comparable to the largest European cities (Paris, London,

Seville). In 1650, the population was some 160,000 and consisted of some 40,000–50,000 Spaniards (creoles and *peninsulares*), about 10,000 blacks and mulattoes, and the rest Indians or mestizos. With the exhaustion of the silver deposits at the end of the eighteenth century, Potosí would wither to some 8,000 inhabitants in the early nineteenth century!

The English cities in North America were much smaller than those of Latin America, and later in developing. By the late seventeenth century, New York City, Boston, and Philadelphia had emerged as the leading port cities, with Charleston a distant fourth. Philadelphia and New York City did not pass a population of 100,000 until the second decade of the nineteenth century. Boston and Baltimore were about one-third the size of Philadelphia and New York City. Charleston, the largest city in the southern colonies in the late seventeenth century, had a population of less than 10,000. Less than 5 percent of the population of the British North American mainland lived in cities at the end of the seventeenth century, a bit lower than the percentage who did so in Latin America. But, again, we should keep in mind that what would become the United States in the late eighteenth century was a small and very underdeveloped set of colonies in the seventeenth century. The most sophisticated, cosmopolitan, urban—and urbane—centers in the Americas in 1650 were all in Latin America.

Mexico City was the center of urban America in the seventeenth century. As Gage's description conveys, it awed even the European traveler who knew London, Paris, and Rome. Mexico City had its own viceregal court, theater, music, and institutions of high culture. In 1650, Harvard College (the oldest university in the United States) was in its infancy. Santo Domingo, Mexico City, and Lima all have universities whose origins date back at least to the 1550s. (Each currently claims to have the oldest university in the Americas.) Brazil, with its late start, compared to Spanish America, did not develop these institutions until the beginning of the nineteenth century. While the Portuguese colony was well in place decades before the English in North America, it was still decades behind in comparison with Mexico and Peru.

In Mexico City and Lima in the mid-seventeenth century, high culture was still largely derivative of Spain. (Given its later development, elite culture in Brazil was even less developed and more derivative of Iberian culture than was the case in Spanish America.) The poets, musicians, artists, and writers of the viceregal courts mostly produced works imitating the great literary and artistic achievements of the Spanish Golden Age (roughly 1550–1650). The great poetry, plays, and novels, from Cervantes' great Western classic *Don Quixote* (1609) to the plays of Calderón de la Barca (d. 1681) quickly crossed the Atlantic and dominated the artistic and literary high culture of *españoles americanos*. Yet, by the late seventeenth century there was already emerging a creole culture that would develop in the eighteenth century into an increasingly powerful sense of creole identity. In a sense, creole culture begins to come of age in the mid-seventeenth century in Spanish America as "American Spaniards" begin to fashion their own identity and distinctive variations of Iberian culture in the New World. This creole identity emerged during the so-called Baroque period in the seventeenth century. A reaction to the clarity, logic, and linearity of the Classical style of the Renaissance, the Baroque era was dominated by allusion, allegory, the ornate, and the technically intricate. Baroque architecture in the great Spanish American cathedrals of the seventeenth century sports facades filled with highly elaborate and complex artwork. In Baroque literature, intricacy and complexity prevail, the ornate metaphor triumphs over straightforward prose.

The finest example of this creole high culture in the seventeenth century is the writer Sor Juana Inés de la Cruz, the greatest literary figure of the Americas in the colonial era. Born Juana de Asbaje on the outskirts of Mexico City in 1651, she was the illegitimate daughter of a landowner with connections to the viceregal court. Still short of her third birthday, she accompanied an older sister to school, quickly learning to read, not only in Spanish, but also in Latin. In a famous autobiographical letter, she described her burning desire to learn: "I began to study Latin . . . And my interest was so intense, that although in women (especially in the very bloom of youth) the natural adornment of the hair is so esteemed, I would cut off four or six finger lengths of my hair, measuring how long it had been before. And I made myself a rule that if by the time it had grown back to the same length I did not know such and such a thing that I intended to study, then I would cut my hair off again to punish my dull-wittedness . . . for I did not think it reasonable that hair should cover a head so bare of facts—the more desirable adornment."

Juana became a protégée of the viceroy's wife and a star of the court with her great beauty and prodigious learning. With her genius, wit, and beauty, she must have been an intimating figure for any male contemporary. She was clearly too strong and assertive a woman for the men of her time. She became a nun (thus she is known as Sister or Sor Juana) because she was not interested in either of the other two principal options open to a woman of her station at the time: to marry or become a lady of the court. The poetry of Sor Juana is some of the greatest literature produced in Spanish and outshines any other writing produced in Latin America in the colonial era. Although she was clearly not a feminist by modern standards (she did not believe in the modern notion of equal rights for women, but accepted a hierarchical universe), she spoke out for the right of women to receive an education and follow intellectual pursuits. Some of her greatest poetry laments the unwillingness of men to take women's minds seriously, and bitterly criticizes men's treatment of women. Her most famous poem begins, "You foolish and unreasoning men/who cast all blame on women,/not seeing you yourselves are cause/of the same faults you accuse . . ." Sor Juana was eventually silenced by the Church for her outspokenness. She sold or gave away her library (reputed to be one the greatest in the Americas) and her scientific instruments and lived her last years in seclusion in her order's convent. She died of the plague in Mexico City in 1695 at the age of 44.

Sor Juana's life provides us with a glimpse not only of creole culture, but also into a Catholic ethos built on ideals of organic social unity, hierarchy, male domination, patriarchy, family, and procreation. These ideals had been preached and promoted by both church and State for centuries in Spain and Portugal before the conquerors and colonists brought them across the Atlantic. In this Iberian Catholic vision, a male God commanded the universe, kings reigned over their subjects, fathers ruled over their families, and women served their men as faithful wives and mothers. As in many societies, the family formed the basic social unit, the foundation of a patriarchal social order where men were all powerful and their women and children were legally dependent. Although women did have important legal rights and protections, the legal system was entirely staffed and administered by men. Widows seem to have had the greatest opportunities for exercising some freedom in decision making, especially elite women who took up the financial and business affairs of their families after the death of their husbands. Ideally, the family included not only husband, wife, and children, but also relatives on both the mother's and father's sides, as well as across several generations. While this extended family may have been the exception rather than the rule, it was very clearly the ideal of the affluent and the powerful. The ability to construct a clan across generations and through intermarriage with other families has long been a mark of power in Latin American society. Small or fragmented families were a sure sign of lack of resources (political or economic), and large extended families a visible demonstration of power.

The Iberian practice of long, multiple surnames reflects this exceptional concern about family ties. One's identity depends on who one's relatives are and to whom one is connected, and those who cannot demonstrate family lineage surely are unimportant. Like the serfs of the Middle Ages, slaves and the rural poor had no need for surnames, for they had no familial power to display. Those who aspired to be like the elite attempted to emulate their families and their concern for kinship. Only in the last century have all Latin Americans been given the dignity of full names. Iberians and Ibero-Americans of all classes (especially the middle and upper classes) have long placed great emphasis on names as a way of placing an individual (and his or her importance) through kinship networks. Unlike North Americans, who normally retain only the surname of the father,

Latin Americans have at least two surnames to indicate the family of both father and mother. In this male-dominated society, the father's surname normally assumes the greatest importance and persistence. Despite the concern for tracing family through both the father's and mother's lineages, the bias is clearly patrilineal. (In Spanish America, the general practice for children is for the surname of the father to come first, followed by the surname of the mother. In Brazil, the reverse is true.)

Ritual kinship reinforces and builds on the biological kinship that binds the family network together. In this Roman Catholic society, godparenting (*compadrio* in Portuguese, *compadrazgo* in Spanish) has long been an essential social institution. Parents try to choose allies and protectors as godparents for their children when the children are baptized. Among the elite, the choice of godparents serves to reinforce powerful social and family networks. Those of lower social standing (Indians and slaves) often attempt to persuade the more powerful to serve as godparents. Generally, however, parents turn to those of their own social world to serve as godparents. Family networks often expand (particularly among the affluent) through the custom of treating associates and dependents as kin. Powerful landowners sometimes informally adopted the families of servants and attendants. (This custom is still practiced today in rural areas.) At times, ties were established through ritual kinship, as servants and subordinates turned to the patron as a godparent. More often, the powerful patriarchs simply assumed a paternalistic responsibility for their distant relatives, servants, and associates (known in Portuguese as *agregados*, "the attached ones").

As in the extended family, sexual attitudes and behavior developed within this Catholic, corporatist ethos. The Euro-American colonists inherited the patriarchal values and attitudes of the European colonizers. In the devoutly Catholic culture of Iberia and Ibero-America, male domination and female submission were fundamental features of the social and cultural order. Females rarely had access to education, political power, or economic opportunity. As in other European societies, a "respectable" woman could become a wife and a mother, but little else. In addition to her duties as a mother and wife, a woman had to maintain a very low profile in Iberian society. While in most of Europe she was to be seen and not heard in public, in Portugal and Spain she was rarely seen. (Sor Juana's high visibility becomes even more striking in this context.)

The view that men should dominate and rule, and that women should submit and accept, is known as *machismo* in Spanish and Portuguese. This overweening male pride is characterized by an emphasis on the aggressivity of the male and the passivity of the female. In its classic form, machismo stresses diametrically opposed male/female roles. Men are tough, aggressive, and worldly, and destined to rule family, community, and nation. Women are weak, passive, and ignorant, and born to bear and raise children, and to care for the family and the home. This rigid division in roles leads men to pride themselves on virility, as demonstrated by sexual conquests, numerous offspring, and heterosexuality. Men shun any displays of femininity, and the worst possible insult is to question a man's heterosexuality.

Men not only had the dominant role, but they also were not held up to as high a moral standard as women. Premarital sex and adultery (particularly in the higher social classes) could destroy a woman's honor, raise the specter of violent retribution by husbands and brothers, and end all chances for a "normal" social existence. It was expected that men would stray from celibacy and marital fidelity—generally with few negative consequences. Women were expected to emulate the Virgin Mary and maintain a cult of virginity. Men followed their hormones and a cult of virility. Although these were the norms, research over the last three decades has shown that males and females of all social classes and races repeatedly strayed from the ideal.

The enormous demographic imbalance between the sexes, along with the domination of slaves and Indians, intensified this double standard in Latin America. Few white women immigrated to the Iberian colonies during the first century of conquest and colonization, and the domination of Indians and African slaves presented white males with ample opportunity to find sexual satisfaction among Indian and African women. By the eighteenth century, the large racially mixed populations of Brazil, Mexico, and Peru offered living testimony to the extent of sexual relations between white males and African and Indian females.

The masters generally did not encourage the formation of stable family relations among slaves and Indians. Business and profits took precedence over conjugal ties. In the slave quarters and among the free poor, marriage in the Church was a rarity. In indigenous communities the faithful very often could not afford the fees required to marry within the Church. Among the masses, consensual unions became more common than legal marriage. Much more so than in North America, sex outside of formal matrimony became commonplace, out of necessity for the masses and out of convenience for elite males. Among the poor, illegitimate births became commonplace and held little social stigma. Probably the majority of those born in Latin America during the colonial period were born out of formal Christian wedlock. This produced a pattern that has been common in many preindustrial societies across the globe of large families through what we would call today cohabitation and common law marriage.

These large families formed the primary social safety net, or one could turn to the charity of the Church. More children meant more workers and, one would hope, assistance in the parents' old age. The government did not provide social services as we see them today, but rather the Catholic Church built orphanages, homes for unwed mothers, hospitals, and the like. The Holy House of Mercy (*Santa Casa da Misercórdia*) built hospitals, for example, throughout the Portuguese empire from Macao to Brazil. Among the elite, the sexual dalliances of males produced illegitimate children, who were incorporated into the family as secondary members. Although not full-fledged family members, these "natural" children (as they are called in Spanish and Portuguese) were recognized and brought into the already extensive family network. The multilineal Iberian family became multileveled.

Although the cities of colonial Latin America were vital and vibrant centers, the social life and labor of most "Americans" took place in the countryside. The vast majority of all Americans lived and worked in rural areas and in small villages and towns. Throughout the colonial period in Latin America and the Caribbean, the vast majority of the population was composed of Indians and Africans. The high culture of Sor Juana and the small Iberian and Ibero-American elites may have revolved around the great centers of Mexico City, Lima, Havana, and Salvador, but the population in these orbits was a tiny fragment of the peoples of Latin America. At the close of the colonial era in the early nineteenth century, probably only one-fifth of all the inhabitants of Latin America were immigrants from the Iberian peninsula or their "European" descendants. In Brazil and the Caribbean islands, the majority of the population was of African descent, while in Mesoamerica and the Andean region (the old Inca Empire) the vast majority of the population was still Indians. After the process of conquest and consolidation, the largest and fastest growing groups were the racially mixed—mestizos and mulattoes.

In comparison, in the southern colonies of British North America, some 30 to 40 percent of the population consisted of slaves, while in the northern colonies the figure was below 10 percent. A racial divide was already taking shape that would eventually help bring the United States to war in the 1860s. New England and the Middle Atlantic colonies were largely white, and engaged in small farming, commerce, and shipping. The southern colonies were increasingly focused on plantation agriculture, slavery, and had large slave populations (although never as large a percentage as Brazil or some of the British Caribbean). Life was hard, with very high mortality and birthrates, and low life expectancy. In the Chesapeake Bay region of British North America in the mid-seventeenth century, life expectancy for colonists was in the 40s. This was slightly lower than back in England. Life expectancy for the nonwhite masses in all regions of the Americas was much lower.

Most people worked in agriculture, but occupations were extraordinarily diverse. In the Caribbean and Brazil the majority of the population was enslaved and the rural workers were overwhelmingly slaves. In Mexico and the Andes the same statement could be made, substituting "Indians" for "slaves." Northern British North America was the great exception and this would have powerful long-term consequences. Both the free and the enslaved worked in every conceivable kind of occupation, urban and rural. Throughout the centuries of colonial rule, the free people of the lower classes gradually assumed greater degrees of flexibility in their work arrangements, as the early stranglehold of the *encomienda* and *repartimiento* receded and the use of contracted wage labor expanded. Freedom of mobility varied enormously across region, class, and race, with slaves and indebted workers at one end of the scale and highly mobile merchants and mine workers at the other end. Diversity of experience characterized the working lives of Latin Americans by the end of the seventeenth century.

For the majority of the population, leisure was constrained by the long hours and hard work of the agricultural cycle. Nonetheless, common people always found ways to celebrate and ease the burdens of tough working conditions. In Latin America, the most notable examples were the collective festivals and rituals of the Catholic Church, especially those that by the seventeenth century blended European and American cultural traditions, such as the Day of the Dead and celebrations of patron saints. A Catholic calendar full of feast days and religious holidays marked the passage of time. Religious brotherhoods, organized around patron saints, formed one of the most powerful and influential vehicles for social solidarity and collective celebrations in communities all across Latin America. These festivities provided rare opportunities for the majority of Latin Americans to gain a respite from their grueling daily work, to seek the collective comfort of their families and friends, and (however briefly) to forget about the enormous power the elite exerted over their lives.

At the close of the seventeenth century, Latin America had become an ever larger and more visible reality. From its creation in the islands of the Caribbean in the 1490s, it had expanded across the core regions of Mesoamerica, the Andes, and the Brazilian coast. By 1700, the devastated population of indigenous peoples had begun to recover from its disastrous decimation from disease and conquest. In New Spain in the mid-seventeenth century (out of a population of around three million), Indians probably accounted for 85 percent of the population with the racially mixed (*castas*) making up about 5 percent, and "Spaniards" the rest. Probably no more than a few thousand of these were *peninsulares*. The vast majority of whites lived in the major cities. The population of Peru probably did not begin to increase until the 1730s and most likely did not pass one million until the second half of the eighteenth century. Brazil had perhaps 1.5 million inhabitants in the early seventeenth century—the majority were slaves, many African-born. As in Spanish America, whites probably made up less than 10 percent of the population. After two centuries of conquest and colonization, the basic social patterns of Latin America were in place. A small white elite (the *gente decente* in Spanish, the *homens bons* in Portuguese) stood atop the social pyramid, dominating a huge population of Indians, African slaves, and the racially mixed. A small but significant portion of the population composed primarily of lower-status whites and the most Europeanized nonwhites formed the middle of the pyramid. These small, but growing, white and racially mixed populations formed the core of the continually emerging new society. The forces of Europeanization constantly increased, drawing more and more Indians and Africans into a racially and culturally mixed society and culture that formed the very essence of Latin America, one that drew on Iberian, Indian, and African cultures and traditions. By the early eighteenth century, Latin America had emerged as a diverse and mature society unlike any other in the world.

11

Reforms and Revolutions

Powerful and far-reaching forces profoundly transformed and reshaped the Atlantic world in the eighteenth century. Just as overseas expansion, the Reformation, and the Scientific Revolution had made the sixteenth century a period of sweeping changes, the Enlightenment, the Industrial Revolution, and the political revolutions (American and French) of the eighteenth century marked a watershed in the history of the West, the Atlantic world, and, indeed, the history of all peoples on the planet. By the early eighteenth century, Latin America had clearly emerged as a large and complex region with well-developed political institutions, social structures, and economic activities. The Iberian colonies in the Americas had reached a high level of maturity and consolidation after more than two centuries of conquest, colonization, and internal struggles. In the mid-eighteenth century, new rulers in Spain and Portugal set out to revamp and reform their empires and they triggered a century of remarkable changes, most notably the wars for independence and the collapse of the American empires they had set out to revitalize.

For some historians, the changes in the mid-eighteenth century were so important that they would divide the history of Latin America into three acts: pre–1750, 1750–1850, and post–1850. They see the century from 1750–1850 as a great, drawn-out watershed dividing the colonial era and modern (or postcolonial) Latin American history. The more traditional interpretation has long seen the history of the region in two acts: colonial rule and then the so-called "national" or "modern" period after the wars for independence in the 1810s and 1820s. For these historians, the transformations of the second half of the eighteenth century form the last gasp of the colonial systems and the prelude to independence and nationhood.

For those who argue for a "middle period," the transformations of the mid-eighteenth century do not completely unfold until the wars for independence are complete, the first steps of nation-building have been taken, and Latin America has fully entered into the Western economic system in the mid-nineteenth century. Both approaches, however, recognize the fundamental importance of the powerful new forces emerging in the Atlantic world in the eighteenth century and the changes that begin to move Latin America from European colonies to independent nations pursuing their own destinies.

In the eighteenth century, the monarchies of Spain and Portugal set out to reorganize their empires in direct response to the rising challenges from other European powers—the Dutch, English, and French. The rulers of Spain and Portugal were acutely aware that they had lost ground throughout the seventeenth century to these newer powers and that they had to act decisively to respond to their declining power on both sides of the Atlantic (and in the Far East as well). As we have seen, the Atlantic world became a battlefield for contending European powers in the seventeenth century as the Dutch, English, and French ended the Iberian colonial monopoly in the Americas. They repeatedly defeated the Spanish and Portuguese on the high seas, and made ever more difficult the maritime connections between Iberia and the New World and among Iberian possessions in Africa, the Indian Ocean, and the Pacific. One of the most important consequences of the rise of these maritime challenges was a relaxation of the imperial grip on the American colonies. Many historians have described the seventeenth century in Latin America as something of a turn inward, or involution, as the colonies developed their own economies, and as creoles increasingly occupied more and more administrative positions, especially in the *audiencias* of Spanish America. By 1700, Spanish Americans (even more so than Portuguese Americans) had become accustomed to a growing sense of autonomy as a result of the looser imperial rule. The emergence of a sense of creole identity accompanied this process of maturation, an increasing sense of autonomy, and a relaxation of Iberian control. The reassertion of imperial authority in the eighteenth century would come as a rude shock to the creole elites, and would be a driving force in the emergence of independence movements at the beginning of the nineteenth century in Spanish America.

A new royal family in Spain (the Bourbons) and an extraordinary nobleman in Portugal (the Marquis of Pombal) reorganized the stagnating Iberian empires with a vengeance. In the sixteenth century, the great Hapsburg kings, Charles I (V) and his son Philip II, had made Spain the greatest power on earth. Their descendants—Philip III, Philip IV, and Charles II—presided over Spain's decline throughout the seventeenth century. When Philip IV died in 1665, he was succeeded by his four-year-old son, Charles II, described by one historian as a "rachitic and feeble-minded weakling, the last stunted sprig of a degenerate line. . . . This last pallid relic of a fading dynasty was left to preside over the inert corpse of a shattered Monarchy, itself no more than a pallid relic of the great imperial past." When Charles II (also known as the "Bewitched") died in 1700, he left no heir to the throne and this set off an international struggle known as the War of Spanish Succession (1701–1714). This war pitted the English, Dutch, and Austrians (the other branch of the Hapsburgs) against France and Castile. At stake was control of the American colonies and their wealth (especially silver) and the balance of power in Europe. Before his death, Charles II had chosen Philip of Anjou, the grandson of Louis XIV of France (1638–1715), as his successor.

Several of the old Spanish kingdoms rose up in revolt against Philip and allied with foreign invaders. Civil war wracked the peninsula, and invading English and French armies occupied the major cities of Spain. After fighting across Europe (and several other continents and oceans) was inconclusive, the war ground to a stalemate. In the end, a series of treaties allowed Philip to keep the Spanish throne (becoming Philip V) and he initiated the Spanish branch of the Bourbons (still the royal family of Spain), but he had to give up any claim to the throne of France to keep the French Bourbons from effectively absorbing Spain and its empire.

The price for the Spanish throne was high. Spain gave up Minorca and Gibraltar to England. Austria took control of the Netherlands, Naples, Milan, and Sardinia. Sicily went to the House of Savoy. Perhaps even more damaging in the long run, the peace treaties gave Britain exclusive rights—for 30 years—to the *asiento de negros*, a monopoly on the right to sell African slaves to the Spanish colonies. The English also gained the right to send an annual shipload of goods to Portobelo, Panama. Both the *asiento* and Portobelo ships would increase the opportunities for the English to engage in smuggling. These concessions provided the British with a lucrative gateway into the commercial system in Spanish America and more direct access to American silver. The Peace of Utrecht (1712–13) marked the end of Spain's reign as a major European power, and the Bourbon Reforms that followed the war would mark a brief plateau before the beginning of a long economic and political decline that would not end until the late twentieth century.

THE BOURBON AND POMBALINE REFORMS

Three principles drove both the Bourbon Reforms in the Spanish Empire and the Pombaline Reforms in the Portuguese Empire: rationalize, centralize, nationalize. In an age when the British monarchy would see its domestic political power gradually erode as the power of the parliament grew, the Iberian monarchies moved in the opposite direction, striving to become truly absolutist regimes ruled by "enlightened" monarchs. Following the lead of Louis XIV in seventeenth-century France, the Spanish Bourbons set out to reorganize their imperial systems to make them more rational and efficient. By doing this, they hoped to direct all power back to the crown through a steady process of centralizing authority. They also understood that the source of their power would ultimately hinge on their ability to generate greater and greater resources, especially through taxation on agriculture, mining, and commerce. Much of the thrust of the mid-eighteenth-century economic reforms was aimed at reasserting Iberian control over the enormous transatlantic trading networks that the French and British had so deeply penetrated and challenged over the previous century. In a sort of early form of economic nationalism, the Iberian rulers attempted both to open up the economic and trading system within the empires, while simultaneously seeking to close the empires to outsiders.

Although the Bourbon Reforms began in bits and pieces under Philip V (1701–46) and Fernando VI (1746–59), they are most closely associated with the reign of Charles III (1759–88). In Portugal, the driving force behind reform was Sebastião José de Carvalho e Mello, better know as the Marquis of Pombal (in power 1750–77). Something like an early version of a super-prime minister, Pombal became a virtual dictator, serving José I, a monarch seemingly more interested in the good life of the court than the burdensome details of imperial administration. Years of service in the diplomatic corps on the continent and in England provided Pombal with a much broader perspective on power politics and imperial rivalries than most of his contemporaries in the Portuguese nobility. Pombal and Charles III were contemporaries, and it was under their guidance that both Iberian empires made concerted efforts in the 1750s, 1760s, and 1770s to reverse the long decline in Spanish and Portuguese power and to counter the ever-growing global might of the English and the French. Given the very long and tight diplomatic and commercial relations between the English and the Portuguese (dating back to the fourteenth century), and the close relationship between the monarchies of Spain and France, the Anglo-French threats presented both of the Iberian monarchies with enormous challenges.

While the French and English presented the most powerful external challenges to the Bourbons and Pombal, the nobility and the Church posed the most formidable internal obstacles to reform. As had Louis XIV, these "enlightened despots" moved to create a new nobility that would owe its success and loyalty to the Crown; the Iberian monarchies would also move to weaken the power of the traditional nobility. After a purported assassination attempt on the king in 1758, Pombal arrested and severely punished some of the most powerful nobles in Portugal. The fate of the Távora family became a lesson for all who might challenge royal authority. In what one historian has called "a carefully orchestrated display of unbridled power," royal executioners brutally and systematically broke the bones of the Marquis of Távora on the torture wheel, then killed each of his children as his wife watched—before her own execution. Pombal imprisoned hundreds, exiled others to the colonies, and confined the king's illegitimate siblings to a monastery. Both Pombal and the Bourbons sought to check the influence of the traditional nobility by appointing members of the lesser nobility and the middle class to positions of influence and power. The reformers brutally suppressed the rambunctious traditional nobles who opposed them and systematically rewarded and elevated new nobles who supported them.

The Bourbons and Pombal also moved forcefully to curb the power of the Church, especially the religious orders, and most particularly, the Jesuits. The process was more dramatic and emphatic in Portugal than in Spain. Asserting even greater royal control over a Catholic Church that had long been an arm of the state, Pombal took over the Inquisition (and repeatedly used it against his political opponents) and he singled out the Jesuits for special treatment. By the mid-eighteenth century, the Society of Jesus had become a very wealthy and politically influential religious order. Their influence within the Catholic Church was so pronounced that the head of the Jesuits had become known as the "Black Pope" (a reference to their black clerical robes). In 1759, Pombal expelled the Jesuits from the Portuguese empire and Charles III followed suit, banishing the Jesuits from the Spanish empire in 1767. Much like the Reformation of Henry VIII in sixteenth-century England, the move deprived the empires of exceptionally talented individuals, but provided the Iberian monarchs with vast resources (farms, vineyards, ranches, buildings, and other properties) they could dole out to their friends and allies.

The efforts to revamp the administration of Spanish America began in the early eighteenth century, and continued for decades. After two centuries of colonization, population growth, and increasing economic activity, the old colonial administrative units no longer reflected the realities on the ground. In 1718–19, the Spanish Crown tried to create a new (third) viceroyalty in northern South America, largely in response to growing economic activity, especially gold production, in what today is Colombia, and growing English and Dutch challenges in the Caribbean. (The fortified port city of Cartagena is a legacy of this effort.) The attempt failed (in part because the first viceroy was a disaster) but the Crown then tried again in the 1730s, and the Viceroyalty of New Granada was created. (The new unit included what today are Venezuela, Colombia, and Ecuador.) In the 1770s, the crown carved out a fourth viceroyalty in southern South America, the Viceroyalty of La Plata, taking in what today are Argentina, Uruguay, Paraguay, and Bolivia (Upper Peru in the colonial era). As in the case of New Granada, this move reflected the growth of commerce around the La Plata River basin (mainly around Buenos Aires), the need to counter English contraband in the region, and a recognition that a logical route for silver exports was down across the Argentine plains and across the Atlantic, rather than westward over the Andes, up the Pacific coast to Panama, and then through the Caribbean.

Pombal understood that Brazil had become by the mid-eighteenth century the most important Portuguese possession and the engine of the imperial economy. Although Portugal retained most of its trading posts around the globe, the English and Dutch had effectively wrested from them control of the trading networks in Asia and the Indian Ocean during the seventeenth century. With the rise of Brazilian sugar production in the seventeenth century and the gold and diamond boom of the first half of the eighteenth century, Brazil had become the center of revenue in the empire. It had become, in the words of one astute Jesuit observer, "the milk cow" of the empire. Just as the Bourbons focused on their American colonies as "those lands from which we seek to extract the juice," Brazil was at the economic center of the Pombaline Reforms.

Pombal reorganized Brazil, with the northern region (the Amazon and northern coast) reporting directly back to Lisbon. He created the state of Grão Pará and Maranhão in the north, and the rest of Brazil came under the control of a viceroy. In 1763, he shifted the colonial capital from Salvador (Captaincy of Bahia) to Rio de Janeiro. The shift reflected both geopolitical and economic realities similar to those in the creation of the new Spanish American viceroyalties. Rio de Janeiro was more centrally located, to contend with the rise of Spanish and English activity in the La Plata region, and the flow of gold from the interior had made Rio de Janeiro the most important commercial center in Brazil. From a tiny, backward settlement in the seventeenth century, Rio had become the gateway for Portuguese colonists, African slaves, and supplies to the gold and diamond fields in Minas Gerais, and the main legal exit for gold production.

The Spanish and Portuguese reformers redrew not only administrative boundaries, but also lines of bureaucratic power within the imperial systems. While they centralized the lines of power back to Madrid and Lisbon, they decentralized the colonial administrative units. The Council of the Indies in Spain and the Overseas Council in Portugal lost their long hold on imperial administration. In Spain, a Minister of the Indies took over from the Council and reported directly to the king. In addition to the creation of two new viceroyalties in Spanish America and the reorganization of Portuguese Brazil, the Bourbons elevated a number of regions to the status of *audiencias* and captaincies-general. Regions on the periphery of the American empire such as Buenos Aires, Caracas, Guatemala (meaning all of Central America), and Chile thrived as the viceregal centers saw their authority diminished. Copying the pattern in seventeenth-century France, the Spanish Bourbons sent out "intendants" in the second half of the eighteenth century as directly appointed royal authorities to rule over a number of regions and to report back directly to the king. Understandably, the viceroys fought this move bitterly. Royal inspectors began to make *visitas generales* (general visits or reviews), checking up on colonial officials. José de Gálvez, the most famous of these inspectors, served the king for two decades (1765–87) and exerted enormous influence in Madrid. Like many other peninsular Spaniards, he had great disdain for the creoles.

By the 1760s, creoles had become the majority (among whites) in a number of *audiencias*, including Mexico City, Lima, and Santiago de Chile. Throughout the previous century and a half, the percentage of creoles in the *audiencias* of Spanish American had risen steadily, especially as imperial control relaxed in the seventeenth century. Throughout the eighteenth century, the Bourbon kings systematically discriminated against the creoles when making imperial appointments. This pattern was pronounced, enduring, and widely noticed. It would become one of the principal grievances of the creole elites and a seed that would eventually blossom into open revolt against Spain.

Freer trade (i.e. with merchants other than those of Spain) eventually became the second great grievance of the creoles. Both Pombal and the Bourbons worked long and hard to revamp their colonial economic systems. They understood that the ability to generate greater and greater wealth within the empire would determine the political destiny of Spain and Portugal. Pombal, in particular, had watched from London the rise of England's manufacturing and commercial revolutions. In the age of Adam Smith, all "enlightened" rulers believed that the economic health of the nation depended on the ability to produce and trade more and more goods, and generate trade surpluses with one's commercial partners. This capitalist trading ideology drove the English and Dutch to the far reaches of the globe seeking more goods and new markets. The officially closed trading systems in Spanish and Portuguese America frustrated the Dutch and English and spurred them to seek access (legal or otherwise) to potentially enormous markets. Both Iberian monarchies undertook a series of economic reforms to generate more economic production, more trade, and great tax revenues. In retrospect, they attempted too little and too late to meet the English economic challenge.

Fortunately for both Spain and Portugal, silver and gold production rose dramatically in the eighteenth century, reviving the imperial economies and stimulating the expansion of the European economy, especially England's. (Brazilian gold moved quickly through Lisbon to London to pay for Portugal's trade deficit with England.) The long decline in silver production in seventeenth-century Spanish America ended by the early eighteenth century, as mining entrepreneurs employed new technology (blasting), and as they gained access to greater quantities of mercury (from Huancavelica in Peru and Almadén in Spain) to refine their ore. By the end of the seventeenth century, Mexican silver production finally caught up with Peru's and continued to rise until, in 1800, Mexican production outstripped Peru's by a ratio of 3:1. In the words of the historian Peter Bakewell, "Silver remained to the last, as always, the prime metallic product, and the main export, of the [Spanish] American empire."

By 1700, the Portuguese had begun to realize the extent of gold strikes in Minas Gerais in the interior to the north of Rio de Janeiro. Brazilian gold production steadily rose until around 1760 and then declined rapidly in the 1770s and 1780s. By 1790, the great Brazilian gold rush was over. (By one estimate, Brazil produced 80 percent of the gold in the Western world in the eighteenth century.) As if this were not luck enough for the Portuguese monarchy, prospectors discovered diamonds to the north of the gold fields and Brazil replaced India as the principal supplier of diamonds to Europe (until the discoveries in South Africa in the 1860s). By the time José I assumed the throne in 1750, Brazilian precious metals and gemstones had made Portugal one of the richest nations on earth.

The English presented the greatest economic threat to Spain and Portugal. By the end of the seventeenth century, the English had defeated the Dutch in a series of naval wars and had emerged as the greatest naval and maritime power in the history of the world. English traders crisscrossed the globe in search of goods and markets. The emergence of England as the world's first industrial nation in the second half of the eighteenth century consolidated its economic might and commercial power. Spanish American silver, Brazilian gold and diamonds, and millions of potential consumers made the Spanish and Portuguese colonies in the Americas an enticing target for the English. In the seventeenth century, the Dutch, French, and English raided and plundered Spanish possessions across the Caribbean as they planted their own colonies in the islands (Jamaica, Barbados, Saint Domingue, and Curaçao, for example) and on the mainland (British and French Guiana, Surinam, and Belize). In the eighteenth century, these colonies became the staging grounds for infiltrating the Ibero-American empires with contraband. The Caribbean, especially the coast of northern South America, and the La Plata River basin became lively centers for smuggling throughout the eighteenth century.

As the English pressed other nations for more and more open trade and access to markets throughout the eighteenth century, the Spanish and Portuguese monarchies moved to control the trade with the outside world, while freeing up trade within their closed systems. The movement of the Spanish fleets across the Atlantic had been sporadic, at best, in the seventeenth century. In the eighteenth century, the old fleet system sputtered to a slow and drawn-out death. When the last fleet of galleons sailed to New Spain in 1776, it was only the fifth to have crossed the Atlantic in nearly thirty years. In the words of the English maritime historian J. H. Parry, the old fleet system "had long outlived its usefulness; in war it had become inadequate, in peace unnecessary." Throughout the eighteenth century, the Spanish crown moved toward the use of officially licensed "register" ships to replace the massive and vulnerable galleons. The Portuguese had never developed a fleet system to Brazil and were perpetually short on merchant ships. Throughout the seventeenth and eighteenth centuries, more and more Dutch and English ships carried goods within the Portuguese Atlantic system.

Both Pombal and the Bourbons attempted (with some success) to increase trade within their Atlantic empires by allowing trade among the colonial ports and (in the case of Spain) with a number of Spanish port cities. The old heavily controlled Spanish system of fleets from Seville and Cádiz to the selected group of Spanish American ports gradually gave way in the late eighteenth century to a more open system allowing intercolonial trade and (by 1789) free trade between all Spanish and Spanish American ports. The so-called decree of free trade (1778), the closing of the old *Casa de Contratación* (Board of Trade) (1789) after nearly three hundred years of operation, and the end of the Seville/Cádiz merchant monopoly marked a gradual but profound change in imperial commercial policy. This more open system, along with the rise of silver production and the emergence of new centers of production (especially sugar in Cuba), did lead to the higher volume of trade the Bourbons had sought. (In the last decade of the eighteenth century, however, more than 85 percent of trade still moved through Cádiz.) A series of special deals with merchant companies to produce cacao, tobacco, cotton, and other products in both the Spanish and Portuguese colonies also helped stimulate new trade, although many of the ventures failed.

Despite these changes in the commercial trading systems of the two Ibero-American empires, the reforms failed in a profound sense. The volume of trade crossing the Atlantic and moving within the Americas escalated dramatically (perhaps by as much as 700 percent, according to some estimates). The efforts to exclude outsiders, especially the English, however, failed. By the end of the eighteenth century, English merchants remained the dominant presence in Lisbon. Although they could not sell directly to the Brazilians, in effect they became the main suppliers of the traders to Brazil, and Brazilian gold did not remain in Portugal. Instead, the gold bullion usually ended up in London to pay for British goods flowing into Portugal and the Portuguese empire. Brazilian gold helped make London the first *global* financial center and provided a powerful stimulus to the

Industrial Revolution. When José I died in 1777 and Pombal fell from power, Brazilian gold production was rapidly declining and the move to continue the commercial reforms largely ended. English merchants swarmed throughout the Spanish and Portuguese colonies by the end of the eighteenth century as the Iberian monarchies were unable to fight them off, or to supply their own American possessions adequately. The Bourbon and Pombaline reforms had managed to rationalize and centralize the power of the crowns, but they had failed to revitalize and nationalize failing colonial trading empires. The reforms were too little, and too late—the last desperate efforts of two long-declining empires to reclaim their former power and glory before they began a sustained slide into decay and chaos.

CREOLE DISCONTENT

The shifting tides of the Atlantic world in the eighteenth century set the stage for the wars for independence in Latin America in the early nineteenth century. England's accelerating Industrial Revolution at home, and the ships it sent out on the high seas, formed the epicenter of the economic transformation of this eighteenth-century world and its rippling effects across the globe. The Bourbon and Pombaline Reforms attempted and failed to counter the rising trading pressures on the Ibero-American empires. While English goods penetrated the empires, Enlightenment ideas (especially via France and the newly independent United States) circulated throughout Latin America, altering the intellectual and political landscapes. These waves of economic, intellectual, and political change reshaped Latin America gradually throughout the eighteenth century but, by themselves, were not enough to unleash fundamental challenges to Spanish and Portuguese control of their American colonies. Ironically, the spark that ignited the wars for independence came not in the Americas, but at the center of the empires. The convergence of these long-term intellectual and economic transformations in the Atlantic world, *along with* the Napoleonic invasions of Spain and Portugal in 1807–8, unleashed the political earthquakes that toppled Iberian rule throughout Latin America, leaving the Ibero-American empires in shambles by the 1820s.

Creole discontent lay at the heart of the wars for independence, and creole unhappiness had grown throughout the previous century. The strength and persistence of the Ibero-American empires are testimony to the ability of the Spanish and Portuguese monarchies to assuage the creoles for so long and through many crises. Portuguese and Spanish colonists, as a rule, rarely chose to challenge the system. On the contrary, Iberian immigrants sought success by rising through the hierarchical bureaucracy of the Spanish and Portuguese monarchies. Their religious and political preferences reinforced the power of king and church rather than challenging or questioning them. Although the so-called Thirteen Colonies shared many of the same problems as the Portuguese empire in Brazil and the Spanish American colonies, they had already begun to follow a distinct historical path by the late eighteenth century. Many of the English colonists had left Britain fleeing religious and political persecution. Even those who had not fled Britain for fear of persecution already shared the values of a political culture that, since the late Middle Ages, had increasingly placed checks on royal power and recognized individual rights.

In nearly all the American colonial societies, the efforts by the monarchies to impose taxation without significant political representation produced revolts among the colonists. In the Thirteen Colonies in the 1770s, the war for independence succeeded. In the Iberian colonies, the wars for independence did not come until the 1810s and 1820s. With little to exploit in either agriculture or raw materials, the British colonies in New England developed a substantial population of small farmers and merchants, as well as a vigorous shipping trade with Europe and the Caribbean. After dominating or driving back the relatively sparse native peoples of eastern North America, the southern British colonies looked very similar to the core regions of Latin America—plantation agriculture, a large unfree labor force, and a white landowning elite. The commercial dynamism of New England, and the lack of a plantation past, enabled it to become a vibrant economic center that emerged by the early nineteenth century as the engine of the new country's economy. The new states of the southern United States, and the Spanish and Portuguese colonies, however, would enter the nineteenth century burdened with the social and political inequities of slave plantation economies.

By the nineteenth century, well-entrenched and sophisticated colonial elites had emerged in many parts of Latin America, largely concentrated around the *audiencia* centers in Spanish America. In Brazil, the wealthy planters and merchants coalesced around the old sugar plantation centers in the northeast, and around the gold mining region in the southeast. They increasingly sought greater economic autonomy and political representation in Portugal and Spain. The Enlightenment, the American and French Revolutions, and the growing economic power of England's Industrial Revolution deeply impressed these American elites. Many of the sons of the privileged who sought a university education had crossed the Atlantic, and they experienced firsthand the seismic economic, intellectual, and political shifts that were reshaping Europe.

The lack of greater economic opportunities and the absence of a stronger role in the administrative and political system became the great grievances of the Spanish and Portuguese Americans by the beginning of the nineteenth century. Economic opportunity meant the ability to trade with greater freedom, primarily with the English. A greater political and administrative role did not mean representation in a parliament (as was the case in the Thirteen Colonies), but rather an end to the systematic discrimination against creoles in royal posts throughout the colonies. As in British North America, it was the unwillingness of the Crown to accept their American cousins as equals that eventually goaded Spanish and Portuguese Americans into breaking from the colonial system. In Spanish America, in particular, the creoles had emerged and matured in the seventeenth century, rising to many positions of prominence and power in the royal bureaucracy. Bourbon kings systematically discriminated against the creoles, favoring peninsular Spaniards throughout the royal administrative structures in Spanish America in the eighteenth century. The tension between creoles and *peninsulares* intensified throughout the eighteenth century and provided the most powerful impetus to war by the beginning of the nineteenth century.

REBELLIONS OF THE MASSES—AND SOME ELITES

Although not direct causes of the wars of independence, serious social and racial uprisings in the second half of the eighteenth century certainly helped set the stage for the wars for independence across Spanish and Portuguese America. The greatest fear of white Europeans, creole or peninsular, was social rebellions and race wars. Haiti, as we shall see in the next chapter, was their worst nightmare come to vivid life. A series of rebellions broke out in the eighteenth century from Venezuela and Colombia to Paraguay and Peru. The most spectacular and notorious of these rebellions exploded across Peru in 1780 and 1781. It was led by José Gabriel Condorcanqui, an educated Indian leader who claimed to be a direct descendant of the Inca royal family. He adopted the name Túpac Amaru (*Royal Serpent* in Quechua) and declared a war to the death on all Spaniards. The rebellion began near Cuzco in November 1780, eventually spreading as far as modern-day Bolivia. Creoles and *peninsulares* closed ranks and suppressed the rebellion after some 100,000 (mostly Indians) had died. Túpac Amaru was captured, tortured, and brutally executed in 1781 as a warning to others who might challenge royal authority. (He was forced to watch as his wife and children were killed. After cutting out his tongue, Spanish authorities then tied his arms and legs to horses and, quite literally, tore him apart.)

Although the Túpac Amaru Rebellion ultimately failed after massive bloodshed, it was the most infamous of a series of rebellions across late eighteenth-century Latin America. Like their Quechua-speaking neighbors in Peru, the Aymara speakers in Upper Peru (later Bolivia) also rose up in the 1770s and 1780s, also led by a charismatic indigenous leader—who took on the name Túpac Catari. In both rebellions, fear of a race war eventually alienated most of the creole support for the uprisings and they were both brutally suppressed. Royal officials executed Túpac Catari in January 1781, just months before the bloody demise of Túpac Amaru. At nearly the same time, a tax revolt broke out in towns in Colombia. The rebels managed to assemble an army of 20,000 and compelled terrified royal officials to make significant concessions. The Comunero Revolt was a classic move to invoke traditional rights from within the system—not to break with it.

In contrast to what we have seen in Spanish America, the division between peninsular Portuguese and those born in Brazil was neither very wide nor profound. In part, this was due to the cultural backwardness of Brazil. While the Spanish had created universities in Mexico City, Santo Domingo, and Lima in the sixteenth century, Brazil had no institutions of higher learning. The sons of the Brazilian elite invariably crossed the Atlantic to attend Coimbra University with the sons of Portugal's elite. The absence of cultural societies, museums, and learned academies also meant that the Brazilians became members of those institutions in Portugal. In short, the sense of Brazilian identity was not as strong or as locally rooted as that of creoles in Spanish America.

Not everyone in Brazil, however, was satisfied with the monarchy. Revolts did arise periodically, beginning as early as the 1780s. The influence of France, the United States, and republican ideals affected all social groups. In 1789, a group of powerful men in the rich gold mining province of Minas Gerais, plotted to kill the royal governor and create an independent republic. The leaders of the Minas Conspiracy (*Inconfidência Mineira*) had read, among other things, the Articles of Confederation and the constitutions of U.S. states (in French translation, of course). The plot was betrayed, its members imprisoned, tried, and then banished to Angola. One military officer—best known by his nickname, *Tiradentes* (Toothpuller)—was hung and then drawn and quartered, becoming the first great martyr for Brazilian independence.

In 1798, mulatto artisans in the northeastern province of Bahia also plotted to create an independent republic. Inspired by the Haitian slave revolt and the French Revolution, they called for the people to throw off the "detestable metropolitan yoke of Portugal." "The happy time," they declared, "of our liberty is about to arrive, the time when all will be brothers, the time when all will be equal." Another republican revolt of the lower classes erupted in 1817, again with strong condemnations of racial and social injustice in the kingdom. Royal authorities dealt severely with the abortive republican revolts. The rebellions helped to bind Brazilian planters even more tightly to the monarchy and to refrain from any serious questioning of the status quo. Brazilian elites needed royal protection and assistance to maintain social peace.

To the contrary, the Túpac Amaru Rebellion, the Comunero Revolt, and other rebellions persuaded the Spanish American creoles that the crown was less and less capable of protecting the social and racial order and that they would have to learn to defend themselves. Increasingly, they hoped to assert their voices within the system, appealing to the king, seeking greater autonomy and control over their political and economic affairs, and their own internal security. The *Inconfidência Mineira* of 1789, and other rebellions led by the masses, helped persuade both the Portuguese monarchy and the Brazilian elites of the need to seek closer ties and greater cooperation. The path of Portuguese America, then, differed from that of Spanish America (and even more so from that of the French Caribbean). While the Portuguese and Brazilian elites sought ways to maintain social peace through collaboration, the Spanish and Spanish American elites increasingly diverged in their views, creating ever greater transatlantic animosity among themselves.

The Bourbon Reforms failed to save an aging empire. The reassertion of imperial control, as in British North America, angered and alienated many of the creoles. The continuing inability of creoles to trade freely with the English also produced great dissatisfaction. The growing military might of the British and the revolts by the masses like that of Túpac Amaru highlighted the growing weaknesses of Spanish royal authority. These efforts to modernize Spain and Spanish America, however, did not lead the creoles to break with Spain. Most Spanish American subjects continued to work toward reforming the system rather than breaking from it. Few openly advocated a break—until events in Europe abruptly forced the issue.

12

The Onset of the Wars
for Independence

By 1800, the Spanish and Portuguese empires in the Americas had been in place for three centuries—and were straining to survive. Latecomers to empire-building in the Americas, the French and English had carved out their own colonies largely in the seventeenth and eighteenth centuries. The English "creoles" on the coast of the North American mainland, dissatisfied and disillusioned with British rule, had successfully rebelled in the 1770s, and the United States became the first American colony to achieve independence. African and African-American slaves on the Caribbean island of Saint-Domingue would rise up in the 1790s and seize their independence from the French. In 1804, Haiti became the second independent nation in the New World. The Spanish and Portuguese colonies moved more slowly and cautiously toward their break with the Iberian monarchies. In Spanish America, the revolts were many and varied, and in some cases, unsuccessful. In Portuguese America, the revolt could hardly be called a "war," given its brevity and lack of bloodshed. When surveying the wars for independence in Latin America, however, one should always keep in mind that these wars formed part of a larger series of rebellions leading to the independence of some twenty new nations across all of the Americas between 1776 and 1836—and the failure of other colonies and regions to achieve their independence.

CREOLES AND PENINSULARES

In Spanish America, a growing division had emerged among those at the top of the social hierarchy, between creoles and *peninsulares*. In the words of the great scientist Alexander von Humboldt, who traveled throughout Spanish America in the early nineteenth century, "The lowest, least educated and uncultivated European believes himself superior to the white born in the New World." A sense of creole identity had begun to emerge in Spanish America by the mid-seventeenth century (and to a lesser extent the same process was emerging more slowly in late eighteenth-century Brazil). Much like their English counterparts in North America, the creoles increasingly saw themselves as the best judges of how to rule the colonies. After centuries of experience and deep knowledge of local conditions, they resented the condescending cultural and social attitudes of *peninsulares* who (fresh off the boat) wanted to tell them what was best for their homeland. By 1800, the term "we Americans" and "our America" became frequent among the creole leadership. By the end of the eighteenth century, these creoles began to challenge the Spanish Empire just as the English "creoles" had challenged Great Britain.

Already in the mid-seventeenth century, vibrant regional elites had emerged, especially in Mexico and Peru, and they modeled the viceregal courts and social life to imitate the royal court in Madrid. Although the literature, art, and theater in these centers imitated that of Spain, they had already begun to take on an American flavor. A small group of white European elites living in a sea of indigenous, African, and racially-mixed peoples produced a high culture that was an increasingly American—a creole—version of Iberian culture. The blatant disdain *peninsulares* often showed for creoles, and the discrimination creoles suffered at the hands of the *peninsulares*, reinforced a growing sense of local pride. By 1800, these Americans had begun to produce literature and history that reveled in the unique features of their "country" or *patria*, as they often called their locale or region. Some historians would argue that a new sense of Americanism played a greater role in the move to independence than the ideas of the Enlightenment. By 1800, many of the Spanish in the New World had begun to see themselves as Mexicans, or Peruvians, or Chileans. (A similar process was taking place, but much more slowly, in Brazil.)

The Spanish American empire was older, richer, and more populous than the empires of the Portuguese, British, French, or Dutch. Columbus had arrived in the Caribbean in the 1490s, and by the 1530s the Spanish had conquered Mexico and Peru. By the 1570s, Spain had imposed imperial structures in the core regions: central Mexico, Peru, and the Caribbean. In Brazil, the core region around Bahia on the northeastern coast did not emerge until about 1600, and the core region in the southeast (Minas Gerais and Rio de Janeiro) would not emerge until the mid-1700s. The Spanish core colonies had been evolving for about a century before the English established a foothold on the eastern coast of North America and a half-century before the Portuguese in Brazil. Spanish America was also far more populous than British North America. In 1500, there may have been some 75 to 80 million people in the Americas, about the size of the population of all of Europe. Even after the demographic catastrophe caused by conquest and disease, the indigenous population of Spanish and Portuguese America in 1800 was probably about 14 to 15 million (the population of Spain was about 12 million). Nearly half of the Spanish Americans lived in Mexico (or, more precisely, New Spain). After centuries of the slave trade, some 1 to 2 million people of African descent lived and worked in the Spanish colonies. About 3 to 4 million people were classified as racially mixed, known generically as *castas* or castes. "Whites" or Europeans probably numbered about 3 million and only about 40,000 of them were *peninsulares*. These numbers and percentages varied from region to region. In Mexico, Central America, and the Andes, Indians formed a large majority of the population. Blacks and mulattoes were the single largest group in the Spanish Caribbean and Brazil.

The Spanish American colonies were also the richest in the Americas, and would remain so for nearly 300 years. The silver mines of northern Mexico and what is now Bolivia (Upper Peru) supplied most of the precious metals in Europe, especially in the sixteenth and seventeenth centuries. The colonies were also rich exporters of sugar, tobacco, chocolate, dyes, leather, and other goods to Europe. Imagine the tobacco wealth of Virginia and multiply it, while adding in silver and a much larger traffic in slaves, and you have a sense of the wealth of colonial Spanish America. (The gold and diamond boom in eighteenth-century Brazil made it the engine of the Portuguese global empire, and also a hugely rich colony.) Spain's and Portugal's colonies in the Americas were the core of their global empires while the Thirteen Colonies were a less significant and smaller piece of Britain's truly global empire. While the English scrambled in the 1760s to find ways to tax the Americans to pay for the costs of their empire, Spain and Portugal extracted enormous profits from their American colonies. In Mexico alone, royal income rose by a factor of five in the eighteenth century, and nearly half this income was pure profit, after paying the costs of administration and defense.

THE HAITIAN REVOLUTION

The first successful war for independence in Latin America took place not in Spanish or Portuguese colonies, but in the tiny French possession of Saint-Domingue. The Haitian Revolution was the bloodiest struggle in the "age of revolution" in the Americas, and it was the only successful slave rebellion in the history of the New World. As a social revolution in a Franco-American colony, the Haitian Revolution is unlike any of the other independence movements. As a precursor to the Ibero-American revolts, it became a polarizing symbol for those who might contemplate colonial rebellion. It demonstrated to would-be rebels that colonial uprisings against the European metropolis could succeed, while also confirming the darkest nightmares of those would-be rebels about the dangers of unleashing the wrath of the lower classes. For creole leaders throughout Latin America, the Haitian uprising served as a cautionary tale. A war of creole elites against peninsular elites could easily lead to race or class warfare that might consume the creoles in the process. To use the imagery preferred by Bolívar, the creoles would be riding a tiger, and they could not afford to fall off. As would be the case in Spanish and Portuguese America in 1807–8, it was events in Europe, and more specifically, the French Revolution, that triggered war in Saint-Domingue and, eventually, led to the independence of France's most profitable overseas colony.

Haiti today occupies the western third of the island of Hispaniola, the original staging ground for the Spanish conquest in Latin America. Columbus himself had founded Santo Domingo on the eastern end of the island in 1493, but the Spanish had neglected the western end of Hispaniola. In the seventeenth century, French buccaneers (*boucaniers*) began to operate from coastal enclaves and by the end of the century (1697), Louis XIV had compelled Spain to recognize French control of what became known as Saint-Domingue. Hispaniola, like many other islands in the Caribbean, was drawn into the booming sugar plantation economy in the seventeenth century. In the first half of the eighteenth century, Barbados and Jamaica (now under English control) had become major sugar plantation centers. By the last quarter of the eighteenth century, Saint-Domingue had eclipsed all the colonies in the Caribbean to become the world's great sugar plantation center, exporting more than 100 million pounds of sugar to Europe each year.

As with all the other great plantation colonies in the Americas, the French sugar plantations swallowed up tens of thousands of African slaves. In the late eighteenth century, more than 30,000 African slaves flowed into Saint-Domingue every year, making the colony one of the most Africanized societies in all the Americas. In the late 1780s, the colony's population consisted of about 25,000 whites (mainly French), about 20,000 mulattoes (*gens de couleur*), and more than 400,000 slaves, most of them African or the children of Africans. Slaves formed not only a majority of the colony's population, they accounted for 90 percent of Saint-Domingue's inhabitants! Most of the slaves came from Angola or Congo and while they worked primarily on sugar plantations, the colony also produced cotton, coffee, and indigo for export. Saint-Domingue alone accounted for one-third of all of France's foreign trade. By the late 1780s, Saint-Domingue was a plantation society built on the brutal repression of hundreds of thousands of slaves by less than 50,000 whites and mulattoes, a repression that produced enormous profits for the white planters and French traders.

The enormous concentration of Africans, and the seemingly ceaseless influx of new African slaves, created a powerful blending of African cultures with French Catholic touches. A new language (Creole) spoken by the masses emerged that blended African and French linguistic patterns. By the eighteenth century, vodun had emerged as a potent underground religion among the slaves. A mix of rites and symbols that originated in Africa, it was an animistic religion (like *candomblé* in Brazil) built around the invocation of a series of deities. The faithful attempted to influence the course of events through appeals to these deities. Some of the most serious resistance to the slave regime came from vodun priests. Runaway slaves (known as *maroons* in English) established communities deep in the hills and forests of the interior of the island. In 1758, a substantial rebellion led by François Macandal (a charismatic maroon leader) failed and he was brutally executed, although adherents of vodun believed that he turned himself into a flying bug and escaped the executioner at the last minute. (The legendary Cuban writer, Alejo Carpentier, recreates this episode in his evocative novel, *El reino de este mundo* (*The Kingdom of this World*), 1949.)

As in Spanish America, it would be divisions among the elites that opened up the possibility of lower-class uprisings and unleashed the masses. Social and ethnic gradations divided the white and mulatto populations in Saint-Domingue. Among the whites, the French-born looked down on the whites born in the Americas (much like the creole-*peninsular* split in Spanish America). The so-called *grand blancs* dominated the island society and the *petits blancs* powerfully resented their treatment by their French-born compatriots. Much of the mulatto population aspired to success in French society, learning the language, adopting Catholicism, and assimilating to French customs and dress. They often became the intermediaries between white and slave society, serving as the agents of repression, yet the whites looked down upon the *gens de couleur*.

When the revolution broke out in France in 1789, and French revolutionaries published the Declaration of the Rights of Man and Citizen, it did not take long for the *gens de couleur* in Saint-Domingue to assert their rights to full citizenship. (Virtually no one, of course, considered slaves as worthy of the rights of citizenship.) When the *gens de couleur* read the classic phrase from the Declaration that "men are born and remain free and equal in rights," they took these powerful words to heart. The new National Assembly in France created positions for six representatives from Saint-Domingue, Guadeloupe, and Martinique, making France the first European colonial power to extend representation to colonials. As factionalism and civil war convulsed France, so in the island colony, various factions of the free population began to fight for control of Saint-Domingue. Most wanted some form of autonomy from France, and wanted to maintain the slave system. Most whites refused to accept the mulattoes as equal citizens and, in fact, whites were angered by moves in France to enfranchise some mulattoes. Disillusioned mulattoes planned an uprising that was uncovered in 1790. The leaders were quickly executed.

Amidst this increasingly bloody infighting among the 50,000 free inhabitants of the colony, the slave population did not sit idly by; indeed, they plotted an uprising of their own for months. Led by the vodun high priest (*papaloi*) Boukman, thousands of slaves rose up simultaneously around Le Cap Français, sweeping across the North Plain burning plantations, killing whites, and plundering. Boukman would soon die in the revolt, but it spread like wildfire through the colony as tens of thousands of slaves joined the rebellion and thousands of whites died at their hands. The lucky ones fled to neighboring colonies and to the United States.

Over the next decade, Saint-Domingue became one of the bloodiest battlegrounds in the history of the Americas. French, English, and Spanish armies invaded and occupied on multiple occasions as the island became a theater for struggles among European powers. Tens of thousands of European troops died, mostly of malaria and yellow fever, an ironic reversal of the demographic catastrophe that ravaged Native Americans on the island in the sixteenth century. In June 1793, the French revolutionary commission led by Léger Sonthonax abolished slavery in Saint-Domingue (the first decree to abolish slavery anywhere in the Americas). Meanwhile, the fighting spread to the surrounding French and British islands in the Caribbean as slave rebellions and invading European armies moved from colony to colony.

Out of the midst of shifting alliances and loyalties among different groups arose one of the greatest figures of the age of revolution in the Americas: François Dominique Toussaint L'Ouverture (eventually know simply as Toussaint Louverture), born in 1743. An American-born slave, he eventually became a slave steward, a key position in the plantation hierarchy. Literate in French and conversant with Catholicism, he was very similar to the *gens de couleur* whose ranks he joined when freed by his master. Toussaint was a complex figure. He brilliantly shifted alliances and loyalties for several years among many groups that fought for control of the revolution and the island, and rather than fighting for independence from France, he sought to become the governor of the French colony of former slaves. Bloody struggles ensued between rival black military leaders and their followers. With the help of his two key lieutenants, Jean-Jacques Dessalines (1758–1806) and Henri Christophe (1767–1820), Toussaint took control of the colony and in 1801 invaded Spanish Santo Domingo on the eastern side of the island. They hoped to guarantee their work by controlling the entire island.

In the words of the great West Indian historian, C. L. R. James, "For nearly ten years the population, corrupt enough before, had been trained in bloodshed and soaked in violence. Bands of marauders roamed the countryside. The only disciplined force was the army, and Toussaint instituted a military dictatorship." To revive the shattered economy, Toussaint failed in an attempt to reinstitute the old plantation system. Although a former slave himself, he failed to see that other former slaves no more wanted to work in the sugar fields as forced laborers than they did as slaves. During an interlude in warfare on the European continent, the new French Emperor Napoléon decided to regain control of the once-rich sugar colony, sending troops to the island in early 1802 under the command of his brother-in-law General Charles Leclerc. Within months, Leclerc reasserted French control, defeating Christophe and Dessalines, and then Toussaint. Leclerc then invited Toussaint to dinner, seized and shackled him, and sent him off to a French prison where he died in April 1803.

The ferocity of the French tactics (executing entire brigades of black troops, for example) forged an uneasy alliance between blacks and mulattoes. In what became a war of near total extermination, the French would fail to hold the island. Yellow fever (which killed General Leclerc), renewed war with the British across the Atlantic world, and the tenacity of the black and mulatto armies finally forced the French to withdraw in late 1803. On January 1, 1804, after nearly fifteen years of savage and bloody fighting, Jean-Jacques Dessalines and his fellow generals declared the independence of the new nation of Haiti (from an indigenous name for the island meaning "land of the mountains"). Ravaged, burned, and bloodied, the Haitians had succeeded in liberating more than 400,000 slaves, a third of whom had probably died in the conflict. Few whites remained on the island. Tragically, the Haitians would now face decades of dictatorship and repression under a series of leaders (black and mulatto) who fought among themselves for supreme control of the first independent nation in Latin America.

THE SEEDS OF REBELLION

As the British historian John Lynch has noted, the Spanish version of the Enlightenment shoved aside most of its philosophy and reduced it to a program of modernization. From the perspective of the king, this meant modernizing administration and the imperial economy: "To bring my royal revenues to their proper level," in the words of Charles III. In America, the Spanish Enlightenment was, according to Lynch, "little more than a programme of renewed imperialism." For Spanish Americans, the Enlightenment did not so much produce revolutionary sentiments as it generated a more critical attitude toward authority, tradition, and monarchy. Creoles began to rethink their relationship with the Spanish monarchy, especially with the profoundly different approaches of the Bourbons after they succeeded the Hapsburgs at the beginning of the eighteenth century. As with the many different peoples in the other European colonies, they saw their first loyalty as being not to nation or to assemblies or governments, but to their king. This was an intensely direct and personal relationship in European societies dating back to the Middle Ages. When the Bourbons replaced the Hapsburgs, they instituted an important shift in the nature of the relationship between king and subjects. Bourbon monarchs and their advisors moved the empire toward a more bureaucratic and rational system and away from the more personalistic ethos of the Hapsburgs.

Many Spaniards and Spanish Americans also began to question the power and authority of the Catholic Church, the most important cultural institution in Spanish America. While the Enlightenment philosophers provided intellectual reasons to question the authority of the Church, increasingly royal authorities also challenged the authority of the Church for very practical political and economic motives. Enlightened monarchs and their counselors saw the Catholic Church as a powerful competitor to royal authority in their emerging nation-states and they chose to attack, weaken, and restrict the representatives and the power of the Church in Iberia and Ibero-America.

The radicalism of the French and American Revolutions also had a profound impact on the creoles. The Anglo-Americans in the United States showed that it was possible to challenge colonial rule—and win. They also provided a living, breathing example of a republic that worked. Although the French Revolution proved much too radical, democratic, and anarchic for most creoles, it did (again) provide a sophisticated and powerful political rationale for the ideals of liberalism and republicanism. Liberty, equality, republican government, representation, and free trade were attractive new ideals for the Latin American revolutionaries. As the liberator Francisco de Miranda said in 1799, "We have before our eyes two great examples, the American and the French Revolutions. Let us prudently imitate the first and carefully shun the second."

A trading revolution in the Atlantic world also had a powerful effect on the creoles. The so-called Seventeenth-Century Depression had ended in the first years of the eighteenth century, and all the European powers had dramatically expanded their transatlantic trading networks and volume. England led the way as it entered into the First Industrial Revolution in the second half of the eighteenth century. By 1750, creoles acutely felt the inability to trade with the English and the restrictions on trading within the empire. England had emerged by 1800 as the greatest maritime and commercial power in the world. The colonists wanted access to English goods and English markets, especially manufactured goods—in particular, textiles. Throughout the eighteenth century, the only means to gain access was through smuggling, which had become a widespread and lucrative business, especially in those colonies away from colonial centers (primarily Venezuela and Argentina).

In 1800, the colonies had a larger population than Spain and produced more exports, but they were limited to trading with a few ports in Spain and the trade was heavily regulated and taxed. Under the mercantilist systems that many of the European empires followed, the metropolis attempted to control all trade within its domain and to exclude any outsiders. These colonial trading empires were not unlike the trading blocs that have emerged at the beginning of the twenty-first century. Much more so than in English America, the Spanish system was highly bureaucratized, centralized, heavily taxed at every step, and funneled through a handful of ports in America and Spain. The ideological and economic shifts in the second half of the eighteenth century deeply affected the creole elites in Spanish and Portuguese America. In Spanish America, the Bourbons added to creole discontent with the reassertion of imperial control through their reforms. After 1750, the monarchy practiced open and systematic discrimination against creoles, believing them not to be as loyal to the interests of Madrid as *peninsulares*. Probably three of every four major imperial appointments in the Americas in the second half of the century went to *peninsulares*.

By 1750, Spanish American creoles were anxious to exert greater control over their homelands in the Americas. In most cases, the wars for independence would be driven forward by creole demands for greater autonomy and free trade. The words of Simón Bolívar, the greatest liberator in Latin America, vividly sum up creole discontent in 1815: "Americans today, and perhaps to a greater extent than ever before, who live within the Spanish system, occupy a position in society no better than that of serfs destined for labor." The parallels with the American Revolution and North American "creoles" are striking. This growing sense of "American-ness" reflected the long and steady growth of American populations, especially in the colonial centers.

The old Viceroyalties of New Spain and Peru had subdivided, as population and economic activity had spread outward from the centers since their creation in the 1520s and 1530s. In addition to the extensive Mexico, New Spain included the Kingdom of Guatemala (that is, all of Central America), an area that already had regional elites and centers in Guatemala, El Salvador, Honduras, Nicaragua, and Costa Rica. Northern South America had developed so greatly by the mid-eighteenth century that it had been spun off as a third viceroyalty (New Granada) and it had three developing regional centers: Venezuela, New Granada (Colombia), and Ecuador. The southern tier of the old Viceroyalty of Peru had also spun off in the 1770s as a fourth Viceroyalty (La Plata) including modern-day

Paraguay, Argentina, and Bolivia. Chile, although still part of Peru, had its own well-developed regional elite by 1750 (and remained a part of the Viceroyalty of Peru).

While the discontent of colonial elites had grown dramatically by the beginning of the nineteenth century, unlike their U.S. counterparts, these elites had not forced the issues of political and economic autonomy to the breaking point. War in Europe broke the colonial bonds for them. The processes of modernization and reform set the stage for the wars for independence in Spanish America, but it was the Napoleonic wars in Europe, and more specifically, Napoléon's invasion of Spain, that triggered the wars. After 1799, Napoléon emerged as the strongman in France, and he led his armies across Europe until the Battle of Waterloo in 1815, deposing monarchs and dominating the entire continent. In the first decade of the nineteenth century, Napoléon Bonaparte dominated Europe from the Atlantic to the borders of the Russian Empire. Unable to challenge British control of the seas (after his naval defeat at the Battle of Trafalgar in 1805 off the coast of Spain), he turned to the conquest of the last two continental European regions not under his control: Iberia and Russia. Although he quickly occupied Spain and Portugal, continual warfare in both countries sapped his armies for years. The occupation of Iberia did allow Napoléon to turn in 1812 to the invasion of Russia, where he would face defeat and the collapse of his European empire. Napoléon's control of Spain, and Britain's control of the seas, left the Spanish American colonies adrift and set off a chain reaction that led to the wars for independence. By 1826, all of Spain's colonies in the Americas (except Cuba and Puerto Rico) had broken away. Unlike Britain's North American colonies, which were a minor outpost of a world empire, the Spanish American colonies formed the core of Spain's once-mighty empire. Spain fought fiercely and futilely to retain what it could, with the bloodiest wars taking place in the richest colonial centers: Mexico and Peru.

The Spanish and Portuguese monarchies reacted in dramatically different ways to the Napoleonic invasions in 1807–8. The Portuguese had long been allies of the English and had been preparing for a possible French invasion for more than a decade. The Braganzas became the ruling family in Portugal in 1640, and Maria I had ascended to the throne in 1777. The Portuguese monarchy had become the richest in Europe in the mid-eighteenth century with the discovery of gold and diamonds in Brazil. Maria I married her uncle, Pedro III, and they ruled jointly until his death in 1786. After the executions of Louis XVI and Marie Antoinette in France (1793), Maria became increasingly unstable, convincing herself that she would also die at the hands of a mob and that she would burn in Hell. Maria's son, João (John), began to rule Portugal and he was named Regent in 1799 after his mother was declared "incurably insane." He would rule in her name until she died in 1816, when he would become João VI. His wife, Carlota Joaquina, was a daughter of Carlos IV of Spain.

When the French sent forces across Spain into Portugal in late 1807, the royal family chose to evacuate to Brazil under British escort. Portuguese ships had been ready in the Lisbon harbor for months, and they had been joined by British ships in mid-November. When João gave the order for the royal family to embark on November 24, chaos ensued as thousands of courtiers scrambled to secure a spot on the fleet amidst days of heavy rains. On November 27, the royal family assembled at the docks and the mad Maria had to be dragged kicking and screaming from her coach. By then, some 10,000 people had scrambled aboard the ships, many without their baggage. The fleet set sail only hours before French troops, under General Andoche Junot, swept into Lisbon on the morning of November 30. The monarchy would not return to Portugal for fourteen years!

Compared to the Spanish Bourbons, the Portuguese Braganzas appeared to be one big happy and wise royal family. The Spanish monarch, Carlos IV, had assumed the throne at the age of 40 in 1788 on the death of his father Carlos III, the great Bourbon reformer. Not the most intelligent of men, Carlos IV loved hunting (every day) and was content to leave the affairs of state to the true power behind the throne, Manuel Godoy. Born in 1767 to a humble family, Godoy was serving as a royal bodyguard when in the 1780s he became the lover of María Luisa, the wife of Carlos, then the crown prince. Sixteen years older than Godoy, María Luisa had been a beauty in her youth, but became increasingly ugly with age (as the paintings of the great Spanish artist Francisco de Goya so brilliantly document). Described by one diplomat as a "passionate, unsatisfied woman bursting with ill-restrained desires," she suffered from several illnesses that wrecked her physically. Godoy's control over the queen was total and he became a duke, then secretary of state, and eventually a prince through her favors.

After French troops occupied Portugal, more moved into northern Spain, gradually edging closer to Madrid. Many blamed Godoy for the invasion and in a dramatic turn of events in March 1808, a mob ransacked Godoy's home, he was jailed, and the king chose to abdicate in favor of his son Fernando (who became Fernando VII). Numerous Spaniards, nobles and commoners, saw Fernando as their only hope of salvation from an inept monarchy and the encroachments of Napoléon. The wily Napoléon then "invited" Carlos and Fernando to visit him in southern France in April 1808. Napoléon announced to them that they must renounce the throne in the first days of May. He wrote to his foreign minister Talleyrand that Fernando was "very stupid" and "very wicked," that his father was "very nice," and that María Luisa had "her heart and her past on her face." On May 6, Fernando abdicated the throne, and his father signed a document handing Spain over to Napoléon, who then placed his half-brother Joseph on the Spanish throne. (Carlos IV and María Luisa would die in exile in Italy in 1819.) The Spanish people, in one of the more heroic moments in the nation's history, would have nothing of it, and rose up in the cities and fields. They resisted the French occupation with tenacity and at enormous cost. The great uprisings of May 1808 initiated a six-year-long struggle to regain Spanish independence. Fierce fighting broke out across the peninsula. Goya's paintings of the May uprisings and his terrifying sketches (the *Disasters of War*) during these years are some of the greatest works in Western art.

Across the country, and in the absence of the true king, citizens formed juntas to rule in the name of the imprisoned Fernando VII. Many of these juntas joined together to form a "supreme" central junta. When the French captured Seville in 1810, the junta became a Council of Regency ruling in the name of Fernando VII in Cádiz. In September 1812, the Council was transformed into a parliament, or *cortes*. In the absence of the crown, most of the royal court, and the nobility, the Cortes became a liberal body calling for the end of most of the privileges and rights of feudal society. In 1812, the Cortes produced Spain's first constitution. Across Spanish America, the colonists also formed juntas of self-governance. They were faced with a fundamental dilemma: how to react to the fall of the monarchy, the French occupation, and the end of all direct rule from Spain? For all intents and purposes, the colonists had political and economic autonomy dropped in their laps by the Napoleonic invasion, and the power of the British navy to keep the French from crossing the Atlantic. This was a pivotal shift, with the "people" ruling through the juntas, rather than the king ruling over his subjects. How were the elites to determine who had authority in the absence of direction from the monarch? What was the nature of authority when not blessed by royal will?

The momentous events in Spain triggered the wars for independence in Spanish America. A first set of wars broke out after 1808. Most colonists were reluctant to break with Spain and chose to remain loyal to Fernando, even in his absence. What is most striking about this initial crisis is how *few* chose to challenge the colonial system. Even creoles with deep resentments and grievances largely chose to remain loyal to Fernando and await his return. Some creoles did seize the opportunity of the moment, and called for independence from Spain. The rebellions that broke out were nearly all defeated, with the exception of those in Paraguay and Argentina. Ironically, the return of Fernando VII to power in 1814 would trigger a second set of wars for independence. Fernando disappointed many loyal colonists by attempting to return to the absolutist, colonial regime of the eighteenth century—a stupid and disastrous move on his part. The creoles had quickly become accustomed to self-rule, trade with England, and greater control over their own regions. Combined with the great wounds and social divisions opened by the first set of wars, Fernando's rejection of constitutionalism and the Constitution of 1812 sparked the final collapse of Spain's once mighty empire in the Americas.

13

The Wars for Independence

The wars for independence in Latin America must be seen within the larger context of an "age of revolution" in the Atlantic world. Between 1776 and 1826, ten nations (the United States, Haiti, Mexico, United Provinces of Central America, Gran Colombia, Peru, Chile, Argentina, Paraguay, and Brazil) achieved their independence, arising out of the colonial empires of the British, French, Portuguese, and Spanish in the New World. Some of these emerging nations would fragment further in the aftermath of independence, leading to the creation of another nine new nations within a generation. (Gran Colombia split into Venezuela, Colombia, and Ecuador; Central America split into Guatemala, El Salvador, Honduras, Nicaragua, and Costa Rica; Uruguay split from both Argentina and Brazil; and Texas separated from Mexico. The Dominican Republic would go through a complicated process of independence from Spain and Haiti.) Despite this impressive wave that created so many new nations in the Americas, we should remember that many colonies did not revolt, or failed to achieve their independence. Cuba and Puerto Rico remained under Spanish control until 1898. Panama would not break away from Colombia until 1903. Canada and the British West Indies did not follow their creole cousins in the Thirteen Colonies, and France, Britain, and the Netherlands would hold on to their Caribbean and mainland territories (the Guianas and British Honduras) well into the late twentieth century. The half-century after 1776, however, was the first great "moment" of decolonization and nationalism in the modern world, and the next moment would not come for another century, in the aftermath of the Great War in Europe in the early twentieth century.

As we saw in the previous chapter, a century of change arising out of the Enlightenment, the Industrial Revolution, and the French and American Revolutions had prepared the way for the revolts in early nineteenth-century Latin America. The Napoleonic wars, and the invasion of the Iberian peninsula had provided the opportunity and the incentive for the ambitious and discontented creole elites in Spanish America. Across the region, leaders would arise, some out of the elites, others from the lower classes, to challenge Spanish rule. Eventually, the wars would mobilize all social and racial groups. In some regions, the wars would be bloody, prolonged, and divisive. In others, independence would come with little bloodshed, and no significant social change. By and large, creole elites would replace peninsular elites, leading some historians pessimistically to describe the aftermath of independence as "same mule, new rider."

NORTHERN SOUTH AMERICA

Although he would fail in his efforts to liberate Spanish America, Francisco de Miranda would blaze the path for the creole "liberators" who would succeed in creating sixteen new nations by the 1840s. In the words of his most recent biographer, Karen Racine, Miranda was ultimately important "not because he himself brought independence to his fellow citizens but because he convinced them that they could do it for themselves." He traveled, talked, debated, and propagandized across the Caribbean, the United States, and all of Europe. Miranda was also the epitome of the American revolutionary of the age, in his reading, travels, and friendships on both sides of the Atlantic. Born in Caracas in 1750, Miranda fought in the Spanish army in North Africa and then in Cuba during the 1770s. In the 1780s, he fought in Florida and the Bahamas, and then traveled throughout the young United States, meeting all the major revolutionary leaders. In the fateful year of 1789, Miranda arrived in France as the Revolution began, and he soon became a general in the French Revolutionary Army. Miranda then moved to London and his home became a focal point of activity for some of the greatest figures of the revolutionary era. In 1810, a young Venezuelan, Simón Bolívar, sought out Miranda in London.

Bolívar is the greatest of all the Latin American revolutionary figures, the "George Washington" of a half-dozen South American nations. True to the spirit of his age, Bolívar was an idealist and a romantic. Bolívar was born in 1783 into an elite Venezuelan family that could trace its local roots back to the conquest of the sixteenth century. Orphaned at an early age, he was raised by tutors and his beloved black maid, Hippólita. Between the ages of nine and fourteen, Simón Rodriguez, his most important tutor, took his young charge to the remote countryside and educated him in a mix of what one writer has described as cowboy life and Enlightenment philosophy. In 1799, at the age of sixteen, Bolívar was sent to Spain to complete his education. He fell madly in love with María Teresa Rodríguez y Alaiza and they married in Spain in May 1802. Tragically, María Teresa died of a fever within months of her arrival in Venezuela. Bolívar would never remarry. He later confided to one of his associates, "If I hadn't been widowed, perhaps my life would have been different. . . . The death of my wife placed me on the path of politics very early; it made me follow thereafter the carriage of Mars rather than the arrow of Cupid."

The grieving Bolívar returned to Paris. In December 1804, he attended the coronation of Napoléon and Josephine in Notre Dame Cathedral. He and his old tutor, Simón Rodríguez, embarked on a sort of pilgrimage to Rome in 1805 where they witnessed the coronation of Napoléon as King of Italy. Supposedly, as the sun set on Rome, standing amidst the ancient ruins, Bolívar committed his life to the liberation of Spanish America. According to Rodríguez, Bolívar dropped to his knees and "his eyes wet, his breath heaving, his face red, and with an almost fevered manner he told me: 'I swear that I will not give rest to my arm nor my sword until the day we have broken the chains of Spanish power which oppress us.' "

Bolívar's homeland was one of the first colonies to break with Spain. In 1808, the first news of the overthrow of the Spanish monarchy came to Venezuela from the British governor in nearby Trinidad. Local creole leaders declared the formation of a council in Caracas to rule in the absence of Fernando VII. They stopped short of declaring independence. Caracas was a wealthy commercial center that exported cacao (chocolate) to Spain. Venezuela probably had a population of less than a million, and only 200,000 were whites, with an equal number of Indians, and some half a million blacks. In early 1810, the Venezuelan creoles formed a delegation (led by Bolívar) to seek support for Venezuelan independence in the United States and England. After receiving a cold shoulder from the British government, Bolívar persuaded the charismatic Miranda to lead an invasion of Venezuela. On July 5, 1811, the Venezuelans declared the colony independent from Spain, the first of all the Spanish American colonies to break openly from the empire. Revolts against the new Venezuelan government by Spanish loyalists began to break out, with some towns refusing to submit to the authority of the new regime. As the loyalists regained control of the colony, Bolívar arrested Miranda, and handed him over to Spanish authorities. In exchange, the Spanish authorities gave him a safe conduct passage out of the country and he fled to Curaçao. The Spanish shipped Miranda back to a prison in Cádiz where he spent the last four years of his life, dying in 1816. The Precursor had perished, betrayed by his heir to the leadership of the liberation of Spanish South America.

The liberation of Venezuela and the rest of northern South America were bitter civil wars pitting creole against *peninsulares* and creole against creole with the poor nonwhite masses often divided as well. In early 1813, Bolívar brilliantly defeated the Spanish forces on the eastern side of the Andes mountains at Cúcuta on the Venezuelan border. In this new campaign, Bolívar engaged in a bloody and brutal "war to the death" with the loyalists. With several thousand men, Bolívar swept down the Andes from western Venezuela. In a series of brilliant maneuvers, he defeated the Spanish forces, and in August 1813, Simón Bolívar returned triumphant to Caracas. He was acclaimed the Liberator in October 1813 and Dictator in January 1814. Venezuelans were still divided, as the majority of the "Spanish" forces were, in fact, creoles. In particular, the lower classes (free and slave) had no reason, as yet, to join the struggle, and the creoles feared igniting a racial and class war.

The greatest scourge of Bolívar was not the Spanish, but the cowboys and horsemen (known as the *llaneros* or plainsmen) of the southern part of the country in the Orinoco River basin. The tough, racially mixed people of the plains lived on horseback and their leader was a Spanish immigrant, José Tomás Boves. Bolívar once said of Boves, "He was not nurtured with the delicate milk of a woman but the blood of tigers and the furies of hell. . . . He was the wrath of heaven which hurled its lightning against the *patria* [fatherland] . . . a demon in human flesh which drowned Venezuela in blood." Boves was a classic example of the Latin American *caudillo*—the so-called "man on horseback" who led by the force of his charisma and his ability to relate to the common man. His mounted warriors were known as the Legion of Hell. The Spanish forces and the lancers of Boves defeated Bolívar's rebel forces at La Puerta in June 1814, and then captured Valencia in July, forcing Bolívar, yet again, to retreat into exile—on Curaçao in September 1814.

Bolívar did not tarry long in Curaçao before heading to New Granada. Compared to the complex racial politics of Venezuela, the situation was simpler in New Granada, with a population of about 1.5 million. Some 900,000 were white and about 300,000 Indians. About 140,000 were free blacks and only 70,000 were slaves. In December 1814, allied with a variety of rebel forces, Bolívar took control of Bogotá, the old capital of the Viceroyalty of New Granada. At the same time, Fernando VII had returned to the throne and had sent 15,000 men to "retake" the rebellious colonies. Bolívar left New Granada in March 1815, taking up exile again, this time in Jamaica. With his departure, the Spanish arrived and reestablished control of Venezuela and New Granada.

Bolívar would have to spend two years cooling his heels in Jamaica and Haiti. While in Jamaica he wrote and published his most famous manifesto.

The "Jamaica Letter" is a long indictment of the atrocities Spain had wrought on the colonies since the conquest of the sixteenth century. The Jamaica Letter reviews the state of all of Spanish America and offers his advice for the future new nations of the Americas. He rejects federalism (the United States model), prescribing a strong central government with a powerful executive. "Pure representative government," Bolívar declares, "is not suitable to our character . . . we are dominated by vices which, developed under the guidance of Spain, became weighted with ferocity, ambition, vengeance and cupidity." Always the practical politician, he goes on to say, "Do not adopt the best system of government, but the one most likely to succeed." His most heady call was for a united federation of American states with its capital in the centrally located Panama.

Several events converged to produce success on this final stage of the war for the liberation of northern South America. Bolívar forged a crucial alliance with José Antonio Páez, the charismatic leader of the *llaneros*, and the successor to his old rival Boves. Páez may have had as many as 10,000 men under his command. In one of the most dramatic and daring moves of the revolutionary era, Bolívar marched from eastern Venezuela into Colombia. Moving from tropical lowland jungles up over mountains through snowy mountain valleys above 10,000 feet, thousands of his men died from the cold, exposure, and altitude sickness. It was, as John Lynch describes it, one of the "great feats of the human mind and great exploits of the human will." On August 7, 1819, Bolívar and his forces defeated the Spanish on the plains near Bogotá at Boyacá. Spanish officials fled and New Granada came definitively under the control of the patriot forces. The local leaders declared Bolívar the Liberator and President of New Granada. He headed back to Venezuela, leaving his vice-president, Francisco de Paula Santander, in charge. On the return trip, he met the 25-year-old José Antonio de Sucre. Born in eastern Venezuela, Sucre was destined to become Bolívar's trusted protégé and lieutenant.

Defeating the Spanish forces at the Battle of Carabobo on June 24, 1821, Bolívar effectively achieved Venezuelan independence. At a congress at Cucutá in eastern Colombia, Bolívar dictated a constitution that gave birth to Gran Colombia (Venezuela, Colombia, and Ecuador) and made him its first president. He now turned his attention to Ecuador. Sending Sucre with a large army by sea to Guayaquil, Bolívar headed through the mountains of southern Colombia. Sucre won a decisive battle at Pichincha, fought at an altitude of almost 10,000 feet above sea level near Quito on May 24, 1822. The victories of Sucre and Bolívar in New Granada and Ecuador completed the struggle that had begun a decade before with the declaration of Venezuelan independence.

SOUTHERN SOUTH AMERICA

José de San Martín was the counterpart of Simón Bolívar in southern South America. San Martín was born in 1778 in the interior of Argentina, the son of a Spanish army officer. At the age of seven, José returned to Spain and soon thereafter began a military career, eventually rising to the rank of lieutenant colonel. In September 1811, after 22 years in the army, and having lived most of his life in Spain, San Martín deserted the Spanish army and fled to London. At the old home of Miranda, now occupied by Bolívar's Venezuelan friend Andrés Bello, he met other rebels in exile. Within weeks, he was on a ship for Buenos Aires, where he arrived in March 1812, in the port city he had left 27 years before.

Like Venezuela, the region around the La Plata River basin was on the periphery of the Spanish empire. The pampas (plains) became a breeding ground for cattle and mules, and Buenos Aires, a small center for smuggling. Buenos Aires would eventually become the main port at the mouth of the La Plata River. On the pampas, a strong ranching culture developed around the Argentine cowboy, the gaucho. Racially mixed, living in the rough interior, the gaucho was similar to the *llaneros* of Venezuela. The pampas and gaucho culture stretched through Argentina into southern Brazil on the opposite side of the La Plata. In 1776, Spain created the Viceroyalty of La Plata and Buenos Aires grew to a thriving port with some 40,000 inhabitants by 1800. All of Argentina probably had fewer than half a million inhabitants.

Along with Venezuela, Buenos Aires was one of the early leaders in the break from Spanish rule. Many historians have pointed out that this is no accident. Both areas were later-developing commercial centers on the fringes of the empire, not old core regions like Mexico and Peru. Both had experienced and desperately wanted more free trade, especially with the British. The Argentines also have a legitimate claim to priority as the first of the colonies to break with Spain. Two British invasions triggered the struggle for independence. In 1806, Sir Home Popham and Colonel William Beresford and their fleet, operating out of what is now South Africa, crossed to the La Plata and occupied Buenos Aires. While the Spanish viceroy fled and the elites cowered, the lower classes and some of the creole leadership rallied behind Santiago Liniers, a French officer serving in the Spanish Army. Liniers defeated and captured more than a thousand British troops. He then became the military governor and the effective ruler of the viceroyalty. A second invasion in February 1807 was also repelled under the leadership of Liniers. When notables called for a *cabildo abierto*, or open town meeting, in May 1810, they seized and deported the viceroy and claimed governing authority in the name of the captive Fernando VII. Although the junta did not declare independence, in Argentine history the "Revolution of May 1810" is celebrated as *the* moment of national independence.

While the struggle between Buenos Aires and the interior provinces would hold back the completion of the war for independence in Argentina for some time, the people of the "Eastern Shore" of the La Plata moved to achieve independence from both Spain and Buenos Aires. The area that would become Uruguay had been a contested region between the Spanish and Portuguese empires for centuries. In the Treaty of Madrid in 1750, the two Iberian monarchies agreed to a rough division between their South American possessions. Spain kept the Jesuit missions in what is today Paraguay, and soon expelled the Jesuits. Portugal agreed to cede its rights to the *Banda Oriental*, but both Portugal and then Brazil would continue to claim the region into the 1820s. The major figure in the struggle for Uruguayan independence was José Gervasio Artigas. Born in 1764, Artigas was the son of a wealthy rancher. He had an elite education, and spent long periods on his father's ranches as a youth learning the ways and skills of the gauchos. He was, in some ways, the perfect combination of the skills of the elites and masses, a mixture that made him an astute and formidable caudillo (man on horseback). He served in the Spanish army in the region until deserting in 1811. He rose to become the Chief of the Easterners (*Jefe de los Orientales*) and led an independence struggle with greater and more broad-based participation by the masses than perhaps anywhere else in the Americas, save Haiti. He declared the independence of what he called the *Estado Oriental* (Eastern State), abolishing slavery and calling for land redistribution. The Portuguese and the government in Buenos Aires both attacked the new government. The Portuguese invaded in 1816 and seized Montevideo in January 1817. For the next three years, Artigas fought a guerrilla war, leading his tough gauchos through the interior. He was finally forced into exile in 1820 and he would spend the next 30 years of his life in Paraguay, a virtual prisoner of its dictatorial leaders. Uruguay would not achieve its independence until 1828, after a long struggle between the governments in Buenos Aires and Brazil.

Paraguay was perhaps the most unusual country in the Americas in the nineteenth century. Ostensibly under the control of the Viceroyalty of La Plata at the beginning of the nineteenth century, it was probably the most racially, culturally, and linguistically mixed area in Spanish America. More than 1,000 miles upriver from where the Rio de la Plata empties into the South Atlantic, the Jesuits established an extensive mission system in the region in the seventeenth century to escape the predations of slave hunters. By the mid-eighteenth century, some 30 missions had possibly as many as 100,000 Guaraní Indians concentrated around them. The few Spanish colonists and the numerous Guaraní Indians intermixed, producing a truly bilingual and bicultural society. The colonial economy consisted primarily of subsistence agriculture and some exports, especially a strong tea, yerba mate. With the creation of the Viceroyalty of La Plata in 1776, Paraguay reported to the royal government in Buenos Aires. The key grievance of the local creoles was the taxation of yerba mate exports, shipments that were taxed repeatedly as they made their way to buyers in Buenos Aires.

The Argentines forced the issue of Paraguayan independence. After the May 1810 upheaval in Buenos Aires, an open meeting of more than 200 prominent citizens in Asunción chose to support the Council of Regency in Spain. Although they supported the Regency, they also refused to accept the authority of the leaders of the May Revolution in Buenos Aires. The leaders in Buenos Aires decided to send a military force (of about 700) upriver to assert their authority. Several thousand Paraguayans organized to fight this invading force. In a series of skirmishes and battles, the Paraguayans resisted the Argentine intervention in early 1811. By this time, the principal Spanish official in Asunción had already fled, fearing the defeat of Paraguayan forces. It was the creole-led troops who defeated the Argentines, and a Paraguayan creole officer who negotiated the surrender. The creoles were now in control of the military and local government. With the revolts in Buenos Aires and Montevideo, there was little the royal officials there could do to reassert control over isolated Paraguay. Led by José Gaspar Rodríguez de Francia, local elites declared their independence from Spain and Argentina on May 17, 1811. In 1814, an enormous congress with more than 1,000 members elected Francia "Supreme Dictator of the Republic" for a five-year term. (Asunción, the capital, had just 8,000 inhabitants.) In June 1816, the congress voted to appoint Francia "Perpetual Dictator" and agreed that the congress would only meet "when the dictator requires it." It would not meet again until 1841, after Francia's death. José Gaspar Rodrígez de Francia would rule Paraguay as *El Supremo* from 1814 to his death at the age of 74 in 1840.

The struggle between Buenos Aires and the Argentine provinces complicated the war for independence, and afterward the situation of the new nation. Despite the proud title of the United Provinces of the Rio de La Plata, the provinces and caudillos of the interior effectively refused to recognize that Buenos Aires had any control over them. Although a congress in the northern city of Tucumán would declare the independence of the United Provinces of South America in 1816, it would be many years before any central government in Buenos Aires would establish effective control over the interior of what today is Argentina.

San Martín became a powerful figure in local politics. He began to believe, like Bolívar, that the independence of his own country would not be guaranteed until the rest of Spanish America achieved independence.

For him, the key was to cross the Andes, liberate Chile, and then head north to the viceregal capital in Lima, Peru. In the midst of this battle over centralism versus federalism in Argentina, San Martín secured an appointment in the northern province of Cuyo. From 1814 to 1817, while Argentine political leaders fought over control of the "nation," San Martín recruited and trained an army. He recruited Chileans fleeing Spanish forces, including the future hero of Chilean independence, Bernardo O'Higgins. Often accused of acting too slowly and with little creativity, San Martín assembled a force of some 5,000 men, 10,000 mules, 1,600 horses and 700 head of cattle by the end of 1816. Rather than moving to subdue and unify the provinces of Argentina, he turned instead to an invasion of Chile.

Although on the periphery of the Spanish American empire, Chile was not as isolated as Argentina, Uruguay, and Paraguay, and it had developed into a thriving creole colony by the beginning of the nineteenth century. Santiago, located in a fertile river valley in the center of the country, was the capital of the captaincy. A small but vibrant mestizo society developed in Santiago, built around a Mediterraneanlike climate and agriculture. The population of the captaincy-general of Chile was less than a million, and probably half of the inhabitants were of racially-mixed blood, primarily Indians and Spaniards. There were probably fewer than 20,000 blacks and only about 5,000 slaves. About 100,000 Indians were primarily concentrated in the southern half of the colony in what amounted to virtually an autonomous state. A wealthy and powerful elite was dominated by some two hundred families whose wealth came primarily from the land (farming, ranching, and mining) and commerce. The Bourbon reforms had given the Chileans greater trading opportunities and administrative independence, and a stronger sense of regional autonomy.

As was done in Buenos Aires, in 1810 the Chileans convened a junta of upper-class creoles and Spaniards professing their loyalty to Fernando VII. Chileans now governed themselves, but the junta, and most others, remained loyal to the imprisoned Fernando VII. An invasion force of Spanish troops from Peru landed in March 1813 to take on the rebels. One of the most outspoken proponents of independence was Bernardo O'Higgins, and he quickly emerged as a popular military hero. O'Higgins is one of the most unusual and fascinating figures in that small pantheon of the great liberators of the Americas. His Irish father, Ambrosio O'Higgins, rose through the ranks of the Spanish American bureaucracy, eventually becoming the Viceroy of Peru. (It was not unusual for Catholics from outside Spain to work in imperial administration, but few rose so high in the system.) Born in 1778 in Chillán, Bernardo was educated in England, where he came under the influence of Miranda. Ambrosio O'Higgins died in 1801, and his son received an inheritance of considerable estates. Bernardo returned to Chile in 1802 to the life of the rich landowner. By 1810, he had begun to raise his own militia. O'Higgins viewed the formation of the junta in September 1810 as a "revolution" and he did not use the term lightly. He wrote to a friend that he had not yet "dared to declare openly that . . . independence from Spain and the establishment of republican institutions . . . has been our real aim from the beginning of the revolution."

When the viceroy of Peru sent troops into Chile in 1813, O'Higgins accepted the post of commander-in-chief for the forces of the rebels. Divisions among the Chilean rebels weakened their efforts and after a defeat at the Battle of Rancagua in October 1814, O'Higgins fled across the Andes to Argentina. Fortunately for the rebels, the Peruvian viceroy attempted to reimpose a harsh system that reasserted Spanish control and alienated large numbers of creoles. While O'Higgins helped San Martín train and equip an "Army of the Andes" in Mendoza, the royalists imprisoned creole patriots. The government confiscated their properties, destroyed their homes, and compelled them to make forced loans. Spanish royalists became the most effective force in creating patriots anxious for independence.

The years 1814–16 were tough ones for the rebels all over Spanish America, with the return to power of Fernando VII. He repudiated the Constitution of 1812 and chose foolishly to return to a regime more absolutist and colonial than his father or grandfather had imposed. Fresh troops arrived by the thousands from Spain and, in many colonies, shifted the balance of power against the rebels (as we have already seen in northern South America). In the period 1814–16, in northern South America, Upper Peru, and Chile, the rebel forces were in retreat.

San Martín's march through the Andes and the defeat of the Spanish in Chile is a story of epic proportions. In early January 1817, the Army of the Andes began its ascent in the dead of winter. San Martín's main forces moved through passes around the towering Aconcagua peak. It took them more than three weeks to reach the summit of the pass at more than 12,000 feet above sea level. As they ascended through the Los Patos Pass the cold and altitude sickness began to take their toll—on the men and animals—and San Martín lost nearly half of his supplies and hundreds of men. The battered forces moved into the central valley of Chile, regrouped, and defeated the royalists at Chacabuco (near Santiago) in February 1817. San Martín entered Santiago in triumph. At his insistence, the glory went to Bernardo O'Higgins, who was named Supreme Dictator of Chile. (For most Chileans, O'Higgins is one of the two greatest figures in the creation of the nation.) The royalists regrouped and defeated San Martín in March 1818 before he definitively vanquished them on the plains of Maipó outside Santiago in April 1818. Maipó was, according to San Martín, the battle that "decided the fate of South America." He returned to Buenos Aires, once again, to mobilize funds and men for the final assault on Peru.

PERU

The first wave of wars for independence in Spanish America barely touched Peru, the great prize in South America, the wealthy heartland of the Andean world. Along with Mexico, Peru was one of the two core regions in Spanish America. Although they had been eclipsed by the Mexican silver mines in the eighteenth century, the mines at Potosí in Upper Peru were still rich and productive. The geography of the viceroyalty was imposing and spectacular, from the deserts of the coast to the towering mountains of the interior to the east. The Andean highlands were overwhelmingly Indian. Whites lived primarily on the coast around Lima, with another cluster around the old Inca capital of Cuzco in the highlands. With a population over one million in 1800, the descendants of the Incas probably accounted for 60 to 65 percent of the population. Mestizos probably accounted for about 20 percent and black slaves less than 5 percent. About 10 to 15 percent of the population was white. The Peruvian upper class was notorious for its conservatism and loyalty to the Crown. As in Mexico, the creole elites in Peru feared the specter of Indian uprisings and they were reluctant to challenge Spanish authority. The bloody Túpac Amaru uprising in 1780–81 remained a vivid memory.

In the aftermath of the Napoleonic crisis, Viceroy José Fernando de Abascal worked energetically and effectively to blunt any moves toward independence. Abascal arrived in Peru in 1806, and when the crisis erupted in Spain in 1808, he moved quickly to mobilize troops, both Spanish and creole. Building up his armed forces, he used them repeatedly across the region, and countered every move toward constitutionalism and reform. Peru became a base for countering rebellions in Ecuador, New Granada, Chile, and even Buenos Aires and Montevideo. Abascal had enormous disdain for creoles, calling them "men born to vegetate in obscurity and abasement." The return of Fernando VII to the throne in 1814, and his rejection of the Constitution of 1812, reinforced the authoritarian rule of Abascal and the loyalists.

After his return from Argentina, San Martín finally moved north from Chile in 1820 on the final stage of his strategy to liberate Spanish South America. He was assisted by one of the most colorful of all the figures of the wars for independence, the renegade British naval officer, Thomas Cochrane, the Earl of Dundonald. Cochrane was an exceptionally brilliant naval officer who always managed to create trouble for himself, with his commanding officers, and with powerful politicians. Scandals, military and financial, seemed to follow him throughout his life. He left England in 1818 and was hired by the Chileans to create a naval force for the invasion of Peru. In August 1820, Cochrane sailed with 4,500 troops to the coast of Peru, landing at Pisco, 150 miles south of Lima. Spanish forces eventually retreated from Lima into the mountains. San Martín took control of the Peruvian capital and declared Peru's independence on July 28, 1821. There was no Peruvian equivalent of Sucre or O'Higgins, so San Martín was named the "Protector" of Peru. He was, however, unable to subdue the interior and defeat the Spanish forces. Nearly a year after his triumphant entry into Lima, he sailed north to Guayaquil, Ecuador, to confer with Simón Bolívar.

San Martín's failure to finish off the struggle in Peru led to one of the pivotal moments in the liberation of Spanish South America—a historic meeting of the two principal figures of the wars—the Liberator and the Protector. By the time they met, San Martín's fortunes were in decline and Bolívar's ascending. San Martín had been bogged down in Peru, and forced to retreat from Lima, while Bolívar was coming off the conquest of Quito and the liberation of Ecuador. For several hours on July 26–27, 1822, the two met, alone. Neither of the two left a direct account of the encounter. Afterwards, Bolívar hosted a grand banquet toasting "the two greatest men in South America, San Martín and myself." San Martín withdrew, leaving the liberation of Peru in the hands of Bolívar. "For me," he wrote to Bolívar, "it would have been the height of happiness to end the war of independence under the orders of a general to whom America owes its freedom. Destiny orders it otherwise, and one must resign oneself to it." San Martín later described Bolívar as "a man of extreme fickleness of principle and full of childish vanity." He left South America for Europe, and a self-imposed exile. José de San Martín, the Protector, died in Paris in 1850 at the age of 72.

Having cleared the field of his major rival, Simón Bolívar moved on to complete the liberation of Spanish South America. He sent his trusted lieutenant, José Antonio de Sucre, into Peru. Bolívar arrived in September 1823, but fell deathly ill, possibly his first major bout with tuberculosis. At this very moment, events in Europe took a crucial turn as absolutism reemerged in Spain and Portugal and threatened to reenergize the loyalist cause in Latin America. First England, then the United States, responded, announcing their opposition to European involvement in the Americas. In December 1823, President James Monroe made a statement (written by John Quincy Adams) announcing his opposition to any "foreign" intervention in the Americas. This later became known as the Monroe Doctrine, a bold statement for a young nation—one that was unenforceable without the cooperation of the British Navy.

A series of crucial battles finally broke the back of royalist resistance. In August 1824, Bolívar defeated the royalist forces at Junín after yet another epic march through the Andes. On December 9, 1824, Sucre conclusively defeated the royalist forces at Ayacucho. This was to be the last great battle in the wars for independence in Spanish South America (although the last

Spanish troops on the mainland of South America would not surrender until January 1826). Bolívar was now President of Colombia and Dictator of Peru. He bestowed upon his fellow Venezuelan general the title of "Grand Marshal of Ayacucho." Sucre would move on to liberate Upper Peru in the final battles of the Spanish American wars in April 1825, and he presided over the creation of a new nation, called Bolivia in honor of the Liberator. Bolívar was named president, but left Sucre to rule in his stead, and he returned to Colombia. Sucre was assassinated by enemies of Bolívar in June 1830.

But what of Simón Bolívar in the aftermath of final victory? In early 1826, Bolívar was 42 years old. He had led the liberation of five new nations in 15 years, covering territories larger than Europe. He had established himself as one of the greatest military figures in the modern world. At least in theory, he was the head of state in Bolivia, Peru, Ecuador, New Granada, and Venezuela. Amidst the threat of civil war, he returned to Bogotá in 1826. Waiting for him was the beautiful Manuela Sáenz, the second great love of his life. In September 1828, some of his enemies tried to kill Bolívar, but he was saved at the last minute by the intrepid Manuela, who was beaten badly by the attackers. (He subsequently called her "the liberator of the Liberator.") Bolívar decided to go into exile. As he headed for the Caribbean coast, he received the news of the assassination of Sucre. Devastated by the death of his protégé and his inability to forge a political consensus, he wrote the following famous (pessimistic) lines, "I have arrived at only a few sure conclusions: 1. For us, America is ungovernable. 2. He who serves a revolution ploughs the sea. 3. The only thing we can do in America is emigrate. 4. This country will eventually fall into the hands of the unbridled mob, and will proceed to almost imperceptible petty tyrannies of all complexions and races." It was a bitter conclusion to a life of exceptional achievements. On December 17,1830, he died on the Colombian coast at Santa Marta, probably of tuberculosis. He was 47 years old.

MEXICO AND CENTRAL AMERICA

Mexico and Central America took paths very different from those taken in Spanish South America. Mexico was the richest colony of Spain and its elites had more at stake in the struggle for independence than in any other colony in the Americas. Since the sixteenth century, its large Indian labor force and rich silver mines had produced great wealth for Spain and the colonial elites. With a population of some six million in 1800, the Viceroyalty of New Spain contained *one-third* of all the inhabitants of Spanish America. New Spain covered an immense expanse from Mexico southward to Guatemala, and north into much of what today is the

Southwest of the United States, from Texas to California. Mexico City was the largest urban center in all of the Americas, with a population of nearly 170,000 in 1810. Indians made up 60 percent of the population, another 20 percent were racially mixed (the *castas*), and the rest were whites. European-born Spaniards probably numbered around 15,000, less than one-half of 1 percent of the population, but they controlled the political and administrative machinery of the viceroyalty. Half of those *peninsulares* (or *gachupines*, as they were derogatorily called) were soldiers. New Spain was the classic Spanish American colony, where several thousand peninsular Spaniards ruled over a million creoles who in turn ruled over five million Indians and mestizos.

By the end of the eighteenth century, Mexico provided Madrid with enormous profits and created the richest family fortunes in the Americas. At the same time, the masses suffered greatly through ten major famines in the century before 1810. Terrible drought in 1808–9 and famine in 1810–11 produced conditions very similar to Old Regime France in 1789. Mexico's revolution in 1810, like the one in 1910, had its roots in the hunger and desperation of the poor Indian masses.

In the aftermath of the Napoleonic invasion of Spain in 1808, with the creoles discussing the formation of a junta to rule in the name of Fernando, the *peninsulares* were alarmed that the viceroy was sympathetic to creole wishes. In a conservative coup d'état, they forced him out and sent him back to Spain in September 1808. They proceeded to arrest and imprison the major creole radicals. One had been so daring as to assert that "authority came to the king from God, but not directly, rather through the people." The first wave of revolution was led by a parish priest, Miguel Hidalgo y Costilla. A creole and the son of a hacienda manager, Hidalgo was born in 1753 in Guanajuato. He received a university education in Mexico City, and was ordained a priest in 1788. One of the great Mexican historians of the period described him as a man "of dark complexion, with lively green eyes, rather bald and white-haired." In 1803, he became the parish priest in the town of Dolores in the arid Mexican north. Along with other creoles in nearby Querétaro he hatched a conspiracy to oust the Spanish. They had the radical notion of mobilizing local Indians and mestizos to join their cause, and they (mistakenly) believed the Indians could be controlled.

Hidalgo triggered the war for Mexican independence on September 16, 1810. At mass on Sunday morning, Hidalgo called for rebellion with the so-called *Grito* (or Cry) *de Dolores*. In the following weeks, some 60,000 peasants, primarily Indians, rallied to his call, chiefly armed with bows and arrows, lances, and machetes. Their rallying cry was, "Long live independence and death to the Spaniards!" His call to seize the property of Europeans, abolish Indian tribute, and to invoke the support of the Virgin of Guadalupe had enormous appeal to the poor masses. The Indians were especially devoted to the Virgin and she became the rallying symbol for the assertion of their own identity. This army of poor peasants converged on the mining center of Guanajuato in September 1810, brutally annihilating creoles and *peninsulares* who had barricaded themselves in the massive stone granary in the center of the city.

Hidalgo's agrarian radicalism and the racial and social nature of the revolt alienated both creoles and *peninsulares*. His was a classic revolutionary movement of the masses. Very quickly the cry of revolution became "independence and liberty." Hidalgo called for the abolition of slavery, the end of Indian tribute, and, ultimately, for the redistribution of land to the dispossessed Indians. Hidalgo's radicalism turned creoles into supporters of the colonial government, and as the creoles became more conservative, he became more radical. The fighting became increasingly brutal as both sides executed prisoners. After hesitating on the outskirts of Mexico City with some 80,000 men, Hidalgo was defeated. Betrayed and ambushed, Hidalgo was captured and executed in March 1811. His head and those of three of his fellow key conspirators were hung from the four corners of the granary in Guanajuato as a lesson to those who might seek to challenge royal authority.

With the death of Hidalgo, the leadership of the rebellion passed to another parish priest, José María Morelos, who was even more closely attuned to the life of the Mexican masses than Hidalgo. Born in 1765 in Valladolid, Michoacán (now named Morelia in his honor), he came from a poor mestizo family. Morelos joined up with Hidalgo within weeks of the uprising and, within a year, he had created a small, but highly effective, guerrilla army south of Mexico City. Morelos presented a manifesto that set out the principles of his movement to a rebel congress at Chilpancingo in September 1813. The "Sentiments of the Nation" contains 22 brief articles beginning with one that declares "That America is free and independent of Spain and every other nation." His thought was radically egalitarian, devoutly Catholic, and fiercely nationalist. In one proclamation he declared that, "All the inhabitants except Europeans will no longer be designated as Indians, mulattoes or other castes, but all will be known as Americans."

Unlike Hidalgo, Morelos tried very hard to rally the support of creoles. Like Hidalgo, Morelos was too radical for them. Eventually captured in November 1814, he was handed over to the Inquisition, charged with heresy, defrocked, and then tried and condemned of treason. Morelos's execution by firing squad on December 22, 1815, effectively ended the armed uprising Hidalgo had begun in September 1810. The first wave of the war for Mexican independence, a potential social revolution, died with Morelos. The fear of race war and social revolution had forged a powerful unity among creoles and *peninsulares*. As in the early stages of the revolution in Haiti and Venezuela, race trumped the grievances of the creoles and their anger at the *peninsulares*.

After the defeat of Hidalgo and Morelos, the royalists developed effective means to blunt the thrust of revolution. Royalist forces probably numbered as many as 85,000 by 1820. This was not, however, a peninsular army occupying New Spain, but rather a creole and mestizo force. Ninety-five percent of the royalist military forces were Mexicans. In January 1820, a liberal revolt in Spain forced Fernando VII to restore the Constitution of 1812 and convene a parliament (*cortes*). This new Cortes was more radical in its liberalism than its predecessor in 1812 and it soon angered the powerful in Mexico. In true liberal fashion, the Cortes abolished special privileges that the Church and military had long enjoyed, privileges (such as special courts and tax exemptions) known as *fueros*. At the same time, the Cortes refused to accept the creole proposals for greater political autonomy and free trade. There was something here to alienate everyone with power.

The principal figure in Mexican independence was Agustín de Iturbide. Hardly the equal of Bolívar or San Martín, Iturbide was a tragic and weak character. Born in 1783 (the same year as Bolívar), he came from a wealthy family in western Mexico. He was a model Mexican creole: fearful of social revolution, devoutly Catholic, and staunchly nationalistic. The Spanish appointed Iturbide commander of the royalist army in the south in 1820. Although he was charged with defeating rebels led by Vicente Guerrero, he soon formulated a plan to join forces with them. In what the Canadian historian Timothy Anna calls "a calculated act of treason," Iturbide consulted with rebel and royalist leaders and drew up a document that Guerrero accepted. The two commanders joined forces and others allied with them. There was something for everyone in this brilliant, pragmatic declaration, which was ultimately impossible to fulfill. On February 24, 1821, Iturbide issued his *Plan de Iguala*, a call for constitutional monarchy, and the protection of "union, religion, and independence." The plan was quickly supported by the Church, the army, and the upper classes, as well as liberal creoles.

On September 28, a ruling junta issued a Declaration of Independence of "the Mexican Empire." In a staged demonstration led by Iturbide's own troops, the "masses" pressured the new congress to name him emperor. The congress caved in and "elected" Iturbide "Constitutional Emperor of the Mexican Empire." He crowned himself Agustín I in an elaborate ceremony on May 21, 1822. In the words of the skeptical Simón Bolívar, Iturbide had become "emperor by the grace of God and of bayonets." Iturbide's reign was short-lived. Disgruntled military commanders began to plot a revolt led by one of the truly extraordinary and bizarre characters in Mexican history, Antonio López de Santa Anna. In the words of John Lynch, "short on revenue, allies and ideas, [Iturbide] abdicated on March 19, 1823." Mexican independence was achieved, and social revolution averted.

Stability, however, would be elusive, as centralists and federalists would battle each other for control of the country. For the next 50 years, Mexico would suffer from civil wars, foreign invasions, and the loss of nearly half of its territory.

The independence of Central America is one of the least dramatic and least violent episodes in the age of revolution. Central America had long been one of the most isolated regions of Spanish America. The northern end of the region—Chiapas, Guatemala, El Salvador, and Honduras—had been the center of the ancient Maya empires and had large indigenous populations. At the southern end, Nicaragua and Costa Rica had been conquered by Spanish expeditions launched from Panama and they had sparse Indian populations. In all these regions, the main population centers were inland, often in mountainous highlands away from the coasts of either the Pacific or the Caribbean. By the beginning of the nineteenth century, small but well-developed regional elites and identities had emerged in Guatemala, El Salvador, Honduras, Nicaragua, and Costa Rica. The population of the Kingdom of Guatemala (as Central America was then called) was not much over a million. The majority, especially in the northern regions, was composed of Indians, and most of the rest of the inhabitants were mestizos. The economy was primarily subsistence and export agriculture with some small-scale mining. The region produced cotton, cacao, cattle, and indigo dye for export. The principal preoccupation of the creole elites was access to trade with the British, to sell their products, and to buy cheap British manufactured goods, especially textiles. Contraband was widespread, especially along the Caribbean coast where the British had enclaves at what is now Belize, and on the "Mosquito Coast" of Nicaragua and Honduras.

The creoles of Central America talked of independence even less than the Mexicans. The powerful elite families, especially in the dominant and populous Guatemala, were most concerned with issues of trade and how to stimulate it. They wanted improved transportation, and other infrastructural improvements. Like the Mexican and Andean elites, they had little interest in creating political conflict that might unleash the indigenous and poor masses. José de Bustamante, president of the *audiencia* of Guatemala from 1811 to 17, represented the last surge of Spanish absolutism. Fernando VII attempted to appease rising liberal sentiment in the region by removing Bustamante. The region freely traded with the British by 1818. With the news of Iturbide's proclamation of independence, the Central Americans were compelled to respond. The newly arrived Captain General, Gabino Gaínza, convoked a meeting of local notables on September 15, 1821 in Guatemala City. The assembly voted to approve a declaration of independence written by a Honduran lawyer, José Cecilio del Valle. In a sense, nothing had changed—Spain no longer had the ability to send in troops to challenge the declaration, and the local elites who had controlled power in the region still controlled it.

The other provinces of Central America reacted to the vote in Guatemala. Both El Salvador and Nicaragua declared their independence from Spain *and* Guatemala. A revolt broke out in Honduras, and the Costa Ricans (supposedly under the rule of Nicaragua) declared their own independence. In June 1822, a small army from Mexico marched into the region occupying El Salvador. When Iturbide's Mexican Empire collapsed in March 1823, the invasion fizzled. In July 1823, a constituent assembly declared the creation of the United Provinces of Central America. The five provinces (Guatemala, El Salvador, Honduras, Nicaragua, and Costa Rica) joined together under a federalist constitution in 1824. (Chiapas chose to join its fortunes with Mexico.) For the next 15 years, Liberals and Conservatives would battle across the isthmus until the confederation collapsed into five independent nations.

By 1824, the wars for independence in Mexico and Central America had ended. The social revolution that Hidalgo and Morelos had pursued in Mexico had been crushed, as creoles and *peninsulares* united in a counterrevolution. The conservative actions of the creoles in both Mexico and Central America ultimately moved them to break with Spain, but only when the metropolis could no longer protect them or offer them any visible benefits. Revolution produced counterrevolution, and the result was a conservative coup against an impotent foreign monarch. The social structure remained intact and creole elites replaced peninsular elites in the administration of the new nations.

PORTUGUESE AMERICA

In Portugal and Brazil, the path to independence took a decidedly different turn. As in Spanish America, in Brazil a small white population was at the top of a social and economic pyramid made up overwhelmingly of nonwhite peoples. The Portuguese mixed freely with Africans and Indians, producing a rainbow of peoples with a broader color spectrum than any other region in the Americas. The free mulatto population expanded dramatically and composed perhaps a quarter of the inhabitants of the colony by 1800. The Portuguese colony consisted of a few enclaves along the Atlantic coast, with the exception of the gold mining center of Minas Gerais some two hundred miles to the north of Rio de Janeiro. Bahia on the northeastern coast and Minas Gerais in the southeast were the economic and population centers. Rio de Janeiro had become the colonial capital in 1763 because of its role as the gateway to the gold fields.

In 1789, the reassertion of imperial control and the imposition of new taxes sparked an abortive revolt by colonial elites in Vila Rica, the capital of Minas Gerais. An early sign of Brazilian nationalism, the Minas Conspiracy (*Inconfidência Mineira*) involved very prominent elite figures as well as military officers. Treason was not a crime treated lightly by absolute monarchs, and royal tribunals sentenced most of the conspirators to prison or exile. The only nonaristocratic member of the conspiracy, a military officer by the name of Joaquim José da Silva Xavier, became the scapegoat. Best known by his nickname, *Tiradentes* (Toothpuller), he was hung and then drawn and quartered in 1792. The Crown placed parts of his body on pikes on the road leading into Vila Rica as a warning to others who might contemplate challenging royal authority.

Wisely, Lisbon recognized the roots of colonial discontent and employed persuasion along with power to co-opt as well as crush challenges to the imperial system. Over the next few decades (in contrast to the Spanish and British empires), the colonial elites and the government in Lisbon worked to strengthen their interdependence. Without Brazilian gold and sugar, Portugal faced economic ruin. Without the support of Portuguese troops, Brazilian miners and planters faced the specter of rebellion by the slave majority. The Haitian Revolution gave white planter minorities nightmares throughout the Americas. Brazilian slave owners, living amidst a slave majority, understood the fragile repressive line between order and chaos, and they were not overly anxious to challenge established authority.

For at least a decade, the Portuguese monarchy had anticipated a French invasion, and when it came, in 1807, the Crown did not accept the surrender and imprisonment that would be the fate of the Spanish monarchy. Recognizing that Brazil *was* the Portuguese economy, and preferring exile to imprisonment, the Portuguese monarchy fled Lisbon shortly before French troops entered the city. Ten thousand Portuguese joined the royal family on British ships in November 1807 for an unprecedented voyage across the Atlantic. With the help of their British allies (Napoléon's bitter enemies), the Portuguese monarchy transferred the center of the empire to Rio de Janeiro. For the first—and last—time in Western history, a European monarch would rule his empire from the colonies. Prince Regent (and later King) João arrived in Brazil in early 1808 and for the next 13 years ruled Portugal's Asian, African, and American colonies from the "tropical Versailles" he constructed in Rio de Janeiro. While the Spanish American colonies warred with Spain for their independence, Brazil flourished as the center of the Portuguese empire. João established the cultural and political institutions of an imperial center, institutions that Brazil had sorely lacked. By 1821, 150,000 of Brazil's 3 million inhabitants lived in Rio. Slaves probably comprised half the colony's population, the racially mixed accounted for another quarter of the inhabitants, and the Portuguese-born (known as *mazombos*) probably numbered about 100,000. In 1815, João elevated Brazil to the status of a kingdom, placing it on an equal footing with Portugal. The presence of the monarchy and the court in Rio brought Brazilian and Portuguese elites together, and it paved the way for a gradual transition to independence.

The end of the Napoleonic wars in Europe in 1815 opened the way for the monarchy to return to Lisbon, but João remained in Brazil. In 1821, a new and aggressive Portuguese parliament (the Cortes) produced a constitution that restricted the king's power, and also returned Brazil to colonial status. Threatened with the loss of his crown, João VI reluctantly returned to a divided Portugal. Legend has it that he left his twenty-three-year-old son, Pedro, in Brazil with some sage advice. João recognized the desire of Brazilians for self-rule and saw that the Cortes wanted to return to the old imperial system. Wishing to avoid the bloodshed that had fragmented the Spanish American colonies, he warned Pedro not to fight the rising movement for independence. Instead, he told him to join and lead the movement if it became powerful. The king, in effect, told the crown prince to rebel against the monarchy in the event that conflict emerged. Better to have father and son on two thrones than to lose Brazil to revolutionary leaders.

Pedro followed his father's advice. His refusal to return to Portugal, and his defiance of orders from the Cortes, cemented his role as the leader of independence. On September 7, 1822, while traveling in the interior near São Paulo, Pedro stopped by a small stream (the Ipiranga) for a brief rest. A messenger arrived with letters from the Cortes that once again challenged his authority. With this came a letter from his closest Brazilian advisor urging Pedro to seize the moment and to break with Portugal. According to one witness, Pedro threw down the letter from the Cortes, ground it under his heel, and drew his saber. With a flourish, he waved the sword and declared, "Independence or death! We have separated from Portugal!" The day on which the "Cry of Ipiranga" was uttered has been celebrated by Brazilians ever since as their independence day. With few troops in Brazil, and civil war erupting between absolutists and constitutionalists at home, Portugal could do little to counter Pedro's unilateral declaration.

England acted as the midwife in the birth of this South American nation. The English had long dominated Portugal's economy and its foreign policy, and the split between crown and colony left the British government in a difficult but pivotal role. Wanting to protect its interests on both sides of the Atlantic, Britain handled negotiations between Lisbon and Rio de Janeiro. Pedro secretly agreed to pay Portugal two million pounds sterling (roughly US$10 million) in compensation for royal properties in Brazil. He also made some formal public concessions in exchange for official Portuguese recognition of Brazil's independence. For their part, the British established themselves (through treaties) as Brazil's dominant trading partner.

CARIBBEAN VARIATIONS

We have now seen about a dozen cases of successful wars for independence from Spain, France, and Portugal. Some of the American colonies, however, did not achieve independence in the Age of Revolution. Some chose not to rebel or the uprisings were weak and relatively easily crushed. Canada and most of the West Indies (French, British, and Dutch) would not follow the path of the United States and most of Spanish and Portuguese America. Some of the islands of the Spanish West Indies came close to becoming part of the United States in the early nineteenth century. In one case (Puerto Rico), an island in the Spanish Caribbean *would* eventually become part of the United States. From the eighteenth century on, the greatest ties and connections between the United States and these islands was trade, especially in sugar, molasses, rum, and slaves. On the eve of the American Revolution, one-third of all the ships leaving New York and Boston went to the West Indies.

Slavery and geography directly contributed to the failure of independence movements in Cuba and Puerto Rico. Much like the U.S. South and Brazil, the elites in the slave societies of the Caribbean were reluctant to pursue wars that might trigger another Haitian Revolution. Both Cuba and Puerto Rico had emerged as rich sugar and tobacco plantation economies in the eighteenth century. Puerto Rico and Cuba had been settled in the first years of the Conquest in the sixteenth century. Puerto Rico became a presidio or military outpost, the Indians died off in droves from disease, and the population remained small for centuries. Cuba, on the other hand, as the largest island of the Greater Antilles, became the principal gateway to the Spanish Empire in the Americas, "the pearl of the Antilles." Havana was the entry and exit point for most traffic, and one of the most heavily fortified cities in the Americas. Cuba had a population of 170,000 in the 1770s, blacks and mulattoes accounted for about 40 percent of the population, and about two-thirds of them were slaves. Despite an intensification of the slave trade at the turn of the nineteenth century, the white population in Cuba and Puerto Rico was much larger, proportionally, than in the other West Indian islands, with Saint Domingue at the other extreme. (All the British islands combined at this time had a white population of less than 60,000.) Just 10 percent of Puerto Rico's inhabitants were slaves, but free blacks and mulattoes comprised nearly 45 percent of the entire population. Its population, however, was small—only about 150,000 in 1800.

The first great shock to the colonial system in Cuba was the British capture of Havana in 1762–63. Spain got Cuba back in the Peace of Paris in 1763, but had to give up Florida in exchange. In the twists and turns of the imperial wars and changing alliances of the late eighteenth century, foreign shipping, both legal and illegal, expanded dramatically. The few who chose to speak of serious reform or autonomy in Cuba and Puerto Rico were quickly suppressed in the early nineteenth century. As in the rest of Latin America, the winds of the Enlightenment blew through Cuba and Puerto Rico. Some extraordinary intellectuals produced a vibrant local press and publications. A few even dared to speak of themselves as "children of colonial despotism." The Haitian Revolution, however, shook the elites in the West Indies profoundly. French planters escaping nearby Saint Domingue brought with them hair-raising horror stories of atrocities. They also brought with them capital and expertise. Beginning in the 1790s, the Cuban elites pushed an ambitious, and very successful, program to expand sugar and slavery.

The Napoleonic invasion and the imprisonment of Fernando VII unleashed the same forces in Cuba and Puerto Rico that they did in the rest of Spanish America. As war raged in Spain, the Cubans and Puerto Ricans discussed options, called councils, and formed juntas. The young United States had acquired Louisiana in 1803 and Florida in 1819. Many U.S. political leaders, including John Quincy Adams, believed that Cuba would also eventually be purchased and annexed to the United States. Thomas Jefferson quietly made inquiries about purchasing Cuba from Spain to prevent it from falling under French or English control.

The wars on the mainland also produced a steady flow of loyalists seeking refuge in Cuba and Puerto Rico. Some 20,000 arrived in Cuba in the 1820s, reinforcing the royalist cause on the island. Havana and San Juan also became bases for troops moving from Spain to the wars in the mainland colonies. In the words of one Cuban historian, Cuba and Puerto Rico became "the barns and bastions of the metropolis in the New World." In a sense, the question for the Cubans and Puerto Ricans was threefold: to stay with Spain, to seek independence, or to join the United States. As the mainland colonies of Spain achieved their independence, the government of Fernando VII managed to hold on to Cuba and Puerto Rico. By 1818, they both had achieved, for all intents and purposes, free trade. Spanish troops helped guarantee the social peace, and reassure nervous planters.

The Dominican Republic is perhaps the most complex case of all the movements for independence in the Americas in the nineteenth century. The site of the original Spanish colonial settlements in the Americas, the island of Hispaniola was supplanted by Cuba as the great administrative and commercial center in the Caribbean. After the late seventeenth century, Santo Domingo's history was forged in a tense relationship with Haiti to the west. The rapid growth of the sugar and slave complex in Saint-Domingue overshadowed the less populous Spanish colony on the eastern end of the island. The outbreak of the Haitian Revolution initiated a half-century of struggle in Santo Domingo. From 1791 to 1803, the French, English, and Spanish fought over the entire island. In 1800, Toussaint Louverture occupied

Santo Domingo on two occasions. Although the Haitians ousted the French in 1803, Napoléon's troops remained in Santo Domingo until 1809. The junta in Seville reclaimed the territory in the name of Spain when the French left. The Haitians far outnumbered the Dominicans (nearly ten to one) and they invaded in 1822, led by President Jean Pierre Boyer. Haiti would dominate the entire island until 1843, when Boyer fell from power. Juan Pablo Duarte led the fight for an independent Dominican Republic and is today recognized as its national hero. Independence was proclaimed on February 27, 1844.

The Spanish West Indies—Cuba, Puerto Rico, and Santo Domingo—provide counterexamples to the successes in the wars for independence across the Americas. They clearly demonstrate that, despite the converging forces of intellectual, political, and economic ferment, independence in colonial America in the early nineteenth century was neither inevitable nor unavoidable. The history of this period from the 1770s to the 1820s shares common traits because all of these nations had their roots in a common process of conquest and colonization. The colonial elites all read, discussed, and exchanged the ideas of the age. Yet, despite this shared culture, they went their different ways. While the U.S. revolutionaries engaged in a war of political ideas and principles, the Latin Americans were less interested and engaged in debates over political discourse. This is clear when we look at how we now tell the histories of the wars: the war for independence in the United States is a story of disagreements over political principles. The story in Latin America is not about liberty and equality, or how to define them, but about who will control power. Much of U.S. history in the aftermath of the revolution is about how to implement the political ideals of the founding moment. In Latin America, the discussion of liberal ideals and principles is very weak and minimal, and the focus is on war and maintaining elite control. Despite the liberal principles behind the wars for independence in Latin America, these principles do not flourish in the aftermath of independence.

The wars for independence in most of Latin America ended in the mid-1820s, having lasted nearly two decades. Without significant assistance from outside the region, with a divided colonial elite, and always facing the possibility of race and class warfare, the wars for independence had succeeded in most (but not all) of Spain and Portugal's old American colonies. As the "Americans" took power across the region and Spanish, Portuguese, French, and English control receded, the new nations embarked upon the difficult task of nation-building. The creation of new nations in Latin America would prove to be much more difficult than the wars for independence. Establishing peace would be more difficult than making war.

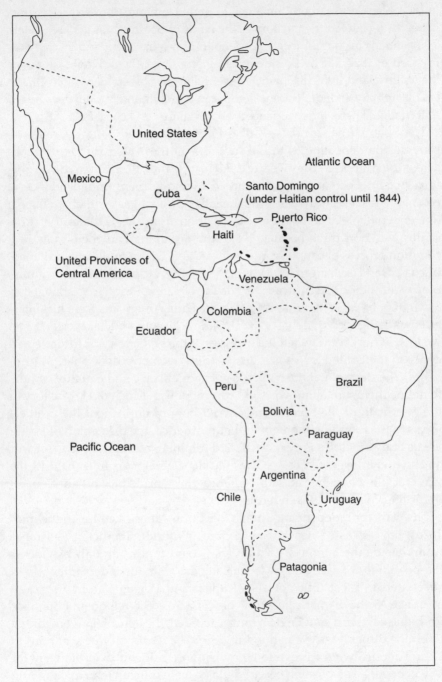

Map 6. Latin America in 1830

Part III

Forging a New Order

14

Liberals, Conservatives, and Disorder

By the 1840s, 18 new nations had emerged out of the wars for independence and the collapse of the Iberian empires in the Americas. (Puerto Rico and Cuba remained Spanish colonies, while Florida was incorporated into the United States in 1819, along with much of northern Mexico in the 1840s.) Much like the people of the United States after the 1780s, the peoples of Latin America faced daunting challenges in the construction of new nation-states, and those in regions incorporated into the United States found themselves in new legal, religious, and political worlds that would produce new cultural paths. In the aftermath of independence, Latin America would be plagued by political factionalism, regionalism, militarism, social unrest, and economic challenges. Stability, both political and economic, had to be achieved to begin a sustained process of nation-building. Even more complicated would be the creation of national communities (what the renowned anthropologist Benedict Anderson has called "imagined communities"). In a region where "white" Europeans and Euro-Americans were a minority (in some cases, a tiny minority), and where the vast majority of the population was composed of non-European peoples (Native Americans, Africans, and their racially and culturally mixed descendants), the task of constructing a sense of national identity as Mexicans, Peruvians, Brazilians, or Argentines would be as complicated and complex as constructing effective political and economic systems. In the first 50 years after independence, most of the new nations of Latin America would face enormous difficulties *beginning* the process of nation-building. In most cases, the process would not be *consolidated* until the twentieth century, especially the construction of national communities.

THE PURSUIT OF A NEW REGIME

In the aftermath of the age of revolution, across all the Americas, perhaps the principal political dilemma was the nature of the relationship between a central government and subnational units (states, departments, or provinces). After 1780, the United States emerged as a vibrant and dynamic new nation, one with a 30- to 40-year head start on the nations of Latin America. Like Latin America, the United States grappled with political instability and the nature of the relationship between central and state authority. This struggle first emerged in the debates over the writing of the Constitution and its passage into law in the 1780s. The Bill of Rights—the first ten amendments to the Constitution—in effect, are concessions to the opponents of centralism. They are guarantees of the rights of individuals and the states against the power of a central, national government. Yet, even this visionary new political order was torn between the full realization of its democratic and republican principles and the continuing growth and importance of slavery in the U.S. South. Slavery would ultimately create an unresolvable impasse that would only be settled by a devastating civil war that killed 600,000 men and women and emancipated four million Africans and African-Americans.

The U.S. South, like many of the regions of Latin America, had emerged out of a common process of conquest and colonization. In the late eighteenth century, nearly all the American colonies were paternalistic and hierarchically structured, with economies geared toward exports to, and profits for, the metropolis (London, Madrid, Lisbon, Paris). Many were built on the exploitation of unfree labor, whether African slaves or indigenous peoples. All the new nations of the Americas struggled (for decades) with their multiracial, hierarchical, and racist colonial heritage. Much of the history of the Americas over the last two centuries has been shaped by the efforts of American nations to dismantle the injustices of these persistent colonial legacies.

The 18 new nations of Latin America embarked on the process of nation-building following many different paths in the early nineteenth century. They all grappled with the central-government-versus-decentralization dilemma and, ultimately, they constructed governments much more centralized than the United States. The great political divide in Latin America in the nineteenth century was between Liberals and Conservatives. Not really political parties in the modern sense of the term, Liberals and Conservatives were ideological groups that very often represented kinship networks and regional loyalties. "Conservatism," in the words of Peter Bakewell, "was not so much a political creed as a form of political inertia, a quite expectable and natural clustering together of many of the rich and eminent who suddenly found themselves deprived of the props that the Spanish presence had provided." At least in theory, Conservatives looked back to the past, hoping to preserve as much of the old colonial order as possible. They looked back to Spain and Portugal for their cultural heritage and roots. Strong, central governments ruled by a powerful executive (a monarch, if possible) was their preference. Conservatives wanted to retain the traditional social structure, hold on to old privileges and hierarchies, maintain slavery and forced Indian labor, and they supported the Catholic Church and its traditional cultural and religious primacy. Finally, they were wary of free trade and hoped to maintain strong government intervention in the economy (i.e., protectionism and monopolies).

Liberals, on the other hand, saw their future in the models provided by England, France, and the United States. In theory, they wanted a decentralized government with a loose confederation of states or provinces. They called for liberty, equality, and the end of social hierarchy, slavery, Indian tribute, and the power of the Catholic Church. They also wanted to open their economies to international commerce through free trade (Adam Smith's *laissez-faire*). I emphasize *in theory* because once Liberals gained power they almost always moved to construct strong central governments, and they rarely made any serious efforts to extend liberty and equality beyond their own small social networks. Once they were in power, it was often difficult to distinguish Liberal from Conservative regimes. Bitter, and sometimes bloody, conflicts between Liberals and Conservative ravaged much of Latin America in the nineteenth century.

Some nations—such as Brazil, Costa Rica, and Chile—fairly quickly achieved political stability and this allowed them to begin the complex process of turning new countries into true nations. All three were able to begin to build their economies and political structures by the 1840s, much sooner than most of Latin America. At the other extreme, countries like Mexico and Peru experienced decades of political instability and they could not begin the process of nation-building for two generations. The other 13 nations of Latin America fell somewhere in between these two extremes on a continuum of political and economic stability. All the nations of Latin America would struggle with two principal problems in the early years of independence. They had to achieve political stability and begin to build a viable economy for the new nation. To do this they first had to resolve the (often bitter) conflict between Liberals and Conservatives.

Latin America would also be plagued by the rise of dictatorial rulers (caudillos) in the aftermath of independence, on the side of both the Liberals and the Conservatives. Militarism and caudillos would cripple much of Latin America in the nineteenth century, and leave an enduring legacy of authoritarianism and dictatorship in many countries. Regional revolts and factionalism would intensify the processes of political fragmentation.

In general, the Conservatives had the upper hand across most of Latin America until the 1870s. It was only in the last third of the nineteenth century that Liberals assumed power just about everywhere, and most of Latin America began to open up to international trade and enter fully into the Atlantic economy. Many economic historians point to the "lost" half-century between independence and "insertion" into the international economy, as *the* primary reason for Latin America's slow economic growth and underdevelopment in the twentieth century.

Latin America, then, became independent later than the United States, started with a weaker economic base, and then fell even further behind in the nineteenth century. The region has strong similarities to the U.S. South, and the U.S. South had the "advantage" of its ties to the dynamic, industrializing U.S. North. The South would not break from its more conservative, hierarchical, slave heritage until forced to do so by the North after the Civil War through what some historians see as the "Second American Revolution." Nothing equivalent to the wrenching economic and political revolution that transformed the U.S. South would take place in the nations of Latin America in the nineteenth century. Independence put new groups into power (primarily the creole elites), but social structures largely remained intact (with the notable exception of Haiti). All of the new nations of Latin America would eventually enter into an Atlantic economic system dominated by England and, to a lesser degree, by the United States. Their late entry compelled the nations of Latin America to seek exports that did not have to compete with British and U.S. manufactured goods. They pursued what economists would call their "comparative advantage"—the export of natural resources and agricultural commodities. By the end of the nineteenth century, most of the nations of Latin America had become single product/crop (monoculture) economies exporting coffee, sugar, bananas, cacao, copper, silver, wheat, or beef.

War and revolution are powerful forces capable of fundamentally transforming societies, but their impact is never predictable. The revolutionaries from North America to southern South America recognized the explosive power war might have on their hierarchical, racially diverse, and elitist social structures. To return to Bolívar's vivid simile, the creole elites knew that unleashing war would be like riding a tiger, and that if they fell off they might be mauled—or devoured. Some of them were ravaged by the tiger they had unleashed. Hidalgo, Morelos, and Sucre are just a few examples. Those leaders who survived and won often became powerful caudillos, and then fought each other for control of the new nations. The United States was fortunate that its first and most powerful caudillo was George Washington and that he was not a Bonaparte or a Bolívar. In the aftermath of independence, the caudillos in Latin America would provide stability—through dictatorial rule—or instability as they fought among themselves for the control of the new nations.

THE LEGACY OF WAR: CAUDILLOS, REGIONALISM, FACTIONALISM

In some countries (Mexico, Peru, Venezuela), the wars for independence and their aftermath ravaged the land, destroying or shutting down mines, haciendas, and towns. In others (Brazil, Chile, Costa Rica, Paraguay), the destruction and devastation were minimal, allowing these new nations to move forward with the project of nation-building. In nearly every new nation, caudillos emerged to dominate politics. This untranslatable term (literally meaning "little chief" in Spanish) is one of the most important in Latin American history. Referring to a strong, charismatic leader, the caudillos of the early nineteenth century primarily emerged out of the military leaders of the wars for independence and their aftermath. Often a local leader, sometimes of nonelite origins, the caudillo embodied the martial virtues of the macho warrior who won the admiration of his men (and women) through his ability to lead on the battlefield. (The term eventually became divorced from its rural, military origins and became a way to denote powerful, personalistic leaders in later decades and the twentieth century.) As Peter Bakewell has observed, the caudillo is one of the chief legacies of the wars for independence: "Before the wars, there were no caudillos; after them, scarcely a country was without them."

Antonio López de Santa Anna (Mexico), Rafael Carrera (Guatemala), Francisco Paula de Santander (Colombia), José Antonio Páez (Venezuela), Juan José Flores (Ecuador), Manuel Isidoro Belzú (Bolivia), Ramón Castilla (Peru), Bernardo O'Higgins (Chile), Juan Manuel Rosas (Argentina), José Artigas (Uruguay), and José Gaspar Rodríguez de Francia (Paraguay) are but a few of the more infamous examples of the "men on horseback" who emerged out of the wars of independence and their aftermath to dominate or devastate the new nations of Latin America. In Paraguay, Argentina, Central America, and Ecuador, these despotic rulers produced stable regimes (whatever one thinks of their politics or personal characteristics). In Mexico, Colombia and Venezuela, Peru, and Bolivia, bloody internal struggles among caudillos condemned the new nations to decades of instability and disorder. Brazil was unusual in that no true caudillos emerged on the national stage, and a monarch provided the nation with stability and leadership. (Even the United States depended heavily on its military heroes for leadership. Presidents Washington, Harrison, Taylor, and Grant all came to the presidency because of their military feats.)

From Mexico to Brazil and Argentina, the powerful forces of regionalism also threatened the nation-building processes. As we have seen, Central America dissolved into five nations by the late 1830s, Gran Colombia split into three, and Mexico lost Texas in the 1830s (and much more in the 1840s) to the United States. In the cases of Central America and Gran Colombia, this regional fragmentation reflected the long development of well-entrenched regional elites in the colonial period. All four of the old Spanish viceroyalties fragmented and splintered after 1808. Although it had developed significant regional elites, the Portuguese colony did not shatter, but remained intact. Spared from a bloody and destructive war for independence, Brazil faced a series of powerful regional revolts from the far north to the far south into the 1840s.

While militarism, caudillos, and regionalism threatened to tear apart much of Latin America in the nineteenth century, bitter political factionalism added to the disorder and chaos of the period. Something of an elite consensus helped hold together the old colonial regimes in the Americas. Colonial elites worked with metropolitan elites for centuries to produce wealth and keep themselves in power over the large masses of non-European peoples who worked the land that yielded up the agricultural and mining wealth. The wars for independence shattered the elite consensus between creoles and *peninsulares*, and among the creoles themselves. Much of the history of Latin America (and the United States and Canada) in the nineteenth century is about the search for a new elite consensus to reestablish a political stability that would allow economic growth to take place. The elites of Brazil, Chile, and Costa Rica were the first to establish a new consensus (built on the converging interests of large landholders and merchants), and they embarked on their nation-building projects by the 1840s and 1850s. Most of the rest of Latin America (and, in some ways, the dis-United States) would not achieve this new elite consensus until the 1870s. In most of Latin America, this elite political consensus hinged on reducing the conflict between the two dominant political "parties"— Liberals and Conservatives.

LIBERALISM, CAPITALISM, AND THE SEARCH FOR ORDER

Whatever its flaws, the old Ibero-American colonial regimes with "legitimate" authority concentrated in the hands of a monarch and his representatives, imbued by a corporatist ethos, buttressed by the Catholic Church, and structured around corporate interest groups (military, clergy, merchants, and others) provided the colonies with order and stability for centuries. The wars for independence shattered the monarchy's authority, and put into question the legitimacy of the entire hierarchical, corporatist structure of society. The first task facing those attempting to construct new nations was how to put into place a new order—a constitutional one—that could reestablish legitimate authority to avoid chaos, disorder, and even social revolution. Inspired by the French and U.S. constitutions of the late eighteenth century, and the 1812 Constitution of Cádiz, both Liberals and

Conservatives in the early national period proposed (and frequently discarded) an array of constitutions. At the close of the "Age of Revolution," Latin America became the first great testing ground for government by constitutional charter. As one historian has written, "No other part of the world had more constitutions or observed them less."

Three nations experimented with monarchy—in Mexico the effort was (twice) short-lived (1822–23 and 1864–67) and in Haiti the institution lasted until 1859—but only in Brazil did it truly function (1822–89). Eventually, all the new nations adopted republican forms of constitutional regimes. Only two of the constitutions promulgated in the first two decades of independence managed to survive into the twentieth century. (Chile's 1833 Constitution lasted until 1925 and Uruguay's 1830 charter lasted until 1918. The longest surviving constitution in Latin America was Argentina's, from 1853 to 1949.) Many countries wrote and discarded constitutions every four or five years before finding one that would endure into the twentieth century. Ecuador had eight in the nineteenth century, Bolivia had nine before 1878, Peru had eight before 1867, and Colombia had seven, before settling on a constitution in 1886 that remained in force until 1991. The most enduring constitutions were those that were strongly centralist (á la Simón Bolívar). In large part, the large number of failed constitutions in nineteenth-century Latin America reflects the instability of many of the new nations and the drawn-out struggle to reestablish any form of legitimate authority.

At the heart of this struggle was a complex (and ongoing) effort to replace the personalistic, corporatist, hierarchical order of Iberian colonialism with the liberalism of the Enlightenment (a struggle that also took place in the United States and Canada). Liberalism assumes the autonomy of the rational individual capable of using reason to make choices in a society governed by a constitutional order that protects individual rights and equality before the law. At least in theory, liberalism spells the end of special privileges, hierarchy, corporate interest groups, and personalistic rule. In the economic marketplace, liberalism promotes the free and unrestricted movement of goods and services, with a minimally intrusive government that guarantees property rights, contracts, and the rule of law. For the founders of the United States, these principles were best articulated by John Locke and Adam Smith. In nineteenth-century Latin America, both Liberals and Conservatives understood the need for a constitutional order that limited power, and eventually (not until 1889 in Brazil) both groups turned to republican forms of government as the best option. The gradual "triumph" of liberalism, however, was superficial in most places, and the old corporatist ethos persisted (and continues to persist in attenuated forms) in all of Latin America. In most countries, Simón Bolívar's views prevailed—a sort of liberalism tempered by a strong, paternalistic executive authority.

Although real ideological differences did separate Liberals and Conservatives, in practice the "differences were by and large more of detail than of substance," and "mainly of tactics and degree," as David Bushnell has observed. The role of the Roman Catholic Church became the most bitterly divisive issue that split the two groups. For more than three hundred years, the Catholic Church had enjoyed a religious monopoly in the Portuguese and Spanish colonies (see chapter 9) through the *patronato real* (*padroado real* in Portuguese). The Church had been virtually an arm of the state and the clergy (like military officers) enjoyed the privileges of the *fuero* that set them apart legally and socially from others in society. Perhaps more important, the various sectors of the Church (parishes, clergy, religious orders, bishops, for example) had accumulated enormous wealth and resources, in Mexico in particular. For Conservatives, the Church had long provided the cultural values and rituals that formed the very basis of cultural and social order. For the most radical Liberals, the Roman Catholic Church represented the epitome of the ills of the old colonial regime: privilege, hierarchy, and outmoded medieval social and political thought. Liberals deplored and attacked the cultural and ideological influence of the Church throughout society and they resented its economic might. The first they saw as obscurantist and morally dangerous, the second presented real challenges to the aspirations of any government to assert its control of the nation-state.

The bitter division between Liberals and Conservatives over the Catholic Church reflected a much more profound cultural conflict in nineteenth-century Latin America. Leadership of both the Conservatives and Liberals was drawn almost exclusively from the upper reaches of society, and this leadership was overwhelmingly light-skinned and culturally European. In the mid-nineteenth century, the vast majority of the 20 million residents of the new nations of Latin America were Indians (especially in Mexico, Guatemala, Ecuador, Peru, and Bolivia), Africans and their descendants (especially in the Caribbean and Brazil), and peoples of racially and culturally mixed heritage. In those regions with large Indian populations, probably the majority of the population did not speak Spanish. After centuries of cultural and racial mixing, most "Latin Americans" either embodied some sort of mix of European, African, and Native American customs, traditions, and values, or they lived apart from Euro-American society and culture (i.e., cities and large towns). The most important European influence on Native Americans, Africans, and the racially mixed quite clearly was Catholicism. Although the spiritual conquest of Latin America had failed to convert the peoples of the region into European-style Catholics, it had infused all the peoples of Latin America with Catholic values, rituals, and beliefs in some form or fashion. Although the forms of Catholicism practiced among the Maya of the Yucatán, the Aymara of Bolivia, Afro-Brazilian slaves, or elite Chilean creoles may have varied drastically, the Catholic Church claimed them all, and formed a part of all of their communities.

In the fight for control of the nascent nation-states in the early decades of independence, the Liberal vision of individualism, private property, economic development, modernization, and "progress" repeatedly provoked powerful resistance from the poor and oppressed masses across Latin America. From the Maya in the Yucatán and Guatemala to the gauchos on the South American pampas, rural peoples fought tenaciously against Liberals and their efforts to bring European "modernity" to the interior of the continent in the form of private property, railroads, foreign investment, and European culture (clothing, food, music, art). Often, Conservative caudillos rallied the poor masses against the Liberals. The mobilizing force was the preservation of "tradition," community, and local culture, and the protection of the Catholic Church was their principal lightning rod. In the Yucatán, Maya peoples rose up and successfully held off the Mexican army and central government throughout the nineteenth century (the Caste War and Cruzobs). Rafael Carrera mobilized the masses in Guatemala against the Liberals, and Dr. Francia closed off Paraguay to the outside world. All of them were resisting the incursion of "modernity" and changes to their way of life, and the Liberals were the principal enemy as the chief proponents of "progress." Ironically, these peoples were sometimes fighting for the "right" to be left alone to choose their own destiny, one that was not liberal, nor modern, nor European.

In many of these cases, the spark for resistance stemmed from the penetration of modern economic life, that is, capitalism, into the interior. The first few decades after independence were frustrating ones for those seeking to modernize and transform the economies of Latin America. The devastation wreaked by the wars for independence in the 1810s and 1820s continued in some nations (Mexico, Peru, and Venezuela, for example) into the 1860s. In Peru and Mexico, silver production did not return to pre-1810 levels until the 1850s. Even those nations that experienced minimal destruction (such as Brazil, Chile, and Costa Rica) faced enormous obstacles in their search to modernize their economies and enter fully into the expanding capitalist economy as it spread across the globe in the nineteenth century. Difficult geography, lack of transportation systems, inadequate port facilities, low levels of technological development, and (most important) the lack of capital investment hindered economic growth in the decades after independence. As the cutting edge of capitalism in the nineteenth century, Great Britain and the United States were best prepared to provide the new Latin American nations the capital, technology, and expertise they so desperately needed to achieve economic growth.

By the 1820s, Great Britain had begun to ride a wave of economic expansion and prosperity growing out of a half-century of industrial revolution and the peace of post-Napoleonic Europe. The British crisscrossed the globe in search of markets for their goods and capital. In the century following the wars for independence, Great Britain flooded the Latin American republics with investments and manufactured goods. British investors pumped more than 25–30 million pounds sterling (US$125–150 million) into Latin America in the early 1820s, but the speculative "bubble" burst in 1825. Speculation ran rampant in London financial markets in 1824–25, as seemingly everyone from clerks to the highest politicians scrambled to invest in the resources (especially gold mines) of the newly independent nations. Burned by the collapse of the stocks of hundreds of companies on the London Exchange in 1825, British investors would not return in force until after mid-century. With the stabilization of many nations in the 1860s and 1870s, British investments rose dramatically, and, by the 1890s, probably totaled more than 550 million pounds sterling (around US$2.5 billion). The lion's share of this investment prior to 1860 went into government loans. Nearly every nation in Latin America took out British loans in the 1820s, and all, except Brazil, defaulted. After midcentury, most British investment funded the construction of railroads, ports, communication systems, public utilities, and the purchase of government bonds.

The power and "preeminence" (to use one scholar's term) of British influence in Latin America in the nineteenth century provoked a debate over the last two centuries about the very nature of Latin American economies in the half-century after independence. In the eyes of some historians, the economic power of Great Britain turned the new nations of Latin America into virtual economic colonies in a system known as neocolonialism or the "imperialism of free trade." Following this logic, Britain did not need to occupy and control Latin American nations (as the British did in its colonies in Africa, Asia, and the Caribbean) to control them. The overwhelming power of British exports, British purchases of Latin American goods, and a dominance via investment, all combined to place the new economies at the mercy of British capitalists and capital. To use the stronger language of theorists of the 1970s, the economies of Latin America were dependent on Britain, and unable to assert control over their destinies. Local elites (landowners, merchants, businessmen) worked with the British in a relationship that condemned their countries to underdevelopment and economic dependency on decisions made in the major financial centers of the North Atlantic world, principally London, and to a lesser extent, New York. In Mexico, Central America, and the Caribbean, the United States eventually assumed this role of economic power and political influence.

While the dependency theorists of the 1960s to 1980s may have overstated the power of the North Atlantic economies in Latin America in the nineteenth century, they do have an important point. The economies of Latin America were weak, with little capital, low levels of technology, and the British (and the United States) did assume a very, very powerful presence in the new nations, shaping their economies. More recent scholarship, by scholars across the political spectrum, has tended to emphasize the agency of Latin Americans, of all social and economic groups, in the formation of the new nations and their economies. Given their lack of modern economic infrastructure in the 1820s, the new nations of Latin America had few options, and the elites pushed them toward the exploitation of raw materials (copper, silver, gold, guano) and agricultural commodities (sugar, coffee, bananas, wheat, beef, dyes). The result was the construction of economies that were highly vulnerable to the fluctuating prices and demand for their goods in the United States and Europe. The Latin Americans may not have been completely dominated by the economies of the North Atlantic, but they had few cards to play in a game of high-stakes economic poker.

Mexico, Chile, Brazil, and Costa Rica provide us with four different paths to nation-building in the mid-nineteenth century. In the 1820s and 1830s, Brazil began to emerge in the role it would play well into the twentieth century, the world's leading coffee producer and exporter. On a much smaller scale, Costa Rica also became one of the first great exporters of coffee in the 1830s. Chile experimented with silver, then copper, and finally nitrates, as it sought an economic niche in the Western economic system. With its enormous natural resources and agricultural lands, Mexico, perhaps better than any new nation in Latin America, should have been positioned to embark on balanced economic growth. Tragically, political chaos, generated by both internal and external forces, crippled Mexico until the 1870s.

MEXICO: INSTABILITY AND CHAOS

Mexico stands out as *the* extreme case of political instability and delayed economic growth in Latin America in the aftermath of independence. In the 50 years after the declaration of independence in September 1821, Mexico would have more than 50 presidents. In the 1830s, rebellious U.S. settlers would wrest away Texas, and then the United States would invade in the 1840s, seizing almost half Mexico's territory. In the 1860s, the French invaded and occupied the country. Conflicts between Liberals and Conservatives tore the country apart until the Liberals finally triumphed and consolidated their power in the 1870s, initiating what would be one of the longest dictatorships in Latin American history.

The wars for independence ravaged Mexico, shutting down its legendary silver mines, halting production on haciendas, and creating enormous insecurity as bands of highway robbers preyed on travelers. Transportation into the interior was precarious, at best. With nearly seven million inhabitants, Mexico was the most populous of the new nations in the Americas, but its economy was entirely based on the production and export of raw materials and agricultural products: silver, gold, tobacco, vanilla, dyes (cochineal), and rope fiber (henequen). The army, with more than 50,000 troops, and the Catholic Church (with hundreds of clergy) were the only truly "national" institutions, and both would fight tenaciously to hold on to their colonial corporate privileges. The Church and army generally supported the Conservatives.

Open warfare between Liberals and Conservatives in the 1820s led to the rise of the caudillo Antonio López de Santa Anna, who would dominate and cripple Mexico from the mid-1830s to the mid-1850s. Although elected president in 1833, he spent much of the next two years on his enormous cattle ranch and allowed his vice-president, Valentín Gómez Farías, and his minister of education, José María Luis Mora, to run the government. They pushed a series of radical Liberal reforms into law: abolition of the *fueros* (making priests and army officers subject to civil courts) and church tithes, downsizing the army, the creation of a civilian militia, and the appropriation of some Franciscan missions. This was the first high point of Liberal reform in Mexico. It provoked, however, a powerful conservative reaction. Santa Anna returned to the capital, tossed out the Liberal reforms and suspended the Constitution of 1824. In 1835, he led the Mexican army north into Texas to quell a rebellion led by settlers from the United States (but cloaked under the guise of federalism and self-rule). After initially routing the rebels at the Alamo, Goliad, and Refugio in February and March, the Texans captured Santa Anna at San Jacinto (the outskirts of present-day Houston) in April 1836 and secured their independence. For a decade, Texas was an independent nation, but in late 1845 it was annexed to the United States. President James K. Polk (a Tennessean) then provoked a war with Mexico in a dispute over the location of the Texas-Mexico border. Forces led by General Zachary Taylor invaded Mexico in April 1846 and moved toward Mexico City via Monterrey. Troops under General Winfield Scott seized Veracruz in March 1847. Santa Anna returned from exile in Cuba and assumed the presidency and command of the army. In late 1847, U.S. forces converged on Mexico City and entered the "halls of Montezuma" as Santa Anna, once again, fled into exile.

The Treaty of Guadalupe Hidalgo in February 1848 very quickly and definitively ceded the northern Mexican borderlands (from Texas to California and Oregon) to the United States and Mexico lost some 40 percent of its territory. As some historians have pointed out, the Conservatives hastened to make a quick peace, preferring to come "to terms with the

United States rather than endanger the interests of the ruling class."
Incorporation into the United States and its legal system would have devastating consequences for "Hispanics" (Californios, Tejanos) and indigenous peoples in what became the U.S. Southwest. Many would lose their
land, legal rights, and even their lives. Incredibly, Santa Anna returned
from exile again in 1853, as the Conservatives searched for a European
monarch to accept a Mexican throne. In August 1855, a Liberal revolt
forced the wily caudillo into exile for a final time and initiated more than
a decade of Liberal reforms and Conservative counterreaction that would
again bathe the country in blood.

CHILE, COSTA RICA, AND BRAZIL: EARLY
STABILITY AND ORDER

The paths of Chile, Costa Rica, and Brazil in the aftermath of independence
were a world apart from the events in Mexico. In all three cases, local
elites forged a new political consensus to replace the old colonial order.
Chilean and Costa Rican elites faced less pressure from social unrest
among the lower classes than the Mexican elites. The Brazilians, however,
would face uprisings and revolts from the lower classes throughout the
nineteenth century. In spite of this continuing disorder, and unlike the
Mexican elites, the Brazilians managed to forge an elite consensus that
allowed them to crush challenges to the new national government.

In many ways, Chile and Costa Rica are very similar. Both were on the
periphery of the Spanish American empire with small populations (one
million in Chile and 100,000 in Costa Rica) with an elite that was concentrated in a central valley around the capital. Under the tough rule of Diego
Portales in the 1830s, Chile very quickly stabilized, achieving economic
expansion and a sort of uneasy cooperation of Liberals and Conservatives.
Although he never served as president, Portales is seen by many Chileans
today as one of the two founders of modern Chile, along with Bernardo
O'Higgins. He did this, however, through authoritarian measures that
only later would give way to power-sharing with both political parties.
This was elitist rule—Portales viewed the masses with disdain. In his
words, "the people is a beast." A wealthy businessman, Portales was the
strongman behind the rulers in the 1830s. Fortunately for Chileans, he was
not a classic caudillo and he was more interested in creating institutions
than in personal power. Although he was executed in 1837 during an
uprising, his views prevailed as the Chilean Conservatives implemented a
system of domination that did not entirely exclude and exile the Liberals.

The 1833 Constitution put into place a very centralized government
with limited suffrage. Rare among the constitutions of the early nineteenth

century, it would endure until 1925. In the 1830s, 1840s, and 1850s, the
pattern was to hold very restricted elections dominated by the elites.
Presidents would serve two five-year terms and then retire from the scene.
Despite its flaws, the Chilean system began a process of regular elections
(with slowly expanding participation), rotation of executives, and a truce
(however uneasy) between Liberals and Conservatives. Rather than an
"all or nothing" struggle between the two factions (as in Mexico), this
Chilean path avoided civil war, economic devastation, and chaos.

Costa Rica followed a very similar path on a smaller scale. Spared the
bloodshed and devastation of a war for independence, and geographically isolated, the small Costa Rican elite located in the Central Valley in
the mountainous center of the country forged a system of uneasy cooperation among Liberals and Conservatives. With a small population,
and very few African slaves or forced Indian laborers, Costa Rica benefited
from its lack of the burdensome colonial legacies of a Mexico, Peru, or
Brazil. Much like Chile's, the small Costa Rican elite rarely allowed any
one individual to remain in power long, or to assume dictatorial authority.
Although the Conservatives dominated in the decades before the 1870s,
they maintained close ties to the Liberals. Centuries of intermarriage
among the small Costa Rican elite, no doubt, helped attenuate the
bitter divisions found in many other (larger) nations. A small, intermarried elite, however, is not a guarantee of more stability, as the case of
Nicaragua demonstrates.

Despite its similarities to Costa Rica, including some elite intermarriage, the Nicaraguan elites were bitterly divided between Liberal and
Conservative factions in the nineteenth century, producing constant civil
war, and even foreign intervention. In the 1850s, the Liberals recruited a
Tennessean, William Walker, and dozens of U.S. mercenaries to their
cause. Incredibly, Walker and his forces briefly took control of the country and he declared himself president. A combined effort by Nicaraguans,
Costa Ricans, and other Central Americans (along with important external
pressure from the shipping interests of Cornelius Vanderbilt) defeated
Walker in 1857. This episode completely disgraced the Nicaraguan Liberals
for decades, began a long history of anti-Americanism in Central
America, and helped unify the Costa Rican elites. Nicaragua would
remain mired in internal conflict for decades, and the Costa Ricans would
move forward with their own process of nation-building.

The Brazilians pursued a path unlike most of Latin America in the
nineteenth century. As we have seen, the "war" for independence was brief
and relatively bloodless, and the Crown Prince of Portugal, Pedro, assumed
leadership of the movement. The presence of the Braganza monarchy
throughout most of the nineteenth century provided Brazil with a system

unique to the Americas. The Constitution of 1824 was strongly centralist, but it put into place an electoral system that evolved into something roughly similar to the limited monarchy in England. From the 1820s to the late 1880s, Liberals and Conservatives alternated power in the Brazilian parliament (with an assembly and a senate) on a regular basis. Again, elites dominated the voting and electoral processes, but they did hold regular elections, and frequently alternated power and politicians. Pedro I put the system in place in the 1820s, abdicated and returned to Portugal in 1831, and then his son, Pedro II, refined the system after assuming power in 1840. Pedro II wisely chose to follow the model of Queen Victoria, to reign rather than rule. An exceptionally well-educated, cosmopolitan, and temperate leader, Pedro II provided Brazil with stability and a leader unlike those of any nation in the Americas in the nineteenth century.

Nevertheless, beneath this surface of elite politics and stability, Brazil was wracked by regional and social revolts through much of the nineteenth century. As many have observed, the problem in Brazil was not achieving independence, but rather holding the new nation together. From the 1830s through the 1840s, separatist revolts threatened the nation from the far north to the far south. Luís Alves de Lima e Silva, eventually the Duke of Caxias, played the central role as the army eventually suppressed and defeated all these revolts. In other Latin American nations, Caxias would have become the caudillo who dominated the nation. In Brazil, he remained the faithful servant of the Emperor (the "most civilian soldier") and a major figure in politics until his death in 1880.

In Brazil, Chile, and Costa Rica, landowning and mercantile elites dominated the new regimes. The political stability they forged allowed them to begin to build export economies linked to European markets. In the 1830s and 1840s, the Costa Ricans and Brazilians constructed the first coffee-export economies in Latin America, sending most of their production to England and Germany. In Brazil, the expansion of coffee cultivation around Rio de Janeiro produced the latest phase in an old system of large landed estates worked by slave labor. In Costa Rica, the landholding patterns remained relatively fragmented, but the elites dominated the purchasing and export of production. In Chile, the landowners and merchants of the Santiago-Valparaíso region began to export wheat and wine (to California in the 1850s), but they also developed mining in the arid northern deserts. In the 1830s and 1840s, copper exports grew until Chile became the world's leading exporter. Nitrates (for fertilizer and then explosives) also became a major export from the northern deserts after midcentury. In all three cases, this new elite consensus in politics paved the way for economic growth after 1830 and a head start on most of the other new nations of Latin America.

15

Liberals, Positivists, and Order

THE IDEA OF PROGRESS . . . AND ORDER

If disorder characterized much of Latin America in the decades after independence, by the 1870s, order prevailed in nearly all the Latin American countries. During the often tumultuous half-century after 1820, the Conservatives dominated politics in the region. By the 1870s, the Liberals had ascended to power in virtually every nation of Latin America. Although these are the clear patterns for the region, the various paths of the nations and areas of Latin America multiplied and diverged from the 1870s to the next momentous economic watershed in the history of the Western world—the Great Depression of 1929. The Liberals established order, and they pursued their vision of progress. For the economy this meant export-oriented economic growth, modernization of infrastructure (railroads, telegraph lines, port facilities, electrification), urbanization, and a welcoming of foreign investment. In social and cultural terms, progress meant Europeanization—attracting European immigrants, aping European culture among the elites, and imposing European culture on the non-European peoples of the region. Politically, the story is more complicated. For many regions (Mexico and most of Central America as the prime examples), liberalism did not produce an expansion of individual rights, civil liberties, or electoral participation. "Liberal" rulers in these regions constructed personalistic dictatorships and brutally repressed the majority of the population. In other regions (Costa Rica, Chile, Argentina, and Uruguay are the best examples), the rise of Liberals expanded political participation and produced an electoral politics that strongly resembled Western Europe and the United States by the 1920s.

The impact of Liberal politics was so powerful and profound across the region that many historians refer to the period as the "Second Conquest," a process that, in many ways, completed the conquest of the sixteenth century. The "First Conquest" imposed Spanish and Portuguese rule on the key cities and towns in the core regions, but most of the interior of Central and South America remained, for all purposes, beyond the reach and direct control of colonial authorities. For centuries, many indigenous communities, and the increasingly racially and culturally mixed peoples of the interior, went about their lives with minimal intervention from metropolitan and imperial officials. Local notables often served as the key intermediaries between their own peoples and the outside world. This changed dramatically in the second half of the nineteenth century. Modernization and economic growth translated into the expansion of "European" culture and power into the interior of most of Latin America in the half-century after 1870. The incipient nation-states began (and I emphasize "began") to extend the power of the state apparatus into the countryside, however slowly and tenuously. The most visible signs of this apparatus were police, the military, courts, and tax collectors.

Modernization produced a monumental cultural and social collision in nineteenth-century Latin America as worlds that had uneasily coexisted for centuries clashed. In many places, the wars for independence had shaken, but not overturned, the fragile cultural structures of the colonial period. Modernization and the Liberals shattered these cultural structures across much of Latin America by the early twentieth century. Only in the most rural and isolated regions of Latin America did the hierarchical, corporatist colonial cultural order survive into the mid-twentieth century (the densely populated highlands of Guatemala and Bolivia are good examples). Ironically, the Liberals and their allies provoked this great cultural clash in the name of progress, modernity, economic growth, and political liberalism. In a few places, they succeeded in producing economic growth and expanding political participation (Argentina, Chile, Uruguay, Costa Rica). In many others, they achieved economic growth, but through authoritarian politics, and the destruction of much of the "traditional" cultures and societies in the interior (Mexico and Brazil, for example). By the 1920s, progress and modernization had won the struggle and, to play on the Brazilian writer Euclides da Cunha's famous phrase, Latin America was "condemned to progress."

The price of progress was high for the majority of Latin Americans. The growth and expansion of state power, urbanization, new transportation networks (especially railways), and increasing foreign investment (for plantations, mines, and infrastructure) brought the "modern" world into the interior of Latin America via the major cities (Mexico City, Buenos Aires, Rio de Janeiro, for example). As the economic and political power of the nation-states increased, indigenous communities shrank or disappeared, and the great masses were slowly integrated into "national communities." Modernization, in effect, initiated an irreversible process of transforming rural peoples (with many languages, traditions, customs, and practices) into Brazilians, Mexicans, Peruvians, and Costa Ricans. In the short term, the price of progress was enormous dislocations and hardships as rural peoples lost their lands, saw their villages disrupted or destroyed, and as the cultural power of the outside world (Europe, the United States, and capital cities) encroached upon the traditions of their small communities. In the long term, modernization may have produced a higher standard of living for the majority of Latin Americans, but the price was cultural homogenization and the annihilation of many languages, customs, and traditions long held sacred by the non-European peoples of the interior.

As early as the first decades after independence, the peoples of the region saw this cultural clash emerging. The political and social elites clearly understood the struggle and fought hard to impose the "civilization" of the cities on the "barbarism" of the countryside. Domingo Faustino Sarmiento (1811–88), an Argentine intellectual who eventually rose to the presidency of his country (1868–74), wrote the most famous and enduring analysis of this collision of cultures. While in exile in Chile, forced from his homeland by one of Latin America's most famous caudillos, Juan Manuel de Rosas (ruler from 1829–52), Sarmiento wrote *Civilización y barbarie* (1845) (translated into English as *Life in the Argentine Republic in the Days of the Tyrants; or, Civilization and Barbarism* [1868]). Although ostensibly about the regional caudillo Facundo Quiroga, the book was an undisguised attack on Rosas. Sarmiento provides extremely sympathetic portraits of the country people of the interior before condemning them as backward. In Sarmiento's words, "two different kinds of civilization existed in the Argentine Republic; one being Spanish, European, and cultivated, the other barbarous, American, and almost wholly of native growth. . . . these two distinct forms of national existence [came] face to face, and gave occasion for a contest between them, to be ended, after lasting many years, by the absorption of one into the other." Absorption was a mild way of saying annihilation or extermination. Sarmiento once told his fellow Liberal Bartolomé Mitre (president from 1862 to 1868), "Do not try to economize the blood of the gauchos. It is fertilizer (like the blood of animals from the slaughterhouse) that must be made useful to the country. Their blood is the only part of them that is human." For Sarmiento, and other Liberals, civilization had to eradicate barbarism for Latin America to become modern, progressive, and developed. In the last third of the nineteenth century, the Liberals embarked upon this crusade with a vengeance.

TRIUMPH OF THE LIBERALS AND POSITIVISTS

Sarmiento and his fellow Liberals in Latin America were strongly influenced by the modernizing and authoritarian philosophy of positivism. The French philosopher Auguste Comte (1798–1857) and the English thinker Herbert Spencer (1820–1904) were the two European writers who most influenced the social thought of nineteenth-century Latin American elites. Known as positivism, Comte's philosophy glorified reason and scientific knowledge and rejected traditional religious beliefs. He believed that humanity had begun to overcome the superstitions and religious beliefs of the past, and with the guidance of science (positive knowledge) would soon enter into a new age where technicians and engineers would run an authoritarian republic, achieving true progress. Comte summed up his beliefs in a catchy epigram: "Love as the base. Order as the means. Progress as the goal." Comte believed in what some might call the imperialism of the scientific worldview, the belief that science will ultimately resolve all significant questions and problems. He coined a new word to describe the scientific study of society—sociology. In Spencer, Latin American elites found a sophisticated scheme of social evolution that not only glorified science and reason, but also provided them with a positivistic rationale to justify their control of the "inferior" racially-mixed lower classes. It was Spencer who coined the phrase "survival of the fittest" and what we usually call social Darwinism would be more accurately described as social Spencerianism. Spencer believed that human races and peoples had evolved unevenly, leaving some inferior to others. He and his followers developed elaborate evolutionary theories showing that white Europeans were the apex of human evolution, with the "lesser" races of Asia, Africa, and Latin America as examples of inferior and less fit peoples.

Although Latin American leaders were often influenced both by classical liberalism and by positivism, the latter was much more authoritarian and elitist. For the true positivist, the best form of government was an authoritarian republic run by scientifically educated experts (technocrats). At least in theory, true political liberals aspired to create a republican form of government with expanding political participation (for adult males). Liberals and positivists converged in their strong belief in a form of progress through science, technology, industrialization, urbanization, and European culture. They looked to Europe (and to a lesser extent, the United States) as the models for the region. They enormously admired and envied the economic and industrial advances in the United States, but often viewed the country as a cultural wasteland. Britain provided an even more powerful example of economic progress and political stability. For most Latin American cultural elites, Paris was the center of their universe from the eighteenth century until the mid-twentieth century. The United States and

Great Britain might offer enticing political and economic models, but neither could compete with France for the cultural affections of the Latin American elites.

No other country in Latin America in the late nineteenth and early twentieth centuries surpasses Mexico in its combination of liberal and positivist ideals, economic growth, brutal authoritarian rule, and imposition of Europeanization and modernity on the non-European peoples of the countryside. For four decades, under the repressive rule of Porfirio Díaz (1876–1911), national elites established political order, impressive economic growth, and a steady process of nation-building. With an impressive zeal, liberals and positivists worked hard to turn the largely Indian peasant majority of the interior into modern, Europeanized, Spanish-speaking citizens of the Mexican nation. Foreign investment, new transportation technology, and industrialization served as the catalysts and the vanguard of their social and cultural transformation. The expansion of capitalism into the Mexican countryside led the way for modernity and progress. By 1910, the results were impressive—a country that was rapidly industrializing, experiencing substantial economic growth, and receiving major foreign investment, especially from the United States. Rapid economic growth, political repression, and social engineering had also produced staggering inequities, social upheaval, and deep divisions in Mexican society. By 1910, Mexico was on the verge of one of the most profound political and social revolutions in modern times.

The Liberals had seized power in the 1850s, led by Benito Juárez, president of Mexico (in theory) from 1858 to 1872. Juárez is one of those extraordinary individuals who rose to great accomplishments despite his extremely humble origins. A Zapotec Indian born in Oaxaca in 1806, Juárez was orphaned at the age of four and worked in the fields of his relatives until the age of twelve. Through his own industriousness and good fortune, he was helped by a Franciscan monk, and pursued an education, eventually receiving a law degree. He joined the side of the Liberals and was elected governor of Oaxaca in 1847. In the mid-1850s, he and his fellow Liberals passed legislation that severely limited the traditional privileges of clergy and military officers. The Lerdo Law called for the forced sale of lands owned by the Catholic Church that were not being used for religious purposes. (Some estimate that the Church owned close to half of all productive lands in Mexico in the 1850s.) The law also barred Indian villages from owning communal lands. The intent was to sell off and privatize Church and village lands to create individual private property holders, thereby expanding the middle class in Mexico. In fact, most of the Church and Indian lands were quickly seized by the powerful, further intensifying the colonial legacy of large landed estates controlled by a small elite. The new Constitution of 1857 proclaimed traditional liberal political ideals, and severely restricted the Catholic Church. This period of Liberal legislation in Mexico is known as the Reform (*la Reforma*).

Civil war broke out (once again) in 1858 and lasted until late 1860. Although elected president in 1862, Juárez was forced to flee northward during the French Intervention (1862–67). Napoléon III of France had ambitions to expand French influence in the region during the U.S. Civil War (1861–65), and sent troops into Mexico. In one of the more bizarre episodes in the history of the Americas, the Austrian archduke Maximilian von Habsburg, younger brother of the Austrian Emperor Franz Joseph, assumed the "throne" of Mexico along with his young wife Carlota (Charlotte, the daughter of Leopold I of Belgium). Led by Juárez, the Liberals eventually reassumed control of the country when Napoléon III withdrew his troops. Maximilian fled north, was captured, and then executed, at Querétaro in June 1867. (Carlota went insane and spent the rest of her long life confined to a castle near Brussels, dying at the age of 87 in 1927.) The tough and dictatorial Juárez unified the Liberals against Maximilian and the French and today he is seen as the greatest symbol of Mexican resistance to foreign intervention. From the defeat of the French in 1867 to his death in 1872, Juárez assumed increasingly authoritarian powers, initiating a long period of stability and Liberal rule.

Porfirio Díaz built a nation on the foundations laid by Juárez, and he did it, in his own words, with "bread and the club" (*pan e palo*). The brutal and repressive *Porfiriato* (1876–1911) forged the national political unity and stability that had eluded Mexico in the decades after independence. Like Juárez, Díaz came from humble origins in the southern state of Oaxaca. A mestizo, Díaz also struggled to study law before joining the military during the War of the Reform (1858–60). He rose to national prominence as a general during the French Intervention, in particular for his role in the Mexican victory against the French at Puebla on May 5, 1862 (now celebrated among Mexican-Americans each year as the "Cinco de Mayo"). After the death of Juárez in 1872, his longtime ally, Sebastián Lerdo de Tejada became president. Claiming that the elections planned for 1876 were fraudulent, Díaz led a revolt that toppled Lerdo de Tejada. His rallying cry, ironically, was "effective suffrage and no reelection." He then ruled Mexico, as president or through subordinates, for the next 35 years, one of the longest personalistic dictatorships in the history of Latin America!

The *Porfiriato* is the quintessential example in Latin America of economic growth under a personalistic dictatorship in the late nineteenth and early twentieth centuries. Beneath a veneer of Liberal politics and economic policy, a centralizing and authoritarian state modernized the Mexican economy, but did not open it up as completely as one would expect under Liberal orthodoxy (free trade, little government intervention, few barriers to the entry of foreign capital). The image of the *Porfiriato* is that Mexico became the "mother of foreigners and the stepmother of Mexicans." On the one hand, foreign capital, primarily from the United States, flowed into Mexico to finance the construction of railroads, port facilities, textile factories, mining enterprises, oil fields, and agribusiness. On the other hand, the Mexican government carefully regulated this capital investment, channeling it into key sectors of the economy, and consciously protected powerful Mexican capitalists who were friends of Díaz. (U.S., British, and French investors expanded Mexican railway lines from less than 500 miles of track in 1876 to more than 15,000 miles in 1911.) Unlike most Latin American countries in this period, Mexico did not fall into export mono-culture, but exported a variety of goods: silver, copper, lead, oil, henequen, tobacco, and sugar. Like many Latin American countries, most foreign investment flowed into the production of raw materials and agricultural commodities, but it also began to fund industrialization, especially around Mexico City. Textiles, metallurgy, and food processing—the classic initial industries during the early phases of industrialization in the developed world—all took shape around the capital, and with it a nascent industrial working class.

The keys to the long-running stability of the regime were the repression of the peasantry, the quiescence of the Catholic Church, a close relationship with the powerful landowners and merchants, and roles for the intelligentsia and small middle class in the government. Díaz bought peace and prosperity by putting everyone on the dole. As he famously remarked, a dog with a bone in his mouth does not kill or steal. Those who refused the "bone" were beaten, persecuted, or jailed. Díaz constructed a national network of regional and local political bosses (*jefes políticos*) who kept the peace in the countryside in exchange for periodic rewards from the central government. The landowners were left to their own devices in the country-side in exchange for loyalty to the central government. In the countryside, the banditry became the rural police (*rurales*). With the help of his wife, Doña Carmen, Díaz quietly forged an alliance with the Catholic Church, despite his "Liberal" credentials. All the anticlerical legislation of the *Reforma* of the 1850s remained in place, but unenforced. The Catholic Church had lost its enormous landholdings, but it was allowed to reopen schools, monasteries, and nunneries. Nevertheless, the Church remained the most powerful cultural force in society, especially among the lower classes and Indian peoples. As did many Latin American caudillos, Díaz found religion a useful tool, an "opium for the people," yet another instrument of social control.

To appease possible opposition from intellectuals, the regime co-opted them with positions as technocrats, bureaucrats, and cabinet ministers. The cluster of positivist intellectuals in the *Porfiriato* who promoted the modernization of Mexico were collectively known as the *científicos* (scientists).

Although the Liberals may have lamented the lack of honest elections and political freedoms, the positivists saw in the authoritarian republic the vehicle for implementing their vision of industrialization, technological advance, and economic growth. While the *científicos* modernized the country's economy, Díaz constructed an elaborate and extensive political network, from the municipalities to the national Congress, that administered the country. A small group of key technocrats led by his father-in-law, Manuel Romero Rubio, and finance minister José Yves Limantour, formed the dictator's "brain trust."

As one historian has noted, "Mexico developed at breakneck speed while minimizing the concern for the liberty and economic security of the vast majority of the people." This is most clearly seen in the impoverishment of the peasants in the countryside. Three-quarters of the 15 million inhabitants of Mexico lived in rural areas engaged in agriculture. The Liberal reforms of the 1850s paved the way for stripping hundreds of thousands of peasants and Indian villages of their lands. Just as the Church lands had been confiscated under the *Porfiriato*, the communal Indian landholdings, many that had been the core of life in indigenous villages for centuries, were privatized, subdivided, and "sold." According to one estimate, 90 percent of the Indian villages on the central plateau were dispossessed of their communal lands. Powerful landowners and foreign companies engaged in an enormous landgrab, leaving three-quarters of the rural population landless by 1910. Some resisted ferociously. The Yaqui Indians of the northern state of Sonora fought back for decades. Ultimately, they were defeated, and thousands shipped off to work on plantations in conditions of virtual slavery in Cuba and the Yucatán. Land concentration reached staggering proportions. The Terrazas family in Chihuahua controlled more than seven million acres by the beginning of the twentieth century. In the state of Morelos (south of Mexico City and named for the hero of independence), some 30 families controlled virtually all the crop land in the state. This stark contrast—between the impressive economic growth during the *Porfiriato* and the drastic impoverishment of the rural masses—had created a powder keg that would explode in revolution in 1910.

EXPORTING PRIMARY PRODUCTS

Like most of Latin America in the late nineteenth and early twentieth centuries, Mexico adopted what some Latin American economists have called "outward-oriented growth"—a turn toward the export of primary products to the United States and Europe as the motor of economic development. Most Latin American economies, however, did not have the diversity of exports that emerged in Mexico. Instead, as we have seen, they became deeply dependent on a single product (monoculture) and Latin American economies would rise and fall, often dramatically and precipitously, with the fluctuating demand and prices for their dominant export. This is the period of the development of what some have slyly referred to as the "economy of desserts"—coffee, sugar, and bananas. (All three of these products so intimately linked in the public mind with Latin America were imported from the Old World—coffee originating in East Africa or the Arabian Peninsula, bananas and sugar in the East Indies.) Central America, Colombia, and Brazil became coffee-exporting economies. Cuba became the world's great sugar plantation. Honduras, Costa Rica, Colombia, and Ecuador became the world's first major banana exporters. In Venezuela (and Mexico), it was oil, in Bolivia, tin, and Chile's fortunes rose and fell with copper prices. On the pampas of Argentina (and Uruguay) wheat, beef, mutton, and wool transformed the plains of South America. Haiti and Paraguay largely remained inwardly-oriented economies with minimal international export sectors.

With the political stability that began to emerge across the region by midcentury, leaders of the new nations could embark upon schemes to pursue their dreams of development. Between 1850 and the onset of the First World War, Latin America's exports grew at a rate of nearly 4 percent per year (an impressive rate sustained in some countries over decades), and increased from $155 million to $1.5 billion annually. As with the drug trade in the late twentieth century, this export boom was driven by escalating demand in the rapidly industrializing economies of Europe and the United States. The factories of the North Atlantic economies consumed Bolivian tin, Chilean copper and nitrates, as consumers in the growing cities and metropolises of Europe and the United States hungered for coffee, sugar, bananas, wheat, beef, mutton, leather, wool, and wine. Over these decades, a slow but clear shift also took shape as the United States emerged as the preeminent market for Latin American exports and as the producer of most of the region's imports. By 1913, the United States had become the principal market for all of the Caribbean, Mexico, and Central America (except Haiti and Guatemala). Great Britain purchased about 20 percent of Latin America's exports, France about 12 percent, and Germany about 8 percent. The United States bought 30 percent, and this figure would continue to rise in the succeeding decades.

This period also witnessed the emergence of the first multinational corporations, and in some Latin American countries, so-called enclave economies. In the 1880s and 1890s, Lorenzo Baker, a ship captain from Boston, began bringing bananas back from Jamaica on his trips. This novel fruit was so successful that Baker formed the Boston Fruit Company. About the same time, a U.S. entrepreneur, Minor C. Keith, who was building a railway in Costa Rica (from San José in the highlands to Limón on the Atlantic coast) began shipping bananas to New Orleans. In 1899, Keith and Baker merged their businesses into the United Fruit Company, one of the first United States–based multinationals in Latin America, and probably the most infamous. In the first decades of the twentieth century, "the octopus" (*el pulpo*, as it was known in the Caribbean and Central America) expanded banana plantations into coastal regions in Central America, the Caribbean, and Ecuador. Typically, these plantations were on the coast, largely unconnected to the economic mainstream in the host countries, and had enormous political influence locally. (Minor C. Keith, for example, married the daughter of the Costa Rican president.) The ability of the companies to influence politics in small, weak economies led to the emergence of the term "banana republic" to refer to nations that were susceptible to the external influence of powerful foreign interests. Nitrates in the northern deserts of Chile, henequen (rope fiber) in the Yucatán peninsula, and rubber in the Brazilian Amazon are other dramatic examples of enclave economies more intimately connected with Europe and the United States than with Santiago or Mexico City or Rio de Janeiro.

The rise of export economies in Latin America from the 1850s to the 1920s produced significant growth in the gross domestic product of many nations, but the socioeconomic chasm between a wealthy elite and an enormous population of poor people (largely of indigenous, African, and racially mixed ancestry) failed to narrow, and many would argue that it widened. For several decades, a fierce debate has raged over the meaning of this growth and its impact on the region. By the early twentieth century, Latin America formed part of an emerging region ("Third World," "underdeveloped nations," "developing world," are some of the usual labels) that by the mid-twentieth century would be dominated by the economies of the "developed nations" of the First World. Socialists and other critics of capitalism have argued that the very development of the First World was built on the underdevelopment of the Third World. (The Soviet Union and its allies formed the so-called Second World.) Bluntly stated, the First World developed by exploiting the resources and economies of the Third World. Development and underdevelopment form two sides of the same coin. By the end of the twentieth century, the proponents of capitalism (especially in the euphoria generated by the collapse of the Soviet Union) have argued that this critique of capitalism is fundamentally wrong. They argue that the problem in nineteenth-century Latin America, and today, has been lack of capital investment, insecure property and contract rights, and protectionist economic policies. In short, the problem has not been the continuing powerful presence of foreign economic interests in Latin America, but rather that those interests have not had enough of a presence.

As every introductory economics student learns, the key factors in any economy are land, labor, capital, and management. Land has long been abundant in Latin America, but controlled by a small elite since the Conquest. Furthermore, much of it was largely inaccessible to the outside world until the transportation revolution of the late nineteenth century. Labor, strangely enough, has always been in short supply, especially outside the dense indigenous population centers in the Andes and Mesoamerica. The response of the elites was to turn to forced Indian labor and to import African slaves. Consequently, free wage labor was late developing and always scarce. Much of the free peasantry of Latin America opted to turn to subsistence agriculture rather than accept the low wages on the haciendas, plantations, and (later) in factories. Capital clearly has been in short supply. The first commercial banks begin to appear in Latin America in the second half of the nineteenth century, but the banking infrastructure was small and weak compared to that in Europe and the United States. Consequently, the main sources of investment were foreign lenders, and (after the 1930s) national governments. Although a long tradition once disparaged the business acumen and abilities of Latin Americans, in recent years it has become very clear that Latin Americans are as entrepreneurial as anyone in the world. What these entrepreneurs have long faced is powerful obstacles: lack of capital, access to markets, shortages of labor, bureaucratic and legal challenges, and an inability to compete with foreign companies.

Whether one believes that capitalism is the problem in the slow economic development of Latin America, or the solution, the principal obstacles to development have been structural. Furthermore, a late entry into the emerging international economy in the nineteenth century put many countries at a huge disadvantage, particularly those with small populations, tiny markets, and few resources. The Mexicans and Brazilians (to single out the two largest economies in the region) have spent a lot of time catching up to the North Atlantic world. As we will see in later chapters, they have industrialized (along with many other countries), but they have done so very late and with little research and development or technological innovation. The result is an increasingly industrialized Latin America, but one that does not seem to have the ability to generate self-sustained growth through domestic innovation and creativity. The region continues to pay for the late start, overwhelming dependence on the export of primary products, and the highly unequal socioeconomic structure inherited from the colonial period.

As odd as it may sound, most of Latin America has been sparsely populated for most of its history. Outside of Mesoamerica, the Caribbean, and the Andes, the indigenous population in 1492 was very sparse. By 1800, the region had perhaps 17–18 million inhabitants in an area covering more than 20 million square kilometers (roughly twice the size of the

United States). Mexico (with some six million inhabitants) and Brazil (with about three million) accounted for half of all Latin Americans. By the beginning of the twentieth century, the population of the region had grown to about 75 million. (The United States over the same period had grown from about 4 million to about 75 million.) Latin America remained overwhelmingly rural, despite significant urbanization. By 1900, Mexico City, São Paulo, and Santiago de Chile had grown to over half a million inhabitants. Buenos Aires and Rio de Janeiro mushroomed to a population of more than a million. (The four largest cities in the United States in 1900 were New York City with 3.5 million, Chicago with 1.7 million, Philadelphia with 1.3 million, and St. Louis with 600,000.) The incipient industry in Mexico, Brazil, and Argentina was largely concentrated around the capital cities (and São Paulo in Brazil). The vast majority of the population remained rural peasants, and the urban working class and middle class formed a small percentage of the population of even the largest and most urbanized countries. In 1850 the ethnic and racial composition of Latin America did not look significantly different than it had in 1800. A powerful wave of immigration, primarily from southern Europe, would change this, but primarily in the southern Cone region (Uruguay and Argentina, and to a lesser extent, in Chile and southern Brazil).

IMPORTING EUROPE

Arguably, no country in Latin America was more profoundly transformed through immigration in the late nineteenth century than Argentina (although Uruguay is a close second). The leadership of Argentina, quite literally, Europeanized the nation through a massive infusion of European "blood," as well as European culture. Juan Bautista Alberdi coined the phrase that summed up the outlook of the Argentine Liberals: "to govern is to populate" (*gobernar es poblar*). The population of Argentina rose from around 1.5 million in 1850 to nearly 8 million in 1914. (At 2.77 million square kilometers, Argentina today is slightly less than one-third the area of the United States.) From 1870 to 1914, nearly 6 million immigrants arrived and more than half settled permanently. Half were from Italy and another quarter from Spain. By the outbreak of the First World War, 30 percent of the inhabitants of Argentina were immigrants, and another 50 percent the descendants of immigrants who had arrived after 1850! The population of Buenos Aires rose from about 90,000 in 1850 to 1.5 million in 1914. One of every six inhabitants lived in Greater Buenos Aires by 1914.

A new and enduring Constitution in 1853, the consecration of Buenos Aires as the national capital in the 1880s, and the presidencies of Mitre (1862–68) and Sarmiento (1868–74) consolidated the transition from

Conservative to Liberal rule, and propelled forward the transformation of the provinces of the Río de la Plata into a federal republic of Argentina. As European immigrants flooded into the nation, the Argentine army under the leadership of General Julio Roca embarked upon a "Conquest of the Desert" (1879–1880) that looked very similar to the U.S. Army's "Conquest of the West." Roca pushed the surviving indigenous peoples southward into the harsh region of Patagonia, or annihilated those who resisted. Roca was rewarded with the presidency (1880–1886) and subsequently passed it on to his brother-in-law, Miguel Juárez Celman (1886–1890). As in the United States, the campaign opened up the plains for an agricultural revolution. Much like the Midwest of the United States, the Argentine pampas became a booming center for the production of wheat and beef in the late nineteenth century. Unlike the United States, in Argentina, powerful landowners (*estancieros*) dominated the countryside.

British-built railroads crisscrossed the pampas as Buenos Aires became the center for meat-packing plants. Most of the immigrants settled in the cities and around the federal capital as small-scale industry sprang up to supply local and regional markets with consumer goods (processed foods, metalworking, textiles, furniture). Along with Mexico City, Rio de Janeiro, and São Paulo, Buenos Aires became one of the first centers for the rise of industry and industrial workers in Latin America. As in Europe and the United States, the rise of an industrial working class in Mexico, Brazil, and Argentina was accompanied by the emergence of socialist and anarchist movements at the turn of the century. (Socialists wanted to seize control of the state for the benefit of the working class, anarchists wanted to destroy it to provide the workers with freedom from government repression.) At the same time, the growing middle classes began to pressure the traditional landed elites for access to power and patronage. In the late nineteenth and early twentieth centuries, the emergence of these new groups was probably more pronounced and powerful than any other country in Latin America (again with the possible exception of Uruguay). In Chile, Argentina, Uruguay (and slightly later in Costa Rica), movements emerged that forged coalitions among the growing working and middle classes, and sectors of the landed and merchant elites. Wishing to avoid the constant political upheavals created by the clash of these new groups and ideologies, these coalitions brought together reformists who pushed through electoral reforms and social legislation that defused political tensions and opened the way for more democratic, representative political systems.

Uruguay (with one million inhabitants, one-third living in Montevideo), Argentina, Chile, and tiny Costa Rica (with 250,000 inhabitants, 50,000 of them in San José) each tentatively and cautiously moved in the first decades of the twentieth century toward the extension of the vote to ever greater numbers of adult males. In all four countries, the elite was composed

primarily of landowners and powerful merchants, and they pursued
political reforms that left intact the land tenure systems they dominated,
but defused the political upheavals produced by the emergence of working
and middle classes in the cities. Uruguay, led by José Batlle y Ordóñez
(president, 1903–1907 and 1911–1915), promulgated some of the most progressive social and labor legislation in the world (eight-hour day, minimum
wage, education for women, pensions). Similar processes developed in
Argentina, Chile, and Costa Rica. In Argentina, the Radical Party (*Unión
Cívica Radical*) under the charismatic leadership of Hipólito Yrigoyen
(1852–1933), pushed the reforms forward through occasional armed
revolts *and* the legislative process in the quarter-century after its formation
in 1890. The great turning point was the passage of the Sáenz Peña Law in
1912 that established universal male suffrage, a legislative action the
historian David Rock has called "an act of calculated retreat by the ruling
class." As in England in the mid-nineteenth century, the combination of
violence and legislative reforms gradually opened up the electoral process
in Argentina (as well as Uruguay, Chile, and Costa Rica) to greater participation by the 1930s. Although the masses may have been numerically the
majority, the landowning and commercial elites, and sectors of the middle
classes, dominated political parties, leadership positions, and national
elections. While Mexico achieved stability through repression and dictatorship, these four countries forged a tentative stability through negotiation,
compromise, and concessions, in particular, by the landowning elites.

THE PRICE OF PROGRESS

Liberals and positivists in Mexico and most of Central America imposed
their versions of modernity and progress on the ethnically non-European
masses in the late nineteenth and early twentieth centuries. In Costa Rica,
Chile, Argentina, and Uruguay, Liberals and positivists forged nation-states
through the promotion of Europeanization, urbanization, industrialization,
and increasing political participation in maturing political systems. The
other regions of Latin America experienced the same forces of transformation but with politics that were neither as continuously dictatorial as in
Mexico, nor as gradually participatory as Costa Rica, Chile, Argentina,
and Uruguay. The Andean republics of Venezuela, Colombia, Ecuador,
Peru, and Bolivia oscillated between periods of electoral politics and personalistic dictatorships. In the cases of Venezuela and Colombia, the periods
of electoral politics were punctuated by repressive personalistic dictatorships
and bloody violence. Liberals and Conservatives engaged in some of the
bloodiest fighting in all of the Americas. The War of a Thousand Days
(1899–1902) left at least 100,000 dead in a country of some three million

people! Although the forces of modernization and Europeanization may have been similar in all of Latin America, the political systems developed in each country ranged from the long-running dictatorship of Porfirio Díaz in Mexico to the Western European–style electoral politics in the Southern Cone. The rest of Latin America fell somewhere in between these two extremes as each nation forged its own path in the century after independence.

"Progress" came at a very high cost across Latin America, especially in those regions where the majority of the population was Indians, Africans, or the racially mixed (mestizos and mulattoes). As cities grew, factories sprang up, and European culture swept across the region, these peoples—who had made up the vast majority of "Latin Americans" for four hundred years—would suffer immensely from the onslaught of modernization and Europeanization. In Argentina, the Liberal-positivistic elite believed that "to govern is to populate," and they Europeanized their nation by importing Europeans and eradicating the peoples and cultures of the interior (Indians and gauchos). Uruguay followed a similar path, but the rest of Latin America could not replenish the gene pool with European immigrants. When the path of genetic transformation through immigration eluded them, they pursued paths of cultural metamorphosis. The largely "white" Liberals across Latin America in the nineteenth century pursued their dreams of building nations in the image of Europe, and this produced an inevitable and tragic cultural clash with the millions of non-European peoples in their midst.

Perhaps more acutely than any other country in the Americas, Brazil suffered from the cultural clashes provoked by the efforts of Liberals and positivists to build a modern nation-state. On the surface, Brazil appeared to be a "peaceable kingdom" in the nineteenth century, an exemplar of stability and growth in comparison to most of Latin America, or the United States. As we have seen (chapter 13), independence was achieved in Brazil with very little bloodshed, and the great challenge came from regional revolts rather than from Portugal. Pedro I (1822–31) had a liberal mind, but a conservative heart. Although he promulgated a constitution in 1824, it was highly centralist, giving the emperor ultimate authority over the judiciary and the legislative process. He clashed repeatedly with powerful sectors of Brazil's elites during the 1820s. Pedro I's greatest contributions were to move Brazil through the process of independence with little violence, and then to abdicate his throne in 1831. He returned to Portugal to engage in a civil war with conservative forces led by his brother Miguel. In 1834, his liberal, constitutional forces defeated Miguel (and his mother Carlota Joaquina), successfully placing his daughter Maria I on the throne. He died months later of tuberculosis at the age of 35.

Throughout the 1830s, a coalition of Liberals and Conservatives shared the powers of the regency before they crowned Pedro II in 1841. The young

Pedro was just a few months past his fourth birthday when his father and family returned to Portugal in 1831. Carefully selected tutors taught the future emperor Latin, Greek, French, German, Spanish, and English, and gave him a broad and profound education in the arts and sciences. Throughout his long life, Pedro would remain an intellectual with a powerful curiosity. In many ways, Pedro became the enlightened monarch envisioned by the philosophers of the eighteenth century.

Despite the declaration of political independence in 1822, the 1840s mark the true transition from colonial to modern Brazil. In politics, the gradual transition began with the transfer of the court in 1808, independence in 1822, abdication in 1831, and comes full circle with the coronation of Pedro II in 1841. After twenty years of independence, a Brazilian-born monarch finally ruled over the regime put into place in the 1820s. The government definitively crushed the last of the major regional revolts in the 1840s, consolidating nationhood. By midcentury, the central government and the economic and political elites of the coast had achieved control (even if somewhat tenuous) over the most populated areas of the country. Finally, the 1840s also mark the emergence of coffee cultivation as the engine of economic growth that would transform Brazil for the next century.

In the eighteenth century, the Portuguese planted coffee in northern Brazil, and, in the following decades, cultivation spread, reaching the fertile valleys near Rio de Janeiro in the 1820s and 1830s. During the next century, coffee cultivation spread rapidly in the area north and west of Rio, in southern Minas Gerais and (most prominently) in the province of São Paulo. The rapid expansion of coffee fields quickly made Brazil the world's leading exporter. Revenue generated by the coffee economy drove the Brazilian economy until the Great Depression in the 1930s, and definitively established southeastern Brazil (principally the states of Rio de Janeiro, Minas Gerais, and São Paulo) as the economic and political core of the nation. Export taxes on coffee provided the vast bulk of government revenue for expansion of the bureaucracy, and building roads, ports, and communications systems. Coffee exports allowed Brazil to maintain a favorable trade balance throughout much of the nineteenth century (and provoked economic crises when coffee prices fell in the early twentieth century).

As with sugar in the seventeenth century and gold in the eighteenth century, the coffee economy ran on slave labor. Brazil imported half a million slaves in the seventeenth century to toil on the sugar plantations of the northeast. In the eighteenth century, the gold fields of Minas Gerais absorbed another 1.5 million Africans. In the first half of the nineteenth century alone, Brazil imported another 1.5 million slaves to fill the demand for labor on the coffee plantations of the southeast. Between 1550 and 1850, Brazil imported about 35 percent of all the Africans brought in bondage to the Americas. The Caribbean basin devoured around 45 percent, the Latin American mainland about 10–15 percent, and the United States only about 6 percent. The abolitionist movement gained strength in England and the United States in the late eighteenth and early nineteenth centuries. The United States ended slave imports in 1808, as did the British Caribbean. British naval pressure forced Brazil to halt its 300-year-old Atlantic slave trade in 1850, and the final shipments cross into the Caribbean in the 1860s and 1870s.

In 1800, Brazil had the largest slave population in the world (half of its population of three million) and this forced migration created a truly African-American culture in Brazil. (The same process emerged powerfully in the islands of the Caribbean and, to a lesser extent, the US South.) African music, religions, foods, and language patterns blended with the culture of the Portuguese and the Indians to produce a cultural mosaic that was not African, European, or Native American. For nearly four decades after the end of the Atlantic slave trade, the Brazilian elites debated and legislated, slowly chipping away at the slave system. The new nations of Latin America abolished slavery in the 1820s, and the British parliament ended slavery in the British West Indies in the 1830s. Bloody civil war ended slavery in the United States in 1865. The Spanish would finally phase out slavery in Cuba and Puerto Rico in the 1870s and early 1880s. Slavery had been so central to the fabric of life in Brazil and Cuba that dismantling it took much longer in both places than in any other place in the Americas. With the rise of a vocal abolitionist movement in the 1880s (largely in the cities), and the growing tendency for slaves to flee from their masters, the system began to disintegrate. By 1888, unrest on plantations, and the refusal of the army to step in and halt the flight of slaves from their masters, brought the system to the brink of chaos. Ruling in place of her father, who was in Europe for medical treatment, Princess Isabel decreed the end of slavery with the "Golden Law" of May 13, 1888. Rather than face the anarchy and upheaval of massive slave unrest and flight, slave owners grudgingly accepted abolition. Pressure from both above and below doomed Brazilian slavery.

A flood of European immigrants to Brazil also eased the process of abolition. With the supply of new captive labor cut off after 1850, coffee planters turned to European immigration to meet their labor needs. Some 2.7 million immigrants—mainly from Italy, Spain, and Portugal—arrived in southeastern and southern Brazil between 1887 and 1914. By the turn of the century, the majority of the inhabitants of the city of São Paulo were immigrants or the children of immigrants. They gradually replaced slaves as the labor force in the coffee fields, and turned southern Brazil into a branch of European civilization strikingly different from the older mining and plantation regions of Minas Gerais and the northeast.

In stark contrast to the upheaval and instability of countries like Mexico, Brazil developed a power-sharing arrangement between Liberals and Conservatives. The Emperor acted as a "moderating power"—almost a fourth branch of government—calling for new elections when it appeared that the ruling party faced a political crisis. Invariably, the opposition party would win the new (and highly restricted) elections. In 49 years, power shifted hands between the two parties 26 times, a remarkable feat of conciliation and political consensus, even for nineteenth-century Europe. Pedro II reigned over what some viewed as a tropical version of Queen Victoria's parliamentary regime in England.

Although the political elite did not act as a monolithic bloc, they did exhibit extraordinary cooperation. In the 1870s and 1880s, a republican movement emerged that called for the end of the monarchy and the creation of a republic modeled after the United States. The republicans, and other members of the Brazilian elite, were deeply influenced by the writings of Auguste Comte and Herbert Spencer. In Spencer, Brazilian elites found a sophisticated scheme of social evolution that not only glorified science and reason, but also provided them with a positivistic rationale to justify their control of the "inferior" racially-mixed lower classes.

Brazil avoided most of the bloodshed and huge military buildup that plagued the early years of the new Latin American nations. Pedro II strove to keep the military weak and underdeveloped prior to the 1860s, fully conscious of the problems of his Latin American neighbors. For complex reasons, Brazil joined Argentina and Uruguay in a long and costly war against Paraguay in the 1860s. Despite the enormous disparity in resources, the Paraguayans tenaciously resisted the invading armies for six bitter years (1864–70), losing the majority of its adult male population and large chunks of territory in the conflict. Paraguay had been the great anomaly in the decades after independence, turning inward and rejecting outside influence and interference. The country developed a racially mixed rural population speaking both Spanish and Guaraní, and engaged in subsistence agriculture. The war with Brazil and Argentina forcibly dragged isolated Paraguay into the international marketplace.

By 1889, an ailing, 63-year-old Pedro had lost the support of key groups in the imperial power structure, and his heir, Princess Isabel, had few supporters among the elites. A small group of conspirators with key support from high-level army officers initiated a coup d'etat on November 15, 1889. The surprised Pedro found himself with little support and wisely (like his father) chose exile over resistance. A new Constitution (using the U.S. charter as a model) went into effect in 1891, replacing the imperial Constitution that had served the nation for 67 years. A new flag bearing the slogan, "Order and Progress" (*Ordem e Progresso*), reflected the influence of positivism among the leaders of the new regime. From 1889 to 1894, the army dominated politics, but thereafter the political and economic elites of the coffee states of São Paulo, Rio de Janeiro, and Minas Gerais shared political power and the presidency. Nine of the twelve presidents between 1894 and 1930 came from these three states. The three states produced most of Brazil's wealth and accounted for most of its population.

The First Republic was both highly controlled and decentralized. Less than 1 percent of the population could vote, and the coffee oligarchy ran state and national affairs. To appease the less powerful states, and to guarantee stability in the interior, the federal government struck a political deal. Recognizing that the central government had neither the revenues nor the means to extend its power into the interior where 80 percent of all Brazilians lived and worked, the political elite decided not to disrupt traditional power relations in the countryside. For centuries, local landowners (honorifically known as colonels of the local militias) dominated the rural population by controlling local government and local courts, and through the use of hired guns. Under the First Republic, these landowners retained their local power in exchange for allegiance to the state government. The state government provided the colonel with outside support if needed, and the colonel guaranteed local votes for the "official" state-level candidates. In turn, the states pledged support to the federal government in exchange for the right to run their own affairs. Should the state officials require help to crush challenges to their authority, the federal government sent troops and supplies to assist the state militia. The federal government accepted this decentralization, but intervened swiftly when state governments failed to demonstrate the necessary allegiance. This decentralized system permitted the federal government to maintain its authority, states to run their own affairs, and local landowners to maintain their traditional powers. Although Brazil began to experience some industrialization and urbanization accelerated, the traditional Brazil in the countryside remained largely unchanged.

Periodically, this traditional rural society erupted, challenging the emerging, modern, urban Brazil. Banditry and revolts in the interior occasionally reminded politicians in Rio and São Paulo of the "primitive," non-European side of their society. The most spectacular of these eruptions took place in 1897 at Canudos, a village deep in the rugged interior of the northeast. A religious mystic known as Antônio Conselheiro (the Counselor) gathered thousands of followers around him, denounced the secular Republic, and called for its destruction. After the Counselor and his followers routed a local police contingent, then two large state militia expeditions, the federal army stepped in. These poor, rural folk ferociously resisted, holding at bay several thousand federal troops during a military siege lasting months. The Canudos revolt revealed the powerful resistance of traditional rural folk to the encroachment of modern European society and the modern state into their lives. Conselheiro died during the siege, and the army ruthlessly obliterated the town and its inhabitants at the end of the siege. Possibly as many as 25,000 rural people died in the siege.

The destruction of Canudos, the Caste War in the Yucatán, the enslavement of the Yaqui in northern Mexico, the Paraguayan War, and numerous other clashes in the late nineteenth and early twentieth centuries reveal the profound struggles that convulsed Latin America in the Liberal era. Between 1870 and 1930 the Liberals and positivists modernized and Europeanized Latin America. All of the tools of modernity began to spread across the region—railroads, electricity, telegraphs and telephones, steamships, and automobiles. These tools in the hands of the Liberals and positivists expanded the power of central governments, and made possible the conquest of the interior of Latin America. This Second Conquest brought capitalism into the farthest reaches of Latin America, producing economic growth and the emergence of modern economies built largely on the export of raw materials and agricultural products to Europe and the United States. Without a doubt, the economies of Latin America grew dramatically during this period, cities expanded, and even the remote regions of the interior of the continent were drawn into a world community dominated by the North Atlantic world.

Modernity and progress, however, came at a high price, primarily for the poor, rural, racially mixed and indigenous peoples of the countryside. In the aftermath of the conquest of the sixteenth century, these peoples had emerged and pursued their lives in a constant and delicate process characterized by cultural tension and negotiation with the larger world. The onslaught of modernity definitively shattered this fragile cultural interaction as progress overwhelmed, and sometimes completely annihilated, the villages, communities, and traditions of rural peoples. Euclides da Cunha and Domingo Sarmiento saw this conflict emerging and understood that it was a battle for the future of Latin America. By the beginning of the twentieth century, the Liberals and positivists had triumphed, and the nation-states of Latin America had begun to consolidate control over their territories. The creation of the "imagined communities" of Latin America accelerated, and would continue to accelerate, throughout the twentieth century. The vast majority of the peoples of Latin America would gradually become "Latin Americans" while desperately striving to hold on to what they could of their languages, traditions, and communities. They had been "condemned to progress."

16

Great Britain, the United States, and Latin America

THE "EXTERNAL CONNECTION" AND FOREIGN POWER

Created out of a collision of cultures in the aftermath of the Columbian Moment, Latin America has been a battleground of empires, colonies, and nations since its birth. During most of the colonial period, Spain, Portugal, France, and England clashed—among themselves and with Native Americans and African slaves—across much of the Americas, especially in the Caribbean basin and on the North American mainland after 1600. The shifting power and fortunes of these European empires shaped the contours of many of the European colonies, areas that by the late eighteenth century had begun to move toward open warfare with the European powers and, at times, among themselves. By the 1830s, nineteen independent nations had arisen in the Americas. Canada and most of the Caribbean remained under British, French, and Spanish control. On the Central and South American mainland, British Honduras (Belize) and the Guianas (English, Dutch, and French) survived as European colonial enclaves— and territorial legacies of the European imperial wars of the seventeenth century.

In the century after the wars for independence in Latin America, two powers—one preeminent and one emerging—would vie for political and economic influence in Latin America. Great Britain, the preeminent power in the world at the beginning of the nineteenth century, would be the most potent external political and economic influence on most of Latin America into the 1930s. The United States, as it emerged as an industrial and economic powerhouse throughout the nineteenth century, would challenge the British for influence in the region. In the first century after independence in the 1780s, the power and influence of the United States radiated westward and southward from the old Thirteen Colonies. It was on the North American continent and in the Caribbean basin that the United States would truly challenge and then supplant the British throughout the nineteenth century. U.S. influence was minimal south of Central America and the Caribbean. British power in South America began to wane with the First World War and would be completely replaced by the political and economic influence of the United States by the end of the Second World War.

For many Latin Americans, and scholars of Latin America, the so-called external connection has been the single most important factor in the evolution of the region since 1492. Following this line of reasoning, the prime mover during the colonial period was the European metropolis (Spain, Portugal, or France), in the nineteenth century it was Great Britain or the United States, and, finally, the twentieth century was the era of U.S. pre-eminence and power. Nearly all those who study the region would agree on the importance of foreign powers acting on and influencing events in Latin America since the Conquest of the sixteenth century. Generally, those to the left of the political spectrum (and some on the far right) have placed the greatest emphasis on the role of the external connection in determining the destiny of Latin Americans. Those who follow this line of reasoning argue that the power of the European empires, then Great Britain, and then the United States has been *the* determinant factor in the history of the region. At its extreme, this line of argument holds the foreign powers responsible for nearly all the ills of Latin America, in the past and today—in particular, the poverty, socioeconomic inequalities, and underdevelopment of the region. During the Cold War, the preponderant power of the United States in the world, and especially in the Americas, stimulated the production of a large literature that made these arguments with great vigor and passion.

While it is clear that the external connection has been one of the most important factors (and sometimes the most important factor) in the evolution of Latin America, overemphasizing the role of foreign powers too often obscures and negates the role of Americans themselves in shaping their own destinies. The relationship between Latin America and these foreign powers has always been very unequal, but it has not been a straightforward, one-way relationship with the external forces largely determining the fate of Latin Americans. The peoples of Latin America, in many forms and fashions, have collaborated or cooperated with, and reacted against or resisted, foreign influences. Local interactions and processes have often been much more important in regional developments than the external connection. The story of Latin America's relationship with foreign powers is one of enormous asymmetries of power, but not of passivity. In particular, we must resist the temptation to lump all of Latin America into a whole when discussing the external connection. As we shall see, big countries such as Mexico or Brazil have the ability to confront external forces in ways not possible for small nations such as Nicaragua or Cuba, or transition zones like Puerto Rico.

FROM BRITISH PREEMINENCE TO DOLLAR DIPLOMACY

By the beginning of the nineteenth century, Great Britain had emerged as the greatest economic and military power in the history of the world. In the midst of the First Industrial Revolution, Britain was constructing the world's first modern economy built on industrial production and global trade. A modern economy must constantly seek new raw materials for its factories and new markets for its mass-produced goods. The British defeat in the American Revolution was an important anomaly in its surge toward global economic and political domination in the half-century after 1775. In the first decades of the nineteenth century, Latin America appeared to present the British with their most promising new opportunities for access to a region rich in raw materials and with millions of potential consumers. As we saw in chapter 14, these economic hopes failed to materialize in the aftermath of independence in countries plagued by warfare, disorder, little infrastructure, and a risky investment environment. It was not until the last third of the nineteenth century that foreign investors (British, U.S., French, German) finally moved into the region with sustained impact.

Despite the initial economic disappointments, the British ardently pursued an aggressive diplomatic and political agenda in Latin America in the nineteenth century. Although the British military did not participate actively in supporting the wars for independence, many British citizens (Lord Cochrane, for example) joined the rebellions in the 1810s and 1820s. Britain was quick to recognize the new nations, often before any other European country. British diplomats quickly moved to negotiate very favorable trade and investment terms for British merchants and companies. When the Portuguese royal family fled to Brazil in 1807–8, they were escorted by a British fleet, and Lord Strangford, a British diplomatic emissary, accompanied the Braganzas. As soon as the entourage disembarked in Salvador in early 1808, Prince Regent João, with Strangford at his side, announced the opening of Brazilian ports to all friendly nations. This move to "free trade," in effect, opened Brazil to British merchants (for who else in Europe or the United States even got to Brazil in those times of war), and within a year there were hundreds operating in Brazil's main ports. Over the next decade, British diplomats negotiated treaties with Brazil that allowed British imports to enter the country with tariffs lower than any other nation, including Portugal. As in many other South American nations, the British became the principal suppliers to Brazil of imports, technology, technical expertise, and investment in the first half of the nineteenth century. One British firm, the Rothschild family in London, handled all Brazilian government loans throughout the nineteenth century. The British-Brazilian relationship was emblematic of Great Britain's role in the region, a relationship the historian Alan K. Manchester long ago labeled British "preeminence," to emphasize the power Britain exerted in nineteenth-century Brazil.

Great Britain's relationship with Latin America was very different from the British role in Africa or Asia in the nineteenth century. While the European powers carved up and occupied much of Africa and Asia, and then guaranteed their control with British troops, in Latin America the British rarely needed troops or navies. Although British warships occasionally intervened to pressure Latin American governments, Britain's influence was overwhelmingly economic and cultural. Governments and local business communities carefully cultivated strong relationships with British officials and investors to ensure the flow of investment into the region. For those who stress the vital importance of the external connection, this British pressure represented an "informal" colonialism, or what some have called the "imperialism of free trade." Diplomats and money, in effect, were the levers of power and control, rather than armies and navies.

By 1815, at the moment the Napoleonic wars were ending in Europe, and in the midst of the wars for independence in Latin America, the British were already sending one-third of their exports to Latin America. In the 1870s, Latin America accounted for about 10 percent of annual British exports, worth about US$125 million. One-third of these exports went to Brazil alone. British investment in the region exploded in the late nineteenth century, growing from US$1 billion in 1880 to US$5 billion in 1913. About 60 percent went to three countries. One-third of this investment went to Argentina, a quarter to Brazil, and a sixth to Mexico. In return, the British bought more than US$400 million from Latin America in 1913, or about 10 percent of all British imports. Substantial British communities formed in Buenos Aires, Montevideo, Rio de Janeiro, São Paulo, Valparaíso, Santiago, and Lima, with smaller communities scattered across Latin America.

This British preeminence in South America did not face any serious challenge from the United States until after the First World War. United States direct intervention into the political affairs of South American countries was extremely rare in the nineteenth century, and the most notorious episodes took place in the late nineteenth century in Valparaíso and Rio de Janeiro.

Both were isolated incidents involving U.S. naval commanders operating on their own rather than under orders from Washington, D.C. Barroom brawls involving U.S. sailors from the USS *Baltimore* and the Chilean police in Valparaíso provoked an incident in 1891. Eventually, the Chilean government was compelled to apologize to the United States, but there was very little U.S. presence in the country at the time. In the mid-1890s, the new Brazilian republic (dominated by the army) faced a rebellion led by Brazilian naval officers who proceeded to blockade the Rio de Janeiro harbor to bring down the government. The blockade might have succeeded in deposing the government, but a U.S. naval commander broke the naval blockade to allow U.S. merchants to enter the harbor. (He cared little for either side in the conflict.) Although the U.S. State Department had been consulting with the commander, Admiral Andrew Benham, his actions were unilateral and taken on the spot. Again, U.S. investment and business in Brazil were small at the time, and U.S. military presence sporadic, at best.

The Caribbean basin and Central America were a different story. Although the Spanish and French had aided the United States in its war of independence in the 1770s and 1780s, the new republic soon challenged both Spain and France as it moved to expand south of Georgia and westward across the Appalachians and then across the Mississippi River. Napoléon Bonaparte, faced with the costs of his wars in Europe, sold Louisiana to the United States in 1803 for $15 million (equivalent to about $300 billion in today's currency), nearly doubling the size of the country. (Louisiana stretched from the Gulf of Mexico to Canada, covering more than 800,000 square miles and containing parts of what today are 14 different states.) During the War of 1812 with the British, U.S. troops moved into Florida, a territory that stretched from the Mississippi River to the Atlantic Ocean. Eventually, the beleaguered Spanish sold Florida to the United States in 1819.

Although the United States officially maintained neutrality during the wars for independence in Spanish America, after 1821 (and the independence of Mexico) the United States moved toward recognition of the new regimes. Many prominent figures in the United States opposed this move, believing Latin Americans had little in common with North Americans. Edward Everett, one of the great New England intellectuals of the period, wrote, "We are sprung from different stocks, we speak different languages, we have been brought up in different social and moral schools, we have been governed by different codes of laws, we profess radically different codes of religion." In March 1822, President James Monroe asked Congress to extend recognition to the new Latin American republics. Congress agreed and moved to establish diplomatic missions across the region. In December 1823, Monroe sent his annual message to Congress and it contained a few paragraphs stating his Latin American policy (written by

John Quincy Adams). What became known as the Monroe Doctrine stated that the Americas would "henceforth not be considered as subjects for colonization by any European powers." The statement went on to warn the Europeans (he was aiming his words at the Spanish, French, and Russians) that "we should consider any attempt on their part to extend their system to any portion of this hemisphere as dangerous to the peace and safety." In effect, the young United States declared the Americas off-limits to European intervention, a statement that was meaningless without British cooperation. The Monroe Doctrine would carry little weight for most of the nineteenth century, but would become the cornerstone of U.S. policy in the twentieth century.

By the 1830s, the United States stretched from the Great Lakes to the Gulf of Mexico and from the Atlantic to what today are Montana, Wyoming, and Colorado. In the 1840s, the Mexican War (1846–48) filled in the continental map from San Francisco to New York City. Many in the United States viewed this westward expansion as inevitable and blessed by divine sanction. In the words of one of the most ardent expansionists of the period, newspaper editor John L. O'Sullivan, the United States had the "manifest destiny to overspread the continent allotted by Providence to the free development of our yearly multiplying millions." Many of these expansionists envisioned the continued "overspread" reaching across the Caribbean and Central America.

The Central American isthmus offered the most advantageous route from the East Coast of the United States to the West Coast. The trip from New York City to San Francisco through the treacherous Straits of Magellan and Tierra del Fuego took months and covered 14,000 miles. With the discovery of gold in California in 1848, the isthmus became the quickest and safest way from coast to coast (less than half the distance of the sea voyage at 6,000 miles). The 3,000-mile trip across the United States still required crossing forbidding terrain and hostile Indian territories in the West. The Transcontinental Railroad was not completed until 1869. Great Britain and the United States clashed over the rights to build a trans-isthmian canal, but resolved in the Clayton-Bulwer Treaty (1850) jointly to construct and control a canal. In the early 1850s, the so-called Forty-Niners primarily crossed the Central American isthmus by shipping up the San Juan River (dividing Nicaragua and Costa Rica) and then taking a stagecoach the last few miles on land from Lake Nicaragua to the Pacific coast. As we saw earlier, the William Walker intervention in the mid-1850s disrupted this route and provoked shipping magnate Cornelius Vanderbilt to intervene against Walker. In 1855, a group of New York financiers opened the Panama Railway, a 47-mile line connecting the Atlantic and the Pacific. For the next 60 years, this would be a heavily traveled route, and the precursor of the Panama Canal. Some 50,000 travelers would cross the isthmus on this train each year in the 1850s and 1860s (along with hundreds of millions of dollars worth of gold bullion from California heading to New York City). The route squarely placed Panama in a prominent position on the geopolitical map of U.S. global strategists.

In the late nineteenth century, the United States began to flex its growing economic and military power to confront British interests in the region, as well as assert its self-appointed role as the leader of all the Americas. Britain and the United States clashed in the late 1890s over the ill-defined boundary between Venezuela and British Guiana. The British, who had their hands full with the Boer War in South Africa, eventually accepted negotiations over the boundary, and agreed to recognize the validity of the Monroe Doctrine. In 1879, Chile went to war with Peru and Bolivia over the rich nitrate deposits in the Atacama Desert. U.S. Secretary of State James G. Blaine proposed a Pan-American conference to negotiate an end to the conflict. Eventually, the Chileans invaded Peru and seized Lima in one of the few major wars between Latin American nations. In the peace settlement, Chile seized three provinces from Peru and one from Bolivia. The war left Bolivia landlocked, without an outlet to the sea. The War of the Pacific left deep scars and powerful resentments in Peru, Chile, and Bolivia—resentments that continue to effect contemporary relations among all three nations. Secretary Blaine would not get his conference until 1889, and suspicious Latin American delegates resisted what they saw as U.S. efforts to dominate the region. The Argentine delegate and future president of his country, Roque Sáenz Peña, remarked that Blaine "wished to make Latin America a market, and the sovereign states tributaries." This would become a regular complaint over the next century.

COLONIALISM, IMPERIALISM, AND FOREIGN INFLUENCE

The Spanish-American War in 1898 marks a watershed, not only in the role of the United States in Latin America, but also the U.S. role in the world. In many ways, 1898 marks the emergence of the United States on the world stage, and the beginning of more than a century of a rise to global supremacy that continues in the twenty-first century. Throughout the nineteenth century, the United States marched across the North American continent, conquering, colonizing, and creating one of the largest domestic markets the world had ever seen. By 1898, the Second Industrial Revolution was in full swing in the United States, built on iron and steel, the internal combustion engine, petroleum, electric power, and a revolution in chemistry that would produce (among other things) fertilizers and explosives that would transform agriculture and warfare. The Civil War in the 1860s had briefly and brutally halted expansion and integration of the continent. In the decades after the war, railroads crisscrossed the nation binding the regions together, and steamships carried U.S. troops and exports outward across the oceans.

The Latin Americans felt the impact of growing U.S. power and expansion most acutely in the Caribbean basin and Central America, in Cuba and Panama, in particular. Throughout the nineteenth century, Cuba had become the greatest sugar plantation in the world, and U.S. investment in the sugar industry had accelerated over the decades. The industry and landholding had become increasingly concentrated as foreign investors built railroads and steam-powered sugar mills across the island. At the same time, slave rebellions and creole revolts against Spain wracked the island. The Ten Years' War (1868–78) decimated the creole landowning class, and provided greater opportunities for U.S. investors to buy up more land. To a lesser degree, the same process was taking place in the sugar industry in Puerto Rico. In spite of their status as Spanish colonies, both islands had been drawn into the U.S. economic sphere by 1898.

Another revolt against Spain broke out in Cuba in 1895. José Martí, one of the greatest Latin American writers of the era, had played a key role in organizing the uprising from his long exile in the United States. Martí died in a minor skirmish in the initial stages of the invasion in 1895, but he would become revered by all Cubans in the twentieth century as one of the great martyrs of independence and one of the founders of the nation. For nearly three years, a very brutal and bloody struggle consumed the island, and East Coast newspapers (led by William Randolph Hearst and Joseph Pulitzer) graphically highlighted Spanish atrocities, while calling for U.S. intervention. Hearst's *New York Journal* described the Spanish General Weyler as a "fiendish despot . . . a brute . . . pitiless, cold an exterminator of men . . . there is nothing to prevent his carnal, animal brain from running riot with itself in inventing tortures and infamies of bloody debauchery." In February 1898, the USS *Maine* exploded and sank in the harbor in Havana, killing more than 250 servicemen. Although the exact cause of the explosion has never been determined, the U.S. government blamed Spain, made extraordinary demands of the Spanish government, and then declared war on April 25, when Spain did not comply with the demands.

What Theodore Roosevelt called a "splendid little war" lasted just four months as an emerging world power quickly defeated a long declining Spanish empire. U.S. naval forces destroyed Spanish fleets in the Philippines and Cuba. Although ostensibly about the revolt in Cuba, the United States used the declaration of war to seize control of the Philippines. In the treaty that formally concluded the war in December 1898, the United States took control of the Philippines, Guam, and Puerto Rico, and the U.S. Army occupied Cuba. The war effectively ended four hundred years of Spanish imperial presence in the Americas, which had begun with the voyage of Columbus in 1492, and announced the emergence of the United States as an imperial power in the world as it entered the twentieth century.

In the months leading up to the outbreak of war, Theodore Roosevelt served as Assistant Secretary of the Navy, positioning U.S. fleets in strategic locations in the Caribbean and the Pacific. Once the war broke out, he resigned his office, helped organize a group of volunteers (who became known as the "Rough Riders"), and took part in the brief hostilities. In 1900, President William McKinley, who had given the orders to go to war against Spain, was reelected with Roosevelt as his vice president. While vice president, Roosevelt declared in a speech that the United States should "speak softly and carry a big stick." When an anarchist assassinated McKinley in September 1901, Roosevelt became the youngest president in U.S. history at the age of 42. He would be elected president in his own right in 1904. Under Roosevelt, the United States became increasingly bold and aggressive, pursuing a foreign policy in the Americas sometimes referred to as Big Stick Diplomacy. After Germany, Italy, and Great Britain blockaded the Venezuelan coast in 1902–1903 to force the government to honor its foreign debts, Roosevelt issued what became known as the Roosevelt Corollary to the Monroe Doctrine. The latter, as we saw, declared the unilateral "right" of the United States to protect the hemisphere from foreign "interference". The corollary announced the unilateral "right" of the United States to intervene in Latin American nations to prevent European intervention. Over the next three decades, the United States would repeatedly invoke this "right" to invade Cuba, the Dominican Republic, Haiti, Venezuela, Nicaragua, and Mexico.

The most spectacular and enduring of Roosevelt's "interventions" was in Panama. Since Balboa first crossed the isthmus in 1513, foreign powers had contemplated proposals to build an interoceanic canal across Panama. Ferdinand de Lesseps, the great French engineer who had built the Suez Canal in the 1860s, failed disastrously in the 1880s in an attempt to construct a sea-level canal in Panama. Mismanagement, and high mortality due to malaria and yellow fever, doomed the enterprise. Roosevelt's administration negotiated a treaty with Colombia in 1903 to take over the failed French effort, but the Colombian Congress rejected the treaty. A supremely irritated Roosevelt then conspired with a small group of Panamanians and the French canal company agent, Philippe Bunau-Varilla, to declare Panamanian independence. U.S. warships offshore, and the assistance of the United States-owned railway, neutralized any effort by the Colombians to halt the revolt. Bunau-Varilla and Secretary of State John Hay quickly signed a canal treaty before the Panamanian officials even arrived in Washington, D.C. After briefing his cabinet on his actions in the episode, Roosevelt reportedly asked them if he had adequately defended

himself. Supposedly, Secretary of War Elihu Root replied, "You certainly
have. You have shown you were accused of seduction and you have conclusively proved that you were guilty of rape." The treaty gave the United
States virtual sovereignty over a ten-mile-wide strip of land that cut across
Panama from northwest to southeast. The treaty became one of the most
infamous examples of U.S. power and hegemony in Latin America.

Over the next decade, the United States constructed one of the great
engineering achievements of the modern world—a 51-mile-long ship
canal that operates on rainfall and gravity. A set of locks near Colón on the
Atlantic side raises ships more than 80 feet, they then sail across the
artificially-created Lake Gatun, and then two sets of locks on the Pacific
side (near Panama City) lower the ships back down to sea level. The massive isthmian rainfall continually refills the lake, which, in turn, fills the
continually emptying locks. Roosevelt—the first U.S. president to travel
abroad—personally traveled to Panama in November 1906 to observe the
construction works. Despite massive engineering and logistical challenges, the canal opened a year ahead of schedule, in 1914, primarily due
to the managerial skills of Colonel George Washington Goethals, the chief
engineer on the project and then Governor of the Canal Zone. Dr. William
Crawford Gorgas of the U.S. Army went to Cuba in 1898, and then in 1904
to Panama, where he virtually eliminated the scourges of yellow fever and
malaria through public health campaigns to eradicate the breeding
grounds of the mosquitoes that carry the deadly diseases. The U.S. Army's
control over both Cuba (1898–1902) and the Panama Canal Zone (after
1904) allowed it to embark upon construction and public health projects
that would never have been feasible in the rough-and-tumble politics of
the United States. The United States recruited tens of thousands of
English-speaking workers from the British West Indies to build the canal,
and more than 25,000 of them died in Panama (mainly of yellow fever
and malaria). The massive influx of English-speaking West Indians also
transformed the racial and cultural landscape of tiny Panama.

Between 1898 and the early 1930s, the United States sent military troops
(the Army or the Marine Corps) into Cuba, Puerto Rico, Haiti, the
Dominican Republic, Panama, Nicaragua, and Mexico. More so than at
any other time in U.S. foreign policy, these interventions were often explicitly to protect U.S. investment and businesses. During the administration
of William Howard Taft (1909–13), the policy became generally known as
Dollar Diplomacy. As Taft once said, referring to Latin Americans, he
believed the United States should have the "right to knock their heads
together until they should maintain peace." The usual practice was to
send in the Marines to establish order, take control of the customs houses,
and then use the tariffs on imports and exports to guarantee payments to

foreign creditors. The U.S. Army occupied Haiti (1915–34), the Dominican Republic (1916–24), and Nicaragua (1909–25), to cite the most notable examples.

When Woodrow Wilson became president in 1913 (after defeating both Taft and Roosevelt in the 1912 election), he sought to imbue U.S. foreign policy with a strong moral dimension fed by his own Christian idealism and faith in the United States as the democratic and capitalist model for the rest of the world. He rejected Dollar Diplomacy as driven by crass, material, and commercial motives. Wilson announced his desire to improve relationships with Latin America, and he assured Latin Americans that the United States would "never again seek one additional foot of territory by conquest."

During his first days in office in March 1913, upheaval in Mexico presented Wilson with his first major foreign policy decisions. The first great social revolution of the twentieth century had exploded in Mexico in 1910, ending the decades-long reign of Porfirio Díaz (more on this in chapter 19). For a decade, civil war would convulse all of Mexico, leaving one million dead in a country of fifteen million inhabitants. When Díaz left for exile in Europe, Mexicans elected Francisco Madero president in 1911. From a prominent landholding family in the north, Madero was an unlikely leader—a spiritualist and a vegetarian, with an unimpressive speaking presence. He was definitely not caudillo material. Throughout 1911–12, civil upheaval spread across all of Mexico, and the United States stationed tens of thousands of troops along the Mexican border. On the eve of Woodrow Wilson's inauguration, General Victoriano Huerta (with the encouragement of the U.S. ambassador in Mexico) deposed and executed Madero. Wilson took office and refused to recognize the Huerta government, calling the new regime "a government of butchers." Instead, he announced that he was "going to teach the South American republics to elect good men!" In April 1914, U.S. troops seized Veracruz (to cut off Huerta's revenues) and occupied the city until November (when Huerta was deposed).

The outbreak of the First World War in Europe in August 1914 raised U.S. fears of German influence in Mexico, Central America, and the Caribbean. In part, the occupations of Haiti (1915) and the Dominican Republic (1916) were spurred by these fears. When the Mexican revolutionary, Pancho Villa, looted the border town of Columbus, New Mexico, in March 1916, killing 17 U.S. citizens, Wilson sent General John J. Pershing and 7,000 troops into northern Mexico in search of Villa. After a futile pursuit across northern Mexico, an intervention that dismayed and angered the Mexican government, Wilson withdrew the troops from Mexico in February 1917 and turned his attention to the U.S. entry into the

First World War (with an expeditionary force led by Pershing). A month later, Wilson recognized the government of Venustiano Carranza, the revolutionary general who had managed to establish control of most of the country and stage his election to the presidency. In the end, Wilson's high-minded efforts in Mexico continued the pattern of direct U.S. military intervention in the region, and reminded Latin Americans that the U.S. government (under Republicans or Democrats) would not relent in trying to teach their southern neighbors how to "elect good men" and organize their governments.

Even more emblematic of U.S. policy toward Latin America in the early twentieth century was the United States' actions in the tiny Central American nation of Nicaragua. As we have seen, Nicaragua was wracked by the Liberal-Conservative battles of the nineteenth century, invaded by the U.S. filibuster William Walker in the 1850s, and fought over as the best site for a sea-level interoceanic canal throughout much of the century. (The Machiavellian maneuvers of the notorious Philippe Bunau-Varilla at the turn of the century had wrested the canal route from Nicaragua to Panama.) The Liberal dictator, José Santos Zelaya, seized power in 1893 and dominated the country until he was overthrown (with U.S. support) in 1909–a coup that initiated decades of political instability and renewed fighting between Liberals and Conservatives. U.S. Marines intervened in 1912 and thus began two decades of intermittent guerrilla warfare and civil war. In the 1920s, Augusto César Sandino led a guerrilla movement that continually frustrated and harassed the U.S. Marines. A working-class figure who had traveled widely in Mexico and Central America, Sandino had forged a vision of antiimperialism that directly challenged the U.S. presence in Nicaragua through armed struggle.

Beginning under Herbert Hoover (1929–33) and then under Franklin D. Roosevelt (1933–45), the United States began a policy of disengagement from the region that became known as the Good Neighbor Policy. Instead of direct military intervention, the U.S. approach was to create, train, and equip nonpartisan, local security forces (police, national guard, army) that could replace the U.S. troops and allow them to withdraw. The expectation was to have this nonpartisan force guarantee the peace in Nicaragua (National Guard), the Dominican Republic (National Guard), Haiti (Gendarmerie), and Cuba (Army). The stability provided, so the thinking went, would allow these countries to build national institutions, democracy, and pursue economic development. After the United States withdrew, it provided loans, military equipment and training, and private investment to assist in the nation-building project in each country. In the first decades of the twentieth century, these Caribbean and Central American countries were the first in which the United States attempted to guide nation-building (along with the Philippines in the Pacific).

Unfortunately, for both the United States and the Latin Americans, the policy produced unintended consequences—dictatorship and repression. As the United States withdrew troops in the 1930s, whoever gained control of the "nonpartisan" security forces then dominated the country: in Cuba, Fulgencia Batista; in Nicaragua, Anastasio Somoza García; in the Dominican Republic, Rafael Leónidas Trujillo; and, in Haiti, (though later) François Duvalier. Rather than building democracies and strong partici-patory institutions, by the late 1930s, the United States had put into place and supported personalistic dictatorships in Cuba, Haiti, Nicaragua, and the Dominican Republic. Reportedly, when someone commented on this ironic turn of events to Franklin D. Roosevelt, he is supposed to have replied, "They may be sons of bitches, but they are our sons of bitches!" Rather than creating gradual and progressive reforms, U.S. policies served to reinforce repressive regimes that would rule these countries into the 1960s and 1970s.

By the end of the nineteenth century, this rising U.S. influence was already provoking strong reactions from Latin American intellectuals. The greatest Latin American poet of the turn of the century, the Nicaraguan Rubén Darío, summed up the fears and anxieties of many Latin Americans in a poem in his collection *Songs of Life and Hope (Cantos de vida y esperanza*, 1905).

> You are the United States
> You are the future invader
> Of the native America that has native blood
> That still prays to Jesus Christ and still speaks Spanish . . .
>
> The United States are powerful and large.
> When they shake, a deep trembling
> Passes through the huge backbone of the Andes . . .
>
> Long live Spanish America!
> A thousand cubs of the Spanish lion are afield.
> You, Roosevelt, would need to become, by command of God Himself,
> The terrible sharpshooter and the mighty Hunter,
> To hold us in your iron claws.

By the 1930s, several patterns were clear. The British preeminence in nineteenth-century Latin America (especially South America) was rapidly disappearing and U.S. power in the region was growing dramatically. U.S. investment in the region moved past that of Great Britain, the United States had decades of direct economic and military involvement across the Caribbean basin and the Gulf of Mexico, and U.S. policy-makers were hard at work on forging a Pax Americana in which the United States would "lead" the rest of the hemisphere. The Second World War would accelerate all of these processes, opening an era of unprecedented U.S. power and influence in Latin America after 1945. As the peoples of the region forged their identities, as Mexicans, Nicaraguans, Chileans, Brazilians—as Latin Americans—they did so in a complex and deeply conflicted relationship with the Colossus of the North.

17

The Pursuit of Identity

FROM IBERIAN TO AMERICAN

Since the wars for independence, the pursuit of identity has been one of the most powerful forces at work in Latin America. In the new nations created in the century between Haitian independence in 1804 and Panamanian independence in 1903, the pursuit has been about the creation of a national community constructed around a common set of symbols, traditions, and values. The Liberals of the nineteenth century, in particular, forged nation-building projects that sought to create an "imagined community" built around a European model. They confronted the extraordinary linguistic, racial, cultural, and social diversity of Latin America with a single-minded goal—to homogenize and standardize, in the image of Europe. As we shall see, the European vision of the nineteenth century gave way in the early twentieth century to national visions that extolled the racially and culturally mixed heritage of the nations of the region, and explicitly rejected the nineteenth-century elite fixation on Europeanization. By the 1920s and 1930s, the leading intellectual and cultural figures in Latin America had proclaimed the cultural independence of Latin America from Europe and defined their national identities as "American" rather than European. For countries like Mexico and Brazil, this vision of the nation was built on racial and cultural mixture—José Vasconcelos's "cosmic race" (*la raza cósmica*) in Mexico or Gilberto Freyre's "luso-tropical civilization" in Brazil.

To return to the central theme of this book, Latin America (and Mexico, Brazil, Peru, Cuba . . .) did not exist in 1491. The region and nations were created out of the collision of cultures that Columbus ignited in October 1492. For more than five hundred years, the region has encompassed many, many groups and identities—thousands of groups of Native American peoples, many different groups from the European continent, hundreds of ethnicities from the African continent, and countless mixtures of these three colliding peoples that conquest and colonization produced over centuries of interaction. The difficult task of imperial rulers (from Spain, Portugal, and France) was to impose some (however tenuous) sense of unity and control over the peoples within their American domains. In a sense, they did this by creating local imperial elites who worked with the leaders of the many indigenous, slave, and *casta* communities that existed or emerged out of the collisions of the conquest. Imperial identity was superficially superimposed over the multiple ethnic and cultural identities within the occupied territories.

In a very real sense, the most important of these identities was that of the creoles, an identity that had begun to emerge in Spanish America by the seventeenth century. Clearly, by the late eighteenth century, creoles had come to see themselves as distinct from Spaniards—as Americans. Although the wars for independence (especially in Haiti) were complex and had many causes, it was creole leadership that became central to the direction of the struggle, and to the construction of the new order in the aftermath of independence. It would be the creoles who would assume control of the nation-building projects of the nineteenth century, and dominate in the struggle to forge one national identity out of the many identities and peoples within the presumed boundaries of the new nations. Although Haiti and Brazil are somewhat different than Spanish America, in both countries a new elite emerges that is the equivalent of the Spanish American creoles, driving the process of nation-building. In the regions that come under the political control of the United States (the borderlands, Puerto Rico, and, in different ways, Cuba and Panama), creole nationalism takes on very different forms from the rest of Latin America. It emerges, sometimes successfully, sometimes not, as a sort of counterpoint to U.S. power and control over territories that are clearly under U.S. control (the borderlands and Puerto Rico) or in nations that are not fully sovereign (Cuba and Panama).

It is also important to remember that other forms of identity formation are taking place alongside the creation of these national communities. Within these nations, regional (subnational) identities (e.g., Buenos Aires vs. the interior, regional identities within Mexico) continue to coalesce, and the creation of supranational communities also proceeds. The promotion of larger, imagined entities such as Central America, the Caribbean, or Latin America, take shape alongside the process of nation-building. To a large degree, the creation of this sense of something called Latin America, emerges in opposition to the emerging power and influence of the United States. I want to emphasize, however, that the formation of these identities is neither inevitable nor unilinear. These identities are often fragile, complex, and shifting. Texas's identity, for example, is initially a regional identity within Mexico, then a nation-building project, then a regional identity within the United States, then within the failed Confederacy, and, finally, a regional subset of the United States once again. The identity of "Mexican" is not only shifting, due to cultural and social struggles within the national political boundaries, but those boundaries are also shifting throughout the nineteenth century. We must be careful not to make the presentist mistake of reading back from today to assume that all roads inevitably led to the creation of the current national states. They did not, and the complex identities of the current nations and the region of Latin America, which have been in constant formation and transformation, will continue to shift and evolve.

For most of the three centuries of colonial rule in Latin America, indigenous peoples (especially in Mesoamerica and the Andes) tenaciously resisted Europeanization, although their cultures evolved and changed in a complicated dance with the world of the Spaniards in the Americas. The transatlantic slave trade uprooted millions of peoples from the African continent, spread them across the Americas (especially Brazil and the Caribbean), and brought them into complex interactions among different African ethnicities, indigenous peoples, and Europeans. The creoles (and their Luso-Brazilian and Franco-American equivalents) were tiny enclaves living within this sea of non-European peoples. As we have seen, these colliding peoples and cultures produced rich and varied cultural and social groups from the 1490s to the 1790s. Latin America, as it entered the nineteenth century, was largely a conglomeration of numerous non-European peoples and cultures living in a world dominated by Europeans and Euro-Americans. The creoles and *peninsulares* had worked for centuries to construct the institutions that would help foster and recreate European culture in the Americas. Along the way, the creoles (sometimes consciously and, at times, unconsciously) began to foster the emergence of American cultures that combined the influences of all the peoples of Latin America. The Europeans and Euro-Americans may have dominated the process of creating and fostering what would become national cultures and identities, but the process involved a complex interaction of all the peoples and cultures of the region.

THE ROMANTIC TRADITION

As the Iberian empires crumbled, then collapsed, in the late eighteenth and early nineteenth centuries, a major cultural shift swept across the Atlantic world as a powerful Romantic movement emerged to challenge the neoclassical Enlightenment culture of the eighteenth century. The Enlightenment—with its emphasis on rationality, logic, linearity, science, technology, and industrial progress—turned to classical antiquity for its inspiration in art, architecture, and literature. The founding fathers in the United States are sublime examples of these influences, which are visible in the literary style of the Declaration of Independence, in the architecture of the new capital in Washington D.C., and in the conscious comparison of George Washington with the Roman soldier/politician Cincinnatus. By the 1790s, a reaction to the Enlightenment had begun to appear in Europe, a movement that stressed intuition, emotion, and a skepticism about science and technology. The Romantics glorified the individual and freedom, especially the heroic individual. They stressed the overwhelming power of nature over human creations, and turned to history to understand the "spirit" of peoples and nations. The practice of serious history and historical writing, in a very real sense, begins with the Romantics. In many ways, Romanticism was the "counterculture" of the late eighteenth and early nineteenth centuries. Jean-Jacques Rousseau (1712–78) is one of its most important philosophers, William Blake (1757–1827) one of its great poets, and Francisco Goya (1746–1828) one of its greatest painters. The rationality of the Enlightenment and the emotional and spiritual forces of the Romantic Movement, two sides of the same coin and the human spirit, both formed crucial pieces of the Age of Revolution and its aftermath in nineteenth-century Latin America. Both cultural movements are still with us today in more contemporary forms.

The Romantic Movement in Latin America lasted roughly half a century, flourishing from the 1820s to the 1870s. The novel was its principal vehicle, the tragic romance its standard plot. In its American incarnation, Romanticism also glorified the Indian heritage of Latin America, reinforcing the stereotype of the Noble Savage. The so-called Indianist novel was common in many countries. In Brazil, José de Alencar (1829–77) was the greatest Romantic novelist, and wrote the classic Indianist novel, *Iracema* (an anagram of America, 1865). The story of the love between the Indian princess, Iracema, and the Portuguese soldier, Martim, the novel is written in the Portuguese of the Brazilians of the period rather than the language of the metropolis. Iracema dies, sacrificing herself for Martim, shortly after the birth of their child, Moacyr, who represents the blending of the two races. Jorge Isaacs (1837–95), a Colombian, produced what most consider the classic Romantic novel in Spanish America, *María* (1867). Again, a love story, this time between María and her lifelong friend, Efraín, the "beautiful and transitory" María suffers from epilepsy and dies suddenly before Efraín can declare his love for her. A weepy tearjerker, the novel has all the features of the classic Romantic novel—unrequited love, a frail heroine, and a rich and exotic backdrop that illustrates the local customs of the period.

These Romantic literary works reflect the desire of the cultural elites of the new nations to define and defend the very notion of something called

Mexico or Peru or Ecuador. Literary critic Doris Sommer has called these Romantic novels the "foundational fictions" of the new nations of Latin America. Much like James Fenimore Cooper's *Last of the Mohicans* (1826) or Mark Twain's *Adventures of Huckleberry Finn* (1884), Romantic novels and poetry began to stake out claims to the "essence" of national identity. Sarmiento's *Facundo* (1845) and *Recuerdos de provincia* (*Provincial Recollections*, 1850) or José Hernández's epic poem, *Martín Fierro* (1872–79) define the Argentine reality in Romantic terms. Ironically, the latter is a nostalgic lament for the world of the gaucho that is passing, largely due to the policies of Liberals like Sarmiento. *Martín Fierro* became one of the great iconic works of Argentine literature not only because it captured the essence of the way of life of the gaucho, but also because it blended the popular ballad poetry of the common people with the national literary traditions of the cultural elites. The poem, often recited from memory by balladeers in bars, became a fundamental cultural icon for the Argentine masses, literate and illiterate, urban and rural.

Perhaps the greatest intellectual figure of Spanish America in this period was Andrés Bello (1781–1865) a brilliant Venezuelan who tutored Simón Bolívar and accompanied him to London in 1810. He edited some of the most influential Spanish American literary journals in the 1820s, before moving to Chile in 1829. Bello wrote poetry, authored the Chilean civil code, published a grammar of the Spanish language ("for the use of Americans"), and served as the first rector of the University of Chile. This extraordinary genius with such exceptional intellectual range helped found national intellectual cultures in both Venezuela and Chile, and his work and travels made him a truly Latin American intellectual.

REALISM AND NATURALISM

At roughly the same time as the Liberals and positivists gained the upper hand in Latin America, new literary and artistic forms known as Realism and Naturalism emerged. In some ways, Realism and Naturalism were the logical cultural companions of Liberal and positivistic political ideologies. Following the lead of the French writers Honoré de Balzac (1779–1850), Gustave Flaubert (1821–80), and Émile Zola (1840–1902), Latin American novelists produced works that moved away from naive, emotional depictions of their nations to gritty depictions of the bleak conditions of daily life, especially for the lower classes. Much like the novels of Frank Norris (1870–1902)—*The Octopus* (1901)—or Upton Sinclair (1878–1968)—*The Jungle* (1906)—in the United States, the Realist and Naturalist writers in Latin America often exposed and denounced the racism, oppression, and inequalities of their societies. Rather than naively glorify the Indian or the gaucho as the Romantics had, the Realists and Naturalists laid bare the exploitation and destruction of indigenous cultures and the gaucho way of life, using literature as a form of social protest.

The novels of the Chilean Alberto Blest Gana (1830–1920) and the Peruvian Clorinda Matto de Turner (1854–1909) reflect the shift from Romanticism to Naturalism as the two genres mix within the same works. Blest Gana was the son of an Irish physician who emigrated to Chile in the aftermath of independence and a Chilean creole from an important landed family. His writings span the nineteenth century and offer something of a history of the emergence of the Chilean nation, especially seen through the eyes of the middle class. His most notable novel, *Martín Rivas* (1862), traces the social ascent of an ambitious, but impoverished, young man who eventually marries well. Blest Gana's work is almost a chronicle of the life and customs of Chile in the mid-nineteenth century, especially of the Chilean middle class. Matto de Turner was one of the first major female writers in nineteenth-century Latin America. A Peruvian creole from Cuzco, she married an Englishman (who died in 1881), worked in journalism, and produced one of the most notable novels of the nineteenth century, *Aves sin nido* (*Birds without a Nest*, 1889). Like many Romantic novels, it is a tragic love story, but it also vividly depicts the exploitation of the Indians of the Peruvian highlands. An unflinching critique of the corruption of the Catholic Church, Matto de Turner presents the tale of two young lovers, Manuel and Margarita, amidst the social upheaval, political corruption, and racism of a small mountain village. The novel climaxes with the revelation that the local bishop is the father of both Manuel and Margarita, calling a halt to their intended marriage and romance.

Race and social oppression are major themes for many of the writers at the end of the nineteenth century. In Brazil, the novels of Aluísio de Azevedo (1857–1913) graphically reveal the prejudices of color and class. In *Mulatto* (1881), Azevedo scathingly portrays the prejudices of his own hometown of São Luís in the northern coastal state of Maranhão. The young, handsome, and European-educated Raimundo returns to São Luís, falls in love, and then is shunned and scorned when it is revealed that he is the illegitimate child of his white father's liaison with a slave woman. In Cuba, Cirilio Villaverde's (1812–94) *Cecilia Valdés* (1882) and Gertrudis Gómez de Avellaneda's (1814–73) *Sab* (1841) also used literature to critique race relations and slavery in their society. The former slave Juan Francisco Manzano (1797–1853) published one of the few slave autobiographies ever written in Latin America. It was published as "Life of the Negro Poet," in England with the help of British abolitionists in 1840.

Perhaps the most brilliant and enduring example of Naturalism, Realism, and national identity formation is the work of the Brazilian writer, Euclides da Cunha (1866–1909). Trained as a military engineer, da Cunha worked as a journalist and witnessed the crushing of one of the great social uprisings in late nineteenth-century Brazil at Canudos in the backlands of Bahia. Led by a religious mystic, Antônio Conselheiro, the thousands of inhabitants of Canudos fought with local authorities in a series of skirmishes that eventually escalated into a major uprising. The determination and tenacity of these backlanders who wanted to be left alone proved too much for local and state authorities, and a tough test of the Brazilian army. A six-month siege and thousands of wounded and dead was the price to crush the rebellion and its leader. Da Cunha wrote a long epic account of the uprising that combines journalism with social commentary and ruminations on the nature of Brazilian identity. Published in 1902, *Os sertões* (*Rebellion in the Backlands* in the English translation, 1944) is a window into the psyche of the Brazilian intelligentsia at the turn of the century as they grappled with how to reconcile their European fixation with their American and African heritage. Da Cunha has enormous admiration for the racially-mixed people of the interior, and he recognizes that *they* are the true Brazilian. Yet, he desperately wants Brazil to be European, and that would mean the gradual elimination of the racially-mixed people of the backlands and their replacement with European immigrants. "We are condemned to civilization," he declared. "Either we shall progress or we shall perish. So much is certain, and our choice is clear." Da Cunha and other intellectuals were trapped in what seemed to be an inescapable dilemma: to be "progressive" and "modern" meant turning their backs on their own heritage and to stop being Brazilian.

TWO FORMS OF MODERNISM

Parallel to the Naturalist and Realist movements in Spanish America was the emergence of another sort of Romantic counterculture in the last decades of the nineteenth century. Much as the Romantics had rejected the prevailing intellectual currents of the Enlightenment, with its emphasis on rationality, science, and technology, the proponents of Modernism in Spanish America countered the late nineteenth-century positivist trends that worshipped science, technology, and reason. The Spanish American modernists turned to emotion, mysticism, spirituality, and the magical. They felt alienated from the positivistic, scientific ideology of the Second Industrial Revolution and the machine age. While the Liberals and positivists sought the material transformation of the world through science and technology, the Modernists declared themselves cosmopolitan aesthetes in pursuit of beauty and truth as they sought "art for art's sake." Modernists rebelled against what they believed to be conventional—in society, morality, and in art—and they emphasized experimentation.

While the novel was the principal instrument of the Romantic writers, poetry became the great art form of the Modernists. Truth, in their eyes, was spiritual, mystical, and revealed the harmonies of the universe, especially through the musicality of poetry. Strongly influenced by French poets of the period, this was a poetry full of symbolism and references to classical mythology.

For most scholars of Spanish American Modernism, its greatest and defining figure was the Nicaraguan poet, Rubén Darío (1867–1916). According to Cathy Jrade, one of the most eminent scholars of the period, "in Spanish, his name divides literary history in a 'before' and 'after'"; Modernism is born and dies with him. From very humble, racially mixed origins in one of the most isolated regions of Latin America, Darío emerges in the late nineteenth century as one of the greatest poets of the Spanish language. His collections of poems and prose, *Azul* (*Blue*, 1888), *Prosas profanas* (*Profane Prose*, 1896), and *Cantos de vida y esperanza* (*Songs of Life and Hope*, 1905) remain some of the great landmarks in Spanish produced on either side of the Atlantic. Like many of the Modernists, he traveled widely in Latin America, the United States, and Europe. In the words of the Colombian intellectual, Germán Arciniegas, Darío "absorbed all cultures and gave them his own accent. . . . He was the greatest Spanish-speaking poet of his time, and will dominate the panorama of Castilian letters for centuries."

Two other major figures, one a poet and journalist, the other a philosopher, define the Modernist literary moment. As we have already seen, the Cuban patriot, José Martí (1853–95) died fighting to liberate the island from Spain. Known best for the excellence of his prose, Martí's poetry, especially the *Versos sencillos* (*Simple Verses*, 1891) beautifully illustrates the Modernist emphasis on musicality. (When some of the verses were translated and put to music by Pete Seeger and others in the early 1960s, the song "Guantanamera" helped revive and perpetuate Martí's influence.) Martí spent much of his adult life in New York City (1881–95) writing in the Spanish-language press. He came to know the United States well, witnessing and fearing its growing economic and political power. He had lived, as he once said, "in the belly of the beast." Many of the Spanish American Modernists saw the United States as the embodiment of what they believed to be the worst evils of their times: unchecked materialism and a utilitarian approach to life.

Like many Spanish and Spanish American intellectuals, the young Uruguayan philosopher, José Enrique Rodó (1871–1917), was shocked by the rapid triumph of the United States over Spain in 1898. Fearing the growing influence of the United States throughout Latin America, he wrote an essay, *Ariel*, published in 1900, as a plea to the youth of Latin America to resist this influence. Rodó identified the United States with

Caliban, the giant slave beast in Shakespeare's *The Tempest*. The narrator of the essay, the teacher Prospero, portrayed Caliban as the epitome of crass materialism and the pursuit of utility. Although Rodó claimed to admire the material accomplishments of the United States, he ardently deplored its populist egalitarianism, which he believed constantly leveled society, holding back true genius and producing mediocrity. For Rodó, living in the completely Europeanized Uruguay, the true heritage of Latin America was its "Latin" heritage. He fixated on French culture, and ancient Greece. Instead of accepting U.S. materialism, he called for the youth of Latin America to follow the ethereal spirit Ariel (also from *The Tempest*) and to seek out beauty, spirituality, and truth. This stereotypical depiction of a materialistic and imperialistic United States versus a more spiritual and noble Latin America has remained a constant theme in the intellectual and cultural currents in Latin America over the past century. Rodó's essay is a cultural landmark, as Latin Americans had begun to define themselves as something distinctly American, and as a region unlike the United States.

Spanish American Modernism had experienced its greatest strength by the advent of the First World War, at the very moment that another Modernist movement emerged in Portuguese-speaking America. Brazilian Modernism has much in common with the Modernist movement in early twentieth-century Europe. This variety of Modernists rejected what they saw as the smug, complacent, bourgeois culture of the late nineteenth century, and they advocated what the art critic Robert Hughes has called "the shock of the new." Although Modernism also found its expression in architecture, music, and literature, its most notable form was painting. Picasso, Matisse, and Renoir are but three of its most famous exponents in Europe. Although Brazilian artists and intellectuals began their own Modernist movement inspired by their European counterparts, they refashioned the movement to adapt it to their own society. During the centennial of Brazilian independence in 1922, a group of avant-garde artists and intellectuals, inspired by Modernism, declared their cultural independence from Europe. These intellectuals argued that they had no desire to be European; they simply wanted to be Brazilian. "Let us forget the marble of the Acropolis and the towers of the Gothic cathedrals," Ronald de Carvalho exclaimed. "We are the sons of the hills and the forests. Stop thinking of Europe. Think of America." In essence, they recognized that "European" was not synonymous with "progress" or "modernity," something Euclides da Cunha had not been able to see just a few years earlier when he wrote about the "rebellion in the backlands" at Canudos. These artists organized a "Modern Art Week" of exhibitions and lectures in São Paulo and Rio de Janeiro in February 1922 to announce their break with the past. Led by the versatile musicologist and writer Mário de Andrade (1893–1945), the Brazilian "Modernists" set out to create an authentically Brazilian art, literature, and culture.

The most striking image in Brazilian Modernism was anthropophagy, or cannibalism. One of the leading Modernists, Oswald de Andrade (1890–1954), issued a "Cannibal Manifesto" (1928). The Brazilian intellectuals wished to consume or devour all influences—European, African, indigenous—and then digest and produce something new, something uniquely Brazilian. They sought to end the old process of aping Europe. Instead, they called for the creation of a Brazilian civilization that incorporated features of the three great peoples who had long populated Brazil. In the Caribbean, similar movements that stressed the African influences in the formation of Caribbean cultures paralleled the cultural movements in Brazil. The Cuban anthropologist Fernando Ortiz (1881–1969) and the poet, Nicolás Guillén (1902–89) are but two outstanding examples of this turn to the non-European roots of Latin American cultures. In the words of Guillén, "And now that Europe strips off/to toast its flesh under the sun,/and goes to Harlem and Havana for jazz and *son*, /flaunt your blackness while the chic applaud/and to the envy of the whites/speak out as a true black." In the Andes and Mesoamerica, intellectuals created the foundations of a movement that became known as *indigenismo*, a pro-Indian nativism that stressed the indigenous roots of Andean nations. The novels of Miguel Ángel Asturias (1899–1974) in Guatemala (especially *Men of Maize*, 1949), and the incisive and brilliant essays (*Seven Interpretive Essays on Peruvian Reality*, 1928) of the Peruvian Marxist, José Carlos Mariátegui (1894–1930), also reflect the Modernist influence on the redefinition of Latin American "reality."

A DEFINING MOMENT

For four centuries, the intellectual and cultural elites of Latin America largely emulated and imitated the elite cultural trendsetters in Europe. Throughout the colonial period (with the spectacular exceptions of Sor Juana's poetry in Mexico and Aleijadinho's art in Brazil) Latin American art, music, and literature were largely derivative and second-rate versions of European elite culture. At the same time, the popular culture of the Americas percolated upward into the art, music, and literature of the elite. Indigenous peoples in Mesoamerica and the Andes, Africans and their descendants in the Caribbean and Brazil, and the rich mixes of the colliding cultures were constantly evolving and producing art, music, and oral traditions. For many of the condescending Europeans who viewed this cultural production in Latin America, it was precisely the "American" influences that made it unworthy of praise.

In the century after independence, Latin American writers, artists, and musicians became increasingly bolder in the incorporation of the local and the popular into their work. For the Romantics, this often meant acknowledging the contributions of indigenous peoples, but in naive and idealized ways. The Realists and Naturalists placed all of the peoples of the Americas into their narratives, recognizing that the "essence" of Latin America arose out of the collision of cultures and peoples. The Modernists took the final step and announced that what defined their peoples and nations was not European, but American—and America was defined by the mixing of Native Americans, Africans, and Europeans. The modernists, especially in Brazil, seized on this realization, and declared the cultural independence of Latin America from Europe nearly a century after political independence had been achieved.

Anxious to counter the sudden and powerful emergence of the United States, Rodó sought to define Latin America in stark contrast to the United States and its Protestant, egalitarian, materialist, utilitarian culture. As an intellectual living in one of the most Europeanized corners of Latin America, Rodó attempted to define Latin America with an emphasis on the "Latin" heritage of the region. Like most nineteenth-century Latin American intellectuals, he ignored, or chose to reject, the reality of most of Latin America—that the vast majority of its peoples for four centuries were racially and culturally non-European. The more powerful and enduring declarations of what it meant to be Latin American—and not from the United States—came from intellectuals in nations with deep roots in African and Native American cultures. The two most notable examples of this "cultural turn" that recognized, and glorified, the non-European heritage of Latin America were Gilberto Freyre (1900–87) in Brazil and José Vasconcelos (1882–1959) in Mexico.

Mexico produced perhaps the most dramatic shift in Latin America toward a powerful cultural nationalism built on a recognition of the indigenous roots of the nation. In the aftermath of the Mexican Revolution (chapter 19), the new regime pursued a nation-building project that aimed to create a sense of national identity that openly depicted the Spanish as the evil conquerors and the Aztecs as the noble, vanquished peoples. The greatest architect of this cultural nationalism was José Vasconcelos, the Minister of Education in the early 1920s. Vasconcelos initiated a government-sponsored cultural project that would endure for decades, one that utilized art and aesthetics to promote a new sense of Mexican identity. He fervently believed that the world was gradually moving toward a fusion of all races, and that Latin America was on the cutting edge of this cultural and biological trend. In Mexico, this "cosmic race" was emerging out of the fusion of the Indian and the Spaniard, but the same fusion was taking place across the Caribbean, Brazil, and the rest of Spanish-speaking America. "That is why," he wrote, "in Mexico we teach not only Mexican patriotism but Latin American patriotism, for here is a vast continent open to all races and all colors of skin, to all humanity, so that they may organize a new experiment in collective living: an experiment founded not only on utility but above all beauty, on that beauty which our southern races instinctively seek, as if in it they had discovered the supreme divine law."

Beginning in the 1920s, Mexico embarked upon what has been perhaps the most forceful form of cultural nationalism in twentieth-century Latin America. Reminiscent of the Liberal project of the nineteenth century, the Mexican revolutionaries set out to create schools, libraries, theaters, museums, publications, radio programs, and films that would serve the didactic purposes of teaching everyone in Mexico what it meant to be "Mexican." It was an ironic reworking of the old Liberal pattern—the revolutionaries also wanted to refashion all the inhabitants of the land, regardless of culture, ethnicity, or language—but not to turn them into Europeans. Instead, they wanted to mold them into believers in the cosmic race, a racially and culturally mixed people primarily rooted in the pre-Columbian cultures of Mesoamerica. A powerful irony has long pervaded this nation-building project. Despite its glorification of the indigenous past, the objective was the same as the Liberals, to homogenize the inhabitants of Mexico, to turn them all into Spanish speakers who would participate in a Western political system built (at least, in theory) on individual rights and equality before the law. (Furthermore, the gap between the propagandistic pronouncements, and the continuing poverty and oppression of Indian peasants became more and more striking as the decades passed.) The most famous means of official propaganda was the commissioning of Diego Rivera (1886–1957), David Alfaro Siqueiros (1896–1974) and others to paint a series of stunning murals in public buildings. The muralists, deeply influenced by modern art as well as socialist social realism, portrayed the history of Mexico with the Spanish and the United States as villains and the noble Indians and peasants as heroes. Rarely has a revolutionary political movement been more brilliantly served by its artists. The works of Rivera and Siqueiros are some of the great works of modern art in the twentieth century.

In Brazil, the cultural nationalism of the Modernists was (at least initially) less state-directed. At the turn of the century, the consequences of Brazil's African heritage obsessed intellectuals, and most despaired over its powerful impact. Most believed racial mixture had condemned their society to backwardness, if not utter hopelessness. In the 1920s, the work of Gilberto Freyre began fundamentally to reshape the debate over race and the national psyche. In his many books and articles, Freyre turned the debate over race around. The African influence in Brazil had not held the nation back, he declared, it had made it stronger. Without the African mixture, the Portuguese would never have survived or thrived in the tropics. The Portuguese created a "new world in the tropics," and the mixture of African, Indian, and European made Brazil unique, even superior. According to

Freyre, this "luso-tropical" civilization had produced a racial democracy where blacks, whites, Indians, and the racially-mixed mingled harmoniously. (Educated at Baylor University and Columbia University, Freyre had witnessed firsthand race relations in the United States and consciously drew the distinction between the two countries.) Freyre even argued forcefully in his voluminous writings that Brazil represented a unique civilization in world history, a "luso-tropical" civilization. He believed that this mixture of Portuguese (Lusitania to the Romans, hence "luso") and tropical cultures made Brazil uniquely capable of bridging the chasm between the European industrial societies of the Northern Hemisphere and the nonwhite agrarian societies of the Southern Hemisphere. For Freyre, Brazilians could take great pride in their racially and culturally mixed heritage as an example for other nations and societies to follow.

By 1930, a clear pattern had emerged across Latin America. The elite nation-building projects of the nineteenth century would continue, but their principal message (in most places) was now the unique racial and cultural mixture that defined most of Latin America. Mexico hailed itself as a mestizo nation, and Brazil began to assume an identity of racial mixture. With the continually growing economic, political, and cultural power of the United States, many countries also self-consciously sought to define themselves as distinct and different from the "colossus of the North." The brilliant and eloquent José Martí summed up this sentiment when he referred to "our America" (*nuestra América*), an America he starkly contrasted to the United States. "However great this America may be," he wrote about the United States, "and however consecrated it may be to the free men of the America in which Lincoln was born, to us in the depths of our hearts, the America in which Juárez was born is greater, and no one can blame us for it, nor think ill of us for it, because it is ours, and because it has been more unfortunate."

Part IV

Democracy, Development, and Identity

18

Diverging Paths: Many Latin Americas

UNITY AND DIVERSITY: NEW RIVERS AND STREAMS

Throughout this book I have returned frequently to the image of Latin America as a collision of three powerful streams converging to produce a roaring river that mixed three peoples into a dazzling variety of combinations that were new and unique in world history. As we have seen, over centuries the turbulent river gradually diverged into many different streams, but all had their origins in the great river formed by the initial clash of Native Americans, Europeans, and Africans. Many Americas took shape within the political and cultural construct we now call Latin America, and that construct has always been a work in progress. By the beginning of the twentieth century, the "story" of Latin America becomes more difficult for the historian to narrate coherently. The collisions of the fifteenth and sixteenth centuries gave birth to a series of patterns with variations, but the narrative of conquest, colonization, and the emergence of new societies has a coherence that is lacking when we look at the region over the last century. The colonial era has a powerful unity created primarily by European conquest and colonialism and the multiple reactions to these wrenching transformations. By the end of the eighteenth century, the mighty river of Latin America had already begun to split off into many distinct streams, a trend that the wars for independence accelerated. The similar processes of independence, early nation-building, and entry into the international economy, however, provide the historian with a new set of common patterns even as the newly emerging nations pursue increasingly divergent paths.

These paths become even more divergent in the twentieth century, but we can still discern common patterns in the twentieth century in politics, economics, society, and culture. The final section of this book surveys these patterns, focusing on the themes of "democracy, development, and identity." Much of the story of twentieth-century Latin America is the slow (sometimes excruciatingly slow) and uneven evolution of a region as it has become increasingly democratic, more economically developed, and much more assertive and secure about its identity/identities as peoples, nations, and a region. Chapters 19–22 focus on the political patterns of the last century. Chapter 23 turns to the struggle to achieve economic development, and chapter 24 turns to issues of race, culture, and identity. At the beginning of the twenty-first century, it is still possible to speak of Latin America as a region with common characteristics, and a common history. Nevertheless, the divergences across the region have increased notably over the last one hundred years. Many of the streams have emerged out of the mighty river of the sixteenth century, and some may diverge so markedly by the end of the twenty-first century that it will be difficult to continue to consider all of them part of the same cultural and political region. In another century, it may be very difficult to write a synthetic history of Latin America with common patterns and characteristics for the twenty-first century—or that region will consist of fewer peoples and a smaller geographic setting.

POLITICS: HIERARCHY AND POWER

Despite an enormously wide range of variations, the pattern in all of Latin America over the last century has been a move toward greater political participation by larger and larger numbers of people from all sectors of society. Although Latin America continues to be a society characterized by a deeply rooted, hierarchical culture and the concentration of power in the hands of a relatively small sector of the population, these long-standing historical patterns have been substantially attenuated by the growing participation of the vast majority of Latin Americans in electoral politics over the last century. This process has not moved at the same pace in all places, and it has encountered enormous setbacks nearly everywhere (especially in the 1960s and 1970s), but the pattern is clear: at the beginning of the twenty-first century, as a whole, Latin America is more participatory, representative, and democratic in its politics than at any time in its long history. This process has been very uneven and halting, across the region, and Latin America has experienced cycles of repression and democratization throughout the century. The tendency in many (but, again, not all) countries in the early twentieth century was toward greater political opening and the extension of the vote to larger and larger numbers of adult males. The outstanding examples of this pattern are Costa Rica, Chile, Argentina, and Uruguay. In some places, representative institutions and elections take place on a fairly regular basis, but with a tiny percentage of the population participating (Brazil is a good example). The shattering effects of the Great Depression across the Atlantic world set back the process of democratization after 1929. In Central America and much of the Caribbean, dictators took power and initiated decades of repression. The rise of Anastasio Somoza García (1936–56) in Nicaragua, Rafael Leónidas Trujillo (1930–61) in the Dominican Republic, and Fulgencio Batista (1933–44, 1952–59) in Cuba are illustrative of this pattern. Even in the countries with the most highly developed electoral, representative politics (Argentina and Chile, for example), these institutions were seriously shaken and, at times, temporarily disrupted by the shock waves of the economic crisis of the 1930s.

In general, the cycle in the region moved back toward political opening in the aftermath of the Second World War. By the late 1950s, most countries in Latin America had some sort of electoral systems in place and at least the mechanisms and procedures of representative politics. Only in the repressive, personalistic dictatorships in Central America and the Caribbean were representative politics completely lacking (Cuba, Dominican Republic, Haiti, Nicaragua, Guatemala). In the mid-1960s, revolutionary leftist movements, and the United States-led response to them, initiated a new phase of dictatorship and repression. The triumph of Fidel Castro and the Cuban Revolution in 1959 produced one of the great turning points in the history of the Americas, indeed, the history of the world. For a brief moment, it appeared that Castro had initiated a phase of leftist revolution that would challenge the capitalist United States and swing Latin America in a radically anticapitalist, anti-United States direction. Ironically, the success of Castro in seizing power and surviving United States efforts to crush him and his revolution instead touched off a wave of right-wing military coups that brought the armed forces to power in most of Latin America. This wave began with a military coup in Brazil in 1964 and reached its zenith with the military coups in Uruguay and Chile in 1973. In the late 1970s, Costa Rica, the Dominican Republic, Colombia, and Venezuela were the last functioning representative, electoral systems left standing in Latin America. (Mexico had a representative, electoral system, but one that had been controlled by one political party since the 1920s.) The late 1970s was one of the darkest moments in the political history of modern Latin America.

Another major economic crisis, one as devastating as the 1930s, ravaged Latin America in the 1980s and severely shook the military regimes.

This economic crisis, and the end of the Cold War, set off the latest political cycle, one characterized by the reemergence of representative, electoral politics in nations where the long history had been disrupted by the military dictatorships (Uruguay, Argentina, Chile), and the emergence, for the first time, of these institutions in many countries where they had been virtually unknown (Guatemala, El Salvador, Honduras, Nicaragua, Haiti, Bolivia). By the year 2000, Cuba stood alone as the last country in the region without meaningful electoral, representative political institutions. Despite some serious challenges, for the last quarter century, Latin America has experienced the longest, strongest, and most meaningful period of representative, electoral politics in its history. Although this is a clear pattern, the variations are great—from the long, durable, and impressive electoral history of the Costa Ricans to the fragile and chaotic electoral politics of the Bolivians.

The next four chapters concentrate on two major political pathways in the twentieth century—reform and revolution. In Mexico (1910), Guatemala (1944), Bolivia (1952), Cuba (1959), and Nicaragua (1979) men and women challenged the status quo through armed struggle, took power, and sought to eliminate the profound social and economic inequities that have plagued Latin America since the Conquest. These nations took the path of revolution—a fundamental transformation of a nation's social structure, political system, and economy through an often violent (and relatively rapid) seizure of political power. Uruguay, Argentina, Chile, and Costa Rica, on the other hand, pursued the path of reform, gradually creating political systems that share many features with the social democratic politics in Western Europe. These nine cases are the clearest examples of sustained reform or fundamental revolution in twentieth-century Latin America. Although revolutionary movements arise nearly everywhere in Latin America, they succeed in seizing power only in these five nations. Reform movements take place nearly everywhere, but with less sustained and impressive success than those in Uruguay, Argentina, Chile, and Costa Rica.

Costa Rica, Chile, Argentina, and Uruguay managed to build long-term, reformist movements that usually avoided bloodshed, civil war, and coups d'état, allowing them to develop strong, representative, electoral systems that gradually extended the vote to most adults by the mid-twentieth century. Even these countries, however, periodically experienced breakdowns. A brief, but very violent, civil war convulsed Costa Rica in 1948. Extremely violent and repressive military dictatorships brought an end to electoral politics in Chile, Argentina, and Uruguay in the 1960s and 1970s. At the other end of the political spectrum were countries with elites who bitterly fought all efforts at gradual reform. These countries became pressure cookers, as the reformists became increasingly frustrated. Eventually, many of them turned to armed struggle as the only option to change the system. In five countries, these revolutionaries managed to overthrow governments, seize power, and initiate profound social and economic reforms, all with varying results. The earliest example was Mexico (1910–20), followed by Guatemala (1944–45), Bolivia, (1952), Cuba (1956–59), and Nicaragua (1977–79).

In the rest of Latin America, the variations on these two patterns are less clearcut and sustained. Some countries experience a series of dictatorships punctuated by brief moments of reform (El Salvador, Honduras, Ecuador, Peru). Others fall under the rule of long-term, personalistic dictatorships (Nicaragua, 1936–1979; Dominican Republic, 1930–1961; Haiti, 1957–1985; Paraguay, 1954–1989) that eventually give way in the 1980s to the wave of democratization and electoral politics. Still other countries—Brazil, Colombia, Venezuela—have a history of some form of representative electoral politics, but struggle to maintain social and political stability over the last half-century. In the cases of Colombia and Venezuela, they finally manage to put into place a regular system of electoral, representative politics in the late 1950s. In the case of Brazil, its representative, electoral political system is very restrictive before 1930, falls to a dictatorship in the 1930s and early 1940s, then experiences two decades of true electoral politics before succumbing to a military coup in 1964. Only in the late 1980s do true electoral, representative politics reemerge. Finally, there is the unique case of Puerto Rico. Incorporated into the United States after 1898, Puerto Ricans become U.S. citizens in 1917, and the island becomes a "free associated state" in 1948. Although clearly Latin American in their history, culture, and language, Puerto Ricans have repeatedly voted overwhelmingly to remain within the U.S. system, despite their awkward and anomalous status.

From the late 1940s to the late 1980s, the Cold War, unfortunately, overshadowed all politics in Latin America. The centuries-old struggle between the impoverished masses and a wealthy (primarily landholding) elite was transformed in the post-World War II period into a struggle between East and West, between communism and capitalism. Both the Soviet Union and the United States saw the global struggle as a "zero sum" contest between two (and only two) power blocs. From the perspective of the United States, "the enemy of my enemy is my friend," and intransigent political elites in Latin America learned to play the anticommunism card very effectively. They portrayed all efforts at reform and change as the ploy of communists and leftists to seize power. In most cases, they were successful in mobilizing U.S. help to crush these reform movements, whether they were inspired by socialism or not. With the dramatic exception of Cuba (1959) and the less successful example of Nicaragua (1979), all the revolutionary, leftist movements in Latin America during the Cold War were soundly defeated.

The polarization of the world produced by the Cold War left little room for those who promoted democratic reform and an economic path that would begin to alter the long-standing socioeconomic inequities of the region. Even in countries with long traditions of representative, electoral politics (Chile, Argentina, Uruguay), the Cold War transformed the pursuit of social justice and equality into a struggle between East and West. For nearly half a century, the Cold War turned this struggle (seemingly) into a battle between capitalism and socialism. The Cuban Revolution became the extreme example of what appeared to be an either/or choice: a capitalist economy aligned with the United States and continuing socioeconomic inequities, or a socialist economy aligned with the Soviet Union and the elimination of these inequities through state intervention and authoritarianism. The experiments with socialism—whether in authoritarian Cuba or in the collapsing democracy in Chile in the early 1970s—fell victims to the polarization of the Cold War.

The United States emerged out of the Second World War with the strongest economy on the planet. While the war left Europe, Japan, and China in ruins, the U.S. industrial economy came out of the war at full production. The United States had forged close strategic, economic, and military relations with nearly all of Latin America during the war to secure the region and to guarantee access to its markets and raw materials. In the immediate aftermath of the war, the Organization of American States became the successor to James G. Blaine's late nineteenth-century Pan American Union. Across the Americas, the United States forged a military alliance with the armed forces in each nation, supplying expertise, arms, training, and equipment. The Monroe Doctrine of the early nineteenth century evolved into the ideological wall against communist influence in the hemisphere. Although Latin American nations continued to develop trade and diplomatic relations with other areas of the world, especially Europe, the "Pax Americana" settled over the region as the United States asserted its right to guide the Americas in the second half of the century.

Events in Europe in 1989 profoundly altered the course of politics in the Americas. For the last quarter century, Latin America has experienced a period of unprecedented political transformation. Although the experiences have varied widely, the end of the Cold War brought (nearly everywhere) the end of radical polarization, the emergence of electoral, representative politics (again, nearly everywhere), and the end of leftist, revolutionary movements (with the odd exceptions of Peru and Colombia). For decades, the Left in Latin America had been the most prominent proponent for social justice, human rights, and the end of socioeconomic inequities. In the words of the Mexican diplomat and political scientist Jorge Castañeda, the Left had fought for utopia. With the rise of electoral politics across the entire region, the Left no longer needed to pursue armed struggle to make its voice heard. Instead, they turned to the ballot box and campaigning. Again, in the words of Castañeda, they now had to pursue "utopia unarmed."

Paradoxically, the great fear of the conservative elites in Latin America has not come to pass. They tenaciously fought (more tenaciously in some countries than others) the reforms that would give the vote to the poor masses, fearing that the impoverished majority would bring to power radical, leftist demagogues who would use governments to nationalize the economy, redistribute wealth, and eradicate the Right. In short, they feared another Cuban Revolution—through the ballot box. Instead, elections in Latin America over the last quarter century have more often than not elected centrist or right-wing candidates. When elections have brought the Left to power, these leftist leaders and their parties have done little to alter the economic policies favored by the Right. Despite their professions of allegiance to the ideals of social justice, human rights, and the elimination of the enormous socioeconomic inequities in their societies, when leftists have come to power, they have offered few new ideas as alternatives to the global capitalism of the late twentieth and early twenty-first centuries.

The emergence of electoral politics has coincided with the collapse of the socialist bloc, the powerful expansion of capitalism, and the rise of the neoliberal (new liberal) model. This economic model (most closely associated with the rise of Ronald Reagan in the United States and Margaret Thatcher in England in the 1980s) returns to the roots of classical liberal economics in the nineteenth century, promoting less government intervention in the economy, free trade, and open markets. After the horrific decade of economic crisis in Latin America in the 1980s, all governments (in varying degrees) have turned to this neoliberal model. By the 1990s, neoliberal economics had become the dominant trend in all of Latin America (except Cuba). The social revolution that the old elites had so feared did not take place. In the heat of the revolutionary upheavals of the 1960s, could anyone have imagined that, just three decades later, leftists would come to power in Brazil or Chile through democratic elections, and then follow capitalist economic policies that did little to address the poverty of most Latin Americans?

ECONOMICS: INTERVENTION AND OPENING

Despite the persistent image of underdevelopment, Latin America (as a whole) experienced impressive economic growth through most of the twentieth century—an annual average of about 4 percent—but that growth was not enough to improve significantly the lives of the majority of Latin Americans. At the beginning of the twenty-first century, despite impressive changes, Latin America remains a "rich land of poor people." As has been the case throughout most of the history of the region, the role of government has been the most important factor in the economic lives of Latin Americans in the twentieth century. The economic history of the last century has been one of cycles of rising and falling government intervention. As in politics, the countries of the region offer a broad spectrum of cases as the region moves between greater and lesser intervention. The twentieth century began with most economies pursuing fairly open, export-oriented growth. From the 1930s to the 1980s, most countries then "turned inward" behind protectionist policies and sought to develop diversified and industrialized economies. They sought to move away from the excessive dependence on monoculture and the dominance of a single export crop or mineral. The century closed with a dramatic reduction of protectionism and government intervention, a new phase of export-oriented growth, and significant moves toward regional integration. In very different ways, Mexico and Brazil became the two largest economies in Latin America (and among the ten largest in the world), and offered two very distinct models for the smaller countries in the region.

All the nations of Latin America faced the daunting legacies of the colonial period and the outward-oriented growth of the nineteenth century: agrarian economies that primarily produced and exported agricultural commodities and raw materials to Europe and the United States. Latin Americans imported most of their industrial goods from the industrial nations of the North, paying for them with the revenues generated by commodities and raw materials exports. As they entered the twentieth century, most Latin American nations relied almost exclusively on a single crop or mineral: sugar in Cuba; coffee in much of Central America, Colombia, and Brazil; bananas in Ecuador and Honduras; tin in Bolivia; copper in Chile; wheat and beef in Argentina. Monoculture made these nations extremely vulnerable to the rise and fall of commodity prices in Europe and the United States. In the early twentieth century, they experienced an increasingly precarious economic roller-coaster ride with the shifting demand for their products in the North Atlantic world. The Great Depression devastated most of the economies of Latin America as the demand for their exports—be they bananas or copper—plummeted.

In nearly all of Latin America, most noticeably in the larger nations, political and economic elites turned the economies inward, and from the 1930s to the 1970s the general pattern in the region was increasing state intervention to promote diversification and industrialization. Protectionism through tariffs and duties on imports, the creation of state-controlled enterprises to guide and develop vital industries, and large-scale government financing of key sectors of the economy became the principal means to develop national economies. By the 1960s, this policy of "import substitution industrialization" (replacing imported manufactured goods with domestically produced ones, or ISI) had stimulated significant industrial growth in the larger nations—Brazil, Mexico, Argentina—and to a lesser extent in many other countries in Latin America. By the late 1960s, however, ISI had largely run its course, creating a domestic industrial base, but one that was heavily protected from international competition. The oil shocks of the 1970s and the debt crisis in the 1980s brutally brought an end to this half-century-long cycle of intervention and protectionism.

Wars in the Middle East (between Israel and Arab nations in 1973, and between Iraq and Iran in 1979) provoked two major oil shocks in the 1970s that sent most of the world into recession as the price of petroleum skyrocketed. In Latin America (and much of the developing world) the escalating price of oil crippled economies and sent them in search of loans from international banks to get them through the crises. At the beginning of the 1980s, as a major economic recession swept across the capitalist world, the second oil shock and dramatically rising interest rates forced nearly all of Latin America into near-default on hundreds of billions of dollars of foreign loans. Latin America's total foreign debt had risen from $2 billion in 1900 to more than $500 billion by 1985. (Mexico and Venezuela suffered the curse of too much oil and too-rapid economic expansion built on huge loans they could not repay in the early 1980s when oil prices eventually fell!) For at least a decade, international banks and lending agencies effectively shut down the capital pipeline and Latin America went into a series of recessions and economic contractions. For more than a decade, most countries struggled mightily to renegotiate their foreign debt and reopen the flow of international financial resources. Financially strapped governments cut their budgets drastically. It was a "lost decade" for most of Latin America as government spending on basic social programs dried up and the standard of living of most Latin Americans declined to the levels of the 1960s. In effect, Latin America lost ground after decades of economic growth.

In the 1990s, the debt crisis finally subsided, new capital investment returned to Latin America, and nearly all the nations of the region made a pronounced move toward more open economies with fewer trade barriers. Latin American economies became more globalized. Governments substantially reduced their intervention in the economy, and privatized hundreds of state-controlled corporations. This return to the classical liberal economics of the early nineteenth century has been accompanied by a paradoxical parallel trend, the creation of trading blocs through regional integration: the North American Free Trade Agreement or NAFTA (Canada, the United States, Mexico), the "Southern Market" or *Mercosul/Mercosur* (Brazil, Argentina, Uruguay, Paraguay, and Venezuela), as well as others. As nations bind together, reducing barriers to trade within their regional blocs, they make it more difficult for those nations outside the trading bloc to gain entry. In effect, the blocs reduce trade barriers internally and raise them externally to nonmember nations, a form of protectionism among global blocs rather than individual nations. For many of the smaller nations of Latin America (the Caribbean islands or the nations of Central America, for example), these regional trading blocs offer the opportunity to seek an economic future (that is, economies of scale) that would not be possible with small national markets and few resources. Although recent electoral victories for presidential candidates in Venezuela, Ecuador, and Bolivia have brought vocal opponents of neo-liberalism to power, it remains to be seen if this "pink tide" will offer a sustained and viable alternative to the neoliberal model. At the beginning of the twenty-first century, neoliberalism and regional integration dominate the economic landscape in all of the Americas. Globalization has become the mantra of economic gurus and free-market capitalism for all countries their goal.

SOCIETY: POVERTY AND PLENTY

The stubborn persistence of pronounced socioeconomic inequities remains the most striking feature of all Latin America. Neither the interventionist policies of the middle of the twentieth century nor the neoliberal model of the last quarter-century have managed to alter significantly the gap between rich and poor in the region. In fact, the gap appears to have widened over the last generation. By some estimates, Latin America has the most unbalanced distribution of resources of any region in the world. Wealthy Brazil, with its enormous resources, in the 1990s had the most unequal distribution of income of any country in the world! (It currently ranks in the top five.) The huge social, economic, and cultural divide between a relatively small elite and masses of impoverished peoples that emerged out of the Iberian conquest in the sixteenth century, has not only persisted for centuries; it has intensified. Contrary to what many would expect, economic growth and the emergence of democracy in Latin America have not done much to close this enormous social and economic divide. Capitalism and democracy may be dominant across the region, but they have not yet begun to eradicate poverty and inequality. They have been the most powerful constants in Latin American history across the continually changing political and economic regimes.

Although the socioeconomic inequities are clear, analyzing them has always been complicated. Social scientists have grappled for decades to come up with clear definitions of social class, with little consensus. Economists tend to use income distribution as a convenient substitute for class, providing statistics on the distribution of national income by deciles.

They split the population of a country into ten groups, from those in the upper tenth to the bottom tenth of society, showing how much of the national income each tenth controls. A standard measure of inequality is to compare the income controlled by the upper 20 percent versus that controlled by the bottom 20 percent of a country. The pattern across all of Latin America (with significant national variations) is clear: the upper group controls 15 to 20 times the income of the lower group. Again, Brazil is the extreme, with the upper 20 percent controlling 64 percent of national income against 2 percent for the bottom 20 percent—a factor of 32 times! (The comparable figure for the United States is 8, among the highest in the developed world.) Across the region, there are variations. Cuba, with its radical redistribution of wealth in the 1960s is clearly the most equitable, but ten million Cubans share scarce resources, living in a society with excellent social services (health care, education) and little disposal income. In the other countries of the region, the factor ranges from 11 in Costa Rica to 30 in Honduras. These inequities affect different groups and regions disproportionately. The industrial economies of Brazil and Mexico, for example, are in a different economic universe from the impoverished, (still) largely agrarian economies of Haiti or Honduras. Chile, Argentina, Uruguay, and Costa Rica have attenuated the socioeconomic divide more successfully than most of the nations of Latin America in societies that are overwhelmingly of European descent. Haiti, after nearly two decades of political turmoil, is among the poorest nations on the planet. Within nations, regional disparities stand out. The drought-stricken interior of northeastern Brazil (the so-called "polygon of drought") is perhaps the most impoverished subregion in all of the Americas. In the Andean countries, the capital cities of the coast have much higher standards of living than the poor villages of the sierra. In Mexico, the rural, largely indigenous population in the south (especially Chiapas) lives in a very different world than that of the highly industrialized megalopolis of the federal capital with its 22 million inhabitants.

The darker-skinned peoples of Latin America, most notably, overwhelmingly remain at the bottom of the socioeconomic pyramid that has characterized Latin America since the sixteenth century. The pattern is clear across countries. The lower echelons of the socioeconomic pyramid are composed primarily of Indians and the dark-skinned, and the upper echelons by the light-skinned. The large indigenous populations of Guatemala, Ecuador, Peru, and Bolivia continue to face grinding poverty and discrimination. Rough estimates by sociologists place the upper class in Latin America at around 5–10 percent of the population, the middle class around 10–15 percent, the working class at about 35–40 percent, with about 40–50 percent of the population living in poverty and working in the informal sector of the economy. (As a point of reference, the

U.S. Census Bureau classifies about 65 percent of the U.S. population in the middle class with about 15–20 percent as below or near the poverty level.)

These striking inequities, as we have seen, have been one of the defining features of Latin America for centuries. Although it was popular in the 1960s and 1970s to blame poverty and inequality in Latin America on a "population explosion," poverty and inequality have been common features of the region since its creation. The enormous expansion of the population of Latin America has not created poverty and inequality; rather it has increased its scale. At the beginning of the twentieth century, the population of Latin America was probably around 60 million, with Mexico (14 million) and Brazil (18 million) accounting for half of all Latin Americans. Chile, Argentina, Peru, and Colombia each had some 3 to 5 million inhabitants, and Uruguay, Bolivia, Ecuador, Haiti, Cuba, El Salvador and Guatemala each had 1 to 2 million. The rest of Central America and the Caribbean and Panama all ranged from 300,000 to 600,000. By 1950, the population of the region had grown by 250 percent to 160 million—again, with half of the region's inhabitants in Brazil (53 million, tripling in size) and Mexico (28 million, doubling). Argentina had become the third most populous country in the region with some 20 million inhabitants, and Colombia, the fourth largest, with 12 million inhabitants. Cuba, Chile, Venezuela, and Peru followed with 4–7 million each, followed by Honduras, El Salvador, Nicaragua, Guatemala, Puerto Rico, the Dominican Republic, Haiti, Bolivia, Ecuador, Uruguay, and Paraguay all in the range of 1–3 million inhabitants. Little Panama and Costa Rica each had about 800,000 inhabitants.

Two powerful and dramatic patterns characterize demographic changes in Latin America in the last half-century: the rapid and explosive growth of the population of the region, and the massive movement of people from the countryside to cities. Between 1950 and 2000, the population of Latin America more than tripled—to just over half a billion people. With a population of 175 million in Brazil, one of every three Latin Americans was a Brazilian. At 100 million in Mexico, one of every five Latin Americans was a Mexican. The populations of Colombia (42 million), Argentina (37 million), Peru (26 million), and Venezuela (24 million)—the next four largest countries—accounted for another quarter of all Latin Americans. Chile, Cuba, Ecuador, and Guatemala each had some 11 to 15 million inhabitants. Bolivia, the Dominican Republic, El Salvador, Haiti, Honduras, Nicaragua, and Paraguay ranged from 5 to 8 million each. The smallest countries—Costa Rica, Panama, and Uruguay—each had 3 to 4 million citizens. The Commonwealth of Puerto Rico was similar in size, with another million people of Puerto Rican descent on the U.S. mainland. Clearly, at the beginning of the twenty-first century, the countries of Latin America ranged from among the largest in the world in population—Brazil (5th largest), Mexico (11th)—to some of the smallest.

Accompanying this explosive population growth has been the dramatic shift of people from rural to urban areas—especially in the decades after 1950. At the beginning of the twentieth century, probably 10 to 15 percent of Latin Americans lived in urban areas (towns and cities with a population over 20,000). At the close of the century, the region as a whole was 75 percent urban, and the figure was 90 percent in Chile, Argentina, Uruguay, and Venezuela. Although the absolute number of rural dwellers had begun to decline in these countries after 1960, more than 125 million Latin Americans resided in rural areas in the year 2000—more than double the entire population of Latin America in 1900! This urban explosion created enormous cities (usually capital cities) across Latin America, cities that could not absorb the massive influx of rural migrants. At the beginning of the twenty-first century, the metropolitan areas of São Paulo and Mexico City were among the five largest in the world (20–23 million inhabitants), and Buenos Aires (13), Rio de Janeiro (12), Lima (9), Bogotá (8), and Santiago (6) had become major world cities.

As we have seen, indigenous peoples, Africans, and the racially mixed formed the vast majority of the peoples of Latin America from the sixteenth century to the beginning of the twentieth century. With the beginning of the last great wave of immigration in the late nineteenth century, the ethnic composition of Latin America began its most important shift since the collisions of the sixteenth century. The indigenous population, although slowly rising for centuries, now faces new challenges as more and more Native Americans leave their communities to move to cities where they very often leave behind their language and traditional culture, assimilating into the world of the Europeanized mestizos. The influx of Africans ended in the mid-nineteenth century, and has not resumed. A massive wave of Europeans, mainly from southern and eastern Europe transformed southern Brazil, Uruguay, Argentina, and Chile at the end of the nineteenth and the beginning of the twentieth centuries. Finally, in the twentieth century, new ethnic groups have arrived: Japanese, Chinese, Koreans, East Indians, and peoples from the Middle East, especially from Syria and Lebanon in the region of the old Ottoman Empire. Although these waves of immigrants have been comparatively small, they have changed the complexion of many Latin American societies over the past century. Descendants of these immigrant communities now play significant roles in Latin America. (In Peru, Ecuador, and Argentina, Latin Americans of Japanese or Lebanese descent have served as presidents in the last twenty years.) These new waves of immigrants have further enriched and diversified the cultural mix produced over the centuries by the collisions of Africans, Native Americans, and Iberians. Over the last century, this rich melting pot of peoples has made Latin America one of the most culturally and ethnically diverse regions on the planet.

CULTURE: MANY IMAGINED COMMUNITIES

The peoples of Latin America have emerged out of five centuries of common historical processes and patterns, yet many nations, regions, and groups within Latin America now pursue their own sense of identity and distinctiveness. Most of the peoples of the traditional twenty nations, and many others beyond their borders, see themselves as "Latin Americans." At the beginning of the twenty-first century, close to half a billion people identify themselves as participants in, and the descendants of, a common history and heritage. As I have tried to emphasize throughout this book, this thing called Latin America, and the nation-states of the region, have been constructed over centuries through complex and contested processes that have not inevitably led to the "imagined communities" that have emerged at the beginning of the sixth century since the region's birth. Latin America has multiple identities, as a region, as nations, as subnational regions, and as peoples and cultures that cross political boundaries. While the sense of Latin American solidarity, and the strength of nationalism, are stronger than at any time in the history of the region, many other "imagined communities" (indigenous peoples and Afro-descendants, to cite but two examples) are thriving and asserting their place within the many communities that make up Latin America today.

This paradox—of a strong sense of national and supranational identity at a time when many, many communities are asserting their own identities apart from the nation—makes Latin America both coherent as a region and as an idea, while making the task of describing that regional identity ever more problematic. Ironically, the nineteenth-century nation-building projects of the Liberals and positivists finally succeeded by the end of the twentieth century. The lack of national integration—infrastructural and cultural—in the late nineteenth century had been largely remedied by the end of the twentieth century, due in large part to improved transportation networks and the telecommunications revolution. In this sense, nationalism and nations came of age in Latin America over the last two generations. Nationalism is one of the most potent forces in Latin America (indeed, the world) today, a force that binds together many diverse peoples and cultures around loyalty to an idea that was merely an elite dream in the nineteenth century. Even as Indians, the descendants of African slaves, and the racially mixed assert their identities as distinct communities, they also ferociously defend the idea and national reality of a Bolivia or a Mexico or a Brazil.

Now, more than at any time in the history of Latin America, the rich and diverse races, ethnicities, and cultures of the region are recognized, honored, and nurtured. Beginning in the 1920s and growing over the century, nearly all Latin American nations have gradually recognized the diversity of their populations, and many have made that diversity central to the process of creating a sense of national identity and consciousness. Racial mixture in Mexico and Brazil, indigenous culture in the Andes and Mesoamerica, are now at the core of official rhetoric about national identity. Although a large gap remains between official rhetoric and the reality of daily life, this nationalism, national discourse, and nation-building are a world apart from the racist, eliminationist nationalism of the late nineteenth century. Sarmiento and da Cunha's racist Euro-centrism have given way to ideologies of inclusion, racial mixture, and "Americanness" as national strengths.

Across the last half-century, Latin America has also become an important exporter of culture to the rest of the world. Gone are the days when the Latin American elites anxiously aped the Europeans as the creators of all cultural value. The many vibrant varieties of cultural creation in Latin America have emerged primarily out of the collision of cultures, and the blending of cultural traits those collisions have produced over the last five hundred years. The art, music, and literature created in Latin America in the twentieth century has been extraordinarily rich and varied—and influential. Whether Brazilian bossa nova, Argentine tango, or Cuban dance music, Latin American rhythms have emerged out of cultural mixing and moved beyond the region to enrich and influence world culture.

This coming of age of Latin American culture is seen more clearly than anywhere else in the vibrant and influential literature that came out of the region in the second half of the twentieth century. By the 1960s and 1970s the so-called "boom" in Latin American literature made it the most influential in the world. Writers like Jorge Luis Borges (Argentina), Mario Vargas Llosa (Peru), Octávio Paz (Mexico), Gabriel García Márquez (Colombia), and Alejo Carpentier (Cuba) forged a literature that was both self-consciously Latin American *and* universal. By the end of the twentieth century, Latin Americans no longer sought to define themselves through cultural models imported from Europe and the United States. Instead, they helped redefine world culture by grappling with the meaning of the collision of peoples in the Americas. In each country and region of Latin America, writers, artists, and composers created new cultural contributions that had their roots in the collisions that began in the late fifteenth century. The feature that has long formed the core of Latin America as a region, the often violent clash of cultures, had become the very source of its cultural strength and influence as it began its sixth century.

19

The Path of
Revolution—Before 1959

Historians and social scientists have debated for decades the meaning of the term "revolution," and they have failed to reach a consensus definition. In popular language, people often use the term very loosely to refer to any violence, upheaval, or change of government. In this loose sense, Latin America has experienced many, many revolutions. My use of the term in this book, however, is much more rigorous and selective. As used here, the term *revolution* means a relatively rapid and fundamental transformation of the basic structures of society, politics, and economics, usually accompanied by violence. There are several key words here: violent, fundamental, and rapid. In all the cases in this chapter (and the next), violence and change take place, and within a relatively short time period. But to qualify as truly revolutionary, there must be more than rapid change and violence—that change must be profound, sweeping, fundamental. The classic revolutions in modern times have been very few—the United States in 1776, France in 1789, Haiti in 1791, Russia in 1917, China in 1949—are the most notable. Countless revolutionary movements have failed to take power.

Many revolutionary movements have emerged in Latin America during the twentieth century, but only a handful have succeeded in seizing power in a country and fundamentally transforming the nation. The Haitian Revolution is the earliest example of a profound and sweeping transformation, freeing hundreds of thousands of slaves, bringing blacks and mulattoes to power, and creating the second independent nation in the Americas (and the first in Latin America). The most successful revolutionaries have been those who managed to stay in power more than a brief period—as in Mexico and Cuba. In both cases, the initial revolutionary upheaval and transformation, however, ran its course fairly quickly, and the hopes for more enduring and successful change faded over decades as authoritarian regimes settled into place. Mexico and Cuba became—to steal the title of a famous documentary— "frozen revolutions." Both revolutions, especially the Cuban, also faced powerful pressures—including military intervention—from the United States. In Guatemala and Nicaragua, the initial revolutionary triumph was blunted by the quick and powerful intervention of the United States as it moved to thwart what appeared to be the rise of Soviet-backed regimes in Central America. U.S. intervention in Guatemala in 1954 halted revolutionary change in its tracks and touched off decades of brutal and deadly civil war that would eventually kill tens of thousands. U.S. intervention in Nicaragua in the 1980s also produced bloody civil wars that extended across Honduras and El Salvador. Today, Nicaragua is one of the poorest and most blighted countries in the hemisphere, and the revolution ground to a halt. The Bolivian Revolution in the 1950s put into place one of the most sweeping land reforms in Latin America, but within a decade the revolutionary leadership had become increasingly cautious. They were overthrown by a United States-supported military coup in 1964.

For better or for worse, the revolutions in all five countries fundamentally altered the lives of nearly everyone in these societies. Armed conflict produced upheaval and profound consequences. At their core, all five revolutions sought to transform the nation through an assault on the most important economic institution in Latin America—land tenure. For nearly the entire history of Latin America, those who have controlled the land (and the labor on it), have dominated the colonies and nations of the region. For centuries, a small landholding elite dominated the economies, political systems, and social structures of Latin America through its stranglehold on the most important and productive lands. By the twentieth century, absentee foreigners (primarily U.S. corporations) had become an important addition to the traditional landholding elite. The key to revolutionary transformation, consequently, was land reform—seizing control of the landholdings, and redistributing wealth to the poor through state control of land, or through land redistribution projects. Land reform struck at the very heart of power in any Latin American society, and it was the key to any revolutionary transformation. No revolution could succeed without land reform, and few believed that land reform could take place without sustained violence and bloodshed. The bloodiest and most sweeping of all of these modern revolutions exploded in Mexico in 1910.

MEXICO: A FROZEN REVOLUTION?

The first great social revolution of the twentieth century took place in Mexico—before the explosion of the Russian Revolution (1917) and nearly three decades before the triumph of the Chinese Revolution (1949). For a full decade (1910–20), civil war and rebellion engulfed the entire nation. Between one and two million Mexicans died in the conflict, in a population of about 15 million. (About 10 percent of the Mexican nation perished in the conflict. As a point of comparison, 620,000 died in the U.S. Civil War between 1861 and 1865 in a population of 31 million, or about 2 percent of the nation.) When the major civil violence ended in 1920 (although significant violence would continue for some time afterward), Mexico had the first socialist constitution of the twentieth century—a constitution that prohibited foreign control of national resources, guaranteed rights to workers, and practically banned the Catholic Church from its historic public role. The Revolution had toppled the 35-year dictatorship of Porfirio Díaz, and put into place a political party (the *Partido Revolucionario Institucional* or PRI) that would rule Mexico for the rest of the century (a one-party regime that lasted as long as the Communist Party in the Soviet Union). The Mexican regime after 1920 would elevate the Indian to the status of a national icon and declare the Spanish (and the United States) as the great villains in Mexican history. Gone was the official Eurocentrism of the nineteenth century. (The last Aztec ruler, Cuauhtémoc, became the symbol of the new Mexico.)

Much like the French or Russian Revolutions, the Mexican Revolution moved through a series of phases. In the first phase (1910–13), the *Porfiriato* collapsed and reformers led by Francisco Madero took power, hoping to institute a truly representative, democratic society. The enemies of change, led by General Victoriano Huerta, overthrew and executed Madero, and initiated a phase of counterrevolution (1913–14). With the overthrow of Huerta in 1914, the fiercest and bloodiest phases of the revolution began, as the revolutionary leaders—Pancho Villa, Emiliano Zapata, Venustiano Carranza, and Alvaro Obregón—turned their armies on each other to gain control of the country and the revolution (1914–17). Carranza (temporarily) triumphed, promulgated a new constitution (1917), and became president. His efforts to impose a handpicked successor in 1920 led to his overthrow and death, and the triumph of Obregón. This final phase (1917–20) marked the end of the major upheavals and the beginning of revolutionary consolidation in the 1920s led by President Obregón. From the 1920s to the late 1930s, Mexican presidents carried out sweeping social reforms, including land reform, a phase that culminated with President Lázaro Cárdenas (1934–40). In the following decades the leadership of this one-party regime increasingly turned to government-led economic growth as its focus on social reforms faded into the background. By midcentury, many Mexican intellectuals and politicians had already begun to ask if the revolution had "died" a bureaucratic death.

As in France in 1789 and Russia in 1917, the revolution began with a reform movement, followed by the collapse of the regime, and then full-scale armed conflict. In all three of these classic revolutions, the previous decade had been one of famine and economic crisis. All three were agrarian societies with a brutally repressed peasant majority living, and starving, in the countryside in the years leading up to the explosion. Famine, repression, and economic troubles, however, are not enough to produce a revolution. For most of the history of humanity, the majority of the world's population has lived in desperate conditions of poverty, injustice, and oppression. Revolutions arise from hope—the stubborn belief that people may be able to change the desperate conditions of their lives for something better, but at the risk of losing everything, including their lives. This desperate and powerful hope emerged in Mexico when a crisis divided the ruling political elites and provided an opportunity for audacious revolutionary leaders to rise up and successfully challenge a powerful state in crisis. This crisis at the highest levels of the *Porfiriato* in 1910–11 opened the door for reformers (Francisco I. Madero) and revolutionaries (Pancho Villa and Emiliano Zapata).

Ironically, the very economic success of the *Porfiriato* had sowed the seeds of its demise. The rapid and sustained economic growth under Porfirio Díaz produced a growing, urban middle class that admired the economic success, but increasingly lamented the lack of democratic, representative politics. The world economic crisis that began in 1907 severely damaged the fragile wealth of this middle class, producing rising dissatisfaction with the regime. For decades, Díaz muffled this dissent by bringing this educated and cosmopolitan group into government in key positions—his technocratic *científicos*. At the same time, the rapid influx of foreign capital (mainly from the United States) modernized and integrated the country, in particular, through the construction of a national railway network. Díaz carefully controlled the flow of foreign imports and capital to foster the creation of a network of Mexican industrialists, merchants, bankers, and companies—all beholden to him for their growing wealth. By 1910, this modernization spelled disaster for rural communities, especially indigenous communities, as Mexican and foreign capitalists seized control of more and more land—for their plantations, ranches, and mining enterprises. The Yucatán Peninsula is an extreme example of this process, as the International Harvester Company (based in Chicago) practically turned this hot, humid limestone plain into a gigantic henequen plantation to produce twine and rope, largely for farmers in the U.S. Midwest. Hundreds of thousands of impoverished peasants toiled for large plantations in conditions appallingly similar to those of rural Russian and Chinese peasants. South of Mexico City, in the state of Morelos (named after the heroic priest of the wars for independence), the rapid expansion of sugar plantations had deprived many traditional communities of their lands and livelihood.

The trigger for the revolutionary explosion was the election of 1910. Díaz was approaching the age of 80, and many reformers had hopes that he would finally step aside in 1910, after ruling Mexico since the 1870s. Díaz initially appeared to be willing to retire to Europe and allow open elections, and this unleashed a wave of reform campaigns and candidates, most prominently, that of Francisco I. Madero (1873–1913). An unlikely character for the role of revolutionary, Madero was a small, thin man from a wealthy ranching family in the northern state of Coahuila (bordering Texas). Educated in Baltimore, Paris, and Berkeley, Madero was a spiritualist and a vegetarian. In 1908, Madero published a small book (*The Presidential Succession of 1910*) laying out the essential reformist platform: effective suffrage and no reelection. (Ironically, this had been Díaz's very platform when he first ran for president in the 1870s.) Retreating from his promises, Díaz instead arrested Madero, and then rigged the election to give himself a massive victory. Madero escaped from his jail in San Luis Potosí, and fled north to San Antonio, Texas, where, in November 1910, he issued a "plan" calling for a revolution to overthrow Díaz.

In the words of one of the great historians of the Mexican Revolution, John Womack, it is a story "about country people who did not want to move and therefore got into a revolution." In the northern deserts and the fertile south, armed bands rose up in 1911 to challenge the regime. The cowboys from the arid northern ranches flocked around charismatic caudillos—Pascual Orozco and Pancho Villa, most notably. In Morelos, thousands of poor peasants and ranchers joined up with Emiliano Zapata (1879–1919), a respected horse wrangler from the village of Anenecuilco. The ninth of ten children, Zapata had been a village leader trying desperately to persuade the Mexican government to return ancestral lands to his people, lands that had been gobbled up by large sugar haciendas. After failing to achieve their aims through the "system" controlled by Díaz and his lieutenants, these frustrated, poor, country people rose up in March 1911 against the government, seizing the city of Cuautla (just 50 miles south of Mexico City). "Land and liberty" (*tierra y libertad*) became the rallying cry of Zapata's movement. In the north, Orozco and his forces took control of Ciudad Juárez (across the border from El Paso, Texas) at the same time. In the face of rising rebellion, and with his army in disarray, Díaz resigned, and left for exile in Paris (where he died peacefully in 1915).

Madero and his advisors had brokered a deal with the Díaz regime for a calm transition of power. What they had unleashed was civil war and revolution. After a triumphant return to Mexico City, Madero held a national election to confirm his mandate to rule. He was, however, a weak figure overwhelmed by the surging forces of revolution and counterrevolution. With the old regime still largely intact (Congress, landed elite, army, industrialists), Madero and the reformists accomplished little in his brief rule of sixteen months. For the insurgent peasants, the one great issue was land reform, and Madero (from a powerful ranching family) had little to offer them. The forces of Zapata in the south, and Villa and others in the north, seized larger and larger territories, pushing the powerful stalwarts of the *Porfiriato* into action against an increasingly ineffective Madero. With the close assistance of the U.S. Ambassador to Mexico, Henry Lane Wilson (no relation to Woodrow Wilson), General Victoriano Huerta deposed Madero in February 1913 and had him murdered in a supposed escape attempt. For his actions, Henry Lane Wilson was quickly recalled by the new U.S. President Woodrow Wilson (inaugurated in March 1913). President Wilson became a bitter enemy of Huerta, eventually sending U.S. troops into Tampico and Veracruz. From the north, Venustiano Carranza (1859–1920), led the so-called Constitutionalist forces. Another son of the landed class in the north, Carranza was older, and more conservative, than either Villa or Zapata. He turned his forces on Huerta after the death of Madero. With his two principal ports under U.S. occupation, Huerta was unable to resupply his troops. In July 1914, the "usurper" (as he is known in Mexican history) fled the country. (After some time in Europe and the United States, Huerta was arrested in west Texas, attempting to return to Mexico. He died in jail at Fort Bliss, Texas, in January 1916 of cirrhosis of the liver.)

What had begun as a reform movement in 1910 unleashed the forces of revolution that were countered in 1913–14 by the forces of reaction under Huerta. With his departure, the revolutionary factions were now virtually unchallenged by forces of the old regime, and fought among themselves for control of the country. Although the three main revolutionary leaders—Villa, Zapata, and Carranza—formed a loose alliance against Huerta, after his flight Villa and Zapata split off with their much more radical program of land redistribution, something Carranza did not support. Through astute political alliances, and the military successes of Alvaro Obregón, Carranza effectively isolated and neutralized Zapata and Villa. Zapata and his followers took control of Morelos and contented themselves (for the time being) with carrying out their long-desired land reform. Obregón defeated Villa and his forces repeatedly in a key series of battles north of Mexico City between April and June 1915. In October, the United States recognized Carranza as de facto president of Mexico. A constitutional convention (largely controlled by radicals) produced the Constitution of 1917 and, following elections, Carranza was sworn in as president in May 1917. Thus began the last phase of the ten-year struggle.

Between 1917 and 1920 the new constitutional regime took shape, Carranza attempted to impose a new sort of Porfirian regime, and he was overthrown in a rebellion that closed the cycle of revolutionary violence. Carranza largely ignored the radical, socialist pillars of the new Constitution: state control of subsoil and mineral rights, a labor code for workers, virulent anticlericalism, and land reform. In April 1919, one of Carranza's officers lured Zapata into an ambush and assassinated the greatest symbol of peasant revolution in modern times. Villa, in an effort to draw the United States into the conflict and destabilize Carranza, attacked the town of Columbus, New Mexico in March 1916. President Wilson sent a "punitive expedition" of 10,000 U.S. forces into northern Mexico under the command of General John J. "Black Jack" Pershing. The Germans, with their hands full on the eastern and western fronts in Europe, worked on both Villa and Carranza to attack the United States in hopes of keeping it out of World War I. Pershing spent a futile year chasing Villa before returning (with his troops) to Washington to assume command of the U.S. Army expeditionary force to France after Wilson declared war on Germany in 1917. After the military defeats in 1915, Villa was never again a major threat to the central government, and he died at the hands of assassins in 1923.

In a scene reminiscent of the 1870s, Carranza tried to impose his own candidate as his successor in the 1920 election, provoking the last major rebellion of the revolutionary decade. Alvaro Obregón, Carranza's brilliant general from the northern state of Sonora, marched on Mexico City, and forced Carranza to flee. After the rail line to Veracruz was blocked, Carranza fled into the mountains, where he was tracked down and killed in May 1920. Obregón was victorious in the 1920 presidential elections, and initiated the next phase in Mexican history—the consolidation of the revolutionary regime. Over the next two decades, many of the ideals of the radical revolutionaries—land redistribution, labor reform, nationalization of key sectors of the economy—would be put into place. In the decades after 1940, however, the focus of the Mexican leadership would shift from social reforms to economic growth. By the beginning of the twenty-first century, little remained of the revolutionary ideals of the 1910s and 1920s.

The true architects of modern Mexico were Alvaro Obregón and Plutarco Elías Calles, both from middle- and lower-class backgrounds in the northern state of Sonora (bordering on Arizona). Obregón had been a farmer and ranch hand before 1910 and Calles was a school teacher. Both rose through the ranks of the revolutionary armies in the north. Both were pragmatists. In the 1920s, they struck a deal to share power. Calles would become president in 1924 when Obregón's term ended, and then would step aside for Obregón in 1928. Together they forged a new political party that eventually became the PRI. Obregón wryly observed that he had ended the disorder and lawlessness by bringing all the bandits to Mexico

City to keep them out of trouble. He and Calles completely reorganized a new military, and kept it firmly under civilian control (keeping Mexico free in the twentieth century from the military coups that would plague other nations). They used a new ministry of labor to organize the working class and provide it with unions, benefits, and better wages, but at the price of independence. For decades, the urban Mexican labor force would be unionized, controlled, and a key pillar of the new regime. The labor unions also became incredibly corrupt.

In the 1920s, most of the intellectuals and advisors of Zapata were brought into the government to carry out the long-awaited land reform. In the 1920s and 1930s, the Mexican government gave millions of acres to peasants, most notably, in the form of communal landholdings (*ejidos*). Unfortunately, many of these lands were of poor quality, and the peasants received little in the way of credit and technical assistance. Consequently, productivity did not rise on the *ejidos*. At the same time, a powerful new landholding class, with close political ties to the new regime, took shape. It was often noted that no Mexican president retired from office without large estates. In short, land reform did take place, but it was ineffective. Modernization of agriculture took place, but as a sort of continuation of the trend of the *Porfiriato*, with larger and larger estates in the hands of rich Mexicans and foreigners.

Although Mexico and the United States were at odds in the aftermath of the revolution over the new Constitution's assertion of control over minerals and subsoil rights, both countries eventually reached a working relationship. The high point of the conflict took place in 1938 when President Lázaro Cárdenas declared the expropriation of Mexico's vast petroleum reserves (among the largest in the world, and the largest offshore in the Gulf of Mexico). With war looming in Europe, President Franklin Roosevelt chose quietly to negotiate a compensation package for foreign firms who lost their assets. In general, the pattern by the 1930s and 1940s was for Mexico to proclaim loudly Mexican control over national resources, while quietly allowing and protecting growing foreign investment, especially from the United States. (Ninety percent of mining operations, for example, were still under foreign control.)

The Constitution of 1917 also carried the nineteenth-century Liberal program of Juárez to its logical conclusion—severely restricting the power and presence of the Catholic Church. The Constitution banned the Church from its traditional role in education, prohibited priests and nuns from wearing their clerical garb in public, and made it impossible for the Church to accumulate wealth. In the late 1926, Calles chose to enforce these restrictions rigorously, provoking an internal religious civil war. The Catholic Church excommunicated Mexican leaders—en masse—and devout believers took up arms against the government in the Cristero Revolt around the cry, "Viva Cristo Rey!" ("Long live Christ the King!") For two years, the Church was forced to go underground, public masses ended, and (in some states) the new revolutionary leadership tracked down, jailed, or shot priests and nuns. (This brief and bitter conflict was immortalized in novelist Graham Greene's *The Power and the Glory* [1940].) Although the government remained openly anticlerical for decades, behind the scenes, politicians and Church officials worked out compromises that brought an end to the rebellion, and restored social peace. The revolt revived the old saying (often attributed to Porfirio Díaz), "Poor Mexico, so far from God, and so close to the United States!"

Not long after his reelection in 1928, a fanatic follower of the Cristero movement assassinated Obregón. Unwilling to provoke another uprising by taking on a second consecutive term, Calles ruled the country for the next six years through intermediaries. His handpicked successor for president in 1934 surprised Calles by emerging as a powerful leader in his own right. In 1936, Lázaro Cárdenas exiled Calles to Los Angeles, and became the first of a series of one-term "dictators." The presidency of Cárdenas was pivotal for twentieth-century Mexico. He made the PRI into a machine (the revolutionary family) that effectively became the battleground for political power and influence. (Everything through the PRI, nothing outside the PRI.) After the 1930s, the main interest groups in Mexico—industrialists, military, peasants, workers—learned that the road to power was through the internal debates and discussions within the PRI. Although opposition parties existed and contested elections, it was a foregone conclusion that the PRI candidates would always win the presidency, governorships, and control of the Congress. The PRI became a massive political machine with an organization that stretched into every municipality in the nation.

Cárdenas also put into place the standard operating procedure for Mexican presidents until the 1990s. He picked his successor, helped him get elected, and then stepped aside. From 1934 to 1994, ten Mexican presidents followed this pattern. Beginning with Manuel Ávila Camacho in 1940 (Cárdenas's chosen successor, who received 99 percent of the votes cast), Mexican presidents increasingly moved away from serious social reforms and focused on developing the Mexican economy through foreign investment and protection of Mexican industry—their own form of import substitution industrialization. After the revolutionary upheaval, Mexico after 1940 became one of the favorite destinations for U.S. investors, and the economy grew at a steady and stable pace for three decades. The oil shocks of the 1970s rocked Mexico, but in ways unlike the ways they affected the non oil producing nations of Latin America. As a major oil exporter, Mexico experienced a rapid and massive influx of capital in the 1970s, over borrowing and over spending. When oil prices dropped in the early 1980s and interest rates soared, the country effectively declared bankruptcy, unable to pay off more than $100 billion of foreign loans. Despite its huge oil reserves, Mexico suffered through the "lost decade" of the 1980s along with the rest of Latin America. Like the rest of Latin America, Mexico began to make the shift toward neoliberalism in the late 1980s and early 1990s.

At the same time, the one-party regime began to crumble under growing pressure internally. In 1968, the government had brutally repressed massive student uprisings, killing and wounding hundreds in Mexico City. The 1988 election was the most contested in the history of the regime, with the PRI managing to hold on to power and defeat the powerful opposition challenge from Cuauhtémoc Cárdenas, the son of former president Lázaro Cárdenas. Although many different groups were challenging the PRI grip on power by the 1990s, the most spectacular challenge came from Indians in the southern state of Chiapas. On January 1, 1994, a rebellion broke out in Chiapas, led by a radical former university professor known as Subcomandante Marcos. Much to the world's surprise, the Mexican government was unable to suppress the revolt, and the rebels in Chiapas survived, held on to many parts of southern Mexico, while helping to force the PRI to open up the regime. By the late 1990s, the PRI was struggling to hold on to political power, at all levels of government, amidst its own fragmentation, a series of economic crises, and strong challenges from opposition political parties. In the 2000 election, Vicente Fox, the former governor of Guanajuato, and the candidate of the *Partido Acción Nacional* (National Action Party), defeated the PRI at the polls. After three-quarters of a century, the one-party regime founded by Obregón and Calles had finally crumbled.

So what are we to make of the Mexican Revolution and its impact? Clearly, it was a profound, relatively rapid, and violent transformation of the nation. The old regime (the *Porfiriato*) was overthrown, and much of the nineteenth-century elite wiped out by the revolution. A new elite, largely emerging out of the mestizo middle class emerged, often with close ties to sectors of the old landholding and industrial elites. (The great Mexican novelist, Carlos Fuentes, brilliantly and cynically captures this transformation in *The Death of Artemio Cruz* [1959].) Indeed, recent work on Mexican economic history shows that the Revolution temporarily disrupted the economic modernization of the *Porfiriato*, and that the new regime essentially continued and accelerated this modernization after 1920. Millions of workers were given social and labor benefits, but at the cost of a government-controlled and corrupt unionization. The PRI made Emiliano Zapata the icon of the Revolution, and never missed an opportunity to invoke his name and cause. Millions of peasants received the land that they had hungered and fought for in the armies of Zapata and Villa. After decades, however, this land reform now looks superficial and corrupted as well. Along with the one-party regime, this disillusionment with land reform casts a dark shadow over Zapata's cry for "Land and liberty!"

The Mexican Revolution profoundly transformed Mexico in ways more dramatic and violent than the revolutions in any other country in Latin America. Perhaps the most visible change was ideological—the official glorification of the indigenous past and of Mexico's racially mixed (mestizo) heritage. The revolutionaries created a vast educational system that, despite its inadequacies, made huge strides in creating a sense of national integration around the "myths" of the revolution. The great murals of Diego Rivera, David Alfaro Siqueiros, José Clemente Orozco, and Rufino Tamayo forged a new art and sense of Mexican identity. The creation of a new political and economic elite in the 1920s and 1930s, however, derailed the ideals of the revolution—land, liberty, and social justice—as the revolutionary fervor of the 1910s and 1920s gave way in succeeding decades to the institutionalization, and slow death, of the hopes and dreams of revolutionaries.

GUATEMALA: A REVOLUTION STIFLED

The Mexican Revolution was decades ahead of its time. The next wave of revolution in Latin America would not emerge until the 1940s and 1950s, followed by another wave in the 1970s and 1980s. All of the later revolutionary movements would take place within the context of the global struggle between the United States and the Soviet Union. Although U.S. politicians and presidential administrations were wary of the socialist tendencies of the new Mexican regime after 1914, the ideological differences between the United States and Mexico played out in the 1920s and 1930s, before the emergence of the Cold War in the late 1940s. Throughout the twentieth century, Mexico espoused a foreign policy rhetoric that strove to be antiimperialist, often antagonistic to the United States, and sensitive to revolutionary movements (while maintaining very conservative and repressive policies in the domestic realm). By the late 1940s, the United States viewed the world as divided between two (and just two) camps—its allies and its enemies (those aligned with or sympathetic to the Soviet Union). All the successful revolutionary movements in twentieth-century Latin America were propelled by economic nationalism, challenges to U.S. political and economic hegemony, and the drive to modernize economies and political systems. Those holding power in Latin American countries were quick and adept at portraying these movements—and any talk of social justice, land reform, and social change—as the work of the Soviet Union, its lackeys, and a world Communist conspiracy. This bipolar worldview (shared by the United States and the Soviet Union) left little ground for non-communist reformers within Latin American politics.

In the cases of Mexico and Cuba, revolutions arose in the most economically advanced countries of the region. Guatemala, Bolivia, and Nicaragua were among the poorest, most rural, and agrarian societies in the Americas. Guatemala and Bolivia also had indigenous majorities dominated by mestizo and white minorities. In all five cases, the staggering socioeconomic inequities and brutal repression became the central targets of the revolutionaries intent on creating societies that would be more democratic, representative, and equitable. In all five cases, control of land (and labor) held the key to control of power, and to transforming the enormous inequities in these nations. In Guatemala, elite control of land and power was intimately linked to U.S. business interests and U.S. power in the region.

Guatemala in the 1940s seemed almost a feudal society, a poor, rural nation where an Indian majority scratched out a subsistence growing corn and beans while compelled to work on the landed estates of the white and mestizo (known as *Ladinos* in Guatemala) minority. About 10 percent of Guatemala's two million inhabitants lived in the capital (Guatemala City), and the next largest city had fewer than 30,000 inhabitants. Along with the rest of Central America, Guatemala had become a coffee exporter in the nineteenth century, noted for its high-quality beans grown on the slopes of the volcanic mountains that stretched across the country from northwest to southeast. The remnants of the once powerful Maya empires were rural villages containing indigenous groups speaking some two dozen Mayan languages. The indigenous population was highly fragmented by language, local customs, and religious rituals. All practiced forms of Catholicism deeply imbued with pre-Columbian religious symbols and rituals. This folk Catholicism helped the poor cope with their oppressive living conditions, and helped the elites maintain social order. Nearly all the indigenous population was illiterate in the 1940s, life expectancy was under 40 years, infant mortality was above 50 percent (the highest in the Americas at that time), and they comprised two-thirds of all Guatemalans. This Indian majority probably controlled less than 10 percent of arable land. Two percent of the population owned more than 70 percent of the arable land. The poor had small plots known as *minifundios*, while the rich controlled enormous landed estates referred to as *latifundios*. These are the inequities that formed the core of Guatemalan (and most of Latin American) society in the 1940s.

The inequities in Guatemala were magnified by the presence of what became in twentieth-century Latin America the most notorious U.S. corporation in the region—the United Fruit Company (UFCO). Formed in 1899 with the merger of newly-emerging banana exporting companies in the Caribbean and Central America, *la Frutera* (as it was often called in Central America) became a powerful transnational corporation under the leadership of Samuel Zemurray in the 1930s. In Guatemala, UFCO built and controlled the only railway in the country (from the Atlantic coast to Guatemala City and then on to the Pacific coast and El Salvador) and it became the largest landholder (with most of its holdings concentrated on the Atlantic coast). During the Depression, UFCO negotiated a deal with dictator Jorge Ubico (who came to power in 1931) that exempted the company from virtually all taxation and export duties. The depression hit the country hard as the value of coffee and banana exports dropped by two-thirds. With its extensive landholdings, railway, power plants, trucking company, shipping fleet, and other firms, the company was often referred to by Central Americans as *el pulpo*—the octopus. The *Ladino* elite controlled the coffee plantations and through "vagrancy" laws compelled the indigenous majority to work on their estates (*fincas*) under abysmal conditions. The banana export business, largely located on the eastern coast, operated as a virtual enclave, contributing little to the larger national economy. (Coffee exports generated 77 percent of export revenue and bananas 13 percent.)

The most striking feature of the revolution in Guatemala is the relative absence of violence, at every stage of the process, especially in a country that had long been ruled by dictators (Justo Rufino Barrios, 1873–85; Manuel Estrada Cabrera, 1898–1920; Jorge Ubico, 1931–44). University student protests in June 1944 touched off a brief crisis that mobilized reformist military officers, intellectuals, and middle-class reformers leading the army to force Ubico to step down, but the military high command remained in power. In October, the reformers within the military forced the generals to resign, and they held national elections in December 1944, the first truly open elections in the history of Guatemala. A philosophy professor, Juan José Arévalo, who had spent years in exile in Argentina, returned home and easily won the presidential election as the candidate of the reformers, receiving 85 percent of the nearly 300,000 votes cast. He was sworn in for a five-year term as the first president elected in a truly open election in the history of Guatemala in March 1945. At this point, the beginning of the Guatemalan Revolution looked very much like Mexico and Madero in 1910–11.

Contrary to its restraint in Mexico, the United States would intervene in Guatemala in 1954 to halt the revolution in its tracks. In retrospect, the social transformations that the revolutionaries tried to implement between 1945 and 1954 were precisely the reforms the United States would back vigorously in El Salvador in the midst of a leftist revolutionary uprising in the 1980s. The Guatemalan Revolution had two phases: under Arévalo (1945–51) the new regime cautiously initiated a labor code, a mild effort at land reform, rural literacy campaigns, and mild economic nationalism. Unfortunately, Arévalo described his program as "spiritual socialism," not a wise choice of words, given the temper of the times. The Communist Party was banned (as were all parties with international linkages). The most open and fair election in Guatemalan history elected Jacobo Arbenz (his father was Swiss), an army officer, to succeed Arévalo, and the transfer of power at the inauguration of Arbenz in March 1951 was the first peaceful transfer of power from one democratically-elected president to another in the history of the country (and the last for more than three decades).

Arbenz touched the most sensitive nerve of all in Guatemalan politics and U.S. foreign policy when he pushed land reform to a new stage. The very mild land reform legislation called for the expropriation (with compensation) of large, "unproductive" landholdings. Although the law would affect very few landowners, the government singled out United Fruit as a major target, calling for the expropriation of more than 15 percent of the company's 650,000 acres (land that was not under cultivation). The government offered to pay the company the value UFCO had officially declared for the lands on its 1950 tax return—just over $600,000. The company immediately claimed the land was worth nearly $16 million. United Fruit lobbied very successfully in Washington for action from the U.S. government. John Foster Dulles (Secretary of State), his brother Allen (Director of the Central Intelligence Agency), and many other powerful figures in the Eisenhower administration had close ties to the company (John Foster Dulles had worked for the law firm representing UFCO and he was a stockholder, along with his brother).

In June 1954, the CIA staged a coup that quickly deposed Arbenz and sent him into exile. He was replaced by Carlos Castillo Armas, an army officer flown into Guatemala to head the coup and the new government. The counterrevolution now triumphed, with a vengeance. The reforms of the previous decades were tossed out, and Castillo Armas initiated nearly four decades of military-dominated rule in Guatemala. By the late 1950s, leftist guerrilla movements had begun to emerge, and for decades the military and various guerrilla movements would battle in the countryside, leaving two hundred thousand dead. In the 1980s, the fighting became incredibly intense and the *Ladino*-dominated military regime carried out a war in the countryside, annihilating entire villages of indigenous peoples. In many ways, the "low-intensity" conflict in Guatemala in the 1980s was an even more intense version of the U.S. experience in the Vietnamese countryside in the 1960s. As one political scientist has noted, "the intervention in 1954 opened a new political era in which almost every effort at reform was stalled by a ruling class determined to protect its economic and social interests at any cost."

The 1954 intervention is one of the most studied episodes in U.S.-Latin American relations. For many, it is the most blatant example of the use of U.S. power to protect U.S. business abroad (in this case, United Fruit). For others, it was simply a logical reaction to a perceived Communist threat in "our own backyard." The two are not mutually exclusive. Protecting U.S. interests (the "American way of life") very often meant not only geopolitical interests, but also economic/business interests. After all, capitalism is at the very core of the "American way of life." At the time, very few realized that the CIA had directly engineered the coup ("Operation Success"). Along with the successful overthrow of a nationalist regime in Iran (1953), the Guatemalan intervention became the model for other covert U.S. operations in the coming years.

Along with El Salvador, Honduras, and Nicaragua, the Guatemalans suffered throughout the 1980s from revolutionary upheavals and U.S.-supported counterrevolutionary movements. Only after years of intense, regional negotiations did Guatemala finally see the end of civil conflict in the early 1990s, and the return to truly open elections. For the past two decades, Guatemala (along with the rest of Central America) has held regular elections, and hesitantly moved to more open politics amidst the persistence of civil violence by both the Right and the Left. With nearly eight million inhabitants, and the dogged persistence of very high rates of poverty, Guatemala continues to face the difficulties of solving the "social question." Indigenous peoples still comprise nearly 40 percent of the population, and they are more vocal and organized than ever. Many of the Indian activists speak of creating a truly indigenous Guatemalan nation, but the ethnic divisions (especially between Indians and Ladinos) remain a sensitive and volatile issue. One wonders what Guatemala might look like today, had the dramatic reforms of the 1950s managed to run their course, and had the country not been subjected to decades of brutal counterrevolutionary violence and warfare. At the beginning of the twenty-first century, the Guatemalans can at least begin to confront their problems in a more open political process, and attempt to make up for the lost years and lives.

BOLIVIA: REVOLUTION GONE ASTRAY

The Bolivian Revolution of 1952 was much more radical and nationalistic than the Guatemalan Revolution of 1944–45, but it met with much less drastic and dramatic reactions from the United States. The Bolivian revolutionaries nationalized the tin mining industry—the most important economic sector in the country—and carried out a land reform more sweeping than Mexico's. Within a decade, however, the leadership of the revolution had become increasingly conservative, cautious, and pro-United States, and in 1964, a military coup ended the revolutionary process. Rather than use direct or covert military intervention, the Eisenhower administration made Bolivia the biggest recipient (per capita) of U.S. foreign aid in the 1950s, effectively using foreign loans and assistance to move Bolivia toward a more moderate path. A series of military rulers and populists since the 1960s have failed to raise the majority of Bolivians out of poverty. Bolivia today is one of the poorest countries in Latin America.

Bolivia, Peru, and Ecuador, the heartland of the Andean region, looked very similar to Guatemala at the beginning of the twentieth century. With indigenous majorities, long histories of forced labor, and grinding poverty, these Andean nations were by no means integrated nation-states or "imagined communities." Bolivia has long been the poorest of the trio. Home of the rich silver mines of Potosí in the colonial period, Bolivia's silver deposits had been exhausted—unlike Mexico's—by the twentieth century. Tin mining had become the new core of the economy, providing the bulk of the government's revenue and most of the country's export earnings. A mestizo and foreign elite dominated this overwhelming rural, agrarian society with near-feudal conditions of debt servitude and patron-client ties. Tin mining and miners formed the most developed sector of the national economy. A small group of powerful landowners controlled the countryside (6 percent of landowners controlled more than 90 percent of all cultivated land), and three families (Patiño, Arayamo, and Hochschild) controlled the tin mining industry on the eve of the revolution.

In the 1880s, Bolivia had lost its access to the sea—becoming a land-locked country—with its defeat (along with Peru) in the War of the Pacific against Chile. A bloody war with Paraguay over the inhospitable Chaco region (1932–35) killed nearly 60,000 Bolivians and 40,000 Paraguayans, and did little for either country. (Paraguay ended up with most of this tropical lowland region where Brazil, Paraguay, Bolivia, and Argentina converge. The Chaco War did produce serious changes within the Bolivian military and army officers dominated politics, usually through military coups, in the late 1930s and the 1940s. These governments often brought together a variety of reformers from a wide range of political positions (socialists, Communists, fascists, among others).

In 1941 a number of reformers founded the Nationalist Revolutionary Movement (*Movimiento Nacionalista Revolucionario* or MNR), most prominently two sons of the wealthy Bolivian elite—Víctor Paz Estenssoro (1907–2001) and Hernán Siles Suazo (1915–96). (Siles Suazo's father was president from 1926–30.) The MNR attracted a dynamic group of figures who sought to bring fundamental changes to Bolivia. The MNR won national elections in May 1951 with Paz as the candidate for president and Siles as his running mate. They received 39,000 of the 54,000 votes cast, but the army stepped in and annulled the elections. In early April 1952, the MNR armed large numbers of civilians and a popular uprising left hundreds dead, but put Paz, Siles, and the MNR in control of the country. Largely dominated by radical figures from the middle and upper classes, and the highly militant tin miners, the MNR put into motion a sweeping transformation of this nation of some three million inhabitants.

Three fundamental transformations defined the Bolivian Revolution: nationalization of the tin mines, land reform, and the complete renovation of the army. Bolivia was the world's largest producer of tin (accounting for 15–20 percent of world production), and the metal provided 60–70 percent of government tax revenues. The extraordinarily wealthy (and largely absentee) Patiño, Aramayo, and Hochschild families controlled 75 percent of production. The revolutionary regime nationalized the tin mines, created a state-controlled corporation (COMIBOL) to run the mines, and strongly supported the tin miners's union, making their leaders powerful figures in the new government. As in the case of any true revolution, the army was practically disbanded and recreated, a process that reduced a powerful potential counterrevolutionary uprising. In effect, the country's economic and political elite had been weakened by two decades of political and economic instability, and the MNR seized power while the elites were weak and their power to repress was low.

Along with the nationalization of the tin mines, the most sweeping legacy of the regime was a profound land reform that surged up from below. The rural (largely Indian) peasantry had not played much of a role in the April revolt, but in its aftermath, peasants rose up in the countryside, taking control of lands (especially from absentee landowners) and destroying tax and property records. The government was forced into action and was, in effect, pulled along by the more aggressive approach of the rural peasantry. The peasants also organized into unions (*sindicatos*) that became very powerful throughout the countryside. Ironically, once the peasantry gained control over land, they became a very conservative force in the nation's politics. In the words of Herbert Klein, the foremost historian of Bolivia in the United States, "The appeasement of their land hunger turned the Indians inward so that for the next two generations the primary concern of the communities and their sindicatos was the delivery of modern facilities of health and education and the guaranteeing of their land titles." Unfortunately, and, as in Mexico, once the peasants gained control of their own lands, they had little access to credit or technical assistance to help them modernize their small farms.

Although these sweeping and radical changes took shape at the very moment the United States was carefully plotting its covert intervention in Guatemala to halt a much less radical land reform, the Eisenhower administration took a much more flexible and less aggressive approach to the Bolivian Revolution. Unlike the Guatemalans, the Bolivian leaders were able to persuade the United States that they were not Communists, but rather homegrown nationalists. The revolutionaries had more breathing space than the Guatemalans, partly because Bolivia was so isolated and distant, because the MNR had developed a reputation in the 1940s for fascist (rather than communist) tendencies, and because the United States had so little investment in the country. A key group of U.S. advisors in the State Department and the Foreign Service (including Milton

Eisenhower, the president's brother) argued that the revolutionaries were a non-Communist alternative to Marxist revolutionaries, who were active all over Latin America in the 1950s.

Finally, the revolutionary leadership became increasingly conservative. Under intense pressure, the Bolivian government agreed to compensate the owners of the confiscated tin mines. Paz Estenssoro made clear his pro-United States and anti-Soviet sentiments, and he found himself increasingly dependent on U.S. aid in an economy devastated by the consequences of land reform and nationalization of the tin mines. By 1960, Bolivia was the largest single recipient of U.S. foreign aid in Latin America. This aid also helped rebuild, train, and equip the new Bolivian military that became very pro-United States and anti-Communist. Siles Suazo was elected president in 1956 and faced enormous economic problems. Rather than continuing the revolutionary social reforms that would have been necessary to begin to address the enormous socioeconomic inequities in Bolivia, Siles opted for more U.S. assistance and compliance with international lending agencies (in particular, the International Monetary Fund).

During the second presidency of Paz Estenssoro (1960–64), and in the aftermath of the Cuban Revolution (1959), the MNR fragmented and divided, and the United States-assisted military grew more professional and powerful. As the struggle between leftist guerrilla movements and United States-supported governments heated up in the 1960s, the Bolivian military stepped in and took power in 1964. The army had power, the peasants had their land, and the government repressed and isolated the militant miners. Bolivian politics would be bitterly divided and fragmented, suffering through a series of military coups and dictators until the 1990s. By the 1980s, many peasants had turned to the lucrative business of coca production as cocaine trafficking emerged (especially in Colombia) as one of the biggest businesses in the Americas.

In the 1980s, with Bolivia suffering from astronomical inflation (over 25,000 percent per year) and recession, Siles Suazo (1982–85) and Paz Estenssoro (1985–89) were returned to the presidency after elections in which no candidate received anywhere near fifty percent of the vote. Paz implemented a drastic neoliberal economic plan that ended inflation and stabilized the economy, but the free-market economics in the following years have not been able to generate economic growth or jobs for a country that remains impoverished and with little to export other than coca and (recently discovered deposits of) natural gas. The tin mines have played out, but the unions remain strong. Peasants, especially the coca growers, are well organized and militant. Politics remain deeply fragmented and racially divided. In 2006, Evo Morales, the leader of the coca-growers union, was elected president. The first president of indigenous ancestry, Morales vowed to reject the neoliberal policies of the past two decades and return to social reforms, government intervention, and the nationalization of the natural gas resources.

Bolivia's revolution rapidly and violently transformed the nation, but the revolutionary leadership became more cautious and did not follow up the transformations with continuing social and economic changes. In a sense, it was a revolutionary leadership that lost its nerve and backed away from radicalism. They had the bad fortune to nationalize aging and inefficient tin mines, and to fragment the landholding structure into small and unproductive farms that could not be modernized and made more efficient. The truly dramatic social reforms needed by a country as incredibly poor as Bolivia could only have come with external aid, but that assistance came from the United States, a superpower that worked to stymie radical social change in the 1950s and 1960s. While the Mexican Revolution lost its impulse over decades and became increasingly conservative, and the Guatemalan Revolution was stopped in its tracks by U.S. intervention, the Bolivian Revolution ran out of steam within a decade, bought out—in a very real sense—with U.S. foreign aid.

20

The Path of
Revolution—Since 1959

The three major revolutions in Latin America before 1959—Mexico, Guatemala, and Bolivia—were all influenced by various forms of socialism, communism, and Marxism. The Mexican Revolution exploded before the Russian Revolution, and long before the era of the Cold War (1947–91). Although seen as socialist (and even "bolshevik") by its critics, the Mexican Revolution had already settled into its more conservative phase before the Cold War broke out in the late 1940s. The Guatemalan Revolution arose almost simultaneously with the emergence of the Cold War superpower-struggle between the United States and the Soviet Union, and it became a casualty of the East-West conflict. The Bolivian Revolution produced an odd mix of ideologies (including socialism), but the revolutionary leadership worked hard to persuade the United States that, in the event of a global conflict, Bolivia would be in the US camp against the Soviet Union. With the Cuban Revolution, revolutionary movements across Latin America entered into a new phase, one profoundly shaped by Marxism-Leninism and the East-West conflict.

The great ideologies that would clash in the twentieth century were born in the eighteenth century, and then came of age in the nineteenth century. Liberalism, socialism, and capitalism are all children of the Enlightenment, with their emphasis on autonomous individuals making rational choices in a system that guarantees equality before the law. Liberalism and capitalism, although they are distinct, have historically converged in Western Europe and the United States. As we have seen, classical liberalism stresses individual rights and minimal government intervention in the lives of citizens. Capitalism is an economic system that emerged in the late Middle Ages and the Renaissance before reaching full flower after 1750. Capitalism is built on the central principle of private property, and thrives best when contracts and property rights are guaranteed, and when the flow of goods, services, capital, and labor faces few restrictions. From the mid-eighteenth century on, the convergence of liberalism's political ideology and the economics of capitalism have produced extraordinarily successful democratic, capitalist regimes in North America and Europe, regimes that have dominated the world's economy and politics led by Great Britain in the nineteenth century and the United States in the twentieth century.

Socialism is both a political ideology and an economic system. It also emerges out of the Enlightenment, coming of age in the 1830s and 1840s in Europe. Private property is anathema to socialism, a system that is built on collective ownership of the "means of production" (that is, the economic infrastructure that produces wealth such as factories and farms). In practice, this has usually meant government control of the key sectors of the economy. Socialism is also built on the notion of individuals acting rationally, but in a system that emphasizes the rights of the collective over the individual. In the words of Karl Marx (1818–83), capitalism operates on the principle, "from each according to his ability, to each according to what he owns," while socialism functions on the principle, "from each according to his ability, to each according to his needs." In short, the wealth produced in a capitalist economy goes to those who have ownership (capitalists) based on how much they own of the means of production. Under socialism, wealth is distributed by the state on the basis of the needs of everyone, not on the basis of ownership of property. Consequently, the objective of capitalists in the eighteenth and nineteenth centuries was to gain control of states to make sure they guaranteed individual property rights, while socialists sought to take control of states to abolish private property and to use the government to distribute production based on the collective needs of the population.

Although socialism comes in many forms, historically Karl Marx's version of socialism has had the greatest influence in world history. (Marx distinguished his version of socialism from others he saw as less practical by calling it "communism," hence, The Communist Manifesto [1848].) Marx believed that capitalism would generate increasing contradictions between the workers/proletariat (who produced all wealth through their labor) and the capitalists/bourgeoisie (who dominated the economy and the state in order to control wealth). In Marx's view, the day would come when the increasingly exploited workers would rise up in the most industrialized nations (i.e., Europe) and overthrow the capitalist bourgeoisie, take control of the state, and create a society built on the collectivist principles of socialism. Marx's violent workers' revolution in the industrial nations of central and Western Europe did not materialize, largely because these nations extended their economic and political might across the globe in the late nineteenth century. As the Europeans built empires, the living standard of the working class slowly improved, and the vote was gradually extended to all adult males. (Thus, the "immiseration" of the European proletariat did not take place as Marx had predicted.) The intense exploitation of labor was, in effect, transferred to the colonies, in what would become known in the mid-twentieth century as the Third World. Surprisingly, the Marxist revolutionaries who did succeed took power in the most rural and least industrialized part of Europe (and the section considered least culturally European)—the Russian Empire.

Vladimir Lenin (1870–1924) became a devoted Marxist, led the Bolsheviks to power in Russia after 1917, and then began to propagate his own version of Marxism that had powerful repercussions in Latin America, and the rest of the world, in the twentieth century. Lenin added (or built on) three key ideas to classical Marxism. Following Marx, he argued that the revolution could only triumph if led by a small, disciplined, and committed vanguard party (in his case, the Bolsheviks, who later became the Communist Party of the Soviet Union). Furthermore, once this vanguard took power, they would need to impose a "dictatorship of the proletariat" to eradicate the last vestiges of capitalism, the bourgeoisie, and to prevent counterrevolution. Marx had written about both points, but only briefly. Finally, Lenin argued that imperialism had shifted the locus of capitalist exploitation, and that the revolution would come in less developed countries as workers and peasants united to overthrow the capitalist minority that controlled the state.

Part of the power of what became known as Marxism-Leninism was the success of the Bolsheviks in Russia. The vanguard successfully seized power, took complete control of the nation, and carried out a radical, socialist revolution—in a country considered backward, with little industry, and a small proletariat amidst a peasant majority. Lenin's success became a powerful example for the Chinese (Mao Zedong) and socialist revolutionaries in the largely agrarian colonies and nations in Asia, Africa, and Latin America. With the formation of the Communist International (Comintern) in the Soviet Union in the 1920s, the USSR became a very powerful and persuasive advocate of a particular version of socialist revolutionary ideology—Marxism-Leninism. For the next 75 years, the most powerful and successful leftist revolutionary movements in Latin America were nearly all Marxist-Leninist, or deeply influenced by Marxism-Leninism. (The most prominent exception is the Shining Path movement in Peru in the 1980s and 1990s, which was inspired by the Chinese Revolution and Mao.) The Cuban Revolution is the most emphatic and expressive example of Marxist-Leninist revolution in twentieth-century Latin America.

CUBA: REVOLUTIONARY SOCIALISM

It is difficult to overstate the importance and impact of the Cuban Revolution on Latin America, the Americas, and the world. After his rebel army toppled the dictatorship of Fulgencio Batista in January 1959, Fidel Castro and his *compañeros* transformed Cuba from a capitalist ally of the United States into a fully socialized economy closed linked to, and heavily subsidized by, the Soviet Union. The Cuban revolutionaries carried out one of the most sweeping land reforms in Latin American history, radically redistributed wealth, providing all Cubans with basic health care, education, and social services, and became an important inspiration and ally in the export of Marxist revolution to other parts of the Americas—and the Third World. The United States organized a failed attempt to invade Cuba and overthrow Castro in April 1961, and the bitter conflict between the United States and Cuba brought the world to the brink of nuclear war in October 1962. It is hard to imagine another country of its size (seven million inhabitants in 1960) that has played such a pivotal role in world politics in the last half century.

One of the most striking aspects of the Cuban Revolution was the triumph of such a radically anti-United States, Marxist revolution in a country so close to the United States (90 miles off the coast of Florida) and with such a long history of integration into the US economy. Observers have often noted that the extreme anti-Americanism of the Cuban regime was a direct result of decades of US cultural, political, and economic domination of this small island nation. (The same holds true for the anti-Americanism of the Nicaraguan Revolution of 1979.) As we saw earlier, the strong economic ties between Cuba and the United States go back to the eighteenth century. The rapid expansion of sugar cultivation in the nineteenth century made Cuba the great sugar exporter of the world, and much of that production was controlled by US investors and corporations. Sugar dominated Cuba, and the United States dominated Cuban sugar. The sudden and dramatic US intervention in the Cuban-Spanish War in 1898 temporarily derailed Cuban independence, as the US Army occupied and ran Cuba until 1902. For the next three decades, the US Marines intervened repeatedly to "stabilize" Cuba and "to protect American lives and property." After 1934, the United States strongly supported Fulgencio Batista, an army sergeant/stenographer who rose to power and maintained it through his control of the Cuban Army.

Batista dominated Cuban politics from 1934 until he fled the island for Santo Domingo on New Year's Eve 1958. In the late 1940s, he went into semiretirement in Miami, and Cuban politics experienced a period of political opening, debate, and reform movements. In 1952, Batista returned to power in a military coup. For most of the 1950s, Cuba gained a reputation as a playground for North Americans with its beautiful beach resorts, luxury hotels and casinos, as well as its corruption and Mafia presence (immortalized on film in Francis Ford Coppola's brilliant *The Godfather II* [1974]). Cuba in the 1950s had become almost a showcase for the inequities in Latin America. Alongside the affluence and opulence that catered to foreign tourists, Cubans lived in a very unequal world. As a whole, Cuba ranked among the top five countries in Latin America in most social indicators— low infant mortality, high literacy rates, and long life expectancy. Within the country, however, an enormous gap divided rural and urban Cubans. In the sugar-producing countryside, infant mortality and illiteracy rates were very high, life expectancy low, and basic services (running water, sewerage, electricity) virtually nonexistent. There were two Cubas in the 1950s, the wealthy, educated, healthy, urban Cuba (primarily Havana) and the impoverished rural countryside. The sugar economy was seasonal and cyclical, with periods of intense labor demand followed by months of unemployment. The modernization and expansion of the sugar economy over the previous century had, ironically, dispossessed many peasants of their land and left them in precarious conditions as they lived from harvest to harvest, in boom years and bust, as a transient labor force.

During a brief moment of reformist enthusiasm, a progressive group of Cuban politicians had managed to created a new constitution in 1940, calling for greater national control over the sugar economy and social reforms. Although Batista promulgated the Constitution of 1940, it was a dead letter. In the late 1940s and early 1950s, many of the Cubans calling for reforms made the true implementation of the Constitution of 1940 their central objective. Ultimately, the most important of these reformers was Fidel Castro Ruz. Born in 1926, Fidel was the oldest child of a newly affluent father (an immigrant from Galicia, Spain). Castro (and his younger brother Raúl, b. 1931) enjoyed the benefits of the *nouveaux riches* and suffered from their lack of social acceptance by the traditional Cuban elite. Although he was a child of the eastern part of the island (*Oriente*) Fidel attended the famous Jesuit-run Belén College in Havana (it now operates in Miami), where he was a standout athlete and a leader among the students. As a law student at the University of Havana in the 1940s, he became involved in politics, married, fathered a son, and seemed destined to settle into a fairly typical life as a lawyer after his graduation in 1950.

In his early political involvement, Castro was a staunch nationalist, inspired by the writings of the legendary José Martí. He was with a university student delegation in Bogotá, Colombia, in April 1948, when the assassination of a prominent populist politician sparked days of riots, and then years of deadly violence between Liberals and Conservatives. This experience amidst a massive, popular uprising left a deep impression on Castro. He became a follower of Eddie Chibás, one of the most prominent reformist politicians in Cuba, and Castro ran for congress in 1952. After the dramatic suicide of Chibás (while he was broadcasting on the radio) in 1951, and the Batista coup in March 1952, Castro gave up on reforming the political system, and turned to armed struggle as the only possible path to real change. On July 26, 1953, Castro led a poorly planned assault on the Moncada army barracks in Santiago that led to the deaths and imprisonment of hundreds of his coconspirators and allies. Put on trial, Castro gave a powerful speech, "History Will Absolve Me," that was circulated widely and secured his reputation as a prominent opponent of Batista. The key ideals expressed in his speech were not that radical—a call for true democracy, a diversification of the economy, and a nationalism that would diminish the overwhelming influence of the United States in Cuba. In short, he called for the implementation of the ideals of the Constitution of 1940.

After nearly two years in prison on the Isle of Pines, Batista released Castro, along with the other conspirators, under an amnesty. Fidel, his brother Raúl, and a number of others went into exile in Mexico, where a young Argentine trained in medicine joined the group. His name was Ernesto Guevara, but he became better known by his nickname—Che (a frequently used nickname in Argentina that translates roughly as "buddy"). Guevara had wandered up through South and Central America, and was in Guatemala in 1954 when the CIA deposed Jacobo Arbenz. Like Fidel's experience in Bogotá in 1948, Che's presence at this crucial historical moment helped forge a committed antiimperialist, anti-United States revolutionary. Ever under the surveillance of the FBI and Batista's agents, the group trained for an invasion of Cuba, and raised money among Cuban exiles in the United States. In early December 1956 (and imitating José Martí's 1895 expedition), 81 men and their munitions headed for Cuba on a rickety and overloaded boat they had purchased (named *Granma*). The Cuban army was waiting for them when they arrived. Like Martí's invading force, most of Castro's was killed or captured almost immediately. (Reportedly, as Castro waded ashore, he told the first peasant he came across, "I am Fidel Castro and we have come to liberate Cuba.") Che, Fidel, Raúl, and a few others survived and regrouped in the Sierra Maestra at the eastern end of the island, forming the nucleus of a guerrilla movement that two years later would march triumphantly into Havana.

While Fidel and his small band slowly built a guerrilla army in the mountains, other opponents of Batista organized an urban resistance movement, especially in Havana. Castro became the most internationally recognized foe of the regime in early 1957, when Herbert L. Matthews published articles about him and his men in the *New York Times*. Castro had smuggled Matthews into the Sierra and proceeded to persuade him that he had a sizable force controlling the Sierra, even though he controlled no territory and had just eighteen men who had survived the invasion, landing, and ambushes. (The adjustment to life in the mountains was very tough on this bunch of urban, university-educated, middle- and upper-class young men.) Although sometimes portrayed as a peasant rebellion (especially by the followers of Che and Fidel), the uprising that overthrew Fulgencio Batista was a general insurrection led by Castro in the Sierra and many others in the cities. Exiles in the United States also played key roles in mobilizing international support for the opponents of Batista. By late 1958, the regime was collapsing, as the poorly managed Cuban army disintegrated. The guerrillas became bolder, moving from ambushes and small fights, as they came down from the mountains and attacked cities. On New Year's Eve 1958, Batista flew to exile in the Dominican Republic. Over the next week, Fidel made his way to Havana like a conquering hero.

For nearly half a century a debate has raged over Fidel Castro's motives and ideology before January 1959. Was he a Marxist or Communist who disguised his true colors to take power and then "steal" the revolution from its broad-based constituencies? Was his conversion to Marxism something that took place in the Sierra under the influence of Raúl and Che? Was he somehow persuaded to adopt Marxism in his first months in power after seeing liberal resistance to fundamental change? In short, how long had Castro known that he would impose a sweeping Marxist revolution and not simply a liberal, democratic one? We will probably never know. Although Castro carefully emphasized his nationalist, and anti-Batista, prodemocracy objectives before January 1959, by early 1960, he and his closest allies had pushed aside nearly all those who had fought to overthrow Batista, except those who were committed to an anti-United States and socialist agenda. In December 1961, he declared in a speech that he was—and always had been in—a Marxist-Leninist. By then, reformists in the rebellion had been completely shoved aside, and the revolutionary vanguard had begun the complete transformation of the country. Hundreds of Batista's cronies died in front of firing squads in 1959, and those who were not Castro's close allies were imprisoned or exiled.

The United States, of course, was not about to sit idly by and observe. Suspicious of Castro since his days in the Sierra Maestra, the Eisenhower administration began to plan an invasion of Cuba to overthrow Castro, and passed along the project to John F. Kennedy when he was inaugurated in January 1961. The ill-fated invasion at the Bay of Pigs (*Playa Girón*) in April 1961 was poorly planned, badly executed, and failed miserably. Mistakenly assuming this was another Guatemala, the CIA and other planners created one of the great foreign policy disasters of postwar US politics. The United States subsequently tried to isolate Castro through different forms of economic and diplomatic retaliation, and then blockaded the island in October 1962 when reconnaissance photographs showed the Russians building missile launchers on the island. After two weeks of brinkmanship between Kennedy and Soviet Premier Nikita Khrushchev, the Soviets agreed to remove the missile launchers (and Kennedy secretly promised to remove NATO missiles from Turkey). Castro was sorely disappointed that the Soviets had backed down, but the United States had also secretly promised to refrain from any further plans to invade the island. (For many years afterward, the CIA and Cuban exile groups, however, continued to harass Castro and failed in many attempts to assassinate him.)

The most radical phase of the revolution came in the first five years. Castro assumed complete control over the political and judicial systems, the military, and other security forces. The Cuban army was completely reconstructed with revolutionary leadership. Castro, in effect, instituted Lenin's dictatorship of the proletariat. (The Cuban Communist Party had opposed Castro's movement and revolt before 1959, and in the early 1960s he simply took control of the party and remade it to his own designs.) The regime eventually confiscated nearly all foreign businesses (including the assets of the United Fruit Company) and the assets of most of the Cuban upper and middle classes. Before 1959, nearly all Cuban exports (most importantly, sugar) had gone to the United States. The Eisenhower administration, responding to expropriations, suspended sugar imports, and Castro then arranged to sell Cuba's sugar to the Soviet bloc. By the end of 1960, the revolutionaries had seized $1 billion in assets. Eventually, the Cuban government assumed control of more than 85 percent of the economy. Rather than follow the path of fragmenting landed estates into small subsistence plots for peasants (as in Mexico, Guatemala, and Bolivia), Castro created collective farms with the intention of maintaining productive export agriculture, and modernizing and diversifying the nonsugar sectors. By the mid-1960s, Cuba had moved from a capitalist economy tightly integrated into the United States to a socialized economy integrated into the Soviet bloc.

Equally dramatic was the redistribution of wealth in Cuba by 1965. The revolutionaries essentially leveled wealth in Cuba by seizing the assets of the wealthy and foreign companies and using that revenue to provide schools, clinics, social services, running water, sewerage, and electricity for all Cubans. (The literacy rate rose from 76 to 96 percent.) This produced a massive shift in resources from the cities to the countryside, ending the enormous and long-standing inequities so characteristic of all Latin American societies. By the 1970s, Cuba had the most egalitarian distribution of wealth in the Americas, but paid for by the upper and middle classes (who largely fled into exile, especially in Florida and New Jersey), by confiscated foreign businesses, and then through massive subsidies from the Soviet Union (in the form of high prices for sugar exports and low prices for oil imports).

Castro was not content just to revolutionize Cuba. From the Bay of Pigs invasion (April 1961), the Missile Crisis (October 1962), and the ongoing efforts of exiles and the United States to bring him down, Castro became convinced that the revolution could only survive and thrive in the long term if it spread to the rest of Latin America and the Third World. In the 1960s, 1970s, and 1980s, Cuba became one of the most important supporters of leftist revolutions throughout the Third World, with moral support, training, equipment, and logistical assistance. In an era defined by revolutionary upheaval from the rice paddies of Vietnam, to the streets of Chicago and Paris, to the farms and fields in Mozambique, Cuba became an important and highly visible player on the world stage. In part, this was made possible with support from the Soviet Union, but it also reflected the deep and abiding commitment of Fidel Castro and the Cuban revolutionaries to the spread of Marxist revolution worldwide.

Che Guevara would become the most powerful and enduring symbol of this revolutionary zeal. Although he held many important posts in the new regime, Che fought with Fidel and some of his key *compañeros* over the ideological direction of the revolution. In the 1960s, many leftist revolutionaries around the world split over their preference for a Soviet-versus a Chinese-style revolution. Che favored the ideological fervor of the Chinese and was soon disillusioned with what he saw as the bureaucratic and conservative tendencies of the Soviet model. (He argued for using "moral" incentives to create the "new socialist man," rather than following the Soviet model of using material incentives.) In a major international conference in Havana in 1967, Che's speech called for the creation of "two, three, many Vietnams." In the mid-1960s, Che led a dedicated group of Cubans in an effort to promote and assist guerrilla revolutionaries in the Congo and then Bolivia. Much as the CIA foolishly assumed that Cuba in 1961 would be like Guatemala in 1954, Che mistakenly believed that he could translate the success of the urban, middle-class Cuban revolutionaries to Africa and the heavily indigenous Bolivia. He paid for the error with his life. Tracked down by a special unit of the Bolivian army (trained and assisted by the CIA), Che was captured and executed in the Bolivian highlands in October 1967. He was thirty-nine. In succeeding decades, the image of Che—with flowing locks, scraggly beard and mustache, and beret (taken from a Alberto Korda photograph)—has become one of the most widely reproduced images in the world.

Although Castro would continue to support revolutionary movements in the 1970s (especially in Ethiopia, Mozambique, and Angola), he concentrated on consolidating the revolution at home through the construction of a repressive, authoritarian political system (very similar to the Soviet Union), and many failed attempts at industrialization and economic diversification. Cuba became increasingly dependent on Soviet aid to subsidize the remarkable array of social programs and services made available to all Cubans. By the late 1970s, the rise of right-wing military regimes across the region and the steady antagonism of the United States had isolated Cuba and made it even more dependent on the Soviet Union. This became even more severe during the debt crisis of the 1980s.

With the fall of the Berlin Wall and the collapse of the Soviet Union in the late 1980s and early 1990s, Fidel Castro had to become ever more resourceful to keep himself in power. Castro has been in power longer than anyone in the history of Latin America (with the exception of Pedro II of Brazil, 1840–89) and the Cuban regime is largely built around the charisma of one man. When serious illness forced Fidel to step aside and "temporarily" hand over power to Raúl in late 2006, speculation raged over the fate of the regime, and whether it would survive what appeared to be the imminent death of Fidel. At the same time, the great social achievements of the 1960s have faded with the impoverishment of the country. Cuba remains largely a sugar exporter, with little industrialization and economic diversity, and no petroleum. Cuba today still ranks among the top five countries in Latin America when one looks at social indicators—literacy, life expectancy, infant mortality. The difference between Cuba in the 1950s and at the beginning of the twenty-first century is the great equalization of wealth and services carried out in the early years of the revolution in the 1960s. Unfortunately, the great antagonism of the United States and the dependence on the Soviet Union gradually limited the options of this small island nation of ten million. In the end, it did become impossible to have a "socialist revolution in one country."

Ironically, the Cuban Revolution also helped propel forward another fundamental change—this one in the United States. Although Cubans had long moved back and forth between the United States and Cuba, in the early 1960s some 250,000 Cubans fled into exile, mainly to south Florida and the New York-New Jersey areas. These exiles were largely middle- and upper-class Cubans who were well educated. They transformed the politics of both regions and created a very powerful political lobby in Washington that has played a key role in US politics over the last fifty years (as swing votes in three important states). In the early 1980s, facing internal political and economic challenges, Castro allowed another 125,000 Cubans to flee the island, and most again went to south Florida. The so-called *Marielitos* (named after the key port of departure in Cuba) were largely darker-skinned, poorer, and less educated than the 1960s wave. Their arrival created serious rifts within the Cuban community in the United States. The hundreds of thousands of Cuban exiles have also played a prominent role in the growing "Latinamericanization" of US culture and society. The bilingual and bicultural Cubans have been incredibly successful in academia, government, and the private sector. One of the great unintended consequences of the Cuban Revolution has been the diversification and enrichment of US society and culture as the country has become "Hispanicized."

NICARAGUA: NO MORE CUBAS

In spite of the spectacular example of the Cuban Revolution in 1959, it would be twenty years before another revolutionary movement in Latin America was able to replicate the successful seizure of power that Fidel Castro and his rebel army had achieved. In part, this was the result of bitter divisions within revolutionary leftist movements over strategy and tactics, and the strength of the regimes in power, especially military dictatorships. More important, the United States used every possible means to prevent the emergence of any more Cubas in the Americas. The United States would use both the carrot and the stick to block the rise of leftist revolution. Throughout the 1960s, US military assistance (training and equipment) to nearly all the military forces in the region would rise dramatically, to promote "counterinsurgency" training. The United States and its military allies across Latin America would wield a very "big stick," crushing leftist movements from the Dominican Republic to Brazil (including Che Guevara in Bolivia). In 1961, in direct response to the Cuban challenge, President Kennedy created the Alliance for Progress (a sort of mini-Marshall Plan for the hemisphere) to provide $20 billion in aid and expertise to Latin American countries over a decade. The logic was simple, if misguided. Poverty and oppression, so the logic went, create the conditions for leftist revolution. The Alliance would help promote economic development, end poverty, force repressive governments to become more democratic, and thereby create a capitalist, democratic, pro-United States Latin America. Kennedy admonished the right-wing regimes that resisted US pressure to compel them to change their ways, declaring, "those who make peaceful revolution impossible, make violent revolution inevitable."

Strangely enough, the success of the Alliance for Progress and other forms of capitalist development may have made revolution "inevitable" in Central America precisely because United States-supported dictators made peaceful revolution impossible. Much to the surprise of both the Right and the Left, one of the least developed, poorest, and most rural regions of Latin America became the locus of the next wave of violent, leftist revolution, some twenty years after the seemingly isolated example of Cuba. The overthrow of the dictatorship of Anastasio Somoza Debayle in 1979 and the emergence of the Sandinista Revolution, the rise of a powerful leftist revolutionary movement and civil war in El Salvador in 1980–81, and the deadly escalation of civil war and leftist insurgency in Guatemala in the early 1980s combined to produce a wave of leftist revolutionary upheaval after nearly a decade of right-wing repression and military dictatorships had seemingly crushed leftist revolution across the continent. The resurgence of revolution coincided with the rise of Ronald Reagan in the United States, Margaret Thatcher in England, and neoliberal economics worldwide. Within a decade, the prospect of armed revolution had faded as neoliberal economics triumphed and as nearly all of Latin America turned to some form of open, electoral politics. Central America in the 1980s may have experienced the last wave of violent, Marxist revolutionary movements in Latin America.

In the early 1970s, Nicaragua appeared to be an unlikely place for the rise of revolution. Although it is the largest country in Central America, Nicaragua is slightly smaller than the state of Arkansas and in 1970 had fewer than three million inhabitants (about the current population of Arkansas). A backwater of the Spanish Empire in the colonial period, its population (like that of neighboring Costa Rica) was around a quarter of a million in the early nineteenth century, largely a mix of Indians, mestizos, and a few whites, with a small Afro-Caribbean population on the isolated Atlantic coast. Throughout the nineteenth and early twentieth centuries, the elite families of Nicaragua divided between Liberals and Conservatives in a series of bloody civil wars and conflicts that included foreign interventions— William Walker in the 1850s, the US Marines after 1900. With the withdrawal of US troops in the 1930s, Anastasio Somoza García (1896–1956) seized control of the United States-trained National Guard and began a family dictatorship that would last for more than four decades.

Throughout the late 1920s and early 1930s, the US Marines had futilely attempted to track down and defeat Augusto César Sandino (1895–1934) and his guerrilla band. Although originally an ally of the Liberals, Sandino had refused to accept the Liberal-Conservative arrangement (1927) that was supposed to bring political peace to Nicaragua, but with US troops as the guarantor of the peace. From a poor, working-class background, Sandino had wandered through the region, working in Mexican oil fields and a Nicaraguan gold mine. He had forged an eclectic personal philosophy influenced by Marxism, anarchism, spiritualism, indigenism, and anti-imperialism (he once called the United States the "enemy of our race"). For Sandino, the presence of US troops in Nicaragua was unacceptable, and he refused to accept any political arrangement that did not include the departure of the US forces. For years, he harassed US troops in a guerrilla war in the countryside. Juan Bautista Sacasa was elected president in 1932, and the Marines departed in early 1933. Before leaving, the United States helped create, train, and equip a National Guard that would, in theory, be nonpartisan and guarantee political peace and stability. Sandino agreed to lay down his arms. With the help of US diplomats, Anastasio Somoza García became the head of the National Guard. Somoza arranged to meet with Sandino, and then had him kidnapped and assassinated as he was returning home from the meeting in February 1934.

For nearly half a century, Somoza and his sons built a family dynasty and fiefdom in Nicaragua through their control of the National Guard, manipulation of the political system, and domination of every important sector of the national economy. When pressured by the United States to hold elections, the Somozas would periodically comply, electing themselves or puppets to run the country. A poet assassinated the elder Anastasio in 1956. His sons, Luis and Anastasio ("Tacho") Somoza Debayle would share power until Luis's death from a heart attack in 1967. A supremely egotistical megalomaniac, Tacho dominated Nicaragua until 1979, while maintaining extremely close relations with the United States. His philosophy, as he once put it, was "ballots for my friends, bullets for my enemies." Educated in US schools and at West Point, he cultivated very close ties in the US Congress and lobbied presidents and congressmen assiduously. He prided himself on how pro-United States he was, once saying, "Who else votes with the US in the United Nations 1000 percent of the time?" In 1961, the CIA used Nicaragua as the training and staging grounds for the Bay of Pigs invasion. In 1965, Somoza sent National Guard troops to assist in the United States invasion of the Dominican Republic. National Guard officers were trained in the United States and the Panama Canal Zone, and Nicaragua had the highest per capita military expenditures of any country in Latin America in the 1960s and 1970s. The Guard (around 7,000 men) served internal police and security functions, ran Nicaraguan customs operations, and controlled the post office and telecommunications systems.

By the 1970s, Nicaragua was a very poor country controlled by a small clique around Anastasio Somoza Debayle. Life expectancy in this population of 2.5 million was barely 50, the literacy rate was scarcely 50 percent (and half that in rural areas), and less than half the population had indoor plumbing. These figures did not improve through the sixties and early seventies, as the Alliance for Progress helped the Nicaraguan gross domestic product grow by 250 percent. The economic prosperity was limited to the 15–20 percent of the population in the middle and upper classes—in particular, those closely connected to Somoza. He and his family dominated the construction and meat-packing industries, tobacco and rice farming, fishing, real estate, the media, automotive sales, and the local airline. Somoza's greed was unbounded, and contributed to his undoing. After a massive earthquake leveled Managua in December 1972, Somoza and his cronies took control of more than half a billion dollars in relief funds and used it to enrich themselves. As he expanded his control over ever-greater sectors of the economy in the aftermath of the earthquake, Somoza pushed aside many of the middle-class businessmen who had thrived over the previous decade. (As the old center of Managua remained in ruins, Somoza profited by developing the suburbs and his control of the construction and cement industries as well as real estate.) He appointed himself head of a Junta for Reconstruction, and then was "elected" president for a seven-year term in 1974. To nearly everyone, he seemed to have a permanent iron grip on the fate of the nation.

Somoza's behavior in the aftermath of the earthquake, however, was the beginning of the unraveling of the family dynasty. Three converging forces had begun to take shape by 1974 that would produce a revolutionary upheaval and general insurrection in 1977–79. The first was the growing disaffection of the middle-class business community, which had prospered in the 1960s and was increasingly anxious to have a voice in politics. Much like their counterparts in the Mexican *Porfiriato*, they were happy with the economic growth they saw, but they wanted more gradual political and economic reforms to produce a more prosperous and democratic nation that would eventually ease the drastic social inequalities in Nicaragua. The second force was the emergence of a powerful grassroots movement known as liberation theology, a movement that motivated many poor Nicaraguans to seek better lives through spiritual and social change. Finally, a small group of dedicated young men and women (largely from urban, middle-class families) created and nurtured a Marxist guerrilla movement that called for the overthrow of Somoza and the creation of a new Nicaragua built on socialist economics and nationalism (i.e., less United States economic dominance). The leaders of the movement took the martyred Augusto César Sandino as their inspiration and called their movement the *Frente Sandinista de Liberación Nacional* (Sandinista National Liberation Front or FSLN).

Although it was formed in 1961, the FSLN was unable to mobilize more than a few dozen trained fighters until the mid-1970s. Throughout the 1960s, each time they tried to mount any sort of offensive against the government, they were badly beaten and forced to retrench. In December 1974, they managed to take a large number of diplomats and prominent Nicaraguans hostage at a holiday party. The publicity from this incident, a $5 million ransom, and the release of some of their colleagues from prison, instantly made the FSLN a viable, armed adversary of Somoza. By 1975, the FSLN probably had some 150 trained guerrillas in the cities and the countryside of Nicaragua. Although a number of the founders and leaders were trained in Cuba and received assistance from the Soviet Union, the FSLN split into three distinct ideological wings in the mid-1970s, each with its own tactical approach. Fidel Castro personally persuaded the three groups to unite in a common struggle against Somoza, and to worry about their ideological differences after they took power. By 1977, the FSLN was growing, and Somoza's son (Anastasio Somoza Portocarrero, or Tachito) was leading a brutal counterinsurgency campaign that drove more and more young men and women into the ranks of the Sandinistas.

As the armed struggle slowly emerged in the 1960s and 1970s, another grassroots movement, one that was much broader and more powerful, began to transform Nicaraguan society. The movement, known as "liberation theology," began to emerge slowly in the 1950s across Latin

America, and then experienced explosive growth in the 1960s in the aftermath of Vatican II (1961–63) and the Latin American bishops' conference at Medellín, Colombia in 1968. Both of these meetings of Catholic bishops, archbishops, and cardinals solidified the fundamental features of the movement: an emphasis on working with the poor (a "preferential option for the poor"), and the combination of a message of worldly redemption with the traditional message of spiritual salvation. Many in the Latin American Catholic Church in the fifties and sixties argued that the Church was not constituted by the institution and the hierarchy, but rather the community of faithful. In Latin America (and especially Nicaragua), that clearly meant the impoverished masses. The long spiritual conquest had made Latin America the largest concentration of Catholics on earth, numbering several hundred million by the 1960s (85 percent of all Latin Americans).

Breaking with the traditional message of the Latin American Catholic Church, activist priests and nuns began to emphasize Jesus, the revolutionary figure of the Sermon on the Mount, the Christ of the poor, the oppressed, and the downtrodden. ("The Spirit of the Lord *is* upon me, because he hath anointed me to preach the gospel to the poor; he hath sent me to heal the brokenhearted, to preach deliverance to the captives, and recovering of sight to the blind, to set at liberty them that are bruised . . ." Luke 5:18) Rather than telling the poor masses to accept their suffering and the status quo, and to await their reward in heaven, the activists worked to help the masses change their lives in this world. They argued that salvation or liberation was not simply spiritual, but also temporal. In a message eerily reminiscent of Calvin and the Protestant Reformation, these priests argued that to be a good Christian one had to behave like a good Christian. Belief required action. The effort to carry out Jesus's message that "the meek shall inherit the earth" would be radical in any society. In the context of Latin America, with its enormous impoverished masses, the message was revolutionary.

Activist priests and nuns organized what became known as Christian Base Communities (or CEBs, the acronym for *comunidades eclesiales de base* in Spanish) to bring the faithful together to study and work together in a Christian environment. This work had both spiritual and practical aims. Priests have always been in short supply in Latin America, and one thrust of the pastoral work with these communities was to delegate some of the traditional responsibilities of the clergy to laypersons. From a practical standpoint, responsibilities had to be delegated to the laity if the Church was going to restore and maintain an active presence among the masses. The Church had a need to empower the laity in a ritual sense, or risk losing them.

Inevitably, this work also carried a political message: the poor do not have to accept powerlessness. Activist priests, nuns, and lay workers sought to empower the masses through the creation of CEBs. Committed Christians in the CEBs worked to understand biblical lessons, and to translate those lessons into the transformation of their daily lives. These communities focused on giving the poor access to land and housing, and to help them develop basic services—water, health care, education. Along with Brazil, Central America was one of the most important foci of the development and expansion of CEBs. Although not a promoter of liberation theology, the Archbishop of Nicaragua (after 1968), Miguel Obando y Bravo, was a vocal critic of Somoza and a supporter of social change in the country. This religious transformation in Nicaragua (and other countries) helped politicize and mobilize many Nicaraguans of all social classes.

As Somoza and his cronies tightened their grip on the economy in the years after the 1972 earthquake, as political challenges to the regime emerged, and as repression intensified, Nicaragua became increasingly polarized. After 1977, the Jimmy Carter administration became more critical of Somoza, but refused to intervene to force him from power. By the beginning of 1978, middle-class, pro-United States capitalists would find they had their options increasingly narrowed to just two choices: continue to support the dictatorship or ally with the armed struggle to take a chance on change. One dramatic event shifted the balance of the struggle in January 1978—the assassination of Pedro Joaquín Chamorro. From one of the oldest and most distinguished families in Nicaragua, and the long-time editor of the major Nicaraguan newspaper, *La Prensa*, Chamorro was also long a bitter opponent of Somoza. Everyone in Nicaragua immediately assumed the Somoza family was behind the killing (and all indications pointed toward Tachito). The message for the reformers was clear—Somoza would do anything to retain power and the only way to remove him was through force.

From early 1978 to mid-1979, the insurrection grew more widespread and intense as young people flocked to the Sandinistas in droves and as the National Guard became more and more brutal and repressive. In August 1978, the Sandinistas seized the National Palace while congress was in session. The televised publicity, the multimillion dollar ransom, and release of political prisoners and their departure from the Managua airport were a powerful public relations blow to Somoza. By early 1979, Somoza's National Guard was fighting its way through the streets and neighborhoods of the major cities of the country as thousands died and whole urban neighborhoods were destroyed. Fidel Castro was supplying the guerrillas with arms, with the help of the governments of Panama and Costa Rica. The Carter administration failed in its efforts to mediate the conflict, and virtually the entire country was calling for Somoza's departure, including major business leaders, the Catholic Church, and most professional organizations. On July 19, 1979, Somoza fled into exile (first in Miami, then in Paraguay) and the Sandinista rebels triumphantly marched into Managua in a scene reminiscent of Cuba in January 1959. (Somoza would die in Paraguay in 1980, assassinated by leftist Argentine guerrillas.)

Nicaragua lay in ruins, decimated by two years of civil war and insurrection. Some 40,000–50,000 people had died in the conflict, the country was in default on nearly $2 billion in debt (after Somoza looted the treasury), and 10 percent of the population was displaced, half of those across the borders in Costa Rica, Honduras, and El Salvador. The Junta for National Reconstruction that took shape in the final moments of the war included a broad-based group of figures from the opposition who called for a new Nicaragua with a more pluralist politics, social change, and an end to corruption. The Sandinistas had led the armed revolt, and quickly asserted their control over the new political regime. Creating what was like a more moderate version of Cuba in 1959–61, the Sandinistas began their effort to transform Nicaragua. Castro, after his bitter struggles and experiences with the United States, counseled the FSLN leadership to move more slowly than he had in Cuba. The United States, first under Jimmy Carter and then under Ronald Reagan, was not going to allow the creation of another Cuba in the Americas and was not about to accept even a moderate version of Castro's Cuba.

As the Sandinistas consolidated their control over the new Nicaraguan regime, more moderate figures (such as Pedro Joaquín Chamorro's widow, Violeta) left the government in protest. Some of those who had fought and led the insurrection also split from the FSLN leadership, most notably, Edén Pastora, one of the key Sandinista commanders. The country began to split into opposing camps and to polarize. The process was hastened and heightened as the Reagan administration (1981–89) fomented internal troubles (political and economic), and as the CIA began to mount a counterrevolution (using the so-called contras), based across the northern border in neighboring Honduras. In something of a small-scale replay of Cuba and the United States after 1959, the United States and Nicaragua became locked in a bitter struggle after 1979. As the United States stepped up the (not-so-covert) war against Nicaragua, the country became more deeply polarized and the FSLN turned increasingly to Cuba and the Soviet Union for assistance.

As it was for John F. Kennedy, Latin America became the first foreign policy challenge for Ronald Reagan when he took office in January 1981. In the aftermath of the fall of Somoza in 1979, civil war had erupted in neighboring El Salvador. Poor, rural, and even more underdeveloped than Nicaragua, El Salvador had been dominated by a succession of dictatorships, military regimes, and short-lived civilian governments since the 1930s. The so-called "Fourteen Families" who dominated the national economy (largely coffee and cotton production) were less visible and not quite the lightning rod that Somoza had provided the opposition in Nicaragua. A group of reformist military officers took power in 1980, and unleashed civil war. A series of leftist revolutionary groups rose up in a protracted guerrilla war. The Sandinistas, seizing on the sudden opportunity, began to supply the insurgents with arms. Ronald Reagan's first important foreign policy decision was to provide military aid and assistance to El Salvador, a move that probably prevented the guerrillas from seizing power in early 1981.

Central America suffered deeply in the 1980s as guerrillas supplied and financed by the United States fought a drawn-out "low-intensity" conflict to bring down the leftist Sandinista regime, and as leftist revolutionaries supported by Nicaragua and Cuba tried to bring down a rightist regime in El Salvador, financed and supported by the United States. The Reagan administration spent billions of dollars in Central America in the 1980s building military bases in Honduras as the staging ground for the conflicts in El Salvador and Nicaragua. Meanwhile, the long civil war in Guatemala intensified as the United States-backed regime engaged in a "scorched earth" campaign against leftist guerrillas. For the first time ever, the struggle in Guatemala began to engage the Maya peoples of the countryside. The massive repression destroyed many of their communities, killing thousands, and drove many into the ranks of the armed rebellion.

This region-wide conflict became one of the showcases for Ronald Reagan's declaration that he would draw the line of the Communist advance in the world, and then roll it back (the Reagan Doctrine). In what later became a major political scandal in the United States, the Reagan administration secretly financed its "covert" contra operation by selling arms to the fundamentalist Islamic regime of the Ayatollah Khomeini in Iran. For many observers of Central America, the massive US response to the Sandinistas was an overreaction. Unlike the revolutionaries in Cuba, the Sandinistas never moved to socialize the entire Nicaraguan economy, just key sectors. Probably less than half the economy came under state control, the land reform efforts were very moderate, and the large landed estates (except for those belonging to the Somoza family) were largely left intact. The FSLN did nationalize the banking system, water and electrical services, and the insurance business. These were fairly tame moves (not unlike those undertaken in Scandinavia or Western Europe) compared to those effected in Cuba in the early 1960s.

More important, the Sandinistas never implemented a "dictatorship of the proletariat." Despite some rather clumsy efforts to dominate politics, the FSLN held regular, open, and competitive elections, including ones in 1984 that the Reagan administration opposed, pressuring anti-Sandinista political parties to boycott the vote. The ironies, once again, were powerful. In El Salvador, the United States spent much of the 1980s trying to support and promote open elections in the midst of a leftist insurrection and civil war. It spent hundreds of millions of dollars to promote the Christian Democrat Party and its leader, José Napoleón Duarte—to elect him and keep his party in power as Marxist revolutionary guerrillas tried to bring down the regime. The United States helped formulate and promote land reform, and Duarte nationalized the banking system. As one long-time observer of Central America noted at the time, what the United States needed in El Salvador was a Jacobo Arbenz to provide a reformist alternative to Marxist revolutionaries! In Nicaragua, the Reagan administration (in the mirror image of the Salvadoran revolutionaries) employed the contras to wreak havoc and try to bring down the Sandinistas, even after elections had confirmed their leadership.

Throughout the 1980s, tens of thousands died in these civil conflicts in Guatemala, El Salvador, and Nicaragua, with the violence spilling over into Honduras and even Costa Rica. The Central Americans, especially through the diplomatic efforts of Costa Rican President Oscar Arias spent years negotiating among themselves and in the late 1980s and early 1990s finally managed to broker peace accords that gradually ended the wars. (The Reagan administration mocked Arias and did everything in its power to block the negotiations.) Nicaragua, El Salvador, Honduras, and Guatemala reached the end of the century with elected governments and regular elections in place in all four countries. The end of the Cold War and the collapse of the Soviet Union helped resolve the conflicts, defusing the intensity of the ideological struggles, and returning everyone's attention to the root causes of the conflicts—the enormous poverty and inequities in the region.

In 1990, the Sandinistas lost the national elections and handed over power to their opponents (Violeta Chamorro was elected president). Since then, most of the social and economic reforms of the Sandinistas have been dismantled, and the electoral process in Nicaragua has been spirited, often chaotic, and hotly contested. Unfortunately, all of Central America has been plagued over the past twenty years by corruption and political scandals. Today, Nicaragua has not recovered from the immense damage produced by the war against Somoza and the long conflict with the contras. After Haiti, Nicaragua is the poorest country in the Americas. Unlike Cuba's revolutionaries, the Sandinistas were unable to level wealth, equalize access to social services, or build strong health care and educational systems. Unlike Cuba, Nicaragua never received massive aid and assistance from the Soviet bloc. Much like Guatemala's revolution in the early 1950s, the Nicaragua Revolution ran into the potent opposition of the United States, and the end result was a social and economic transformation halted, not by a CIA coup, but by a CIA-supported guerrilla war that sapped Nicaragua of its meager resources and left death, destruction, and ruins in its wake.

UTOPIA DISARMED

For most of the twentieth century—from Mexico in the 1910s to Central America in the 1980s—the path of revolution provided a viable, but violent, option to those who sought social and economic change in Latin America. In many countries, the harsh and repressive regimes that resisted any and all significant reforms seemed to leave no option but armed struggle for the proponents of social justice, human rights, and economic opportunity for all. The staggering inequalities, and centuries of repression, in countries like Mexico, Guatemala, Bolivia, Cuba, and Nicaragua polarized politics and left the proponents of change with few options: accept the glacial pace of change or take up arms. When the revolutionaries in all five countries seized power, they had noble ideals, principally to improve the lives of the impoverished masses of peasants in overwhelmingly agrarian countries. To promote real change, they had to take on the most deeply rooted and important structure in their societies, the control of land and labor by a small elite. In the twentieth century, as the United States and the Soviet Union divided the world into opposing camps, most revolutionaries blamed the long development of capitalism for the construction and maintenance of these structures of inequality. Socialism and Marxism, logically, provided the humane alternative to the inequities of capitalism.

In all five cases, the revolutions failed to produce the economic transformation necessary to provide the material development that would make possible a higher standard of living for the majority. In Mexico, the land reform withered, and the country industrialized, but under a system that was more capitalist than socialist. In Guatemala, Bolivia, and Nicaragua, the transformations failed to take place either because of direct US opposition or co-optation. Although Cuba carried out the most sweeping and complete transformation of its economy and society, the benefits of socialization were possible (in this small, agro-exporting economy) only with massive foreign subsidies. In effect, full-blown socialism was never implemented, except in Cuba, a country that did not have the economic base to generate the self-sustaining growth needed to make socialism a viable social and economic model. In Mexico and Cuba, the two countries where the revolutionaries were able to attempt a complete restructuring of their societies (despite US opposition), the long-term results proved disappointing. The revolutions did not produce new paths to economic development.

With the exception of Nicaragua, the revolutions also did not produce more open and participatory politics. The PRI in Mexico, in effect, established a one-party regime. US intervention in Guatemala halted the political opening, and helped trigger decades of military repression, civil war, and tens of thousands of violent deaths. In Bolivia, the revolution did initiate decades of gradual political mobilization and participation, interrupted frequently by United States-supported repression and dictatorship. In Cuba, Fidel Castro created a Soviet-style regime that has failed to provide Cubans with truly open and democratic politics. Only in Nicaragua did the revolution initiate a true political opening, with elections, representative politics, and mass mobilization. Unfortunately, 20 years of elections and representative politics have not helped Nicaraguans resolve the long-standing and bitter divisions in their society.

The path of revolution, at best, helped nudge forward the modernization of Mexico and Cuba, and at worst helped create authoritarian political regimes. In Mexico, Guatemala, Bolivia, and Nicaragua the dream of social equity and justice withered through the increasing conservatism of the regimes, or as a result of US opposition to the leftist governments. The aspirations for development, economic equity, and social justice faded as leaders betrayed the dreams of their peoples or as conservative forces crushed and blocked fundamental and enduring change. With the end of military dictatorships, and the rise across the region of increasingly democratic and representative politics in the 1990s, the appeal and need for armed revolution appears to have passed from the scene. Should these structural changes persist and endure, the struggle for economic development, social justice, and democracy will be unfolding with ballots and not bullets. The path to progress will be through reform, and not revolution.

21

The Path of Reform

Despite major setbacks and obstacles, the path of reform in twentieth-century Latin America has produced more sustained and enduring changes than the path of revolution. All the nations of Latin America have experienced reform movements in some form or fashion. The most successful have been in countries where the reforms have been gradual, cumulative, and substantive—over many decades. While revolutionaries—having given up on changing the system from within—challenge governments and regimes through violence and armed struggle, reformists choose to work within the existing system while continuing to cling to the stubborn belief that true change can be initiated and sustained from within—short of armed struggle and widespread destruction. While the path of reform may be less dramatically and explosively violent than revolution, successful reformist movements are also accompanied by periodic outbreaks of violence. Indeed, brief episodes of violence (strikes, failed revolts, massacres, demonstrations, government repression) often provide the needed push to propel reforms to the next stage of progress. The civil rights movement in the United States is an outstanding example of this pattern. Lynchings, assassinations, and violent street confrontations played key roles in pushing legislation forward in the 1950s and 1960s, legislation that profoundly changed U.S. society. Reform movements also experience setbacks and defeats, and it often takes many, many efforts to consolidate and institutionalize true change. In some ways, a long-term, successful reform movement is a revolution in very slow motion.

In the nineteenth and twentieth centuries, Uruguay, Argentina, Chile, and Costa Rica managed to build long-term reformist movements that generally avoided bloodshed, civil war, and coups d'état, allowing them to develop strong, representative, electoral systems that gradually extended the universal, secret vote to most adults by the mid-twentieth century. Even these countries, however, periodically experienced breakdowns. A brief, but very violent, civil war convulsed Costa Rica in 1948. Extremely violent and repressive military dictatorships brought a (temporary) halt to electoral politics in Chile, Argentina, and Uruguay in the 1960s and 1970s. The gradual, cumulative, and substantive reforms in these societies have endured, however, even surviving the brutal military regimes that (for a time) nearly erased the gains of decades.

While these four countries stand out as the most successful examples of long-term reform movements, many other nations in Latin America have been shaped by reformism. The pattern, however, has been less gradual and cumulative, and shorter in duration. These changes, especially in recent decades, may ultimately prove to be as enduring as those in Uruguay, Argentina, Chile, and Costa Rica. The key point is that Mexico, Guatemala, Bolivia, Cuba, and Nicaragua are the most clear-cut examples of revolution, while Uruguay, Argentina, Chile, and Costa Rica offer the definitive patterns of reform. The rest of Latin America falls somewhere in between these cases, mostly as examples of nations that do not follow steady paths toward either revolution or reform. For many decades, Guatemala, El Salvador, Honduras, Nicaragua, the Dominican Republic, Haiti, Ecuador and Peru appeared to be resistant to true reform. In most of these cases, reforms were minimal and these nations were dominated for most of the last two centuries by repressive authoritarian regimes. The pattern of the past generation, in nearly all Latin America, has been toward gradual, substantive reforms. Ultimately, the structural changes in the Americas have helped foster a new era in which all the countries of Latin America now appear to have greater possibilities for true reform than at any time in the past. Yet, we should be cautious, given the reformist moments in the past, moments that were followed by setbacks, authoritarian governments, and repression. The political experiences of the countries of Latin America in the twenty-first century will be increasingly diverse, but those with the longest and strongest reformist traditions should be best positioned to build the more enduring and successful paths toward democracy and representative politics.

URUGUAY: THE WESTERN EUROPEAN MODEL

Uruguay may be the least studied and least noticed country in Latin America. Along with Argentina, Uruguay is one of the two most ethnically European nations in Latin America (with about 95 percent of the population of European descent and only about 5 percent nonwhite). About the size of Oklahoma, tiny Uruguay is squeezed uncomfortably between the two largest countries in Latin America—Brazil and Argentina. For most of the colonial period, the so-called Cisplatine (bordering the La Plata River) region was sparsely populated and developed a ranching and gaucho culture very similar to that found on the pampas of Argentina (to the west) and southern Brazil (to the east). Mainly rolling prairie with large stocks of cattle and sheep, the region was long a contested area on the borders of the Spanish and Portuguese empires (with fewer than 100,000 inhabitants in the 1820s). In 1828, Uruguay definitively achieved its independence, although it would continue to suffer from the political meddling of its larger and more powerful neighbors. With just 3.5 million citizens today, more than half living in metropolitan Montevideo, Uruguay is today one of the smallest and least visible countries of Latin America.

In many ways, Uruguay in the nineteenth century followed the general Latin American pattern. Cattle and sheep ranching became the core of an agro-export economy. At first, the country exported hides, wool, and salted beef. With the advent of refrigerated ships in the late nineteenth century, beef and mutton became the principal exports and sources of revenue for the country. Liberals and Conservatives formed the two major, contending political parties, the latter known as the *Blancos* (Whites) and the former as the *Colorados* (Reds). As in the rest of Latin America, the Liberals/*Colorados* emerged as the ruling party in the 1870s and would dominate Uruguayan politics in the first half of the twentieth century. The Liberals promoted and expanded the export economy (essentially an enormous meat-packing operation) and brought in waves of European immigrants who completely transformed the ethnic composition of the country. These immigrants generally arrived earlier than the wave of immigrants in Argentina, and had very high birthrates. At the beginning of the twentieth century, the one million inhabitants of Uruguay were more ethnically and culturally European than any national community in Latin America.

The key to successful reform movements, anywhere in the world, is to create a political arena that allows for increasing participation, and avoids the extreme polarization that has characterized so much of Latin American history in the nineteenth and twentieth centuries. People and political parties with a stake in the system, and a belief that they can work and achieve results within it, do not take up arms and rebel. In Uruguay, as in the other nations we will examine in this chapter, the primary key to successful, long-term reform is the creation and cultivation of a political system that provides for participation and access to power for major interest groups. In Uruguay, despite the dominance of the *Colorados*, the *Blancos* were always key participants in the process of governance and decision-making. Unlike, say, in Nicaragua, the political process was not a winner-take-all, zero-sum game. Another key to success was enlightened and visionary leadership. In Uruguay, the key figure was José Batlle y Ordóñez (1856–1929).

Batlle came from the upper class, had an excellent education, and had traveled abroad. A *Colorado*, his father also served as president (1868–72). Although he served just two terms (1903–7 and 1911–15), Batlle was the dominant presence in national politics during the first quarter of the twentieth century. He built on an already long tradition of power-sharing. (The 1830 Constitution remained in force until 1919.) With the ascendancy of the *Colorados* in the last quarter of the nineteenth century, the *Blancos* had settled for control of a minority of the departments (states) in the interior. Batlle brokered an arrangement in the early twentieth century that kept the powerful, conservative ranching interests satisfied by giving them a fixed proportional representation in government offices. The ranchers also dominated the agro-export economy. In effect, the *Colorados* and *Blancos* struck a power-sharing deal: the *Blancos* would control the economy and a major share of political power while conceding political dominance to the *Colorados*. (This consensus was not easily forged. Batlle faced a serious civil revolt in 1904 led by powerful landowners.) The *Colorados* then constructed a modern social welfare state that defused class conflict and purchased social peace. It was a masterpiece of political balancing. It was also politically complicated and unwieldy. To avoid the Latin American pattern of the strong, centralized executive and caudillos, the Uruguayans split presidential powers (along a Swiss model). The president handled foreign affairs, external and internal defense. A National Council (of nine men) handled the rest of the affairs of the executive branch. The role of religion in society was severely weakened and divorce legalized.

As the Uruguayans built a durable social peace, they also extended the vote to all adult males (and then females, who gained the vote in 1932). By the 1920s, Uruguayans had put into place a Western European-style social welfare state. The government controlled the public utilities, mortgage banks, insurance companies, and even some of the meat-packing companies. Hefty tariffs protected the small, local industrial base. As Montevideo gradually grew to include more than half the population, workers organized, achieved the eight-hour day, minimum wage, accident insurance, pensions, and social security. While a massive revolution convulsed Mexico, and frequent coups or dictatorships plagued many Latin American nations in the early twentieth century, Uruguayans built a vibrant export economy, a social welfare state, and a highly educated and sophisticated citizenry. The Uruguayan elite liked to envision the country as the "Switzerland of South America."

The Achilles heel of the Uruguayan economy, as has been so common in Latin America, was an agro-export sector dependent on foreign demand.

Batlle died in 1929, just as the Great Depression erupted across the Western world. Demand for beef, mutton, wool, and hides dropped by 80 percent in just a few years. Political upheaval was the result, and a new constitution in 1934 reestablished a more centralized presidential system. Rising demand during World War II and the Korean War seemed to rescue the Uruguayan economy, while the United States replaced the Europeans as the major purchaser of the nation's exports. As with many Latin American countries, the leadership of Uruguay in the 1930s and succeeding decades moved toward economic protectionism in an effort to foster local industry. The country did experience industrial growth, but largely to provide consumer goods for a very small internal market, and Uruguayan industry was not competitive in the international marketplace. In the late 1940s and mid-1950s, Luis Batlle Berres (the nephew of José Batlle) served two presidential terms before the bottom once again fell out of the agro-export economy.

As the terms of trade (the growing difference between the cost of imported manufactured goods and the revenues from the export of agricultural and ranching products) continually deteriorated in the late 1950s and the 1960s, the Uruguayan economy could no longer support a modern European social welfare state. The gross domestic product in 1967 was smaller than it had been a decade earlier. By 1968, rampant inflation (approaching 200 percent) had driven real wages down to levels below those of 1950. The Uruguayan agro-export economy was unraveling, and 90 percent of the national wealth was produced on 10 percent of the land. Economic decline and rising dissatisfaction coincided with the Cold War revolutionary upheavals of the 1960s. The powerful and conservative *Blanco* ranching interests reasserted themselves in the 1960s, while the *Colorados* were increasingly discredited after decades of leadership. An armed guerrilla movement emerged as a potent challenge to both *Blancos* and *Colorados*.

Taking as their icon the eighteenth-century Inca rebel, Túpac Amaru II, these urban revolutionaries called themselves *Tupamaros*. Overwhelmingly, these urban guerrillas were university-educated, middle-class, young people inspired by Marx, Lenin, Che Guevara, and the Cuban Revolution. Vividly depicted in Costa Gavras's 1973 film, *State of Siege*, the *Tupamaros* robbed banks to finance their operations, kidnapped diplomats, and (in 1970) kidnapped and executed a U.S. official who was training local security forces. As in many Latin American countries in the 1960s, the rise of leftist revolutionary movements spurred the powerful emergence of the military and counterinsurgency campaigns supported by the United States. The result was a vicious cycle of leftist insurrection and right-wing, military repression. In February 1973, the Uruguayan military seized power in a coup and instituted one of the most brutal and repressive dictatorships in the history of Latin America.

A highly developed vision known as National Security Doctrine (NSD) guided the military's plan of action in the 1960s and 1970s. NSD had its origins in the military schools of Latin America as an offshoot of the Cold War. Deeply influenced by training in the United States, and by the work of U.S. instructors in Latin America, Latin American officers developed a sophisticated view of how their country fit into the superpower struggle. In essence, they saw the world as divided between two contending camps, one Christian and democratic, the other atheist and communist. Third World nations stood on the front line of the conflict between these two camps led by the United States and the Soviet Union. According to their logic, these two camps were engaged in a world war vying to destabilize the allies of their enemies through internal subversion. This was not a conventional war, but an unconventional struggle of "subversives" attempting to spark leftist revolutions against the allies of the United States. The generals watched the brewing turmoil in Latin America in the early sixties and saw the nightmare of more Vietnams, or more precisely, other Cubas, in the making. Their political objective was to halt the drift toward revolution, and to exterminate completely any forms of internal subversion. And crush the Left they did—with a deadly vengeance.

By the mid-1970s, the *Tupamaros* had been virtually eradicated and the military regime had imprisoned more than 5,000 people. Uruguay, the "Switzerland of South America," had become the penal colony of the Americas with one political prisoner for every 600 inhabitants. The military closed the legislature, took control of universities, imposed censorship on the media, and systematically tracked down, tortured, imprisoned, exiled, or killed anyone deemed to be a "threat" to the regime. Perhaps 15 percent of the Uruguayan people went into exile. By the beginning of the 1980s, the threat of leftist revolution had disappeared (along with many Uruguayans), and the major challenge facing the regime was a massive economic crisis and the specter of bankruptcy.

The economic crisis of the 1980s, the end of any serious leftist revolutionary threat, and broad-based reform movements very gradually pushed the Uruguayan military to disengage from power in the early 1980s. In 1984, Uruguayans returned to the polls for the first time in more than a decade and elected Julio Sanguinetti (a *Colorado*) as their president (1985–89). (He was later elected for a second term [1995–2000].) As in Argentina, Brazil, and Chile in the same years, the Uruguayans in the 1980s engaged in a delicate process of rebuilding civilian politics and sending the military back to their barracks. A 1986 general amnesty freed both rebels and military officers from prosecution for their actions during the military regime. The Uruguayans also formed a "truth commission" to investigate the fate of political prisoners and those who "disappeared" during military rule. This process of national reconciliation has been fraught with anguish, recriminations, and political land mines. Although the Uruguayan economy has remained weak and stagnant for much of the past two decades, the Uruguayans have managed to reestablish democratic, representative politics and move beyond the violence, repression, and wounds of the 1960s and 1970s. In the 2004 national elections, Tabaré Vásquez Rosas became the first elected president since the nineteenth century who is neither a *Colorado* nor a *Blanco* (now the National Party). Elected with a clear majority (in an election with a 90 percent turnout) as the candidate for a broad coalition of forces, Vásquez Rosas (an oncologist) continues the process of rebuilding one of the oldest, strongest, and most enduring democracies in the Americas. The reformers have once again established their primacy in Uruguayan politics, but they still must confront the legacies of an agro-export economy that has long been in decline.

ARGENTINA: THE PUZZLE OF PROGRESSIVE REFORM

Argentina is a mystery. How can a country so rich, well educated, and cosmopolitan have failed to stabilize one of the oldest representative political systems in Latin America to produce prosperity, sustained economic growth, and stable democratic processes? By the 1920s, the Argentines seemed to be on their way to entering the First World and emerging as the dominant power—the "United States"—of South America. Superficially, Argentina looked very much like the powerful "United States of North America." By one estimate, Argentina in 1930 had the seventh largest economy in the world, with a per capita income nearly as high as that in the United States.

Sparsely populated, with largely nomadic Indians, the region evolved in the colonial period on the periphery of Spain and Portugal's empires in the Americas. One of the "advantages of backwardness" was the failure to develop the notorious colonial legacy of the large landed estate exploiting forced Indian labor or African slave labor. Enlightened leadership in the second half of the nineteenth century put into place the liberal, constitutional project, and then (quite literally) populated Argentina with Europeans. Several million Europeans poured into Buenos Aires and its hinterland between 1870 and 1914, mainly from Italy and Spain. In the brothels and bars of Buenos Aires, this rapid and dramatic mixing of Europeans, gauchos, and (a few Afro-Argentines) gave birth to the tango (the music and the dance). The massive migration of millions of poor workers from southern Europe also produced a powerful labor movement and potent pressures to open up the political system.

The Argentine equivalent to Uruguay's José Batlle was Hipólito Yrigoyen (1852–1933). Unlike the upper-class Batlle, Yrigoyen arose from humble origins. He was the illegitimate son of a blacksmith. He built a career, like Batlle, on brilliant maneuvering in the back rooms of politics, and through his ability to mobilize the masses behind the banners and slogans of social reforms. Batlle and Yrigoyen are among the breed of twentieth-century Latin American politicians often labeled "populists" because of their ability to move the masses (and substantial sectors of the middle class) through a rhetoric of economic growth, political reforms, and social welfare programs. Most populists are charismatic public speakers. Yrigoyen was an exception to this pattern. Usually described as "enigmatic," he shunned public speaking and had poor oratorical skills. At the beginning of the twentieth century, Yrigoyen assumed control of the Radical Party (*Unión Cívica Radical* or UCR) and made it the machine of political change. In 1912, the Argentine legislature passed the Sáenz Peña Law extending the vote (and the secret ballot) to all males over the age of 18. In 1916, Yrigoyen won the presidency for a six-year term.

The Radicals, Yrigoyen, and powerful grassroots movements (especially of workers) transformed Argentina in the early decades of the twentieth century. Building on decades of steady reforms, by the 1920s, Argentina had universal male suffrage, the secret ballot, modern schools and universities, labor legislation, unionization, and the foundations of a social welfare state along the lines of western Europe. These progressive reforms did not come easily. Bitter and bloody strikes often led by anarchists and socialists pushed the elites and reformers hard in the early twentieth century. Despite his populist credentials, Yrigoyen brutally repressed a national strike in January 1919. The police and military (with Yrigoyen's full support) killed hundreds, wounded thousands, and imprisoned tens of thousands. The Tragic Week (*Semana Trágica*) demonstrated the continuing power of the military and landed elites, the depth of the desire for reforms by the working class, and the pressing need for the middle class to support reforms that would avoid future tragedies. Unfortunately, Yrigoyen and his successors relied heavily on personalism and political patronage to mobilize votes, building a system that is so common in Latin America—the state controls much of the national patrimony, and the objective of politicians is to win public office to gain access to the patronage that will get them reelected and increase the influence of their party and their personal political profile.

A "revolution on the pampas" had transformed Argentina in the late nineteenth and early twentieth centuries as foreign investment (primarily British) built a dense railway system across the pampas, as wheat cultivation and cattle ranching spread (along with wine production on the eastern slopes of the Andes around Mendoza). According to some estimates, wheat and beef exports, and the industrialization of Buenos Aires, made Argentina one of the wealthiest countries in the world by the First World War. Much like Australia, Canada, and the U.S. Midwest, Argentina built a vibrant and expanding economy that helped ease the transition to a more partici-patory politics and social reforms. The Great Depression, however, bat-tered the Argentine export economy, temporarily brought the military to power (they forcibly ended Yrigoyen's second presidency 1928–30), but World War II reinitiated the prosperity of the export sector.

The political problems and military interventions of the 1930s gave way in 1943 to the rise of Juan Domingo Perón (1895–1974), along with his second wife Eva (1919–52), easily the most contested and controversial figures in Argentine history. The ultimate populist politician, Perón astutely recognized the emerging power of the Argentine working class, and he built his political base on labor unions, first as the secretary of labor (1943–45) and then during two terms as president (1946–55). In many ways, the charismatic Evita (popularized in musicals and films) became his most important publicist, ally, and political partner. The two Peróns built large voting majorities in the national elections in 1946 and 1951 through the patronage they channeled to workers (the "shirtless ones" or *descamisados*), the poor, and other key sectors of society. Staunchly nation-alistic, vaguely fascistic, and at times anti-United States, Perón polarized Argentina and his legacy dominated national politics for decades.

With the death of the glamorous and charismatic Evita in 1952 (from uterine cancer), Juan Perón lost a major political asset. The decline of the Argentine agro-export economy in the early 1950s, as well as increasing political polarization, radicalized society. In 1955, the military overthrew Perón and initiated a half-century of economic decline and political crises. Much to the dismay of many, this cosmopolitan and highly educated soci-ety experienced increasingly bitter political and ideological polarization in the 30 years after the fall of Perón. A series of military coups punctuated by short-lived civilian presidencies characterized Argentina from the 1950s to the 1980s. The aging Juan Perón continued to cultivate his supporters from exile in Panama and then Spain. Amazingly, he led both the Right and Left to believe that he would be their champion on his return to power. When the military relinquished power in 1973 and allowed Perón to return, Argentine politics became further polarized and radicalized. (Deadly gun battles broke out between left-wing and right-wing Peronists among the hundreds of thousands of supporters surrounding the Ezeiza Airport awaiting his plane. Dozens died.)

Perón returned to the presidency in 1973, winning more than 60 percent of the vote, and his third wife, Isabel, was elected vice-president. Aging and ineffective, Juan Perón died in July 1974, his wife assumed power, and Argentina quickly descended into political and economic chaos. The bitter ideological struggles that wracked all of Latin America reached one of their most stunning crescendos in Argentina in the late 1970s. The Argentine military deposed Isabel Perón in March 1976, embarking upon what became known as the Dirty War (1976–79). The National Security Doctrine of the Argentine military (tinged with some Nazi influence and anti-semitism) turned the country into a living hell. The military "stabilized" the nation and restored "order" at a high cost. Some 9,000–10,000 persons "disappeared" as torture became systematic and widespread among all types of security forces—from the police to the army. (Jacobo Timerman, a prominent newspaper publisher and Zionist, chillingly depicts his imprisonment and the military mentality, in his controversial 1981 bestseller, *Prisoner without a Name, Cell Without a Number*.)

As the economy collapsed and political opposition to the military intensified in the early 1980s, the armed forces sought to rally support by attacking the Falkland Islands (the Malvinas Islands, for the Argentines), long under British control but claimed by Argentina. Much to the surprise of General Leopoldo Galtieri (head of the military regime), British Prime Minister Margaret Thatcher immediately mobilized the British people and military, quickly defeating the Argentine invasion forces. About a thousand British and Argentine troops died in the brief conflict. The stunning defeat brought down the military regime, forced them to hold national elections, and set the nation on a quarter-century of efforts to strengthen democratic, representative politics, and somehow to rebuild the once powerful Argentine economy.

The last 25 years have seen the redemocratization of Argentina, but the country has experienced repeated economic crises, hyperinflation, and political instability. Raúl Alfonsín (1983–89) failed to address the expanding debt crisis that devastated all of Latin America in the 1980s, and he left office (six months early) with inflation reaching 200 percent per month! The Peronist Party returned to power led by Carlos Saúl Menem (1989–99), the charismatic provincial politician born to Syrian Muslim parents in the northwest province of La Rioja. (Menem had been jailed between 1976–81 by the military regime.) Much to the surprise of everyone, including his Peronist followers, Menem embarked upon a dramatic, neoliberal economic program that privatized state-controlled corporations, opened the Argentine economy to foreign investment, downsized the government through massive layoffs, and broke the powerful political influence of labor unions. He also pardoned the leaders of the military regime, gaining the support of the armed forces and defusing a powerful political tension. During Menem's first term (1989–95), foreign investment surged, inflation went from 5,000 percent per annum to near zero, and the economy began to grow. He was reelected in 1995 with a large majority.

Argentina—like Brazil, Uruguay, and Chile—also grappled with the atrocities of the military rule with the return of democratic politics. The Mothers of the Plaza de Mayo, a human rights group that had been a vocal critic of the military regime, demanding information about the "disappeared" (*desaparecidos*), began demonstrating each week in front of the presidential palace in 1977. They and other groups successfully pressed for the formation of a commission to investigate the crimes of the Dirty War. Entitled *Nunca Más* (*Never Again* [1984]), the report of the National Commission on the Disappearance of Persons estimated the number of disappeared between 1976–83 at 11,000. Argentines continue to grapple with the atrocities of the period and the wounds they have produced in their society. (The anguish and tensions are beautifully re-created in the 1985 Oscar-winning film, *La história oficial* [*The Official Story*].)

Unfortunately, the neoliberal reforms did not produce sustained economic growth and unemployment in Argentina has remained high. Corruption escalated dramatically during Menem's presidency and his economic reforms unraveled by 2001. Argentina's democracy was shaken severely as five presidents came and went between 2001 and 2003, none able to address some of the worst economic problems in Argentine history. Néstor Kirchner, born in Patagonia to Swiss-Croatian parents, was elected president in 2003. Kirchner, Hugo Chávez in Venezuela, Evo Morales in Bolivia, and Tabaré Vásquez in Uruguay, have emerged as the "new" populists in Latin America and vocal critics of the neoliberal reforms of the past quarter-century. Kirchner has helped stabilize the Argentine economy and politics, but continues to face the central challenges of revitalizing the economy to provide stable economic growth, a return to the prosperity of the past, and to consolidate Argentine democracy. The crises of the last half-century—and especially of the last decade—have only made more bewildering the puzzle of progressive reform in Argentina. The Argentines (and Argentine watchers) continue to ask themselves: how is it that a nation so richly endowed, so highly educated and cosmopolitan, cannot stabilize its democracy and produce sustained economic growth?

CHILE: THE POLITICS OF COMPROMISE

Even more so than Uruguay or Argentina, Chile is a story of the triumph of progressive reforms, the nightmare of military dictatorship and repression, and the revival and triumph of a new wave of progressive reforms. With a long history of developing representative and pluralistic politics, alternation of power among different political parties, rare moments of military intervention, and renewed economic growth, Chile is one of the long-term successes in Latin America. By the 1960s, Chile was a model of stability, democratic politics, and social reforms for the rest of Latin America. As we saw in chapter 14, the Chilean elite forged a consensus in the nineteenth century that allowed for relative political peace and economic growth built on the export of minerals, wheat, and wine. The principal weakness of the Chilean economy was its excessive dependence on revenue from nitrates (before World War I) and then copper. Foreign firms (Anaconda and Kennecott especially) dominated the mining sector. Chile also experienced the European immigrant wave at the end of the nineteenth century, albeit on a much smaller scale than Uruguay or Argentina. The mix of Europeans, the Native Americans of the south (Mapuche), and Spanish colonists produced a population that is slightly more mestizo than Argentina or Uruguay, but still overwhelmingly European in its ethnicity and cultural habits. (Ninety-five percent of all Chileans identify themselves as "white.")

Politics in Chile developed along lines closer to European parliamentarism than U.S. presidentialism. Multiple parties, coalition governments, and a broad political spectrum characterized twentieth-century Chilean politics. As in Uruguay and Argentina, enlightened social reforms beginning in the nineteenth century gradually produced very high literacy rates, low infant morality rates, long life expectancy, and a highly educated citizenry. Like many reformist movements (including those in Europe) the system occasionally faced serious crises, the most severe a brief civil war in 1891. From the 1890s to the 1970s, Chileans gradually forged a democratic, representative political process built on universal suffrage (the vote for women came in 1931), the secret ballot, universal education, and increasingly competitive and frequent elections. By the 1950s, Chileans could choose among political parties from the extreme Right to the extreme Left, with many parties in between.

In the early twentieth century, numerous leftist parties emerged in Chile, especially among the working class and middle-class intellectuals. In 1916, Luis Emilio Recabarren (1876–1924) founded what would become the Communist Party of Chile (eventually linked to the Communist International in Moscow). As in most countries in Latin America, leftist parties and unions were bitterly repressed before the 1930s, but they had established their place in the political process by the Second World War, and a coalition of leftist and centrist parties governed Chile for brief periods in the late 1930s and early 1940s. Chile had effectively brought the working class and middle class into the political process, defusing the political tensions that so characterized Mexico, Guatemala, Bolivia, and Nicaragua before the eruptions of revolutions in those nations. By the 1950s, the most prominent leftist politician was Salvador Allende Gossens (1908–73) a physician and leader of the Socialist Party.

Beginning in the 1960s, the strongest centrist party was the Christian Democrats (*Partido Demócrata Cristiano* or PDC), like many of the socialist and communist parties, a movement with roots in Europe. Christian Democrats in Europe and Latin America (strongest in Costa

Rica, El Salvador, Colombia, and Venezuela) combined ideological components from both the Left and the Right. (The movement emerged along with, and had close ties to, fascism in Europe.) Built on a bedrock of Catholic religiosity, Christian Democrat beliefs promote communitarian values, and interest group cooperation, while rejecting communism and its emphasis on class conflict. In common with leftists, the Christian Democrats have collectivist values and an emphasis on social justice. It is a movement, however, that vehemently rejects what its followers see as the godless atheism of communism and socialism and the narcissistic materialism of both socialism and capitalism. Some Christian Democrats have referred to their political philosophy as "capitalism with a human face." Although its Chilean roots go back much earlier, the PDC was officially founded in 1957 and its standard bearer in the 1960s was the enormously popular Eduardo Frei Montalva (1911–82).

By the 1950s, Chilean electoral politics had developed a pattern of multiple parties competing in frequent elections at the municipal, state, and national levels. The PDC became the strongest centrist party, the Left normally formed a coalition around a single presidential candidate, and the Right (when unified) rallied round the National Party (largely a fusion of the old Liberal and Conservative parties). In four consecutive elections (1952, 1958, 1964, and 1970), Salvador Allende was the candidate for the leftist coalition. (Allende sometimes joked that his tombstone would read, "Here lies the next president of Chile.") In each election he gained about one-third of the vote. In all but the 1964 election, the winning candidate garnered little more than 30 percent of the vote. In 1964, a Right-Center coalition elected Eduardo Frei Montalva with a clear majority (56 percent versus 39 percent for Allende). During these two decades, the number of voters in Chile rose rapidly and dramatically—from 500,000 in the late 1930s to three million by 1970. Frei's sweeping victory for his "revolution of liberty" in 1964 was touted by the U.S. government as the democratic alternative to armed, leftist revolution in Latin America. Frei had strong support (overt and covert) from the United States during his campaign and presidency. True to his Christian Democrat ideological roots, Frei embarked upon social reforms that included housing for the poor, a mild land reform program, and the nationalization of Chile's copper mines (much to the dismay of U.S. business). Although he had a clear majority in the presidential vote, the Chilean congress remained fragmented in three parts—Right, Center, and Left. Congressmen and senators on the Right and Left often voted together to block Frei's programs. Both the Right and the Left anticipated winning the 1970 election and collaborated to weaken Frei and the Christian Democrats.

The early 1970s are some of the most hotly contested and tragic moments in the history of social and political reforms in Latin America.

On his fourth try, Salvador Allende finally won the presidency in the 1970 election. During the campaign, the United States (especially via the Central Intelligence Agency) had done everything possible to block Allende's election. His *Unidad Popular* (Popular Unity) coalition secured 36.5 percent of the vote, while former President Jorge Alessandri (the candidate of the Right) finished second with 35.2 percent, and the Christian Democrat candidate Radomiro Tomic finished third with just 28 percent of the vote. Allende won by just under 40,000 votes out of three million cast. Although this was not unusual in Chilean elections, given the ideological intensity of the campaign (and the revolutionary upheaval in Latin America), the Chilean Congress compelled Allende to agree to an extraordinary set of constitutional guarantees before it would certify his victory. Salvador Allende became the first democratically elected, socialist president to take office in the history of the Americas, and he promised his followers that he would progressively move the country forward through constitutional processes on the "Chilean road to socialism" (*la vía chilena al socialismo*).

Over the next three years, Chilean politics (with the strong intervention of the United States government under Richard Nixon and Henry Kissinger) polarized dramatically, eventually producing the complete collapse of Chilean democracy and the rise of one of the most authoritarian military regimes in Latin American history. As soon as Allende took office, the Nixon administration embarked upon a covert project to "destabilize" the regime and help topple it. (Nixon instructed CIA Director Richard Helms to make the Chilean economy "scream.") As much as the U.S. played a crucial role in undermining democracy in Chile, ultimately, it was Chileans (in particular, their political leaders) who bear the brunt of responsibility for the catastrophe that would envelope the country. Allende found himself moving too slowly for his more radical supporters on the Left, who demanded the rapid socialization of the Chilean economy and society. The extreme Left called for arming the workers and peasants to seize complete control of the country. Allende moved to nationalize larger and larger sectors of the economy, increase government social programs, and initiate a more aggressive land reform program. In effect, he sought to accelerate Frei's "revolution of liberty," while trying not to alienate centrist constituencies. Allende at times found himself trying to persuade factory workers and peasants *not* to seize control of factories and farms. As the government asserted greater control over the media and the schools, opposition to Allende grew among the middle class. A long and highly visible visit by Fidel Castro in November 1971 provided a powerful negative image of Allende's socialist project for many Chileans.

In many ways, Allende's greatest problem was the steady deterioration of the Chilean economy. World copper prices fell in the early seventies, severely damaging the economy. U.S. businesses (AT&T, ITT, Anaconda) and the Nixon administration aggressively blocked credits and international capital, and the CIA carried out a covert campaign of economic sabotage. As government spending accelerated, Allende printed more currency, and inflation rose rapidly to 300 percent per annum. By early 1973, the Chilean economy was in shambles, further accelerating the political polarization. *Unidad Popular* candidates managed to gain 44 percent of the (3.6 million) votes in the municipal elections of March 1973, the coalition controlled 30 of the 50 seats in the Senate, and more than half the seats in congress. Negotiations between the Christian Democrats and the *Unidad Popular* coalition failed and by mid-1973, the country had clearly moved toward complete political polarization. When a contentious legislature blocked reform, Allende began to resort to executive decrees and constitutionally questionable maneuvers to keep the socialist project moving forward. Throughout 1973, Allende and his coalition moved further to the left, and the center in Chilean politics (principally the Christian Democrats) moved to the right. The center—that core so crucial to the continuity and durability of democratic, representative politics—evaporated. Allende's balancing act—trying to appease his leftist coalition and maintain support from centrist voters—failed completely and miserably.

The highly professionalized Chilean military had become increasingly politicized, and a group of generals and admirals led by Augusto Pinochet Ugarte (1915–2006) led a bloody coup d'état on September 11, 1973. Allende barricaded himself in the presidential palace and died (probably by his own hand) after the air force bombed the palace and troops invaded the building. In the succeeding days and weeks, a Pinochet-led junta systematically searched out anyone they believed to be a threat to the new regime. Tens of thousands were rounded up and jailed in makeshift prison camps across the country. Thousands were summarily executed. Thousands more fled the country or sought asylum in foreign embassies. The junta dissolved the congress, banned all political parties, took control of the universities, and censored the media. The ferocity of the coup and its aftermath shocked the world, and took the Right and center in Chile by surprise. They had expected, even openly called for, the armed forces to intervene, crush the Left, and then return governance to right-wing and centrist politicians. Much as in Brazil in 1964, Uruguay in 1973, and Argentina in 1976, the armed forces effectively told civilian politicians, "a plague on all your houses," and then set out to show the civilians how to run the country. They sought political stability and economic growth—without the debate, discussion, and dissent of liberal, democratic politics. The technocrats took charge.

As he closed down politics, Pinochet opened up the economy, blessing the policies of a group of economists who became known as the "Chicago Boys." Many had been trained at the University of Chicago by

Milton Friedman and they became early apostles of the neoliberal economics that would sweep across the Atlantic world in the 1980s. Reversing a half-century of government interventionism, they sold off state companies (including the state copper companies), reduced trade barriers, cut government spending, encouraged foreign investment, and deregulated much of the economy. This economic shock plan made Chile perhaps the most open economy in the world, resulting in foreign control of most of the key industries, utilities, and services in the country. It was a radical and dramatic transformation, arguably a right-wing economic revolution as sweeping as Cuba's leftist economic revolution in the 1960s. The results have been hotly debated, as wealth in Chile has become increasingly concentrated, the country has deindustrialized in the face of international competition, and poverty levels have increased.

Unlike the generals in the so-called "bureaucratic-authoritarian" military regimes in Argentina, Uruguay, and Brazil (where the military rulers were constantly rotating and changing), Pinochet became the dominant figure and icon of the "new" Chile. The repressive apparatus he created was used to hunt down and kill opponents of the regime, not only in Chile, but around the world (including on the streets of Washington, D.C.). Chile became a pariah state in the international community, even drawing the criticism and censure of the Reagan administration in the 1980s. Despite the brutal and repressive tactics of the regime, concerted and widespread opposition began to emerge by the early 1980s. To institutionalize his rule, Pinochet had pushed through a new constitution in 1980 that called for a plebiscite in 1988, a vote that he expected would reconfirm his rule for another eight years. With a stable and growing economy, and the end of nearly all serious violent opposition to the regime (the repression was very effective), many Chileans across the political spectrum gradually forged a broad coalition (the *Concertación*) that defeated Pinochet in his own plebiscite with 55 percent voting against the continuation of his rule. It was an extraordinary moment in Latin American politics. A dictator with complete power organized and held a completely fair and open election that (to his great surprise) he lost! Much to his credit, Pinochet carried out the constitutional provisions and allowed the first direct presidential election since 1970 to take place in December 1989. Patricio Aylwin (his father was of Welsh ancestry), a Christian Democrat supported by a broad coalition of forces, won 55 percent of the vote over two conservative candidates. He took office in early 1990.

Although the process of redemocratization has not been without its difficulties, Chile has returned to sane and reasonable politics. Since 1989, Chileans have elected four presidents (Aylwin, Eduardo Frei Ruiz-Tagle [son of Eduardo Frei Montalva], Ricardo Lagos, and Michelle Bachelet). The first two were Christian Democrats. Lagos and Bachelet come from

Allende's Socialist Party. All four have been elected as candidates of the coalition of forces and parties that emerged out of the 1988 plebiscite. These presidents have had to deal with the conservative institutional checks that Pinochet included in the 1980s constitution. These have led to the overrepresentation of the Right in congress (including the lifetime appointment of some senators, including Pinochet), and the ongoing struggle to come to grips with the scars of military rule. Chile's Commission on Truth and Reconciliation initiated an ongoing process to identify human rights violations in the 1970s and 1980s, and to recover the memories and remains of the disappeared. Legal actions against former members of the regime, including Pinochet, will go on for years to come. Chileans remain deeply divided over Pinochet and his legacy. On his death in December 2006, his staunch supporters staged public demonstrations to honor their hero while Pinochet's opponents rallied to condemn him, his regime, and his legacy.

The election of Michelle Bachelet (b. 1951) in late 2005 confirms Chile's return to the forefront of progressive reformism in Latin America. Bachelet's father was an air force general. While growing up, she lived all over Chile and in the United States. Her father was imprisoned in the aftermath of the 1973 coup and tortured, dying of "cardiac arrest" in prison in early 1974. Bachelet and her mother were also imprisoned, tortured, then exiled—first to Australia, then East Germany. She returned to Chile in 1979, completed a medical degree and studied military strategy at the Inter-American Defense College in Washington D.C. and at the National Academy for Strategic and Policy Studies in Chile. Appointed Minister of Health under Ricardo Lagos in 2000, two years later she became the first woman to serve as Minister of Defense in any Latin American country. Her victory over two conservative candidates in the 2005 presidential election made her the first woman elected president (who was not riding on the political legacy of a husband) of any country in the Americas.

The key to the successful return of progressive reformism in Chile has been a consensus—in politics and economic policy. With some tinkering, the neoliberal policies of the 1970s and 1980s have been maintained since 1989. Chile is one of the most prosperous countries in Latin America today, although income distribution has worsened and poverty has increased. The political consensus, no doubt, arises out of the desire of everyone to avoid the cataclysmic polarization and collapse that nearly destroyed Chile in the 1970s. Out of the ashes of the firestorm of the early 1970s, Chile has arisen anew, and once again provides a model of reform for the rest of Latin America. Three decades after the violent overthrow of a democratically-elected socialist president, Chile is now led by another democratically-elected socialist president, and the country is thriving.

COSTA RICA: AN ENLIGHTENED ELITE

Over the last half-century, Costa Rica may have been the most democratic and socially progressive country in Latin America. Since the early 1950s, Costa Ricans have enjoyed universal suffrage (with the secret ballot) voting in fourteen national elections (every four years) and regularly alternating the political party in power. Voter participation rates have long been above 85 percent in very competitive elections. Beginning with the Liberals in the late nineteenth century, the Costa Ricans have constructed an educational system that serves the entire population and has produced literacy rates (96 percent) equal to those in Western Europe. Costa Rica's four million citizens today enjoy the benefits of a modern social welfare state including pensions, labor legislation, national health care, and a life expectancy of 77. With no army since the late 1940s, the Costa Ricans love to say that they have "more teachers than soldiers, more schools than barracks." These social and political reforms are especially striking when compared with the conditions of Costa Rica's Central American neighbors. Nicaragua, just across the northern border, is one of the poorest countries in the hemisphere. Per capita income in Costa Rica is more than double that in Honduras.

The indigenous population in Costa Rica was nowhere near as dense as in northern Central America (Guatemala and El Salvador) and the demographic catastrophe of the Conquest decimated it. Spanish colonists (via Panama) settled Costa Rica and Nicaragua in the late sixteenth century with the most important nucleus in the Central Valley (around 1000 meters up) surrounded by volcanoes. Although the Costa Ricans like to emphasize the poverty and equality of the settlers, colonial society was stratified and hierarchical, as in the rest of Latin America. Costa Rica did benefit from the "advantages of backwardness"—that is, the lack of a coerced indigenous labor force and large landed estates meant Costa Rica entered nationhood with a lighter imprint from the pernicious colonial heritage than Guatemala or the core regions of Mexico, Peru, the Caribbean, and Brazil. With few Indians and Africans, the population (just 60,000 in the 1820s) developed largely out of European immigrants and some mestizos. (Today some 95 percent of Costa Ricans are white or light-skinned mestizos.)

As we saw in chapter 15, Costa Rica was at the forefront of the development of the agro-export economy in the nineteenth century, emerging as one of the first major coffee exporters (primarily to England and Germany). The expansion of coffee production further stratified Costa Rican society, but landholding was widespread and fragmented. The Costa Rican elite developed their economic power through the purchasing and export of coffee production. Something of a small-scale version of Chile (without the nitrates and copper), Costa Rica modernized in the late nineteenth century. By 1900, coffee exports provided 90 percent of the value of all export revenues and nearly all government tax revenues. Minor C. Keith's United Fruit Company on the Atlantic coast operated largely apart from the world of the Central Valley, and developed as a West Indian enclave using English-speaking peoples brought in from the British Caribbean. By the beginning of the twentieth century, the population had grown to about 300,000, overwhelmingly concentrated around the capital, San José, in the Central Valley.

As in the other notable cases of social and political reform movements, Costa Rica's achievements have depended on an enlightened political elite that has taken advantage of periods of economic growth to institute reforms, while largely resisting fratricidal conflicts in moments of economic and social crisis. (The great exception to the rule was 1948, as we shall see.) For reasons that cannot be quantified or scientifically tested, the Costa Rican economic and political elites developed a consensus in the late nineteenth century that has gradually evolved for nearly 150 years. Coffee provided the wealth of this elite. Although they contended for political power, they rarely resorted to violence, and they gradually incorporated larger and larger numbers of people into an evolving system of representative politics. In general, the elite preferred to negotiate and alternate among the positions of power, including the presidency. It was a classic "old boys' network," but with enlightened leadership. (Between 1906 and 1936, two men—Cleto González Víquez and Ricardo Jiménez Oreamuno—served in the presidency for 20 years, but never for more than four years at a time.) Briefly, in 1917–19, the consensus broke down and a coup interrupted the electoral system. By 1920, however, the elites had resolved their differences and resumed electoral politics. By the 1940s, Costa Rica had nearly a half-century of experience with regular elections, and a steadily increasing number of voters.

From the 1880s, the government had begun to build an educational system and to institute modest social reforms. As in the rest of Latin America, socialism and communism emerged as significant forces after the First World War, especially among workers on the banana plantations of the Caribbean coast. Although the Catholic Church has never been a powerful force, a very influential Catholic social action movement emerged in the Central Valley in the 1920s and 1930s. During the presidency of Rafael Ángel Calderón Guardia (1940–44), the government put into place a series of social reforms to protect the rights of workers and to provide them with greater social benefits (social security, national health care). As was true of nearly all Costa Rican presidents, Calderón Guardia came from an old and well-established elite family. A physician by training, his reformist vision largely derived from Catholic social thought, although he entered into an alliance with the (very) small Costa Rican Communist Party to pass his reforms in the legislature.

Unfortunately, Calderón Guardia attempted to manipulate the electoral process and violate the unwritten rules of the elite consensus. Claims of electoral fraud were widespread in the 1944 election won by Calderón Guardia's handpicked successor, Teodoro Picado. Calderón Guardia ran for president again in 1948 in a bitterly contested election. After losing the vote (60,000 to 45,000), the government annulled the results, igniting a two-month-long civil war that left 1,200 dead (out of a population of 750,000). The rebel forces were led by an outsider to Costa Rican politics, José (Pepe) Figueres (1906–90), the son of Catalan immigrants. Figueres played the central role in the renovation and direction of Costa Rican reformism in the post-World War II decades. A self-styled small businessman, Figueres was largely self-educated. As a teenager, he moved to Boston for some time, reading widely and sitting in on classes and lectures at local universities (including MIT). Figueres developed a social and political philosophy that was an eclectic mix from his readings of Locke, Martin Luther, Voltaire, Karl Marx, and John Maynard Keynes among others. (In the 1970s, Figueres published his most important work, *The Poverty of Nations*, playing on Adam Smith's classic, *The Wealth of Nations* [1776].) He was essentially what is normally labeled a "social democrat"—espousing a form of nonviolent, nonrevolutionary socialism, although in Figueres's case, it was blended with a belief in reforming and retaining the strengths of capitalism. He returned to Costa Rica (with a flawless Boston-accented English) and developed a rope and twine business. In 1943, he gained national notoriety after a radio speech criticizing the government. Sent into exile, he developed ties with leaders of the social democratic left in the Caribbean basin. During the 1948 civil war, he emerged as the leader of the rebel forces and the junta that took power.

An unusual set of circumstances favored reform in Costa Rica. Calderón Guardia (although a Catholic social reformer) had allied with the small Communist Party and his opposition was fervently anti-Communist, but largely social democratic in their political philosophy. In effect, the civil war took place among two contending groups of reformers and not the reformers/revolutionaries versus the guardians of the status quo as has so often been the case in twentieth-century Latin America. As a result, when Figueres and his junta took power in May 1948, quite ironically, they confirmed and extended the social reforms of the Calderón Guardia years, but with a firmly anti-Communist ideology. Although the United States government was wary of Figueres (and had its hands full at that very moment with the Guatemalan Revolution), his anti-Communist credentials were impeccable. (In the aftermath of the revolt, the new junta outlawed the previously legal Communist Party.)

José Figueres took control of Costa Rica in May 1948 as the head of a rebel army that had toppled the government. He then embarked upon a path unprecedented in Latin American history. Figueres vowed to rule for 18 months, then step aside, handing over power to Otílio Ulate, the newspaper publisher who had won the February 1948 election. In November 1949, Figueres—true to his word—stepped aside and voluntarily relinquished control of the country. In his year and a half in power he guided through the series of reforms that are the foundations of modern Costa Rican politics and society. He abolished the army, nationalized the nation's banks, imposed a 10 percent tax on private property to finance the government, restricted the powers of the president, limited the presidency to one term, decentralized power through the creation of autonomous and semiautonomous government agencies, and extended the vote to women. These were bold reforms that built on a long tradition of reformism, and their strength and endurance came from the participation of many groups in their formulation and implementation. Figueres also strengthened the reforms by stepping aside and refusing to become a dictator.

Instead, he created his own political party, *Liberación Nacional*, a party that would dominate Costa Rican legislative politics for the next three decades, helping guarantee the endurance and continuation of social reforms. In the 1953 election, Figueres easily won the presidency. When his party lost in 1958, he then handed over the presidency to the opposition in a pattern that would be repeated many times over the next half-century. Not until 1970 and 1974 was *Liberación Nacional* able to win back-to-back presidential elections. In a testament to the strength of Costa Rican democracy, the Communist Party and its longtime supporters began to compete openly in elections in the 1970s, garnering about 5 percent of the national vote.

Ironically, the creation of a modern social welfare state is the culmination, in a sense, of the reforms that Calderón Guardia pushed so hard in the 1940s, but were carried out by those who took up arms against him in 1948. In effect, 1948 marked an extraordinary moment in Costa Rican history, when the elite consensus broke down, but the civil war became a struggle between two visions of reform. Despite mass democracy and political participation, the old elite families (many dating back to the colonial period) continue to dominate Costa Rican political leadership. Nearly all the presidents since 1949—Figueres is the notable exception—have come from the traditional elite families. Ironically, Figueres's son, José María Figueres Olsen (b. 1954), was elected president in 1994, taking the presidential sash from Calderón Guardia's son, Rafael Ángel Calderón Fournier (b. 1949), who was president from 1990–94.

Despite the long-developing and strong reformism in Costa Rica, the country has faced serious challenges over the last quarter-century. The rise of revolution in Nicaragua created serious internal problems as war and rebels spilled over into Costa Rica. (The Costa Ricans aided and supported the Sandinistas with arms and logistical support against the Somoza dictatorship.) Nicaragua's economic problems in the last decade have pushed many Nicaraguans into Costa Rica, creating social unrest and problems. The oil crises of the 1970s (Costa Rica imports all of its petroleum), and the debt crisis of the 1980s also put enormous pressures on Costa Rica. The country continues to be a major exporter of coffee, bananas, sugar, chocolate, and beef, but ecotourism has now become the major source of foreign currency. With about one-fifth of this astonishingly beautiful and ecologically diverse country under the protection of the national park system, Costa Rica has become a major tourist destination in the last 20 years for North Americans and Europeans. With only small-scale industry (textiles, food processing), the political leadership has sought to built a high-tech economic sector with electronics assembly plants.

Even more so than the Chileans, Uruguayans, and Argentines, the Costa Ricans have built a prosperous society on decades of gradual social and political reforms. On the periphery of the Spanish Empire in the colonial period, they avoided most of the debilitating legacies of unfree labor and large landed estates. With the rise of the classic coffee-export economy in the nineteenth century, they again avoided the most damaging features of the Latin American land-and-labor complex. Most important, the small and intermarried elites had the foresight and savvy to incorporate gradually other sectors of society into the political process beginning in the late nineteenth century. Finally, when the political process and the elite consensus did break down in the 1940s, the society regrouped and advanced the social and political reforms of earlier generations. As a result, at the beginning of the twenty-first century, tiny Costa Rica has become a highly educated, prosperous, and democratic society, arguably the most democratic and participatory in all the Americas.

DILEMMAS OF REFORMISM

Uruguay, Argentina, Chile, and Costa Rica stand out as the most successful and enduring examples of the path of reform in Latin America. For much of the last half–century, they have been the Latin American nations with the highest levels of social development as measured in literacy rates (above 95 percent), low rates of infant mortality (below ten deaths per 1,000 live births), long life expectancy (above 77), and many other indicators such as levels of educational attainment, access to health care, and access to basic services. The only other country in Latin America to reach comparable levels has been Cuba, after the 1959 revolution. For much of the twentieth century (and now the twenty-first), these four nations have generally had the highest levels of democratic, representative, electoral politics of any of the nations of the region.

Despite these success stories, as we have seen, the path of reform has not been without its major obstacles and failures. The brutal and repressive military regimes in Uruguay, Argentina, and Chile in the 1960s and 1970s nearly ended decades of progressive reforms. The 1948 civil war in Costa Rica stands out as a bloody moment in a long history of gradual reforms. Despite the problems these four countries now face (especially Uruguay and Argentina), all have survived the bloody challenges to progressive reform and, once again, are among the strongest examples of democratic electoral politics in Latin America.

Perhaps the most striking lesson from these successes is the continuing difficulty of finding a sustainable economic base for social and political reform. As in the cases of revolution in chapter 20, strong and enduring reforms must be built on more than an agro-export economy. Uruguay has learned this painfully and today grapples with how to construct a viable alternative to the old ranching economy. Argentina seemed to be on the path to overcoming its reliance on the fruits of the land (wheat, beef, wine) as it industrialized, but that industrial base has faced near-complete collapse in the era of neoliberal reforms. The Costa Ricans learned the problems of building social reform on the export of coffee and bananas, and they have turned to ecotourism and the informatics industry as the means to build a stronger economy. With its dramatic turn to neoliberalism, Chile appears (for the moment) to have moved toward a new economic model, but it remains unclear how strong and sustained it will be over the long run. It has diversified its economy, made it more global, but also more vulnerable to the fluctuations of the international marketplace.

The reformist path in Latin America has been neither smooth nor without its setbacks, but these four cases demonstrate the importance of building a consensus within a society, and strengthening it over decades. The four countries have been blessed (at times) with political leadership that had the wisdom to seek gradual reforms over decades rather than to block any real change at all cost. This pattern clearly sets apart the nations of sustained reform from the nations that experienced dramatic revolutions. These reforms came at the cost of decades of debate, confrontations, and sometimes violence, as the various social groups struggled to gain access to power—or to hold on to it. In all four countries (although much earlier in Costa Rica), the political consensus developed over decades collapsed, violence and repression ensued, and the social groups have since faced a delicate process of reconciliation and the rebuilding of consensus. The lessons here are clear. Democracy, economic growth, and national identity do not emerge fully formed out of sudden and cataclysmic upheaval. They are cultivated, consolidated, and constantly refined over long periods, and they are always fragile. Nation-building takes time, and decades of negotiation, conflict, and compromise, in Latin America, or any other region of the world.

22

Between Reform and Revolution

DICTATORSHIP AND DEMOCRACY: OTHER PATHS

As this survey has repeatedly stressed, a series of patterns and similarities allow us to speak of something called Latin America. Yet, this vast and fascinating region has also been marked by great diversity. The previous three chapters traced the clearest and most pronounced patterns of reform and revolution in twentieth-century Latin America. This chapter briefly sketches the paths of reform and revolution in the rest of Latin America, paths that are less clear-cut and tidy. In many ways, these regions (fully half of Latin America) provide the messier and more complicated cases. These countries have often moved between dictatorship and democracy, sometimes repeatedly—in many cycles. In some cases, they experienced very little democratic, representative politics until the last generation. They range in size from some of the smallest countries in Latin America (Panama, El Salvador, Honduras, Haiti, the Dominican Republic) to the largest (Brazil). Some have a long history of isolation, grinding poverty, and repressive regimes (Honduras, Haiti, Paraguay) while others are resource-rich nations (Brazil, Venezuela, Peru). Those in the Caribbean and Central America (El Salvador, Honduras, Haiti, Panama, Dominican Republic, Puerto Rico) have lived in the powerful shadow of the United States. The nations of South America (Brazil, Colombia, Venezuela, Ecuador, Peru, Paraguay) largely developed free from the power and pressure of the United States until recent decades.

The following survey is very concise and succinct. The goal is not to be encyclopedic, but to provide a glimpse at some of the diverse paths of the many nations of Latin America across the last century. To impose some sort of order and logic on this brief overview, I have placed eleven countries and Puerto Rico into three groups—those countries that have experienced what I call "uneven reformism" (Brazil, Colombia, Venezuela, Ecuador, Peru), those that have largely developed in poverty, isolation and under authoritarian rulers (El Salvador, Honduras, Paraguay), and, finally, those who have lived "in the shadow of the eagle" (Haiti, the Dominican Republic, Panama, and Puerto Rico).

UNEVEN REFORMISM

Brazil

The process of reform in Brazil has been long, very gradual, and not always cumulative. Brazil is more emblematic of the problems and challenges of reform in twentieth-century Latin America than the classic cases of reform we examined in chapter 21. Unlike the other nations of the region, Brazil moved relatively quickly and peacefully from colony to nation in the 1820s, and became a monarchy rather than a republic. The 1824 Constitution endured until the fall of the monarchy in 1889, and the republican Constitution of 1891 would last two generations. From independence in the 1820s to the 1930s, Brazil developed a long experience with elections and representative government. Nevertheless, only about 1–2 percent of the population could vote and the control of nominations and elections was dominated by powerful landowners in the countryside. Not unlike Costa Rica or Argentina, Brazil developed an electoral tradition throughout the nineteenth century, albeit one that was heavily managed.

When the army toppled the Emperor in 1889, it was an unusual moment of military intervention in politics. The military, however, quickly withdrew to the barracks, and the coffee elite resumed control of electoral politics between 1894 and 1930. An informal alliance of the powerful coffee states (São Paulo, Rio de Janeiro, Minas Gerais) provided Brazil with a stability that assured national unity while conceding control of much of rural Brazil to landowners (the colonels or coronéis). A conflict among the elites over the elections of 1930 gave rise to 15 years of increasingly controlled politics dominated by Getúlio Vargas, who took complete control between 1937 and 1945 with the support of the armed forces. The most important political figure in twentieth-century Brazil, Vargas dominated politics for a quarter-century, moving Brazil into the world of industrialization, mass urbanization, working-class politics, and populism. When forced from the presidency in 1945, he was immediately elected to the congress, and then in 1950 to the presidency. This authoritarian dictator quickly made the transition to charismatic advocate of electoral politics.

For 20 years (1945–64), postwar Brazil became an enormous "experiment in democracy." The Constitution of 1946 gave the vote to all Brazilians over the age of eighteen (except illiterates, who were perhaps a third of the population) and the country had its first real experience with mass politics. The populism that characterized so many Latin American countries in the 1950s also permeated Brazilian politics from candidates on both the Right and the Left. During a period of rapid growth of the population (from 40 million in 1940 to 70 million by the mid-1960s), a massive shift of people from the countryside to the cities, and an industrial surge (especially under President Juscelino Kubitschek, 1956–61), Brazilian politics were vibrant, highly charged, and constantly unstable. At this moment of Cold War politics and revolutionary upheaval, Brazil's electoral democracy was on the verge of collapse repeatedly in the 1950s and early 1960s.

Facing high inflation, economic stagnation, and intense ideological battles, Brazilian democracy collapsed in 1964 when the military deposed President João Goulart (1961–64). The Brazilian coup began the wave of military coups and dictatorships across Latin America over the next two decades. Much to the surprise of nearly all civilian politicians (especially the Right, which had called for military intervention), the armed forces remained in power and attempted to transform Brazil through brutal repression of dissent (especially on the Left) and a massive national economic development project. Hundreds "disappeared" and thousands were jailed and tortured. The generals (and admirals) ruthlessly eradicated any leftist threat, and successfully industrialized Brazil, albeit with massive government intervention. In the process, they accumulated a staggering foreign debt, and bankrupted the country. Facing constantly rising pressure from all sectors of Brazilian society in the early 1980s, the military handed over power to a civilian president in 1985, the Congress wrote a new constitution (1988), and in 1989, the country held its first national presidential election since 1960.

For the past 20 years, Brazil has returned to electoral, representative politics. Everyone over the age of 16 has the right to vote (including illiterates). With more than 100 million voters in presidential elections, Brazil has become the third largest democracy in the world (after India and the United States). Five successive presidential elections, a multiparty system, and mass communications have consolidated Brazilian democracy. In 2002, Brazilians elected Luis Inácio "Lula" da Silva to the presidency. The founder and leader of the Workers' Party (*Partido dos Trabalhadores* or PT), from truly poor, working-class origins, Lula's election, in many ways, marks the consolidation of mass, electoral politics in Brazil. Unfortunately, he and his immediate predecessor (the eminent sociologist Fernando Henrique Cardoso, 1995–2003) have both confronted the substantial structural obstacles that make it difficult to deal with Brazil's enormous socioeconomic inequities through electoral politics. Both Cardoso and Lula followed neoliberal economic policies, and neither has been able to mobilize the resources of a reduced state as instruments of social change. Reelected with more than 60 percent of the vote in late 2006, Lula faces the difficult challenge of all the leaders of contemporary Latin America: how to address the massive social problems effectively while pursuing neoliberal economic policies?

Brazil's path to electoral mass politics has a long history, but not one that has been gradual and continual. Its history has been (again, not unlike Costa Rica) one of elite controlled electoral politics for the century after independence, and an elite consensus that rarely collapsed. When it did collapse in 1889 and 1930, the resulting civil violence was very brief. The military became a potent force in politics, but not until 1964 did the armed forces assume complete control of the nation. In this sense, the military dictatorship was a striking and dramatic anomaly. The resumption of electoral mass politics in the late 1980s paralleled events across the rest of Latin America. Brazilian electoral, democratic politics today are the strongest at any time in the country's history, but the path has been long, often tightly controlled, and not without its moments of acute crisis and violence (1889, 1930, 1964, to name the most important examples). Brazil has moved along a political path over the last two centuries that has skirted revolution and embraced reform, but with great hesitancy.

Colombia

Despite its recent troubles, Colombia offers another example of moderation and slow, but eventual, progress toward social reform and democratic politics. With a long history that oscillates between periods of brutal violence and political moderation, Colombia is one of the most puzzling cases of reform in Latin America. In the century after independence, the Colombians moved between bloody wars and elite controlled electoral politics. More so than in most of Latin America, the Liberals and Conservatives endured, and have fought astoundingly bloody wars interspersed with moments of electoral politics. The so-called War of the Supremes (1839–41) in the nineteenth century, and the War of a Thousand Days (1899–1902) are the two most striking examples of this violence. Probably as many as 100,000 died in the latter struggle in a nation with under 4 million inhabitants. Yet, in the peaceful interludes, the Colombian political elite (Liberals and Conservatives) managed to put into place a constitutional order that allowed for (controlled) electoral politics.

For much of the early twentieth century, the Liberals and Conservatives managed to settle their differences through elections, but the system broke down in the late 1940s, resulting in two decades of fratricidal bloodshed as Liberals and Conservatives killed each other wantonly. During the *Violencia*, hundreds of thousands of Colombians died in this brutal civil war. In the late 1950s, the two parties agreed to a power-sharing arrangement that would alternate the presidency and political offices. Known as *convivencia* (getting along), the arrangement gave the country stability, regular elections, and the *Violencia* largely subsided by the mid-1960s. Unfortunately, this also coincided with the rise of leftist revolutionary movements in the countryside, and in the 1980s a dramatic escalation of drug trafficking. Even with the formal end of the *convivencia* in the 1970s, electoral politics have survived in Colombia, although in the midst of some of the most harrowing and widespread violence in the world.

Colombian politicians over the last two decades have run for office and served at enormous personal risk. Drug trafficking has become so lucrative and pervasive that it permeates all aspects of life in Colombia. The revenues from the multibillion dollar drug trade help provide the country with a favorable trade balance, provide employment for thousands, and finance politicians of all types. (The coca leaves from which cocaine is derived are largely grown in Bolivia and Peru, processed in Bolivia and Colombia, and then marketed by the Colombians. The enormous and lucrative traffic is driven by demand in Europe and the United States.) The Colombians have been known for their astute moderation in economic policy-making over the last half-century, yet drugs have now completely distorted Colombian society and politics, making it unlike any other country in Latin America. The drug lords have entered into arrangements for military security and protection with the "revolutionary" movements that control much of the countryside. Today, perhaps as much as one-third of the national territory of Colombia is outside the control of the state, and in the hands of drug lords and armed insurgents (both "leftist" guerrillas and right-wing paramilitary forces). Somehow the Colombians have managed to maintain electoral politics amidst very high levels of endemic violence, and to survive what is, in effect, a civil war lasting a generation. As long as demand for cocaine continues to be strong in the United States and Europe, the drug trade will continue to be profitable, and Colombia will be condemned to live with the tragic violence and instability it produces on a daily basis in this beautiful country.

Ecuador

The other two nations to emerge out of Simón Bolívar's New Granada have also had trouble developing a long, gradual, and cumulative reform tradition. Although Ecuador and Venezuela have not experienced the exceptional violence that has plagued Colombia, they have a long history of military coups, personalistic politics, and regional conflict. The old northern core of the Inca Empire, Ecuador had a dense indigenous

population pressed into forced labor during the colonial period. In addition
to the development of large landed estates, Ecuador became a major textile producer and then (in the late eighteenth century) an exporter of
cacao. By the early nineteenth century, powerful creole landowners and
textile merchants in the highlands around Quito and the coast around
Guayaquil had come to dominate Ecuador and its Indian majority. In the
late nineteenth century, the Liberals dominated politics, promoted cacao
(a coastal product) exports, and used the revenues to modernize the country's infrastructure. By the mid-twentieth century, bananas had become
the dominant export, and after the Second World War, banana exports
became the key to the country's revenue stream.

Regionalism (especially the coast versus the highlands) has repeatedly
divided national politics. Personalism, and the lack of strong political
institutions, have also been at the core of a long history of instability. Since
independence, Ecuador has had seventeen constitutions, and only brief
periods of electoral continuity and stability—in the early 1920s, from
1948–60, and in the 1980s. Presidents who finished their elected term in
office have been few in the last two centuries. Even fewer have been the
instances of elected presidents succeeding each other and completing
their terms. (The prosperity of the banana export sector helped produce
unusual stability between 1948–60 when three consecutive presidents
completed their elected terms before a fourth was toppled in a military
coup in 1961.)

In the nineteenth century, charismatic caudillos dominated national
politics as factionalism, regionalism, and personalism prevented the
development of the kind of strong, institutional political structures that
developed in Costa Rica, Chile, Uruguay, and Argentina (or Brazil). In the
twentieth century, military coups and military juntas have too often
deposed and ruled in the place of civilian politicians. The populism that
spread across so much of Latin America from the 1930s to the 1960s, also
affected Ecuador. The charismatic José María Velasco Ibarra (1893–1979)
was elected president five times (1934, 1944, 1952, 1960, 1968), but was
chased from office four times (1935, 1947, 1961, 1972) by military coups.
Famed for his public speaking skills, he supposedly asserted, "Give me a
balcony, and I will be president!" This highly personalistic, populist style,
however, did not help foster the creation and development of political
institutions and stability.

Since the late 1970s, Ecuador has experienced, along with much of the
rest of Latin America, the emergence of mass electoral politics and frequent elections. (The Ecuadorian economy has also been bolstered with
the discovery and exploitation of oil in the Amazonian lowlands.)
Between 1984 and 1996, three consecutive elected presidents served out
their terms. Unfortunately, the country has experienced serious instability

since 1996 with some seven different presidents. Two of them have been the descendants of Lebanese immigrants, one was a woman. The indigenous population has become a force within national politics as well in the last two decades. Mass politics have arrived and diversified the political scene. Clearly, Ecuador has entered fully into the re-democratization of Latin American politics in the last quarter-century, but the lack of a long tradition of institution-building has made its recent politics chaotic and fragile.

Venezuela

The third piece of the fragmented Gran Colombia, Venezuela has suffered from the curse of abundant petroleum, an enormous asset that has completely distorted its economy and politics for nearly a century. Simón Bolívar's dream of Latin American unity, or even the unity of Gran Colombia, died quickly as his old ally, the cowboy caudillo José Antonio Páez, took Venezuela on an independent path after 1829. Caudillos dominated nineteenth-century Venezuela, first under the "Conservative Oligarchy" (1830–47) and then under a "Liberal Oligarchy" (1848–65). Páez, from the eastern plains, dominated the politics of the period, as president or military leader on various occasions. He became the leader of the Conservatives. His protégé, José Tadeo Monagas (from the western mountains), turned against him and became the leader of the Liberals in the late 1840s. Another caudillo, Antonio Guzmán Blanco (1829–99), dominated politics in the 1870s and 1880s. Coffee and cacao became the main exports and sources of revenue under the Liberals in the late nineteenth century.

Dictators and petroleum dominated Venezuelan politics and its economy in the first half of the twentieth century. Under General Cipriano Castro (1899–1908) and then under Juan Vicente Gómez (1908–35), politics remained personalistic and carefully controlled. The exploitation of vast oil reserves (especially in the west around Lake Maracaibo) made Venezuela the world's largest oil exporter by the 1920s. Although the production was initially monopolized by powerful multinational oil companies through government concessions, over the succeeding decades, the Venezuelan government gradually extracted larger and larger shares of profits, and eventually nationalized production. In the late 1950s and 1960s, Venezuela was at the forefront of the creation and growth of the Organization of Petroleum Exporting Countries (OPEC), a group that would shock the world economy in the 1970s with its oil embargoes. As in Nigeria or several Middle Eastern nations, oil became a powerful force— a sort of megaprimary export product—dominating and distorting the national economy with its price swings since the 1970s.

In the 1930s and 1940s, a series of military officers dominated the presidency. Two political parties emerged in the 1940s and 1950s that would dominate national politics: *Acción Democrática* (Democratic Action or AD) and COPEI (the Social Christian Party). Rómulo Gallegos, a renowned novelist, became the first popularly elected civilian president in Venezuelan history in 1948, but was overthrown within months and the country experienced a decade of military rule dominated by the caudillo General Marcos Pérez Jiménez. Finally, in the late 1950s, an agreement between AD, COPEI, and other parties initiated a quarter-century of stability and electoral politics. Much like the Liberals and Conservatives in Colombia, the AD and COPEI dominated national politics and alternated the presidency repeatedly between 1959 and 1993. After a century of authoritarianism, this power-sharing politics seemed to promise a new era in Venezuelan politics.

Unfortunately, corruption scandals and the roller-coaster-like price fluctuations for petroleum discredited both COPEI and AD. In 1993, Rafael Caldera, a former president from COPEI (1969–74) broke from the party and was elected president (1994–98). Dissatisfaction with the two parties was widespread, and a coup attempt in 1992 led by Hugo Chávez Frías, a young army officer, failed, but helped make Chávez a national symbol of change. With the disarray and discrediting of AD and COPEI, Chávez emerged as a powerful, charismatic, populist figure. Although he has very strong support, especially among the masses, Chávez has polarized Venezuelan politics. First elected president in late 1998, he has held a series of elections and plebiscites to generate public legitimacy for his government, including a new constitution and measures to concentrate greater and greater power in the hands of the president. He has allied himself closely with Fidel Castro and opponents of neoliberal economics. With oil prices at record levels, Chávez has become a powerful presence in Latin America, and a thorn in the side of U.S. foreign policy in the region. Much like Fidel Castro in the 1960s and 1970s, Chávez has sought an international presence as a leader of countries in Latin America, Africa, Asia, and the Middle East who resist and resent U.S. power and influence in the world. After decades and decades of caudillos who paid no attention to electoral politics, Chávez has expertly and astutely built his own populist *caudillismo* through the constant mobilization of the machinery of electoral mass politics.

Peru

Like its neighboring Bolivarian republics, Peru has not been blessed with a history of gradual and progressive political reform. While Venezuela and Colombia are largely white and mestizo nations with small populations of African and indigenous heritage, Ecuador, Peru and Bolivia (the core of the old Inca Empire) have had indigenous majorities for most of their history. Over the last century, the percentage of mestizos has grown

as the percentage of "Indians" has slowly declined. (About 65 percent of
Ecuador's 15 million people are of indigenous descent with the figure at
about 45 percent for 30 million Peruvians.) Both Ecuador and Peru have
significant groups of African and Asian descent along the Pacific coast.
Both societies have deep ethnic, social, and regional divisions, in particular,
the highlands (sierra), the arid coast, and the jungle on the eastern slopes of
the Andes. In the 1840s, the Peruvians imported many indentured laborers
(probably over 100,000) from China and the Polynesian islands. Slavers
captured and sold many Polynesians to Peruvian contractors.

Peru also suffered through a series of caudillos in the nineteenth century.
In the 1840s, a small group of offshore islands became the key to economic
growth and modernization. For tens of thousands of years, flocks of birds
nesting on the islands had left droppings, and this manure (guano) provided a rich source of fertilizer for Europe, and by the 1860s, 80 percent of
government revenues. As in most of South America, the British provided
the expertise, technology, and financing for economic modernization. The
Irish immigrant Michael Grace (whose brother William later became the
mayor of New York City in the 1880s) signed a contract with the Peruvian
government to finance its foreign debt and handle its external financial
obligations. The Grace Contract also gave (what eventually became the
multinational) W. R. Grace Company control of Peru's railroads, guano
export rights, and free use of Peruvian ports. This pattern of foreign multinational corporations gaining control of national resources continued for
the next century and included foreign control of Peru's copper, silver, lead,
and oil deposits. (As noted in chapter 16, Peru also lost its claim to the rich
nitrate deposits of the northern Atacama Desert when it lost the War of the
Pacific to Chile in 1883.) The guano deposits were practically exhausted by
the 1890s and for the next few decades, sugar, cotton, and mining became
the revenue producers at the heart of the export-oriented economy.

Elections were rare and authoritarian regimes common in Peru from the
mid-nineteenth to the mid-twentieth century. An oligarchy of powerful
landowners and political bosses dominated the national economy, along
with the multinational corporations. The politics of personalism have characterized Peru rather than the consolidation of parties and institutions. In
the 1920s, two figures of special note emerged in Peru, José Carlos
Mariátegui (1894–1930), a journalist and writer who produced some of the
most influential Marxist writings on Latin American reality, and Raúl Haya
de la Torre (1895–1979). Mariátegui's *Seven Interpretive Essays on Peruvian
Reality* (1928) is one of the earliest and most brilliant analyses of the role
played by the large landed estate and the exploitation of Indian peoples in
the creation of the enormous inequities in Latin American societies.
"Socialism," he wrote, "preaches solidarity with and the redemption of the
working classes. Four-fifths of Peru's working classes consist of Andean

Indians. Therefore, socialism means the redemption of these Indians."
Influenced by socialism, anarchism, and spiritualism, Haya de la Torre
founded the *Alianza Popular Revolucionario Americano* (Popular Revolutionary
American Alliance, or APRA), the most enduring political party in twentieth-
century Peru. Although it gradually became increasingly conservative,
APRA and Haya de la Torre in the 1920s and 1930s rejected U.S. power (read
imperialism) in the region *and* Soviet Communism. Haya de la Torre spoke
often not of "Latin" America, but rather "Indo" America. His movement
paralleled the rise of *indigenista* movements in the Andes and Mexico that
attempted to place the region's indigenous past and culture at the center of
Latin America's development. During an uprising in 1932 in which a group
of military officers were executed, Haya de la Torre and APRA earned
the enduring enmity of the Peruvian armed forces who would oppose his
presidential aspirations for the next half-century.

From the 1930s to the 1950s, the military dominated Peruvian politics,
either through direct rule or behind-the-scenes pressure on civilian politicians. In contrast to most of Latin America, Peru (under General Manuel
Odría, 1948–56) moved away from government economic intervention and
into two decades of greater openness to foreign investment and export-led
growth. By the 1960s, leftist guerrilla movements inspired by the Cuban
Revolution had begun to emerge in the highlands, and they were brutally
suppressed, leaving thousands of peasants dead, displaced, or in prison. In
1968, the Peruvian military seized power, yet again, deposing President
Fernando Belaúnde Terry (1912–2002). Belaúnde was a reformist politician
educated in France and the United States. At first, the overthrow of
Belaúnde appeared to be yet another in the series of right-wing military
coups that had begun with the Brazilians in 1964. Much to the surprise of
nearly everyone, the Peruvian military under the leadership of General
Juan Velasco Alvarado (1910–77) embarked upon a sweeping series of
social and economic reforms including the nationalization and expropriation of most of Peru's natural resources (petroleum, copper, fishing). The
regime seized the large sugar plantations on the coast and created workers'
cooperatives to run them. It was one of the most sweeping land-reform
movements in twentieth-century Latin America. Close relationships with
the Soviet Union and Cuba also brought new capital into Peru. The new
regime proclaimed it would pursue a path that would be "neither capitalist nor communist." The "Peruvian Revolution" led by leftist generals
stood in stark contrast to the wave of right-wing military regimes that were
opposing and dismantling social and economic reforms. In the words of
Fidel Castro, it was "as if a fire had broken out in the firehouse."

This corporatist regime, despite its extraordinary social and economic
reforms, faced increasing opposition as the economy declined in the late
1970s. Following the pattern of military regimes across the region, the

Peruvian military disengaged from power and the country returned to full-scale electoral politics. Fernando Belaúnde Terry, deposed by the military in 1968, won the presidential election of 1980. He was succeeded in 1985 by the 36-year-old Alan García, the charismatic new leader of APRA. Both Belaúnde (1980–85) and García (1985–90) had little success facing the enormous debt crisis of the 1980s, and, in the late 1980s, the Peruvian economy effectively collapsed as the GDP shrank by a third and inflation surpassed 3000 percent per annum. Even more tragic was the emergence of one of the most brutal and enigmatic leftist insurgencies in Latin American history, the Shining Path (*Sendero Luminoso*). Founded in southern Peru by a university philosophy professor, Abimael Guzmán (Comrade Gonzalo), *Sendero* followed a "prolonged popular war" strategy inspired not by Marx and Lenin, but by Mao Zedong. Incredibly secretive, highly disciplined, and ruthless, *Sendero*'s influence spread through the highlands and into the cities of Peru by the late 1980s.

Out of this political and economic crisis emerged an unlikely caudillo, Alberto Fujimori (b. 1938), the child of Japanese immigrants to Lima. An agricultural engineer educated in France and the United States, Fujimori was the rector of the *Universidad Nacional Agraria*. In a stunning surprise, he defeated the world-renowned Peruvian novelist Mario Vargas Llosa in the 1990 election. Vargas Llosa had campaigned as the man who would transform Peru with a neoliberal economic shock plan and Fujimori had taken a populist stance. In a stunning turn of events, Fujimori stabilized the national economy by implementing a radical neoliberal plan that became known as the Fujishock. He privatized the sectors of the economy that had been nationalized by the military, and reduced trade barriers while welcoming foreign capital back to Peru. At the same time, he embarked upon a dramatic and ruthlessly effective counterinsurgency campaign that nearly destroyed *Sendero Luminoso* and its leadership. (Abimael Guzmán was captured and imprisoned in 1993.) A so-called "self coup" gave Fujimori extraordinary executive powers and brought the military into close collaboration with his regime and made possible the successful campaign against *Sendero*. By 1995, Fujimori easily won re-election. Over the next five years, however, the economy worsened, and major corruption scandals forced Fujimori to resign in 2000. President Alejandro Toledano (b. 1946) won the election of 2001, but faced continual economic problems and social protests. In spite of his disastrous presidency in the 1980s, Alan García won the presidential election in 2006 and returned to power.

Like many of the countries discussed in this chapter, Peru has a long experience with electoral politics, but ones often dominated by oligarchic elites, the military, and often interrupted by military coups. It has experienced the redemocratization of the past quarter-century, but (like Colombia) has faced serious leftist guerrilla insurgencies. Despite its rich natural resource base, Peru's economy has been too dependent on the vagaries of primary-product export cycles. The challenges Peru faces are similar to those of Ecuador and Colombia: how to institutionalize electoral, democratic politics, and consolidate a national economy in this era of globalization. These are formidable challenges in a country with a long history of deep ethnic and social cleavages and little experience with reform and truly open and participatory electoral politics.

POVERTY AND PROGRESS?

Honduras

Central America was one of the poorest and most isolated regions of the Spanish American empire. As we have seen, independence was practically dropped in the laps of the regional elites as Mexico moved from rebellion to civil wars and foreign interventions in the first half of the nineteenth century. The effort by Liberals to create a United Provinces of Central America failed in the late 1830s with the rise of the Conservatives to power. The emergence of the Guatemalan Conservative caudillo, José Rafael Carrera (1814–65), in the late 1830s and the death of the great leader of Liberalism and unity, the Honduran Francisco Morazán (b. 1792) in front of a firing squad in Costa Rica in 1842, spelled the end of Central American unity. For most of the nineteenth century, caudillos dominated Central America—from Guatemala to Costa Rica—creating centralized governments and heavily managed elections. (As we have seen, Costa Rica began to diverge from these patterns in the late nineteenth century.)

The five nations of Central America became prime examples of the agro-export economy, especially after the rise of Liberals in the 1870s. Coffee cultivation grew rapidly in all five nations, but especially in Guatemala and Costa Rica. At the beginning of the twentieth century, banana plantations controlled by United States-based multinational corporations took shape on the Caribbean coast, especially in Honduras and Costa Rica. Throughout most of the twentieth century, coffee and bananas dominated the Central American economies, accounting for 60–90 percent of exports. Honduras, in particular, became the epitome of the so-called "banana republic," as foreign corporations dominated the economy and occasionally toppled unfriendly governments. (The great short story writer, O. Henry, brilliantly captured the expatriate life at the turn of the century on the Honduran coast in his famous collection *Cabbages and Kings* [1904].) Well into the twentieth century, the countries of Central America remained overwhelmingly rural and dominated by a landed elite. Unlike the large nations of Latin America (Mexico, Argentina, Brazil), no significant challenge to landowners arose from an emerging group of industrialists.

Both Honduras and El Salvador were plagued by a series of authoritarian regimes, often led by military officers. In Honduras, in particular, the military became the dominant force in national politics. In many ways, the military became a career path to power and influence, especially for young men who did not come from the traditional landowning elites. Throughout much of the middle of the twentieth century, the country alternated between military regimes and brief periods of civilian-led reforms. During the civil insurgencies and conflicts in Central America in the 1970s and 1980s, the United States made Honduras the staging ground for U.S. military operations in Nicaragua, El Salvador, and Guatemala. This substantial U.S. military presence reinforced the power of the Honduran armed forces and no serious guerrilla insurgency ever took shape in this most underdeveloped country in a very underdeveloped region. Honduras also participated in the cycle of democratization that took shape in Latin America in the 1980s, but in a context very different from that of the more developed nations of the region. Slightly larger than Tennessee, half of Honduras's seven million inhabitants live in poverty and nearly a quarter remain illiterate. In Latin America, only Nicaragua and Haiti are poorer. (Per capita income in Honduras is one-fifth that of Argentina.) The Hondurans have been spared the tragic excesses of the civil wars and revolutions that wracked its Central American neighbors in the last half-century, but its (recent) fragile electoral democracy confronts some of the most serious economic underdevelopment in the hemisphere.

El Salvador

Like Honduras, El Salvador has become a largely mestizo nation over the last two centuries with a peasant majority ruthlessly exploited by a small and powerful landowning elite (the so-called "fourteen families"). In 1932, peasants rose up to challenge the brutal oppression they faced. The dictatorship of General Maximiliano Hernández Martínez responded with one of the great bloodbaths in Latin American history. During the "Massacre" (*La Matanza*) some 10–20,000 peasants were killed and often buried in mass graves. The message from the military and the landowning elite was clear: no reforms, no challenges, and death to those who attempt to question our power. In the late 1970s, nearly 80 percent of Salvadorans still lived in the countryside, and nearly half of the peasants were landless, working on the plantations of the wealthy. From the 1950s to the 1970s, liberation theology became a potent force promoting social change, much as it did in Brazil and Nicaragua. This Catholic reformist movement had pervasive grassroots support throughout the countryside, and right-wing paramilitary groups began to kill lay workers, priests, and nuns who supported this activist wing of the Church. The Archbishop of El Salvador,

Óscar Romero (b. 1917), began to speak out powerfully against right-wing violence, and he was assassinated, gunned down while saying mass in March 1980.

In 1979–80 another revolt erupted as reformist military officers took power. The Salvadoran state effectively collapsed and the country entered into nearly a decade of civil war. By late 1980, the Salvadoran army and right-wing paramilitary groups were brutally, and often senselessly, killing thousands of civilians. A series of leftist revolutionary groups formed a relatively united front and were close to taking power in early 1981. Ronald Reagan's first major foreign policy decision in January 1981 was to "draw the line" in El Salvador. There would be no more Cubas, no more Nicaraguas. Massive U.S. military aid and assistance kept the rebels from taking power, but could not defeat them. As in Nicaragua, the 1980s in El Salvador were a bloody period of "low-intensity conflict," as the United States-backed military held the leftist revolutionaries at bay. There were no winners in this conflict, only losers. Somewhere between 70,000 and 80,000 people died in more than a decade of conflict. This grinding and bloody civil war destroyed the country's basic infrastructure and drove hundreds of thousands of Salvadorans northward—seeking shelter in the United States. By the 1990s, the Salvadoran exile community in Los Angeles made it the second largest urban concentration of Salvadorans.

The Central American peace process (led by Costa Rica's President Oscar Arias) finally brought an end to the conflict in the early 1990s. Incredibly, the Salvadorans were able to forge an open, electoral, democratic process in the 1980s and 1990s out of the chaos and ashes of civil war. Former leaders of right-wing paramilitary groups and death squads and armed leftist rebels eventually gave up their weapons and now compete for power through an extremely active political process. The destruction of the war, however, has made reconstruction costly and El Salvador depends heavily on billions of dollars of remittances from Salvadorans living and working in the United States. The repatriation of thousands of Salvadorans who had developed gangs in southern California has led to the rise of gangs and a crime problem in El Salvador, an unexpected and ironic cultural consequence of the exile provoked by civil war. Along with the rest of Central America, the Salvadorans have moved toward regional economic integration, and closer economic ties with the United States, as the path to economic growth. As in Honduras, Guatemala, and Nicaragua, the good news is that highly participatory electoral politics are stronger now than at any time in the history of these nations. Unfortunately, they all face enormous economic challenges to overcome their long dependence on the export of coffee and bananas. Even more acutely and severely than Mexico or Brazil, with their huge economies, the nations of

Central America must find ways to strengthen and cultivate electoral politics while addressing enormous socioeconomic problems.

Paraguay

Paraguay has suffered for much of its history from long dictatorships and little experience with truly open electoral, democratic politics. For the first half-century of independence, Paraguay was ruled first by José Gaspar de Rodríguez de Francia (1814–40) then by Carlos Antonio López (1844–62) and his son, Francisco Solano López (1862–70). A disastrous war with Brazil and Argentina (1864–70) devastated the country and perhaps a fifth of the population died in the conflict and many, many more were injured and displaced. In the late nineteenth and early twentieth centuries, Liberals and Conservatives (*Colorados*) fought over power, but certainly did not build stable, open, and representative politics. The *Colorados* dominated politics in the late nineteenth century, and then the Liberals from the 1910s to the 1930s. Factionalism, elitism, and instability characterized the period. The widespread mixing of Spaniards and the Guaraní Indians produced a nation that, by the twentieth century, was overwhelmingly mestizo, bilingual, and bicultural. (The Jesuits in the colonial period created a written alphabet for Guaraní and the Paraguayans have produced a flourishing literature in this indigenous language.)

In the 1930s, Paraguay and Bolivia fought a war over the semiarid plains (Gran Chaco) that straddle southern Bolivia and northern Paraguay. Although Paraguay defeated the Bolivians and gained control of most of the region, the Chaco War (1932–35) ushered in a period of regimes dominated by military officers, many of whom sympathized with European fascism and, specifically, with the Nazis in Germany. In 1954, General Alfred Stroessner (of German descent), seized power and gradually established (through the *Colorado* Party) one of the more enduring dictatorships in Latin American history. This personalistic regime turned Paraguay (and its two million inhabitants) into a virtual family fiefdom. Cronyism, corruption, and personal networks linked to the Stroessner family defined Paraguay politics from the 1950s to the General's overthrow (by a fellow general and relative) in 1989.

The Paraguayans drew up a new constitution (1991) and in 1993, Juan Carlos Wasmosy became the first freely elected president in Paraguayan history. After Wasmosy left office in 1998, a series of murders, assassinations, and corruption scandals disrupted national politics. In 2003, Nicanor Duarte Frutos (b. 1956) was elected president with just 37 percent of the vote. All presidents since Stroessner have been from the *Colorado* Party in its various reformed versions. With some six million citizens in 2006, and a GDP of just over $30 billion and per capita GDP of just over $5,000, Paraguay today is one of the smallest countries in Latin America, and one of the poorest. As the last two decades have shown, the Paraguayans will face a great deal of political instability as they construct the institutional infrastructure of mass, electoral, democratic politics. The challenges are even more daunting than those faced by most of Latin America, given the long and frequent periods of authoritarianism and personalism over the last two centuries. Political reformism is very new and untested in Paraguay.

IN THE SHADOW OF THE EAGLE

While the nations of South America largely avoided the power and influence of the United States until the post-1945 period, Central America and the Caribbean (as we saw in chapter 16) have long lived in the "shadow of the eagle." The determined resistance of the United States to the revolutions in Guatemala and Cuba was but the latest chapter in a long history of (direct and indirect) intervention in the region. In the last four cases to be discussed in this chapter—Haiti, the Dominican Republic, Panama, and Puerto Rico—the power and influence of the United States have been (and continue to be) decisive in the development of their politics and economies. In all four cases, the United States has intervened militarily, occupied, and (sometimes) partially absorbed these regions into the U.S. "empire."

Haiti

Haiti is one of most tragic stories in the Americas over the last century. In the aftermath of the only successful slave revolt in the Americas, Haiti was ruled by a succession of autocratic despots. Jean Jacques Dessalines (1804–06), Henri Christophe (1806–20), Alexandre Pétion (1806–18), and Jean Pierre Boyer (1818–43) bequeathed to this tiny nation a legacy of tyranny, ethnic tension (between mulattoes and blacks), and an economy based on small landholders who gradually degraded the environment. The invasion and occupation (1822–44) of the eastern end of the island of Hispaniola also served to create a lasting enmity between Haiti and the Dominican Republic. From the mid-nineteenth century to the First World War, Haiti experienced periodic dictatorships punctuated by shortlived "elected" governments. The United States intervened in Haiti in 1915 as a part of the wave of gunboat diplomacy in the early decades of the twentieth century. For twenty years, Haiti became a U.S. protectorate (much like Nicaragua, Cuba, and the Dominican Republic). Although the U.S. occupation forces engaged in what today we call nation-building projects (roads, communication systems, courts, port facilities), the occupation did not contribute to the institutionalization of representative, electoral politics or an independent judiciary. For two decades after the withdrawal of U.S. troops in 1934, Haiti had a series of weak, short-term governments and petty dictators.

In 1957, François Duvalier, a physician with long experience in public health work, was elected president. He quickly moved to establish a totalitarian regime. Duvalier (or Papa Doc, as he was known) organized a brutal and sinister security force known as the *Tontons Macoutes* (bogeymen). The long developing Afro-Haitian religion of Voudun had become central to national culture by the 1950s, and Duvalier used it as a powerful psychological weapon to intimidate the population. As Duvalier terrorized Haitians in the 1960s and 1970s, ironically, the country became a very stable and safe haven for foreign tourists, and foreign investors in search of a docile and cheap labor force (with the lowest wages in the Americas). When Papa Doc died in 1971, his nineteen-year-old son, Jean-Claude (Baby Doc), succeeded him. Without the iron will or political skills of his father, Jean-Claude Duvalier was eventually forced into exile in 1986. A reformist Catholic priest, Jean-Bertrand Aristide, won the first truly free elections ever in Haiti in 1990, but was deposed in a military coup in early 1991. In the aftermath of the coup, thousands of Haitians fled on homemade boats to the United States, creating a substantial exile population, especially in south Florida.

The U.S. military invaded the island (once again) in 1994, forcing out the military regime and restoring Aristide to power. He was succeeded as president in 1996 by René Préval, who served until early 2001, when Aristide assumed the presidency again after winning reelection. Tragically, Haiti's political and economic institutions have gradually disintegrated over the last decade. For all intents and purposes, no national government or security forces have functioned in Haiti since 2003. The United States forced Aristide into exile in 2004, and a series of leaders have failed to impose order and stability. The single most important source of stability in recent years has been a United Nations peacekeeping force (led by Brazil). Haiti today is the most impoverished country in the Americas with a per capita GDP of barely $2,000, a life expectancy of 50, and a literacy rate of just 50 percent. With no functioning national institutions, massive unemployment and underemployment, constant illegal immigration to the Dominican Republic and the United States, Haiti can barely claim to be a functioning nation-state some two hundred years after it became the first independent nation in Latin America.

Dominican Republic

Electoral democracy and representative government have been the exception rather than the rule in the Dominican Republic for most of its history. From the 1810s to the 1930s, the country had more than 120 rulers, ranging from Spanish and French officials to Haitian presidents. As political scientists have often pointed out, political instability was the norm in the Dominican Republic until the late 1960s. Much like impoverished Nicaraguans, the Dominican people have been poorly served by their political leaders for much of their history. After subjugation to Haiti (1822), then independence (1844), then resubjugation by Spain (1861), the Dominican Republic finally achieved its lasting independence in 1865. In 1870, the caudillo Buenaventura Báez held a fraudulent plebiscite (16,000 in favor, 11 against!) and then signed a treaty to annex the country to the United States, but the annexation treaty died in the U.S. Senate after a contentious debate. In the 1880s and 1890s, General Ulises Heureaux dominated the nation. Heureaux (1899) and his successor, General Ramón Cáceres (1911) both died at the hands of assassins.

The United States (under President Theodore Roosevelt) intervened in 1905 to establish a receivership that guaranteed the repayment of foreign creditors through control of the customs houses in the ports (invoking the so-called Roosevelt Corollary to the Monroe Doctrine). When civil war broke out in 1916, the United States sent in troops and occupied the country until 1924. U.S. interests were both economic and strategic. As war raged in Europe in 1916, the United States sought to blunt the German presence in the key shipping lanes of the Caribbean. As in Cuba and Haiti, the U.S. military built roads, schools, communication systems, and gradually trained and equipped a police force. (The Dominicans also took up baseball and soon—like the Cubans, Nicaraguans, and Panamanians— were producing some truly exceptional players, and they continue to do so today.) Like Batista in Cuba, and Somoza in Nicaragua, Rafael Leónidas Trujillo Molina (1891–1961) established a long-lasting, personalistic dictatorship by assuming control of the "nonpartisan" security forces created by the U.S. Marines. The racially-mixed Trujillo trumpeted "Hispanism" and the "white" Spanish heritage of the country while putting in place a brutal and repressive regime complete with secret police, torture, assassinations, and massacres. In October 1937, Trujillo ordered the execution of some 25,000 Haitians living in the Dominican Republic. (Trujillo's maternal grandmother was Haitian.) Much like the Somozas in Nicaragua, the Trujillo family amassed a phenomenal fortune (estimated at $800 million) by turning the country into their own personal business fiefdom.

During the 1950s, Trujillo closely aligned himself with the anti-Communist foreign policy of the United States. Despite his close relationship with the United States, and the use of expensive lobbyists in Washington, President John Kennedy personally ordered the Central Intelligence Agency to assist in the assassination of Trujillo in 1961, to make way for moderate reformers rather than leftist revolutionaries, or so he thought. Between 1961 and 1965, however, reform failed. In September 1963, the Dominican military deposed Juan Bosch, elected president in December 1962. As the country floundered in 1965, President Lyndon Johnson, fearing a possible leftist uprising, sent in the U.S. Marines and the 82nd Airborne to take control of the country. Within two weeks, more than 20,000 U.S. troops had landed. Although this invasion (along with many other U.S. military interventions in the region) has been roundly condemned over the last 40 years, the Dominican Republic is the rare case of electoral reform and stability eventually emerging out of U.S. military intervention.

From 1966 to 1978, one of Trujillo's old associates, Joaquín Balaguer (1906–2002), was elected president for three consecutive terms (1966, 1970, 1974). Balaguer's Reformist Party lost the 1978 and 1982 elections to the Dominican Revolutionary Party (PRD), but both of these administrations were plagued by corruption scandals. Amazingly, the 78-year-old Balaguer won the 1986 election and was elected again in 1990 and 1994. He was forced from power in 1996 (at the age of ninety and completely blind), although he ran again for the presidency in 2000 (gathering a quarter of the vote). Despite the dominance of Balaguer, and frequent complaints of electoral irregularities, Dominicans have now voted in ten consecutive presidential elections, and have alternated power among competing political parties. Whatever the flaws of Dominican democracy, the country has gradually evolved into an open, competitive, electoral democracy, and the process began more than a decade earlier than the majority of Latin America in the 1980s.

Panama

Geography has shaped the destiny of Panama. Since Balboa first gazed upon the "Southern Sea" in 1513, the world has come to Panama as a vital transit point to move between the Atlantic and Pacific Oceans. For centuries, Spanish mule trains carried goods across the isthmus to Peru, and carried back from Potosí the silver that financed the world's first great global empire. Although separated from the South American mainland (even today) by impassable mountains and jungles, Panama was long a province of the Spanish American viceroyalties—first Peru, then New Granada—beginning in the eighteenth century. In the nineteenth century, the Colombians, British, French, and United States all made plans to dig an interoceanic canal across the isthmus. The need became more pressing with the discovery of gold in California in 1848. (The distance from New York to San Francisco via Panama is about 6,000 miles, via Cape Horn the trip is more than 14,000 miles.)

In the 1850s, U.S. investors built a railway across the isthmus that flourished, and Colombia granted the United States the right to intervene to protect the facilities. Over the next half-century, the United States intervened thirteen times. In the 1880s, the French attempted to build a sea-level canal across Panama, led by Ferdinand de Lesseps, the famed architect of the Suez Canal. Malaria and yellow fever killed more than 20,000 workers (largely black West Indians) and the project collapsed in the early 1890s. In the aftermath of the Spanish-American War of 1898, the United States felt even more pressed to build a canal to move its navy more easily between the Atlantic and Pacific. In one of the more unsavory episodes in the history of the Americas, the Frenchman Philippe Bunau-Varilla, working with President Theodore Roosevelt, Secretary of State John Hay, and a small group of Panamanian elites combined to declare independence in November 1903, protected and supported by U.S. troops and ships. Although the Panamanians had attempted to secede from Colombia several times in the nineteenth century, they had been defeated on each attempt. This time, the military might of the United States guaranteed success. In the infamous words of Theodore Roosevelt, "I took the Canal Zone."

Over the next decade, the United States constructed one of the great engineering feats of modern times. The Panama Canal Zone sliced the isthmus, and the nation, in half for the rest of the twentieth century. The effective sovereignty that the United States exercised over the Canal Zone made Panama a virtual protectorate and completely distorted national politics. In the early twentieth century, Panama had a population of fewer than 500,000, and more than 150,000 immigrants (largely from the British West Indies) flowed into Panama to build the canal, transforming the cultural and ethnic composition of the country. With a "white" population of less than 50,000, and about 200,000 mestizos and mulattoes, a small group of powerful families (whose wealth was largely based on sugar, cattle, and commerce) dominated Panamanian politics in the early twentieth century. In the Canal Zone, the United States constructed a highly segregated "Jim Crow" system, paying blacks with silver coin and whites with gold coin.

The United States tried (with little success) throughout the twentieth century to shape Panamanian politics to protect the canal, described by one observer as "a body of water entirely surrounded by trouble." In the words of the eminent historian of U.S. foreign affairs, Walter LaFeber, very early on during the building of the canal, Panama entered into an "era of fragmented, personalized political parties that lasted until 1969." Although the Canal would flourish throughout the century, "political life became stagnant and corrupt." In the infamous 1903 treaty that Bunau-Varilla had written and signed (before the Panamanian representatives arrived in Washington), the United States reserved the right to "reestablish public peace and constitutional order" in Panama. For much of the twentieth century, the United States regularly labored to ensure elections and representative government in Panama, but also frequently intervened (through diplomacy, economic pressure, or troops) to guarantee stability.

Despite frequent elections throughout the twentieth century, Panamanian politics have been dominated by elite families, and by a few key leaders who have emerged out of the military (often from humble origins). Two brothers, Arnulfo and Harmodio Arias Madrid, exemplify the personalistic, populist politics in twentieth-century Panama. Both played key roles in a coup that deposed President Florencio Arosemena in 1931. In the 1920s, the Arosemena and Chiari families had dominated national politics. The Arias brothers had made their wealth in the countryside, and they were mestizos, making them outsiders to the elite families. Harmodio (1886–1963) had studied at the London School of Economics, and Arnulfo (1901–88) was trained in medicine at Harvard. Harmodio served as president (1932–36) and was succeeded by a member of the Arosemena family. Arnulfo was elected president in 1940 and his staunch nationalistic programs, appeals to the masses, vocal anti-United States and profascist positions transformed national politics. (Arnulfo was known throughout Panama as "El Hombre.") His appeals to *panameñismo* (Panamanianism) mobilized the masses around the call for social reforms and control over the nation's destiny (i.e., the Canal).

The National Guard (really a national police force) deposed Arnulfo Arias in 1941 and emerged as a powerful force in politics thereafter. The commander of the Guard in the 1940s, José Antonio Remón, dominated politics until his assassination in 1955. From 1956 to 1968, three successive elected presidents served and peacefully handed over power to their successor. Once again the elite families produced the presidents (Guardia, Chiari, Robles Méndez). At the same time, the tensions between the United States and Panama increased. After student-led demonstrations (the so-called Flag Riots) in 1964 left two dozen dead, serious talks began under President Lyndon Johnson to renegotiate the status of the Canal Zone. The return of Arnulfo Arias, and his large electoral victory in 1968, however, produced a quick reaction from the National Guard, who deposed Arias during his second week in office. (Arias, with his broad appeal among the Panamanian masses, would remain a force in national politics until his death in 1988.) Very quickly, Colonel Omar Torrijos (b. 1929) emerged as the leader in the new regime.

Torrijos was a personalistic populist who ruled by force and by offering social reforms to the masses (land reform, in particular). He also made Panama into an offshore banking haven. Torrijos, ever the master of public relations, managed to negotiate a new set of canal treaties with the United States and, after bitter and contentious debates, the treaties were approved by the narrowest of margins in the United States Senate in 1978. Thus began a two-decade process of gradually returning control of the Canal Zone to Panama, a process completed on December 31, 1999. Torrijos, however, would not live to see this final transfer of control. He died in a plane crash in 1981, and, for the rest of the decade, Manuel Antonio Noriega would control the National Guard and the country. Noriega became involved in the Colombian drug trade, arms trafficking to rebels in El Salvador (fighting the United States) and in Nicaragua (fighting for the United States), and he was on the payroll of the Central Intelligence Agency and the U.S. Army as an informer. In December 1989, after a long and contentious war of words between Noriega and the Reagan and Bush administrations, the United States sent 12,000 troops into Panama ("Operation Just Cause"), destroying several neighborhoods in Panama City, and capturing Noriega. (He was later taken to Miami, convicted on drug trafficking charges, and has been in prison ever since.) The United States, once again, took Panama.

Since 1989, Panama has experienced contentious, fragmented, and scandal-plagued politics. Elected months before the invasion, but denied power by Noriega, Guillermo Endara (b. 1936) took over in the aftermath of the overthrow of Noriega. Endara had helped form the Arnulfista Party after the death of Arnulfo Arias. In a highly partisan and fragmented election in 1994, Ernesto Pérez Balladares, a banker, won the election with just one-third of the vote. Mireya Moscoso, the widow of Arnulfo Arias, came in second with 25 percent of the vote. Moscoso won the presidency in 1999—becoming the first female president of Panama—but left office in 2004 amidst corruption scandals. Martín Torrijos (b. 1963), the son of Omar, defeated Guillermo Endara in the elections of 2004, winning 47 percent of the vote. Torrijos has made ambitious plans to construct a new canal that will accommodate the enormous supertankers that are too wide for the old canal. In the early twentieth century, Panama's politics and destiny remained tied to its strategic geographic position as the transit point between the Atlantic and the Pacific. Spain, Britain, France, and then the United States all shaped Panama's past through their interest in controlling that transit. In this century, China and Japan will also play a key role in shaping Panama's future.

Puerto Rico

Neither a colony nor a nation, Puerto Rico is unlike any other region of Latin America. By any standard—other than national political sovereignty—Puerto Rico has been a part of Latin America since the moment of creation in the early sixteenth century. One of the first Spanish colonial outposts in the Americas, it was also one of the last. After the conquest of Cuba, and then Mexico and Peru (in the 1530s and 1540s), Puerto Rico's principal role in the empire was to serve as a strategic military garrison protecting the Caribbean shipping lanes, the lifelines of the Spanish Empire in the New World. In the early nineteenth century, it had a population of just over 100,000 and a small but thriving sugar plantation economy. Morro Castle looming above San Juan on the northern coast of the island formed one part of the ring of Spanish fortifications around the Caribbean basin in Havana, Cartagena, Portobelo (Panama).

Like Cuba, Puerto Rico remained under Spanish political control, and came under increasing U.S. economic hegemony, after the wars for independence on the American mainland. (By the 1820s, the United States was purchasing all of Puerto Rico's sugar exports.) Slave rebellions and creole revolts against Spain periodically shook the island throughout the nineteenth century. (Slavery was finally abolished in 1873.) The most famous of the creole revolts broke out in 1868, led by Ramón Betances. On September 23, the rebels issued their manifesto for independence in the small town of Lares (hence the declaration is known as the *Grito*, or Cry, of Lares). The rebellion was quickly crushed, but pressure steadily increased on Spain to extend greater autonomy to the colony. In 1898, Spain finally conceded this autonomy, allowing Puerto Ricans to create a legislature, vote by secret ballot, and send representatives to the Spanish parliament. Elected governor general, Luis Muñoz Rivera (1859–1916), was scheduled to assume office in May 1898. In early 1898, however, the intervention of the United States into the Cuban war against Spanish control abruptly ended this stillborn move to autonomy. In early May 1898, the United States bombarded San Juan (and the Morro Castle), occupied the island, and seized control of it in the treaty that ended the Spanish American War.

Since 1898, the legal status of Puerto Rico has evolved, but remains unresolved. The Foraker Act (of the U.S. Congress) in 1900 granted Puerto Ricans the ability to create an elected chamber of deputies, but made clear that the island would remain under the control of the United States (similar to the Philippines, Hawaii, Guam, and other territories). The Jones-Shafroth Act in 1917 made (the roughly one million) Puerto Ricans citizens of the United States. The island's population was largely racially mixed, 80 percent rural, and the principal exports were sugar and coffee. Puerto Rico looked very much like other Caribbean islands or Central American nations. Nearly 60 percent of the island's wealth was controlled by three powerful United States-based sugar corporations. A key difference was the ability of Puerto Ricans, as U.S. citizens, to move more freely between the island and the North American mainland. After the Second World War, a growing and vibrant Puerto Rican community began to take shape in the United States, especially in the New York City metropolitan area.

On the island, three separate political movements and options gradually emerged—those supporting independence, statehood, or some sort of intermediary status. In 1938, Luis Muñoz Marín (the son of Luis Muñoz Rivera) founded the Popular Democratic Party (PPD), and he would dominate Puerto Rican politics for the next three decades. Muñoz Marín and the PPD pursued reformist policies to increase Puerto Rican autonomy and to promote economic development. Pedro Albizu Campos (1893–1965) emerged as the leader of the Puerto Rican Nationalist Party, seeking independence through the legislative process and armed uprisings. President Harry Truman appointed the first Puerto Rican-born governor in 1947 and, in 1948, Luis Muñoz Marín (1898–1980) became the first elected governor (serving from 1949–65). Public Law 600 paved the way for the writing of a constitution, and the creation of the commonwealth of Puerto Rico on July 25, 1952 (commonwealth was translated into Spanish as *Estado Libre Asociado*, or Associated Free State). In the 1950s, "Operation Bootstrap" actively and aggressively sought investment in Puerto Rico to promote industrialization (much like the efforts of southern U.S. states in recent decades). The island experienced a dramatic transformation. Per capita income rose from $121 in 1940 to $900 in 1965, and literacy rose from 60 to 85 percent. By the 1970s, the industrial surge had waned, however, and immigration to the mainland increased.

Since the 1960s, the legal status of Puerto Rico has formed the backdrop of all politics. Muñoz Marín's PPD has long supported the status quo (commonwealth), the New Progressive Party (PNP) has supported a move to statehood, and the Puerto Rican Independence Party (PIP) has long advocated full independence. In 1950, two nationalists tried to assassinate President Truman, and in 1954, four nationalists opened fire with automatic pistols from the visitors gallery during a session of the U.S. House of Representatives. (Most of them spent the next quarter-century in federal prisons until their pardon by President Jimmy Carter in 1979.) In 1967, 1993, and 1998, plebiscites in Puerto Rico have resulted in votes in favor of maintaining the status quo. To some extent, the two main political parties have become proxies for the two principal positions—of statehood (the PNP, closely associated with the Republican Party) and the status quo (the PDP, closely associated with the Democratic Party). Throughout much of the last four decades, most elections and opinion polls show a clear pattern in Puerto Rico with about 48 percent in favor of statehood, 48 percent in favor of the status quo, and a small percentage in favor of independence.

The four million Puerto Ricans on the island and the three million on the U.S. mainland, then, are the most unusual Latin Americans—they are both a part of the United States (as citizens), but culturally and linguistically part of Latin America. Puerto Rico has autonomy in its internal affairs, yet it is part of the U.S. economy. Puerto Ricans (on the island) cannot vote in presidential elections (much like residents of Washington D.C.), but those on the mainland can. They pay federal payroll taxes, but not a federal income tax. They receive many of the social and welfare benefits that citizens receive on the mainland, but not all. Per capita GDP in Puerto Rico today is approaching $19,000 per year, a figure that is nearly double that of Mexico or Chile or Costa Rica ($10,000–11,000)—the countries with the highest figures in Latin America. With high levels of literacy, health care services, education, and bilingualism, Puerto Rico is simultaneously a poor U.S. state, and a very developed Latin American nation.

BETWEEN REFORM AND REVOLUTION

This brief survey of eleven nations (and one "free associated state") highlights the enormous diversity of political paths in Latin America over the last century. It should be apparent that the path of a continental nation like Brazil, with its enormous resources and population, has been and will continue to be very different than the past and future of a Haiti or a Honduras. At the same time, the challenges facing Panama or Puerto Rico are worlds apart from those of Venezuela or Peru. As the next chapter will show, the economic paths and destinies of the various parts of Latin America also highlight a great diversity within the region. Yet, despite this range of paths, it is still possible (at least for now) to speak of patterns and commonalities that bind the region together.

Whether a massive social revolution in Mexico or Cuba, a long history of authoritarianism in Paraguay or Haiti, or long histories of gradual reform in Costa Rica or Chile, all of Latin America continues to bear the burdens of history—its colonial legacy. In some countries that burden remains heavy, and in others, much of the colonial legacy has been transformed fundamentally over the centuries. The colonial legacy of large landed estates, a largely non-European labor force compelled to work for a small elite, corporatist and hierarchical social and political structures, and the often embittered collision of peoples will always form the core of the identities of Latin American peoples. These four chapters on politics have shown the many ways Latin Americans have confronted, challenged, and transformed that burdensome colonial legacy. They have created twenty-one distinct paths, yet each has its roots in a common past.

23

Poverty and Progress

THE STRUGGLE FOR DEVELOPMENT

One of the hard lessons social scientists and policy-makers have learned over the last half-century is that political and economic development must take place in tandem for nations to prosper and move forward. Democratic, representative politics may collapse into chaos if they are not built on a strong, sustainable economic base. Conversely, a strong and dynamic economy does not guarantee the development of democratic, representative politics. The most successful countries in modern history are those nations that have managed to promote and sustain economic and political development—together—over long periods. In Latin America, the pursuit of democratic, representative politics has been fraught with perils. The pursuit of economic development has presented even greater challenges than democratization for most of the region.

Without a doubt, the single most striking feature of Latin America is the enormous poverty amidst such great wealth. To return to one of the central themes of this book, Latin America is a rich region filled with enormous numbers of poor people. In many ways, the central question in the history of the region has been: How have these staggering inequalities taken shape and persisted? The central challenge for nearly all Latin Americans is: How can we reduce these inequalities? Economic and political theorists of all persuasions for the last two hundred years have offered a dazzling variety of explanations and solutions to these two fundamental questions and the answers remain controversial and elusive. Much of the blood that has been spilled, and the political struggles of the last century, arose out of the clashes between groups with contending views of how to deal with these questions and the solutions they proposed.

During the centuries of colonial rule, the Iberian monarchies chose to isolate, exploit, and control the resources and people of the region, all for the benefit of the underdeveloped economies of Spain and Portugal (and, to a lesser extent, France). In the early decades after independence, one important facet of the struggle between Liberals and Conservatives was how slow or how fast to integrate Latin America into the emerging industrial capitalism of the North Atlantic world. Economic historians in recent years have made persuasive arguments that the enormous gap between Latin America and the developed world first emerged in the eighteenth century and widened significantly in the nineteenth century. In effect, Latin America "fell behind" during the troubled decades between 1810 and 1870. The triumph of the Liberals in the late nineteenth century led them to try to integrate their nations into the Atlantic commercial and industrial world as quickly as possible through the export of agricultural commodities and raw materials. In the early twentieth century, socialism emerged as a serious alternative to the capitalist model, but (with the partial exception of Mexico) socialists were unable to achieve power to pursue the countercapitalist option. In the aftermath of the Great Depression, in nearly all the countries of Latin America, governments employed the tactics of "managed" capitalism. In the last half of the twentieth century, many of the reformist, and most of the revolutionary, movements in the region offered powerful socialist challenges to the capitalist economic model. The driving force behind the radical challenges to the capitalist model was the powerful desire to remedy the social and economic problems of the region, and the belief that centuries of capitalism had created those problems.

Throughout the last century, the high levels of inequality in Latin America have been persistent and fairly stable. Created out of the collision of cultures during the Conquest, the patterns have largely survived through colonial rule, monarchy, republics, dictatorships, and democratic governments. In the two centuries since independence in the early nineteenth century, Latin America has grown from some 15–18 million inhabitants to more than 500 million today. Despite the industrialization in some countries (in particular, Brazil and Mexico) and economic growth across much of the region, one-quarter of all Latin Americans live on less than $2 a day. By some definitions, nearly 40 percent of Latin Americans live in poverty. The richest 10 percent of the population controls 30–45 percent of all household income while the poorest 40 percent receives just 10–20 percent. Despite decades of economic "progress" in many (but not all) countries of the region, poverty and inequality continue to define Latin America. According to several World Bank studies, Latin America has the highest income inequalities in the world, rivaled only by a few desperately poor countries in sub-Saharan Africa. It should not be surprising that many governments in Latin America in the twentieth century intervened aggressively to promote national economic development. Since the 1930s, all political leaders in Latin America have been compelled to address the pressing economic needs of their societies.

NATIONALISM AND STATE INTERVENTION

As we saw in chapter 15, the Liberal triumph in the last quarter of the nineteenth century definitively moved nearly all of Latin America into the commercial and industrial economy of the North Atlantic world. In the words of economists, the Liberal leaders "inserted" their economies into the dynamic, industrial, capitalistic economic system dominated by Europe (primarily England) and the United States. Desperately in search of economic growth and tax revenue, the Liberals turned (quite logically) to what economists call their "comparative advantage"—the fruits of the land. The Latin American nations could not, by any stretch of the imagination, embark upon a process of industrialization to compete with the already industrialized (and industrializing) North Atlantic economies. They could produce and provide agricultural goods and raw materials for those economies. Between the 1870s and the 1920s, most of Latin America developed highly productive mining and agricultural sectors that exported the goods that most people probably tend to associate with the region: coffee, bananas, sugar, chocolate, copper, tin, silver, oil, and beef.

A new wave of foreign investment, primarily from Great Britain and the United States, financed the intense development of the plantations, ranches, and mines of Latin America. U.S. investment predominated in Mexico, Central America, and the Caribbean. British capital prevailed in South America, especially in Brazil and Argentina, the two largest economies of the region. Foreign capital brought economic and technological "modernity" and financed the Second Conquest, fully "integrating" the peoples of the interior of Latin America into the Western world and its economic system. By the 1920s, the larger economies of Latin America–Brazil, Argentina, Mexico—had begun to develop some industry around major cities, especially the capital cities. This industry was, at times, a spin-off from the export economy. The new wealth from coffee and beef, for example, created more jobs and demand for more consumer goods. Typically, the first wave of industrialization entailed the rise of textiles, food processing, wood and metal working—largely to supply consumer goods for the growing urban populations and the growing middle class. Yet, even in 1900, 75 percent of all Latin Americans still lived in the countryside, 70 percent were illiterate, life expectancy was 40 years, and industry accounted for just 5 percent of the GDP of the region.

In the 1920s, after nearly a half-century of this "outward-oriented" growth, it appeared to many that the agro/minerals export model was Latin America's destiny and its future. Prices for sugar, coffee, and copper, for example, reached record highs in the 1920s. In Cuba, for example, the sugar economy reached phenomenal highs in the early 1920s and those controlling the sugar plantations and the export sector engaged in the "dance of the millions" as their revenues reached unthinkable heights. Although signs of overproduction and periodic crises had already appeared in the early twentieth century, coffee prices had rebounded and revenues were strong and growing in the 1920s, good news (seemingly) for Brazil, Colombia, and Central America. By the 1920s, the export economies of Latin America had already experienced the ups and downs of rising and falling commodity prices for several decades. They were acutely aware of their dependence on foreign markets, foreign capital, tax revenues generated by exports, and the vulnerability of their economies. Even in small countries like Costa Rica, the political and economic elites had experimented with economic diversification, but that usually meant planting other crops or seeking out other mineral resources that could generate export revenues in the event of the decline in coffee prices. Probably most economic policymakers in the 1920s remained firmly convinced that Latin America would remain raw materials and agro-exporters, exploiting their comparative advantage well into the future. They had experienced the severe world economic downturns in the 1870s and 1890s, but had survived them.

The great watershed for Latin American economies, indeed, for all the economies of the Western world, was the Great Depression that spread like a plague across the capitalist world beginning in 1929 and 1930. The greatest economic crisis in modern history, the Depression severely shocked the capitalist economies of the Atlantic world, and not until the industrial escalation needed for fighting the Second World War (1939–45) would the Western world finally return to economic expansion. In the United States, nearly 40 percent of the workforce was unemployed, and industry in Europe and the United States virtually ground to a halt. The severity of the crisis in Europe fueled the rise of fascism in Italy, Nazism in Germany, and very strong government intervention in the economies of Scandinavia and northwestern Europe. In the United States, the Depression brought Franklin D. Roosevelt to office for an unprecedented four terms (1933–45). Governments turned to economic protectionism and high tariffs to survive. As demand dropped dramatically, and as nations closed their ports to foreign goods, the shock waves crippled the economies of Latin America—these economies that had become so dependent on the markets of the North Atlantic world. Consumers in the United States and Europe could survive with less coffee, sugar, bananas, chocolate, and beef, and industry required less copper and tin.

The experience of Brazil is illustrative of the path of the larger economies in the first half of the twentieth century. Brazil, like tiny Costa Rica, had become one of the world's great coffee exporters in the mid-nineteenth century. Despite Brazil's overwhelming reliance on coffee exports (accounting for as much as 90 percent of the value of all exports in some years in the nineteenth century), rather than falling into an inescapable form of economic dependency, the coffee economy generated what economists like to call "spread effects" and "linkages." Entrepreneurs reinvested profits from coffee into banking, commerce, and industry, stimulating the growth of various sectors of the economy. Many of the early industrial entrepreneurs came from landholding families, and the foreign immigrants attracted to southeastern Brazil played a fundamental and catalytic role in the origins of industrialization. Coffee also helped expand the use of free wage labor and the growth of a domestic market.

Until the twentieth century, the Brazilian government normally intervened to protect coffee interests and agriculture, not to foster the creation of new industry. In the nineteenth century, the interests of landowners and those tied to the export agriculture economy took precedence over the interests of the tiny industrial sector. Foreign manufactured goods, principally British manufactures, dominated the Brazilian market. The British could mass-produce cheap, quality goods and ship them around the globe, and still undersell local producers. The enormous advantages from "economies of scale" and the political backing of their government helped the British sweep away local competition. In spite of the tremendous competitive pressures from foreigners, domestic producers survived and grew, albeit slowly and in limited sectors of the economy. Throughout the nineteenth century, Brazilian manufacturing grew slowly, producing goods for consumption in local and regional markets: textiles and clothing, iron, furniture, and processed foodstuffs. In these areas, principally what economists call nondurable consumer goods, local producers retained something of an advantage over foreigners. These goods could be produced with relatively simple technology, in cottage industries, and to satisfy markets (especially in the interior) that were not easily accessible from major ports. By the end of the nineteenth century, Brazil had a small, but growing, industrial base.

Most of this production developed in the southeast. The industrial growth in the cities of Rio de Janeiro and São Paulo easily overshadowed the industrial growth in all other regions of the country. As the national capital and principal port, Rio de Janeiro became the logical location for early industry. By 1890, the city had a population of more than a half a million inhabitants, a considerable consumer market. The spectacular growth of the city of São Paulo, and its emergence as the largest industrial center in the Third World, could not have been predicted by anyone in the nineteenth century. A rustic town just over the high coastal escarpment, São Paulo had fewer than 30,000 inhabitants in the 1850s. With the expansion of coffee cultivation into the surrounding hinterland in the late nineteenth century, the city became a dynamic and booming entrepôt, connected to the port of Santos by a railway. Between 1890 and 1900 the city's population grew from about 70,000 to nearly 240,000. Much like Buenos Aires and Montevideo, tens of thousands of immigrants—Italians, Germans, and many others—flooded into the city and the state. The entrepreneurial talents of coffee planters, Brazilian industrialists, and immigrants transformed the city, creating a dynamic pole of industrial growth. By the 1930s, the state of São Paulo had become the most populous in Brazil, the city of São Paulo had a population over a million, and it moved past Rio de Janeiro as the most important industrial center in the nation.

Brazil's industrialists benefited somewhat from the disruptions that World War I produced in the western economy. The war disrupted the normal trade flows from the North Atlantic, making it difficult for manufacturers to import essential technology. The scarcity of imports helped local producers of consumer goods who expanded output of textiles, clothing, shoes, and processed foods. The war also demonstrated to many of the elite the nation's economic vulnerability. They could see how dependent their economy was on European markets for Brazil's coffee, and how much they depended on European and North American imports. (The smaller economies in Latin America were not as well positioned to develop this local industry and the closing of European markets during the war was a rude shock.)

In the 1920s, the Brazilian economy continued to expand and diversify, but its dynamism still hinged on coffee exports. In the mid-twenties, coffee accounted for three-quarters of the value of all exports, and nearly 10 percent of the gross domestic product. The political elite carefully protected the coffee economy. Confronting a glutted world market, the government set up a price-support system to buy excess production. The government hoped that this interventionist measure would be temporary, keeping producers in business during low-price periods, driving up prices by keeping supplies off the market. The coffee "valorization" plan forced the government into deficit spending, external borrowing to finance it, and ultimately failed. Overproduction was not a temporary phenomenon, and many of the stocks had to be destroyed rather than eventually placed on the market.

The Great Depression sent powerful shock waves through the Brazilian economy and forced the elites to rethink and reorient economic policies. Between 1929 and 1932, the value of exports dropped by 60 percent as world trade nosedived. The influx of foreign capital halted and essentially forced Brazil to suspend payments in 1931 on more than $1.3 billion in external debt. As in the United States, the shattering economic effects of the Depression forced the government to take interventionist measures that had been unthinkable just a few years earlier. Although the first impulse of political leaders was to prop up and protect the coffee economy, the 1930s do begin a shift toward increasingly supportive moves to stimulate and develop domestic industry. The movement toward economic diversification built on industrialization using government intervention begins in these years across nearly all of Latin America. For the first time, the government made important efforts at economic planning and a systematic assessment of the state of the economy. Policy-makers resorted constantly to tinkering with all the fiscal and monetary measures at their disposal, creating new agencies and mechanisms for intervention. Just as in the United States and Europe, "priming the pump" with interventionist economic policies became standard procedure.

As the head of state from 1930 to 1945, Getúlio Vargas played a central role in the new interventionism. Vargas, however, was a reluctant interventionist who kept one foot in the old liberal school of economic theory. Although many of the measures taken by the Vargas governments during these years stimulated industrial production, much of the resulting industrial expansion came as side effects of policies that did not directly aim at stimulating domestic industry. This has been called "spontaneous import-substitution industrialization," as compared with the more managed and directed efforts to substitute imports with domestic production in the post-World War II period. By the end of the war, Brazil imported just 20 percent of its industrial products, with domestic industry producing 80 percent of national needs. In the area of light consumer durables such as furniture, household goods, and clothes, national industry supplied close to 100 percent of domestic demand. As goods produced by domestic industry gradually replaced previously consumed foreign manufactures, Brazil's balance of payments picture improved. Fewer imports and growing exports produced a positive balance of payments and allowed the government to build up a substantial surplus of foreign exchange reserves. By 1945, Brazil's economy had become more diversified and industrialized, but it remained heavily dependent on agricultural exports. The agricultural sector accounted for 28 percent of the gross national product (versus 20 percent for the industrial sector) and more than *60 percent* of the economically active population still worked in agriculture. Agricultural exports (coffee, sugar, cocoa, cotton, tobacco) still accounted for the bulk of Brazil's exports.

DEVELOPMENTALISM AND INDUSTRIALIZATION

Despite being the largest country in Latin America, Brazil's experience was emblematic of the other countries in the region from the 1920s to the

1940s. Mexico, Argentina, Colombia, and Chile followed a very similar pattern, and even the smaller, more agrarian nations of South and Central America reacted to the shock of the Depression with new forms of government interventionism. (In much of Central America and the Caribbean, the dictatorships of the Somozas, Trujillo, Batista and the like, made the intervention more personalistic than institutional. These economies also remained extremely dependent on agro/mineral exports and, in some cases, on one primary export such as coffee, bananas, sugar, oil, or tin.) By the late 1940s, policy-makers in many Latin America nations (especially the larger countries) recognized that future economic growth hinged on increased dynamism in the industrial sector, and less dependence on agricultural exports and industrial imports. They sought to change the nature of their economies by consciously promoting "import-substitution industrialization" (ISI). After 1945, economic policy-makers in nearly all of Latin America pursued these goals, albeit with very diverse approaches and ideological agendas. The drive to industrialize has often transcended divisions among political parties and regimes. In the late 1940s, the creation of the United Nations Economic Commission on Latin America (ECLA) gave rise to a very influential critique of the economies of the region, and promoted a vision of interventionism to break from the old formula of exporting commodities and importing manufactured goods.

In the 1950s, the move toward state intervention to promote industrialization and economic growth crystallized. Many of the Latin American elites shared this mentality, known as developmentalism. They often disagreed violently on how to achieve development, but virtually all elite groups believed that the region's future depended on the promotion of industrialization. The debate over the extent of government intervention in the economy became an issue that bitterly divided groups in many nations. In general, those to the Left in politics favored more nationalistic, protectionist, and interventionist policies, while those to the political Right favored more traditional laissez-faire approaches to industrial promotion. (At times, very right-wing military officers also promoted the nationalistic, protectionist, and interventionist policies, most notably in Brazil from 1964–85.) Throughout the 1950s and early 1960s, nationalism and interventionism prevailed among many politicians and policy-makers. Across Latin America, governments formed state-controlled enterprises to manage key sectors of the economy. The principal targets were public utilities, petroleum, mining, iron and steel, and transportation networks. Many major enterprises (such as iron, steel, automobiles) became joint ventures between public and private (multinational) investment.

Economic nationalism, state intervention, planning by technocrats, and foreign investment all converged to produce very high economic and industrial growth rates. From the Second World War until the oil shocks of the mid-1970s, Latin America grew at a faster rate than any other region in the world—at an annual rate of more than 5 percent. Again, Brazil is the outstanding example of this pattern. From 1940 to 1980, the Brazilian economy grew at a rate of 7 percent a year. Not only did the gross domestic product grow, real GDP per capita quintupled in the same period, one of the highest rates of growth in the world during these four decades. President Juscelino Kubitschek (1956–61)—a brilliant political improvisor—juggled the interests and methods of both Left and Right to pursue his plan of moving Brazil forward "fifty years in five." Kubitschek placed technocrats and planners in positions of power in his administration. As soon as he took office, he created a National Development Council, and his technocrats issued a "Target Program" (*Programa de Metas*). The program identified key sectors of the economy and set growth targets for both government and the private sector.

Under Kubitschek in the late fifties, overall industrial production rose by 80 percent, while in several key industries (steel, mechanical, electrical and communications, and transportation equipment) growth rates ranged from 100 to 600 percent. Brazil moved dramatically from being mainly a producer of nondurable consumer goods toward the goal of producing its own intermediate and capital goods. By 1960, manufacturing accounted for a greater share (28 percent) of the GDP than agriculture. Even when adjusted for an annual population growth rate of 3 percent, Brazil's per capita real growth in the 1950s was about three times that of the rest of Latin America in a period when the region had the highest growth rates in the developing world. Brazilian industry in the early sixties supplied nearly 100 percent of the country's consumer goods, about 90 percent of its intermediate goods, and close to 90 percent of its capital goods.

Although they did not achieve results as spectacular as Brazil's, other countries in the region (especially the larger ones—Argentina, Mexico, Colombia) pursued similar policies. This state-led process of industrialization transformed institutions and infrastructure, and promoted urbanization and the growth of the middle and working classes. It helped create an industrial sector and business interests tied to industrialization. Unfortunately, the policies of Kubitschek, and others like him, tended to avoid the hard issues. Industrial promotion tried to finesse the structures of power and inequality through economic growth that would gradually alleviate the problems of the past. ISI did not challenge the traditional prerogatives of the landed class or the other powerful groups in society and did not impose direct taxes on them. Furthermore, the capital intensive nature of industrialization did not produce jobs rapidly enough to accommodate the massive movement of peoples from rural to urban areas, and did virtually nothing to address income inequalities.

Kubitschek's expansionary program, however, clearly exposed the Achilles heel of this pattern of interventionism. It was primarily financed through deficit spending, and government debt was often financed by printing more currency and foreign borrowing, both inflation-generating measures. By 1960, inflation rates had passed 20 percent per annum in Brazil and the nation faced a severe balance of payments crisis. International lenders and lending agencies pressured Kubitschek to impose an economic austerity program to lower inflation, cut imports, expand exports, and cut government spending. Brazil's external debt had reached (for then) record levels by the mid-1960s: $2.5 billion. By the 1960s, the ISI model had reached its limits, in Brazil and elsewhere in Latin America. It had helped foster impressive economic growth, a larger urban, middle and working class, but built upon a protected, and increasingly limited, national industrial base.

One of the most interesting and unusual cases of ISI is tiny Puerto Rico. In a project that became known as "Operation Bootstrap," Puerto Rico embarked in the 1950s on something of a unique version of ISI. As a "free associated state" and a part of the United States, Puerto Rico sought to industrialize by attracting firms to the island with the incentives of very cheap labor and tax breaks. Because of its unusual political status, these companies were, in a sense, foreign corporations, but also domestic (U.S.) enterprises. Puerto Rico became a powerful magnet for industrial operations in the 1950s and 1960s, but the process of industrialization did not create as many jobs as expected, as was common across Latin America. In the case of Puerto Rico, this led to the growth of migration to the United States (especially the greater New York City area). It was an odd version of the later failure of ISI to produce adequate employment in Mexico and Central America, leading to (illegal) migration into the United States. Unlike the effects it had in the rest of Latin America, this industrialization in Puerto Rico led to a "domestic" industrial sector dominated (nearly 100 percent) by core industries controlled by non-Puerto Ricans.

THE IDEOLOGY OF THE FREE MARKET

The two great waves of economic expansion in Latin America—from the 1850s to the 1920s and from the 1940s to the 1970s—have both been followed by periods of severe recessions and policy transitions. In the 1930s, the recession was an enormous one, the Great Depression, and the policy transition moved the countries of the region into a half-century of protectionism, government interventionism, and ISI. The oil shocks of the 1970s and the debt crisis of the 1980s produced another devastating period of rolling recessions, and the policy transition moved Latin America from government interventionism, ISI, and protectionism into a neoliberal economic model of trade liberalization, privatization, and a reduced role for government. (Again, liberalism is used here in its classic meaning—as a belief in free markets and minimal government intervention in the market-place, what in the United States is seen, ironically, as conservatism.) As with the earlier phase of interventionism, not all the countries of the region have fully adopted the new model. Across the region, countries have opted for a variety of paths along the spectrum between full-scale neoliberalism and the old interventionism. Chile has moved most dramatically toward an open, privatized economy with a downsized role for the state. Some of the Andean nations (Venezuela, Bolivia, and Peru, in particular) have been increasingly resistant to the neoliberal shift. (Cuba, of course, remains the most protected and statist economy in the Americas with Fidel Castro's continuing commitment to his own version of socialism.)

A series of events in Latin America, the United States, and the rest of the world propelled the shift from ISI to neoliberalism from the early 1970s to the late 1980s. Already by the late 1960s, a number of scholars and policy-makers had begun to question the continuing viability of the ISI model. As democratic regimes collapsed in Brazil (1964), Argentina (1966), Uruguay (1973), and Chile (1973), scholars on the Left and the Right, at times, agreed that a momentous shift had begun to take place in the political economy of Latin America. For some, ISI had reached the limits of growth and expansion, and the regime crises were the result of the exhaustion of an economic model and social crises produced by the inability of ISI to continue to move forward with economic growth. Many, on both the Right and Left, called for even greater interventionism—for authoritarian regimes that would guide the next stage of industrialization. Ironically, they believed that even greater government intervention—minus the political dissent and debate characteristic of liberal democracies—was the only way to combat the growing power of multinational corporations and the world market. In a sense, the bureaucratic-authoritarian military regimes of the 1960s and 1970s represented the last gasp of many Latin American nations to resist through strong state intervention what we now glibly refer to as globalization.

Despite what appeared to be impressive economic growth in some countries in the late 1960s and early 1970s, oil and massive debt would bring down the military regimes, discredit government interventionism, and help fuel the rise of neoliberalism. Again, Brazil is the most dramatic example of these trends. Under a dictatorial regime after 1964, the nation experienced a spectacular industrial spurt that became known as the Brazilian "miracle." In the early 1950s, Brazil's economy was the 50th largest in the world. By the late 1970s, it had become the tenth largest. Under the military, the Brazilian economy initially stagnated, then experienced an unprecedented boom, followed by continued high growth accompanied by growing problems, and then slipped into a prolonged crisis. As Brazil rode this economic roller coaster, the generals loudly proclaimed their faith in capitalism while continually extending the role of the state in the economy. The nationalistic right-wing generals created the most statist economy in the noncommunist world. By the 1980s, the state accounted for more than 60 percent of Brazil's gross domestic product.

From 1967 to 1973, the spectacular growth of Brazil truly seemed "miraculous" to many observers. In addition to the very high growth rates (averaging nearly 11 percent per year), dropping inflation rates (to around 17 percent per year), and continually rising domestic demand and output, the traditional problem with the balance of payments seemed to have been solved. In 1969, Brazilian banks had accumulated about $650 million of foreign exchange holdings. This amount grew by a factor of ten by 1973 to nearly $6.5 billion, a phenomenal increase. Export promotion dramatically increased the total value of exports from $2.7 billion in 1970 to $7 billion in 1973. The influx of foreign capital that had come to a virtual halt in 1964 surpassed $4 billion in 1973. Then the oil shocks of 1973 and 1979 rocked the world economy.

With the outbreak of the Arab-Israeli conflict in 1973 and the Iran-Iraq War in 1979, world oil prices skyrocketed, more than quadrupling in 1973–74 (from $3 to $12 per barrel) and more than threefold in 1979–80 (from $13 to $40). The economies of Latin America and the rest of the world had two choices: buy less oil, reduce consumption, and go into recession, or keep buying the oil and pay the higher prices. Most countries, including most of Europe and the United States, followed the first path and went into a series of economic recessions in the late 1970s and early 1980s. Some small Latin American countries (Costa Rica, for example) could not stop importing oil completely, and they began to run up large trade deficits. (Costa Rica imports 100 percent of its petroleum needs.) Ironically, the steep price increases created an enormous capital flow into the oil-producing nations, who then deposited these "petrodollars" into international banks, which then "recycled" them as loans (which is, after all, the basic function of a bank). Suddenly, bankers were offering very cheap loans to all takers. Some Latin American countries (unwisely) resolved their deficit problems with this easy money. Mexico and Venezuela (huge oil producers) suddenly found themselves awash in oil revenue and embarked on impressive spending programs that exceeded even their own revenues and were financed with massive credit. (After all, many reasoned, Mexico and Venezuela had oil and that would always provide the collateral to pay back the loans.) Brazil, alone of all the non-oil-producing nations in Latin America, chose to borrow its way through the 1973–74 and the 1979–80 crises. Brazil's foreign debt rose from less than $5 billion in 1970 to nearly $100 billion by 1980. Between 1979 and 1982, Latin American total external debt escalated rapidly from $184 to $314 billon.

To the great disillusionment of the Mexicans and the Venezuelans, the price of oil did drop dramatically by the early 1980s from the historic highs, leaving them with much smaller revenue streams and massive foreign debt. At the same time, international interest rates rose substantially in 1980–81 (to 16–20 percent on bank loans) as the United States went through a recession. Nearly all of Latin America had accumulated large foreign debts (from the bankers gladly handing out cheap petrodollar loans), and the rising interest rates now made those loans (and interest payments) drastically more expensive. In late 1982, Mexico initiated a chain reaction that became the debt crisis of the decade. Rising interest rates, still-high oil prices, falling prices for Latin American export commodities, and the rash lending effectively made most Latin American nations insolvent. They simply did not have the cash (dollar) reserves to pay the banks. Many of the leading international banks had seriously overextended themselves, lending over $70 billion to Latin America, or more than 100 percent of their own equity! Over the next decade, the international banks, multilateral lending agencies (such as the World Bank) and Latin American governments were locked into constant negotiations and re-negotiations of hundreds of billions of dollars of loans. (Only in Colombia, where politicians and policymakers had exhibited calm and restraint in the 1970s, was the true brunt of the debt crisis avoided.)

Hundreds of creditor banks gathered together in a cartel to confront the crisis and renegotiate hundreds of loans. The International Monetary Fund and the World Bank (both set up in the aftermath of World War II) became the principal intermediaries pressuring governments to put their finances in order. The solution was simple and simplistic, a recipe for all countries regardless of local conditions: cut imports, export more, cut the government's budget, and use the resulting surpluses to pay down the debt. Unfortunately, the world recession and low commodity prices made it difficult to accelerate exports, putting more pressure on governments to reduce spending and cut imports. With such massive debt, international lenders shut down the flow of capital and billions of dollars of capital streamed out of the region, starving Latin American countries of new resources. The effects were devastating across the region. Real wages declined, government social expenditures dropped, unemployment and poverty rose, and many Latin Americans were forced into the increasingly large "informal" sector of the economy (i.e., outside formal employment, doing everything from washing cars on the street to selling cigarettes on street corners).

The oil shocks and debt crisis helped discredit the military regimes that had promised economic development and security from leftist revolutionaries in the 1970s. The economic crisis hastened the process of redemocratization from Mexico to Argentina and Brazil. The generals in Brazil and

Argentina, for example, could no longer claim to have a formula for economic growth that was somehow better than the plans of civilian politicians. The military regimes had also effectively crushed nearly all the leftist revolutionary movements in the region. The need to have a strong military to crush leftist subversion had become much less persuasive by the mid-1980s. Finally, the collapse of the Soviet bloc—and the Soviet Union itself—in the late 1980s and early 1990s effectively moved Latin America into a new era of geopolitics. As we have already seen, all across Latin America in the 1980s, grassroots movements seized the moment and helped move nearly all of the region back to civilian-controlled, electoral politics. The armed forces returned to the barracks discredited.

This momentous political and economic transition in Latin America coincided with the rise of Ronald Reagan in the United States and Margaret Thatcher in the United Kingdom. Reagan and Thatcher became the most visible and important figures in the so-called "Conservative Revolution," a revolution that in fact was a return to classical liberal economics of the nineteenth century: the promotion of laissez-faire (trade liberalization), a reduced role for government in the economy, a downsized government, balanced budgets (fiscal orthodoxy), and a near sanctification of the "marketplace" and the private sector. As Reagan and Thatcher's governments dismantled 50 years of interventionism and social policies in the United States and the United Kingdom, they also became the powerful advocates for what would become known as the "Washington Consensus." The World Bank, the International Monetary Fund, the Inter-American Development Bank, and other international agencies became the means to pressure countries around the world to sign on to this "consensus": balanced budgets, reduced role of the state, more open trade, and privatization of the economy. (Although this economic model has been labeled "conservative" in the United States, in most of the rest of the world, it is known as neoliberalism, because it returns to classical liberal economics.)

Neoliberalism swept across Latin America in the 1980s and 1990s. Chile, as we have seen, anticipated the Reagan-Thatcher revolution with the policies of the Chicago Boys beginning in the mid-1970s. With the obvious exception of Cuba, the rest of the nations of Latin America all have adopted some form of neoliberalism (although some countries have been less enthusiastic than others, and some have recently returned to greater government interventionism). Latin America has certainly become much less interventionist and more open to international trade than at any time since the end of the nineteenth century. The average level of tariffs in the region dropped from 45 to 13 percent between 1975 and 1995. In many ways, the era after the 1970s strongly resembles the period after the 1870s—a period of outward-oriented, export-led growth with fairly open trade, dominated by the private sector and reduced government intervention in the economy. Unfortunately, the growth rates have been erratic and low compared with a century ago—only about 2 percent per year over the last 15 years.

REGIONAL INTEGRATION

As Latin America slowly and fitfully recovered from the debt crisis of the 1980s, the new version of export-led growth also led to the revival of the regional integration schemes that had emerged in the 1950s and 1960s in the era of ISI. On a regional level, this movement reflected the larger, global trend best exemplified in the 1990s by the consolidation of the European Union, with its drive toward a single market, currency, and customs union. The most important move in this direction was the decision by Mexico to join the North American Free Trade Agreement in 1994. (Canada and the United States had initiated the agreement in 1989 as the Canada-United States Free Trade Agreement or FTA.) Over a decade, Mexican trade with the United States and Canada tripled, reinforcing Mexico's longstanding economic orientation toward North America and away from Central and South America. Eighty-five percent of Mexico's exports now go directly to the United States. Exports from Mexico to the United States now account for one-quarter of the Mexican GDP and fully half of all trade between Latin America and the United States is between Mexico and the United States. (The most dramatic opposition to NAFTA in Mexico has been the Zapatista Rebellion that broke out in Chiapas in January 1994.)

During the 1990s, the nations of Central America (1990), the Andean region (1995), and the Caribbean (1992) revived common markets begun in the 1950s and 1960s that had all but disappeared by the 1980s. The most interesting of these regional groups has been the *Mercado Común del Sur/Mercado Comum do Sul* (*Mercosur*, or *Mercosul* in Portuguese). Begun as a customs union between Argentina, Brazil, Uruguay, and Paraguay (with Bolivia and Chile as associate members), *Mercosur* has been seen by many as an effort to counterbalance the rising power of the United States and its efforts to construct a hemispheric customs union—a Free Trade Area of the Americas (FTAA).

FTAA began to emerge with the Enterprise of the Americas Initiative of President George H. W. Bush in 1990. His goal was to create a hemispheric free trade zone by 2000. In a series of "summits" of presidents, foreign ministers, and finance ministers between 1994 and 2005, 34 countries have struggled to bring FTAA into existence. Opposition has emerged in many countries from grassroots organizations fighting the impact of globalization on farmers, workers, and the environment, and and other issues.

These groups have also resisted many of the free-trade initiatives of the World Trade Organization, the principal global group promoting trade liberalization. This opposition became violent and strident in demonstrations during the summit in Quebec City, Canada in April 2001. The rise of Hugo Chávez in Venezuela, Néstor Kirchner in Argentina, and Evo Morales in Bolivia, and (to a lesser extent) Luis Inácio "Lula" da Silva in Brazil has put a significant brake on FTAA from the highest political ranks in several of the most important economies of the region. Their resistance to moving FTAA forward during the November 2005 summit in Mar del Plata, Argentina has effectively halted plans for the moment. The United States has aggressively pursued a "second track," signing agreements with countries that are ready to move forward. (Twenty-six of the thirty-four participants at Mar del Plata were in agreement on the next stage in hemispheric economic integration.) This strategy may gradually produce a larger and larger free-trade zone in the Americas that lacks just a few countries—most notably the large and significant economies of Brazil, Argentina, and Venezuela.

NAFTA, *Mercosur*, and other "common markets" will remain, however, much less developed than the European Union. Even in NAFTA and *Mercosur*, important sectors of the economies retain tariffs and restrictions. Legal differences on environmental issues and labor rights still must be worked out among countries. Most importantly, a true common market is built on the free movement of capital, goods, services, and labor. Even if the United States and Canada are able to iron out differences with other American nations on tariffs and environmental issues, it seems highly unlikely that the restricted flow of labor will be eased in North America at any time in the near future. Recent battles over immigration into the United States (legal and illegal) highlight the enormous difficulties facing any discussion of reducing restrictions on the flow of labor between the United States and Latin America.

BIG NATIONS, LITTLE NATIONS

An assessment of Latin America's economies at the beginning of the twenty-first century suggests both good news and bad news, change and continuity, when compared with the beginning of the twentieth century. Over the last century, Latin America has experienced a revolution in infrastructure and national integration. By and large, the countries of the region have drawn their subregions into national markets through railroads, highways, telecommunications, and commerce. The continually expanding reach and power of modern commercial networks of exchange have proven to be one of the most potent instruments in the creation of true national communities. At the same time, these forces have drawn national and subnational communities into a global community. In the late nineteenth century, the peoples of the backlands and the interior of Latin America were confronted with the encroachment of the central state (of the capital cities and ports) into their lives and villages. At the beginning of the twenty-first century, they are faced with the encroachment of the world into their communities and ways of life. Just as the expansion inward of the late nineteenth century became a sort of Second Conquest, the globalization at the turn of the twenty-first century has become something of a Third Conquest. Compelled to enter into the world of the "nation" by 1900, the tens of millions of Latin Americans of the vast interior have now been compelled to enter into the "global community."

Although still behind the developed nations, Latin America has not stood still over the last century. Since 1900, the region has grown at a rate of about 4 percent per year (although that growth has been just about 2 percent per year since the early 1980s). Despite a population explosion after 1940 and the massive movement of peoples from the countryside into cities, Latin America's economies grew rapidly after the Second World War. Latin Americans, who numbered 70 million in 1900, now number more than 500 million. Seventy-five percent rural in 1900, Latin America is now 65 percent urban. The illiteracy rate has dropped from 70 to 15 percent, and per capita income has multiplied fivefold. Life expectancy has nearly doubled, from 40 to 70+ years. Industry has risen from 5 to 25 percent of the GDP. In short, Latin America today is more industrialized, more developed, and has much better social indicators than it did at the beginning of the twentieth century. Economic growth has taken shape, but it has been modest, and it has not been as strong as in other regions of the world (such as East Asia), *and* the massive income inequalities that have long characterized Latin America have not diminished. Latin America has achieved significant economic progress in comparison with many areas of the world, but that progress has not been enough to meet the basic needs of tens of millions of Latin Americans. By the more conservative estimates, two of every five Latin Americans today live in poverty. In spite of the fivefold growth of per-capita income over the last century, Latin American per-capita incomes are only 30 percent of the per-capita income of the developed countries.

This brief survey has also highlighted the diversity within the larger patterns of Latin American economic history. The many nations have generally experienced similar patterns: periods of export-oriented growth, depression, growth through a turn inward, oil and debt crises, and then a new phase of export-oriented growth. They have responded to these long-term trends in a variety of ways. The strongest industrializers have been Brazil, Mexico, Argentina, Uruguay, Colombia, and Chile. Other nations have remained largely dependent on the primary-product export model: Venezuela, Ecuador, Peru, Bolivia, Paraguay, and Central America. While Argentina, Mexico, Chile, and Uruguay were the fastest growing economies in the early twentieth century, Brazil and Mexico emerged in the second half of the century as the two largest economies (probably the 10th and 12th largest economies in the world at the beginning of the twenty-first century). Puerto Rico remains anomalous as a "free associated state" within the United States. Were it a separate nation, it would be the richest country in Latin America, yet it remains one of the poorest states in the United States.

The neoliberal transition has also varied greatly across the region. Chile is the great success story and the most open economy in Latin America. (Chile is the only country in Latin America whose economic growth since 1980 has surpassed its growth in the 1950s.) Fidel Castro's Cuba remains the most closed and statist economy in the Americas. The failure of neoliberal economics to produce significant improvement in living standards in some nations has fueled a new populism that has taken Argentina, Bolivia, and Venezuela (however, tentatively) back in the direction of government interventionism, economic nationalism, and protectionism. What appeared to be an inevitable wave of regional integration in the early 1990s that would lead to the creation of a unified hemispheric common market by 2000 (FTAA), has now stalled with the opposition from these more populist leaders and grassroots movements that are also against the move toward trade liberalization and globalization.

Globalization and regional integration have highlighted the clear differences between the larger and smaller economies. Mexico has effectively moved toward full integration into the U.S. economy and has grown dramatically. At the other end of Latin America, Brazil has resisted U.S. power, dividing its trade between Europe, Asia, the United States, and Latin America. It has tried to use *Mercosul* as an instrument to hold off U.S. domination of a hemispheric trading bloc. Seemingly always on the verge of a move into the ranks of the developed economies, Brazil has experienced good, but erratic, growth over the last 15 years. It remains on the verge of fulfilling its economic potential. The smaller nations of Central America and the Caribbean have largely opted to join the United States-led bloc, seeking the advantages of access to larger markets and avoiding isolation and the tiny and unviable national economies they believe will no longer be able to survive as "autonomous" national units. Nearly everywhere in the region, the debt crisis has passed, capital is once again flowing into Latin America, and direct foreign investment is at all-time highs. Trade has expanded dramatically over the last generation alongside the nearly 5 percent per year expansion in world export volume since the 1970s. Nevertheless, as a trade revolution has taken place around the globe over the last generation, Latin America's share of world trade has declined over the last century (from 7 to 3 percent).

The differences among the economies of Latin America have also become more pronounced. Although high levels of income inequality and poverty continue to characterize the region as a whole, the range is wide. In 2000, the percentage of households in Latin America below the poverty line was the same as 1980, 35 percent. The figure was lowest in those nations with long, reformist traditions—Uruguay (6 percent), Argentina (16), and Chile (18)—and highest in the long-impoverished and undemocratic countries of Central America and the Caribbean—Nicaragua (65), Honduras (74), and Haiti (probably above 85 percent). In many ways, the Haitians and Nicaraguans live in a different economic universe from the Chileans or the Uruguayans. The small economies of Central America and the Caribbean have very little in common today with the enormous economies of Mexico or Brazil.

Although the last quarter-century looks very similar to the end of the nineteenth century, with its waves of foreign investment, infrastructural modernization, and export-orientation, the pattern this time around is, in fact, very different. Over the last generation, a revolution in communications technology and knowledge-based industries (informatics, in particular) has transformed the world (just as an industrial, chemical, and energy revolution transformed the world a century ago). Capital is much more mobile and volatile, and countries experience greater vulnerability to sudden economic shifts than they did a century ago. To some extent, the move toward regional integration has been motivated by the desire to reduce volatility and uncertainties, especially for the small nations of Latin America. The answer to economic development today is no longer simply to industrialize. Although industrialization and diversification remain important, economic development in this century will depend on the mastery of knowledge-based sectors of the economy. The bad news for much of Latin America is that it continues to lag behind North America, Europe, and East Asia in the electronic, digital knowledge revolution. The good news is that the most important resource in economic development will be human capital, not natural resources or heavy industry. Those countries in Latin America (indeed, in the world) that invest in human capital will be the best positioned in the coming decades to innovate, succeed, and grow in a global economy driven forward by the knowledge revolution.

Over the last century, the economies of Latin America have become increasingly diverse, in spite of their common colonial and nineteenth-century heritage. As millions of people have moved from the countryside to the cities, the legacy of the large landed estate remains powerful. The enormous income inequalities it helped create over centuries, however, have now largely become an urban problem. After five hundred years, the control of land (and labor) are no longer central to social and economic development, especially in the more developed economies. The struggle for justice in the countryside remains a potent issue, but not the foremost one in social and economic life. The challenges for Latin Americans in the twenty-first century, in many ways, remain the same as they were in 1900: economic diversification, the creation of good jobs, fostering the creation of savings and capital formation, and developing ways of lowering levels of poverty and income inequalities. The larger and more developed economies of Latin America clearly have more options than the smaller, primary-product exporters. Yet even the larger economies will continue to face the pressures to combine into regional trading blocs, whether *Mercosul* or FTAA. In a world that daily becomes more integrated and interconnected, the future of "national" economies and "national" development will continue to take on much more complex meanings. Ironically, the globalization and regional integration may lead to a sort of reunification of Latin America into a more integrated set of economies with a common future.

24

Race, Culture, Identity

LATIN AMERICA, LATIN AMERICAS

A shared set of political, economic, and cultural processes has shaped, defined, and redefined Latin America for more than five centuries. The collision of peoples and cultures during the first century of conquest and colonization forged structures of hierarchy, power, inequality, and exploitation that, initially, were largely imposed by European conquerors (and in Mesoamerica and the Andes with collaboration of the elites of the conquered indigenous empires). In the next two centuries, the ongoing conflicts and struggles among Europeans, Indians, and Africans forged colonial societies ("American" or "creole" societies) with a common core of political, economic, social, and cultural patterns. As we have seen in chapters 18–23, much of the history of Latin America over the last two centuries has been the story of efforts to overcome, shed, and transform the heritage of three centuries of colonialism. One of the most striking and enduring legacies of the colonial era has been the structures of race and culture that have so deeply and profoundly defined Latin American identity.

As with politics and economics, Latin America shares common patterns of race, culture and identity, while at the same time the region displays remarkable variations on those patterns. To some degree, the history of all of the Americas has been forged out of the collision of Indians, Europeans, and Africans before 1800. Yet, as the first half of this book shows, the patterns of interactions among these peoples evolved very differently in Anglo America. In Latin America, corporatism, widespread racial mixing, the survival of substantial indigenous communities, large communities of African descent, and elite control of land and labor produced societies and cultures with deeply entrenched racial and social hierarchies dominated by a small (primarily white) elite. Similar structures emerged in what became the U.S. South and the British West Indies. The profound impact and influence of English (and then Anglo-American) legal and political culture on these regions sets them apart from Latin America, and provides the most powerful rationale for arguing that the former Spanish colonies in the Caribbean basin gradually evolved out of Latin America after they were seized by Britain (and the Netherlands).

The influx of large numbers of Europeans (from southern and eastern Europe) in the late nineteenth century, of East Asians (principally Chinese, Japans, and more recently, Koreans), and peoples from the Middle East (especially from what are now Syria and Lebanon) has enriched the cultural collisions in Latin America over the last century. These "new" additions to the mix of Latin American cultures have added to the variations on the colonial heritage and further diversified and complicated any notions of "a" Latin American identity. In the last half-century, the massive movement of Latin Americans—especially from Mexico, Central America, and the Caribbean—into the United States has also enriched and complicated efforts to define Latin American identity/ies. The globalization of popular culture has both enriched and impoverished Latin America, and it has made efforts to define the region culturally increasingly problematic—but not impossible. As I have argued throughout this book, Latin America has always been an evolving and shifting notion and place. There was no Latin America before 1492. The defining features of the region in 1600 were not exactly the same as in 1800 or 2000, and they will, no doubt, have shifted again by the end of this century. Yet, as the Uruguayan writer Eduardo Galeano asserts (in the epigraph of this book), Latin America is more than a geographical reality; it consists of peoples "made of assorted clays from the same multiple earth." This chapter looks at how Latin Americans have sought to define themselves over the last century through their visions of the mixing and remixing of these "assorted clays."

THE PURSUIT OF IDENTITIES

"Latin" Americans have grappled with these complicated issues of identity, race, and culture for centuries. Over the last century, within Latin America, there have been efforts to single out at least four major Americas. Rodó and the Hispanophiles emphasized the "Latin" heritage of the region, a categorization that, at best, applies perhaps to Argentina, Uruguay, Chile, and Costa Rica. With the rise of *indigenismo* in the early twentieth century, writers like Mariátegui liked to speak of an "Indo" America, a term that best applies to Mexico, Guatemala, Ecuador, Peru, and Bolivia. Parallel to the rise of *indigenismo*, the move in the 1920s and 1930s to emphasize the African roots of the Americas (*négritude*, to use the term of the Francophone Caribbean writers), was the search for "Afro" America. Again, this term would only apply to some countries in Latin America, most notably, Brazil, Cuba, the Dominican Republic, Haiti, and Puerto Rico. Probably the most powerful and influential movement has been to describe Latin America as a racially mixed or "Mestizo" America. In national terms, Paraguay, Honduras, Nicaragua, El Salvador, and Mexico come closest to this description. Using mestizo in the broader sense of racially mixed (not just Indian and European), the term applies comfortably to nearly all of Latin America, except the most "European" countries (Uruguay and Argentina).

Clearly, over five centuries, one of the defining features of Latin America has been the racial and cultural mixtures arising out of the collisions of peoples—first the Indians, Europeans, and Africans, and later Asians and Middle Easterners. This extraordinary cauldron of mixing has created a cultural dynamism across Latin America that has produced efforts (especially by intellectuals and writers) to define the region around this central feature. Much (but not all) of the cultural and artistic excellence in Latin America since the 1930s has emerged out of an ongoing conversation about cultural and racial mixing. In much of Latin America today, this notion of mixture has become the official ideology promoted by governments and image-makers. This is a world apart from the nineteenth-century Liberals and Conservatives who saw their new nations as little Europes and (in the case of the Liberals like Sarmiento) drove them to annihilate the non-European peoples and cultures in their societies. This shift, from defining the region as "Europe in the Americas" to a "Mestizo" America began to take place in the early decades of the twentieth century, and is seen best in the rise and triumph of Latin America literature.

THE TRIUMPH OF LATIN AMERICAN LITERATURE

Much of the driving force behind the most creative literature and art in Latin America over the last century has been the efforts of writers and artists to define and forge a sense of identity, whether local, regional, national or transnational. Since the 1920s, arguably, the central theme of Latin American cultural production has been the search for identity. Novelists, poets, dramatists, and artists have placed the collision of cultures and peoples at the center of much of their work. By the middle of the twentieth century, the themes of mixture and "hybridity" had become central to the creative production of Latin Americans from Mexico to Chile. Although this creativity appears in all forms of art, drama, and popular culture, I will concentrate in the following pages primarily on literature as a window into the efforts of Latin Americans to define themselves over the last century. (Again, as throughout this book, this brief section is meant to be illustrative rather than encyclopedic.)

As we saw in chapter 17, by the 1930s, Latin American writers and artists had begun self-consciously to define themselves and their peoples as unique—as the products of the unusual racial and cultural mixture that characterizes most of Latin America. José Vasconcelos hailed Mexico as a mestizo nation peopled by a "cosmic race," and Gilberto Freyre glorified the racial and cultural mixture that defined Brazil and Brazilians—what he called a "luso-tropical civilization." Latin American intellectuals, quite often resenting the continually growing economic, political, and cultural power of the United States, also sought to define themselves as distinct and different from the "colossus of the North." In Spanish-speaking regions, the interaction among Spanish poets, intellectuals, and writers and their Latin American counterparts intensified after the First World War and accelerated during the Spanish Civil War (1936–39). The impact of this exchange was most pronounced in Mexico and Argentina, as Mexico City and Buenos Aires emerged as the dominant cultural and publishing centers in Latin America (outside Brazil). The flight of many Spaniards into exile after the triumph of Francisco Franco in 1939 also profoundly affected intellectual life, especially in Mexico City and Buenos Aires. As in the nineteenth century, the allure and influence of Paris also played a powerful role in the cultural interaction among writers and artists. Although these tendencies climaxed in the 1950s and 1960s, they had been developing for decades, first with the Naturalist and Realist literature of the late nineteenth century, and then with the Vanguardist and Regionalist writers after the First World War.

From the 1910s to the 1940s, Latin American poetry flourished as writers who saw themselves at the vanguard of cultural creation—an *avant-garde*—drew upon European Modernism, especially the loss of faith in progress, reason, and liberalism. (The senseless mass slaughter of the First World War—facilitated by modern science and technology—deeply shocked Europeans and Latin Americans alike.) Much like the Europeans (especially the French), the Latin American *vanguardistas* turned to forms of poetry that reflected an "anguish at the loss of faith in a transcendent reality." Its greatest figure was the Chilean poet Vicente Huidobro (1893–1948). From an aristocratic Chilean family, Huidobro traveled widely in Europe and Latin America, promoting a poetic style he labeled "creationism." At the same time, the Peruvian César Vallejo (1892–1938) produced what some consider the most original poetry of the period. From humble origins in the Andes, Vallejo lived in poverty in Paris for the last 15 years of his life, largely immune to the influences of the Modernist movement around him. Much like the European philosophical movements of the post-World War II period, an existential dread and emphasis on the irrational and the absurd permeate Vallejo's work. Two of the greatest writers of the century emerged in this period as advocates of the avant-garde, but later went in very different directions. The Chilean poet, Pablo Neruda (1904–73), and the Argentine, Jorge Luis Borges (1899–1986), gradually moved in very different directions (both aesthetically and politically) and would emerge in the 1960s and 1970s as two of the most honored and admired literary figures in the world.

The Modernist movement in Brazil after the First World War (unlike the Modernism in Spanish America at the turn of the century) paralleled the movements in Europe. Profoundly antibourgeois, antagonistic to middle-class culture, and consciously rejecting traditional art forms, the Brazilian Modernists (mostly from upper-class families) visited and lived in Paris, imbibing its powerful cultural influences. Mário de Andrade's extraordinary novel, *Macunaíma* (1928), stands out as the emblematic work of the period in Brazil. Strongly influenced by his own work as a poet, dramatist, and musicologist, the novel is a fascinating mix of the fantastic and the surreal, as well as a commentary on Brazilian reality. The novels of João Guimarães Rosa (1908–67), especially *Grande sertão veredas* (*The Devil to Pay in the Backlands*, 1956), reflect the profound influence of Modernism. Highly creative, innovative, and original, Guimarães Rosa turns language into a powerful tool in ways reminiscent of James Joyce and *Ulysses*. Set in the arid interior (*sertão*), his novels and short stories employ this quintessentially Brazilian setting to speak of some of the universal themes of human existence.

The Modernist turn toward the "authentically" national gave rise to what have often been referred to as "regional" novels. These works, preceded by the naturalist novels of the late nineteenth century and their social realism, illuminate life in the interior of Latin America, often in the most traditional and rural regions. In Brazil, the novels of José Lins do Rego (1901–57) are perhaps the best example of this trend. Set on the sugar plantations of the northeast, Lins do Rego's series of novels, in what has been called the "sugarcane cycle," reflect both a condemnation of, and a nostalgic longing for, the paternalistic rural social world of the impoverished and decadent sugar plantation society of the Brazilian northeast. The drought-ridden *sertão* provided the setting for many of these regional novels. One of the greatest was Graciliano Ramos' (1892–1953) *Vidas sêcas* (*Barren Lives*, 1938). Immortalized in neorealist film (1963) by the brilliant director Nelson Pereira dos Santos, the novel recounts the trek of an impoverished family from the interior to the coast during one of the brutal droughts that so characterize the interior of northeastern Brazil.

A whole series of excellent writers emerged around this northeastern movement. Eventually, the most famous were Jorge Amado (1912–2001) and Gilberto Freyre (1900–87). From the cacao planting region of Itabuna, Amado moved to the port of Ilhéus as an infant. He began his career with a series of realist novels about power, injustice, and society in this traditional social order. By the 1950s, he had emerged as the greatest popular writer in Brazil with a series of works that, for many, helped shape and define national identity. His *Gabriela, cravo e canela* (*Gabriela: Clove and Cinnamon*, 1958) revolves around the central character of the sensual *mulata* Gabriela, the bar of Nacib (the "Turk") and the men in her life in Ilhéus. For many Brazilians and non-Brazilians, Gabriela eventually came to symbolize the essence of the stereotypical Brazilian female sex symbol. In *Dona Flor e seus dois maridos* (*Dona Flor and Her Two Husbands*, 1966) and *Tenda dos milagres* (*Tent of Miracles*, 1969), Amado confirmed his role as the greatest contemporary chronicler of the lush image of Brazil as a mix of races, foods, sounds, and religions filled with a mystical and sensual people. As Brazil's best-known and most successful author for decades, Amado's work played a powerful role in forging images and stereotypes of Brazilian identity both among Brazilians and foreigners.

Perhaps the greatest writer Latin America has produced, Jorge Luis Borges began his writing life during the Modernist movement, but defies categorization. One of the most original writers of the twentieth century, Borges is best known for his clever and provocative short stories. Fluent in English, Spanish, and French from childhood, and deeply influenced by the works of British and German writers and philosophers, Borges foreshadows both existentialism and postmodernism. His short stories are small gems—carefully crafted "microworlds"—in which he often creates characters who find themselves in worlds of infinite complexity and uncertainty, a universe where personal identity is unstable, fragile, and constantly in question. In the 1930s and 1940s he produced most of his greatest work, most notably his collection of short stories, *Ficciones* (1944). Although his themes and work are universal, the settings are often Argentine—Buenos Aires, the pampas, gauchos. Blind from glaucoma by the mid-1950s, Borges became the head of the National Library, and increasingly conservative in his politics. Although considered a leading contender for the Nobel Prize in Literature from the 1960s to his death in the 1980s, Borges received nearly every other literary prize in the Western world except this one. Many literary critics in Europe and the Americas consider him the greatest writer Latin America has ever produced.

The first Latin American to win the Nobel Prize in Literature was a woman, the poet Gabriela Mistral (1889–1957). From a provincial town in the north of Chile, Mistral (born Lucila Godoy Alcayaga) worked as a schoolteacher all over the country. (At one point, the young Pablo Neruda was her student in the provincial town of Temuco in southern Chile!) Her poetic style is natural, colloquial, intensely passionate and, in her words, carries "the rural lilt in which I have lived and in which I will die." For the last 30 years of her life, she traveled widely, serving in the Chilean diplomatic corps. She helped found the United Nations Cultural and Educational Fund (UNICEF). She was awarded the Nobel Prize in 1945.

In 1967, a Guatemalan became the second Latin American to win the Nobel Prize in Literature. Like Borges, the Guatemalan novelist, Miguel Ángel Asturias (1899–1974), forms a literary bridge between Modernism and the so-called "boom" of the 1960s. In his two most famous novels—*El Señor Presidente* (1946) and *Hombres de maís* (*Men of Maize*, 1949)—the fantastic, magical, and mystical permeate all of his prose. The latter novel draws its inspiration and narrative techniques from Maya myths. In the words of the literary critic, Edwin Williamson, this novel "is one of the first works of magical realism, because it introduced non-rational material into the fabric of the novel as a valid expression of an alternative reality."

Alejo Carpentier (1904–80), a Cuban born to a French father and Russian mother, usually gets credit for first formulating the notion of what later became known as "magical realism." Carpentier lived in Paris in the 1910s and again in the 1930s, and was deeply moved by a visit to Haiti in 1943. His work seeks out the *real maravilloso*—the "marvelous real"—as he attempted to reconcile rationalism and the spiritual. *El reino de este mundo* (*The Kingdom of this World*, 1949) has as its setting the Haitian slave revolt of the 1790s, taking the culture of voodoo seriously and presenting alternative, nonrational realities. In the 1940s and 1950s, Carpentier lived and worked in Venezuela and traveled extensively. His widely celebrated novel, *Los paso perdidos* (*The Lost Steps*, 1953, published in English in 1956) reflects the influence of his travels in Amazonia. After the triumph of the Cuban Revolution in 1959, Carpentier became a major figure in national cultural policies. He spent the last 12 years of his life in a diplomatic post in Paris.

Two other outstanding writers of this period also contributed to the growing international reputation of Latin American literature—Octávio Paz (1914–98) and Pablo Neruda (1904–73). With a career spanning more than a half-century, beginning with the Modernist movement of the 1920s, Neruda is the most widely translated and read Latin American poet of all time. Born in a small, provincial town in southern Chile, he joined the diplomatic corps, serving in what today are Myanmar, Sri Lanka, and Indonesia as a young man. His *Veinte poemas de amor y una canción desesperada* (*Twenty Poems of Love and a Song of Despair*, 1923) are lyrical and erotic poems that have been enormously popular for decades. His diplomatic post in Madrid in the 1930s brought him into direct contact with some of the greatest poets in the Spanish language, including Federico García Lorca. A lifelong Communist, Neruda helped many Spaniards escape into exile after the triumph of the fascist dictator Francisco Franco. Neruda's *Canto general* (1950), an epic poem that retells the history of Latin America

is widely considered a poetic masterpiece. García Márquez has called
Neruda "the greatest poet of the twentieth century in any language." A
staunch supporter of socialist President Salvador Allende, Neruda was
awarded the Nobel Prize for Literature in 1971, and he died just days after
the overthrow of Allende in September 1973.

Although friends in their youth, Paz and Neruda took very different
directions, poetically and politically, by the 1950s. While Neruda became
an ardent Communist, and a Stalinist in the 1940s, Paz became increasingly conservative. Although he built his reputation as a poet, Paz was
also a brilliant essayist. His collection of essays, *The Labyrinth of Solitude*
(1950) is a meditation on Mexican identity and culture deeply influenced
by his years as a consular official in southern California. His essays on
Mexican-American culture are some of the earliest (and most influential)
efforts by an intellectual to probe the interconnected cultures and lives of
Mexicans on both sides of the Mexican-United States border. The book
deeply probes the duality of Mexican identity, as children of both indigenous and Spanish societies, of both La Malinche and Cortés. Paz brilliantly employs the image of masks and mixture. Mexicans, he asserts,
carry the shame of Malinche's betrayal of her people, and behave "like
persons who are wearing disguises, who are afraid of a stranger's look
because it could strip them and leave them stark naked." He was also
awarded the Nobel Prize for Literature (in 1990) for his "impassioned
writing with wide horizons, characterized by sensuous intelligence and
humanistic integrity."

International recognition for Latin American literature had been slowly
building from the 1930s to the 1950s. In the 1960s, Latin American writers
suddenly emerged as some of the most admired, copied, and feted in the
world. This sudden explosion of interest in Latin American literature
became known as the "boom" (even the Latin Americans use the English
word). Although a large number of excellent writers are associated with
this vibrant and fertile period, the signature mode was the novel, and four
men—a junta—achieved international celebrity status towering above all
others: Julio Cortázar (1914–1984, Argentina), Mario Vargas Llosa (b. 1936,
Peru), Carlos Fuentes (b. 1928, Mexico), and Gabriel García Márquez
(b. 1928, Colombia). Their lives and work—like those of Carpentier,
Borges, and Mistral—reflect a cosmopolitan experience and intellectual
exchange ultimately grounded in a Latin American reality.

Slightly older than the other three, Cortázar was also the most daring
and experimental in his work. Like Borges, much of his influence and reputation come from his brilliant and evocative short stories. All of his writing, however, employs innovative narrative techniques blending the
fantastic with the "real," often producing complicated plots that invite
multiple interpretations and perspectives on the story lines. His most

famous novel, *Rayuela* (*Hopscotch*, 1963) reflects Cortázar's disillusionment with bourgeois culture and rationality and an emphasis on the erotic. Born in Paris, Cortázar settled there permanently in the early 1950s. Although considered one of the quintessential Latin American writers of the mid-twentieth century, he spent most of his life abroad, deeply influenced by European intellectual currents and, in turn, profoundly influencing world literature after the 1950s.

Carlos Fuentes has been one of the most prolific and visible figures of this quartet. The child of a Mexican diplomat, Fuentes grew up in Europe, the United States, and Latin America. With the publication of *La muerte de Artemio Cruz* (*The Death of Artemio Cruz*, 1962), Fuentes emerged as one of the young stars of Latin American literature. Much like the classic film *Citizen Kane* (1941), the novel has a complex and difficult narrative structure that moves back and forth in time, beginning with Artemio Cruz on his hospital deathbed. The novel follows the life and death of Cruz—a mulatto child of a powerful landowner and his black servant—as he flees the ranch, joins the rebels in the Mexican Revolution, marries the daughter of a once powerful landowner, and then rises to power, cynicism, and corruption in the 1930s, 1940s, and 1950s. The story of the rebirth of a nation and the rise of the racially mixed to power, it is a tale of disillusionment and the betrayal of the ideals of the Revolution. Multilingual, cosmopolitan, and constantly traveling, Fuentes became an international literary superstar over the past four decades. His numerous novels have been widely (and immediately) translated into many languages, becoming bestsellers around the world. An adamant supporter of the Cuban Revolution in the 1960s, and long a harsh critic of the United States, Fuentes's novels in the last twenty years have become much less political, and much more concerned with interpersonal relations, eroticism, and alienation.

Mario Vargas Llosa's career parallels that of Fuentes, but his politics do not. His remarkable narrative skills have influenced writers worldwide over the last half-century. Trained in a military academy, Vargas Llosa's first book, *La ciudad y los perros* (*The Time of the Hero*, 1962) takes place in a military school and draws on his personal experiences, as does his *La tía Julia y el escribidor* (*Aunt Julia and the Scriptwriter*, 1978), the story of a very young aspiring writer who marries his (much older) aunt. *La casa verde* (*The Green House*, 1966) and *Conversación en la catedral* (*Conversation in the Cathedral*, 1969) are two of the classic novels of the boom. Vargas Llosa has been a prolific writer, speaker, traveler, and publicist. His name has been frequently mentioned as a possible Nobel Prize winner. Increasingly conservative, in 1990 he ran for the presidency of Peru, to be defeated by the (then) unknown Alberto Fujimori. Ironically, Fujimori implemented many of the neoliberal policies advocated by Vargas Llosa during the electoral campaign.

The most celebrated writer of this group is Gabriel García Márquez, the fourth Latin American writer to win a Nobel Prize for Literature (1982). Born in the small town of Aracataca near Colombia's Caribbean coast, García Márquez worked for many years as a journalist in Latin America, the United States, and Europe. Deeply influenced by the work of William Faulkner, his early writings were brilliant short stories that became the basis for some of his novels. His first novel *La hojarasca* (*The Leaf Storm*, 1955) resembles Faulkner's *As I Lay Dying* (1930). A novella (really a series of short stories), *El coronel no tiene quien le escribe* (*No One Writes to the Coronel*, 1961) introduces characters and scenes that would later form the basis for his most famous book, *Cien años de soledad* (*One Hundred Years of Solitude*, 1967) widely considered *the* great Latin American novel. (Some would say that it is only surpassed in the world of Spanish letters by Cervantes's *Don Quixote*.)

Cien años (as it is known in shorthand by the *literati*) is an astonishingly compelling and complex tale of seven generations of the Buendía family from the town of Macondo (obviously based on Aracataca) in an unnamed country (that seems very much like Colombia, but could easily be anywhere in Latin America). Wracked by civil violence, struggles between Liberals and Conservatives, the power of foreign corporations, and bad governments, Macondo becomes a microcosm of the Latin American experience combining the mythical, magical, the comic, and the tragic. Drawing on indigenous mythology, Western literature, the Bible, and deeply immersed in the literature and history of Latin America, *Cien años* creates a virtually self-contained universe (á la Borges) with a biblical genesis and Armageddon. Had García Márquez written this novel, and nothing else, his reputation would have been made. In addition to his brilliant earlier works, his novels afterward have also been international critical and commercial successes. *El otoño del patriarca* (*The Autumn of the Patriarch*, 1975), *El amor en los tiempos del cólera* (*Love in the Time of Cholera*, 1985), and *El general en su labirinto* (*The General in His Labyrinth*, 1989)—to cite just three of his later novels—are all major literary achievements. Living in Mexico since the early 1960s, García Márquez is the supernova in this immensely talented constellation of stellar writers.

As many critics have observed, the best-known writers of the boom largely have been men. Despite the fascination and fixation with the large array of (outstanding) male writers, the last half-century has also seen the emergence of a brilliant and influential group of female writers across Latin America, and even in the United States. While Clorinda Matto de Turner (Peru, 1852–1909), Gertrudis Gómez de Avellaneda y Arteaga (Cuba, 1814–73), and Juana Manuela Gorritti (Argentina, 1818–96) were shining exceptions to a male-dominated literature in the nineteenth century, by the mid-twentieth century, female writers had become more numerous and their work more widely read and respected.

One of the greatest of these early figures was the Mexican writer, Rosario Castellanos (1925–74). She spent her early years in the heavily indigenous southern state of Chiapas before moving to Mexico City, where she pursued a career in journalism. Her writings have been widely influential, in particular, two novels that offer a highly empathetic, but unromanticized view of the Indians of Chiapas—*Balún-Canan* (*The Nine Guardians*, 1957) and *Oficio de tinieblas* (*Book of Lamentations*, 1962). Her tragic, accidental death while serving as the Mexican ambassador to Israel cut short the life of a truly innovative writer. The Brazilian writer Clarice Lispector (1925–77) was a contemporary with an equally short life. Born in Ukraine, Lispector's family emigrated to Brazil when she was a small child. Best known as a writer of short stories, Lispector wrote newspaper columns (*crônicas*), children's books, and translated many works into Portuguese (she also spoke Yiddish, English, and French). Her works are all deeply psychological, filled with interior monologue, alienation, angst and the pursuit of self-awareness. Plot takes a back seat to the exploration of the human psyche. Her early novel, *Perto do coração selvagem* (*Near to the Wild Heart*, 1942) represented a major break from the narratives typical of the regionalist novels of the 1920s and 1930s. Discovered by French feminists and literary critics in the 1980s, Lispector may well be the most admired and studied female Latin American writer of the last half-century.

With the rise of new waves of feminism in the Western world in the 1960s and 1970s, female writers gradually began to receive the attention they deserve. Politics and art, at times, converged as some writers became equally famous for their writing as for their political engagement. In Mexico, Elena Poniatowska (b. 1932) exemplifies this trend. Born in Paris to a father descended from the Polish aristocracy and a Mexican mother from an elite family, Poniatowska also attended schools in the United States. Blending journalism, oral history, and politics, her *La noche de Tlatelolco* (*Massacre in Mexico City*, 1971) reconstructs the tragic murder of hundreds of young students protesting in Mexico City in 1968. It is a brilliant window into a generation, an era of political upheaval, and of disillusionment. Her widely praised novel, *Querido Diego, te abraza Quiela* (*Dear Diego*, 1978) is based on the letters of the wife of the famous Mexican muralist Diego Rivera, a notorious womanizer who abandoned her. The Nicaraguan poet, Gioconda Belli (b. 1948) comes from the same generation as the students Poniatowska portrays in *La noche de Tlatelolco*. Born into an elite Nicaraguan family, Belli joined the Sandinista Revolution in the 1970s, just as her poetry began to gain attention. Her poetry and prose are something of a celebration of female sexuality. Several volumes of her poetry were gathered together and published as *Poesía reunida* (1989). Her novel, *La mujer habitada* (*The Inhabited Woman*, 1988) and her autobiography, *El país bajo mi piel* (*The Country Under My Skin*, 2001) are beautifully written, powerful statements about women in contemporary Latin America.

Women have also played a powerful role in the emergence of a new form of literature that bridges the political and linguistic borders of the Americas. Latino/a literature has blossomed over the last generation with female authors at the forefront. Written in English (although often with a great deal of Spanish mixed in), this literature illuminates the lives of writers and their subjects living between and in two worlds, in English and Spanish. The works of Cristina García (*Dreaming in Cuban*, 1992), Esmeralda Santiago (*When I Was Puerto Rican*, 1993), Sandra Cisneros (*The House on Mango Street*, 1984), Julia Alvarez (*In the Time of the Butterflies*, 1995; *How the Garcia Girls Lost Their Accents*, 1991), and Oscar Hijuelos (*The Mambo Kings Play Songs of Love*, 1989) (among others) have been wildly successful among both English-speaking critics and readers. Identity has been a common theme running through these works as the authors grapple with the meaning of the lives of peoples of Latin American origin who spend much of their lives in the United States. These themes have also been brilliantly explored in the essays and memoirs of Gustavo Pérez-Firmat (*Life on the Hyphen*, 1994; *Next Year in Cuba*, 1995) and Ilan Stavans (*The Hispanic Condition*, 1995).

These works form something of a literary borderland between the United States and Latin America, a zone of transition that makes it increasingly difficult to speak of Latin America and the United States as separate spheres separated by political borders. The memoirs and novels of Santiago, the essays of Pérez-Firmat, and the novels of Alvarez offer windows into the emergence of a new, transnational, bicultural, bilingual world fostered through the emergence of globalization, a telecommunications revolution, and the mass movements of peoples across the continents of the Americas. Many of these writers were born in Latin America, raised in the United States, and they write mainly in English. Their works are then translated and sold to Spanish-speaking audiences in Latin America, and the United States.

Both Latino/a literature and Latin American literature have emerged out of the continuing and most recent collisions of cultures in the Americas. These writers have produced works that have received international recognition over the last half-century, very often for their sensitive and nuanced treatment of identities forged out of the many streams that have converged to form Latin America, the Caribbean, and the United States. Galeano's "multiple earths" have nurtured and given birth to a rainbow of peoples, cultures, and identities that these writers have so brilliantly and evocatively explored. Whatever the political, economic, or social challenges Latin America has faced over the last century, the region has confronted its cultural and racial collisions with eyes wide open. As they have dissected and pondered the meanings of these collisions, the writers of the region have given birth to some of the greatest literary works ever produced. In the nineteenth century, Latin Americans imitated the culture and literature of Europe. No longer imitative, the literature of the past century has become increasingly original and innovative, and widely imitated by writers around the globe.

Epilogue

Latin America in the Twenty-first Century

In the 500 years since the initial collisions of peoples from three continents gave birth to Latin America in the islands of the Caribbean, the region has become an extraordinarily diverse collection of peoples and cultures with a shared past. It is this collective experience that defines a region that has become increasingly diverse over centuries, as the clashes among peoples and cultures have become more complex, varied, and distinct. As I have emphasized repeatedly throughout this book, this shared set of experiences allows us to see the region as a whole, despite the enormous variations across regions, peoples, and cultures. The violent encounters of the fifteenth and sixteenth centuries gave birth to Latin America. The continuing and increasingly varied collisions over the past 500 years will also make it more and more difficult to find a unity in the coming decades. The definition of Latin America, in short, becomes more complex and difficult the more distance the region moves from the colonial heritage. I close this concise, interpretive history of Latin America where I began it, reflecting on the very nature and definition of the region.

As we have seen, it was not until the early seventeenth century that peoples of Spanish descent in the Americas began to see themselves as some sort of collective entity defined by the geography of the "New World." An emergent "creole identity, a collective consciousness that separated Spaniards born in the New World from their European ancestors and cousins" was taking shape within a century after the Columbian voyages. By the mid-seventeenth century, the conquest and early processes of colonization had been completed and the population of "Spanish" Americans had been in place long enough and had reached sufficient levels in "central areas" (New Spain, Peru, the Caribbean) to create some nascent sense of rootedness. Small pockets or enclaves of "new" Spains had taken root in the Americas. In Brazil, this sense of an "American" identity emerged even later.

Yet these enclaves were just that, small islands of Europeans in a vast sea of Indians and Africans. Quite clearly the native peoples of the Americas did not see themselves as part of a larger society or culture (Indian or European) across the growing regions of the Spanish American and Portuguese colonies. The Africans, mainly concentrated in the islands of the Caribbean and on the northeastern coast of Brazil, had even less of a sense of belonging, given their traumatic dislocation from their homelands in Africa to strange lands, cultures, and languages in the New World. Some of these Indian and African peoples, and their descendants, were slowly being drawn into the cultural and linguistic world of the neo-Spains (and neo-Portugals) by the end of the seventeenth century. From the first moments of conquest, racial and cultural mixture had begun to produce intermediate groups who did not fit the "ideal types" of the racial hierarchy. Their very presence and influence, in fact, meant that the neo-Spaniards were forced to define themselves and their newly emerging societies as distinct from (even though very strongly identified with) Spain. To complicate matters further, the very tiny Portuguese presence in Brazil, even in the late seventeenth century, meant that the development of a neo-Portuguese sensibility was even weaker than the process taking shape in the Spanish colonies. Any sense of connectedness with their Spanish American counterparts was also very weak, and to some extent the experience of the so-called "Babylonian Captivity" (1580–1640) had possibly even heightened a sense of difference.

By the late eighteenth century, this sense of creole identity, of Spaniards in the New World, had been spurred forward both by the growth of creole populations in Spanish America, but also by the impact of the Bourbon Reforms. Ironically, these imperial reforms spurred on creole "nationalism" and helped create a stronger sense of connectedness among the creole elites from Mexico to Argentina. This sense of common identity, promoted and spurred on by creole elites, played a powerful role in the wars for independence in Spanish America. (Perhaps its greatest statement is Bolívar's "Jamaica Letter.") Yet, as Bolívar himself learned so bitterly, local and regional roots in the collapsing Spanish colonies too often were more powerful in their attraction than any greater sense of identity as Americans or Spanish Americans. Trying to unite these similar, yet disparate, peoples—Peruvians, Mexicans, Chileans—into a single community exhausted even the extraordinary talents of Bolívar, leading to his famous despairing quote, "America is ungovernable. He who serves the revolution ploughs the sea."

The wars for independence and the processes of nation-building in the nineteenth century helped forge a sense of a collective past and present throughout the former Spanish and Portuguese colonies (and to a lesser extent among the new leadership in Haiti). In the midst of the bloody struggle, the optimistic Simón Bolívar could speak of "the hearts of all the peoples of Spanish America." By the 1890s, José Martí (writing from exile in North America) could speak of "our America" and José Enrique Rodó (writing from southern South America) could address the "youth of America" in 1900, both clearly speaking of Spanish or Hispano-América. Ironically, this collective identity would arise partly in response to the growing power of the United States throughout the nineteenth and twentieth centuries. In the writings of both Martí and Rodó, this was quite conscious and deliberate. Both saw the construction of a Latin American identity as a means to combat the growing imperial power of "América del Norte" and a way to avoid the "delatinization" of "Hispano-América."

Latin American intellectuals like Martí and Rodó were reacting to the efforts of the United States to extend its sphere of influence throughout the hemisphere. In many ways, the "creation" of "Latin America" in the minds of the citizens of the United States takes place at the end of the nineteenth century. The Pan American movement, despite its efforts to forge a hemispheric alliance of nations, did so by identifying the United States as a nation with a heritage and history distinct from the "other" America. Since the nineteenth century, much of the discussion of hemispheric solidarity has been built upon a discussion of how to "overcome" the differences between the United States and Latin America. In this long tradition, the "problem" has been how to overcome Latin America's history (read culture) by making its people more like U.S. citizens (i.e., having them adopt "our" values).

Throughout much of the twentieth century, especially after 1945, Latin Americans developed their sense of collective identity in opposition to U.S. power and imperialism in the region, and scholars in the United States too often defined Latin America out of an experience shaped by the Cold War and government funding efforts designed to fight that war in the academic arena. This oppositional approach has been fuzzy from both directions, and the linguistic terminology has contributed to the fuzziness. Citizens of the United States, calling themselves "Americans," have never been very clear on what exactly is to the south, and the term "Latin America" has been left vague and poorly defined. Those who have consciously taken on the identity of "Latin Americans" (usually from Brazil and Spanish-speaking nations) have often taken to calling those from the United States "North Americans," a vague term that should include Mexicans and Canadians. Both perspectives tend to leave out or avoid those areas of the Americas that make definitions the most problematic and interesting: most of the islands of the Caribbean (especially those where Spanish is not the principal language), Belize, the Guianas, and regions of "overlap" (what Herbert Eugene Bolton called the Spanish Borderlands). One could also include much of the Caribbean coastal zone of Central America. It is precisely in these "transitional zones" that the definition of Latin America and the United States becomes most difficult and challenging.

As I have argued throughout this book, the very essence of any notion of Latin America emerges primarily from the view that the region and peoples arose out of the process of conquest and colonization by European powers, primarily the Spanish and Portuguese. The "Latin" in Latin America derives primarily from this vision of the creation out of European conquest. These processes of conquest and colonization, the complex struggles between conqueror and colonized, are at the very essence of any definition of Latin America. This is, if you will, the touchstone of Latin American history. This perspective has been around for centuries. What the English historian David Brading has called colonial creole "first Americans" defined themselves as the products of this process of conquest and colonization in the sixteenth century. In the nineteenth century, the first wave of historians wrote about the drive to create new nations in Latin America as the triumphal struggle of European "civilization" over the "barbarism" of native peoples and Africans. (Sarmiento, of course, is the foundational text in this genre.) The so-called "Second Conquest" of the late nineteenth century was rationalized by many Latin American intellectuals and elites as the completion of the "First Conquest" in the sixteenth century.

This tale of European conquest and colonization was a reductionist tale from its beginnings. It was really the story of the conquest of the "central areas"—the Caribbean, Mexico, and Peru. By the end of the sixteenth century, the fringes of the two Spanish viceroyalties were just that—frontiers sparsely settled by Europeans (or by anyone else in many places). In the case of Brazil, it is even difficult to speak of a "conquest" of the small enclaves on the Atlantic coast. The vast majority of what is now Brazil lay beyond the pale of European conquest and colonization. When creole identity began to emerge in the Spanish American colonies in the seventeenth century, most of what we would include today in any definition of Latin America lay beyond the reach of European power and control. Most of the lands remained fragmented pieces of an *indigenous* "America." Even in the central areas, the Spaniards and Portuguese constituted small islands of Europeans in a sea of non-European peoples.

In these core regions, we see unfold the basic elements of the features that I have employed to define Latin America: the imposition of European political and legal structures, languages, religions, and cultures. Until the

1960s, traditional historians generally saw this process as unilinear, often inevitable, and desirable. Much of the "story" of the field of Latin American history since the 1960s has been challenges to this powerful and enduring paradigm. Although many today would probably acknowledge that the process of Europeanization has been overwhelming and ongoing, the approach over the past 40 years has been to emphasize the resistance of non-European peoples to the juggernaut of Europeanization, and to highlight the give-and-take in the process. Conquest and colonization, to put it another way, was not a unilineal and complete process, but rather a bitter struggle among Europeans and non-Europeans that has produced a complex cultural mix that defines contemporary Latin Americans: they live in nation-states formed out of western and southern European political and legal traditions; speak Romance languages as the dominant tongues; overwhelmingly they practice varieties of Christianity (especially Roman Catholicism); and they are integrated into the capitalist system that arose out of the North Atlantic world.

If political, cultural, and economic boundaries have been constantly shifting since 1492, how then do we pin down this elusive notion of something called Latin America? Here I come back full circle to the moments of origin and my image of the river, of converging and diverging streams. At its most basic, we must begin any definition of the region with the initial collisions and convergences. Few would disagree with that assertion. For the first century of its existence, Latin America was Ibero-America, with Spain and Portugal as the driving forces in the collision of peoples. The commonality, it seems to me, is in the *Iberian* heritage and its transformation through struggles with non-Iberian peoples in the Americas. When the French, English, and Dutch appear on the scene in the seventeenth century they also become part of the non-Iberian collisions and mixtures. In this sense, the Caribbean continues to be part of Latin America, but most of the islands under English, Dutch, and French control gradually take their own distinct path. Politically, many of the islands of the Caribbean may fall under the sway of the British, French, and Dutch, but culturally and socially these islands and enclaves will carry with them a powerful Ibero-American heritage: the spiritual conquest of the Catholic Church, racial mixture, profound social inequities, slavery, and the cultural mix of Iberian, Native American, and African peoples. As the centuries pass, the cultural and political influences of the British, French, and the Dutch eventually supplanted the Ibero-American heritage. The societies continue to be racially and culturally mixed, slavery persists, as do the profound social inequities, but the influence of different political and cultural traditions reshaped these former regions of Latin America.

This means that there are no easy dates that demarcate the entry and exit of regions into and out of Latin America. Instead, there are gradual transitions, and this complicates the task of the historian. Latin America has shared an ever-evolving set of core characteristics and each country or region must be measured on a sort of continuum to gauge its convergence or divergence from the set of characteristics. Jamaica does not suddenly stop being Latin American in 1655 with the English conquest, but gradually evolves away under the demographic, political, and cultural influences from England. Conversely, the borderlands of northern Mexico only gradually are drawn into Latin America, and (after 1848) gradually drawn out. The non-Spanish-speaking Caribbean then gradually evolves away from Latin America, despite the strong similarities (slavery, social structure, racial and cultural mixture). Puerto Rico, and even more so, places like California, Texas, and Florida also evolve away (in varying degrees) from their Latin American cousins under the influence of U.S. political culture, economic development, and new types of cultural and linguistic mixtures.

If we are to speak of something called Latin America, it must have some common core elements that allow us to group different geographies together into a single unit. There must be a core, but we also must recognize that the core elements continually evolve. That core is neither static, nor uniform. The enormous variety of collisions across Latin America produces multiple hybrids. The beauty of Latin America is that there is enough unity of features that we can, in fact, define the region, yet there is enough diversity that we are always watching the pieces of that region diverge from their origins. Geographically, Latin America has had four core regions—Mexico, Peru, Brazil, and the Caribbean—and a constantly shifting series of peripheries (U.S. borderlands, much of the Caribbean). If there is a "classic" moment in Latin American history it is in the core regions in the late sixteenth and early seventeenth centuries, before the arrival of the other European powers, yet long enough after the initial conquest to have created societies that are not European, Native American, or African. They are truly American. After roughly 1700, the great roaring river of collisions begins to spin off a series of streams. By the twentieth century, the non-Hispanic Caribbean has diverged enough that it no longer has many connections with its (distant) Ibero-American cousins.

Ironically, most of the peoples of the region begin to become aware of a shared Latin American identity over the last half-century, even as the forces of divergence and complexity make it increasingly difficult to speak of "a" Latin American identity. While telecommunications and the electronic, digital revolution have drawn the peoples of Latin American nations together as Mexicans, Costa Ricans, or Brazilians, the increasing ease of migration (internal and external) has made the notion of "a" national identity ever more problematic. The three converging streams of the late fifteenth and sixteenth centuries (Africans, Europeans, Native Americans) collided, mixed, and produced a great river that by the twenty-first century had branched into diverging streams that are fed by new streams and collisions (Asians and peoples from the Middle East). The old colonial legacy and the core features of Latin America continue to evolve and take on new configurations.

In the twenty-first century some of the nations that have long been a part of Latin America may diverge enough that historians in the twenty-second century will no longer include them in Latin America. In fact, the divergences from the cultural core may have become so profound by the sextacentennial that we may no longer be able to speak of "a" Latin America, except in the past tense. Latin America may have a common past, but not a common future. The greatest irony of hemispheric economic integration, should it prove successful over the long haul, is that it may bring all the Americas back toward convergence and greater unity. The patterns of conquest, colonization, migration, and independence that shaped all of the early history of the Americas, may give way to new patterns of cultural, social, political and economic integration. If this does happen, the proper question may no longer be "does Latin America have a common history," but rather "do all of the Americas have a common future?"

Historians are notoriously bad prophets, so I will not make any predictions about the future of Latin America. It has grown from a few outposts in the islands of the Caribbean (in the sixteenth century) to European colonies stretching from Tierra del Fuego to western North America (by the beginning of the seventeenth century). British, Dutch, French, and U.S. challenges then reduced the region to its current political boundaries by the beginning of the twentieth century. The region has moved from European colonies, ruled by absolute monarchs, powered by African slave or coerced indigenous labor, dominated by an elite landholding class who controlled nearly all local power. The processes leading up to the wars for independence in the early nineteenth century began to attack, reshape, and (sometimes) obliterate the colonial heritage, a process that has continued for nearly two hundred years. As Latin America opened up to influences beyond Spain, Portugal, and France, the region experienced another profound conquest at the end of the nineteenth century.

Much of the "story" of the twentieth century has been the transformation of the colonial heritage of large landed estates, governed by a light-skinned elite who controlled a largely nonwhite slave or free labor force, and often employing authoritarian methods of political control. By the beginning of the twenty-first century, Latin America has become an overwhelmingly urban society characterized (in most countries) by racial and cultural mixture. The economies of the region have moved in very diverse paths. While some places remain heavily dependent on the export of agricultural products and raw materials, Latin America is the most industrialized region of what used to be called the Third World. After centuries of monarchs and dictators, democratic regimes prevail nearly everywhere. The most enduring legacy of the colonial collisions is the staggering socioeconomic inequity in nearly every country. As Latin America moves further and further away from the legacies created out of the collisions of the sixteenth-century Conquest, the so-called "social question" remains the largest challenge facing Latin Americans. These inequities form one of the key features of Latin American identity. The central challenge for Latin Americans in the twenty-first century is how to mobilize its citizens through democratic, representative politics to elect leaders who will pursue forms of economic development that will some day diminish substantially the enormous socioeconomic inequities that have so long plagued Latin America. In many ways, the current challenge of Latin America is finally to dismantle this vicious legacy of the colonial heritage that helped define the region. Ironically, those countries that are most successful in this pursuit of development and equity will, no doubt, redefine what it means to be Latin American.

Time Line

PRE-COLUMBIAN AMERICA

12,000–30,000 B.C.	Arrival of first humans to the Americas
6000–3000 B.C.	Emergence of agriculture in Mesoamerica and the Andes
1200–400 B.C.	Beginnings of Olmec civilization
A.D. 150–900	Maya Classic Period
A.D. 900–1200	Rise of Toltecs in Mesoamerica
1300–1500	Emergence of Aztec and Inca empires

EARLY LATIN AMERICA

1492	Columbus lands in Caribbean
1494	Treaty of Tordesillas
1500	Pedro Alvares Cabral lands on coast of Brazil
1503	Board of Trade created in Seville
1513	Formulation of the Requirement
1519	Charles I of Spain elected Charles V of Holy Roman Empire
1519–1522	Spanish expedition circumnavigates the globe
1521	Fall of Tenochtitlan
1524	Council of the Indies created in Spain
1528–1536	Cabeza de Vaca wanders through Texas and Southwest
1532	Conquest of Peru begins
1535	First printing press in Mexico
1537	*Sublimus Deus*, Pope Paul III declares Indians are men
1540s	Spanish discover silver in New Spain and Peru
1542	New Laws promulgated
1550	Debate between Bartolomé de Las Casas and Juan Ginés de Sepúlveda in Valladolid on treatment of Indians
1556	Philip II becomes King of Spain

1569	Inquisition established in Mexico and Peru
1580	Spain and Portugal united under Philip II
1583	First printing press in Peru
1610	Jesuits begin work in what today is Paraguay
1620s–1654	Dutch occupation of northeastern Brazilian coast
1640	Portugal splits away from Spanish rule Braganzas become royal family
1655	English seize Jamaica
1690s	Gold discovered in Brazilian interior (Minas Gerais)
1692	Uprisings in Mexico City
1695	Sor Juana dies in Mexico City
1700	Philip V becomes first Bourbon ruler of Spain
1701	Beginning of War of Spanish Succession
1713	Treaty of Utrecht ends War of Spanish Succession
1739	Viceroyalty of New Granada created
1750	Treaty of Madrid sets out borders between Brazil and Spanish Empire in South America
1759	Jesuits expelled from Brazil
1767	Jesuits expelled from Spanish America
1776	Creation of Viceroyalty of La Plata
1780–1781	Túpac Amaru uprising in Andes
1789	Minas Conspiracy (*Inconfidência Mineira*) in Brazil

FORGING NEW NATIONS

1791–1804	Haitian Revolution
1803	U.S. purchases Louisiana
1807	Napoléon invades Portugal; flight of royal family to Brazil
1808	Napoléon invades Spain; Braganzas arrive in Brazil
1810	Buenos Aires declares independence from Spain *Grito de Dolores* in Mexico
1811	Venezuela declares independence
1812	Constitution of Cádiz
1814–1815	Pumacahua Revolt
1818	Chile declares independence
1819	Creation of Republic of Colombia; U.S. purchases Florida
1821	Declaration of Mexican independence
1822	Crown Prince Pedro declares Brazilian independence
1823	Monroe Doctrine declared; Central America declares independence
1824	Last major battle of Spanish American independence (Ayacucho)

1825	Bolivia declares independence
1828	Uruguay declares independence
1829	Venezuela declares independence from Republic of Colombia
1830	Ecuador declares independence from Republic of Colombia
1830	Simón Bolívar dies
1831	Pedro I abdicates Brazilian throne
1836	Texas independence from Mexico
1839	Central American union collapses
1841	Pedro II crowned Emperor of Brazil
1844	Dominican Republic declares independence from Haiti
1845	Publication of Sarmiento's *Facundo*
1846–1848	War between Mexico and the United States
1855	Panama railway completed across isthmus
1855–1856	William Walker intervenes in Nicaragua
1862–1867	French Intervention in Mexico
1864–1870	War of Triple Alliance (Brazil, Paraguay, Argentina, Uruguay)
1868–1878	Ten Years War in Cuba
1879–1883	War of the Pacific (Chile, Peru, Bolivia)
1886	Slavery abolished in Cuba
1888	Abolition of slavery in Brazil
1889	First International Conference of American States
	Emperor dethroned in Brazil, proclamation of republic
1895	Cuban War for Independence begins
1896	Rubén Darío publishes *Prosas profanas*
1897	Brazilian Army destroys Canudos
1898	United States declares war on Spain
1899–1901	War of a Thousand Days in Colombia
1903	Panama declares independence
1904	Roosevelt Corollary

DEMOCRACY, DEVELOPMENT, AND IDENTITY

1910	Mexican Revolution begins
1914	Opening of Panama Canal
1922	Modern Art Week in Brazil
1927–1933	Augusto César Sandino fights U.S. Marines in Nicaragua
1929	Great Depression begins
1932–1935	Chaco War between Bolivia and Paraguay
1944	Jorge Luis Borges publishes *Ficciones*
	Guatemalan Revolution begins

1946   Gabriela Mistral awarded Nobel Prize in Literature
            Miguel Ángel Asturias publishes *El Señor Presidente*
1948   Civil War in Costa Rica
            Beginning of *La Violencia* in Colombia
1952   Puerto Rico become a Free Associated State
            Bolivian Revolution begins
1954   U.S. intervention to overthrow President Arbenz in
            Guatemala
1959   Overthrow of Batista, Cuban Revolution begins
1961   Bay of Pigs Invasion
1962   Cuban Missile Crisis
1965   U.S. invades Dominican Republic
1967   Miguel Ángel Asturias awarded Nobel Prize in Literature
            Gabriel García Márquez publishes *Cien años de soledad*
            Che Guevara captured and executed in Bolivia
1971   Pablo Neruda awarded Nobel Prize in Literature
1973   Military coup deposes Salvador Allende in Chile
1979   Anastasio Somoza Debayle overthrown by Sandinista
            Revolution
1982   Falklands/Malvinas War between England and Argentina
            Gabriel García Márquez awarded Nobel Prize in Literature
1990   Octavio Paz wins Nobel Prize in Literature
1994   North American Free Trade Agreement goes into effect in
            Mexico, United States, and Canada
2000   PRI loses presidential election in Mexico for first time
            Panama Canal returns to control of Panama
2003   Census Bureau announces that Hispanics have surpassed
            African Americans as largest minority in U.S.

Bibliography

The following is a selective list of books in English. I have chosen works that I believe are accessible to the general reader. Consequently, I have not listed the vast and impressive list of publications aimed primarily at an audience of academic specialists.

GENERAL WORKS

Ades, Dawn. *Art in Latin America: The Modern Era, 1820–1980*. New Haven: Yale University Press, 1989.

Anderson, Benedict. *Imagined Communities: Reflections on the Origin and Spread of Nationalism*. Revised edition. London: Verso, 2006.

Andrews, George Reid. *Afro-Latin America, 1800–2000*. New York: Oxford University Press, 2004.

Bakewell, Peter. *A History of Latin America: Empires and Sequels 1450–1930*. Malden, MA: Blackwell, 1997.

Bethell, Leslie M., ed. *The Cambridge History of Latin America*. 11 vols. Cambridge: Cambridge University Press, 1985–.

Bulmer-Thomas, Victor. *The Economic History of Latin America Since Independence*. Cambridge: Cambridge University Press, 1994.

Chasteen, John Charles. *Born in Blood and Fire: A Concise History of Latin America*. 2nd ed. New York: W. W. Norton, 2005.

Collier, Simon, Thomas E. Skidmore and Harold Blakemore, eds. *The Cambridge Encyclopedia of Latin America and the Caribbean*. 2nd ed. Cambridge: Cambridge University Press, 1992.

Dean, Warren. *With Broadax and Firebrand: The Destruction of the Brazilian Atlantic Forest*. Berkeley: University of California Press, 1995.

Diamond, Jared. *Guns, Germs, and Steel: The Fates of Human Societies*. New York: W. W. Norton, 1999.

Fernández-Armesto, Felipe. *The Americas: A Hemispheric History*. New York: The Modern Library, 2003.

Fitz, Earl E. *Rediscovering the New World: Inter-American Literature in a Comparative Context*. Iowa City: University of Iowa Press, 1991.

Fuentes, Carlos. *The Buried Mirror: Reflections on Spain in the New World*. New York: Houghton Mifflin, 1992.

Galeano, Eduardo. *Memory of Fire*. 3 vols. Translated by Cedric Belfrage. New York: Pantheon, 1985.

———. *Open Veins in Latin America: Five Centuries of the Pillage of a Continent*. New York: Monthly Review Press, 1997.

Holy Bible, King James Version. Cleveland: World Publishing Company, 1964.

Keen, Benjamin and Keith Haynes. *A History of Latin America*. 7th ed. Boston: Houghton Mifflin Company, 2004.

Lockhart, James and Stuart B. Schwartz. *Early Latin America: A History of Colonial Spanish America and Brazil*. New York: Cambridge University Press, 1983.

Longley, Kyle. *In the Eagle's Shadow: The United States and Latin America*. Wheeling, IL: Harlan Davidson, 2002.

Morse, Richard M. *New World Soundings: Culture and Ideology in the Americas*. Baltimore: Johns Hopkins University Press, 1989.

Rock, David. *Argentina, 1516–1987: From Spanish Colonization to Alfonsín*. Berkeley: University of California Press, 1987.

Tenenbaum, Barbara A., ed. *Encyclopedia of Latin American History and Culture*. 5 vols. New York: Scribner's, 1996.

Williamson, Edwin. *The Penguin History of Latin America*. New York: Penguin, 1992.

Wolf, Eric R. *Europe and the People Without History*. Berkeley: University of California Press, 1982.

THREE PEOPLES CONVERGE

Boxer, Charles R. *The Portuguese Seaborne Empire, 1415–1825*. New York: Alfred A. Knopf, 1969.

Brown, Jonathan C. *Latin America: A Social History of the Colonial Period*. Fort Worth: Harcourt College Publishers, 2000.

Burkholder, Mark A. and Lyman L. Johnson. *Colonial Latin America*. 5th ed. New York: Oxford University Press, 2003.

Carrasco, David and Scott Sessions. *Daily Life of the Aztecs: People of the Sun And Earth*. Westport, CT: Greenwood Press, 1998.

Clendinnen, Inga. *Ambivalent Conquests: Maya and Spaniard in Yucatán, 1517–1570*. Cambridge: Cambridge University Press, 1991.

Coe, Michael. *The Maya*. 5th ed. London: Thames and Hudson, 1993.

Columbus, Christopher. *The Four Voyages*. Translated and edited by J. M. Cohen. New York: Penguin, 1969.

Conrad, Robert Edgar, ed. *Children of God's Fire: A Documentary History of Black Slavery in Brazil*. University Park: The Pennsylvania State University Press, 1994.

Cook, Alexandra Parma and Noble David Cook. *Good Faith and Truthful Ignorance: A Case of Transatlantic Bigamy*. Durham, NC: Duke University Press, 1991.

Cook, Noble David. *Born to Die: Disease and the New World Conquest, 1492–1650*. Cambridge: Cambridge University Press, 1998.

Cortés, Hernán. *Letters from Mexico*. Translated and edited by Anthony Pagden. New Haven: Yale University Press, 1986.

Crosby, Alfred W., Jr. *The Columbian Exchange: Biological and Cultural Consequences of 1492*. New York: Praeger, 2003.

Díaz del Castillo, Bernal. *The Conquest of New Spain*. Translated and edited by J. M. Cohen. London: Penguin, 1963.

Dillehay, Thomas D. *The Settlement of the Americas: A New Prehistory*. New York: Basic Books, 2000.

Elliott, John H. *Empires of the Atlantic World: Britain and Spain in America, 1492–1830*. New Haven: Yale University Press, 2006.

———. *The Old World and the New, 1492–1650*. Cambridge: Cambridge University Press, 1970.

Hemming, John. *The Conquest of the Incas*. New York: Harcourt Brace Jovanovich, 1970.

————. *Red Gold: The Conquest of the Brazilian Indians, 1500–1760*. Cambridge, MA: Harvard University Press, 1978.

Heyerdahl, Thor. *Kon-Tiki (Six Men Cross the Pacific on a Raft)*. Translated by F. H. Lyon. Chicago: Rand McNally, 1950.

Kolata, Alan. *Valley of the Spirits: A Journey into the Lost Realm of the Aymara*. Boston: John Wiley, 1996.

Landa, Diego de. *Landa's Relación de las cosas de Yucatan, a Translation*. Translated by C. P. Bowditch and Eleanor P. Adams. Cambridge, MA: Peabody Museum, 1941.

Lane, Kris. *Blood and Silver: A History of Piracy in the Caribbean and Central America*. Armonk, NY: M. E. Sharpe, 1998.

————. *Quito 1599: City and Colony in Transition*. Albuquerque, NM: University of New Mexico Press, 2002.

Las Casas, Bartolomé de. *A Short Account of the Destruction of the Indies*. Translated and edited by Nigel Griffin. London: Penguin Books, 1992.

Leon-Portilla, Miguel, ed. *The Broken Spears: The Aztec Account of the Conquest of Mexico*. Boston: Beacon Press, 1962.

Léry, Jean de. *History of a Voyage to the Land of Brazil*. Translated by Janet Whatley. Berkeley: University of California Press, 1993.

Minta, Stephen. *Aguirre: The Recreation of a Sixteenth-Century Journey Across South America*. New York: Henry Holt, 1994.

Núñez Cabeza de Vaca, Alvar. *Castaways: The Narrative of Alvar Núñez Cabeza de Vaca*. Edited by Enrique Pupo-Walker. Translated by Frances M. López-Morillas. Berkeley: University of California Press, 1993.

Prescott, William Hickling. *History of the Conquest of Mexico*. New York: Modern Library, 2001.

Restall, Matthew. *Maya Conquistador*. Boston: Beacon Press, 1998.

————. *Seven Myths of the Spanish Conquest*. New York: Oxford University Press, 2003.

Rouse, Irving. *The Tainos: Rise and Decline of the People Who Greeted Columbus*. New Haven: Yale University Press, 1992.

Thomas, Hugh. *Conquest: Montezuma, Cortés, and the Fall of Old Mexico*. New York: Touchstone, 1993.

Thornton, John M. *Africa and Africans in the Making of the Atlantic World, 1400–1800*. 2nd ed. New York: Cambridge University Press, 1998.

Van Sertima, Ivan. *They Came Before Columbus: The African Presence in Ancient America*. New York: Random House, 2003.

Wood, Michael. *Conquistadors*. Berkeley: University of California Press, 2000.

BUILDING EMPIRES AND SOCIETIES IN THE NEW WORLD

Andrien, Kenneth, ed. *The Human Tradition in Colonial Latin America*. Wilmington, DE: SR Books, 2002.

Bell, Madison Smartt. *All Souls' Rising*. New York: Penguin, 1995.

————. *Toussaint Louverture: A Biography*. New York: Pantheon, 2007.

Bergamini, John D. *The Spanish Bourbons: The History of a Tenacious Dynasty*. New York: Putnam, 1974.

Bolton, Herbert Eugene. *The Spanish Borderlands: A Chronicle of Old Florida and the Southwest*. New Haven: Yale University Press, 1921.

Boxer, Charles R. *The Golden Age of Brazil, 1695–1750*. Berkeley: University of California Press, 1962.

Brading, D. A. *The First America: The Spanish Monarchy, Creole Patriots, and the Liberal State, 1492–1867*. Cambridge: Cambridge University Press, 1991.

Conniff, Michael L. and Thomas J. Davis. *Africans in the Americas: A History Of the Black Diaspora*. New York: Bedford/St. Martin's, 1994.

Dubois, Laurent. *Avengers of the New World: The Story of the Haitian Revolution*. Cambridge, MA: Harvard University Press, 2005.

Elliott, J. H. *Imperial Spain, 1469–1716*. London: Penguin, 1990.

Equiano, Olaudah. *The Interesting Narrative and Other Writings*. Edited by Vincent Carretta. New York: Penguin, 1995.

Freyre, Gilberto. *The Masters and the Slaves: A Study in the Development of Brazilian Civilization*. Translated by Samuel Putnam. Berkeley: University of California Press, 1986.

James, C. L. R. *The Black Jacobins*. London: Penguin, 2001.

Klein, Herbert S. *African Slavery in Latin America and the Caribbean*. New York: Oxford University Press, 1999.

Maxwell, Kenneth. *Pombal: Paradox of the Enlightenment*. Cambridge: Cambridge University Press, 1995.

Merriman, Roger Bigelow. *The Rise of the Spanish Empire in the Old World and the New*. 4 v. New York: Macmillan, 1918–1924.

Parry, J. H. *The Establishment of the European Hegemony: 1415–1715*. New York: Harper Torchbooks, 1966.

Sor Juana Inés de la Cruz. *The Answer/La Respuesta*. Translated and edited by Electa Arenal and Amanda Powell. New York: The Feminist Press, 1994.

Stein, Stanley, and Barbara H. Stein. *The Colonial Heritage of Latin America: Essays on Economic Dependence in Perspective*. New York: Oxford University Press, 1970.

Thomas, Hugh. *The Slave Trade: The Story of the Atlantic Slave Trade: 1440–1870*. New York: Simon and Schuster, 1997.

Von Humboldt, Alexander. *Political Essay on the Kingdom of New Spain*. Translated by John Black. Norman: University of Oklahoma Press, 1988.

Weber, David J. *The Spanish Frontier in North America*. New Haven: Yale University Press, 1992.

Wolf, Eric R. *Sons of the Shaking Earth: The People of Mexico and Guatemala–Their Land, History, and Culture*. Chicago: University of Chicago Press, 1959.

FORGING A NEW ORDER

Barman, Roderick J. *Citizen Emperor: Pedro II and the Making of Brazil, 1825–91*. Stanford: Stanford University Press, 1999.

Burns, E. Bradford. *The Poverty of Progress: Latin America in the Nineteenth Century*. Berkeley: University of California Press, 1980.

Bushnell, David. *Simón Bolívar: Liberation and Disappointment*. New York: Pearson, 2004.

Calderón de la Barca, Frances. *Life in Mexico*. Berkeley: University of California Press, 1982.

Graham, Richard. *Independence in Latin America: A Comparative Approach*. 2nd ed. New York: McGraw-Hill, 1994.

Hemming, John. *Amazon Frontier: The Defeat of the Brazilian Indians*. London: Macmillan, 1987.

Kinsbruner, Jay. *Independence in Spanish America: Civil Wars, Revolutions, and Underdevelopment*. Albuquerque: University of New Mexico Press, 1994.

Langley, Lester D. *The Americas in the Age of Revolution, 1750–1850*. New Haven: Yale University Press, 1996.

Levine, Robert M. *Vale of Tears: Revisiting the Canudos Massacre in Northeastern Brazil*. Berkeley: University of California Press, 1992.

Lynch, John. *The Spanish American Revolutions, 1808–1826*. 2nd ed. New York: W. W. Norton, 1987.

Racine, Karen. *Francisco de Miranda: A Transatlantic Life in the Age of Revolution*. Wilmington, DE: SR Books, 2003.

Rodó, José Enrique. *Ariel*. Translated by Margaret Sayers Peden. Austin: University of Texas Press, 1988.

Sarmiento, Domingo F. *Facundo: Civilization and Barbarism*. Translated by Kathleen Ross. Berkeley: University of California Press, 2004.

Skidmore, Thomas E. and Peter H. Smith. *Modern Latin America*. 6th ed. New York: Oxford University Press, 2004.

Turner, Clorinda Matto de. *Birds without a Nest*. Translated by J. G. H. Emended by Naomi Lindstrom. Austin: University of Texas Press, 1996.

DEMOCRACY, DEVELOPMENT, AND IDENTITY

Allende, Isabel. *The House of the Spirits*. Translated by Magda Bogin. New York: Bantam, 1986.

Alvarez, Julia. *In the Time of the Butterflies*. Chapel Hill, NC: Algonquin Books, 1994.

Amado, Jorge. *Gabriela, Clove and Cinnamon*. Translated by James L. Taylor and William Grossman. New York: Avon, 1988.

Anderson, Jon Lee. *Che Guevara: A Revolutionary Life*. New York: Grove/Atlantic, 1998.

Assis, Joaquim Maria Machado de. *Dom Casmurro*. Translated by John Gledson. New York: Oxford University Press, 1997.

Asturias, Miguel Ángel. *Men of Maize*. Translated by Gerald Martin. Pittsburgh: University of Pittsburgh Press, 1995.

Balfour, Sebastian. *Castro*. 2nd ed. London: Longman, 1995.

Belli, Gioconda. *The Country Under My Skin: A Memoir of Love and War*. Translated by Kristina Cordero. New York: Alfred A. Knopf, 2002.

Bergquist, Charles. *Labor in Latin America*. Stanford: Stanford University Press, 1986.

Borges, Jorge Luis. *Borges: Collected Fictions*. Translated by Andrew Hurley. New York: Penguin, 1999.

Cabezas, Omar. *Fire from the Mountain: The Making of a Sandinista*. Translated by Kathleen Weaver. New York: Plume, 1985.

Castañeda, Jorge G. *Utopia Unarmed: The Latin American Left after the Cold War*. New York: Vintage, 1993.

Crandall, Russell. *Gunboat Democracy: The United States Interventions in the Dominican Republic, Grenada, and Panama*. Lanham, MD: Rowman and Littlefield, 2006.

Feinstein, Adam. *Pablo Neruda: A Passion for Life*. New York: Bloomsbury, 2004.

Fuentes, Carlos. *The Death of Artemio Cruz*. Translated by Alfred Mac Adam. New York: Farrar, Straus and Giroux, 1991.

García Márquez, Gabriel. *Living to Tell the Tale*. Translated by Edith Grossman. New York: Vintage, 2003.

———. *One Hundred Years of Solitude*. Translated by Gregory Rabassa. New York: Avon, 1971.

Gleijeses, Piero. *Shattered Hope: The Guatemalan Revolution and the United States, 1944–1954*. Princeton: Princeton University Press, 1992.

Gonzales, Michael J. *The Mexican Revolution, 1910–1940*. Albuquerque: University of New Mexico Press, 2002.

Gorriti Ellenbogen, Gustavo. *The Shining Path: A History of the Millenarian War in Peru*. Chapel Hill: University of North Carolina Press, 1999.

Guillermoprieto, Alma. *Looking for History: Dispatches from Latin America*. New York: Vintage, 2002.

———. *Samba*. New York: Vintage, 1991.

Gutiérrez, Gustavo. *A Theology of Liberation: History, Politics and Salvation*. Maryknoll, NY: Orbis Books, 1988.

Hemming, John. *Die If You Must: Brazilian Indians in the Twentieth Century*. London: Macmillan, 2003.

Jesus, Carolina Maria de. *Child of the Dark: The Diary of Carolina Maria de Jesus*. Translated by David St. Clair. New York: Signet, 2003.

LaFeber, Walter. *The Panama Canal: The Crisis in Historical Perspective*. New York: Oxford University Press, 1990.

Lewis, Oscar, Ruth Lewis, and Susan M. Rigdon. *Living the Revolution: An Oral History of Contemporary Cuba*. 3 vols. Urbana: University of Illinois Press, 1977.

Mariátegui, José Carlos. *Seven Interpretive Essays on Peruvian Reality*. Translated by Marjory Urquidi. Austin: University of Texas Press, 1988.

McCullough, David. *The Path Between the Seas: The Creation of the Panama Canal, 1870–1914*. New York: Touchstone, 1977.

McGowan, Chris, and Ricardo Pessanha. *The Brazilian Sound: Samba, Bossa Nova, and the Popular Music of Brazil*. New York: Billboard Books, 1991

Nazario, Sonia. *Enrique's Journey*. New York: Random House, 2006.

Neruda, Pablo. *Memoirs*. Translated by Hardie St. Martin. New York: Farrar, Straus and Giroux, 2001.

Paz, Octavio. *The Labyrinth of Solitude: Life and Thought in Mexico*. Translated by Lysander Kemp. New York: Grove Press, 1961.

Pérez-Stable, Marifeli. *The Cuban Revolution: Origins, Course, and Legacy*. 2nd ed. New York: Oxford University Press, 2003.

Soto, Hernando de. *The Other Path: The Invisible Revolution in the Third World*. New York: Harper & Row, 1989.

Thorp, Rosemary. *Progress, Poverty and Exclusion: An Economic History of Latin America in the Twentieth Century*. Baltimore: Johns Hopkins University Press and The Inter-American Development Bank and the European Union, 1998.

Timerman, Jacobo. *Prisoner without a Name, Cell without a Number*. Madison: University of Wisconsin Press, 2002.

Weschler, Lawrence. *A Miracle, a Universe: Settling Accounts with Torturers*. New York: Penguin, 1990.

Winn, Peter. *Weavers of the Revolution: The Yarur Workers and Chile's Road to Socialism*. New York: Oxford University Press, 1986.

Index